Longmans Annotated English Poets

GENERAL EDITOR: F. W. BATESON

MATTHEW ARNOLD
c. 1860

THE POEMS OF
MATTHEW
ARNOLD

EDITED BY
KENNETH
ALLOTT

1724

LONGMANS

LONGMANS, GREEN AND CO LTD
48 Grosvenor Street, London W I
Associated companies, branches and representatives
throughout the world

© *Longmans, Green & Co. Ltd.*, 1965
First published 1965

Made and printed in Great Britain by
William Clowes and Sons, Limited,
London and Beccles

To
Stephen Tait

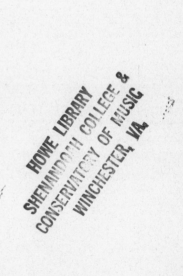

Contents

CONTENTS

JUVENILIA, UNFINISHED POEMS, AND FRAGMENTS

1*

CONTENTS

APPENDICES

Illustrations

Preface

The first object of this edition is annotation. For the great majority of Arnold's poems the text is based on the *textus receptus*, that is to say, the text of *Poems* (1885), which was the last collected edition to have the benefit of the poet's supervision; for the remainder the textual authority is a variety of printed and MS. sources. The text has been slightly modernized in spelling and punctuation in accordance with editorial policy for the series to which this edition belongs, but the only frequent change is the printing of the silent 'e' in such words as 'danced' where Arnold usually, though not invariably, prefers 'danc'd'. Unlike the editors of the standard edition, *The Poetical Works of Matthew Arnold* edited by Messrs. C. B. Tinker and H. F. Lowry (1950), I have not attempted to produce a textually definitive edition by recording all the variant readings of the printed editions and MSS., but I believe that I have included all that on a generous interpretation are of real interest or significance, and I have given all the MS. variants where, as in some instances, the standard edition fails to do so. By the inclusion of most of Arnold's poetic *juvenilia* from early note-books and the *Fox How Magazine*, of his poetic drafts and fragments from the Yale MS., letters and other sources, and of his translations of passages from the *Iliad*, which he published only in *On Translating Homer* (1861), this edition can claim to be more nearly complete than any earlier edition of his poetry. 'The River' is printed for the first time in an unmutilated text. Arnold omitted the first six stanzas of the poem, probably because he felt that they were too intimate a self-revelation, when he published it in 1852.

The order of the poems in this edition is, as nearly as I can establish it, their order of composition. Positive evidence for the dating of many of Arnold's poems is lacking, so that my order is only very approximately correct, but it is close enough to the real order, I hope, to preserve what S. T. Coleridge called 'the interest which arises from watching the progress, the maturity, and even the decay of genius'. The *juvenilia*, poetic drafts and fragments have not been inserted in this order, because they might be felt to be intruders among the pieces with which Arnold was satisfied, or, in the case of cancelled poems, which at some time he had been willing to print. They are given in a chronological order of their own after the rest of Arnold's poems.

The commentary, which is divided between headnotes and footnotes, should be self-explanatory. Textual comments are not separated from the rest. Greek and German quotations in the notes have been translated (again in accordance with editorial policy for the series), but exact references to the originals of translated passages have been given. For references to Goethe's prose I have cited the German edition which Arnold himself possessed. Translations of Greek are usually taken from those in the Loeb Classics. For German writers I have used whatever translations I could find, or, with the assistance of friends better informed than myself, made my own. I have explored a little further than earlier commentators Arnold's poetic debt to the Greek and Latin classics and to German literature, but I have no doubt that in these fields much remains to be done. An annotated edition of a Victorian poet is still perhaps something of a novelty, but the feeling that we can read the Victorians without the props to understanding recognized to be necessary when we read (let us say) an Augustan poet is very largely an illusion. There is a sense in which all good poetry is contemporary, but it is equally true that good poetry belongs firmly to its own time and that any poem over fifty years old has to be 'translated'.

In preparing this edition I have enjoyed the generous assistance of many persons and institutions. My principal debt – and one which it is a special pleasure to acknowledge – is to the members of Matthew Arnold's family for the loan of and permission to print MS. material (poems, letters, diaries, etc.). I must mention by name Mr. Arnold Whitridge and Major Peter Thwaites, the poet's grandson and great-grandson respectively, the late Miss Dorothy Ward, Rear-Admiral Delafield Arnold-Forster, Mrs. Barnett and Miss Florence Vere O'Brien. Among other items, for example, Mr. Whitridge entrusted me with Arnold's 1851 diary and an unpublished general note-book begun in 1847; Miss Ward with the nine issues of the *Fox How Magazine* preserved in five small note-books; Mrs. Barnett with the MSS. of Arnold's poems 'The River' and 'Separation'. Next in order of importance is my debt to the officials of Yale University Library and in particular to Miss Marjorie Wynne, Curator of the Rare Book Room at Yale. Through their generosity I have been able to consult and make full use of their remarkable Arnold collection, which includes, apart from books, the Yale MS. and the Yale Papers. The Yale MS., a group of poetic drafts and prose notes, might be described as Arnold's poetic workshop in the 1840s and early 1850s. The Yale Papers contain Arnold's autograph copies of various poems, almost all his diaries and note-books from 1845 to 1888, and many unpublished letters. It is natural enough that university libraries should be jealous of their MS. treasures, and I take this opportunity of saluting the generous

decision of Yale University Library to open their rich Arnold collection
to scholars all over the world. I am indebted to Mr. J. H. Broderick for
assistance on several occasions and especially for his kindness in providing
me with a transcription of Arnold's 'Lucretius' fragments from photostats
of the original MS. made for Dr. H. F. Lowry before 1940 (the location
of the MS. containing these fragments is now unknown). Acknow-
ledgements are also owed by me to the officials of the Bodleian Library,
Oxford, and of the Alexander Turnbull Library, Wellington, New
Zealand, for allowing me to consult their holdings of unpublished letters
by the younger Thomas Arnold. For supplying me with references or
answering other queries I am grateful to Professor Kathleen Tillotson,
Mr. Fraser Neiman, Professor J. C. Maxwell and Mr. C. Rawson. What
I owe to the writings of Arnold scholars and commentators such as
Professor Kathleen Tillotson, Professor Louis Bonnerot and Professor
R. H. Super cannot be acknowledged in detail – the notes in this edition
make some partial acknowledgement – but the work of Dr. H. F. Lowry,
from whom I have also had kind personal encouragement, is in a special
category. I have spoken of him elsewhere as the 'onlie begetter' of
modern Arnold scholarship, and the phrase is not too strong. Without
his edition of *Matthew Arnold's Letters to Clough* (1932), and without *The
Poetry of Matthew Arnold: A Commentary* (1940) and the later editions of
The Poetical Works (1950) and *The Note-books* (1952), in the production
of which he was associated with the late Mr. C. B. Tinker (for the first
two titles) and then with Professors K. Young and W. H. Dunn (for
The Note-books), this edition would have been an impossibility. I must
also thank him and his fellow editors, and the Oxford University Press of
London and New York, for permission to quote from these books.

Finally, I have to express my gratitude to Mr. F. W. Bateson, general
editor of the series of Annotated English Poets, and to some of my col-
leagues at Liverpool University. Mr. Bateson, who invited me to edit
Arnold, has read my commentary with scrupulous attention and made
many suggestions from which I have profited. At Liverpool I have had
the advice and assistance of Messrs. W. H. Fox, D. Barker and L. Harri-
son and of Miss Erika Wirtz of the Department of German; of Mr. G.
Townend of the School of Classics; and of Professor Kenneth Muir, Dr.
G. K. Hunter, Dr. E. Schanzer, Mrs. I.-S. Ewbank and Mr. R. T. Davies
of my own Department of English Literature. Much of my commentary
has been talked over, item by item, with my wife, Miriam Allott, who
teaches in the same department. For typing carefully the whole manuscript of the edition I am grateful to Miss Margaret Burton, Departmen-
tal Secretary; and I have also to thank Mr. A. N. Ricketts and Miss E.

Whelan of the Harold Cohen Library in the University of Liverpool for
dealing so efficiently and amiably with the various demands I made on
them. The photograph of Matthew Arnold which appears as a frontis-
piece is reproduced by the kind permission of the Trustees of Dove Cottage, Grasmere. It is the only portrait of Arnold known to me that shows
him at an age when he was still as much the poet as the critic or school-
inspector. The autograph MS. of his poem 'The River' is reproduced
by the joint permission of its owner, Mrs. Barnett, and of the owner
of the copyright, Major Peter Thwaites.

KENNETH ALLOTT

Liverpool
August 1963

Chronological Table of Matthew Arnold's Life and Chief Publications

1822   (*24 December*) Born at Laleham-on-Thames, eldest son of Rev. Thomas Arnold and Mary Arnold (*née* Penrose).

1828   (*August*) Arnold's family move to Rugby on his father's appointment as Headmaster of Rugby School.

1831   (*January*) Pupil of his uncle, Rev. John Buckland, at Laleham until December 1832.
       (*August*) First visit to the Lake District on a tour of England and Scotland with his family.

1833   (*May*) Herbert Hill, a cousin of Southey, engaged by Dr. Arnold as a tutor for his sons.

1834   (*July*) Fox How (nr. Ambleside) completed and becomes the permanent holiday home of the Arnolds in the Lakes. Wordsworth a neighbour and frequent visitor.

1836   First attempts at writing verse.
       (*September*) Accompanied by his brother Tom enters Winchester College, his father's old school, as a Commoner.

1837   Wins verse-speaking prize at Winchester with a speech from Byron's *Marino Faliero*.
       (*August*) First visit to France.
       (*September*) Removed from Winchester and enters the Fifth Form at Rugby.

1838   (*January*) First number of the manuscript *Fox How Magazine*, which he brought out twice a year with his brother Tom's help until January 1842.
       Fifth Form prize for Latin verse.
       (*August*) Removed to the Sixth Form under his father.

1840   (*June*) School prizes for English essay and English verse. His prize-poem, 'Alaric at Rome', printed at Rugby.
       (*November*) Wins open scholarship to Balliol College, Oxford.

1841   (*June*) Shares school prizes for Latin essay and Latin verse.
       (*August*) His father appointed Regius Professor of Modern History at Oxford.
       (*October*) Goes into residence at Oxford. Beginning of intimacy

with A. H. Clough. Impressed by the artistry of Newman's preaching at St. Mary's, but little affected by the ideas of the Oxford Movement.

1842   (*March*) *Proxime accessit* for Hertford Latin Scholarship.
(*12 June*) Sudden death of his father of heart disease at Rugby.

1842–5 Reads and is influenced by Carlyle, Emerson and George Sand; at a slightly later date by Goethe and Spinoza. Member of the 'Decade', an undergraduate society on the pattern of the Cambridge 'Apostles'.

1843   Newdigate prize-poem *Cromwell* printed.

1844   (*June*) A. P. Stanley's *Life and Correspondence of Thomas Arnold*.
(*November*) B.A. (Second Class in 'Greats').

1845   (*February–April*) Temporary assistant-master at Rugby.
(*28 March*) Elected Fellow of Oriel College, Oxford.

1846   (*July*) Visits France and meets George Sand at Nohant.
(*December*) Visits Paris at the end of the month to see Rachel act and remains there until 11 February 1847.
Probably begins to read Senancour and Sainte-Beuve about this time.

1847   (*April*) Private secretary to the Marquis of Lansdowne, Lord President of the Council and Whig elder statesman.
(*November*) His brother Tom emigrates to New Zealand in the hope of finding 'Liberty, Equality, Fraternity'.

1848   (*February*) His brother William Delafield leaves Oxford to go out to India as an Ensign in the Bengal Army of the East India Company.
(*September*) Visits Switzerland and meets 'Marguerite' at Thun.
(*November*) Clough publishes *The Bothie of Toper-na-Fuosich* after resigning his Oriel fellowship in October because of his conscientious difficulties about religious subscription.

1849   (*February*) Publishes *The Strayed Reveller, and Other Poems*.
(*September*) Visits Switzerland and meets 'Marguerite' at Thun for the second and last time.

1850   (*23 April*) Death of Wordsworth.
(*June*) Publishes 'Memorial Verses' in *Fraser's Magazine*.
(*August*) His eldest and favourite sister, Jane ('K'), is married to W. E. Forster. His own courtship of Frances Lucy Wightman is interrupted because of his lack of worldly prospects.

His brothers Tom (at Hobart, Tasmania) and William (at Lahore in the Punjab) also marry during this year.

1851 (*15 April*) Appointed Inspector of Schools by Lord Lansdowne.
(*10 June*) Marries Frances Lucy, daughter of Sir William Wightman, Justice of the Queen's Bench, at Hampton.
(*September–October*) Delayed honeymoon on the Continent (France, Italy, Switzerland) during which he visits the Grande Chartreuse.
(*11 October*) Begins work as school-inspector. From this time forward spends much time in travelling both on inspectorial duties and for some years as Marshal to Judge Wightman on circuit.

1852 (*October*) Publishes *Empedocles on Etna, and Other Poems.*

1853 (*November*) Publishes *Poems. A New Edition* (a selection from his two earlier volumes with a critical preface and, among new poems, 'Sohrab and Rustum' and 'The Scholar-Gipsy').

1854 (*December*) Publishes *Poems, Second Series* (a further selection from his first two volumes, 'Balder Dead' being the only important new poem; title-page dated 1855).

1855 (*April*) Publishes 'Stanzas from the Grand Chartreuse' in *Fraser's Magazine.*
(*May*) Publishes 'Haworth Churchyard' in *Fraser's Magazine.*

1857 (*5 May*) Elected Professor of Poetry at Oxford.
(*August*) Visits Switzerland with his wife.
(*14 November*) Inaugural lecture, 'On the Modern Element in Literature', at Oxford. (Arnold, the first Professor of Poetry to lecture in English, was re-elected at the end of his first term of five years.)
(*December*) Publishes *Merope* (title-page dated 1858).

1858 (*February*) Settles at 2, Chester Square, London ('. . . it will be something to unpack one's portmanteau for the first time since I was married, now nearly seven years ago').
(*August–September*) On a walking holiday in Switzerland with his friend Theodore Walrond.

1859 (*March–August*) Abroad in France, Holland and Switzerland as Foreign Assistant Commissioner to the Newcastle Commission on elementary education.
(*9 April*) Death of his brother William at Gibraltar.
(*August*) Publishes *England and the Italian Question.*
(*19 August*) Meets Sainte-Beuve (with whom he had exchanged letters in 1854 and 1855) in Paris.

1861   (*January*) Publishes *On Translating Homer*.
        (*May*) Publishes *The Popular Education of France* (with the intro-
        ductory essay 'Democracy').
        (*13 November*) Death of Clough at Florence.

1862   (*March*) Risks official hostility by publishing in *Fraser's Magazine*
        'The Twice-Revised Code', a strong attack on Robert Lowe's
        new method of distributing government grants for education
        ('Payment by Results').
        Publishes *On Translating Homer: Last Words*.

1864   (*June*) Publishes *A French Eton*. Most of his work in prose from
        now on appears in magazines before being published in book
        form.

1865   (*February*) Publishes *Essays in Criticism* (First Series).
        (*April–November*) Abroad in France, Italy, Germany and Switzer-
        land as Foreign Assistant Commissioner to the Taunton (*Schools
        Enquiry*) Commission.

1866   (*March*) Applies unsuccessfully to be appointed a Charity Com-
        missioner.
        (*April*) Publishes 'Thyrsis', his elegy on Clough, in *Macmillan's
        Magazine*.

1867   (*April*) Applies unsuccessfully for the Librarianship of the House
        of Commons.
        (*June*) Publishes *On the Study of Celtic Literature*.
        (*July*) Publishes *New Poems* (which includes 'Empedocles on
        Etna' reprinted, at Browning's wish, for the first time since 1852).
        From this time forward writes very little verse but is increasingly
        widely known for his controversial social and religious writings.

1868   (*January*) Death of his infant son Basil.
        (*April*) Moves to Byron House, Harrow.
        (*November*) Death of his eldest son Thomas, aged sixteen, then a
        Harrow schoolboy.

1869   (*January*) Publishes *Culture and Anarchy*, his chief work in social
        criticism.
        (*June*) Publishes the first collected edition of his *Poems* (two
        volumes). Applies unsuccessfully for appointment as one of the
        three Commissioners under the Endowed Schools Act.
        (*October*) Publishes his essay on '*Obermann*' in *The Academy*.
        (*13 October*) Death of Sainte-Beuve.
        (*November*) Publishes his essay 'Sainte-Beuve' in *The Academy*.

1870 (*May*) Publishes *St. Paul and Protestantism*.
(*June*) Receives the honorary degree of D.C.L. at Oxford.
Promoted Senior Inspector of Schools during this year.

1871 (*February*) Publishes *Friendship's Garland*, a series of letters 'half serious, half playful' on English life and culture originally contributed to the *Pall Mall Gazette* (1866-7, 1869-70).
(*August*) Visits France and Switzerland with his wife and his son Richard.

1872 (*February*) Death of his son William Trevenen, aged eighteen.

1873 (*February*) Publishes *Literature and Dogma*, the most important of his writings on religion.
(*February–May*) Spends a holiday leave from school-inspection with his wife in Italy.
(*June*) Moves to Pains Hill Cottage, Cobham, Surrey.
(*30 September*) Death of his mother at Fox How.

1875 (*November*) Publishes *God and the Bible*, a review of objections to *Literature and Dogma*.

1876 (*9 June*) Death of George Sand.
(*December*) Reprints 'The New Sirens' in *Macmillan's Magazine*.

1877 (*February*) Declines re-nomination for the Professorship of Poetry at Oxford.
(*March*) Publishes *Last Essays on Church and Religion*.
(*April–May*) Portrayed as 'Mr. Luke' in W. H. Mallock's satirical *The New Republic*.
(*June*) Publishes his essay 'George Sand' in *The Fortnightly Review*.
(*November*) Declines nomination for the Lord Rectorship of St. Andrews' University.

1878 (*June*) Publishes *Selected Poems of Matthew Arnold* (Golden Treasury Series).

1879 (*c. March*) Publishes *Mixed Essays*.
(*August*) Publishes his selected *Poems of Wordsworth*.

1880 (*12 May*) Attends the reception in London given in honour of Cardinal Newman by the Duke of Norfolk 'because I wanted to have spoken once in my life to Newman'.
(*September*) Visits Switzerland and Italy on holiday.
Contributes three essays – 'Introduction' (later called 'On the Study of Poetry'), 'Thomas Gray' and 'John Keats' to T. H. Ward's *The English Poets*.

1881   (*June*) Publishes his selected *Poetry of Byron*.
        (*18 July*) Death of A. P. Stanley, Dean of Westminster.

1882   (*January*) Publishes 'Westminster Abbey', his elegy on Stanley,
        in *The Nineteenth Century*.
        (*March*) Publishes *Irish Essays*.

1883   (*August*) Accepts Civil List pension of £250 a year 'in public
        recognition of service to the poetry and literature of England'.
        (*October*) Arrives in the U.S.A. to begin a lecture-tour lasting
        until March 1884.

1884   Becomes Chief Inspector of Schools.

1885   (*June*) Publishes *Discourses in America*.
        (*c. August*) Publishes three-volume collected edition of *Poems*
        (Library Edition).
        (*October*) Again declines re-nomination for the Professorship of
        Poetry at Oxford (in spite of a memorial from Oxford heads of
        colleges and tutors, and another from four hundred undergradu-
        ates). 'Every one is very kind as one grows old . . .'
        (*November–December*) Abroad in Germany for the Royal Com-
        mission on Education.

1886   (*February–March*) Abroad again in France, Switzerland and Ger-
        many for the Royal Commission on Education.
        (*30 April*) Retires from Inspectorship of Schools.
        (*May–August*) Second visit to U.S.A.

1888   (*15 April*) Dies suddenly of heart failure at Liverpool while await-
        ing the arrival of his married daughter from America.
        (*November*) Posthumous publication of *Essays in Criticism* (Second
        Series).

Abbreviations

1849 = *The Strayed Reveller, and Other Poems* (1849).

1852 = *Empedocles on Etna, and Other Poems* (1852).

1853 = *Poems.* A new edition (1853).

1854 = *Poems.* Second edition (1854).

1855 = *Poems.* Second series (1855).

1857 = *Poems.* Third edition (1857).

1867 = *New Poems* (1867).

1869 = *Poems* (1869). First collected edition (2 volumes).

1877 = *Poems* (1877). Collected edition (2 volumes).

1881 = *Poems* (1881). Collected edition (2 volumes).

1885 = *Poems* (1885). Collected *Library* edition (3 volumes).

1890 = *Poetical Works of Matthew Arnold* (1890). Globe edition.

1950 = *Poetical Works of Matthew Arnold* ed. by C. B. Tinker and H. F. Lowry (1950).

E in C I = *Essays in Criticism* (1865).

E in C II = *Essays in Criticism* Second series (1888).

Works = *The Works of Matthew Arnold* (1903–4). De luxe edition (15 volumes).

L = *Letters of Matthew Arnold, 1848–88* ed. by G. W. E. Russell in 2 volumes (1895).

CL = *The Letters of Matthew Arnold to Arthur Hugh Clough* ed. by H. F. Lowry (1932).

UL = *Unpublished Letters of Matthew Arnold* ed. by A. Whitridge (Yale University Press: New Haven, 1923).

Note-books = *The Note-books of Matthew Arnold* ed. by H. F. Lowry, K. Young and W. H. Dunn (1952).

Baum = *Ten Studies in the Poetry of Matthew Arnold* by P. F. Baum (Duke University Press: Durham, N.C., 1958).

Bonnerot = *Matthew Arnold – Poète: Essai de biographie psychologique* by L. Bonnerot (Paris, 1947).

Buckler = *Matthew Arnold's Books: Towards a Publishing Diary* written and edited by W. E. Buckler (Geneva and Paris, 1958).

Commentary = *The Poetry of Matthew Arnold: A Commentary* by C. B. Tinker and H. F. Lowry (1940).

Correspondence of A.H.C. = *Correspondence of Arthur Hugh Clough* ed. by F. L. Mulhauser in 2 volumes (1957).

Life of J.D.C. = *Life and Correspondence of John Duke, Lord Coleridge* . . . written and edited by E. H. Coleridge in 2 volumes (1904).

Neiman = *Essays, Letters, and Reviews by Matthew Arnold* ed. by F. Neiman (Harvard University Press: Cambridge, Mass., 1960).

Obermann = *Obermann*, by E. P. de Senancour, ed. by G. Michaut, in 2 volumes (Paris, 1912–13).

Parrish = *A Concordance to the Poems of Matthew Arnold* ed. by S. M. Parrish (Cornell University Press: Ithaca, N.Y., 1959).

Remains of A.H.C. = *The Poems and Prose Remains of Arthur Hugh Clough, with a selection from his letters and a memoir*, ed. by his wife in 2 volumes (1869).

Russell = *Matthew Arnold* by G. W. E. Russell (Literary Lives series, second edition 1904).

Sells = *Matthew Arnold and France: The Poet* by I. E. Sells (1935).

Trilling = *Matthew Arnold* by L. Trilling (New York, 1939).

Vict. Poetry = *Victorian Poetry: A Critical Journal of Victorian Literature* (West Virginia University, Morgantown, W.Va.).

Vict. Stud. = *Victorian Studies: A Quarterly Journal of the Humanities, Arts, and Sciences* (Indiana University, Bloomington, Indiana).

Yale MS. = A collection of notes, poetic drafts, etc. by Matthew Arnold, which are preserved as a poetic note-book at Yale.

Yale Papers = The larger collection of Arnold's poetic MSS., note-books diaries, letters, etc. preserved at Yale.

(This list excludes familiar abbreviations such as *OED, DNB, N & Q,* etc.)

THE POEMS

1 Alaric at Rome

Written 1840: A.'s first published poem, 'recited in Rugby School, June XII, MDCCCXL' – 1840 title-page, which is without author's name but E. H. Bradby records, 'When I was a small boy at Rugby I heard Arnold recite the poem' with a 'roll and vigour . . . unlike the timid utterance of the ordinary school poet' (*Pall Mall Gazette* 2 Jan. 1892); *Rugby Register* (second edition – undated, probably 1847) ascribes it to A.; and A. acknowledges authorship in a letter of 9 Feb. 1888 to Edmund Gosse, 'Yes! "Alaric at Rome" is my Rugby prize-poem, and I think it is better than my Oxford one, "Cromwell"; only you will see that I had been very much reading *Childe Harold*' (*Athenaeum* no. 3157 (28 April 1888) 533–4). A.'s stanza, the Spenserian stanza shortened by omitting fifth, sixth and seventh lines, recalls Byron, but the melancholy of Alaric, the first of A.'s solitary contemplatives, is already distinctive.

Published Rugby 1840; not reprinted by A.; type-facsimile reprint by T. J. Wise 1893.

> 'Admire. exult, despise, laugh, weep, for here
> There is such matter for all feeling.'
> > Childe Harold.

I

Unwelcome shroud of the forgotten dead,
Oblivion's dreary fountain, where art thou?
Why speed'st thou not thy deathlike wave to shed
O'er humbled pride, and self-reproaching woe?
5   Or time's stern hand, why blots it not away
The saddening tale that tells of sorrow and decay?

II

There are, whose glory passeth not away –
Even in the grave their fragrance cannot fade:
Others there are as deathless full as they,
10   Who for themselves a monument have made
By their own crimes – a lesson to all eyes –
Of wonder to the fool – of warning to the wise.

¶ 1. *Motto. Childe Harold* iv st. 109, part of Byron's description of Roman decay.
7–8. Cp. *Childe Harold* iii st. 67,

> But these are deeds which should not pass away,
> And names that must not wither . . .

III

Yes, there are stories registered on high,
Yes, there are stains time's fingers cannot blot,
15   Deeds that shall live when they who did them, die;
Things that may cease, but never be forgot:
Yet some there are, their very lives would give
To be remembered thus, and yet they cannot live.

IV

But thou, imperial City! that hast stood
20   In greatness once, in sackcloth now and tears,
A mighty name, for evil or for good,
Even in the loneness of thy widowed years:
Thou that hast gazed, as the world hurried by,
Upon its headlong course with sad prophetic eye.

V

25   Is thine the laurel-crown that greatness wreathes
Round the wan temples of the hallowed dead –
Is it the blighting taint dishonour breathes
In fires undying o'er the guilty head,
Or the brief splendour of that meteor light
30   That for a moment gleams, and all again is night?

13–14. The figure is a favourite with Byron in *Childe Harold* and was also used by A. in his mature work – cp., for example, 'The Scholar-Gipsy' 211–12 (p. 342 below),

> Still nursing the unconquerable hope,
> Still clutching the inviolable shade . . .

19–22. Byronic apostrophe. Cp. *Childe Harold* iv sts. 42 and 78,

> Italia! oh, Italia! thou who hast
> The fatal gift of Beauty, which became
> A funeral dower of present woes and past –
> On thy sweet brow is sorrow ploughed by shame . . .

> Oh, Rome! my Country! City of the Soul!
> The orphans of the heart must turn to thee,
> Lone Mother of dead Empires! . . .

23–4. Rome looks on the world's 'headlong course' as in 'Obermann Once More' 105–12 (p. 524 below) the 'brooding East' looks on Roman activity. The position of detached onlooker is congenial to A. – cp. the role assigned to the poet in 'Resignation' 144–98 (pp. 89–92 below).

VI

Fain would we deem that thou hast risen so high
Thy dazzling light an eagle's gaze should tire;
No meteor brightness to be seen and die,
No passing pageant, born but to expire,
35   But full and deathless as the deep dark hue
Of ocean's sleeping face, or heaven's unbroken blue.

VII

Yet stains there are to blot thy brightest page,
And wither half the laurels on thy tomb;
A glorious manhood, yet a dim old age,
40   And years of crime, and nothingness, and gloom:
And then that mightiest crash, that giant fall,
Ambition's boldest dream might sober and appall.

VIII

Thou wondrous chaos, where together dwell
Present and past, the living and the dead,
45   Thou shattered mass, whose glorious ruins tell
The vanished might of that discrownéd head:
Where all we see, or do, or hear, or say,
Seems strangely echoed back by tones of yesterday:

IX

Thou solemn grave, where every step we tread
50   Treads on the slumbering dust of other years;
The while there sleeps within thy precincts dread
What once had human passions, hopes, and fears;
And memory's gushing tide swells deep and full
And makes thy very ruin fresh and beautiful.

47–8. Cp. *Childe Harold* iv st. 81,

> But Rome is as the desert – where we steer
> Stumbling o'er recollections . . .

49–50. Cp. *Childe Harold* iv st. 144,

> Heroes have trod this spot – 'tis on their dust ye tread.

51–2. Cp. *Childe Harold* iv st. 112,

> . . . and in yon field below
> A thousand years of silenced factions sleep . . .

X

55   Alas, no common sepulchre art thou,
     No habitation for the nameless dead,
     Green turf above, and crumbling dust below,
     Perchance some mute memorial at their head,
     But one vast fane where all unconscious sleep
60   Earth's old heroic forms in peaceful slumbers deep.

XI

     Thy dead are kings, thy dust are palaces,
     Relics of nations thy memorial-stones:
     And the dim glories of departed days
     Fold like a shroud around thy withered bones:
65   And o'er thy towers the wind's half-uttered sigh
     Whispers, in mournful tones, thy silent elegy.

XII

     Yes, in such eloquent silence didst thou lie
     When the Goth stooped upon his stricken prey,
     And the deep hues of an Italian sky
70   Flashed on the rude barbarian's wild array:
     While full and ceaseless as the ocean roll,
     Horde after horde streamed up thy frowning Capitol.

XIII

     Twice, ere that day of shame, the embattled foe
     Had gazed in wonder on that glorious sight;
75   Twice had the eternal city bowed her low
     In sullen homage to the invader's might:
     Twice had the pageant of that vast array
     Swept from thy walls, O Rome, on its triumphant
            way.

57–8. A reminiscence, probably unconscious, of Gray's 'Elegy written in
a Country Church-yard'.

68. *stooped*] Pounced like a hawk.

73 *ff*. 'The sieges of Rome by the Goths under Alaric were three in
number. The first was commenced A.D. 408, and concluded A.D. 409 by
Alaric's accepting a ransom. In the second Alaric entered the city in
triumph, and appointed Attalus Emperor. After again degrading this new
monarch of his own creation he finally captured and sacked the city, A.D.
410.' A.'s note.

XIV

Twice from without thy bulwarks hath the din
80   Of Gothic clarion smote thy startled ear;
Anger, and strife, and sickness are within,
Famine and sorrow are no strangers here:
Twice hath the cloud hung o'er thee, twice been
        stayed
Even in the act to burst, twice threatened, twice de-
        layed.

XV

85   Yet once again, stern Chief, yet once again,
Pour forth the foaming vials of thy wrath:
There lies thy goal, to miss or to attain,
Gird thee, and on upon thy fateful path;
The world hath bowed to Rome, oh! cold were he
90 Who would not burst his bonds, and in his turn be free.

XVI

Therefore arise and arm thee! lo, the world
Looks on in fear! and when the seal is set,
The doom pronounced, the battle-flag unfurled,
Scourge of the nations, wouldest thou linger yet?
95   Arise and arm thee! spread thy banners forth,
Pour from a thousand hills thy warriors of the north!

XVII

Hast thou not marked on a wild autumn day
When the wind slumbereth in a sudden lull,
What deathlike stillness o'er the landscape lay,
100   How calmly sad, how sadly beautiful;
How each bright tint of tree, and flower, and heath
Were mingling with the sere and withered hues of
        death?

82. '"That unfortunate city gradually experienced the distress of scarcity
and at length the horrid calamities of famine ... The miseries of which
were succeeded and aggravated by the contagion of a pestilential disease." –
Gibbon.' A.'s note. See *Decline and Fall* ed. J. B. Bury (1900–2) iii 309,
referring to Alaric's first siege.
96. Cp. *Paradise Lost* i 351–4,

> *A multitude, like which the populous North*
> *Pour'd never from her frozen loins, to pass*
> *Rhene or the Danaw, when her barbarous Sons*
> *Came like a Deluge on the South ...*

100. calmly sad] See *n* to 'Cromwell' 186 (p. 20 below).

XVIII

And thus, beneath the clear, calm vault of heaven
In mournful loveliness that city lay,
105   And thus, amid the glorious hues of even
That city told of languor and decay:
Till what at morning's hour looked warm and bright
Was cold and sad beneath that breathless, voiceless
          night.

XIX

Soon was that stillness broken: like the cry
110   Of the hoarse onset of the surging wave,
Or louder rush of whirlwinds sweeping by,
Was the wild shout those Gothic myriads gave,
As towered on high, above their moonlit road,
Scenes where a Cæsar triumphed, or a Scipio trod.

XX

115   Think ye it strikes too slow, the sword of fate,
Think ye the avenger loiters on his way,
That your own hands must open wide the gate,
And your own voice[s] guide him to his prey?
Alas, it needs not; is it hard to know
Fate's threat'nings are not vain, the spoiler comes
120   not slow?

XXI

And were there none, to stand and weep alone,
And as the pageant swept before their eyes
To hear a dim and long forgotten tone
Tell of old times, and holiest memories,
125   Till fanciful regret and dreamy woe
Peopled night's voiceless shades with forms of long Ago?

XXII

Oh yes! if fancy feels, beyond to-day,
Thoughts of the past and of the future time,
How should that mightiest city pass away
130   And not bethink her of her glorious prime,
Whilst every chord that thrills at thoughts of home
Jarred with the bursting shout, 'They come, the Goth,
          they come'!

115. '"They (the Senate) were unable to guard against the secret conspiracy of their slaves and domestics." "At the hour of midnight the
Salarian gate was silently opened and the inhabitants were awakened by the
tremendous sound of the Gothic trumpet." – *Gibbon*.' A.'s note. See
Decline and Fall ed. *cit.* iii 321.

X...

The trumpet swells ye... ...der: they are here!
Yea, on your fathers' ... ...s the avengers tread;
135 Not this the time to v... ...upon the bier
That holds the ashes ... ...ur hero-dead;
If wreaths may twin... ...you, or laurels wave,
They shall not deck yo... ...e, but sanctify your grave.

...V

Alas! no wreaths a... ...re. Despair may teach
140 Cowards to conqu... ...d the weak to die;
Nor tongue of ma... ...r fear, nor shame can preach
So stern a lesson a... ...essity;
Yet here it speak... ...Yea, though all around
Unhallowed feet a... ...mpling on this haunted
        ground,

...XXV

145 Though every ... ...t feeling, every tie
That binds th... ...t of man with mightiest power,   *word swells*
All natural lo... ...human sympathy
Be crushed, a... ...traged in this bitter hour,
Here is no ec... ...he sound of home,
No shame that... ...hould rise to light a conquered
150   Rome.

XXVI

That trou... ...light is over: on the brow
Of thy ste... ..., thou mighty Capitol,
One form... ...s gazing: silently below
The mor... ...ists from tower and temple roll,
155 And lo!... ...rnal city, as they rise,
Bursts, in... ...c beauty, on her conqueror's eyes.

XXVII

Yes, t... ...e stood, upon that silent hill,
And... ...eneath his feet his conquest lay:

---

133. "'Adest ... ...s, trepidam urbem obsidet, turbat, irrumpit." –
Orosius Lib. ... ...39.' A.'s note, quoted with 'urbem' substituted for
'Romam' fro... ...bon's footnote, *Decline and Fall* ed. *cit.* iii 322.

2+M.A.

Unlike that ocean-city, gazing still
160   Smilingly forth upon her sunny bay,
     But o'er her vanished might and humbled pride
Mourning, as widowed Venice o'er her Adrian tide.

XXVIII

Breathe there not spirits on the peopled air?
Float there not voices on the murmuring wind?
165   Oh! sound there not some strains of sadness there,
To touch with sorrow even a victor's mind,
And wrest one tear from joy? Oh! who shall pen
The thoughts that touched thy breast, thou lonely con-
     queror, then?

XXIX

Perchance his wandering heart was far away,
170   Lost in dim memories of his early home,
And his young dreams of conquest; how to-day
Beheld him master of Imperial Rome,
Crowning his wildest hopes: perchance his eyes
As they looked sternly on, beheld new victories,

XXX

175   New dreams of wide dominion, mightier, higher,
Come floating up from the abyss of years;
Perchance that solemn sight might quench the fire
Even of that ardent spirit; hopes and fears
Might well be mingling at that murmured sigh,
180   Whispering from all around, 'All earthly things must
     die'.

159. *that ocean-city*] 'Naples –

> *Stabiasque, et in otia natam*
> *Parthenopen . . .*

Ovid, *Metamorphoses* xv 711–12.' A.'s note. The tomb of the siren Par-
thenope was shown at Naples; Stabiae was destroyed A.D. 79.

162. Cp. *Childe Harold* iv st. 11.

> *The spouseless Adriatic mourns her Lord,*
> *And annual marriage now no more renewed . . .*

169–70. Like the dying gladiator's, *Childe Harold* iv st. 141.

169 and 177, 181. Cp. the repetition in *Childe Harold* iv sts. 102 and 103,

> *Perchance she died in youth – it may be, bowed*
> *With woes . . .*
> *Perchance she died in age – surviving all . . .*

XXXI

Perchance that wondrous city was to him
But as one voiceless blank; a place of graves,
And recollections indistinct and dim,
Whose sons were conquerors once, and now were
185   It may be in that desolate sight his eye   [slaves:
Saw but another step to climb to victory!

XXXII

Alas! that fiery spirit little knew
The change of life, the nothingness of power,
How both were hastening, as they flowered and grew,
190   Nearer and nearer to their closing hour:
How every birth of time's miraculous womb
Swept off the withered leaves that hide the naked tomb.

XXXIII

One little year; that restless soul shall rest,
That frame of vigour shall be crumbling clay,
195   And tranquilly, above that troubled breast,
The sunny waters hold their joyous way:
And gently shall the murmuring ripples flow,
Nor wake the weary soul that slumbers on below.

XXXIV

Alas! far other thoughts might well be ours
200   And dash our holiest raptures while we gaze:

---

193. 'Alaric died after a sudden illness, while engaged in attempting the invasion of Sicily, A.D. 410, the very year of the third siege of Rome by his forces.' A.'s note.

195–8. 'For an account of the death and singular burial of the Gothic monarch, see Gibbon [*Decline and Fall* ed. *cit.* iii 333]. "By the labour of a captive multitude they forcibly diverted the course of the Busentinus, a small river that washes the walls of Consentia. The royal sepulchre, adorned with the splendid toils and trophies of Rome, was constructed in the vacant bed; and the waters were then restored to their natural channel; and the secret spot, where the remains of Alaric had been deposited, was for ever concealed by the inhuman massacre of the prisoners who had been employed to execute the work".' A'.s note corrected. Alaric's burial is described in 'The Grave of Alaric', a poem which A. could have seen in *Rugby Magazine* (No. 5 July 1836).

Energies wasted, unimprovéd hours,
The saddening visions of departed days:
And while they rise here might we stand alone,
And mingle with thy ruins somewhat of our own.

XXXV

205 Beautiful city! If departed things
Ever again put earthly likeness on,
Here should a thousand forms on fancy's wings
Float up to tell of ages that are gone:
Yea, though hand touch thee not, nor eye should see,
210 Still should the spirit hold communion, Rome, with
  thee!

XXXVI

Oh! it is bitter, that each fairest dream
Should fleet before us but to melt away;
That wildest visions still should loveliest seem
And soonest fade in the broad glare of day:
215 That while we feel the world is dull and low,
Gazing on thee, we wake to find it is not so.

XXXVII

A little while, alas, a little while,
And the same world has tongue, and ear, and eye,
The careless glance, the cold unmeaning smile,
220 The thoughtless word, the lack of sympathy!
Who would not turn him from the barren sea
And rest his weary eyes on the green land and thee!

XXXVIII

So pass we on. But oh! to harp aright
The vanished glories of thine early day,
225 There needs a minstrel of diviner might,
A holier incense than this feeble lay;
To chant thy requiem with more passionate breath,
And twine with bolder hand thy last memorial wreath!

201–2. Byronic lament – see, for example, *Lara* (1814) 325–6,

> *With thoughts of years in phantom chase misspent.*
> *And wasted powers for better purpose lent . . .*

217. Probably an unconscious echo of *John* xvi 16, 'A little while, and ye shall not see me: and again, a little while, and ye shall see me.'

2 Cromwell

A.'s Newdigate prize-poem completed by Feb. 1843: see his letter to J. D. Coleridge 2 March 1843 confessing the 'great stiffness' of what had been written slowly: 'This is a great fault in my poem, and is, ludicrously enough, united with the fault of over-rapidity in the last part, which I had to finish in two or three days. However, some of it, I think, is fairly good ... there are faults in the construction which alarm Stanley terribly ...' (*Life of J.D.C.* i 124). The subject reflects interest in Carlyle's defence of Cromwell in *Heroes and Hero-Worship* (1841) and his projected edition of *Cromwell's Letters and Speeches* (1845), but was probably aimed by the Professor of Poetry, James Garbett, at Tractarianism and specifically at the cult of Charles the Martyr in the university. The original title-page claims 'Cromwell' was 'recited in the Theatre, Oxford; June 28 1843', but see *Commentary* 325-6 (quoting *The Times* report of 29 June) for the uproar at Commemoration preventing the poem's delivery; also G. V. Cox's *Recollections of Oxford* (1868) 329-30: 'The Honorary Degrees ... were conferred in dumb-show. The Creweian Oration ... was read, but not a word of it was heard. Tired out and disgusted ... the Vice-Chancellor dissolved the Convocation, - the Prize Compositions being left unrecited.' The heroic couplet was traditional for the Newdigate; A.'s historical sources, except for Carlyle's lecture, are cited in his notes; the borrowings from Carlyle are discussed in K. Tillotson's Warton Lecture, *Matthew Arnold and Carlyle* (British Academy, 1956).

Published Oxford 1843 (second ed. 1863); reprinted without author's name in *Oxford Prize Poems* (1846); not reprinted by A.

SYNOPSIS

Introduction – The mountains and the sea the cradles of freedom – contrasted with the birth-place of Cromwell – His childhood and youth – The germs of his future character probably formed during his life of inaction – Cromwell at the moment of his intended embarkation – Retrospect of his past life and profligate youth – Temptations held out by the prospect of a life of rest in America – How far such rest was allowable – Vision of his future life – Different persons represented in it – Charles the First – Cromwell himself – His victories and maritime glory – Pym – Strafford – Laud – Hampden – Falkland – Milton – Charles the First – Cromwell on his death-bed – His character – Dispersion of the Vision – Conclusion.

> Schrecklich ist es, deiner Wahrheit
> Sterbliches Gefäss zu seyn.
> SCHILLER.

¶ 2. *Motto.* 'It is awful to be the mortal vessel of thy truth', Schiller's 'Kassandra' 63-4. Her complaint to Apollo is apt for the Carlylean hero 'elected' to a life of troubles and misunderstanding.

High fate is theirs, ye sleepless waves, whose ear
Learns Freedom's lesson from your voice of fear;
Whose spell-bound sense from childhood's hour hath
Familiar meanings in your mystic tone: [known
5   Sounds of deep import – voices that beguile
Age of its tears and childhood of its smile,
To yearn with speechless impulse to the free
And gladsome greetings of the buoyant sea!
High fate is theirs, who where the silent sky
10   Stoops to the soaring mountains, live and die;
Who scale the cloud-capped height, or sink to rest
In the deep stillness of its shelt'ring breast;
Around whose feet the exulting waves have sung,
The eternal hills their giant shadows flung.

15   No wonders nursed thy childhood; not for thee
Did the waves chant their song of liberty!
Thine was no mountain home, where Freedom's form
Abides enthroned amid the mist and storm,
And whispers to the listening winds, that swell
With solemn cadence round her citadel!
20   These had no sound for thee: that cold calm eye
Lit with no rapture as the storm swept by,
To mark with shivered crest the reeling wave
Hide his torn head beneath his sunless cave;
25   Or hear 'mid circling crags, the impatient cry
Of the pent winds, that scream in agony!

14. 'This is in allusion to the idea expressed in the twelfth of Mr. Wordsworth's Sonnets [dedicated] to Liberty [*title* 1845 and thereafter: Poems
Dedicated to National Liberty and Independence]: –

> *Two Voices are there: one is of the sea,*
> *[One of the mountains; each a mighty Voice:*
> *In both from age to age thou didst rejoice,*
> *They were thy chosen music, Liberty!]*

contrasting it with the fact of Cromwell's birth-place having been the fen
country of Huntingdonshire, where he lived till he was forty years old.'
A.'s note.

15–26. Cp. *The Oxford Ars Poetica* (1853) in *Three Oxford Ironies* ed. G.
Gordon 114 and *n.*

> *If there's no moss, 'no columns crown the scene,*
> *Clasped by pale ivy, decked with myrtles green,'*
> *To twenty verses NO prefixed should be,*
> *Minutely telling all you didn't see . . .*

and Gordon's preface 26–9: 'It is a method, of course, not confinable to

Yet all high sounds that mountain children hear
Flashed from thy soul upon thine inward ear;
All Freedom's mystic language – storms that roar
30   By hill or wave, the mountain or the shore –
All these had stirred thy spirit, and thine eye
In common sights read secret sympathy;
Till all bright thoughts that hills or waves can yield,
Decked the dull waste, and the familiar field;
35   Or wondrous sounds from tranquil skies were borne
Far o'er the glistening sheets of windy corn:
Skies – that, unbound by clasp of mountain chain,
Slope stately down and melt into the plain;
Sounds – such as erst the lone wayfaring man
40   Caught, as he journeyed, from the lips of Pan;
Or that mysterious cry that smote with fear,
Like sounds from other worlds, the Spartan's ear,
While, o'er the dusty plain, the murmurous throng
Of Heaven's embattled myriads swept along.

45   Say not such dreams are idle: for the man
Still toils to perfect what the child began;

Ruins, but capable of infinite application. There is a palmary example ...
in Matthew Arnold's *Cromwell* ... He has written twenty-six lines about
the sea and the mountains, which he was determined in any case to
describe, and he has done so because Cromwell lived remote from either ...
It is an ancient game ... known in Greece as τὸ 'Ἀντιμάχου: The Dodge
of Antimachus.' For Gordon's reference to Antimachus see Aristotle,
Rhetoric iii 6 (7).
36 and *114* below. Cp. Tennyson, 'Ulysses' 17,
          Far on the ringing plains of windy Troy.
'Ulysses' first appeared in *Poems* (1842).
39–40. See Herodotus vi 105: 'The general sent as a herald to Sparta
Phidippides, an Athenian ... a runner of long distances ... This man ...
when he was in the Parthenian hills above Tegea, met with Pan; who,
calling to Phidippides by name, bade him say to the Athenians, "Why is it
that ye take no thought for me ...?"' A.'s reference.
41–4. 'The vision of Demaratus on the plain of Eleusis. – Herodotus viii
65.' A.'s note. Demaratus saw a cloud of dust 'as it were raised by the feet
of about thirty thousand men' and heard a cry like 'the Iacchus-song of the
mysteries'.
45–6. Cp. Wordsworth, 'My heart leaps up' 7,
          The Child is father of the Man
(used by W. with following two lines as motto of the 'Immortality
Ode').

And thoughts, that were but outlines, time engraves
Deep on his life; and childhood's baby waves,
Made rough with care, become the changeful sea,
50   Stemmed by the strength of manhood fearlessly;
And fleeting thoughts, that on the lonely wild
Swept o'er the fancy of that heedless child,
Perchance had quickened with a living truth
The cold dull soil of his unfruitful youth;
55   Till, with his daily life, a life, that threw
Its shadows o'er the future, flowered and grew,
With common cares unmingling, and apart,
Haunting the shrouded chambers of his heart;
Till life, unstirred by action, life became
60   Threaded and lightened by a track of flame;
An inward light, that, with its streaming ray,
On the dark current of his changeless day,
Bound all his being with a silver chain –
Like a swift river through a silent plain!

65   High thoughts were his, when by the gleaming flood,
With heart new strung, and stern resolve, he stood;
Where rode the tall dark ships, whose loosened sail
All idly fluttered in the eastern gale;
High thoughts were his; but Memory's glance the while
70   Fell on the cherished past with tearful smile;
And peaceful joys and gentler thoughts swept by,
Like summer lightnings o'er a darkened sky.
The peace of childhood, and the thoughts that roam,
Like loving shadows, round that childhood's home;
75   Joys that had come and vanished, half unknown,
Then slowly brightened, as the days had flown;

58. *shrouded*] A Carlylean epithet.
59–64. Cp. Carlyle, *Heroes and Hero-Worship* (1841), *Works* ed. H. D.
Traill v 217, 'An outer hull of chaotic confusion . . . and yet such a clear
determinate man's energy working in the heart of that . . . The ray as of
pure starlight and fire . . .' Note A.'s first and confusing use of river
imagery. Cromwell's outward life is first a 'dark current' and then 'a
silent plain' through which the swift river of inward life flows.
65–8. '"Eight ships, lying in the Thames, and ready to sail, were detained
by order of the council; [and in these were embarked Sir Arthur Hazelrig,
John Hambden, John Pym, and Oliver Cromwell, who had resolved for
ever to abandon their native country]." – Hume [*History of England*, 1819
ed.] vi 309.' A.'s note, which refers to Cromwell's supposed intention to
emigrate to New England in 1637, corrected and expanded.

Years that were sweet or sad, becalmed or tossed
On life's wild waves – the living and the lost.
Youth stained with follies: and the thoughts of ill
80   Crushed, as they rose, by manhood's sterner will.
Repentant prayers, that had been strong to save –
And the first sorrow, which is childhood's grave!
All shapes that haunt remembrance; soft and fair,
Like a green land at sunset, all were there!
85   Eyes that he knew, old faces, unforgot,
Gazed sadly down on his unrestful lot,
And Memory's calm clear voice and mournful eye
Chilled every buoyant hope that floated by;
Like frozen winds on southern vales that blow
90   From a far land – the children of the snow –
O'er flowering plain and blossomed meadow fling
The cold dull shadow of their icy wing.
    Then Fancy's roving visions, bold and free,
A moment dispossessed reality.
95   All airy hopes that idle hearts can frame,
Like dreams between two sorrows, went and came:
Fond hearts that fain would clothe the unwelcome truth
Of toilsome manhood in the dreams of youth,
To bend in rapture at some idol throne,
100   Some lifeless soulless phantom of their own;
Some shadowy vision of a tranquil life,
Of joys unclouded, years unstirred by strife;
Of sleep unshadowed by a dream of woe;
Of many a lawny hill, and streams with silver flow;
105   Of giant mountains by the western main,
The sunless forest, and the sealike plain;
Those lingering hopes of coward hearts, that still
Would play the traitor to the steadfast will,
One moment's space, perchance, might charm his eye
110   From the stern future and the years gone by.
One moment's space might waft him far away
To western shores – the death-place of the day!
Might paint the calm, sweet peace – the rest of home,
Far o'er the pathless waste of labouring foam –
115   Peace, that recalled his childish hours anew,
More calm, more deep, than childhood ever knew!
Green happy places – like a flowery lea
Between the barren mountains and the stormy sea.

106. *sealike plain*] Cp. Shelley, 'Lines written among the Euganean Hills'
90–1,

> *Beneath is spread like a green sea*
> *The waveless plain of Lombardy . . .*

2*

O pleasant rest, if once the race were run!
120   O happy slumber, if the day were done!
Dreams that were sweet at eve, at morn were sin;
With cares to conquer, and a goal to win!
His were no tranquil years – no languid sleep –
No life of dreams – no home beyond the deep –
125   No softening ray – no visions false and wild –
No glittering hopes on life's grey distance smiled –
Like isles of sunlight on a mountain's brow,
Lit by a wandering gleam, we know not how,
Far on the dim horizon, when the sky
130   With glooming clouds broods dark and heavily.

Then his eye slumbered, and the chain was broke
That bound his spirit, and his heart awoke;
Then – like a kingly river – swift and strong
The future rolled its gathering tides along!
135   The shout of onset and the shriek of fear
Smote, like the rush of waters, on his ear;
And his eye kindled with the kindling fray,
The surging battle and the mailed array!
All wondrous deeds the coming days should see,
140   And the long Vision of the years to be.
Pale phantom hosts, like shadows, faint and far,
Councils, and armies, and the pomp of war!
And one swayed all, who wore a kingly crown,
Until another rose and smote him down.
145   A form that towered above his brother men;
A form he knew – but it was shrouded then!
With stern, slow steps – unseen – yet still the same,
By leaguered tower and tented field it came;
By Naseby's hill, o'er Marston's heathy waste,
150   By Worcester's field, the warrior-vision passed!
From their deep base, thy beetling cliffs, Dunbar,
Rang, as he trod them, with the voice of war!
The soldier kindled at his words of fire;
The statesman quailed before his glance of ire!
155   Worn was his brow with cares no thought could scan;

but the phrase occurs in A. P. Stanley's Rugby prize-poem 'Charles
Martel' (1832).
149-51. The places named were battlefields of the Civil War.
151-2. Probably suggested by Tennyson, 'Morte d'Arthur' (1842) 188-90,
          The bare black cliff clang'd round him, as he based
          His feet on juts of slippery crag that rang
          Sharp-smitten with the dint of armed heels.

His step was loftier than the steps of man;
And the winds told his glory – and the wave
Sonorous witness to his empire gave!

     What forms are these, that with complaining sound
160   And slow, reluctant steps are gathering round?
Forms that with him shall tread life's changing stage,
Cross his lone path, or share his pilgrimage?
There, as he gazed, a wondrous band – they came,
Pym's look of hate, and Strafford's glance of flame:
165   There Laud, with noiseless steps and glittering eye,
In priestly garb, a frail old man, went by.
His drooping head bowed meekly on his breast;
His hands were folded, like a saint at rest!
There Hampden bent him o'er his saddle bow,
170   And death's cold dews bedimmed his earnest brow;
Still turned to watch the battle – still forgot
Himself, his sufferings, in his country's lot!
There Falkland eyed the strife that would not cease,
Shook back his tangled locks, and murmured – 'Peace!'

157–8. '"It is just to say, that the maritime glory of England may first be traced from the era of the commonwealth in a track of continuous light." – Hallam's *Constitutional History* [1832 ed.] ii [356].' A.'s note.

164. Pym played the main part in Strafford's downfall.

165–8. 'The [Tractarian] enthusiasm should be borne in mind as we read the description of Laud,' *Commentary* 323. A. is closer to Wordsworth here ('Ecclesiastical Sonnets' xlv where Laud is 'an old weak Man') than to Carlyle or Dr. Arnold.

169–72. '"His head bending down, and his hands resting on his horse's neck, he was seen riding off the field." – Lord Nugent's *Memorials of Hampden* (1831) ii 435.' A.'s note. Hampden died 24 June 1643, six days after being wounded at Chalgrove Field.

173–4. '"In his clothes and habit, which he had minded before always with more neatness, and industry, and expence, than is usual to so great a soul he was not now only incurious, but too negligent." – Clarendon.' A.'s note corrected. See Clarendon's *History of the Rebellion* ed. W. D. Macray (1888) iii 188. 'Falkland' in *Mixed Essays* (1879), *Works* x 197–226, which gives A.'s mature attitude to the issues of the Civil Wars, cites both this and part of the famous passage immediately following (omitted in 1843, probably as too familiar): ' . . . and, sitting amongst his friends, often after a deep silence and frequent sighs, [he] would, with a shrill and sad accent, ingeminate the word *Peace, Peace* . . .' Falkland, the only fully sympathetic public figure of the period to A., would have provided a more welcome Newdigate subject than Cromwell, who was described by A. in 1879 as 'the Philistine of genius of politics'.

175   With feet that spurned the ground, lo! Milton there
        Stood like a statue; and his face was fair –
        Fair beyond human beauty; and his eye,
        That knew not earth, soared upwards to the sky!

        He, too, was there – it was the princely boy,
180   The child-companion of his childish joy!
        But oh! how changed – those deathlike features wore
        Childhood's bright glance and sunny smile no more!
        That brow so sad, so pale, so full of care—
        What trace of careless childhood lingered there?
185   What spring of youth in that majestic mien,
        So sadly calm, so kingly, so serene?
        No – all was changed – the monarch wept alone,
        Between a ruined church and shattered throne!
        Friendless and hopeless – like a lonely tree,
190   On some bare headland, straining mournfully,
        That all night long its weary moan doth make
        To the vexed waters of a mountain lake!
        Still, as he gazed, the phantom's mournful glance
        Shook the deep slumber of his deathlike trance;
195   Like some forgotten strain that haunts us still,
        That calm eye followed, turn him where he will;
        Till the pale monarch, and the long array,
        Passed, like a morning mist, in tears away!

        Then all his dream was troubled, and his soul
200   Thrilled with a dread no slumber could control;
        On that dark form his eyes had gazed before,
        Nor known it then; but it was veiled no more!
        In broad clear light the ghastly vision shone—
        That form was his – those features were his own!
205   The night of terrors and the day of care,
        The years of toil, all, all were written there!

179–80. 'Alluding to the stories of Cromwell's childish intimacy with
Charles the First.' A.'s note.
186. sadly calm] Cp. 'Alaric' 100 (p. 7 above), 'How calmly sad...' and
'Obermann Once More' 48 (p. 521 below), 'sad, tranquil lore...' 'Calm'
and 'sad' are among A.'s favourite epithets.
189–92. Tennysonian vignette. Cp. 'The Palace of Art' (1842) 249–52,

> *A still salt pool, lock'd in with bars of sand,*
>   *Left on the shore; that hears all night*
> *The plunging seas draw backward from the land*
>   *Their moon-led waters white.*

Sad faces watched around him, and his breath
Came faint and feeble in the embrace of death.
The gathering tempest, with its voice of fear,
210 His latest loftiest music, smote his ear!
That day of boundless hope and promise high,
That day that hailed his triumphs, saw him die!
Then from those whitening lips, as death drew near,
The imprisoning chains fell off, and all was clear!
215 Like lowering clouds, that at the close of day,
Bathed in a blaze of sunset, melt away;
And with its clear calm tones, that dying prayer
Cheered all the failing hearts that sorrowed there!

A Life – whose ways no human thought could scan,
220 A life – that was not as the life of man;
A life – that wrote its purpose with a sword,
Moulding itself in action, not in word!
Rent with tumultuous thoughts, whose conflict rung
Deep through his soul and choked his faltering tongue;

209. 'Clarendon mentions a great storm which attended the death of Cromwell.' A.'s note. See *History of the Rebellion* ed. *cit.* vi 91, ' . . . a day very memorable for the greatest storm of wind that had ever been known, for some hours before and after his death . . .'
210. '"He was a great lover of Musick, and he entertained the most skilful in that science in his pay and family." – *The Perfect Politician* [by H. Fletcher, 1681 ed. 210].' A.'s note.
211–12. 'Cromwell died on his fortunate day, the anniversary of Dunbar and Worcester, – September 3rd.' A.'s note (adapted from Byron's note to *Childe Harold* iv st. 85).
214–18. 'There is a remarkable contrast between the perfect clearness of the celebrated prayer Cromwell is recorded to have uttered on his death bed, and the confusedness of the speeches which are attributed to him.' A.'s note.
219–34. A.'s hurried style here illustrates the kind of writing mocked in *The Oxford Ars Poetica* ed. *cit.* 120:

> *Don't spare your dashes – or your semicolons;*
> *(Fools by these aids have often passed for Solons)*
> *And let each sentence, by anticipation*
> *Conclude with full-sized notes of admiration!!*

221–2. Cp. Carlyle, *Heroes and Hero-Worship* (1841), *Works* ed. *cit.* 233, '. . . not used to *speak* the great inorganic thought of him, but to act it rather!'
223–4. Cp. Carlyle, *loc. cit.* 233, 235: 'A helplessness of utterance, in such bursting fulness of meaning . . . *speech* lying imprisoned in these broken rude tortuous utterances . . .'

225   A heart that recked not of the countless dead,
       That strewed the blood-stained path where Empire led;
       A daring hand, that shrunk not to fulfil
       The thought that spurred it; and a dauntless will,
       Bold action's parent; and a piercing ken
230   Through the dark chambers of the hearts of men,
       To read each thought and teach that master mind
       The fears and hopes and passions of mankind;
       All these were thine – Oh thought of fear! – and thou,
       Stretched on that bed of death, art nothing now.

                    *   *   *   *

235   Then all his vision faded, and his soul
       Sprang from its sleep! and lo, the waters roll
       Once more beneath him; and the fluttering sail,
       Where the dark ships rode proudly, wooed the gale;
       And the wind murmured round him, and he stood
240   Once more alone beside the gleaming flood.

239–40. Tennysonian.

3 To a Gipsy Child by the Sea-shore
DOUGLAS, ISLE OF MAN

Date of composition unknown, but probably written *c.* August 1843 or
1844 (the earlier date is the more likely) and revised later before publication
in *1849*: see A.'s letter of 1869 to F. T. Palgrave, ' . . . a very youthful
production . . .' (*Russell* 43) and *Manchester Guardian* 18 May 1888 (unsigned obituary of A., but by Tom Arnold), 'In 1843 or 1844 the family
passed part of the long vacation at Douglas in the Isle of Man. Matthew
and a companion were one afternoon on the pier, watching the passengers
landed from the Liverpool steamer. There was a crowd, and just in front
of them stood a poor woman; she might have been a gipsy . . . she was
looking down at the steamer, and the child in her arms was looking backwards over her shoulder. Its pitiful wan face and sad dark eyes rested on
Matthew for some time without change of expression.' The identity of the
Guardian obituary writer is established by Tom A.'s letter (undated, but
probably 1895) which tells the same story of the poem's origin and adds
that the writer was A.'s 'companion' and that looking at the gipsy child
A. became 'completely abstracted' (see G. C. Macaulay's *Poems by
Matthew Arnold* (1896) 114–15). This letter dates the occasion erroneously
in Autumn 1842 when the Arnold family did not visit Douglas; A. was in
the Isle of Man again in 1845, but Tom A. did not then accompany him.
The poem was extensively revised for *1869*, but within a month (26 June
1869) A. wrote to his mother, 'I suppose I must change back the "Gipsy

Child" to its old form, as no one seems to like the new one' (*L* ii 15); and
in *1877* it was restored to its original shape and classified as an 'Early
Poem'.

A. adopts from Wordsworth's 'Immortality Ode' the idea of the child's
recollection of a pre-natal happiness and of the fading of this recollection
in the course of life, but gives it a tragic significance that is pointedly un-
Wordsworthian. For the unusual 'positive' pessimism, which is also found
in 'Mycerinus', another rejection of a Wordsworthian viewpoint, see
headn. to that poem (p. 26 below).

Published *1849*; reprinted *1855*, *1869*, etc.

> Who taught this pleading to unpractised eyes?
> Who hid such import in an infant's gloom?
> Who lent thee, child, this meditative guise?
> Who massed, round that slight brow, these clouds of
> [doom?

¶ 3. *1–4*. In *1869* only this stanza cancelled and ll. 5–22 rewritten as follows:

> *The port lies bright under the August sun,*
> *Gay shine the waters and the cluster'd pier;*
> *Blithely, this morn, old Ocean's work is done,*
> *And blithely do these sea-birds hover near.*
>
> *Poor child, whom the light air of childish joy*
> *Wafts not from thine own thoughts – of graver strain,*
> *Surely, than those which should thine age employ –*
> *A weight of meditation mixt with pain!*
>
> *Blithe all else stirs, thou stirrest not – averse*
> *From thine own mother's breast, that knows not thee,*
> *With eyes which seek thine eyes thou dost converse,*
> *And thy dark mournful vision rests on me.*
>
> *Glooms that go deep as thine I have not known,*
> *Moods of fantastic sadness, nothing worth!*
> *Musings, that ere they could grow ripe were flown,*
> *And grief that heal'd at every smile of earth.*
>
> *Whose mood shall fancy liken to thy woe?*
> *Some dreamer's, who, far off, a summer's day . . .*

A. also tinkered with the text of later stanzas of the poem in *1869*, but these
experimental changes were with one exception discarded in *1877*.

4. clouds of doom] Cp. 'Memorial Verses' 68 (p. 229 below),

> *The cloud of mortal destiny . . .*

In *1855* only this line reads:

> *What clouds thy forehead, and fore-dates thy doom?*

5   Lo! sails that gleam a moment and are gone;
The swinging waters, and the clustered pier.
Not idly Earth and Ocean labour on,
Nor idly do these sea-birds hover near.

But thou, whom superfluity of joy
10   Wafts not from thine own thoughts, nor longings vain,
Nor weariness, the full-fed soul's annoy –
Remaining in thy hunger and thy pain;

Thou, drugging pain by patience; half averse
From thine own mother's breast, that knows not thee;
15   With eyes which sought thine eyes thou didst converse,
And that soul-searching vision fell on me.

Glooms that go deep as thine I have not known:
Moods of fantastic sadness, nothing worth.
Thy sorrow and thy calmness are thine own:
20   Glooms that enhance and glorify this earth.

What mood wears like complexion to thy woe?
His, who in mountain glens, at noon of day,
Sits rapt, and hears the battle break below?
– Ah! thine was not the shelter, but the fray.

25   Some exile's, mindful how the past was glad?
Some angel's, in an alien planet born?
– No exile's dream was ever half so sad,
Nor any angel's sorrow so forlorn.

9. *superfluity of joy*] A. is glancing at sts. 3 and 4 of Wordsworth's 'Immortality Ode' and at 'the Child among his newborn blisses' (l. 86).
11. *annoy*] Discomfort. A poeticism.
22-3. Cp. Lucretius, *De Rerum Natura* ii 5-6,

> *suave etiam belli certamina magna tueri*
> *per campos instructa tua sine parte pericli.*

and the cancelled first stanza of 'The Lord's Messengers' (p. 452 below).
25-6. The *1869* reading. In *1849*, *1855*,

> *What exile's, changing bitter thoughts with glad?*
> *What seraph's, in some alien planet born?*

Is the calm thine of stoic souls, who weigh
30   Life well, and find it wanting, nor deplore;
But in disdainful silence turn away,
Stand mute, self-centred, stern, and dream no more?

Or do I wait, to hear some gray-haired king
Unravel all his many-coloured lore;
35   Whose mind hath known all arts of governing,
Mused much, loved life a little, loathed it more?

Down the pale cheek long lines of shadow slope,
Which years, and curious thought, and suffering give.
– Thou hast foreknown the vanity of hope,
40   Foreseen thy harvest – yet proceed'st to live.

O meek anticipant of that sure pain
Whose sureness gray-haired scholars hardly learn!
What wonder shall time breed, to swell thy strain?
What heavens, what earth, what suns shalt thou discern?

45   Ere the long night, whose stillness brooks no star,
Match that funereal aspect with her pall,
I think thou wilt have fathomed life too far,
Have known too much – or else forgotten all.

29–32. A.'s early interest in Stoicism had a Byronic element, as 'disdainful' (l. 31) sufficiently indicates. A more genuine interest in Stoic attitudes was probably stimulated by A.'s reading of Senancour's *Obermann* in 1846–7; he studied Epictetus first in 1848 – see headn. to 'To a Friend' (p. 104 below).

33–4. Recollected in writing 'The Scholar-Gipsy' 182–6 (p. 341 below),

> *. . . one,*
> *Who most has suffered, takes dejectedly*
> *His seat upon the intellectual throne;*
> *And all his store of sad experience he*
> *Lays bare of wretched days . . .*

34. many-coloured] An epithet used elsewhere by A. only in 'Resignation' 61 (p. 87 below),

> *Our wavering, many-coloured line . . .*

'Resignation' was probably begun in 1843.

39–40. Cp. 'Resignation' 231–4 (p. 93 below),

> *Blame thou not, therefore, him who dares*
> *Judge vain beforehand human cares;*
> *Whose natural insight can discern*
> *!What through experience others learn . . .*

The Guide of our dark steps a triple veil
50   Betwixt our senses and our sorrows keeps;
Hath sown with cloudless passages the tale
Of grief, and eased us with a thousand sleeps.

Ah! not the nectarous poppy lovers use,
Not daily labour's dull, Lethæan spring,
55   Oblivion in lost angels can infuse
Of the soiled glory and the trailing wing.

And though thou glean, what strenuous gleaners may,
In the thronged fields where winning comes by strife;
And though the just sun gild, as mortals pray,
60   Some reaches of thy storm-vexed stream of life;

Though that blank sunshine blind thee; though the cloud
That severed the world's march and thine be gone;
Though ease dulls grace, and Wisdom be too proud
To halve a lodging that was all her own –

65   Once, ere the day decline, thou shalt discern,
Oh once, ere night, in thy success, thy chain!
Ere the long evening close, thou shalt return,
And wear this majesty of grief again.

55–6. Cp. Wordsworth, 'Immortality Ode' 63–5.
> ... *not in utter nakedness,*
> *But trailing clouds of glory do we come*
> *From God, who is our home* ...

59. *mortals*] all men *1849–69.*
60. *stream of life*] A commonplace with late-Augustan and Romantic poets
that A. made his own and developed variously in 'The Buried Life', 'The
Future' (pp. 271 and 263 below) and other poems. The origin of the
comparison is indicated by Senancour's comment, 'La fuite de l'eau est
comme la fuite de nos années' (*Obermann* (Lettre xc) ii 230).
68. Cp. *Lélia* (1833), *Œuvres de G. Sand* (1855 ed.) i 58 'La majesté pleine
de tristresse qui entourait Lélia...', which probably echoes Pascal's
'misères d'un roi depossédé'.

4 Mycerinus

Date of composition unknown, but (?) 1843–4 with revision and perhaps
addition of some lines *c.* 1848 (see *n.* to ll. 49–54 below). The bitterness of
the stanzaic part of the poem (understandable if written not long after
Dr. Arnold's sudden death in June 1842, particularly as A. had been warned
that he had inherited his father's heart defect), perhaps the source in
Herodotus (translated in family circle by Dr. A., who also set 'Mycerinus'
as a Rugby prize-poem subject in 1831), and some stylistic touches, point

to an early date. J. D. Coleridge remarked in the *Christian Remembrancer* xxvii (1854) 313 on the imitation of Wordsworth's style in 'Laodamia' – the stanza of which A. uses ll. 1–78 – without noticing that A. writes throughout in blunt opposition to Wordsworth's acceptance of heavenly 'justice' in the poem. In *1849* A. indicates his source as Herodotus ii 133; in *1853* substitutes this note (conflating sentences from 129 and 133): 'After Cephren, Mycerinus, son of Cheops, reigned over Egypt. He abhorred his father's courses, and judged his subjects more justly than any of their kings had done. – To him there came an oracle from the city of Buto, to the effect that he was to live but six years longer, and to die in the seventh year from that time.' The rest of the passage used by A. runs (in the Loeb translation):

'The king deemed this unjust, and sent back to the oracle a message of reproach, blaming the God: why must he die so soon who was pious, whereas his father and uncle had lived long, who shut up the temples, and regarded not the gods, and destroyed men. But a second utterance from the place of divination declared to him that his good deeds were the very cause of shortening his life; for he had done what was contrary to fate; Egypt should have been afflicted for an hundred and fifty years . . . Hearing this, he knew that his doom was fixed. Therefore he caused many lamps to be made, and would light these at nightfall and drink and make merry; by day or night he never ceased from revelling, roaming to the marsh country and the groves and wherever he heard of the likeliest places of pleasure. Thus he planned, that by turning night into day he might make his six years into twelve and so prove the oracle false.'

Published *1849*; reprinted *1853* (*1854*, *1857*), *1869*, etc.

> 'Not by the justice that my father spurned,
> Not for the thousands whom my father slew,
> Altars unfed and temples overturned,
> Cold hearts and thankless tongues, where thanks are
> 5   Fell this dread voice from lips that cannot lie,   [due;
> Stern sentence of the Powers of Destiny.
>
> 'I will unfold my sentence and my crime.
> My crime – that, rapt in reverential awe,
> I sate obedient, in the fiery prime
> 10   Of youth, self-governed, at the feet of Law;
> Ennobling this dull pomp, the life of kings,
> By contemplation of diviner things.

¶ 4. *10. self-governed*] Cp. Protesilaus to his wife, Wordsworth's 'Laodamia' 139–40,

> *And Thou, though strong in love, art all too weak*
> *In reason, in self-government too slow . . .*

'My father loved injustice, and lived long;
Crowned with gray hairs he died, and full of sway.
15   I loved the good he scorned, and hated wrong –
The Gods declare my recompense to-day.
I looked for life more lasting, rule more high;
And when six years are measured, lo, I die!

'Yet surely, O my people, did I deem
20   Man's justice from the all-just Gods was given;
A light that from some upper fount did beam,
Some better archetype, whose seat was heaven;
A light that, shining from the blest abodes,
Did shadow somewhat of the life of Gods.

25   'Mere phantoms of man's self-tormenting heart,
Which on the sweets that woo it dares not feed!
Vain dreams, which quench our pleasures, then depart,
When the duped soul, self-mastered, claims its meed;
When, on the strenuous just man, Heaven bestows,
30   Crown of his struggling life, an unjust close!

'Seems it so light a thing, then, austere Powers,
To spurn man's common lure, life's pleasant things?
Seems there no joy in dances crowned with flowers,
Love, free to range, and regal banquetings?
35   Bend ye on these, indeed, an unmoved eye,
Not Gods but ghosts, in frozen apathy?

'Or is it that some Force, too wise, too strong,
Even for yourselves to conquer or beguile,
Sweeps earth, and heaven, and men, and gods along,
40   Like the broad volume of the insurgent Nile?
And the great powers we serve, themselves may be
Slaves of a tyrannous necessity?

16. A. omits the reason given by the oracle for the short reign of Mycerinus.
22. *archetype*] Used this once; and therefore probably owed to A.'s Oxford
reading of Plato, 1843–6.
28–30. These lines could well refer to Dr. Arnold's death. Cp. *English
Review* xiii (March 1850) 211–12, 'The very first longer poem ...,
"Mycerinus", is a kind of apotheosis of despair; it looks as if suggested by
a father's fate. At the same time, it seems almost a profession of atheism.'
39 *Sweeps*] Whirls *1849–57*; Bears *1869–81*. With the original reading cp.
'Resignation' 277 (p. 95 below),

        In action's dizzying eddy whirled ...

40. The *1869* reading. In *1849–57*,

        Like the broad rushing of the column'd [*insurged* 1853–7] *Nile.*

'Or in mid-heaven, perhaps, your golden cars,
Where earthly voice climbs never, wing their flight,
45   And in wild hunt, through mazy tracts of stars,
Sweep in the sounding stillness of the night?
Or in deaf ease, on thrones of dazzling sheen,
Drinking deep draughts of joy, ye dwell serene?

'Oh, wherefore cheat our youth, if thus it be,
50   Of one short joy, one lust, one pleasant dream?
Stringing vain words of powers we cannot see,
Blind divinations of a will supreme;
Lost labour! when the circumambient gloom
But hides, if Gods, Gods careless of our doom?

55   'The rest I give to joy. Even while I speak,
My sand runs short; and – as yon star-shot ray,
Hemmed by two banks of cloud, peers pale and weak,
Now, as the barrier closes, dies away –
Even so do past and future intertwine,
60   Blotting this six years' space, which yet is mine.

47–8. Cp. Lucretius, *De Rerum Natura* ii 646–51,

> omnis enim per se divom natura necessest
> immortali aevo summa cum pace fruatur
> semota ab nostris rebus seiunctaque longe;
> nam privata dolore omni, privata periclis,
> ipsa suis pollens opibus, nil indiga nostri,
> nec bene promeritis capitur, neque tangitur ira . . .

and iii 18–22,

> apparet divum numen sedesque quietae
> quas neque concutiunt venti nec nubila nimbis
> aspergunt neque nix acri concreta pruina
> cana cadens violat semperque innubilus aether
> integit, et large diffuso lumine ridet.

See also Tennyson's 'The Lotos-Eaters' (1842), Choric Song 110–19, where
the Gods in their golden houses enjoy the 'music' of men's lamentations.
49–54. These lines show that 'self-governed' (l. 10) and 'self-mastered'
(l. 28) merely mean obedience to an external law divinely sanctioned.
Mycerinus holds that we should enjoy ourselves if there is no such law.
The contradiction between this position and the picture of him as an
Egyptian Marcus Aurelius in ll. 107–11 is hardly avoided by the repetition
of 'It may be . . .' (ll. 107, 112). Conceivably ll. 100–27 were added *c.* 1848
when A. began to study Stoicism seriously – see *n.* to 'To a Gipsy Child
. . .' 29–32 (p. 25 above) and headn. to 'To a Friend' (p. 104 below) – and
the poem ended originally with the poetic flourish of l. 99.
53. *circumambient*] A Carlylean epithet.

'Six years – six little years – six drops of time!
Yet suns shall rise, and many moons shall wane,
And old men die, and young men pass their prime,
And languid pleasure fade and flower again, ·
65   And the dull Gods behold, ere these are flown,
Revels more deep, joy keener than their own.

'Into the silence of the groves and woods
I will go forth; though something would I say –
Something – yet what, I know not; for the Gods
70   The doom they pass revoke not, nor delay;
And prayers, and gifts, and tears, are fruitless all,
And the night waxes, and the shadows fall.

'Ye men of Egypt, ye have heard your king!
I go, and I return not. But the will
75   Of the great Gods is plain; and ye must bring
Ill deeds, ill passions, zealous to fulfil
Their pleasure, to their feet; and reap their praise,
The praise of Gods, rich boon! and length of days.'

– So spake he, half in anger, half in scorn;
80   And one loud cry of grief and of amaze
Broke from his sorrowing people; so he spake,
And turning, left them there; and with brief pause,
Girt with a throng of revellers, bent his way
To the cool region of the groves he loved.
85   There by the river-banks he wandered on,
From palm-grove on to palm-grove, happy trees,

61. Cp. 'Alaric at Rome' 193 (p. 11 above),

> *One little year; that restless soul shall rest . . .*

and Byron's *Manfred* II ii 173,

> *How few – how less than few – wherein the soul . . .*

79–99. Tennysonian, according to many *1849* reviewers. See, for example
Blackwood's Magazine lxvi (Sept. 1849) 344.
83. revellers] Cp. Protesilaus' dislike of revelry, Wordsworth's 'Laodamia' 110–13,

> *'Ill', said he,*
> *'The end of man's existence I discerned,*
> *Who from ignoble games and revelry*
> *Could draw, when we had parted, vain delight . . .'*

86. happy trees] A Miltonism. See *Baum* 15, quoting *Paradise Lost* i 469,
> *Of* Abbana *and* Pharphar, *lucid streams.*

Their smooth tops shining sunward, and beneath
Burying their unsunned stems in grass and flowers;
Where in one dream the feverish time of youth
90   Might fade in slumber, and the feet of joy
Might wander all day long and never tire.
Here came the king, holding high feast, at morn,
Rose-crowned; and ever, when the sun went down,
A hundred lamps beamed in the tranquil gloom,
95   From tree to tree all through the twinkling grove,
Revealing all the tumult of the feast –
Flushed guests, and golden goblets foamed with wine;
While the deep-burnished foliage overhead
Splintered the silver arrows of the moon.
100   It may be that sometimes his wondering soul
From the loud joyful laughter of his lips
Might shrink half startled, like a guilty man
Who wrestles with his dream; as some pale shape
Gliding half hidden through the dusky stems,
105   Would thrust a hand before the lifted bowl,
Whispering: *A little space, and thou art mine!*
It may be on that joyless feast his eye
Dwelt with mere outward seeming; he, within,
Took measure of his soul, and knew its strength,
110   And by that silent knowledge, day by day,
Was calmed, ennobled, comforted, sustained.
It may be; but not less his brow was smooth,
And his clear laugh fled ringing through the gloom,
And his mirth quailed not at the mild reproof
115   Sighed out by winter's sad tranquillity;
Nor, palled with its own fullness, ebbed and died
In the rich languor of long summer-days;
Nor withered when the palm-tree plumes, that roofed

99. Cp. Shelley, 'To a Skylark' 21–2,

> *Keen as are the arrows*
> *Of that silver sphere . . .*

101. Cp. A. to J. D. Coleridge 28 July 1844, 'I laugh too much and they [friends] make one's laughter mean too much' (*Life of J.D.C.* i 145). Mycerinus as a Stoic disguised by his revelling reminds us of A. in his dandy phase at Oxford and in London. Cp. his sister Mary's letter of 1849, 'I felt there was so much more of this practical questioning in Matt's book than I was at all prepared for . . . it showed a knowledge of life and conflict . . . *strangely like experience* . . . I think that 'Mycerinus' struck me most perhaps, as illustrating what I have been speaking of' (Mrs. H. Ward, *A Writer's Recollections* (1918) 44).

With their mild dark his grassy banquet-hall,
120   Bent to the cold winds of the showerless spring;
No, nor grew dark when autumn brought the clouds.
  So six long years he revelled, night and day.
And when the mirth waxed loudest, with dull sound
Sometimes from the grove's centre echoes came,
125   To tell his wondering people of their king;
In the still night, across the steaming flats,
Mixed with the murmur of the moving Nile.

5 The Hayswater Boat

Date of composition unknown, but stylistically and from its Tennysonian
romanticism of subject probably no later than 1843–5; described by A.'s
brother William in an unpublished letter from India 19 Nov. 1849 as
'. . . one of my favourites . . . which I think I heard some years ago'.
As a young man A. almost certainly fished Hayeswater, a mountain tarn
in the Lake District, and the neighbouring Angle Tarn, both locally
celebrated for their trout.
Published *1849*; not reprinted by A.

A region desolate and wild.
Black, chafing water: and afloat,
And lonely as a truant child
In a waste wood, a single boat:
5   No mast, no sails are set thereon;
It moves, but never moveth on:
And welters like a human thing
Amid the wild waves weltering.

Behind, a buried vale doth sleep,
10   Far down the torrent cleaves its way:
In front the dumb rock rises steep,
A fretted wall of blue and grey;
Of shooting cliff and crumbled stone
With many a wild weed overgrown:
15   All else, black water: and afloat,
One rood from shore, that single boat.

Last night the wind was up and strong;
The grey-streaked waters labour still:
The strong blast brought a pigmy throng
20   From that mild hollow in the hill;
From those twin brooks, that beachéd strand
So featly strewn with drifted sand;

From those weird domes of mounded green
That spot the solitary scene.

25   This boat they found against the shore:
The glossy rushes nodded by.
One rood from land they pushed, no more;
Then rested, listening silently.
The loud rains lashed the mountain's crown,
30   The grating shingle straggled down:
All night they sate; then stole away,
And left it rocking in the bay.

Last night? – I looked, the sky was clear.
The boat was old, a battered boat.
35   In sooth, it seems a hundred year
Since that strange crew did ride afloat.
The boat hath drifted in the bay –
The oars have mouldered as they lay –
The rudder swings – yet none doth steer.
40   What living hand hath brought it here?

6 The New Sirens

Date of composition unknown, but probably first written between
1843–5: see A.'s note to reprint in *Macmillan's Magazine* Dec. 1876, 'To a
work of his youth, a work produced in long-past days of ardour and
emotion, an author can never be very hard-hearted' (*Works* xv 355 *fn.*),
which recalls his 'George Sand' (1877), '. . . agitations more or less stormy
. . . of youth . . . days of Valentine, days of Lélia, days never to return'
(*Mixed Essays* (1879), *Works* x 305) and implies that (1) reprinting was homage to G. Sand, who had died 9 June 1876, and (2) that the poem was begun
and perhaps completed in first draft during A.'s years at Oxford – cp. Mrs.
H. Ward, *A Writer's Recollections* (1918) 12, 'There are many allusions of
many dates in the letters of my father and uncle to each other as to their
common Oxford passion for George Sand.' In support of an early date
see also Tom Arnold's statement, *Manchester Guardian* 18 May 1888
(obituary of A., unsigned but by Tom A.) that 'To a Gipsy Child . . .'
(1843 or 1844) and 'The New Sirens', the latter 'composed while walking
up and down on a soft gloomy day in the field by the Rotha below Fox
How', were early pieces that A. 'had kept by him for a considerable time'.

¶ 6. *Title.* The New Sirens. A Palinode. *1849, Macmillan 1876.* The
original title implies that the poem is a recantation of what A. once
believed in common with the new sirens.

A.'s stanza with its trochaic rhythm may have been suggested by E. B.
Browning's 'The Wine of Cyprus' (1844). The poem was frequently
revised before publication – see A.'s letter to Clough (undated, but March
1849), '. . . your word is quite just – it is exactly a mumble – and I have
doctored it so much and looked at it so long that I am now powerless respecting it' (CL 107). For revision after 1849 see nn. below. The germ of A.'s
distinction between the old and new sirens was probably the debate in
G. Sand's Lélia (1833) chs. xxxiii–xxxviii between Pulchérie (sensuality) and
Lélia (alternating between romantic passion and ennui); and the scene of
the debate, the Villa Bambucci with its 'pavillon d'Aphrodise', is perhaps
recalled in A.'s setting. 'The New Sirens' was admired by Swinburne and
the Pre-Raphaelite poets generally – see Swinburne's 'Matthew Arnold's
New Poems', Essays and Studies (1875) and A.'s letter to G. Smith c.
1 Sept. 1875, 'I don't thoroughly understand it myself, but I believe it is
very fine and Rossetti and his school say it is the best thing I ever wrote'
(Buckler 97).

A.'s 'argument' to his poem is in his letter to Clough of March 1849
(CL 105–7):

'The New Sirens

A lawn stretching away in front of the palace of the New Sirens,
dotted with pines and cedars, and with glimpses to the right and left
over the open country. Time evening.

*   *   *   *

The speaker (one of a band of poets) stands under a cedar, newly
awakened from a sleep: the New Sirens are seen round about in their
bowers in the garden, dejected.

He addresses them, saying he has dreamed they were = the Sirens
the fierce sensual lovers of antiquity. [ll. 1–16]

Yet, he says, this romantic place, and the multitude and distinction
of your worshippers some of them attracted from the service of the
spirit by you, seem to indicate a higher worth in you. Are you then
really something better and more lawfully attractive than the old
Sirens? [ll. 17–48]

– oh, he continues, I perceive the change that gives you an advantage
over them. Your love is romantic, and claims to be a satisfying of the
spirit. [ll. 49–88]

And, he says, I cannot argue against you: for when about to do so,
the remembrance of your beauty and life as I witnessed it at sunrise on
these lawns occupies my mind, and stops my mouth. [ll. 89–104]

– Yes, he continues, that was glorious: and if that could have lasted,
or if we were so made as not to feel that it did not last – (aposiopesis).
[ll. 105–14]

– But, soon after the life and enjoyment I witnessed in you at daybreak, a languor fell upon you as the day advanced: the weather
clouded, your happy groups were broken up, and in lassitude and

ennui you dispersed yourselves thro: the gardens, and threw yourselves dispiritedly down in your bowers where at evening I now see you. [ll. 115–30]

– Does the remembrance of your vivacity of this morning suffice to console you in the void and weariness of the afternoon and evening? or do your thoughts revert to that life of the spirit to which, like me, you were once attracted, but which, finding it hard and solitary, you soon abandoned for the vehement emotional life of passion as 'the new Sirens'? [ll. 131–54]

What, he says, without reply, I see you rise and leave your bowers, and re-enter your palace. And yet do not be angry with me: for I would gladly find you in the right and myself, with my conscientious regrets after the spiritual life, wrong. [ll. 155–70]

(They have re-entered the palace, and night falls.)

– That is right, he continues, away with ennui, and let joy revive amidst light and dancing. [ll. 171–78]

– But (after a pause he continues), I, remaining in the dark and cold under my cedar, and seeing the blaze of your revel in the distance, do not share your illusions: and ask myself whether this *alternation* of ennui and excitement is worth much? Whether it is in truth a very desirable life? [ll. 176–202]

And, he goes on, were this *alternation* of ennui and excitement the best discoverable existence, yet it cannot last: time will destroy it: the time will come, when the elasticity of the spirits will be worn out, and nothing left but weariness.

(This epoch is described under the figure of morning but all this latter part you say is clear to you.)' [ll. 203–76]

Published *1849*; reprinted *Macmillan's Magazine*, Dec. 1876; *1877*, etc.

> In the cedarn shadow sleeping,
> Where cool grass and fragrant glooms
> Forth at noon had lured me, creeping
> From your darkened palace rooms –
> 5 I, who in your train at morning
> Strolled and sang with joyful mind,
> Heard, in slumber, sounds of warning;
> Heard the hoarse boughs labour in the wind.
>
> Who are they, O pensive Graces,
> 10 – For I dreamed they wore your forms –
> Who on shores and sea-washed places
> Scoop the shelves and fret the storms?
> Who, when ships are that way tending,
> Troop across the flushing sands,
> 15 To all reefs and narrows wending,
> With blown tresses, and with beckoning hands?

Yet I see, the howling levels
Of the deep are not your lair;
And your tragic-vaunted revels
20   Are less lonely than they were.
Like those Kings with treasure steering
From the jewelled lands of dawn,
Troops, with gold and gifts, appearing,
Stream all day through your enchanted lawn.

25   And we, too, from upland valleys,
Where some Muse with half-curved frown
Leans her ear to your mad sallies
Which the charmed winds never drown;
By faint music guided, ranging
30   The scared glens, we wandered on,
Left our awful laurels hanging,
And came heaped with myrtles to your throne.

From the dragon-wardered fountains
Where the springs of knowledge are,
35   From the watchers on the mountains,
And the bright and morning star;
We are exiles, we are falling,
We have lost them at your call –
O ye false ones, at your calling
40   Seeking ceiléd chambers and a palace-hall!

Are the accents of your luring
More melodious than of yore?
Are those frail forms more enduring
Than the charms Ulysses bore?
45   That we sought you with rejoicings,
Till at evening we descry
At a pause of Siren voicings
These vexed branches and this howling sky? . . .

*   *   *   *

21–3. 1849,

> In a Tyrian galley steering
> From the golden springs of dawn,
> Troops, like Eastern kings, appearing . . .

A.'s alteration of the text of the poem (see headn. above) was resumed
in 1876. This is one instance of many small alterations made not only in
1876, but in 1877, 1881 and 1885.
31–2. The laurel belongs to poetry and knowledge, the myrtle to love.
40. ceiléd] Ceilinged.
44. Homer's sirens, Odyssey xii 39 ff., 184 ff.

Oh, your pardon! The uncouthness
50   Of that primal age is gone,
And the skin of dazzling smoothness
Screens not now a heart of stone.
Love has flushed those cruel faces;
And those slackened arms forego
55   The delight of death-embraces,
And yon whitening bone-mounds do not grow.

'Ah,' you say; 'the large appearance
Of man's labour is but vain,
And we plead as staunch adherence
60   Due to pleasure as to pain.'
Pointing to earth's careworn creatures,
'Come,' you murmur with a sigh:
'Ah! we own diviner features,
Loftier bearing, and a prouder eye.'

65   'Come,' you say, 'the hours were dreary;
Dull did life in torpor fade;
Time is lame, and we grew weary
In the slumbrous cedarn shade.
Round our hearts with long caresses,
70   With low sighings, Silence stole,
And her load of steaming tresses
Fell, like Ossa, on the climbing soul.

'Come,' you say, 'the soul is fainting
Till she search and learn her own,
75   And the wisdom of man's painting
Leaves her riddle half unknown.
'Come,' you say, 'the brain is seeking,

55. *death-embraces*] fierce embraces *1849*.
61. *earth's careworn*] some world-worn *1849*.
66. *Dull did life in torpor*] Life is long, and will not *1849*; Life without love does but *1877*; Dull, without love, life doth *1881*.
67. *Time is lame*] Vain it wastes *Macmillan 1876, 1877–81*.
72. *climbing*] The *1885* reading. All earlier editions read 'aery'.
77–84. A. never subscribed to the extreme Romantic view of the 'new sirens' that 'Only, what we feel, we know' (l. 84), but he believed with many Victorians that it was a mistake to exalt 'head' over 'heart' – cp. 'Empedocles on Etna' II [i] 90–1 (p. 180 below),

> The brave, impetuous heart yields everywhere
> To the subtle, contriving head . . .

While the sovran heart is dead;
Yet this gleaned, when Gods were speaking,
80   Rarer secrets than the toiling head.

'Come,' you say, 'opinion trembles,
Judgment shifts, convictions go;
Life dries up, the heart dissembles –
Only, what we feel, we know.
85   Hath your wisdom felt emotions?
Will it weep our burning tears?
Hath it drunk of our love-potions
Crowning moments with the wealth of years?'

– I am dumb. Alas, too soon all
90   Man's grave reasons disappear!
Yet, I think, at God's tribunal
Some large answer you shall hear.
But, for me, my thoughts are straying
Where at sunrise, through your vines,
95   On these lawns I saw you playing,
Hanging garlands on your odorous pines;

When your showering locks enwound you,
And your heavenly eyes shone through;
When the pine-boughs yielded round you,
100   And your brows were starred with dew;
And immortal forms, to meet you,
Down the statued alleys came,
And through golden horns, to greet you,
Blew such music as a God may frame.

105   Yes, I muse! And if the dawning
Into daylight never grew,
If the glistering wings of morning
On the dry noon shook their dew,

---

and 'The Scholar-Gipsy' 205 (p. 342 below),

> *It's [modern life's] heads o'ertaxed, its palsied hearts . . .*

For A.'s notion of a proper balance of powers see 'Pagan and Mediæval
Religious Sentiment', *E in C* I (1865), *Works* iii 241, 'But the main element
of the modern spirit's life is neither the senses and understanding, nor the
heart and the imagination; it is the imaginative reason.'
78. *sovran*] The *1885* reading. Earlier editions read 'princely'.
88. *wealth*] The *1885* reading. Earlier editions read 'weight'.

If the fits of joy were longer,
110   Or the day were sooner done,
Or, perhaps, if hope were stronger,
No weak nursling of an earthly sun . . .
Pluck, pluck cypress, O pale maidens,
Dusk the hall with yew!

*   *   *   *

115   For a bound was set to meetings,
And the sombre day dragged on;
And the burst of joyful greetings,
And the joyful dawn, were gone.
For the eye grows filled with gazing,
120   And on raptures follow calms;
And those warm locks men were praising,
Drooped, unbraided, on your listless arms.

Storms unsmoothed your folded valleys,
And made all your cedars frown;
125   Leaves were whirling in the alleys
Which your lovers wandered down.
– Sitting cheerless in your bowers,
The hands propping the sunk head,
Still they gall you, the long hours,
130   And the hungry thought that must be fed!

Is the pleasure that is tasted
Patient of a long review?
Will the fire joy hath wasted,
Mused on, warm the heart anew?
135   – Or, are those old thoughts returning,
Guests the dull sense never knew,
Stars, set deep, yet inly burning,
Germs your untrimmed passion overgrew?

Once, like us, you took your station
140   Watchers for a purer fire;
But you drooped in expectation,
And you wearied in desire.
When the first rose flush was steeping
All the frore peak's awful crown,
145   Shepherds say, they found you sleeping
In some windless valley, farther down.

Then you wept, and slowly raising
Your dozed eyelids, sought again,

Half in doubt, they say, and gazing
150   Sadly back, the seats of men;
Snatched a turbid inspiration
From some transient earthly sun,
And proclaimed your vain ovation
For those mimic raptures you had won. . . .

*   *   *   *

155   With a sad, majestic motion,
With a stately, slow surprise,
From their earthward-bound devotion
Lifting up your languid eyes –
Would you freeze my too loud boldness,
160   Dumbly smiling as you go,
One faint frown of distant coldness
Flitting fast across each marble brow?

Do I brighten at your sorrow,
O sweet Pleaders? – doth my lot
165   Find assurance in to-morrow
Of one joy which you have not?
O, speak once, and shame my sadness!
Let this sobbing, Phrygian strain,
Mocked and baffled by your gladness,
170   Mar the music of your feasts in vain!

*   *   *   *

Scent, and song, and light, and flowers!
Gust on gust, the harsh winds blow –
Come, bind up those ringlet showers!
Roses for that dreaming brow!
175   Come, once more that ancient lightness,
Glancing feet, and eager eyes!
Let your broad lamps flash the brightness
Which the sorrow-stricken day denies!

151. *turbid*] earthly *1849.*
152. *earthly*] human *1849.*
154. After this line in *1849* the refrain (ll. 113–14) is repeated.
168. *sobbing*] throbbing *Macmillan 1876* (only).
169. *Mocked*] Sham'd *1849.*
170. *Mar*] Blame *1849.*
172. *harsh*] hoarse *1849.*

180 Through black depths of serried shadows,
Up cold aisles of buried glade;
In the mist of river-meadows
Where the looming kine are laid;
From your dazzled windows streaming,
185 From your humming festal room,
Deep and far, a broken gleaming
Reels and shivers on the ruffled gloom.

Where I stand, the grass is glowing;
Doubtless you are passing fair!
But I hear the north wind blowing,
190 And I feel the cold night-air.
Can I look on your sweet faces,
And your proud heads backward thrown,
From this dusk of leaf-strewn places
With the dumb woods and the night alone?

195 Yet, indeed, this flux of guesses –
Mad delight, and frozen calms –
Mirth to-day and vine-bound tresses,
And to-morrow – folded palms;
Is this all? this balanced measure?
200 Could life run no happier way?
Joyous, at the height of pleasure,
Passive at the nadir of dismay?

But, indeed, this proud possession,
This far-reaching, magic chain,
205 Linking in a mad succession
Fits of joy and fits of pain –
Have you seen it at the closing?
Have you tracked its clouded ways?
Can your eyes, while fools are dozing,
210 Drop, with mine, adown life's latter days?

---

181. *mist*] The reading of all editions until *1885*, which has 'midst' (presumably a misprint).
182. *kine*] deer *Macmillan 1876, 1877–81*. The original Tennysonian phrase was restored in *1885*.
185–6. The broken lights, like 'the looming kine' above, are Tennysonian properties.
201. *Joyous, at the height*] Happy, at the noon *1849*.
202. *nadir*] midnight *1849*.

3 + M.A.

When a dreary dawn is wading
Through this waste of sunless greens,
When the flushing hues are fading
On the peerless cheek of queens;
215   When the mean shall no more sorrow,
And the proudest no more smile;
As old age, youth's fatal morrow,
Spreads its cold light wider all that while?

Then, when change itself is over,
220   When the slow tide sets one way,
Shall you find the radiant lover,
Even by moments, of to-day?
The eye wanders, faith is failing –
O, loose hands, and let it be!
225   Proudly, like a king bewailing,
O, let fall one tear, and set us free!

All true speech and large avowal
Which the jealous soul concedes;
All man's heart which brooks bestowal,
230   All frank faith which passion breeds –
These we had, and we gave truly;
Doubt not, what we had, we gave!
False we were not, nor unruly;
Lodgers in the forest and the cave.

235   Long we wandered with you, feeding
Our rapt souls on your replies,
In a wistful silence reading
All the meaning of your eyes.
By moss-bordered statues sitting,
240   By well-heads, in summer days.
But we turn, our eyes are flitting –
See, the white east, and the morning rays!

213. *flushing hues*] The *1885* reading. Earlier editions read 'flashing lights'
217–18. The *1885* reading, replacing in earlier editions:

> *While the dawning of the morrow*
> *Widens slowly westward all that while?*

236. *rapt*] sad *1849*.

And you too, O worshipped Graces,
Sylvan Gods of this fair shade!
245   Is there doubt on divine faces?
Are the blessed Gods dismayed?
Can men worship the wan features,
The sunk eyes, the wailing tone,
Of unsphered, discrownéd creatures,
250   Souls as little godlike as their own?

Come, loose hands! The wingéd fleetness
Of immortal feet is gone;
And your scents have shed their sweetness,
And your flowers are overblown.
255   And your jewelled gauds surrender
Half their glories to the day;
Freely did they flash their splendour,
Freely gave it – but it dies away.

In the pines the thrush is waking –
260   Lo, yon orient hill in flames!
Scores of true love knots are breaking
At divorce which it proclaims.
When the lamps are paled at morning,
Heart quits heart and hand quits hand.
265   Cold in that unlovely dawning,
Loveless, rayless, joyless you shall stand!

Pluck no more red roses, maidens,
Leave the lilies in their dew –
Pluck, pluck cypress, O pale maidens,
270   Dusk, oh, dusk the hall with yew!
– Shall I seek, that I may scorn her,
Her I loved at eventide?
Shall I ask, what faded mourner
Stands, at daybreak, weeping by my side?
275   Pluck, pluck cypress, O pale maidens!
Dusk the hall with yew!

243. *worshipped*] weeping *1849.*
246. *blessed*] happy *1849.*
249. *discrownéd*] Used elsewhere only in 'Alaric at Rome' 46 (p. 5 above).
267. *Pluck*] Strew *1849.*

7 Stagirius

Written 1844: the date of the untitled autograph signed 'M.A.' (Yale Papers); *1849* title probably added March 1848 when A. read Saint-Marc Girardin's *Cours de littérature dramatique* i (1843) – see his letter to Clough of that date (*CL* 68) – and noted that 'le démon de Stagyre' paralleled his own romantic malaise: '. . . il y a eu une littérature qui a exprimé l'état de malaise et d'inquiétude que nous ressentons . . . la littérature des Pères de l'Église . . . voyons quel est le démon qui possède Stagyre . . . c'est la tristesse, ou plutôt c'est l'*athumia* . . . c'est le défaut d'énergie et de ressort, c'est l'abattement . . . c'est le néant de l'âme' (*loc. cit.* 105–6). The *1849* title 'Stagyrus' is a careless anglicization of the French 'Stagyre'; the *1855* title 'Desire' connects the poem with G. Sand's *Lélia* (1833) ch. lxvii, 'Vérité! vérité! tu ne t'es pas révélée, depuis mille ans je te cherche et je ne t'ai pas trouvée! Et depuis mille ans, pour toute réponse à mes cris, pour tout soulagement . . . j'entends planer sur cette terre maudite le sanglot désespéré du désir impuissant . . .' – a passage which deeply impressed the youthful A. and which he translated in 'George Sand', *Mixed Essays* (1879), *Works* x 306.

Published as 'Stagyrus' *1849*; reprinted as 'Desire' *1855*; with present title *1877*, etc. The poem and its title-changes are discussed in my 'M.A.'s "Stagirius" and Saint-Marc Girardin', *RES* n.s. ix (1958) 286 ff.

Thou, who dost dwell alone –
Thou, who dost know thine own –
Thou, to whom all are known
From the cradle to the grave –

5   Save, oh! save.
From the world's temptations,
From tribulations,
From that fierce anguish
Wherein we languish,

10   From that torpor deep
Wherein we lie asleep,
Heavy as death, cold as the grave,
Save, oh! save.

¶ 7. *Title.* 'Stagirius was a young monk to whom St. Chrysostom addressed three books, and of whom those books give an account. They will be found in the first volume of the Benedictine edition of St. Chrysostom's works.' A.'s note first added in *1877*.

When the soul, growing clearer,
  Sees God no nearer;
15 When the soul, mounting higher,
    To God comes no nigher,
But the arch-fiend Pride
Mounts at her side,
Foiling her high emprise,
20 Sealing her eagle eyes,
And, when she fain would soar,
Makes idols to adore,
Changing the pure emotion
Of her high devotion,
25 To a skin-deep sense
Of her own eloquence;
Strong to deceive, strong to enslave –
  Save, oh! save.

30 From the ingrained fashion
Of this earthly nature
That mars thy creature;
From grief that is but passion,
From mirth that is but feigning,
35 From tears that bring no healing,
From wild and weak complaining,
  Thine old strength revealing,
    Save, oh! save.
From doubt, where all is double;
40 Where wise men are not strong,
Where comfort turns to trouble,
Where just men suffer wrong;
Where sorrow treads on joy,
Where sweet things soonest cloy,
45 Where faiths are built on dust,
Where love is half mistrust,
Hungry, and barren, and sharp as the sea –
  Oh! set us free.

14–17. MS.,
  When the soul rising higher, to God comes no nigher –
  When the mind waxing clearer sees God no nearer –

33–4. The two lines are transposed in A.'s autograph.
36. *weak complaining*] Cp. the *1849* reading of 'Quiet Work' 10 (p. 107 below),
  Man's weak complainings mingling with his toil ...
40. *wise*] good MS.
43. *treads on*] puts out MS.

<pre>
        O let the false dream fly,
50   Where our sick souls do lie
            Tossing continually!
            O where thy voice doth come
            Let all doubts be dumb,
            Let all worlds be mild,
55   All strifes be reconciled,
            All pains beguiled!
            Light bring no blindness,
            Love no unkindness,
            Knowledge no ruin,
60   Fear no undoing!
            From the cradle to the grave,
                Save, oh! save.
</pre>

8 The Voice

Date of composition unknown, but Shelleyan influence here and in 'To Fausta' suggests both are early; (?) 1844 if the 'voice' belongs to Newman, who resigned his St. Mary's living 18 Sept. 1843 – cp. l. 35 'in the bygone year'. In favour of an early date see also A.'s letter to F. T. Palgrave in 1869 (*Russell* 43), 'In the "Voice" the falsetto rages too furiously; I can do nothing with it; ditto in "Stagirius" [of 1844] . . .'
Published *1849*; reprinted *1877*, etc.

<pre>
        As the kindling glances,
            Queen-like and clear,
        Which the bright moon lances
            From her tranquil sphere
5   At the sleepless waters
            Of a lonely mere,
    On the wild whirling waves, mournfully, mournfully,
                Shiver and die.
</pre>

¶ 8. *1–4.* Cp. Shelley, 'To a Skylark' 21–4,

> *Keen as are the arrows*
> *Of that silver sphere*
> *Whose intense lamp narrows*
> *In the white dawn clear . . .*

and see 'Mycerinus' 99 (p. 31 above), another reminiscence of the same passage.

As the tears of sorrow
    Mothers have shed –
Prayers that to-morrow
    Shall in vain be sped
When the flower they flow for
    Lies frozen and dead –
Fall on the throbbing brow, fall on the burning breast,
    Bringing no rest.

Like bright waves that fall
    With a lifelike motion
On the lifeless margin of the sparkling Ocean;
A wild rose climbing up a mouldering wall –
A gush of sunbeams through a ruined hall –
Strains of glad music at a funeral –
    So sad, and with so wild a start
    To this deep-sobered heart,
    So anxiously and painfully,
    So drearily and doubtfully,
And oh, with such intolerable change
    Of thought, such contrast strange,
O unforgotten voice, thy accents come,
Like wanderers from the world's extremity,
    Unto their ancient home!

In vain, all, all in vain,
They beat upon mine ear again,
Those melancholy tones so sweet and still.
Those lute-like tones which in the bygone year
    Did steal into mine ear –
Blew such a thrilling summons to my will,
    Yet could not shake it;
Made my tossed heart its very life-blood spill,
    Yet could not break it.

34–5. Cp. A.'s 'Emerson', *Discourses in America* (1885), *Works* iv 350, 'Who could resist the charm of that spiritual apparition, gliding in the dim afternoon light through the aisles of St. Mary's, rising into the pulpit, and then, in the most entrancing of voices, breaking the silence with words and thoughts which were a religious music, – subtle, sweet, mournful?' A. 'for a long time regularly attended' Newman's sermons and was 'powerfully attracted' – see T. Arnold's *Passages in a Wandering Life* (1900) 57. The conjecture that Marguerite's voice is referred to is contradicted by the description in 'Parting' 17–22 (p. 118 below).

35. *the bygone year*] long distant years *1849*.

39. *1849*,

       Drain'd all the life my full heart had to spill . . .

9 A Question

TO FAUSTA

Date of composition unknown, but (?) 1844: see previous headn.; the
Shelleyan influence is noted by Swinburne, *Miscellanies* (1886) 112, 'The
echo of Shelley's voice in its fainter but not least exquisite modulations
...' The name 'Fausta', also found in 'Resignation' (p. 84 below), refers
to Jane Arnold, Matthew's eldest sister, usually known in the family
circle as 'K'.
Published *1849* as 'To Fausta'; reprinted with present title *1877*, etc.

Joy comes and goes, hope ebbs and flows
Like the wave;
Change doth unknit the tranquil strength of men.
Love lends life a little grace,
5   A few sad smiles; and then,
Both are laid in one cold place,
In the grave.

Dreams dawn and fly, friends smile and die
Like spring flowers;
10   Our vaunted life is one long funeral.
Men dig graves with bitter tears
For their dead hopes; and all,
Mazed with doubts and sick with fears,
Count the hours.

15   We count the hours! These dreams of ours,
False and hollow,
Do we go hence and find they are not dead?
Joys we dimly apprehend,
Faces that smiled and fled,
20   Hopes born here, and born to end,
Shall we follow?

10 Shakespeare

Dated 1 Aug. 1844 in autograph (Brit. Mus.), which is a fair copy of a
poem first enclosed in a letter to Jane Arnold – see Mrs. H. Ward's *A
Writer's Recollections* (1918) 39. For Shakespeare's inscrutability cp. letter to
Clough (undated but early Dec. 1847), 'Yet to *solve* the Universe as you
try to do is as irritating as Tennyson's dawdling with its painted shell ...
and yet I own that to *re-construct* the Universe is not a satisfactory attempt
either – I keep saying, Shakespeare, Shakespeare, you are as obscure as

life is' (*CL* 63). The sonnet is irregular in form. The octet is Italian with
Wordsworth's favourite variation – used by A. in five of the eleven *1849*
sonnets but never in the later sonnets of *1867* – of a third rhyme in ll. 6–7;
the sestet consists of a Shakespearean quatrain and couplet (though this is
disguised by the lay-out of the sestet in *1869* and subsequent editions, and
by the accidental sight-rhyme). F. R. Leavis discusses the poem searchingly,
if too harshly, in *Education and the University* (revised ed. 1948) 73–6.
Published *1849*; reprinted *1853* (*1854*, *1857*), *1869*, etc.

Others abide our question. Thou art free.
We ask and ask – Thou smilest and art still,
Out-topping knowledge. For the loftiest hill,
Who to the stars uncrowns his majesty,

5   Planting his steadfast footsteps in the sea,
Making the heaven of heavens his dwelling-place,
Spares but the cloudy border of his base
To the foiled searching of mortality;

¶ 10. *1.* Cp. Schiller's *Über naive und sentimentalische Dichtung* (1795) tr.
W. F. Mainland (1951) 19, 'Since I was accustomed by the practice of
modern poets to seek the poet in his work ... I could not bear that the
poet in Shakespeare could never be seized and would never give me an
account of himself [*und mir nirgends Rede stehen wollte*].

3. Out-topping knowledge] Exceeding *our* knowledge, i.e. ability to understand. Goethe's Shakespeare as a Mont Blanc among poets in Eckermann's
Conversations (under 2 Jan. 1824) belongs to an entry first published 1848,
but Emerson in 'The Poet', *Essays* 2nd series (1844) says that the great poet
will 'stand out of our low limitations, like a Chimborazo ...' (*Works*
Riverside ed. iii 14–15). F. R. Leavis thinks the comparison a radically bad
one – 'Had he [A.] realized in the least what purports to be his theme,
Shakespeare's greatness or inscrutability, a mountain could never have
presented itself to him as a symbol for it. There is nothing remote or
austerely and inhumanly exalted about Shakespeare, whose genius is
awe-inspiring by the inwardness and completeness of its humanity ...'
(*Education and the University* 75).

5. A reminiscence of Cowper, 'Light shining out of Darkness' 1–3,

> *God moves in a mysterious way*
> *His wonders to perform;*
> *He plants his footsteps in the sea ...*

The implied parallel is explicit in Schiller (*loc. cit.*): 'Like Deity behind the
universe, he [i.e. the 'objective' poet of Shakespeare's kind] hides himself
behind his work.'

3*

And thou, who didst the stars and sunbeams know,
10   Self-schooled, self-scanned, self-honoured, self-secure,
Didst tread on earth unguessed at. – Better so!

All pains the immortal spirit must endure,
All weakness which impairs, all griefs which bow,
Find their sole speech in that victorious brow.

10. Cp. the deliberate repetitions of 'Mycerinus' III (p. 31 above).
A.'s Shakespeare and Mycerinus both have Stoic characteristics.
11. tread] walk *MS.*, *1849–69.* Cp. Carlyle, *Heroes and Hero-Worship* (1841),
Works ed. H. D. Traill v 113, 'We did not account him a god . . . while he
dwelt with us.'
12–14. Cp. Carlyle, *Heroes and Hero-Worship* (1841) *Works* ed. *cit.* v 108,
'Withal the joyful tranquillity of the man is notable. I will not blame
Dante for his misery: it is as battle without victory . . . I call Shakespeare
greater than Dante, in that he fought truly, and did conquer. Doubt it
not, he had his own sorrows . . . how could a man delineate a Hamlet, a
Coriolanus, a Macbeth . . . if his own heroic heart had never suffered?'
14. sole speech] sole voice *1849–77.* Their only adequate expression.

11 To the Duke of Wellington

ON HEARING HIM MISPRAISED

Date of composition unknown, but (?) 1844: the *1849* group of sonnets
appears to be arranged chronologically, and this sonnet is sandwiched
between two others belonging to 1844. Wellington retired from public
life in 1846. Dissatisfaction with this and the three following pieces may be
suggested by their exclusion from *1869*, the first collected edition of A.'s
poems.
Published *1849*; reprinted *1877*, etc.

Because thou hast believed, the wheels of life
Stand never idle, but go always round;
Not by their hands, who vex the patient ground,
Moved only; but by genius, in the strife

5   Of all its chafing torrents after thaw,
Urged; and to feed whose movement, spinning sand,
The feeble sons of pleasure set their hand;
And, in this vision of the general law,

¶ 11. *8. general law*] That time does not stand still (ll. 1–2). Wellington
would therefore be 'mispraised' in the eighteen-forties by those who

Hast laboured, but with purpose; hast become
Laborious, persevering, serious, firm –
For this, thy track, across the fretful foam

Of vehement actions without scope or term,
Called history, keeps a splendour; due to wit,
Which saw one clue to life, and followed it.

10

regarded him as implacably hostile to all change. Cp. A.'s commendation
in *Culture and Anarchy* (1869) of the Duke's 'strong sagacity' in recognizing
the inevitability after 1832 of a social 'revolution by due course of law'
(*Works* vi 77), and with A.'s view of Wellington cp. J. McCarthy's *History
of Our Own Times* (1882 ed.) ii 108, 'He gave up again and again his most
cherished convictions . . . in order that he might not stand in the way of
the Queen's Government and the proper carrying of it on.'

12 Written in Butler's Sermons

Probably written *c.* 1844 at Oxford where Butler's *Sermons* was a text-
book for 'Greats': see A.'s 'Bishop Butler and the Zeit-Geist' in *Last Essays*
(1877), ' . . . we at Oxford used to read our Aristotle or our Butler with the
same absolute faith in the classicality of their matter as in the classicality
of Homer's form' (*Works* ix 260); and for A.'s criticism of Butler, 'The
truth is, all this elaborate psychology of Butler's . . . is unsatisfying . . .
What he calls our instincts and principles of action, which are in truth the
most obscure, changing, interdependent of phenomena, Butler takes as if
they were things . . . separate, fixed, and palpable . . .' (*loc. cit.* 306–7).
Published *1849*; reprinted *1877*, etc.

Affections, Instincts, Principles, and Powers,
Impulse and Reason, Freedom and Control –
So men, unravelling God's harmonious whole,
Rend in a thousand shreds this life of ours.

Vain labour! Deep and broad, where none may see,
Spring the foundations of that shadowy throne
Where man's one nature, queen-like, sits alone,
Centred in a majestic unity;

5

¶ 12. *Title.* Joseph Butler (1692–1752), Bishop of Bristol 1738 and of
Durham 1750, published his *Fifteen Sermons . . .* in 1726.
5–7. Cp. the passage in Yale MS. (of uncertain date but probably 1848–52)

10 And rays her powers, like sister-islands seen
Linking their coral arms under the sea,
Or clustered peaks with plunging gulfs between

Spanned by aërial arches all of gold,
Where'er the chariot wheels of life are rolled
In cloudy circles to eternity.

which A. drew on for 'Palladium' (p. 494 below), 'Our remotest self
must abide in its remoteness awful and unchanged, presiding at the tumult
of the rest of our being . . . as the moon over the agitations of the Sea.'
9–10. Cp. Clough, 'Truth is a golden thread . . .' (1838) 6–10,

> *Like islands set*
> *At distant intervals on Ocean's face,*
> *. . . but in the depths*
> *The mystic colonnade unbroken keeps*
> *Its faithful way . . .*

The poem was first published in 1865, but Clough showed his unpublished
work to A.
11–14. Shelleyan scenery.

13 Written in Emerson's Essays

Date of composition unknown, but probably written 1844 shortly after
publication of Emerson's *Essays* 2nd series (1844): see A.'s early draft in
Yale MS. on a sheet also containing 'Night comes . . .' (p. 577 below),
the latter quoted in a letter Feb. or March 1845 (*CL* 57); and cp. A.'s
'Emerson' in *Discourses in America* (1885), 'Forty years ago, when I was an
undergraduate at Oxford, voices were in the air . . . a voice also from this
side of the Atlantic, – a clear and pure voice . . . as new, and moving, and
unforgettable, as the strain of Newman, or Carlyle, or Goethe' (*Works* iv
349, 352). *1950* omits the variants of the Yale draft, which is reproduced
Commentary 27.
Published *1849*; reprinted *1853, 1877*, etc.

'O monstrous, dead, unprofitable world,
That thou canst hear, and hearing hold thy way!
A voice oracular hath pealed to-day,
To-day a hero's banner is unfurled;

¶ 13. *1. unprofitable*] An allusion to *Hamlet* I ii 133–4,
> *How weary, stale, flat, and unprofitable*
> *Seem to me all the uses of this world.*

5 Hast thou no lip for welcome?' – So I said.
 Man after man, the world smiled and passed by;
 A smile of wistful incredulity
 As though one spake of life unto the dead –

 Scornful, and strange, and sorrowful, and full
10 Of bitter knowledge. Yet the will is free;
 Strong is the soul, and wise, and beautiful;

 The seeds of godlike power are in us still;
 Gods are we, bards, saints, heroes, if we will! –
 Dumb judges, answer, truth or mockery?

6. *the world smiled and passed by*] they smiléd and passed on *MS.*
7–8. *MS.*,

   A smile of mournful incredulity
  (7) *Each to his labour. And when all were gone*
    As tho men spake of life, a   Joy
  (8) *It chanced, I know not how, My Dream was fled:*

8. *life*] noise *1849–77.*
9. *MS.*,

   So scornful seemed that smile, so strange, so full . . .

11–13. Cp. Emerson's 'History' (1841), 'What Plato has thought, he [man] may think; what a saint has felt, he may feel; what at any time has befallen any man, he can understand' (*Works* Riverside ed. ii 9).
11. *wise*] fresh *MS.*
14. *MS.*,

   O barren boast, o joyless Mockery.

Perhaps unintentionally this reading appears to justify the world's scorn of the enthusiast, whereas A.'s revised line leaves it open whether the world's pessimism may not be due to inertia.

14 In Harmony with Nature

TO A PREACHER

Date of composition unknown, but (?) 1844–7: see headn. to 'To the Duke of Wellington' (p. 50 above). The sonnet seems to contradict 'Quiet Work' (p. 106 below), but note that 'When true' (l. 3) implies a sense in which we can be 'in harmony with Nature' by learning a moral lesson from it. Here A.'s concern is with the distinction between the 'law for man' and the 'law for thing'. See *Literature and Dogma* (1873), *Works* vii 357, 361, 'Ah, what pitfalls are in that word *Nature*! . . . do you mean that

we are to give full swing to our inclinations ... the constitution of things
turns out to be somehow against it ... the free development ... of our
apparent self has to undergo a profound modification from the law of our
higher *real* self, the law of righteousness.'
Published *1849* as 'To an Independent Preacher, who preached that we
should be "In Harmony with Nature"'; reprinted with present title
1877, etc.

> 'In harmony with Nature?' Restless fool,
> Who with such heat dost preach what were to thee,
> When true, the last impossibility –
> To be like Nature strong, like Nature cool!
>
> 5 Know, man hath all which Nature hath, but more,
> And in that *more* lie all his hopes of good.
> Nature is cruel, man is sick of blood;
> Nature is stubborn, man would fain adore;
>
> Nature is fickle, man hath need of rest;
> 10 Nature forgives no debt, and fears no grave;
> Man would be mild, and with safe conscience blest.
>
> Man must begin, know this, where Nature ends;
> Nature and man can never be fast friends.
> Fool, if thou canst not pass her, rest her slave!

15 In Utrumque Paratus

Probably written *1846* when A. was reading Plotinus – see my 'Three
Early Diaries', *Vict. Stud.* ii (1959) 262-3 – whose ideas (the One all-pure,
the overflowing *Fons Deitatis*, the world as emanation, the re-ascent of the
soul by purification) are reproduced ll. 1-14. Coleridge's *Biographia
Literaria* (also read *1846*) is the probable source of A.'s imagery ll. 15-21.
The alternatives of the title are the world as emanation (man has descended)
or as eternal matter achieving consciousness in man (man has ascended).
Published *1849*; reprinted *1869*, etc.

> If, in the silent mind of One all-pure,
> At first imagined lay

¶ 15. *1. One all-pure*] Cp. Plotinus, *Ennead* I vi 7, ' ... that solitary-
dwelling Existence, the Apart, the Unmingled, the Pure, that from Which
all things depend ... the Source of Life and of Intellection and of Being'
(*The Ethical Treatises* tr. S. MacKenna (1917) 86). For the Plotinian origin of
the world see *Ennead* V ii 1, *The Divine Mind* ed. *cit.* (1926) 16-17.

The sacred world; and by procession sure
From those still deeps, in form and colour dressed,
5   Seasons alternating, and night and day,
The long-mused thought to north, south, east, and
                Took then its all-seen way;   [west.

O waking on a world which thus-wise springs!
            Whether it needs thee count
10   Betwixt thy waking and the birth of things
Ages or hours – O waking on life's stream!
By lonely pureness to the all-pure fount
(Only by this thou canst) the coloured dream
                Of life remount!

15   Thin, thin the pleasant human noises grow,
            And faint the city gleams;
Rare the lone pastoral huts – marvel not thou!
The solemn peaks but to the stars are known,
But to the stars, and the cold lunar beams;
20   Alone the sun rises, and alone
                Spring the great streams.

3. *procession*] Used this once in the theological sense of emanation.
11–14. Cp. Plotinus, *Ennead* I vi 8–9, 'What then is our course, what the manner of our flight? . . . when you are self-gathered in the purity of your being . . . call up all your confidence, strike forward yet a step . . . If the eye that adventures the vision be dimmed by vice, impure, or weak . . . then it sees nothing . . . So, mounting, the Soul will come first to the Intellectual Principle . . . and The Good, which lies beyond, is the Fountain at once and Principle of Beauty' (*The Ethical Treatises* ed. cit. 87–9).
13. *coloured dream*] Perhaps suggested by Shelley, 'Adonais' 462–3,

> *Life, like a dome of many-coloured glass,*
> *Stains the white radiance of Eternity . . .*

A. uses the epithet 'many-coloured' twice in *1849.*
15–21. Cp. Coleridge, *Biographia Literaria* (1817) ed. J. Shawcross i 165–6, 'The first range of hills, that encircles the scanty vale of human life, is the horizon for the majority of its inhabitants. On *its* ridges the common sun is born and departs. From *them* the stars rise, and touching *them* they depart. By the many, even this range . . . is but imperfectly known . . . But in all ages there have been a few, who measuring and sounding the rivers of the vale . . . have learned, that the sources must be far higher and far inward.' Coleridge is talking of intellectual exploration in this part of ch. xii.

But, if the wild unfathered mass no birth
     In divine seats hath known;
In the blank, echoing solitude if Earth,
25   Rocking her obscure body to and fro,
Ceases not from all time to heave and groan,
Unfruitful oft, and at her happiest throe
     Forms, what she forms, alone;

O seeming sole to awake, thy sun-bathed head
30   Piercing the solemn cloud
Round thy still dreaming brother-world outspread!
O man, whom Earth, thy long-vexed mother, bare
Not without joy – so radiant, so endowed
(Such happy issue crowned her painful care) –
35   Be not too proud!

Oh when most self-exalted most alone,
     Chief dreamer, own thy dream!
Thy brother-world stirs at thy feet unknown,
Who hath a monarch's hath no brother's part;
40   Yet doth thine inmost soul with yearning teem.
– Oh, what a spasm shakes the dreamer's heart!
     'I, too, but seem.'

36–42. 1869 only:

> *Thy native world stirs at thy feet unknown,*
>   *Yet there thy secret lies!*
> *Out of this stuff, these forces, thou art grown,*
> *And proud self-severance from them were disease.*
> *O scan thy native world with pious eyes!*
> *High as thy life be risen, 'tis from these,*
>   *And these, too, rise.*

The apparent connection here with topical Victorian ideas of evolution seems to have irked A., and the stanza was restored to its original form in later editions. Note that the stanza has much the same meaning in both forms (except that in *1869* the 'brother-world' is also evolving). Man, a monarch because of his consciousness, should not be too proud – his yearning towards the natural world should remind him that he is intimately akin to it and has the same degree of reality. The obscurity is due mainly to the equivocal use of 'dream' and 'dreamer' in the last two stanzas. In l. 31 the brother-world is dreaming because it is without man's consciousness, but in l. 37 man is the 'Chief dreamer' because he falsely imagines that he is a monarch, i.e. that the world really exists for him. Cp. the boasting of the lovers in 'The Youth of Man' 26–7 (p. 251 below),

> *'We are young, and the world is ours;*
> *Man, man is the king of the world!'*

and the sober instruction given to Pausanias, 'Empedocles on Etna' I ii
177–81 (p. 164 below),

> *We mortals are no kings*
> *For each of whom to sway*
> *A new-made world up-springs,*
> *Meant merely for his play;*
> *No, we are strangers here; the world is from of old.*

16 Horatian Echo

(TO AN AMBITIOUS FRIEND)

Written 1847: A.'s signed and dated autograph is among Yale Papers (with
cancelled variants not recorded in *1950*) – see facsimile accompanying A.
Galton's 'Some Letters of Matthew Arnold', *Century Guild Hobby Horse*
no. 18 (April 1890) 47–55 and also the letters of (1) 21 April 1887, '. . . if
I can make anything of a little Horatian Echo, in verse, which has lain by
me for years, discarded because of an unsatisfactory stanza, you shall have
it . . .' and (2) 4 June 1887, 'I send you the thing I promised – a relic of
youth. It is quite artificial in sentiment, but has some tolerable lines,
perhaps' (*loc. cit.* 49, 51). A.'s unpublished 1847 diary notes the purchase of a
Béranger 6 Feb. and in Dec. he bought another for Clough (*CL* 63), but by
29 Sept. 1848 this interest had been outgrown: 'Horace whom he resembles
had to write only for a circle of highly cultivated désillusionés roués, in a
sceptical age: we have the sceptical age, but a far different and wider
audience: voilà pourquoi, with all his genius, there is something "fade"
about Beranger's Epicureanism' (*CL* 92–3). This passage immediately
precedes quotation of the fragment 'Say this of her . . .' (p. 577 below),
which is obviously linked with the last stanza of 'Horatian Echo'. Stanzas
2 and 3 glance at the hopes and fears associated with the rising Chartist
agitation in 1847. The 'ambitious friend' is strictly unidentifiable but may
be John Blackett (1821–56), who wrote for the Whig *Globe* and was
invited to contest a Newcastle-upon-Tyne constituency in 1846.
Published *Century Guild Hobby Horse* July 1887; reprinted *1890*, etc.

> Omit, omit, my simple friend,
> Still to enquire how parties tend,
> Or what we fix with foreign powers.
> If France and we are really friends,
> And what the Russian Czar intends,
>   Is no concern of ours.

5

¶ 16. *1–6.* Cp. Milton, Sonnet xviii 7–8,

> *Let Euclid rest and Archimedes pause,*
> *And what the Swede intend and what the French . . .*

Us not the daily quickening race
Of the invading populace
Shall draw to swell that shouldering herd.
10   Mourn will we not your closing hour,
Ye imbeciles in present power,
        Doomed, pompous, and absurd!

And let us bear, that they debate
Of all the engine-work of state,
15   Of commerce, laws, and policy,
The secrets of the world's machine,
And what the rights of man may mean,
        With readier tongue than we.

Only, that with no finer art
20   They cloak the troubles of the heart
With pleasant smile, let us take care;
Nor with a lighter hand dispose
Fresh garlands of this dewy rose,
        To crown Eugenia's hair.

---

and its source in Horace, *Odes* II xi 1–4,

> *Quid bellicosus Cantaber et Scythes,*
> *Hirpine Quinti, cogitet, Hadria*
> *divisus obiecto, remittas*
> *quaerere . . .*

7–12. A. divides his contempt between populace and aristocracy – with ll. 10–12 cp. his letter 7 March 1848, '. . . still the hour of the hereditary peerage and eldest sonship and immense properties has, I am convinced, . . . struck' (*L* i 4), but the first draft of the stanza in A.'s copy of Eckermann' *Gespräche mit Goethe* (Leipzig, 1837) ii is concerned only with the crowd:

> *Him not the noisy swarming race*
> *Of the invading populace*
> *Mounting to power long denied –*
> *Who will not mount in peace – but love*
> *At such despotic length to prove*
> *That right is on their side . . .*

(see *Commentary* 59). With ll. 1–3 of this cp. another passage of the letter cited above, '. . . the din and whirl and brutality which envelop a movement of the masses . . .'

10. your] *MS.*, over 'the' cancelled.

11. Ye imbeciles in present] *MS.*, over 'Of all the incapables in' cancelled.

12. pompous] *MS.*, over 'solemn' cancelled.

23. this] *MS.*, over 'yet' cancelled.

24. Eugenia] The name is also used in 'Philomela' (p. 347 below).

25   Of little threads our life is spun,
        And he spins ill, who misses one.
        But is thy fair Eugenia cold?
        Yet Helen had an equal grace,
        And Juliet's was as fair a face,
30   And now their years are told.

        The day approaches, when we must
        Be crumbling bones and windy dust;
        And scorn us as our mistress may,
        Her beauty will no better be
35   Than the poor face she slights in thee,
                When dawns that day, that day.

27. The reading of *MS.* over a cancelled and nearly indecipherable earlier
reading, which may be 'Appears [?Assume] Eugenia selfish cold'.
28-32. Cp. Horace, *Odes* IV vii 14-16,

> . . . *nos ubi decidimus,*
> *quo pius Aeneas, quo Tullus dives et Ancus*
> *pulvis et umbra sumus.*

28. Yet] *MS.*, over 'But' cancelled.
30. And] *MS.*, over 'Yet' and 'But' cancelled.
33. And scorn us as our] *MS.*, over 'Disdain thee as thy' cancelled.
35. slights] *MS.*, over 'scorns' cancelled.
36. dawns] *MS.*, over 'comes' cancelled. A.'s discarded first attempt at the
line reads, 'My friend, on that just day'.

17 To George Cruikshank
ON SEEING, IN THE COUNTRY, HIS PICTURE OF 'THE BOTTLE'

Date of composition unknown, but probably 1847-8: Cruikshank's 'The
Bottle', a plea for total abstinence in a series of eight plates showing a
drunkard's progress, was published in 1847.
Published *1849* as 'To George Cruikshank, Esq. on seeing for the first time
his picture of "The Bottle", in the country'; reprinted *1853* (*1854, 1857*);
1869 as 'Human Limits. On seeing George Cruikshank's picture of "The
Bottle", in the country'; with present title *1877*, etc.

        Artist, whose hand, with horror winged, hath torn
        From the rank life of towns this leaf! and flung
        The prodigy of full-blown crime among
        Valleys and men to middle fortune born,

5   Not innocent, indeed, yet not forlorn –
       Say, what shall calm us when such guests intrude
       Like comets on the heavenly solitude?
       Shall breathless glades, cheered by shy Dian's horn,

       Cold-bubbling springs, or caves? – Not so! The soul
10   Breasts her own griefs; and, urged too fiercely, says:
       'Why tremble? True, the nobleness of man

       May be by man effaced; man can control
       To pain, to death, the bent of his own days.
       Know thou the worst! So much, not more, he *can*.'

¶ 17. *10. urged too fiercely*] A fair comment. See *Commentary* 32 for the motto under Cruikshank's last plate, 'The bottle has done its work – it has destroyed the infant and the mother, it has brought the son and the daughter to vice and to the streets, and has left the father a hopeless maniac.'

18 Fragment of an 'Antigone'

Date of composition unknown, but (?) 1847–8: see the praise of Sophocles in 'To a Friend' (p. 104 below), which is probably of 1848, and on Sopho-clean style A.'s letter to Clough (undated but soon after 26 Feb. 1849), 'Nay in Sophocles what is valuable is not so much his contributions to psychology and the anatomy of sentiment, as the grand moral effects produced by *style* . . . But my Antigone supports me and in some degree subjugates destiny' (*CL* 101). A translation of *Antigone* with music by Mendelssohn was performed in London in 1844–5 and again at the Hay-market Theatre in 1847. A. probably saw the latter performance with his admired Helen Faucit in the title-role. The primacy of the 'law, which consecrates the ties of blood' over 'self-selected good' connects the poem with the theme of 'The Sick King in Bokhara'.
Published *1849*; reprinted *1855*, *1869*, etc.

The Chorus
Well hath he done who hath seized happiness!
For little do the all-containing hours,

¶ 18. *1.* A.'s chorus is not an imitation of an actual chorus in Sophocles's *Antigone*, but he follows Sophocles's familiar version of the legend. The titles of this poem and of 'Fragment of Chorus of a "Dejaneira"' (p. 64 below), which was probably composed about the same time, may be taken as indicating how long A. had toyed with the idea of a tragedy on the Greek model before he wrote *Merope* (1858).

Though opulent, freely give.
Who, ~~weighing that life well~~
5   Fortune presents unprayed,
Declines her ministry, and carves his own;
And, justice not infringed,
Makes his own welfare his unswerved-from law.

He does well too, who keeps that clue the mild
10   Birth-Goddess and the austere Fates first gave.
For from the day when these
Bring him, a weeping child,
First to the light, and mark
A country for him, kinsfolk, and a home,
15   Unguided he remains,
Till the Fates come again, this time with death.

In little companies,
And, our own place once left,
Ignorant where to stand, or whom to avoid,
20   By city and household grouped, we live; and many
Our order heaven-ordained   [shocks
Must every day endure:
Voyages, exiles, hates, dissensions, wars.
Besides what waste *he* makes,
25   The all-hated, order-breaking,
Without friend, city, or home,
Death, who dissevers all.

~~Him then I praise, who dares~~
~~To self-selected good~~
30   Prefer obedience to the primal law,
Which consecrates the ties of blood; for these, indeed,
Are to the Gods a care;
That touches but himself.
For every day man may be linked and loosed
35   With strangers; but the bond
Original, deep-inwound,
Of blood, can he not bind,
Nor, if Fate binds, not bear.

But hush! Hæmon, whom Antigone,
40   Robbing herself of life in burying,
Against Creon's law, Polynices,
Robs of a loved bride – pale, imploring,
Waiting her passage,
Forth from the palace hitherward comes.

Hæmon

45   No, no, old men, Creon I curse not!
I weep, Thebans,
One than Creon crueller far!
For he, he, at least, by slaying her,
August laws doth mightily vindicate;
50   But thou, too-bold, headstrong, pitiless!
Ah me! – honourest more than thy lover,
O Antigone!
A dead, ignorant, thankless corpse.

The Chorus

Nor was the love untrue
55   Which the Dawn-Goddess bore
To that fair youth she erst,
Leaving the salt sea-beds
And coming flushed over the stormy frith
Of loud Euripus, saw –
60   Saw and snatched, wild with love,
From the pine-dotted spurs
Of Parnes, where thy waves,
Asopus! gleam rock-hemmed –
The Hunter of the Tanagræan Field.

65   But him, in his sweet prime,
By severance immature,
By Artemis' soft shafts,
She, though a Goddess born,
Saw in the rocky isle of Delos die.
70   Such end o'ertook that love.
For she desired to make
Immortal mortal man,
And blend his happy life,
Far from the Gods, with hers;
75   To him postponing an eternal law.

59–64. The proper names are Boeotian. Euripus is the strait separating Boeotia from Euboea; Parnes, a mountain that forms part of the boundary with Attica; Tanagra, a Boeotian town on one bank of the Asopus.
64. 'Orion, the Wild Huntsman of Greek legend, and in this capacity appearing in both earth and sky.' A.'s note, first added *1869*. Orion was loved by the Dawn-Goddess (Eos, Aurora). One legend is that he was slain accidentally by the arrow of Artemis while swimming off Delos.

Hæmon

But like me, she, wroth, complaining,
Succumbed to the envy of the unkind Gods;
And, her beautiful arms unclasping,
Her fair youth unwillingly gave.

The Chorus

80   Nor, though enthroned too high
To fear assault of envious Gods,
His beloved Argive seer would Zeus retain
From his appointed end

In this our Thebes; but when
85   His flying steeds came near
To cross the steep Ismenian glen,
The broad earth opened, and whelmed them and
    him;
And through the void air sang
At large his enemy's spear.

90   And fain would Zeus have saved his tired son
Beholding him where the Two Pillars stand
O'er the sun-reddened western straits,
Or at his work in that dim lower world.
Fain would he have recalled
95   The fraudulent oath which bound
To a much feebler wight the heroic man.

82. Argive seer] Tiresias. See 'The Strayed Reveller' 135–42, 212–22 and *nn.*
(pp. 70, 73 below); here ll. 84–9 refer to the story of his death when in flight
with the Thebans after their defeat by the Epigoni, the descendants of the
'Seven against Thebes'.
86. Ismenian] The river Ismenus flows through Thebes to Lake Hylica.
90. his tired son] Hercules, son of Zeus and Alcmene, was bound by the
Delphic oracle to serve Eurystheus. In ll. 91–3 A. alludes to two of his
Twelve Labours – the fetching of the golden apples of the Hesperides and
the bringing of Cerberus from Hades.
92. 'Erytheia, the legendary region round the Pillars of Hercules, probably
took its name from the redness of the West under which the Greeks saw
it.' A.'s note, first added *1869*.

> But he preferred Fate to his strong desire.
> Nor did there need less than the burning pile
>   Under the towering Trachis crags,
> 100 And the Spercheios vale, shaken with groans,
>   And the roused Maliac gulf,
>   And scared Œtæan snows,
> To achieve his son's deliverance, O my child!

97–103. Hercules was snatched to heaven by Zeus from his funeral pyre on Mt. Oeta (which he mounted when agonized by the shirt of Nessus innocently sent to him by his wife Deianira). Mt. Oeta is in southern Thessaly where the River Spercheios flows into the Malic gulf. Trachis is a Thessalian town where Hercules lived for a time.

19 Fragment of Chorus of a 'Dejaneira'

Date of composition unknown, but (?) 1847–8: for A.'s interest in Sophocles at this time see headn. to 'Fragment of an "Antigone"' (p. 60 above), which this poem follows in *1869* and later collected editions; '. . . probably, like the preceding [poem], a product of the poet's youth' (*Commentary* 162). In his review of *1867* (*Fortnightly Review*, Oct. 1867) Swinburne wrote, 'We must hope to have more of the tragedy in time; that must be a noble statue which could match this massive fragment' (*Essays and Studies* (1875) 160).
Published *1867*; reprinted (*1868*), *1869*, etc.

> O frivolous mind of man,
> Light ignorance, and hurrying, unsure thoughts!
> Though man bewails you not,
> How *I* bewail you!
>
> 5   Little in your prosperity
>   Do you seek counsel of the Gods.
> Proud, ignorant, self-adored, you live alone.
> In profound silence stern,
>   Among their savage gorges and cold springs,
> 10   Unvisited remain
>   The great oracular shrines.

¶ 19. *Title.* Deianira, the wife of Hercules, is a character in Sophocles's *Trachiniae.* She killed herself in despair when the poisoned shirt of Nessus caused the hero's death.

Thither in your adversity
Do you betake yourselves for light,
But strangely misinterpret all you hear.
15   For you will not put on
New hearts with the enquirer's holy robe,
And purged, considerate minds.

And him on whom, at the end
Of toil and dolour untold,
20   The Gods have said that repose
At last shall descend undisturbed –
Him you expect to behold
In an easy old age, in a happy home;
No end but this you praise.

25   But him, on whom, in the prime
Of life, with vigour undimmed,
With unspent mind, and a soul
Unworn, undebased, undecayed,
Mournfully grating, the gates
30   Of the city of death have for ever closed –
Him, I count *him*, well-starred.

16. the enquirer's holy robe] Clients bathed ceremonially and wore fresh
linen robes when they approached the oracle.
25–31. Cp. Wordsworth's 'At the Grave of Burns' (published 1842) 67–72,

> For he *is safe, a quiet bed*
> *Hath early found among the dead,*
> *Harboured where none can be misled,*
>   *Wronged, or distrest;*
> *And surely here it may be said*
>   *That such are blest.*

Wordsworth is speaking of a son of Burns. The poem is included in A.'s
selected *Poems of Wordsworth* (1879).

20 The Strayed Reveller

Date of composition unknown, but (?) 1847–8 if, as seems likely, A. is
experimenting in this title-poem with the 'natural magic' of Maurice de
Guérin's 'Le Centaure', which he read and was haunted by in 1847 (see
'Maurice de Guérin' (1862), *E in C I* (1865), *Works* iii 87 ff.) and which is
probably echoed in ll. 143–50. The setting is from *Odyssey* x, but the
balancing within the classical frame of the two sets of visions is original
(cp. similar types of structure in 'Resignation', 'The Scholar-Gipsy' and

'Bacchanalia'). Various reviewers of *1849* recognized an attempt to reproduce the effect of Greek lyric measures, but L. Binyon in *Tradition
and Reaction in Modern Poetry* (English Assoc. Pamphlet no. 63, 1923) 12
argues that A. is imitating 'Goethe's and Heine's free-verse poems, which I
imagine were . . . modelled on a misunderstanding of Greek lyrics'.
Published *1849*; reprinted *1853* (*1854*, *1857*), *1869*, etc.

THE PORTICO OF CIRCE'S PALACE. EVENING

A Youth. Circe

The Youth

Faster, faster,
O Circe, Goddess,
Let the wild, thronging train,
The bright procession
5   Of eddying forms,
Sweep through my soul!

Thou standest, smiling
Down on me! thy right arm,
Leaned up against the column there,
10   Props thy soft cheek;
Thy left holds, hanging loosely,
The deep cup, ivy-cinctured,
I held but now.

¶ 20. Stage-direction. *The Portico . . . Evening*] Added *1853*.
3–6. Cp. A. on one type of poetic temperament (i.e. that shared by Guérin
and Keats), 'Maurice de Guérin', *E in C I* (1865), *Works* iii 116–17,
'. . . an extraordinary delicacy of organisation and susceptibility to impressions; in exercising it the poet . . . aspires to be a sort of Aeolian harp
. . . To assist at the evolution of the whole life of the world is his craving . . .'
and his translation from Guérin's journal, 'My imagination welcomes every
dream, every impression, without attaching itself to any, and goes on for
ever seeking something new' (*loc. cit.* 118). In 1863 A. felt that such a
temperament was 'devouring' and that great poetry interpreted life by
its possession of both 'natural magic' and 'moral profundity', but clearly
in one mood at least before 1849 poetic volatility powerfully attracted
him. 'Eddying' (l. 5) is for once without its usual unfavourable significance
– see, for example, 'Resignation' 277 (p. 95 below),

In action's dizzying eddy whirled . . .

7–22. The pictorial vividness here and elsewhere in the poem is unusual
for A.; it may have been worked up partly to compensate for the lack of
rhyme and conventional metre.

Is it, then, evening
15 So soon? I see the night-dews,
Clustered in thick beads, dim
The agate brooch-stones
On thy white shoulder;
The cool night-wind, too,
20 Blows through the portico,
Stirs thy hair, Goddess,
Waves thy white robe!

Circe

Whence art thou, sleeper?

The Youth

When the white dawn first
25 Through the rough fir-planks
Of my hut, by the chestnuts,
Up at the valley-head,
Came breaking, Goddess!
I sprang up, I threw round me
30 My dappled fawn-skin;
Passing out, from the wet turf,
Where they lay, by the hut door,
I snatched up my vine-crown, my fir-staff,
All drenched in dew –
35 Came swift down to join
The rout early gathered
In the town, round the temple,
Iacchus' white fane
On yonder hill.

40 Quick I passed, following
The wood-cutters' cart-track
Down the dark valley; I saw
On my left, through the beeches,
Thy palace, Goddess,
45 Smokeless, empty!
Trembling, I entered; beheld
The court all silent,
The lions sleeping,

---

38. *Iacchus*] A minor deity of the Eleusinian mysteries often identified with Dionysus. The vine-crown and thyrsus (l. 33) are Bacchic insignia.
43–8. Cp. Homer's *Odyssey* x 210–13, 'Within the forest glades they found the house of Circe built of polished stone . . . and round about it were mountain wolves and lions, whom Circe herself had bewitched.'

On the altar this bowl.
50   I drank, Goddess!
And sank down here, sleeping,
On the steps of thy portico.

Circe

Foolish boy! Why tremblest thou?
Thou lovest it, then, my wine?
55   Wouldst more of it? See, how glows.
Through the delicate, flushed marble,
The red, creaming liquor,
Strown with dark seeds!
Drink, then! I chide thee not,
60   Deny thee not my bowl.
Come, stretch forth thy hand, then – so!
Drink – drink again!

The Youth

Thanks, gracious one!
Ah, the sweet fumes again!
65   More soft, ah me,
More subtle-winding
Than Pan's flute-music!
Faint – faint! Ah me,
Again the sweet sleep!

Circe

70   Hist! Thou – within there!
Come forth, Ulysses!
Art tired with hunting?
While we range the woodland,
See what the day brings.

Ulysses

75   Ever new magic!
Hast thou then lured hither,
Wonderful Goddess, by thy art,
The young, languid-eyed Ampelus,
Iacchus' darling –
80   Or some youth beloved of Pan,
Of Pan and the Nymphs?
That he sits, bending downward
His white, delicate neck
To the ivy-wreathed marge

78–9. See Ovid, *Fasti* iii 409–10.

85   Of thy cup; the bright, glancing vine-leaves
That crown his hair,
Falling forward, mingling
With the dark ivy-plants –
His fawn-skin, half untied,
90   Smeared with red wine-stains? Who is he,
That he sits, overweighed
By fumes of wine and sleep,
So late, in thy portico?
What youth, Goddess, what guest
95   Of Gods or mortals?

Circe

Hist! he wakes!
I lured him not hither, Ulysses.
Nay, ask him!

The Youth

Who speaks? Ah, who comes forth
100   To thy side, Goddess, from within?
How shall I name him?
This spare, dark-featured,
Quick-eyed stranger?
Ah, and I see too
105   His sailor's bonnet,
His short-coat, travel-tarnished,
With one arm bare! –
Art thou not he, whom fame
This long time rumours
110   The favoured guest of Circe, brought by the waves?
Art thou he, stranger?
The wise Ulysses,
Laertes' son?

Ulysses

I am Ulysses.
115   And thou, too, sleeper?
Thy voice is sweet.
It may be thou hast followed
Through the islands some divine bard,
By age taught many things,
120   Age and the Muses;
And heard him delighting
The chiefs and people
In the banquet, and learned his songs,
Of Gods and Heroes,

125   Of war and arts,
        And peopled cities,
        Inland, or built
        By the grey sea. – If so, then hail!
        I honour and welcome thee.

                    The Youth

130   The Gods are happy.
        They turn on all sides
        Their shining eyes,
        And see below them
        The earth and men.

135   They see Tiresias
        Sitting, staff in hand,
        On the warm, grassy
        Asopus bank,
        His robe drawn over
140   His old, sightless head,
        Revolving inly
        The doom of Thebes.

        They see the Centaurs
        In the upper glens
145   Of Pelion, in the streams,
        Where red-berried ashes fringe
        The clear-brown shallow pools,
        With streaming flanks, and heads
        Reared proudly, snuffing
150   The mountain wind.

        They see the Indian

130–34. The view of Epicurus. Cp. 'Mycerinus' 47–8 (p. 29 above) and *n.*
quoting Lucretius, *De Rerum Natura* ii 646–51, iii 18–22.
135–42. Tiresias, the blind soothsayer, was involved in the 'doom of
Thebes' from the time of Laius and Jocasta until the Theban defeat by the
Epigoni. He had to witness helplessly the fate of Oedipus and in the next
generation the fate of Oedipus' children, Eteocles, Polynices and Antigone.
143–50. Cp. Guérin, 'Le Centaure', '. . . ma mère rentrait . . . ruisselante
des flots qu'elle fréquentait . . . Je me delassais souvent de mes journées
dans le lit des fleuves . . . Cependant, la tête inclinée au vent qui m'appor-
tait le frais, je considérais la cime des montagnes . . .' (*Revue des Deux
Mondes* xxii (1840) 583, 585, 586).

Drifting, knife in hand,
His frail boat moored to
A floating isle thick-matted
155   With large-leaved, low-creeping melon-plants,
And the dark cucumber.
He reaps, and stows them,
Drifting – drifting; round him,
Round his green harvest-plot,
160   Flow the cool lake-waves,
The mountains ring them.

They see the Scythian
On the wide steppe, unharnessing
His wheeled house at noon.
165   He tethers his beast down, and makes his meal –
Mares' milk, and bread
Baked on the embers; all around
The boundless, waving grass-plains stretch, thick-
With saffron and the yellow hollyhock   [starred
170   And flag-leaved iris-flowers.
Sitting in his cart
He makes his meal; before him, for long miles,
Alive with bright green lizards,
And the springing bustard-fowl,
175   The track, a straight black line,
Furrows the rich soil; here and there
Clusters of lonely mounds
Topped with rough-hewn,
Grey, rain-bleared statues, overpeer
180   The sunny waste.

They see the ferry
On the broad, clay-laden

151–61. Cp. A. Burnes, *Travels into Bokhara* (1834) i 60, 'In the valley of
Cashmeer there are moveable beds of melons, which . . . may be considered
in the light of islands. The ingenious people of that valley spread a thick
mat on the surface of their lake, and sprinkle it over with soil: it soon
acquires a consistency, from the grass growing upon it. In the following
year they sow melons and cucumbers, and reap the harvest from a
boat . . .'
162–80. No source identified, but A. may be embroidering the account of
the Scythians in Herodotus iv 46–82.
181–90. Cp. *Travels into Bokhara* i 249–50, 'The mode in which we passed
the Oxus was singular . . . We were drawn by a pair of horses, who were

                    Lone Chorasmian stream; thereon,
                    With snort and strain,
185   Two horses, strongly swimming, tow
                    The ferry-boat, with woven ropes
                    To either bow
                    Firm harnessed by the mane; a chief,
                    With shout and shaken spear,
190   Stands at the prow, and guides them; but astern
                    The cowering merchants, in long robes,
                    Sit pale beside their wealth
                    Of silk-bales and of balsam-drops,
                    Of gold and ivory,
195   Of turquoise-earth and amethyst,
                    Jasper and chalcedony,
                    And milk-barred onyx-stones.
                    The loaded boat swings groaning
                    In the yellow eddies;
200   The Gods behold them.

                    They see the Heroes
                    Sitting in the dark ship
                    On the foamless, long-heaving.
                    Violet sea,
205   At sunset nearing
                    The Happy Islands.

                       These things, Ulysses,
                    The wise bards also
                    Behold and sing.
210   But oh, what labour!
                    O prince, what pain!

---

yoked to the boat, on each bow, by a rope fixed to the hair of the mane.
The bridle is then put on as if the horse were to be mounted; the boat is
pushed into the stream, and . . . is ferried directly across the most rapid
channel. A man on board holds the reins of each horse . . . urging him to
swim.'

183. Chorasmian stream] The lower Oxus. The Chorasmii inhabited its
banks and islands.

201–6. The Fortunate Isles were vaguely located in the 'streams of Ocean',
which the Argonauts reached according to Pindar, *Pythian Odes* iv 251.

210–11. See *n.* to 'Philomela' 4 (p. 348 below). The Romantic commonplace that the poet's song is bought at the price of his suffering conflicts
violently with the Goethean view of the poet's detachment expressed in
'Resignation' 144–69 (pp. 89–91 below). See *Trilling* 100, '"The Strayed

They too can see
Tiresias; but the Gods,
Who give them vision,
215   Added this law:
That they should bear too
His groping blindness,
His dark foreboding,
His scorned white hairs;
220   Bear Hera's anger
Through a life lengthened
To seven ages.

They see the Centaurs
On Pelion; then they feel,
225   They too, the maddening wine
Swell their large veins to bursting; in wild pain
They feel the biting spears
Of the grim Lapithæ, and Theseus, drive,
Drive crashing through their bones; they feel
230   High on a jutting rock in the red stream
Alcmena's dreadful son
Ply his bow; such a price
The Gods exact for song:
To become what we sing.

235   They see the Indian
On his mountain lake; but squalls
Make their skiff reel, and worms
In the unkind spring have gnawn
Their melon-harvest to the heart. – They see

Reveller" is Arnold's celebration of the painful glories of man's bondage to the strength of the emotions, but "Resignation" is the assertion of the way to human freedom in the abandonment of the romantic temperament . . .'; and, for A.'s awareness of such contradictions in his early poems, his letter to his sister 'K' c. July 1849 (misdated 1853), 'Fret not to make my poems square in all their parts, but like what you can . . . The true reason why parts suit you while others do not is that my poems are fragments – i.e. that I am fragments . . . a person therefore who endeavoured to make them accord would only lose his labour . . .' (UL 18).
220–2. Tiresias was blinded by Hera for deciding that women took more pleasure in the sexual act than men. Zeus extended his life to seven generations.
223–32. The fight between the Centaurs and the Lapiths took place at the wedding-feast of Pirithous. Theseus was present. Hercules also fought the Centaurs during his pursuit of the Erymanthian boar.

4+M.A.

240   The Scythian; but long frosts
            Parch them in winter-time on the bare steppe,
            Till they too fade like grass; they crawl
            Like shadows forth in spring.

            They see the merchants
245   On the Oxus stream; but care
            Must visit first them too, and make them pale.
            Whether, through whirling sand,
            A cloud of desert robber-horse have burst
            Upon their caravan; or greedy kings,
250   In the walled cities the way passes through,
            Crushed them with tolls; or fever-airs,
            On some great river's marge,
            Mown them down, far from home.

            They see the Heroes
255   Near harbour; but they share
            Their lives, and former violent toil in Thebes,
            Seven-gated Thebes, or Troy;
            Or where the echoing oars
            Of Argo first
260   Startled the unknown sea.

            The old Silenus
            Came, lolling in the sunshine,
            From the dewy forest-coverts,
            This way, at noon.
265   Sitting by me, while his Fauns
            Down at the water-side
            Sprinkled and smoothed
            His drooping garland,
            He told me these things.

270   But I, Ulysses,
            Sitting on the warm steps,
            Looking over the valley,

251–53. Burnes caught a fever on the banks of the Oxus – see *Travels* i
258–9 and *n.* to 'The Sick King in Bokhara' 22 (p. 77 below).
258–60. Cp. Ovid, *Metamorphoses* vi 720–1,

> *vellera cum Minyis nitido radiantia villo*
> *per mare non notum prima petiere carina.*

261. Silenus, the satyr companion and instructor of the youthful Dionysus,
is represented as having prophetic powers when drunk. A. here accepts
poetry as an intoxication that is also a true insight into the human condition.

All day long, have seen,
Without pain, without labour,
275   Sometimes a wild-haired Mænad –
Sometimes a Faun with torches –
And sometimes, for a moment,
Passing through the dark stems
Flowing-robed, the beloved,
The desired, the divine,
280   Beloved Iacchus.

Ah, cool night-wind, tremulous stars!
Ah, glimmering water,
Fitful earth-murmur,
285   Dreaming woods!
Ah, golden-haired, strangely smiling Goddess,
And thou, proved, much enduring,
Wave-tossed Wanderer!
Who can stand still?
290   Ye fade, ye swim, ye waver before me –
The cup again!

Faster, faster,
O Circe, Goddess,
Let the wild, thronging train,
295   The bright procession
Of eddying forms,
Sweep through my soul!

286. *golden-haired*] Circe is 'fair-tressed' in Homer (*Odyssey* x 220).

21 The Sick King in Bokhara

Date of composition unknown, but (?) 1847–8. Story and many details from Alexander Burnes's *Travels into Bokhara* . . . (1834), also drawn on for 'The Strayed Reveller' and 'Sohrab and Rustum', but when A. first read it is unknown. In a letter to F. T. Palgrave in 1869 (*Russell* 42) he notes that 'it was the first thing of mine dear old Clough thoroughly liked'. For the incidents on which the poem is based see *Travels into Bokhara* i 307–9:

'I have already mentioned the rigour of the Mohammedan law, which is enforced in Bokhara. . . . About twelve years since, a person who had violated the law proceeded to the palace, and, in the presence of the King, stated his crime, and demanded justice according to the Koran. The singularity of an individual appearing as his own accuser induced the King to direct him to be driven away. The man appeared the following day with the same tale, and was again turned out. He repaired a third time to the palace, repeated his sins, and upbraided the King for his remissness in declining to dispense justice, which, as a believer of Mahommed, he intreated, that it might lead to his punishment in this world instead of the next. The Ulema, or congress of divines, was assembled: death was the punishment; and the man himself, who was a Moollah, was prepared for this decision. He was condemned to be stoned till dead. He turned his face to Mecca, and, drawing his garment over his head, repeated the kuluma, ("There is but one God, and Mahommed is his prophet!") and met his fate. The King was present, and threw the first stone: but he had instructed his officers to permit the deluded man to escape if he made the attempt. When dead the King wept over his corpse, ordered it to be washed and buried, and proceeded in person to the grave, over which he read the funeral service. It is said that he was much affected. . . . An incident similar to the above happened within this very year. A son who had cursed his mother appeared as a suppliant for justice, and his own accuser. The mother solicited his pardon and forgiveness; the son demanded punishment: the Ulema directed his death, and he was executed as a criminal in the streets of Bokhara.'

The subject interested A. for its suggestion that the moral law may transcend rational expediency and yet be sanctioned by the individual conscience. For the mullah as a Raskolnikov figure who insists on retribution to purge his sense of guilt see *Trilling* 104–6.
Published *1849*; reprinted *1855*, *1869*, etc.

Hussein

> O most just Vizier, send away
> The cloth-merchants, and let them be,
> Them and their dues, this day! the King
> Is ill at ease, and calls for thee.

The Vizier

> 5   O merchants, tarry yet a day
> Here in Bokhara! but at noon,
> To-morrow, come, and ye shall pay
> Each fortieth web of cloth to me,
> As the law is, and go your way.

¶ 21. *5–8.* Cp. Burnes, *Travels* i 290, 'The Vizier . . . was levying duties on the merchants . . . The webs of cloth are produced and every fortieth piece is taken in place of duties.'

10 O Hussein, lead me to the King!
Thou teller of sweet tales, thine own,
Ferdousi's, and the others', lead!
How is it with my lord?

Hussein

Alone,
Ever since prayer-time, he doth wait,
15 O Vizier! without lying down,
In the great window of the gate,
Looking into the Registàn,
Where through the sellers' booths the slaves
Are this way bringing the dead man. –
20 O Vizier, here is the King's door!

The King

O Vizier, I may bury him?

The Vizier

O King, thou know'st, I have been sick
These many days, and heard no thing
(For Allah shut my ears and mind),
25 Not even what thou dost, O King!
Wherefore, that I may counsel thee,
Let Hussein, if thou wilt, make haste
To speak in order what hath chanced.

The King

O Vizier, be it as thou say'st!

---

12. *Ferdousi*] The Persian epic poet, whose *Shāhnāma* contains the story of
Sohrab and Rustum.
16–18. Cp. *Travels* i 272–3, '. . . the Registan of Bokhara, which is the
name given to a spacious area in the city, near the palace, which opens
upon it. On two other sides there are massive buildings, colleges of the
learned, and on the fourth side there is a fountain . . . Idlers and news-
mongers assemble round the wares of Europe and Asia, which are here
exposed for sale.'
22. The sickness of the king, vizier and mullah was probably suggested 'by
the account of the Balkh fever . . . which prostrated Captain Burnes and
many members of his party upon their arrival in Bokhara' (*Commentary* 87,
referring to *Travels* i 258–9).

Hussein

30   Three days since, at the time of prayer
A certain Moollah, with his robe
All rent, and dust upon his hair,
Watched my lord's coming forth, and pushed
The golden mace-bearers aside,
35   And fell at the King's feet, and cried:

'Justice, O King, and on myself!
On this great sinner, who did break
The law, and by the law must die!
Vengeance, O King!'

But the King spake:
40   'What fool is this, that hurts our ears
With folly? or what drunken slave?
My guards, what, prick him with your spears!
Prick me the fellow from the path!'
As the King said, so it was done,
45   And to the mosque my lord passed on.

But on the morrow, when the King
Went forth again, the holy book
Carried before him, as is right,
And through the square his way he took;
50   My man comes running, flecked with blood
From yesterday, and falling down
Cries out most earnestly, 'O King,
My lord, O King, do right, I pray!

'How canst thou, ere thou hear, discern
55   If I speak folly? but a king,
Whether a thing be great or small,
Like Allah, hears and judges all.

30–49. For the details cp. *Travels* i 292, 'I . . . repaired to the great mosque
. . . and saw his majesty and his court passing from prayers . . . The Koran
was carried in front of him, and he was preceded by two golden mace-
bearers.'
31. Moollah] A mullah is a Mohammedan theologian and jurist.
49. way] path *1849–77.*

'Wherefore hear thou! Thou know'st, how fierce
In these last days the sun hath burned;
60   That the green water in the tanks
Is to a putrid puddle turned;
And the canal, which from the stream
Of Samarcand is brought this way,
Wastes, and runs thinner every day.

65   'Now I at nightfall had gone forth
Alone, and in a darksome place
Under some mulberry-trees I found
A little pool; and in short space,
With all the water that was there
70   I filled my pitcher, and stole home
Unseen; and having drink to spare,
I hid the can behind the door,
And went up on the roof to sleep.

'But in the night, which was with wind
75   And burning dust, again I creep
Down, having fever, for a drink.

'Now meanwhile had my brethren found
The water-pitcher, where it stood
Behind the door upon the ground,
80   And called my mother; and they all,
As they were thirsty, and the night
Most sultry, drained the pitcher there;
That they sate with it, in my sight,
Their lips still wet, when I came down.

85   'Now mark! I, being fevered, sick
(Most unblest also), at that sight
Brake forth, and cursed them – dost thou hear?
One was my mother – Now, do right!'

58–64. Cp. *Travels* i 301–2, 'Bokhara is very indifferently supplied with
water, the river is fifteen miles distant, and the canal is only opened once
in fifteen days. In summer the inhabitants are sometimes deprived of good
water for months, and when we were in Bokhara the canals had been dry
for sixty days; the snow had not melted in the high lands of Samarcand,
and the scanty supply of the river had been wasted before reaching
Bokhara.'
66–7. Cp. *Travels* i 301, 'The city is intersected by canals, shaded by
mulberry trees . . .'

But my lord mused a space, and said:
90   'Send him away, Sirs, and make on!
It is some madman!' the King said.
As the King bade, so was it done.

The morrow, at the self-same hour,
In the King's path, behold, the man,
95   Not kneeling, sternly fixed! he stood
Right opposite, and thus began,
Frowning grim down: 'Thou wicked King,
Most deaf where thou shouldst most give ear!
What, must I howl in the next world,
100   Because thou wilt not listen here?

'What, wilt thou pray, and get thee grace,
And all grace shall to me be grudged?
Nay but, I swear, from this thy path
I will not stir till I be judged!'

105   Then they who stood about the King
Drew close together and conferred;
Till that the King stood forth and said:
'Before the priests thou shalt be heard.'

But when the Ulemas were met,
110   And the thing heard, they doubted not;
But sentenced him, as the law is,
To die by stoning on the spot.

Now the King charged us secretly:
'Stoned must he be, the law stands so.
115   Yet, if he seek to fly, give way;
Hinder him not, but let him go.'

So saying, the King took a stone,
And cast it softly; – but the man,
With a great joy upon his face,
120   Kneeled down, and cried not, neither ran.

So they, whose lot it was, cast stones,
That they flew thick and bruised him sore.
But he praised Allah with loud voice,
And remained kneeling as before.

116. *Hinder*] Forbid *1849–55*.

125 My lord had covered up his face;
But when one told him, 'He is dead,'
Turning him quickly to go in,
'Bring thou to me his corpse,' he said.

And truly, while I speak, O King,
130 I hear the bearers on the stair;
Wilt thou they straightway bring him in?
– Ho! enter ye who tarry there!

The Vizier

O King, in this I praise thee not!
Now must I call thy grief not wise.
135 Is he thy friend, or of thy blood,
To find such favour in thine eyes?

Nay, were he thine own mother's son,
Still, thou art king, and the law stands.
It were not meet the balance swerved,
140 The sword were broken in thy hands.

But being nothing, as he is,
Why for no cause make sad thy face?
Lo, I am old! three kings, ere thee,
Have I seen reigning in this place.

145 But who, through all this length of time,
Could bear the burden of his years,
If he for strangers pained his heart
Not less than those who merit tears?

Fathers we *must* have, wife and child,
150 And grievous is the grief for these;
This pain alone, which *must* be borne,
Makes the head white, and bows the knees.

But other loads than this his own
One man is not well made to bear.
155 Besides, to each are his own friends,
To mourn with him, and show him care.

Look, this is but one single place,
Though it be great; all the earth round,
If a man bear to have it so,
160 Things which might vex him shall be found.

4*

Upon the Russian frontier, where
The watchers of two armies stand
Near one another, many a man,
Seeking a prey unto his hand,

165　　Hath snatched a little fair-haired slave;
They snatch also, towards Mervè,
The Shiah dogs, who pasture sheep,
And up from thence to Orgunjè.

And these all, labouring for a lord,
170　　Eat not the fruit of their own hands;
Which is the heaviest of all plagues,
To that man's mind, who understands.

The kaffirs also (whom God curse!)
Vex one another, night and day;
175　　There are the lepers, and all sick;
There are the poor, who faint alway.

All these have sorrow, and keep still,
Whilst other men make cheer, and sing.
Wilt thou have pity on all these?
180　　No, nor on this dead dog, O King!

The King

O Vizier, thou art old, I young!
Clear in these things I cannot see.
My head is burning, and a heat
Is in my skin which angers me.

185　　But hear ye this, ye sons of men!
They that bear rule, and are obeyed,
Unto a rule more strong than theirs
Are in their turn obedient made.

In vain therefore, with wistful eyes
190　　Gazing up hither, the poor man,
Who loiters by the high-heaped booths,
Below there, in the Registàn,

161. *Russian*] northern *1849*.
167. *Shiah dogs*] The Shiahs are an Islamic sect. The vizier was a Sunni.
173. *kaffirs*] Infidels. Cp. *Travels* ii 221, '. . . that extraordinary people, the
Siahposh Kaffirs, or Black-vested Infidels . . . This race is entirely confined
to the mountains, and persecuted by all the surrounding nations, who seek
to capture them as slaves . . .'

Says: 'Happy he, who lodges there!
With silken raiment, store of rice,
195   And for this drought, all kinds of fruits,
Grape-syrup, squares of coloured ice,

'With cherries served in drifts of snow.'
In vain hath a king power to build
Houses, arcades, enamelled mosques;
200   And to make orchard-closes, filled

With curious fruit-trees brought from far;
With cisterns for the winter-rain,
And, in the desert, spacious inns
In divers places – if that pain

205   Is not more lightened, which he feels,
If his will be not satisfied;
And that it be not, from all time
The law is planted, to abide.

Thou wast a sinner, thou poor man!
210   Thou wast athirst; and didst not see,
That, though we take what we desire,
We must not snatch it eagerly.

And I have meat and drink at will,
And rooms of treasures, not a few.
215   But I am sick, nor heed I these;
And what I would, I cannot do.

Even the great honour which I have,
When I am dead, will soon grow still;
So have I neither joy, nor fame.
220   But what I can do, that I will.

I have a fretted brick-work tomb
Upon a hill on the right hand,
Hard by a close of apricots,
Upon the road of Samarcand;

195–7. Cp. *Travels* i 259, 277–8, '. . . we quenched our thirst, under a
thermometer of 108°, with sherbet of cherries, cooled by ice . . .'; '. . . one
may purchase "rahut i jan", or the delight of life, – grape jelly or syrup,
mixed up with chopped ice . . . It is a refreshing sight to see the huge
masses of it, with the thermometer at 90°, coloured, scraped, and piled
into heaps like snow . . .'

225   Thither, O Vizier, will I bear
                This man my pity could not save,
                And, plucking up the marble flags,
                There lay his body in my grave.

                Bring water, nard, and linen rolls!
230   Wash off all blood, set smooth each limb!
                Then say: 'He was not wholly vile,
                Because a king shall bury him.'

22 Resignation

TO FAUSTA

Date of composition unknown, but (?) 1843–8: probably partly written
soon after July 1843, date of the poem's second walk – a memorial stone at
Wythburn commemorates 'the two walks from hence over the Armboth
Fells July 1833–43' (*Commentary* 64 *fn.*) – and added to and revised until
first published, as dependence on Goethe's *Wilhelm Meister* (read in Carlyle's translation at Oxford, probably by 1845) and the more general influences of the Stoics, Spinoza, *Obermann*, etc. (1847–8) would indicate.
Like Wordsworth's 'Tintern Abbey' this is a poem addressed to a favourite
sister about revisiting a place and the reflections aroused by the two occasions, and A.'s view that natural objects 'Seem to bear rather then rejoice'
(l. 270) contradicts Wordsworth's claim that it is Nature's privilege
('Tintern Abbey' 124–5),

> *Through all the years of this our life, to lead*
> *From joy to joy . . .*

For further study of the relationship between the two poems see L.
Gottfried's *Matthew Arnold and the Romantics* (1963) 219–23 and U. C.

¶ 22. *Sub-title. Fausta*] Jane Arnold ('K'), Matthew's elder sister – see Mrs.
H. Ward, *A Writer's Recollections* (1918) 39, 'It was to her that "Resignation" was addressed, in recollection of their mountain walks and talks together.' She married W. E. Forster in Aug. 1850, but in 1841–2 she was
engaged to George Cotton (then assistant-master at Rugby), who broke
off the engagement in early May; the breaking of the engagement and
Jane's consequent depression were predisposing causes of Dr. A.'s collapse
17 May and probably of the attack of angina that killed him 12 June 1842
(see N. Wymer, *Dr. Arnold of Rugby* 191–4). The name may be meant to
suggest 'a female Faust' who 'desires poignant experience to relieve the
dullness of her life' (*Trilling* 99), but, equally, with the Latin meaning of
the word in mind, it may hint a gentle rebuke – in spite of her sense of
frustration Jane is 'fortunate'.

Knoepflmacher, *Vict. Poetry* i (1963) 18–21; and for other comments on
'Resignation', *Bonnerot* 284–99 and *Baum* 21–34.
Published *1849*; reprinted *1855*, *1869*, etc.

To die be given us, or attain!
Fierce work it were, to do again.
So pilgrims, bound for Mecca, prayed
At burning noon; so warriors said,
5   Scarfed with the cross, who watched the miles
Of dust which wreathed their struggling files
Down Lydian mountains; so, when snows
Round Alpine summits, eddying, rose,
The Goth, bound Rome-wards; so the Hun,
10   Crouched on his saddle, while the sun
Went lurid down o'er flooded plains
Through which the groaning Danube strains
To the drear Euxine; so pray all,
Whom labours, self-ordained, enthrall;
15   Because they to themselves propose
On this side the all-common close
A goal which, gained, may give repose.
So pray they; and to stand again
Where they stood once, to them were pain;
20   Pain to thread back and to renew
Past straits, and currents long steered through.

But milder natures, and more free –
Whom an unblamed serenity
Hath freed from passions, and the state
25   Of struggle these necessitate;
Whom schooling of the stubborn mind
Hath made, or birth hath found, resigned –
These mourn not, that their goings pay
Obedience to the passing day.
30   These claim not every laughing Hour
For handmaid to their striding power;
Each in her turn, with torch upreared,
To await their march; and when appeared,
Through the cold gloom, with measured race,
35   To usher for a destined space
(Her own sweet errands all forgone)
The too imperious traveller on.
These, Fausta, ask not this; nor thou,
Time's chafing prisoner, ask it now!

23. *unblamed serenity*] Stoic ataraxy or Hindu 'detachment'.

40 We left, just ten years since, you say,
That wayside inn we left to-day.
Our jovial host, as forth we fare,
Shouts greeting from his easy chair.
High on a bank our leader stands,
45 Reviews and ranks his motley bands,
Makes clear our goal to every eye –
The valley's western boundary.
A gate swings to! our tide hath flowed
Already from the silent road.
50 The valley-pastures, one by one,
Are threaded, quiet in the sun;
And now beyond the rude stone bridge
Slopes gracious up the western ridge.
Its woody border, and the last
55 Of its dark upland farms is past –
Cool farms, with open-lying stores,
Under their burnished sycamores;
All past! and through the trees we glide,
Emerging on the green hill-side.
60 There climbing hangs, a far-seen sign,

cf. 79

40–1. 'Those who have been long familiar with the English Lake-Country will find no difficulty in recalling, from the description in the text, the roadside inn of Wythburn on the descent from Dunmail Rise towards Keswick: its sedentary landlord of twenty years ago, and the passage over the Wythburn Fells to Watendlath.' A.'s note added *1869* ('thirty' substituted for 'twenty' *1877*). Cp. Tom A.'s unpublished letter of 28 Aug. 1849 (A. Turnbull Library, Wellington, N.Z.), 'Does Fausta mean K, and is the walk "ten years ago" alluded to in "Resignation" that which we took over Wythburn Fells to Keswick with Captain Hamilton?'; and also Mrs. A.'s unpublished journal July 1833, 'Jane, Matt and Tom will remember their walk to Keswick from Wythburn, and how their poor young legs were tried by the stiff sticks of the heath on the mountain, and how they eat oatcake and bathed to refresh themselves – but how poor Jane was still tired, and obliged to lie down – and was far from well at that comfortless Cockermouth. Mr. Hamilton was with us. And do you recollect how fine the view was from the high ground as we were returning between Whitehaven and Scale Hill.' The best reconstruction of events is that the walk between Wythburn and Keswick was part of a much longer excursion made by carriage. The carriage was left by Dr. A., Captain Hamilton and the three children at Wythburn and rejoined at Keswick. The whole party, which included Mrs. A. and a companion, then proceeded to the coast after a short rest at Cockermouth. The 'wide-glimmering sea' (l. 85) must refer to the Irish Sea.

Our wavering, many-coloured line;
There winds, upstreaming slowly still
Over the summit of the hill.
And now, in front, behold outspread
65   Those upper regions we must tread!
Mild hollows, and clear heathy swells,
The cheerful silence of the fells.
Some two hours' march with serious air,
Through the deep noontide heats we fare;
70   The red-grouse, springing at our sound,
Skims, now and then, the shining ground;
No life, save his and ours, intrudes
Upon these breathless solitudes.
O joy! again the farms appear.
75   Cool shade is there, and rustic cheer;
There springs the brook will guide us down,
Bright comrade, to the noisy town.
Lingering, we follow down; we gain
The town, the highway, and the plain.
80   And many a mile of dusty way,
Parched and road-worn, we made that day;
But, Fausta, I remember well,
That as the balmy darkness fell
We bathed our hands with speechless glee,
85   That night, in the wide-glimmering sea.

Once more we tread this self-same road,
Fausta, which ten years since we trod;
Alone we tread it, you and I,
Ghosts of that boisterous company.
90   Here, where the brook shines, near its head,
In its clear, shallow, turf-fringed bed;
Here, whence the eye first sees, far down,
Capped with faint smoke, the noisy town;
Here sit we, and again unroll,

61. *many-coloured*] See *n*. to 'To a Gipsy Child . . .' 34 (p. 25 above).
86-107. Cp. Clough, 'Blank Misgivings' ix 1-21 and particularly 1-6,

> *Once more the wonted road I tread*
> *Once more dark heavens above me spread,*
> *Upon the windy down I stand,*
> *My station, whence the circling land*
> *Lies mapped and pictured wide below; –*
> *Such as it was, such e'en again . . .*

Clough's lines, which are dated Feb. 1841, probably also suggested A.'s
use of 'station' (= viewpoint) at l. 164 below.

95   Though slowly, the familiar whole.
    The solemn wastes of heathy hill
    Sleep in the July sunshine still;
    The self-same shadows now, as then,
    Play through this grassy upland glen;
100   The loose dark stones on the green way
    Lie strewn, it seems, where then they lay;
    On this mild bank above the stream,
    (You crush them!) the blue gentians gleam.
    Still this wild brook, the rushes cool,
105   The sailing foam, the shining pool!
    These are not changed; and we, you say,
    Are scarce more changed, in truth, than they.

    The gipsies, whom we met below,
    They, too, have long roamed to and fro;
110   They ramble, leaving, where they pass,
    Their fragments on the cumbered grass.
    And often to some kindly place
    Chance guides the migratory race,
    Where, though long wanderings intervene,
115   They recognise a former scene.
    The dingy tents are pitched; the fires

113. *migratory race*] A phrase that cannot be much later than A.'s prize-poem
'Cromwell' (1843).
116–19. Cp. Wordsworth, 'Gipsies' 1–2, 5–8,

> *Yet are they here the same unbroken knot*
> *Of human beings, in the self-same spot!*

> *Only their fire seems bolder, yielding light,*
> *Now deep and red, the colouring of night;*
>   *That on their Gipsy-faces falls,*
>   *Their bed of straw and blanket-walls* . . .

Wordsworth stresses the 'torpid life' of the gipsies as A. does. A. also remembered A. P. Stanley's prize-winning Newdigate, 'The Gypsies' (1837)
157–8, 161–2, 167–70,

>   . . . *but still from year to year*
> *To Nature's voice they turn a dull deaf ear;*

> *Autumn's wan leaves and Winter's death-like snows*
> *To them no solemn truths disclose;*

> *Yea, God and Man, the Future and the Past*
> *Are but to them a chaos dark and vast –*
> *One gloomy Present, one unchanged To-day*
> *Stirred by no storm, and brightened by no ray.*

Give to the wind their wavering spires;
In dark knots crouch round the wild flame
Their children, as when first they came;
120   They see their shackled beasts again
Move, browsing, up the gray-walled lane.
Signs are not wanting, which might raise
The ghost in them of former days –
Signs are not wanting, if they would;
125   Suggestions to disquietude.
For them, for all, time's busy touch,
While it mends little, troubles much.
Their joints grow stiffer – but the year
Runs his old round of dubious cheer;
130   Chilly they grow – yet winds in March,
Still, sharp as ever, freeze and parch;
They must live still – and yet, God knows,
Crowded and keen the country grows;
It seems as if, in their decay,
135   The law grew stronger every day.
So might they reason, so compare,
Fausta, times past with times that are.
But no! – they rubbed through yesterday
In their hereditary way,
140   And they will rub through, if they can,
To-morrow on the self-same plan,
Till death arrive to supersede,
For them, vicissitude and need.

The poet, to whose mighty heart
145   Heaven doth a quicker pulse impart,
Subdues that energy to scan
Not his own course, but that of man.
Though he move mountains, though his day
Be passed on the proud heights of sway,
150   Though he hath loosed a thousand chains,
Though he hath borne immortal pains,

144-69. Cp. Carlyle's translation (1824) of *Wilhelm Meister* ii ch. 2, *Works*,
ed. H. D. Traill xxiii 112, 'Look at men, how they struggle after happiness
and satisfaction! Their wishes, their toil, their gold, are ever hunting restlessly; and after what? After that which the poet has received from nature –
the right enjoyment of the world. . . . Now fate has exalted the poet above
all this [continual agitation], as if he were a god. He views the conflicting
tumult of the passions; sees families and kingdoms raging in aimless commotion. . . . He has a fellow-feeling of the mournful and the joyful in the
fate of all human beings.'

Action and suffering though he know –
He hath not lived, if he lives so.
He sees, in some great-historied land,
155   A ruler of the people stand,
Sees his strong thought in fiery flood
Roll through the heaving multitude;
Exults – yet for no moment's space
Envies the all-regarded place.
160   Beautiful eyes meet his – and he
Bears to admire uncravingly;
They pass – he, mingled with the crowd,
Is in their far-off triumphs proud.
From some high station he looks down,

160. uncravingly] Like an Indian sage the poet mixes with mankind but is
emotionally detached from its concerns. Cp. A.'s letter to Clough 4 March
1848 (*CL* 71), 'The Indians distinguish between . . . abandoning practice,
and abandoning the fruits of action and all respect thereto. This last is a
supreme step, and dilated on throughout the Poem.' A typical instance is
Bhagavad Gita vi 9–10 transl. J. Mascaro (1962) 69–70, 'He has risen on the
heights of his soul. And in peace he beholds relatives, companions and
friends, those impartial or indifferent or who hate him: he sees them all
with the same inner peace . . .' A. probably first encountered the ideas of
the *Bhagavad Gita* at second-hand in 1845 when he read V. Cousin's
account of the poem in the sixth lecture of *Cours de l'histoire de la philosophie au dix-huitième siècle* (2 vols.: Paris, 1829). Cousin refers respectfully
to Humboldt's analysis of the poem; this analysis, 'Über die unter den
Namen Bhagavad-Gita bekannte Episode des Mahá-Bhárata', which appeared in the *Transactions of the Royal Academy of the Sciences, Berlin, 1825*
(1826), occurs as 'Humboldt uber die B.G.' with 'Cousin Cours. vol. ii'
on a reading-list in A.'s 1845 diary and also separately on two 1846 reading-
lists. A. probably read the poem itself first in late 1847 or early 1848 in
C. Lassen's Latin translation (Bonn, 1846), a corrected version of A. W.
Schlegel's Latin rendering of 1823.

164. high station] Cp. Lucretius, *De Rerum Natura* ii 7–10,

> sed nil dulcius est, bene quam munita tenere
> edita doctrina sapientum templa serena
> despicere unde queas aliosque passimque videre
> errare atque viam palantis quaerere vitae . . .

and also *The Thoughts of the Emperor M. Aurelius Antoninus* vii 48, tr.
G. Long (2nd revised ed. 1875) 138, 'This is a fine saying of Plato: That
he who is discoursing about men should look also at earthly things as if he
viewed them from some higher place; should look at them in their assem-
blies, armies, agricultural labours, marriages . . .'; and ix 30 (ed. *cit.* 166),

165 At sunset, on a populous town;
Surveys each happy group which fleets,
Toil ended, through the shining streets,
Each with some errand of its own –
And does not say: *I am alone.*

170 He sees the gentle stir of birth
When morning purifies the earth;
He leans upon a gate and sees
The pastures, and the quiet trees.
Low, woody hill, with gracious bound,

175 Folds the still valley almost round;
The cuckoo, loud on some high lawn,
Is answered from the depth of dawn;
In the hedge straggling to the stream,
Pale, dew-drenched, half-shut roses gleam;

180 But, where the farther side slopes down,
He sees the drowsy new-waked clown
In his white quaint-embroidered frock
Make, whistling, tow'rd his mist-wreathed flock –
Slowly, behind his heavy tread,

185 The wet, flowered grass heaves up its head.
Leaned on his gate, he gazes – tears
Are in his eyes, and in his ears
The murmur of a thousand years.
Before him he sees life unroll,

190 A placid and continuous whole –
That general life, which does not cease,
Whose secret is not joy, but peace;
That life, whose dumb wish is not missed

'Look down from above on the countless herds of men and their countless solemnities . . .' A. quotes this second passage in 'Marcus Aurelius', *E in C I* (1865), *Works* iii 410.

170–85. These lines anticipate the idyllic backgrounds of 'The Scholar-Gipsy', 'Thyrsis', 'Bacchanalia'.

181–3. A.'s 'new-waked clown' whistles because of Milton's 'L'Allegro' 63–4,

> *While the Plowman neer at hand*
> *Whistles ore the Furrow'd Land . . .*

Both poets are describing the countryside at dawn.

191. The life of universal nature, which is one of the peaceful or 'resigned' acceptance of 'eternal change' (l. 222 below and *n.*). A. is here separating himself from the Wordsworthian view – which he adopts elsewhere (see 'Self-Dependence 21, p. 143 below) – of the joy offered in nature.

> If birth proceeds, if things subsist;
> 195   The life of plants, and stones, and rain,
> The life he craves – if not in vain
> Fate gave, what chance shall not control,
> His sad lucidity of soul.
>
> You listen – but that wandering smile,
> 200   Fausta, betrays you cold the while!
> Your eyes pursue the bells of foam
> Washed, eddying, from this bank, their home.
> *Those gipsies, so your thoughts I scan,*
> *Are less, the poet more, than man.*
> 205   *They feel not, though they move and see;*
> *Deeper the poet feels; but he*
> *Breathes, when he will, immortal air,*
> *Where Orpheus and where Homer are.*
> *In the day's life, whose iron round*
> 210   *Hems us all in, he is not bound;*
> *He leaves his kind, o'erleaps their pen,*
> *And flees the common life of men.*
> *He escapes thence, but we abide –*
> *Not deep the poet sees, but wide.*

194. subsist] A favourite word with Senancour. Cp. *Obermann* (Lettre xlviii) ii 19–20, '. . . je vois le caillou soumis à la main de l'homme, et qui existera cent siècles après lui . . . Je m'arrête étonné: j'écoute ce qui subsiste encore; je voudrais entendre ce qui subsistera . . .'; and (Lettre lxxxv) i 199, '. . . les siècles de vie subsisteront quand nous, nos plaintes, notre espérance et nos systèmes auront à jamais passé. . . .'

198. sad lucidity] Cp. A.'s analysis of Empedocles's character in the Yale MS., 'He sees things as they are . . . in their stern simplicity. The sight is a severe and mind-tasking one . . .'

201–2. Cp. ll. 105, 277. Fausta is still drawn towards excitement and action.

203. so your thoughts I scan] Fausta does not speak. The poem is a 'dialogue of the mind with itself' (*1853* Preface, p. 591 below).

206. Deeper] *Deeply* 1849–77.

209–10. A. remembered these lines in speaking of Wordsworth, 'Memorial Verses' 45–7 and *n.* (p. 228 below).

211–12. Added *1881.*

214. Glossed by ll. 186–90. Cp. A.'s letter to Clough Feb. 1849 (*CL* 99), 'I often think that . . . a slight gift of poetical expression . . . is overlaid and crushed in a profound thinker. . . . The trying to go into and to the bottom of an object instead of grouping objects is as fatal to the sensuousness of poetry as the mere painting . . . is to its airy and rapidly moving life. "Not deep the Poet sees, but wide": – think of this as you gaze from the Cumner Hill towards Cirencester and Cheltenham.'

215   The world in which we live and move
        Outlasts aversion, outlasts love,
        Outlasts each effort, interest, hope,
        Remorse, grief, joy; and were the scope
        Of these affections wider made,
220   Man still would see, and see dismayed,
        Beyond his passion's widest range,
        Far regions of eternal change.
        Nay, and since death, which wipes out man,
        Finds him with many an unsolved plan,
225   With much unknown, and much untried,
        Wonder not dead, and thirst not dried,
        Still gazing on the ever full
        Eternal mundane spectacle –
        This world in which we draw our breath,
230   In some sense, Fausta, outlasts death.

        Blame thou not, therefore, him who dares
        Judge vain beforehand human cares;
        Whose natural insight can discern
        What through experience others learn;
235   Who needs not love and power, to know
        Love transient, power an unreal show;
        Who treads at ease life's uncheered ways –
        Him blame not, Fausta, rather praise!
        Rather thyself for some aim pray
240   Nobler than this, to fill the day;
        Rather that heart, which burns in thee,
        Ask, not to amuse, but to set free;
        Be passionate hopes not ill resigned
        For quiet, and a fearless mind.

222. *eternal change*] A frequent idea in M. Aurelius and Senancour. Cp. M. Aurelius ix 28 ed. *cit.* 166, 'Soon will the earth cover us all: then the earth, too, will change, and the things which result from change will continue to change for ever, and there again for ever.'

231–6. Cp. 'To a Gipsy Child' 39–40 (p. 25 above),

    – *Thou hast foreknown the vanity of hope,*
    Foreseen thy harvest – yet proceed'st to live …

and A.'s letter to Clough 29 Sept. 1848 (*CL* 93), 'We know beforehand all they [women] can teach us: yet we are obliged to learn it directly from them.'

237. *life's uncheered ways*] Cp. Lucretius, *De Rerum Natura* ii 15–16,

    qualibus in tenebris vitae quantisque periclis
    degitur hoc aevi quodcumquest.

245 And though fate grudge to thee and me
   The poet's rapt security,
   Yet they, believe me, who await
   No gifts from chance, have conquered fate.
   They, winning room to see and hear,
250 And to men's business not too near,
   Through clouds of individual strife
   Draw homeward to the general life.
   Like leaves by suns not yet uncurled;
   To the wise, foolish; to the world,
255 Weak; yet not weak, I might reply,
   Not foolish, Fausta, in His eye,
   To whom each moment in its race,
   Crowd as we will its neutral space,
   Is but a quiet watershed
260 Whence, equally, the seas of life and death are fed.

   Enough, we live! and if a life,
   With large results so little rife,
   Though bearable, seem hardly worth
   This pomp of worlds, this pain of birth;
265 Yet, Fausta, the mute turf we tread,
   The solemn hills around us spread,
   This stream which falls incessantly,
   The strange-scrawled rocks, the lonely sky,
   If I might lend their life a voice,
270 Seem to bear rather than rejoice.
   And even could the intemperate prayer
   Man iterates, while these forbear,
   For movement, for an ampler sphere,
   Pierce Fate's impenetrable ear;
275 Not milder is the general lot
   Because our spirits have forgot,

253. The image is of the Tree of Life. Those who can distinguish the vanity of life without experience are like 'leaves by suns not yet uncurled'. A. may have had Carlyle's 'Tree Igdrasil' in mind – see *Heroes and Hero-Worship* (1841), *Works* ed. *cit.* v 20–1.
257–60. At every moment men are being born and men are dying.
265–68. These lines are intended to recall ll. 96–105 above.
268. *strange-scrawled rocks*] The scrawls are the striations on erratic boulders transported by glacial action in the Lake District.
270. Perhaps suggested by *Obermann* (Lettre iv) i 28, '. . . je ne prétends plus employer ma vie . . . je ne veux plus en jouir, mais seulement la tolérer . . .'

In action's dizzying eddy whirled,
The something that infects the world.

277. dizzying eddy] Cp. 'The Buried Life' 43 (p. 273 below),

Eddying at large in blind uncertainty . . .

and 'Rugby Chapel' 73-7,

And there are some, whom a thirst
Ardent, unquenchable, fires
Not with the crowd to be spent,
Not without aim to go round
In an eddy of purposeless dust . . .

But see 'The Strayed Reveller' 3-6 and *n.* (p. 66 above) for 'eddying' in a different emotional context.

278. Necessity, which thwarts our Romantic expectations of life. These expectations are 'intemperate' (l. 271), but 'infects' suggests that A. still has some sympathy with them.

23 The Forsaken Merman

Date of composition unknown, but between (?) 1847–Jan. 1849; not earlier than Sept. 1848 if the name Margaret connects the poem with Marguerite and the 'Switzerland' lyrics (against this 'Grethe' in A.'s source is a diminutive of Margarethe). A. probably first met the story in Mary Howitt's translation of Hans Andersen's *The True Story of My Life* (1847) – note Andersen visited England June 1847 – which contains an account of the Danish ballad 'Agnete og Havmanden' (Agnes and the Merman), but he follows the fuller version in George Borrow's review of J. M. Thiele's *Danske Folkesagn, Universal Review* ii (1825) 563-4 (cp. ll. 52 'the youngest sate on her knee', 58 'Easter-time', 68-77 the Merman's calling outside the church – all indicated in Borrow but not in Andersen):

'There lived once two poor people . . . in Jutland, who had one only child, a daughter, called Grethe. One day . . . as she was washing her apron, a merman rose out of the water . . . he spoke to the girl in a kind and friendly tone, and said, "Come with me, Grethe . . ." She let herself be prevailed on, and he took her by the hand, and brought her down to the bottom of the sea, and she in the course of time be-came the mother of five children. When a long time had passed over, and she had nearly forgotten all she knew of religion, one festival morning as she was sitting with her youngest child in her lap, she heard the church bells ringing above, and there came over her mind great uneasiness, and an anxious longing to go to church. And as she sat there with her children, and sighed heavily, the merman . . . enquired what made her so melancholy. She then coaxed him, and earnestly entreated him to let her go once more to church. The merman could not withstand her tears and solicitations, so he set her on the land, and charged her strictly to make haste back to the children. In the middle of the sermon, the merman came to the outside of the church, and cried "Grethe, Grethe!" She heard him plainly, but she thought she might as well stay till the service was over. When the sermon was concluded, the merman came again to the church, and cried, "Grethe, Grethe! will you come quick?" but still she did not stir. He came once more, the third time, and cried, "Grethe! Grethe! will you come quick? your children are crying for you." But when she did not come, he began to weep bitterly, and went back to the bottom of the sea. But Grethe ever after stayed with her parents . . .'

The poem was a favourite with the *1849* reviewers, and was liked by Froude, Clough and Palgrave among A.'s friends and by Tennyson (whose *juvenilia* include 'The Merman' and 'The Mermaid').
Published *1849*; reprinted *1853* (*1854*, *1857*), *1869*, etc.

Come, dear children, let us away;
Down and away below!
Now my brothers call from the bay,
Now the great winds shoreward blow,
5   Now the salt tides seaward flow;
Now the wild white horses play,
Champ and chafe and toss in the spray.
Children dear, let us away!
This way, this way!

10   Call her once before you go –
Call once yet!
In a voice that she will know:
'Margaret! Margaret!'
Children's voices should be dear
15   (Call once more) to a mother's ear;
Children's voices, wild with pain –
Surely she will come again!
Call her once and come away;
This way, this way!
20   'Mother dear, we cannot stay!
The wild white horses foam and fret.'
Margaret! Margaret!

Come, dear children, come away down;
Call no more!
25   One last look at the white-walled town,
And the little grey church on the windy shore,
Then come down!
She will not come though you call all day;
Come away, come away!

30 Children dear, was it yesterday
    We heard the sweet bells over the bay?
    In the caverns where we lay,
    Through the surf and through the swell,
    The far-off sound of a silver bell?
35 Sand-strewn caverns, cool and deep,
    Where the winds are all asleep;
    Where the spent lights quiver and gleam,
    Where the salt weed sways in the stream,
    Where the sea-beasts, ranged all round,
40 Feed in the ooze of their pasture-ground;
    Where the sea-snakes coil and twine,
    Dry their mail and bask in the brine;
    Where great whales come sailing by,
    Sail and sail, with unshut eye,
45 Round the world for ever and aye?
    When did music come this way?
    Children dear, was it yesterday?

    Children dear, was it yesterday
    (Call yet once) that she went away?
50 Once she sate with you and me,
    On a red gold throne in the heart of the sea,
    And the youngest sate on her knee.
    She combed its bright hair, and she tended it well,
    When down swung the sound of a far-off bell.
55 She sighed, she looked up through the clear green
    She said: 'I must go, for my kinsfolk pray   [sea;
    In the little grey church on the shore to-day.
    'Twill be Easter-time in the world – ah me!
    And I lose my poor soul, Merman! here with thee.'
60 I said: 'Go up, dear heart, through the waves;
    Say thy prayer, and come back to the kind sea-
        caves!'
    She smiled, she went up through the surf in the
    Children dear, was it yesterday?   [bay.

        Children dear, were we long alone?
65 'The sea grows stormy, the little ones moan;
    Long prayers,' I said, 'in the world they say;
    Come!' I said; and we rose through the surf in the
    We went up the beach, by the sandy down   [bay.
    Where the sea-stocks bloom, to the white-walled
        town;
70 Through the narrow paved streets, where all was
    To the little grey church on the windy hill.   [still,

From the church came a murmur of folk at their
    prayers,
But we stood without in the cold blowing airs.
We climbed on the graves, on the stones worn with
    rains,
75   And we gazed up the aisle through the small leaded
She sate by the pillar; we saw her clear: [panes.
'Margaret, hist! come quick, we are here!
Dear heart,' I said, 'we are long alone;
The sea grows stormy, the little ones moan.'
80   But, ah, she gave me never a look,
For her eyes were sealed to the holy book!
Loud prays the priest; shut stands the door.
Come away, children, call no more!
Come away, come down, call no more!

85   Down, down, down!
Down to the depths of the sea!
She sits at her wheel in the humming town,
Singing most joyfully.
Hark what she sings: 'O joy, O joy,
90   For the humming street, and the child with its toy!
For the priest, and the bell, and the holy well;
For the wheel where I spun,
And the blessed light of the sun!'
And so she sings her fill,
95   Singing most joyfully,
Till the spindle drops from her hand,
And the whizzing wheel stands still.
She steals to the window, and looks at the sand,
And over the sand at the sea;
100   And her eyes are set in a stare;
And anon there breaks a sigh,
And anon there drops a tear,
From a sorrow-clouded eye,
And a heart sorrow-laden,
105   A long, long sigh;
For the cold strange eyes of a little Mermaiden
    And the gleam of her golden hair.

¶ 23. *96. spindle drops*] shuttle falls *1849–77*. But Clough had pointed out the
error in March 1849 – see A.'s letter, 'I believe you are right about the
shuttle also: but I will look in the technological dict.: one is sadly loose by
default of experience, about spinning and weaving, with a great poetical
interest in both occupations' (CL 107).

Come away, away children:
Come children, come down!
110   The hoarse wind blows coldly;
Lights shine in the town.
She will start from her slumber
When gusts shake the door;
She will hear the winds howling,
115   Will hear the waves roar.
We shall see, while above us
The waves roar and whirl,
A ceiling of amber,
A pavement of pearl.
120   Singing: 'Here came a mortal,
But faithless was she!
And alone dwell for ever
The kings of the sea.'

But, children, at midnight,
125   When soft the winds blow,
When clear falls the moonlight,
When spring-tides are low;
When sweet airs come seaward
From heaths starred with broom,
130   And high rocks throw mildly
On the blanched sands a gloom;
Up the still, glistening beaches,
Up the creeks we will hie,
Over banks of bright seaweed
135   The ebb-tide leaves dry.
We will gaze, from the sand-hills,
At the white, sleeping town;

112–19. An imitation of Byron, *Manfred* I i 76–87,

> *In the blue depths of the waters,*
>   *Where the wave hath no strife,*
> *Where the Wind is a stranger,*
>   *And the Sea-snake hath life,*
> *Where the Mermaid is decking*
>   *Her green hair with shells,*
> *Like the storm on the surface*
>   *Came the sound of thy spells;*
> *O'er my calm Hall of Coral*
>   *The deep Echo rolled –*
> *To the Spirit of Ocean*
>   *Thy wishes unfold.*

> At the church on the hill-side –
> And then come back down.
140   Singing: 'There dwells a loved one,
> But cruel is she!
> She left lonely for ever
> The kings of the sea.'

24 The World and the Quietist
TO CRITIAS

Date of composition unknown, but (?) March 1848 when A. failed to interest Clough in the 'mournful rhymes' (l. 4) of the *Bhagavad Gita* ('I am
disappointed the Oriental wisdom pleased you not', *CL* 69). For Clough's
attitude to A.'s Indian 'quietism' see his censure of A.'s poems in *North
American Review* (July 1853), reprinted *Remains of A.H.C.* (1869) i 377–8,
'. . . for the present age, the lessons of reflectiveness and caution do not
appear to be more needful than . . . calls to action . . . the dismal cycle of
his rehabilitated Hindoo-Greek philosophy . . .' The temperamental differences between A. and Clough are defined by Clough's reproach that A.'s
verse was '*mollis et exspes*' and by A.'s fierce refusal 'to be sucked even for
an hour into the Time Stream' in which, in his view, Clough and other
Oxford friends were plunging (*CL* 95, 126–7).
Published *1849*; reprinted *1855*, *1877*, etc.

> 'Why, when the world's great mind
> Hath finally inclined,
> Why,' you say, Critias, 'be debating still?
> Why, with these mournful rhymes
5   Learned in more languid climes,
> Blame our activity
> Who, with such passionate will,
> Are what we mean to be?'

> Critias, long since, I know
10   (For Fate decreed it so),
> Long since the world hath set its heart to live;

¶ 24. *4–5*. The *Bhagavad Gita*, the 'divine song' from the Indian epic, the
Mahabharata. A. knew of the poem in 1845, but may not have read it until
1847–8 – see *n*. to 'Resignation' 160 (p. 90 above). The mental detachment,
i.e. freedom from the world's 'passionate will', which Krishna preaches
to Arjuna (while urging him to act) supplies one element in A.'s conception of the poet's contemplative role in 'Resignation.'

Long since, with credulous zeal
        It turns life's mighty wheel,
Still doth for labourers send,
        Who still their labour give,
15   And still expects an end.

Yet, as the wheel flies round,
With no ungrateful sound
Do adverse voices fall on the world's ear.
20   Deafened by his own stir
        The rugged labourer
Caught not till then a sense
So glowing and so near
        Of his omnipotence.

25   So, when the feast grew loud
        In Susa's palace proud,
A white-robed slave stole to the Great King's side.
He spake – the Great King heard;
        Felt the slow-rolling word
30   Swell his attentive soul;
Breathed deeply as it died,
        And drained his mighty bowl.

17–24. Cp. 'The Function of Criticism at the Present Time', *E in C I*
(1865), *Works* iii 27, 'The rush and roar of practical life will always have a
dizzying and attracting effect upon the most collected spectator, and tend
to draw him into its vortex . . . But it is only by remaining collected, and
refusing to tend himself to the point of view of the practical man, that the
critic can do the practical man any service . . .' Immediately before this
passage A. speaks of 'the Indian virtue of detachment'.
25–7. Cp. Herodotus v 105. Darius 'charged one of his servants to say to
him thrice whenever dinner was set before him, "Master, remember the
Athenians".' A.'s third stanza explains the bearing of the allusion; paradoxi-
cally, Darius felt the full extent of his power only when reminded of the
single check to it.

25 To a Republican Friend, 1848

Date of composition unknown, but almost certainly *c.* March 1848: the
friend was Clough, who claimed 10 March 1848, 'If it were not for all
these blessed revolutions, I should sink into hopeless lethargy' (*Remains of*

¶ *25. Title.* Date added first *1853.*

A.H.C. i 119); and whose enthusiasm A. mocked by addressing a letter 7 March 1848 to 'Citizen Clough, Oriel Lyceum, Oxford' (envelope in Yale Papers and *Correspondence of A.H.C.* i 216). For A.'s cooler attitude to events in France see his letter to Clough 1 March 1848, 'Certainly the present spectacle . . . is a fine one: mostly so indeed to the historical swift-kindling man, who is not over-haunted by the pale thought, that, after all man's shiftings of posture, restat vivere' (*CL* 68) and the later remark reported by Clough, 'The millennium, as Matt says, won't come this bout' (*Correspondence of A.H.C.* i 243).

Published *1849*; reprinted *1853* (*1854, 1857*), *1869*, etc.

> God knows it, I am with you. If to prize
> Those virtues, prized and practised by too few,
> But prized, but loved, but eminent in you,
> Man's fundamental life; if to despise
>
> 5   The barren optimistic sophistries
> Of comfortable moles, whom what they do
> Teaches the limit of the just and true
> (And for such doing they require not eyes);
>
> If sadness at the long heart-wasting show
> 10 Wherein earth's great ones are disquieted;
> If thoughts, not idle, while before me flow
>
> The armies of the homeless and unfed –
> If these are yours, if this is what you are,
> Then am I yours, and what you feel, I share.

5. *barren optimistic sophistries*] Cp. A.'s letter to Clough 1 March 1848, 'Don't you think the eternal relations between labour and capital the Times twaddles so of have small existence for a *whole society* that has resolved no longer to live by bread alone' (*CL* 68).
8. *they require not*] have no need of *1849*.
10. *earth's great ones*] Probably Carlyle, Emerson, George Sand.

26 [To a Republican Friend]

CONTINUED

Date of composition unknown, but *c.* March 1848: see headn. to previous poem.

Published *1849*; reprinted *1853* (*1854, 1857*), *1869*, etc.

Yet, when I muse on what life is, I seem
Rather to patience prompted, than that proud
Prospect of hope which France proclaims so loud –
France, famed in all great arts, in none supreme;

5   Seeing this vale, this earth, whereon we dream,
Is on all sides o'ershadowed by the high
Uno'erleaped Mountains of Necessity,
Sparing us narrower margin than we deem.

Nor will that day dawn at a human nod,
10   When, bursting through the network superposed
By selfish occupation – plot and plan,

Lust, avarice, envy – liberated man,
All difference with his fellow-mortal closed,
Shall be left standing face to face with God.

¶ 26. 4. Cp. A.'s review (*Academy* 15 Feb. 1872) of Renan's *La Réforme intellectuelle et morale de la France*, 'But, after all, a nation's intellectual place depends upon its having reached the very highest rank in the very highest lines of spiritual endeavour ... More than twenty years ago we said, lovers of France as we are ...

France, famed in all great arts, in none supreme –

and this still seems to us to be the true criticism on her' (*Neiman* 190); and also Wordsworth, 'Poems Dedicated to National Independence and Liberty' xv 'Great men have been among us' 9–10, 12–14,

> ... *France, 'tis strange*
> *Hath brought forth no such soul as we had then.*

> *No single volume paramount, no code,*
> *No master spirit, no determined road;*
> *But equally a want of books and men!*

13. *fellow-mortal closed*] fellow-man compos'd *1849–57*.

27 Religious Isolation
TO THE SAME FRIEND

Date of composition unknown, but (?) July–Aug. 1848, when Clough was about to resign his Oriel fellowship on conscientious grounds: see *CL* 84–9 for A.'s concern at this time and also Alan Harris, 'Matthew Arnold: the "Unknown Years"', *Nineteenth Century* (1933) 500: 'It appears from a letter which he sent, with a copy of the poem, to his elder sister "K" (Jane) ... that the fault in Clough that he was castigating was his inability to act on his convictions without troubling himself with "unanswerable

questions" as to their general validity, an inability which he says produces
fanaticism (he calls Clough "a great social fanatic"), since people try to
force their opinions on others in order to convince themselves.' Cp. A.'s
letter to Clough 12 Feb. 1853, 'You ask me in what I think . . . you wrong:
in this: that you would never take your assiette as something determined
final and unchangeable for you . . . but were always poking and patching
and cobbling at the assiette itself – could never finally, as it seemed –
"resolve to be thyself" . . . you are the most conscientious man I ever
knew; but on some lines morbidly so . . .' (CL 130).
Published *1849*; reprinted *1853* (*1854*, *1857*), *1869*, etc.

> Children (as such forgive them) have I known,
> Ever in their own eager pastime bent
> To make the incurious bystander, intent
> On his own swarming thoughts, an interest own –
>
> 5 Too fearful or too fond to play alone.
> Do thou, whom light in thine own inmost soul
> (Not less thy boast) illuminates, control
> Wishes unworthy of a man full-grown.
>
> What though the holy secret, which moulds thee,
> 10 Mould not the solid earth? though never winds
> Have whispered it to the complaining sea,
>
> Nature's great law, and law of all men's minds? –
> To its own impulse every creature stirs;
> Live by thy light, and earth will live by hers!

¶ 27. *9.* The need to act according to the 'inner light' of conscience. Cp.
'In Harmony with Nature' (p. 53 above); A. rejects as 'unworthy of a
man full-grown' a reluctance to admit that

> *Nature and man can never be fast friends.*

28 To a Friend

Probably written Aug. 1848 – cp. l. 5 on Epictetus '. . . whose friendship I
not long since won' with A.'s letter (undated but Aug.–Sept. 1848), 'I have
been reading with equal surprize and profit lately the short work

> *Of that lame slave who in Nicopolis*
> *Taught Arrian, when Vespasian's brutal son*
> *Cleared Rome of what most sham'd him –*'

(CL 90). The 'friend' of the title is probably Clough.
Published *1849*; reprinted *1853* (*1854*, *1857*), *1869*, etc.

Who prop, thou ask'st, in these bad days, my mind?
He much, the old man, who, clearest-souled of men,
Saw The Wide Prospect, and the Asian Fen,
And Tmolus hill, and Smyrna bay, though blind.

5   Much he, whose friendship I not long since won,
That halting slave, who in Nicopolis
Taught Arrian, when Vespasian's brutal son
Cleared Rome of what most shamed him. But be his

My special thanks, whose even-balanced soul,
10   From first youth tested up to extreme old age,
Business could not make dull, nor passion wild;

Who saw life steadily, and saw it whole;
The mellow glory of the Attic stage,
Singer of sweet Colonus, and its child.

¶ 28. *1. these bad days*] Referring to 1848, but cp. Carlyle, *Past and Present* (1843), *Works* ed. H. D. Traill x 36, '. . . French Revolutions, Chartisms . . . that make the heart sick in these bad days . . .'

2. the old man] Homer.

3. 'The name Europe (Εὐρώπη, *the wide prospect*) probably describes the appearance of the European coast to the Greeks on the coast of Asia Minor opposite. The name Asia, again, comes, it has been thought, from the muddy fens of the rivers of Asia Minor, such as the Cayster or Mæander, which struck the imagination of the Greeks living near them.' A.'s note, which first appeared *1869* and in precisely this form *1877*; in early editions only the Greek word as footnote.

4. Smyrna, at the foot of Mt. Tmolus, was one of the seven cities that claimed to be Homer's birthplace.

6–8. The Stoic philosopher Epictetus taught at Rome until Domitian's expulsion of the philosophers in A.D. 90; and then at Nicopolis in Epirus where Arrian took down his discourses. Of the allusiveness of these lines A. says complacently, 'There's for you but this style is not hard tho: rather taking' (*CL* 90).

9–14. Sophocles was born at Colonus 496 B.C. and died in his ninetieth year; the *Oedipus Coloneus* was his last play. Cp. with l. 12 'On the Modern Element in Literature' (1857), *Complete Prose Works* ed. R. H. Super i (1960) 28, '. . . the peculiar characteristic of the poetry of Sophocles is its consummate, its unrivalled adequacy . . . it represents the highly developed human nature of that age . . . in its completest and most harmonious development . . . the charm of that noble serenity which always accompanies true insight . . . And therefore I have ventured to say of Sophocles, that he "saw life steadily, and saw it whole".'

5+M.A.

29 Quiet Work

Date of composition unknown, but (?) 1848: stylistically, and from its position in *1849*, it is unlikely to be early work; ll. 9–10 may refer to the troubles of 1848, which A. also mentions in the sonnets 'To a Republican Friend, 1848' I and II and 'To a Friend' (pp. 101–2 and 104 above). For the attitude towards nature cp. 'Self-Dependence' (p. 142 below) and 'Spinoza and the Bible', *E in C I* (1865), 'Spinoza first impresses Goethe and then composes him; first he fills and satisfies his imagination by the width and grandeur of his view of nature, and then he fortifies and stills his . . . poetic temperament by the moral lesson he draws from his view of nature . . . of joyful activity within the limits of man's true sphere' (*Works* iii 366). This was the first poem *1849, 1853*; was grouped with other sonnets *1869* – '"One lesson" I have banished from its pre-eminence as an introductory piece', A. to F. T. Palgrave in 1869 (*Russell* 43); and from *1877* was first of 'Early Poems'.

Published *1849* as 'Sonnet'; reprinted *1853* (*1854, 1857*); with present title *1869*, etc.

> One lesson, Nature, let me learn of thee,
> One lesson which in every wind is blown,
> One lesson of two duties kept at one
> Though the loud world proclaim their enmity –
>
> 5   Of toil unsevered from tranquillity!
> Of labour, that in lasting fruit outgrows
> Far noisier schemes, accomplished in repose,
> Too great for haste, too high for rivalry!

¶ 29. 1. *One lesson*] Two lessons *1849*. The 1853 reading (with consequent alterations of *1849* in ll. 2–3) is preferable grammatically. With it cp. Wordsworth, 'Hartleap Well' 177–8,

> *One lesson, Shepherd, let us two divide,*
> *Taught both by what she shows, and what she conceals* . . .

The 'she' is Nature.

5–13. Cp. Coleridge (quoting Plotinus, *Enneads* III viii 4), *Biographia Literaria* (1817) ed. J. Shawcross i 166, 'Should any one interrogate her [Nature], how she works . . . she will reply, it behoves thee not to disquiet me with interrogatories, but to understand in silence even as I am silent, and work without words.' The *Biographia* was read in 1846.

6. *lasting fruit*] one short hour *1849*; still advance *1853–7*.

Yes, while on earth a thousand discords ring,
10   Man's fitful uproar mingling with his toil,
        Still do thy sleepless ministers move on,

Their glorious tasks in silence perfecting;
Still working, blaming still our vain turmoil,
Labourers that shall not fail, when man is gone.

9–12. Cp. Carlyle's quotation of Goethe's epigram in 'Goethe's Works',
Crit. and Miscell. Essays (1839), *Works* ed. H. D. Traill xxvii 432,

> *Wie das Gestirn*
> *Ohne Hast*
> *Aber ohne Rast*
> *Drehe sich jeder*
> *Um die eigne Last*

which he translates, 'Like as a Star / That maketh not haste / That taketh
not rest / Be each one fulfilling / His god-given Hest.' Carlyle's *Essays* are
on the reading-list in A.'s unpublished 1847 diary.
10. fitful uproar] weak complainings *1849*; senseless uproar *1853–77*.
11–12. The 'sleepless ministers' are the stars, as the *1849* reading 'glorious
course' (l. 12) indicates. Cp. Wordsworth, 'Gipsies' 23–4,

> *Life which the very stars reprove*
> *As on their silent tasks they move!*

but 'sleepless' is probably an unconscious reminiscence of 'nature's patient,
sleepless Eremite' in Keat's 'Bright Star' sonnet. If the echo is a real one,
A.'s poem cannot be earlier than Sept. 1848 (when Keat's sonnet was first
published).
12. tasks] course *1849*.
13. blaming] chiding *1849*.

30 A Memory Picture

Written between Oct. 1848–Jan. 1849 (between A.'s first meeting with the
French girl Marguerite at Thun Sept. 1848 – see headn. to 'Meeting', p. 115
below – and publication of *1849* on 26 Feb.). The Yale MS. list of pieces to
be composed in 1849 (undated but not earlier than Oct. 1848) indicates this
poem with 'Thun and vividness of sight and memory compared: sight
would be less precious if memory could equally realize for us'. It became
an 'Early Poem' in *1877*.
Published *1849* as 'To my Friends, who ridiculed a tender Leave-taking';
reprinted *1853* (*1854*, *1857*); with present title *1869*, etc. ('Switzerland' I
1853–69).

Laugh, my friends, and without blame
Lightly quit what lightly came;
Rich to-morrow as to-day,
Spend as madly as you may!
5   I, with little land to stir,
Am the exacter labourer.
    Ere the parting hour go by,
    Quick, thy tablets, Memory!

Once I said: 'A face is gone
10   If too hotly mused upon;
And our best impressions are
Those that do themselves repair.'
Many a face I so let flee,
Ah! is faded utterly.
15   Ere the parting hour go by,
    Quick, thy tablets, Memory!

Marguerite says: 'As last year went,
So the coming year'll be spent;
Some day next year, I shall be,
20   Entering heedless, kissed by thee.'
Ah, I hope! – yet, once away,
What may chain us, who can say?
    Ere the parting hour go by,
    Quick, thy tablets, Memory!

¶ 30. *1–8*. This stanza cancelled *1869*, but restored *1877*. Between sts. 1 and 2 until *1869* the following extra stanza:

> *But my Youth reminds me –* ' *Thou*
> *Hast liv'd light as these live now:*
> *As these are, thou too wert such:*
> *Much hast had, hast squander'd much.*'
> *Fortune's now less frequent heir,*
> *Ah! I husband what's grown rare.*
>   *Ere the parting kiss be dry*   [*hour go by 1857*]
>   *Quick, thy tablets, Memory!*

7. (and first line of refrain in each stanza) *hour go by*] *kiss be dry 1849–54*.
8. Cp. *Hamlet* I v 107,

> *My tablets, – meet it is I set it down* . . .

17. Marguerite] All that is known of her is in the 'Switzerland' poems. See headn. to 'Meeting' (p. 115 below) and, for a fuller discussion, *Commentary* 151–9 and *Baum* 58–84.

25 Paint that lilac kerchief, bound
Her soft face, her hair around;
Tied under the archest chin
Mockery ever ambushed in.
Let the fluttering fringes streak
30 All her pale, sweet-rounded cheek.
　　Ere the parting hour go by,
　　Quick, thy tablets, Memory!

Paint that figure's pliant grace
As she tow'rd me leaned her face,
35 Half refused and half resigned,
Murmuring: 'Art thou still unkind?'
Many a broken promise then
Was new made – to break again.
　　Ere the parting hour go by,
40 　　Quick, thy tablets, Memory!

Paint those eyes, so blue, so kind,
Eager tell-tales of her mind;
Paint, with their impetuous stress
Of inquiring tenderness,
45 Those frank eyes, where deep I see
An angelic gravity.
　　Ere the parting hour go by,
　　Quick, thy tablets, Memory!

What, my friends, these feeble lines
50 Show, you say, my love declines?
To paint ill as I have done,
Proves forgetfulness begun?
Time's gay minions, pleased you see,
Time, your master, governs me;
55 　　Pleased, you mock the fruitless cry:
　　'Quick, thy tablets, Memory!'

Ah, too true! Time's current strong
Leaves us fixed to nothing long.
Yet, if little stays with man,
60 Ah, retain we all we can!
If the clear impression dies,
Ah, the dim remembrance prize!
　　Ere the parting hour go by,
　　Quick, thy tablets, Memory!

31 A Modern Sappho

Date of composition unknown, but (?) 1848-9: A.'s self-indulgence in preserving this 'dramatic lyric' may suggest an autobiographical origin; its position in *1849* after 'To my Friends, who ridiculed a tender Leave-taking' may indicate a 'common origin' for the two poems (*Commentary* 41). G. Saintsbury and H. Paul note the influence of Moore's *Irish Melodies*. Published *1849*; reprinted *1853*, *1869*, etc.

They are gone – all is still! Foolish heart, dost thou quiver?
   Nothing stirs on the lawn but the quick lilac-shade,
Far up shines the house, and beneath flows the river –
   Here lean, my head, on this cold balustrade!

5 Ere he come – ere the boat by the shining-branched border
   Of dark elms shoot round, dropping down the proud
      stream,
   Let me pause, let me strive, in myself make some order,
   Ere their boat-music sound, ere their broidered flags
      gleam.

   Last night we stood earnestly talking together;
10   She entered – that moment his eyes turned from me!
   Fastened on her dark hair, and her wreath of white heather –
   As yesterday was, so to-morrow will be.

   Their love, let me know, must grow strong and yet
      stronger,
   Their passion burn more, ere it ceases to burn.
15 They must love – while they must! but the hearts that love
      longer
   Are rare – ah! most loves but flow once, and return.

   I shall suffer – but they will outlive their affection;
   I shall weep – but their love will be cooling; and he,
   As he drifts to fatigue, discontent, and dejection,
20   Will be brought, thou poor heart, how much nearer to
      thee!

¶ 31. 8. After this line the following cancelled stanza in *1849*, *1853*:

> *Is it hope makes me linger? the dim thought, that sorrow*
> *Means parting? that only in absence lies pain?*
> *It was well with me once if I saw him: to-morrow*
> *May bring one of the old happy moments again.*

For cold is his eye to mere beauty, who, breaking
  The strong band which passion around him hath furled,
Disenchanted by habit, and newly awaking,
  Looks languidly round on a gloom-buried world.

25 Through that gloom he will see but a shadow appearing,
  Perceive but a voice as I come to his side –
But deeper their voice grows, and nobler their bearing,
  Whose youth in the fires of anguish hath died.

So, to wait! – But what notes down the wind, hark! are
     driving?
30 'Tis he! 'tis their flag, shooting round by the trees!
  – Let my turn, if it *will* come, be swift in arriving!
  Ah! hope cannot long lighten torments like these.

Hast thou yet dealt him, O life, thy full measure?
  World, have thy children yet bowed at his knee?
35 Hast thou with myrtle-leaf crowned him, O pleasure?
  – Crown, crown him quickly, and leave him for me!

32 Consolation

Written in part June 1849: see A.'s *1852* note to l. 21, 'Written during the siege of Rome by the French, [1849]' (date added *1877*), but details in ll. 26–40 indicate a final draft after 15 May 1851 (see *nn.* to these lines below and *Commentary* 63). The poem, which was classified as an 'Early Poem' *1877*, is a Stoic attempt to discipline the Romantic ego by 'remembering that we are a part of universal nature and that we follow her order' (*The Ethics* Pt. iv appendix, *Spinoza's Works* tr. R. H. M. Elwes (1891) ii 243). Published *1852*; reprinted *1853* (*1854*, *1857*), *1869*, etc.

¶ 32. *Title.* Followed *1853*, *1854* by this motto (almost certainly composed by A.):

> *The wide earth is still*
> *Wider than one man's passion: there's no mood,*
> *No meditation, no delight, no sorrow,*
> *Cas'd in one man's dimensions can distil*
> *Such pregnant and infectious quality,*
> *Six yards round shall not ring it. –*

Mist clogs the sunshine.
Smoky dwarf houses
Hem me round everywhere;
A vague dejection
5   Weighs down my soul.

Yet, while I languish,
Everywhere countless
Prospects unroll themselves,
And countless beings
10   Pass countless moods.

Far hence, in Asia,
On the smooth convent-roofs,
On the gilt terraces,
Of holy Lassa,
15   Bright shines the sun.

Grey time-worn marbles
Hold the pure Muses;
In their cool gallery,
By yellow Tiber,
20   They still look fair.

Strange unloved uproar
Shrills round their portal;
Yet not on Helicon
Kept they more cloudless
25   Their noble calm.

1–3. In 1849 A.'s London lodgings were in Mount Street, Mayfair.
11–15. Based on the following passage in E. Veuillot's review of R. E.
Huc's *Souvenirs d'un Voyage dans la Tartarie, le Thibet et la Chine* (1850) in
Revue des Deux Mondes 15 June 1850 (nouvelle période vi 1015): 'H'Lassa
est située dans une vallée . . . De nombreux temples aux toits dorés, aux
couleurs brillantes, dominent les maisons. Plusieurs temples . . . sont
groupés autour du temple principal . . . cet édifice est terminé par un dôme
entièrement recouvert de lames d'or.'
21–2. Referring to the siege of Rome by the French forces under Oudinot
in June 1849 – see headn. above. Clough was in Rome throughout the
siege and saw the Vatican marbles on a pass signed by Mazzini; his only
surviving letter to A. (23 June–3 July 1849, *CL* 107–9) describes the last
days of the Roman Republic. A. may have taken a hint for ll. 16–25 from
an earlier letter now destroyed.

                    Through sun-proof alleys
                    In a lone, sand-hemmed
                    City of Africa,
                    A blind, led beggar,
30   Age-bowed, asks alms.

                    No bolder robber
                    Erst abode ambushed
                    Deep in the sandy waste;
                    No clearer eyesight
35   Spied prey afar.

                    Saharan sand-winds
                    Seared his keen eyeballs;
                    Spent is the spoil he won.
                    For him the present
40   Holds only pain.

                    Two young, fair lovers,
                    Where the warm June-wind,
                    Fresh from the summer fields
                    Plays fondly round them,
45   Stand, tranced in joy.

                    With sweet, joined voices,
                    And with eyes brimming:
                    'Ah,' they cry, 'Destiny,
                    Prolong the present!
50   Time, stand still here!'

26–40. Inspired by reading P. Merruau's review of James Richardson's *Travels in the Great Desert of Sahara* (1851) in *Revue des Deux Mondes* 15 May 1851 (n.p. x 745–67).

26–8. Ghadames consisted of 'ruelles obscures, tortueuses' (Merruau, *loc. cit.* 759).

31–3. 'Les Arabes habitant la partie de l'Atlas située entre Tripoli et Ghadamès étaient des voleurs: la Porte les a metamorphosés en gendarmes, qui escortent . . . les caravanes. Certes, leur protection n'est pas bien efficace; mais ne vaut-il pas mieux les avoir pour compagnons . . . sur la route que de les trouver placés en embuscade sur le passage . . .' (Merruau, 758).

36–7. 'Le vent soulève . . . le sable et la poussière . . . pour incommoder les caravanes et pour y propager les opthalmies . . .' (Merruau, 747).

48–50. Cp. Lamartine, 'Le Lac' 21–4,

> *O temps, suspends ton vol! et vous, heures propices,*
> *Suspendez votre cours!*
> *Laissez-nous savourer les rapides délices*
> *Des plus beaux de nos jours.*

The prompt stern Goddess
Shakes her head, frowning;
Time gives his hour-glass
Its due reversal;
55   Their hour is gone.

With weak indulgence
Did the just Goddess
Lengthen their happiness,
She lengthened also
60   Distress elsewhere.

The hour, whose happy
Unalloyed moments
I would eternalise,
Ten thousand mourners
65   Well pleased see end.

The bleak, stern hour,
Whose severe moments
I would annihilate,
Is passed by others
70   In warmth, light, joy.

Time, so complained of,
Who to no one man
Shows partiality,
Brings round to all men
75   Some undimmed hours.

33 Sonnet to the Hungarian Nation

Written mid-July 1849: see A.'s letter 29 July, 'There was a sonnet of mine
in last week's *Examiner* – "To the Hungarian Nation", but as it was not
worth much I do not send it' (*L* i 11). The Hungarian War of Independence
began in Sept. 1848, and Hungary declared itself free under Kossuth's
leadership 14 April 1849; Russian troops arrived in June 1849. An editorial
in *Examiner* (14 July) expressed the English Liberal view that Russian inter-
vention on the Austrian side had converted the war into one of 'defence
against foreign invasion' (*Commentary* 327).
Published *Examiner* 21 July 1849; not reprinted by A.

Not in sunk Spain's prolonged death agony;
Not in rich England, bent but to make pour
The flood of the world's commerce on her shore;
Not in that madhouse, France, from whence the cry
5   Afflicts grave Heaven with its long senseless roar;
Not in American vulgarity,
Nor wordy German imbecility –
Lies any hope of heroism more.
Hungarians! Save the world! Renew the stories
10   Of men who against hope repelled the chain,
And make the world's dead spirit leap again!
On land renew that Greek exploit, whose glories
Hallow the Salaminian promontories,
And the Armada flung to the fierce main.

¶ 33. *4–5. that madhouse, France*] The February revolution in 1848, which led to the creation of the Second Republic, was followed in June by a bloody popular rising in Paris. The aged Archbishop of Paris was killed while trying to mediate between the authorities and the insurgents. The rising was savagely put down by General Cavaignac.
6. Cp. A.'s letter 7 March 1848, 'I see a wave of more than American *vulgarity . . .* preparing to break over us' (*L* i 4).
12–14. The Greeks defeated the Persian fleet of Xerxes off Salamis in 480 B.C.

34 Meeting

Probably written Sept. 1849. 'Switzerland', the sequence of poems (including 'Meeting') given this title *1853* (but added to and subtracted from *1854*, *1857*, *1869*, *1877*), was inspired by A.'s attraction for Marguerite, a French girl whom he met at Thun Sept. 1848 and 1849; in 1849 he arrived there probably after a short holiday with Wyndham Slade at Ischl in the Tyrol. Marguerite's name, nationality and appearance are known only from the poems, but that she existed is proved by A.'s letters to Clough of 29 Sept. 1848, 'Tomorrow I repass the Gemmi and get to Thun: linger one day at the Hotel Bellevue for the sake of the blue eyes of one of its inmates: and then proceed by slow stages . . . to . . . England' and 23 Sept. 1849, 'I am here in a curious and not altogether comfortable state: however tomorrow I carry my aching head to the mountains and to my cousin the Blumlis Alp [here A. quotes an early draft of the 'Switzerland' poem 'Parting' 25–34, ending 'I come, O ye mountains – / Ye torrents, I come'] Yes, I come, but in three or four days I shall be back here, and then I must try how soon I can ferociously turn towards England' (*CL* 91 and 110–11). Further independent confirmation of the love-story is lacking: A.'s diaries for 1848, 1849 and 1850 are missing or inaccessible; and there are no help-ful records at Thun. 'A Memory-Picture' (p. 107 above) relates to A.'s 1848 visit and was part of 'Switzerland' *1853–69*. 'The Terrace at Berne', first published *1867* and as one of the 'Switzerland' series *1869*, concerns A.'s Swiss visit of 1859. The other poems in the final *1877* arrangement of 'Switzerland' were probably all either written or begun in Sept. or early Oct. 1849 – except 'Absence', the last of the series, which may not have been composed until early 1850 (it seems to refer to A.'s first meeting with Frances Lucy Wightman).

A. was first drawn to Switzerland by his reading of *Obermann*, whom he designates 'Thou master of my wandering youth' in 'Obermann Once More' 39 (p. 520 below). The first 'Obermann' poem was begun at Thun in 1849 – like 'Parting' it is quoted in the letter to Clough 23 Sept. 1849 – and clearly for A. 'Obermann et Marguerite sont étroitement unis' (*Bonnerot* 58). A.'s keen nostalgia for Switzerland, which in retrospect, like the Scholar-Gipsy's Oxford countryside, came to stand for emotional free-dom and the poetic life, appears both in his letters, e.g. to his wife March 1853, 'All this afternoon I have been haunted by a vision of living with you at Berne . . . and how different that would be from this incessant grind in schools' (*L* i 26), and in unexpected poetic contexts – see 'Rachel I' 12–14 and 'Rome-Sickness' 1–12 (pp. 483 and 545 below).

Published as 'The Lake' *1852*; reprinted *1853* (*1854*, *1857*); with present title *1869*, etc. ('Switzerland' 2 *1853–69*; 1 *1877*, etc.)

> Again I see my bliss at hand,
> The town, the lake are here;
> My Marguerite smiles upon the strand,
> Unaltered with the year.
>
> 5   I know that graceful figure fair,
> That cheek of languid hue;
> I know that soft, enkerchiefed hair,
> And those sweet eyes of blue.

¶ 34. *2.* Thun, situated on the Aar where the river emerges from Lake Thun to flow down to Berne, was by 1848 a fashionable resort with many English and French visitors. For a description of the old town and the Hotel Bellevue (built 1830) see *Sells* 92–7.

3–4. 'See, among "Early Poems", the poem called *A Memory-Picture*.' A.'s note, added *1877*.

6. Marguerite's pallor is also noticed in 'A Memory-Picture', 'Parting' and 'A Farewell'.

Again I spring to make my choice;
10 Again in tones of ire
I hear a God's tremendous voice:
'Be counselled, and retire.'

Ye guiding Powers who join and part,
What would ye have with me?
15 Ah, warn some more ambitious heart,
And let the peaceful be!

11. Cp. 'To Marguerite – Continued' 22 (p. 125 below),

A God, a God their severance ruled!

13. Ye guiding Powers] Cp. 'Destiny' 4 (p. 144 below),

– Ask of the Powers that sport with man!

and 'Human Life' 26–7 (p. 140 below),

. . . chartered by some unknown Powers
We stem across the sea of life by night . . .

15–16. Cp. A.'s letter to Clough (undated but March 1848, *CL* 76), 'Do not let us forsake one another: we have the common quality, now rare, of being unambitious, I think. Some must be contented not to be at the top.'

35 Parting

Probably written *c.* 23 Sept. 1849: see headn. to 'Meeting' above, quoting A.'s letter to Clough of this date. The poem's metrical changes ll. 1–58 represent A.'s wavering between the desire to give free play to emotion ('storm-winds of Autumn') and the desire for peace and detachment (the stillness of the 'white peaks in air'). A. escaped from Thun for 'three or four days' (*CL* 111) on an expedition to the mountains (perhaps to consider in a less charged atmosphere the confession implicit in ll. 63–70); various verbal links between 'Parting' and 'Obermann' – the latter refers to Leukerbad and was 'conceived, and partly composed, going down from the foot of the Gemmi Pass towards the Rhone' (A.'s *1869* note) – show that the 1849 expedition repeated wholly or in part A.'s 1848 journey over the Gemmi to Leukerbad and then by way of Brig and the Simplon to Domodossola (for this route see *CL* 91).
Published 1852; reprinted *1853* (*1854*, *1857*), *1869*, etc. ('Switzerland' 4 *1853–7*; 3 *1869*; 2 *1877*, etc.)

Ye storm-winds of Autumn!
Who rush by, who shake
The window, and ruffle
The gleam-lighted lake;
5   Who cross to the hill-side
Thin-sprinkled with farms,
Where the high woods strip sadly
Their yellowing arms —
Ye are bound for the mountains!
10   Ah! with you let me go
Where your cold, distant barrier,
The vast range of snow,
Through the loose clouds lifts dimly
Its white peaks in air —
15   How deep is their stillness!
Ah, would I were there!

But on the stairs what voice is this I hear,
Buoyant as morning, and as morning clear?
Say, has some wet bird-haunted English lawn
20   Lent it the music of its trees at dawn?
Or was it from some sun-flecked mountain-brook
That the sweet voice its upland clearness took?
Ah! it comes nearer —
Sweet notes, this way!

25   Hark! fast by the window
The rushing winds go,
To the ice-cumbered gorges,
The vast seas of snow!

¶ 35. *1.* Cp. 'Obermann' 3 (p. 130 below).

The autumn storm-winds drive the rack . . .

11–16. Freely imitating Goethe's 'Sehnsucht' (1802) 5–8,

Wie dort sich die Wolken
Um Felsen verziehn!
Da mocht ich hinuber,
Da mocht ich wohl hin!

(How the clouds there / Drift away past rocks. / Oh, were I but yonder, /
It is there I should like to go.)

25–34. The early draft in A.'s letter to Clough 23 Sept. 1849 (*CL* 110) has
several minor variants not recorded in *1950*: l. 25, Fast, fast; l. 27, Towards
the; l. 28, vast fields; l. 31, And the.

There the torrents drive upward
30   Their rock-strangled hum;
There the avalanche thunders
The hoarse torrent dumb.
– I come, O ye mountains!
Ye torrents, I come!

35   But who is this, by the half-opened door,
Whose figure casts a shadow on the floor?
The sweet blue eyes – the soft, ash-coloured hair –
The cheeks that still their gentle paleness wear –
The lovely lips, with their arch smile that tells
40   The unconquered joy in which her spirit dwells –
        Ah! they bend nearer –
        Sweet lips, this way!

Hark! the wind rushes past us!
Ah! with that let me go
45   To the clear, waning hill-side,
Unspotted by snow,
There to watch, o'er the sunk vale,
The frore mountain-wall,
Where the niched snow-bed sprays down
50   Its powdery fall.
There its dusky blue clusters
The aconite spreads;
There the pines slope, the cloud-strips
Hung soft in their heads.
55   No life but, at moments,
The mountain-bee's hum.
– I come, O ye mountains!
Ye pine-woods, I come!

        Forgive me! forgive me!
60   Ah, Marguerite, fain
        Would these arms reach to clasp thee!
        But see! 'tis in vain.

29–30 and 56 below. Cp. 'Obermann' 33–4 (p. 131 below),

      Yet, through the hum of torrents lone,
      And brooding mountain-bee . . .

In the void air, towards thee,
    My stretched arms are cast;
65 But a sea rolls between us –
    Our different past!

To the lips, ah! of others
    Those lips have been pressed,
And others, ere I was,
70   Were strained to that breast;

Far, far from each other
    Our spirits have grown;
And what heart knows another?
    Ah! who knows his own?

75 Blow, ye winds! lift me with you!
    I come to the wild.
Fold closely, O Nature!
    Thine arms round thy child.

To thee only God granted
80   A heart ever new –
To all always open,
    To all always true.

Ah! calm me, restore me;
    And dry up my tears
85 On thy high mountain-platforms,
    Where morn first appears;

65. Cp. Coleridge's 'Christabel' 423,

    A dreary sea now flows between . . .

and see headn. to 'To Marguerite – Continued' (p. 123 below).
75. A Romantic commonplace to be found, for example, in Chateaubriand
and Lamartine, but cp. Shelley, 'Ode to the West Wind 53,

    Oh, lift me as a wave, a leaf, a cloud!

78. *thy child*] See 'Lines written in Kensington Gardens' 23–4 (p. 256
below),

    But in my helpless cradle I
    Was breathed on by the rural Pan.

79–82. Cp. Wordsworth, 'Tintern Abbey' 122–3,

    Knowing that Nature never did betray
    The heart that loved her . . .

> Where the white mists, for ever,
> Are spread and upfurled –
> In the stir of the forces
90   Whence issued the world.

87. Cp. 'Obermann' 9 (p. 130 below),

> *The white mists rolling like a sea!*

36 Isolation. To Marguerite

Probably written Sept. or early Oct. 1849: see headn. to 'Meeting'
(p. 115 above); the *1852* title, too circumstantial for fiction, of 'To Marguerite – Continued' (which uses the same stanza to continue the argument
about human isolation and is in some sense a sequel to 'Isolation. To Marguerite') implies composition of both poems at Thun. 'Isolation. To
Marguerite' was tactfully excluded from *1852* – sts. 3–5 would have read
oddly so soon after A.'s marriage – but restored to its proper place before
'To Marguerite – Continued' in *1857* and all subsequent editions. For the
lover's special awareness of human isolation see also 'The Buried Life'
12–29 (p. 272 below).
Published as 'To Marguerite' *1857*; reprinted with present title *1869*, etc.
('Switzerland' 6 *1857–69*; 4 *1877*, etc.)

> We were apart; yet, day by day,
> I bade my heart more constant be.
> I bade it keep the world away,
> And grow a home for only thee;
5   Nor feared but thy love likewise grew,
> Like mine, each day, more tried, more true.
>
> The fault was grave! I might have known,
> What far too soon, alas! I learned –
> The heart can bind itself alone,
10   And faith may oft be unreturned.
> Self-swayed our feelings ebb and swell –
> Thou lov'st no more; – Farewell! Farewell!

¶ 36. *1. We were apart*] Between Sept. 1848 and Sept. 1849 – see headn. to
'Meeting' (p. 115 above).
10. may oft be] is often *1857–69*; may well be *1877*.
11. Our feelings are a sea ebbing and swelling under the influence of the
heart. This moon image, which is carried on by 'remote and spheréd
course' (l. 16), prompts the reference to the myth of Luna and Endymion
in ll. 19–30.

Farewell! – and thou, thou lonely heart,
Which never yet without remorse
15   Even for a moment didst depart
From thy remote and spheréd course
To haunt the place where passions reign –
Back to thy solitude again!

Back! with the conscious thrill of shame
20   Which Luna felt, that summer-night,
Flash through her pure immortal frame,
When she forsook the starry height
To hang over Endymion's sleep
Upon the pine-grown Latmian steep.

25   Yet she, chaste queen, had never proved
How vain a thing is mortal love,
Wandering in Heaven, far removed.
But thou hast long had place to prove
This truth – to prove, and make thine own:
30   'Thou hast been, shalt be, art, alone.'

Or, if not quite alone, yet they
Which touch thee are unmating things –
Ocean and clouds and night and day;
Lorn autumns and triumphant springs;
35   And life, and others' joy and pain,
And love, if love, of happier men.

Of happier men – for they, at least,
Have *dreamed* two human hearts might blend
In one, and were through faith released
40   From isolation without end
Prolonged; nor knew, although not less
Alone than thou, their loneliness.

16. See the similar astronomical image in 'A Farewell', 73–6 (p. 128 below),

> And we, whose ways were unlike here,
> May then more neighbouring courses ply;
> May to each other be brought near,
> And greet across infinity . . .

and *n*.

37 To Marguerite – Continued

Probably written Sept. or early Oct. 1849: see headnn. to 'Meeting' and 'Isolation. To Marguerite' (pp. 115 and 121 above). 'Yes' (l. 1) is a link with the concluding lines of the antecedent poem, but in the last stanza A. is thinking as much of his imminent real separation from Marguerite as of the imprisonment in separateness of other lovers. The 'estranging sea' (l. 24) is partly the English Channel, soon to flow between him and Marguerite; partly the sea of 'Parting' 65–6 –

> *But a sea rolls between us –*
> *Our different past . . .*

(p. 120 above); partly the sea that isolates all human beings from each other, i.e. A. from those supposedly closest to him – cp. his letter to his sister 'K' 25 Jan. 1851, '. . . as I become formed there seems to grow a gulf between us, which tends to widen till we can hardly hold any intercourse across it' (L i 14). G. Saintsbury noted the parallel between 'To Marguerite – Continued' and a passage in Thackeray's *Pendennis* (1848–50); and J. D. Coleridge (*Christian Remembrancer* 3 April 1854) saw indebtedness to some familiar lines in 'Christabel' – see particularly ll. 418–23,

> *They parted – ne'er to meet again!*
> *But never either found another*
> *To free the hollow heart from paining –*
> *They stood aloof, the scars remaining,*
> *Like cliffs which had been rent asunder;*
> *A dreary sea now flows between . . .*

These and other literary parallels, some of which may be influences, are discussed by Kathleen Tillotson, 'Yes: in the sea of life', *RES* n.s. iii (1952) 346–64.
Published as 'To Marguerite, in Returning a Volume of the Letters of Ortis' *1852*; reprinted as 'To Marguerite' *1853* (*1854*); as 'Isolation' (*1857*); with present title *1869*, etc. ('Switzerland' 5 *1853*; 6 *1854*; 7 *1857*–*1869*; 5 *1877*, etc.)

¶ 37. Title *1852*. A. may have read Foscolo's *Ultime Lettere di Jacopo Ortis* (1802) in the French translation of A. Dumas (1839; reprinted 1847). Ortis is an unhappy lover and a Wertherian misfit who finds the universe incomprehensible, but the theme of human isolation is not stressed.

Yes! in the sea of life enisled,
With echoing straits between us thrown,
Dotting the shoreless watery wild,
We mortal millions live *alone.*

5 The islands feel the enclasping flow,
And then their endless bounds they know.

But when the moon their hollows lights,
And they are swept by balms of spring,
And in their glens, on starry nights,

10 The nightingales divinely sing;
And lovely notes, from shore to shore,
Across the sounds and channels pour –

Oh! then a longing like despair
Is to their farthest caverns sent;

1–4. Cp. *Pendennis* ch. xvi, 'How lonely we are in the world!... you and
I are but a pair of infinite isolations, with some fellow-islands a little more
or less near to us'. The 'sea of life' occurs several times in A.'s poems and
is usually associated with voyaging – cp. 'Human Life' 27 (p. 140 below),

We stem across the sea of life by night . . .

and 'A Summer Night' 52–3 (p. 269 below),

. . . and depart
On the wide ocean of life anew.

2. echoing] Making communication confused and uncertain.
6. endless] Unending – cp. 'Isolation. To Marguerite' 40–1 (p. 122 above),

. . . isolation without end
Prolonged . . .

The primary meaning is that the individual knows that his isolation is for
life, but 'enclasping' (l. 5) suggests an embrace rather than imprisonment
and, in conjunction with 'shoreless' (l. 3), may imply that the individual
also knows that he belongs to a General Life which seems to him boundless
(i.e. without apparent beginning or end).
7–12. The islands are enchanted by moonlight and nightingales as human
beings fall under the enchantment of love.
13. longing like despair] Cp. 'A Buried Life' 12–15 (p. 272 below),

Alas! is even love too weak
To unlock the heart, and let it speak?
Are even lovers powerless to reveal
To one another what indeed they feel?

15 For surely once, they feel, we were
    Parts of a single continent!
    Now round us spreads the watery plain –
    Oh might our marges meet again!

    Who ordered, that their longing's fire
20 Should be, as soon as kindled, cooled?
    Who renders vain their deep desire? –
    A God, a God their severance ruled!
    And bade betwixt their shores to be
    The unplumbed, salt, estranging sea.

15–16. The 'single continent' is the One or All from which men are divorced in their individual lives; 'once'=before birth. It is only the deepest part of the self –

> *Being one with which we are one with the whole world . . .*

('Empedocles on Etna' II [i] 372) – that retains any sense of the unity of being; and this remote self is difficult, perhaps impossible, to reach. See 'The Buried Life' 30–98 (pp. 272–5 below).
22–4. A. combines two phrases from Horace. For the repetition 'A God, a God' cp. *Epodes* xiv 6,

> *deus, deus nam̄ me vetat . . .*

and for 'estranging' cp. *Odes* I iii 21–3,

> *nequiquam deus abscidit*
> *prudens Oceano dissociabili*
> *terras . . .*

Kathleen Tillotson quotes S. Selfe's *Chapters from the History of Rugby School* (1910) 83–4 to show that A. C. Tait's rendering of 'Oceano dissociabili' as 'with the estranging main' was remembered at Rugby as an example of his skill in oral translation. Tait, later Archbishop of Canterbury, was a tutor at Balliol during A.'s first undergraduate year.

38 A Farewell

Probably written early Oct. 1849: see headn. to 'Meeting' (p. 115 above). The poem refers to A.'s final parting from Marguerite at Thun on his return from the mountain expedition mentioned in the letter to Clough of 23 Sept. 1849 (*CL* 109–11) and in 'Parting' (p. 117 above).
Published *1852*; reprinted (*1854*, *1857*), *1869*, etc. ('Switzerland' 5 *1854–7*; 4 *1869*; 3 *1877*, etc.)

My horse's feet beside the lake,
Where sweet the unbroken moonbeams lay,
Sent echoes through the night to wake
Each glistening strand, each heath-fringed bay.

5   The poplar avenue was passed,
And the roofed bridge that spans the stream;
Up the steep street I hurried fast,
Led by thy taper's starlike beam.

I came! I saw thee rise! – the blood
10   Poured flushing to thy languid cheek.
Locked in each other's arms we stood,
In tears, with hearts too full to speak.

Days flew; ah, soon I could discern
A trouble in thine altered air!
15   Thy hand lay languidly in mine,
Thy cheek was grave, thy speech grew rare.

I blame thee not! – this heart, I know,
To be long loved was never framed;
For something in its depths doth glow
20   Too strange, too restless, too untamed.

And women – things that live and move
Mined by the fever of the soul –
They seek to find in those they love
Stern strength, and promise of control.

25   They ask not kindness, gentle ways –
These they themselves have tried and known;
They ask a soul which never sways
With the blind gusts that shake their own.

I too have felt the load I bore
30   In a too strong emotion's sway;
I too have wished, no woman more,
This starting, feverish heart away.

¶ 38. 5–6. The roofed bridge and the poplars along the Frutigen road were features of Thun at the time of A.'s visits.
10. *Poured flushing*] Came flooding *1852* ; Came flushing *1854–7*.
23–5. Cp. Clough, *Amours de Voyage* ii 293–5,

> *For the woman, they tell you,*
> *Ever prefers the audacious, the wilful, the vehement hero;*
> *She has no heart for the timid, the sensitive soul . . .*

I too have longed for trenchant force,
And will like a dividing spear;
35 Have praised the keen, unscrupulous course,
Which knows no doubt, which feels no fear.

But in the world I learnt, what there
Thou too wilt surely one day prove,
That will, that energy, though rare,
40 Are yet far, far less rare than love.

Go, then! – till time and fate impress
This truth on thee, be mine no more!
They will! – for thou, I feel, not less
Than I, wast destined to this lore.

45 We school our manners, act our parts –
But He, who sees us through and through,
Knows that the bent of both our hearts
Was to be gentle, tranquil, true.

And though we wear out life, alas!
50 Distracted as a homeless wind,
In beating where we must not pass,
In seeking what we shall not find;

Yet we shall one day gain, life past,
Clear prospect o'er our being's whole;
55 Shall see ourselves, and learn at last
Our true affinities of soul.

We shall not then deny a course
To every thought the mass ignore;
We shall not then call hardness force,
60 Nor lightness wisdom any more.

33–6. Cp. 'Courage' 25–6 (p. 142 below),

> *Our bane, disguise it as we may,*
> *Is weakness, is a faltering course.*

56. *affinities*] A.'s use of the word may glance at Goethe's discussion of 'elective affinities' in *Die Wahlverwandtschaften* (1809). *O.E.D.* gives 1868 for 'affinity' in this sense, i.e. a spiritual attraction believed to exist between persons; the subjects of the affinity.

Then, in the eternal Father's smile,
Our soothed, encouraged souls will dare
To seem as free from pride and guile,
As good, as generous, as they are.

65   Then we shall know our friends! – though much
Will have been lost – the help in strife,
The thousand sweet, still joys of such
As hand in hand face earthly life –

Though these be lost, there will be yet
70   A sympathy august and pure;
Ennobled by a vast regret,
And by contrition sealed thrice sure.

And we, whose ways were unlike here,
May then more neighbouring courses ply;
75   May to each other be brought near,
And greet across infinity.

How sweet, unreached by earthly jars,
My sister! to maintain with thee
The hush among the shining stars,
80   The calm upon the moonlit sea!

How sweet to feel, on the boon air,
All our unquiet pulses cease!
To feel that nothing can impair
The gentleness, the thirst for peace –

85   The gentleness too rudely hurled
On this wild earth of hate and fear;
The thirst for peace a raving world
Would never let us satiate here.

73–6. The astronomical image was probably suggested by Clough's letter
to A. 23 June 1849, 'Our orbits therefore early in August might perhaps
cross, and we two serene undeviating stars salute each other once again for
a moment amid the infinite spaces' (CL 108).
81–2. Cp. Keats, 'Ode to a Nightingale' 56,

> To cease upon the midnight with no pain . . .

81. boon] Gracious, benign. Cp. 'Thyrsis' 175 (p. 506 below),

> To a boon southern country he is fled . . .

39 Stanzas in Memory of the Author of 'Obermann'

NOVEMBER, 1849

Written late Sept.–Nov. 1849: ll. 143–4 are quoted in A.'s letter to Clough 23 Sept. 1849 (*CL* 110); 'November, 1849', added to title *1877*, refers to poem's completion, but (?) later revision before publication – see 1852 diary (*Note-books* 552). A.'s *1869* note to l. 5 connects composition with the journey anticipated in 'Parting' and the above-mentioned letter to Clough – see headnn. to 'Meeting' and 'Parting' (pp. 115 and 117 above). The following note on Senancour – with minor changes *1877, 1885* – was first attached to the poem in *1869* (having already appeared as a note to 'Obermann Once More' in *1868*):

'The author of *Obermann*, Étienne Pivert de Senancour, has little celebrity in France, his own country; and out of France he is almost unknown. But the profound inwardness, the austere sincerity, of his principal work, *Obermann*, the delicate feeling for nature which it exhibits, and the melancholy eloquence of many passages of it, have attracted and charmed some of the most remarkable spirits of this century, such as George Sand and Sainte-Beuve, and will probably always find a certain number of spirits whom they touch and interest.

Senancour was born in 1770. He was educated for the priesthood, and passed some time in the seminary of St. Sulpice; broke away from the Seminary and from France itself, and passed some years in Switzerland, where he married; returned to France in middle life, and followed thenceforward the career of a man of letters, but with hardly any fame or success. He died an old man in 1846, desiring that on his grave might be placed these words only: *Éternité, deviens mon asile!*

The influence of Rousseau, and certain affinities with more famous and fortunate authors of his own day, – Chateaubriand and Madame de Staël, – are everywhere visible in Senancour. But though, like these eminent personages, he may be called a sentimental writer, and though *Obermann*, a collection of letters from Switzerland treating almost entirely of nature and of the human soul, may be called a work of sentiment, Senancour has a gravity and severity which distinguish him from all other writers of the sentimental school. The world is with him in his solitude far less than it is with them; of all writers he is the most perfectly isolated and the least attitudinising. His chief work, too, has a value and power of its own, apart from these merits of its author. The stir of all the main forces, by which modern life is and has been impelled, lives in the letters of *Obermann*; the dissolving agencies of the eighteenth century, the fiery storm of the French

---

¶ 39. *Title.* Obermann *1855* only.

Revolution, the first faint promise and dawn of that new world which
our own time is but now more fully bringing to light -- all these are
to be felt, almost to be touched, there. To me, indeed, it will always
seem that the impressiveness of this production can hardly be rated
too high.

Besides *Obermann* there is one other of Senancour's works which,
for those spirits who feel his attraction, is very interesting; its title is
Libre Méditations d'un Solitaire Inconnu.'
Sainte-Beuve included a translation of A.'s poem in *Chateaubriand et son
groupe littéraire . . .* (1860) with the comment, 'Voilà pourtant, si je ne
m'abuse, sur ce tombeau solitaire . . . une immortelle couronne funèbre'
(ed. M. Allem (1948) i 294–8). For A.'s letters to S–B and synopses of the
latter's replies on this subject see *Bonnerot* 520–8; for A.'s 1869 *Academy*
article on Senancour, *Neiman* 156–63; and for Senancour's influence on A.'s
poetry, *Sells* and *Commentary* 253–74. A.'s earliest reference to Senancour
is Nov. 1848 (*CL* 95), but he probably knew of him as early as July 1846
when he met George Sand at Nohant.
Published *1852*; reprinted *1855, 1869*, etc.

In front the awful Alpine track
Crawls up its rocky stair;
The autumn storm-winds drive the rack,
Close o'er it, in the air.

5   Behind are the abandoned baths
Mute in their meadows lone;
The leaves are on the valley paths,
The mists are on the Rhone —

The white mists rolling like a sea!
10   I hear the torrents roar.
— Yes, Obermann, all speaks of thee;
I feel thee near once more!

1–8. Some details of this Alpine setting also occur in 'Parting' (p. 117
above). Both poems are quoted in A.'s letter to Clough 23 Sept. 1849 (*CL*
109–11).
3. rack] See A. to Sainte-Beuve 8 March 1855, '*Rack* est un mot de la
vieille langue anglaise pour signifier les *bords*, la *frange* d'une nuage qui
passe. Shakespeare s'en sert dans la "Tempête" . . .' (*Bonnerot* 525).
5. 'The Baths of Leuk. This poem was conceived, and partly composed, in
the valley going down from the foot of the Gemmi Pass towards the
Rhone.' A.'s note, first added *1869*.
12. once more] A. had made the same journey in Sept. 1848.

I turn thy leaves! I feel their breath
Once more upon me roll;
15   That air of languor, cold, and death,
     Which brooded o'er thy soul.

Fly hence, poor wretch, whoe'er thou art,
Condemned to cast about,
All shipwreck in thy own weak heart,
20   For comfort from without!

A fever in these pages burns
Beneath the calm they feign;
A wounded human spirit turns,
Here, on its bed of pain.

25   Yes, though the virgin mountain-air
Fresh through these pages blows;
Though to these leaves the glaciers spare
The soul of their white snows;

Though here a mountain-murmur swells
30   Of many a dark-boughed pine;
Though, as you read, you hear the bells
Of the high-pasturing kine –

Yet, through the hum of torrent lone,
And brooding mountain-bee,
35   There sobs I know not what ground-tone
Of human agony.

Is it for this, because the sound
Is fraught too deep with pain,
That Obermann! the world around
40   So little loves thy strain?

Some secrets may the poet tell,
For the world loves new ways;
To tell too deep ones is not well –
It knows not what he says.

27. *spare*] See A. to Sainte-Beuve 8 March 1855, 'Les glaciers *prêtent*, *donnent quelque chose* de l'âme de leurs neiges au livre d'Obermann' (Bonnerot 526).
28. *white*] mute *1852*.
44. Cp. *Luke* xxiii 34, 'Then Jesus said, Father, forgive them; for they know not what they do.' Perhaps the implication is that the poet who tells 'deep secrets' is crucified by the world's neglect.

45   Yet, of the spirits who have reigned
        In this our troubled day,
        I know but two, who have attained,
        Save thee, to see their way.

        By England's lakes, in grey old age,
50   His quiet home one keeps;
        And one, the strong much-toiling sage,
        In German Weimar sleeps.

        But Wordsworth's eyes avert their ken
        From half of human fate;
55   And Goethe's course few sons of men
        May think to emulate.

        For he pursued a lonely road,
        His eyes on Nature's plan;
        Neither made man too much a God,
60   Nor God too much a man.

        Strong was he, with a spirit free
        From mists, and sane, and clear;
        Clearer, how much! than ours – yet we
        Have a worse course to steer.

65   For though his manhood bore the blast
        Of a tremendous time,
        Yet in a tranquil world was passed
        His tenderer youthful prime.

49–50. 'Written in November, 1849.' A.'s note *1852–69.* Wordsworth had
been dead for more than two years when 'Obermann' was first published.
51–2. Goethe died in 1832. He is also linked with Wordsworth by A. in
'Memorial Verses' (p. 225 below) and 'Epilogue to Lessing's Laocoön'
26–9 (p. 510 below).
53–4. Cp. 'Heinrich Heine', *E in C I* (1865), *Works* iii 193–4, 'The gravest
of them [the English Romantics], Wordsworth, retired (in Middle-Age
phrase) into a monastery. I mean, he plunged himself in the inward life, he
voluntarily cut himself off from the modern spirit.'
61–2. Cp. 'Heinrich Heine', *E in C I* (1865), *Works* iii 175, 'Goethe's
profound, imperturbable naturalism is absolutely fatal to all routine
thinking . . .'
65–6. Goethe was forty in 1789.
66. a tremendous] Europe's stormiest *1855* only. Cp. A.'s *1869* note on
Senancour (see headn. above), '. . . the fiery storm of the French Revolution . . .' and 'Obermann Once More' 201–8 (p. 528 below).

But we, brought forth and reared in hours
70   Of change, alarm, surprise –
What shelter to grow ripe is ours?
What leisure to grow wise?

Like children bathing on the shore,
Buried a wave beneath,
75   The second wave succeeds, before
We have had time to breathe.

Too fast we live, too much are tried,
Too harassed, to attain
Wordsworth's sweet calm, or Goethe's wide
80   And luminous view to gain.

And then we turn, thou sadder sage,
To thee! we feel thy spell!
– The hopeless tangle of our age,
Thou too hast scanned it well!

85   Immoveable thou sittest, still
As death, composed to bear!
Thy head is clear, thy feeling chill,
And icy thy despair.

Yes, as the son of Thetis said,
90   I hear thee saying now:
Greater by far than thou are dead;
Strive not! die also thou!

79–80. Cp. 'Resignation' 214 (p. 92 above),

Not deep the poet sees, but wide . . .

and *n.*, the point being that a synoptic view is an escape from the Romantic 'personal estimate'. See also J. C. Shairp to Clough 24 July 1849, 'I don't think he [Goethe] will ever be an oracle for me, though Matt says "he saw life steadily and saw it whole" . . .' (*Correspondence of A.H.C.* i 270). A.'s phrase was originally applied to Sophocles – see 'To a Friend' 12 (p. 105 above) and *n.*

85–8. Sainte-Beuve refers to Senancour's 'philosophie glacée' in his 1832 essay included in *Portraits Contemporains* i (1845), but A. is remembering *Obermann* (3$^{me.}$ Fragment) i 148, 'Le vent apporte ou recule ces sons alpestres; et quand il les perd, tout paraît froid, immobile et mort.'

91–2. Cp. Achilles to Lycaon, *Iliad* xxi 106–7, 'Nay, friend, do thou too die; why lamentest thou thus? Patroclus also died, who was better far than thou.'

Ah! two desires toss about
The poet's feverish blood.
95   One drives him to the world without,
And one to solitude.

The glow, he cries, *the thrill of life,*
Where, where do these abound?
Not in the world, not in the strife
100   Of men, shall they be found.

He who hath watched, not shared, the strife,
Knows how the day hath gone.
He only lives with the world's life,
Who hath renounced his own.

105   To thee we come, then! Clouds are rolled
Where thou, O seer! art set;
Thy realm of thought is drear and cold –
The world is colder yet!

93–6. The oscillation of the divided self is typical of A., but these lines probably owe something to Pascal, *Pensées* 205, 'Ils ont un instinct secret qui les porte à chercher le divertissement et l'occupation au dehors, qui vient du ressentiment de leurs misères continuelles; et ils ont un autre instinct secret, qui reste de la grandeur de notre première nature, qui leur fait connaître que le bonheur n'est en effet que dans le repos, et non pas dans le tumulte . . .' (*L'Œuvre de Pascal* ed. J. Chevalier (1941) 878); and *Obermann* (Lettre lxxv) ii 147, 'Soit que les vaines sollicitudes de la vie me fassent oublier les choses naturelles, soit que l'inutile besoin de jouir me ramène à leur ombre, le vide m'environne tous les jours . . .' Cp. also 'Empedocles on Etna' II [i] 220–9 (pp. 184–5 below).
97. The glow, he cries] The glow of thought *1852*. The *1852* reading contradicts l. 107.
103–4. Only the man who has renounced living in the world can really understand its ways. Cp. 'Obermann Once More' 75–7 (p. 522 below),

> *Ah me! we anchorites read things best,*
> *Clearest their course discern!*

For this view that the spectator has the clearest view of events see 'Resignation' 144–69 (pp. 89–91 above) and *nn.* citing Goethe, Lucretius and M. Aurelius.
107. For A.'s belief that 'the service of reason is freezing to feeling' see the passage from Yale MS. quoted in *n.* to 'Progress' 31–2 (p. 262 below).

And thou hast pleasures, too, to share
110   With those who come to thee –
Balms floating on thy mountain-air,
And healing sights to see.

How often, where the slopes are green
On Jaman, hast thou sate
115   By some high chalet-door, and seen
The summer-day grow late;

And darkness steal o'er the wet grass
With the pale crocus starred,
And reach that glimmering sheet of glass
120   Beneath the piny sward,

Lake Leman's waters, far below!
And watched the rosy light
Fade from the distant peaks of snow;
And on the air of night

125   Heard accents of the eternal tongue
Through the pine branches play –
Listened, and felt thyself grown young!
Listened and wept – Away!

Away the dreams that but deceive
130   And thou, sad guide, adieu!
I go, fate drives me; but I leave
Half of my life with you.

109–12. Cp. A.'s 1869 essay on *Obermann*, 'No representation of Senancour can, however, be complete without some of the gleams which relieved this discouragement. Besides the inwardness, besides the sincerity, besides the renouncement, there was the poetic emotion and the deep feeling for nature' (*Neiman* 161).

114. *Jaman*] Jaman overlooks Vevey on the Lake of Geneva. Obermann's chalet 'Imenström' was near Vevey.

121. *Lake Leman*] Another name for the Lake of Geneva.

125–6. Cp. *Obermann* (Lettre xlviii) ii 19–20, 'Et moi aussi, j'ai des momens d'oubli . . . Je m'arrête étonné; j'écoute ce qui subsiste encore; je voudrais entendre ce qui subsistera: je cherche dans le mouvement de la forêt, dans le bruit des pins, quelques-uns des accens de la langue éternelle.'

132. The poetic half of the divided self, but A. is also thinking of Marguerite.

We, in some unknown Power's employ,
Move on a rigorous line;
135   Can neither, when we will, enjoy,
Nor, when we will, resign.

I in the world must live; but thou,
Thou melancholy shade!
Wilt not, if thou canst see me now,
140   Condemn me, nor upbraid.

For thou art gone away from earth,
And place with those dost claim,
The Children of the Second Birth,
Whom the world could not tame;

145   And with that small, transfigured band,
Whom many a different way
Conducted to their common land,
Thou learn'st to think as they.

Christian and pagan, king and slave,
150   Soldier and anchorite,
Distinctions we esteem so grave,
Are nothing in their sight.

133-4. Cp. 'Meeting' 13 (p. 117 above),

> Ye guiding Powers who join and part . . .

and 'Human Life' 26 (p. 140 below),

> . . . chartered by some unknown Powers . . .

and see *n.* to ll. 43-4 of 'The Buried Life' (p. 273 below).

143-4. See A.'s letter to Clough 23 Sept. 1849, 'Marvel not that I say unto you, ye must be born again. While I will not much talk of these things, yet the considering of them has led me constantly to you the only living one almost that I know of

> The children of the second birth,
> Whom the world could not tame –'

(*CL* 109-10); and *John* iii 3, 7, 'Jesus answered and said unto him, Verily, verily, I say unto thee, Except a man be born again, he cannot see the kingdom of God . . . Marvel not that I said unto thee, Ye must be born again.'

They do not ask, who pined unseen,
Who was on action hurled,
155 Whose one bond is, that all have been
Unspotted by the world.

There without anger thou wilt see
Him who obeys thy spell
No more, so he but rest, like thee,
160 Unsoiled! – and so, farewell.

Farewell! – Whether thou now liest near
That much-loved inland sea,
The ripples of whose blue waves cheer
Vevey and Meillerie;

165 And in that gracious region bland,
Where with clear-rustling wave
The scented pines of Switzerland
Stand dark round thy green grave,

Between the dusty vineyard-walls
170 Issuing on that green place
The early peasant still recalls
The pensive stranger's face,

And stoops to clear thy moss-grown date
Ere he plods on again;
175 Or whether, by maligner fate,
Among the swarms of men,

156. Cp. *Epistle of James* i 27, 'Pure religion and undefiled before God and
the Father is this, To visit the fatherless and widows in their affliction, and
to keep himself unspotted from the world.'

161–4. Sainte-Beuve wrote to A. 6 Sept. 1854, 'Vous ne savez peut-être
pas que l'auteur, M. de Senancour, est mort il y a quelques années à Sèvres
près Paris où on l'avait transporté. Il n'a eu à son enterrement que deux
personnes, et on a gravé sur sa tombe ces mots qu'il avait indiqués: "Eter-
nité deviens mon asyle"' (*UL* 68). A. made use of the information in
'Obermann Once More' 268–72 (p. 530 below).

171–4. The 'early peasant' recalls the 'hoary-headed Swain' of Gray's
'Elegy written in a Country Church-yard' 97–116 (the allusion being
suggested by l. 120, 'And Melancholy mark'd him for her own', which A.
must have felt as applicable to Senancour as to Gray).

6+M.A.

Where between granite terraces
The blue Seine rolls her wave,
The Capital of Pleasure sees
180   The hardly-heard-of grave;

Farewell! Under the sky we part,
In this stern Alpine dell.
O unstrung will! O broken heart!
A last, a last farewell!

183–4. It is his own 'unstrung will' and 'broken heart' as much as Obermann's that A. is dismissing. Cp. the letter to Clough 23 Sept. 1849,
'What I must tell you is that I have never yet succeeded in any one great
occasion in consciously mastering myself: I can go thro: the imaginary
process of mastering myself . . . but at the critical point I am too apt to
hoist up the mainsail to the wind and let her drive' (*CL* 110). The lines are
A.'s farewell to youth, insouciance and Marguerite – and also, in the long
run, to the writing of poetry.

40 Absence

Written between Oct. 1849 – early 1850: see headn. to 'Meeting' (p. 115
above). Published *1852*; reprinted *1853* (*1854, 1857*), *1869*, etc. ('Switzerland' 6 *1853*; 7 *1854*; 8 *1857*; 5 *1869*; 6 *1877*, etc.)

In this fair stranger's eyes of grey
Thine eyes, my love! I see.
I shiver; for the passing day
Had borne me far from thee.

5   This is the curse of life! that not
A nobler, calmer train
Of wiser thoughts and feelings blot
Our passions from our brain;

¶ 40. *1*. The stranger was almost certainly Frances Lucy Wightman. Cp.
'Separation' 15–16 (p. 233 below),

Who, *let me say*, is this stranger regards me,
With the grey eyes, and the lovely brown hair?

and 'On the Rhine' 19–20 (p. 236 below),

Eyes too expressive to be blue,
Too lovely to be grey.

3. shiver] shudder *1852–69*.

But each day brings its petty dust
10   Our soon-choked souls to fill,
And we forget because we must
And not because we will.

I struggle towards the light; and ye,
Once-longed-for storms of love!
15   If with the light ye cannot be,
I bear that ye remove.

I struggle towards the light – but oh,
While yet the night is chill,
Upon time's barren, stormy flow,
20   Stay with me, Marguerite, still!

13-20. The light is knowledge of the self and the world leading to self-mastery. The image is of a man struggling through a storm towards a light which will mean safety, but the confusion of A.'s feelings is revealed by 'bear' (l. 16), which implies that he enjoys the storm, and by the plea to Marguerite, who is the cause of the storm, to stay with him until the light is reached. 'Time's barren, stormy flow' (l. 19) extends the image to that of a man struggling ashore through rough seas – cp. 'Obermann' 19 (p. 131 above),

All shipwreck in thy own weak heart . . .

41 Human Life

Date of composition unknown, but between (?) Oct. 1849 – early 1850: it is natural to assume that Marguerite is recalled in l. 16 and that the poem, which was classified as an 'Early Poem' in 1877, was written when A.'s separation from her was still recent. The idea that our behaviour is determined in spite of our apparent freedom occurs again in 'The Buried Life'. The unusual stanza (a³b⁴cacb⁵) is nowhere else used by A.
Published 1852; reprinted 1867, (1868), 1869, etc.

What mortal, when he saw,
Life's voyage done, his heavenly Friend,
Could ever yet dare tell him fearlessly:
'I have kept uninfringed my nature's law;
5   The inly-written chart thou gavest me,
To guide me, I have steered by to the end'?

¶ 41. 5. *The inly-written chart*] Conscience.

Ah! let us make no claim,
On life's incognisable sea,
To too exact a steering of our way;
10   Let us not fret and fear to miss our aim,
If some fair coast have lured us to make stay,
Or some friend hailed us to keep company.

Ay! we would each fain drive
At random, and not steer by rule.
15   Weakness! and worse, weakness bestowed in vain!
Winds from our side the unsuiting consort rive,
We rush by coasts where we had lief remain;
Man cannot, though he would, live chance's fool.

No! as the foaming swath
20   Of torn-up water, on the main,
Falls heavily away with long-drawn roar
On either side the black deep-furrowed path
Cut by an onward-labouring vessel's prore,
And never touches the ship-side again;

25   Even so we leave behind,
As, chartered by some unknown Powers,
We stem across the sea of life by night,
The joys which were not for our use designed;
The friends to whom we had no natural right,
30   The homes that were not destined to be ours.

7–12. This stanza is apparently contradicted by the following one, but A. probably means to imply that our freedom of action is circumscribed, not that it is illusory. A degree of freedom within a general plan determined by 'unknown Powers' is suggested also by 'chartered' (l. 26).

8. For the 'sea of life' see 'To Marguerite – Continued' 1 (p. 124 above) and n.

13–18. The same idea that our behaviour is secretly determined is expressed by a different figure in 'The Buried Life' 30–44 (pp. 272–3 below).

23. prore] An obsolete form of 'prow'.

27. stem] Hold to a fixed course.

42 Courage

Date of composition unknown, but (?) late 1849 or early 1850: A. appears to be glancing retrospectively at his own lack of decision in 'renouncing' Marguerite – cp. 'A Farewell' 13–40 (pp. 126–7 above); the praise of Byron's courage resembles that of 'Memorial Verses' (p. 225 below). Printed 1852; not reprinted by A.

True, we must tame our rebel will:
True, we must bow to Nature's law:
Must bear in silence many an ill;
Must learn to wait, renounce, withdraw.

5 Yet now, when boldest wills give place,
When Fate and Circumstance are strong,
And in their rush the human race
Are swept, like huddling sheep, along;

  Those sterner spirits let me prize,
10 Who, though the tendence of the whole
They less than us might recognize,
Kept, more than us, their strength of soul.

  Yes, be the second Cato praised!
Not that he took the course to die –
15 But that, when 'gainst himself he raised
His arm, he raised it dauntlessly.

¶ 42. *1–4*. The feeling here is Stoic, but 'renounce' has Carlylean and Goethean overtones. Carlyle probably introduced A. to Goethe's 'Entsagen' – cp. *Sartor Resartus* (1838), *Works* ed. H. D. Traill i 153, 'Well did the Wisest of our time write: "It is only with Renunciation (*Entsagen*) that Life, properly speaking, can be said to begin"', but of the various Goethean contexts for the idea available to A. 1849–50 the most likely is *Dichtung und Wahrheit* (Pt. IV) xvi (discussing Spinoza), 'Our physical as well as our social life, manners, customs, worldly wisdom, philosophy, religion, and many accidental happenings, all call upon us to deny ourselves' (tr. M. S. Smith, Bohn's Popular Library ed. (1913) ii 204). For A.'s later familiarity with the passage see *Note-books* 187 where the last phrase in German (*alles ruft uns zu: dass wir entsagen sollen*) is prefixed in 1872 to the quotation of *Faust* Pt. I 1549–53,

> *Renounce! renounce! 'tis all one hears!*
> *That is the song that ceaselessly*
> *Is ringing, ringing in our ears:*
> *That every hour with hoarse insistence*
> *Repeats throughout our whole existence . . .*

(J. Shawcross's translation, 1934.)
13. the second Cato] The great-grandson of Cato the Censor, who killed himself at Utica 46 B.C. to avoid falling into Caesar's hands. Suicide in such a case was permitted by Stoic teaching.

And, Byron! let us dare admire,
If not thy fierce and turbid song,
Yet that, in anguish, doubt, desire,
20   Thy fiery courage still was strong.

The sun that on thy tossing pain
Did with such cold derision shine,
He crushed thee not with his disdain –
He had his glow, and thou hadst thine.

25   Our bane, disguise it as we may,
Is weakness, is a faltering course.
Oh that past times could give our day,
Joined to its clearness, of their force!

17–24. For A. on Byron see 'Memorial Verses' 6–14 (pp. 226–7 below) and *nn.*

25–8. The same wish for force of will is expressed in 'A Farewell' 33–6 (p. 127 above), but in neither case does A. think that energy is a sufficient gift. In 'A Farewell' 40 it is 'far less rare than love'. Here he would welcome it only if it could be joined to 'clearness', i.e. the individual's recognition of his relation to 'the tendence of the whole'.

43 Self-Dependence

Date of composition unknown, but (?) late 1849 or early 1850. As in 'Human Life' (p. 139 above) A. is probably recalling his return by sea to England after his final parting with Marguerite at Thun in Oct. 1849. Published *1852*; reprinted *1853* (*1854, 1857*), *1869*, etc.

Weary of myself, and sick of asking
What I am, and what I ought to be,
At this vessel's prow I stand, which bears me
Forwards, forwards, o'er the starlit sea.

¶ *43. Title.* Perhaps suggested by Emerson's 'Self-Reliance', *Essays* (1st series, 1841). A. would have endorsed Emerson's comment, 'Discontent is the want of self-reliance: it is infirmity of will' (*Works*, Riverside ed. ii 77) – cp. 'Courage' 25–6 above.

1–2. Cp. A.'s note in the Yale MS., 'The disease of the present age is divorce from self'; and also *Obermann* (Letters xlii and i) i 175, 'Je ne sais ce que je suis, ce que j'aime, ce que je veux . . .' and i 5, '. . . ce qui importe surtout à l'homme, c'est d'être ce qu'il doit être . . .'

3. this vessel's prow] Surely the 'onward-labouring vessel's prore' of 'Human Life' 23 (p. 140 above).

5 And a look of passionate desire
O'er the sea and to the stars I send:
'Ye who from my childhood up have calmed me,
Calm me, ah, compose me to the end!

'Ah, once more,' I cried, 'ye stars, ye waters,
10 On my heart your mighty charm renew;
Still, still let me, as I gaze upon you,
Feel my soul becoming vast like you!'

From the intense, clear, star-sown vault of heaven,
Over the lit sea's unquiet way,
15 In the rustling night-air came the answer:
'Wouldst thou *be* as these are? *Live* as they.

'Unaffrighted by the silence round them,
Undistracted by the sights they see,
These demand not that the things without them
20 Yield them love, amusement, sympathy.

'And with joy the stars perform their shining,
And the sea its long moon-silvered roll;
For self-poised they live, nor pine with noting
All the fever of some differing soul.

25 'Bounded by themselves, and unregardful
In what state God's other works may be,
In their own tasks all their powers pouring,
These attain the mighty life you see.'

16–28. A similar lesson is drawn in 'Quiet Work (p. 106 above).
17. Unaffrighted by the silence] Cp. Pascal, *Pensées* 91 'Le silence éternel de ces espaces infinis m'effraie' (*L'Œuvre de Pascal* ed. J. Chevalier (1941) 848). It is unknown when A. first read Pascal, but his remark that twenty-three is 'an age which usually feels Pascal's charm most profoundly' ('Eugénie de Guerin', *E in C I* (1865), *Works* iii 142) may be autobiographical and point to 1846.
21. joy] But cp. 'Resignation' 191–2 (p. 91 above) and *n*.
22. moon-silvered roll] Cp. 'Empedocles on Etna' II [i] 425 (p. 192 below),
     Where the moon-silvered inlets . . .
23. self-poised] alone *1852–7*.
23–8. See A.'s letter to Clough 12 Feb. 1853, 'You ask me in what I think you . . . going wrong: in this: that you . . . could never finally, as it seemed – "resolve to be thyself" – but were looking for this or that experience and doubting whether you ought not to adopt this or that mode of being . . . because it might possibly be nearer the truth than your own' (*CL* 130).
25. unregardful] unobservant *1852–7*.

> O air-born voice! long since, severely clear,
30   A cry like thine in mine own heart I hear:
> 'Resolve to be thyself; and know that he,
> Who finds himself, loses his misery!'

31–2. Cp. Pascal, *Pensées* 81, 'Il faut se connaître soi-même: quand cela ne servirait pas à trouver le vrai, cela au moins sert à régler sa vie, et il n'y a rien de plus juste' (*L'Œuvre de Pascal* ed. cit. 839). A. varies the Socratic precept to 'be thyself' perhaps because of Goethe's and Carlyle's scorn for it – cp. Eckermann's *Conversations of Goethe* (under 10 April 1829), 'Altogether man is a darkened being; he knows not whence he comes, nor whither he goes; he knows little of the world, and least of himself. I know not myself, and God forbid I should' (Bohn's Library revised 1883 ed. 402); and *Sartor Resartus* (1838), '. . . the folly of that impossible Precept, *Know thyself*; till it be translated into this partially possible one, *Know what thou canst work at*' (*Works* ed. H. D. Traill i 132).

44 Destiny

Date of composition unknown, but (?) 1849–50: probably a 'Marguerite' poem cancelled by A. as duplicating the fuller self-analysis of 'A Farewell' 17–36 (pp. 126–7 above).
Published *1852*; not reprinted by A.

> Why each is striving, from of old,
> To love more deeply than he can?
> Still would be true, yet still grows cold?
> – Ask of the Powers that sport with man!

5   They yoked in him, for endless strife,
> A heart of ice, a soul of fire;
> And hurled him on the Field of Life,
> An aimless unallayed Desire.

¶ 44. *1–3.* Cp. 'A Farewell' 17–18 (p. 126 above),

> . . . this heart, I know,
> To be long loved was never framed . . .

5–6. A. makes the same complaint as Obermann and G. Sand's Lélia.
7. Field of Life] Cp. 'Empedocles on Etna' II [i] 365–6 (p. 190 below).

> . . . this meadow of calamity,
> This uncongenial place, this human life . . .

8. Cp. Senancour, *Obermann* (Lettre lxiii) ii 73, '. . . le tourment du cœur insatiable est le mouvement aveugle d'un météore . . . Je sens, j'existe pour me consumer en désirs indomptables . . .'

45 Youth's Agitations

Date of composition unknown, but (?) 1849–50. The Yale MS. list of
poems to be composed in 1849 identifies 'The World's Triumphs' below
and 'Youth's Agitations' as the second and third of a projected group
of five sonnets: '5 sonnets – out thunder – So far – When I have found. –
It may be true that men *cannot* do the best they can *desire*: it is equally
true they *have* never yet done it.' Unlike the rest of A.'s sonnets, these
two, which were brought together in *1869* and classified as 'Early Poems'
in *1877*, are in the Shakespearian form (the other three sonnets of the
projected sequence have not survived, if they were ever composed).
A. is poised anxiously between relief and regret as he feels youth slipping
away – cp. 'Youth and Calm' (p. 224 below) and his letter to his sister
'K' 25 Jan. 1851, 'How strong the tendency is ... as characters take
their bent ... to submit onself gradually to the silent influence that
attaches us more and more to those whose characters are like ours ... and
that detaches us from everything besides, as if we could only acquire any
solidity of shape ... by narrowing and narrowing our sphere and diminish-
ing the number of affections and interests which continually distract us
while young, and hold us unfixed and without energy to mark our place
in the world; which we thus succeed in marking only by making it a very
confined and joyless one. The aimless and unsettled, but also open and
liberal state of our youth we *must* perhaps all leave ... but with most of us
it is a melancholy passage from which we emerge shorn of so many beams
that we are almost tempted to quarrel with the law of nature which
imposes it on us' (*L* i 14).
Published as 'Sonnet' *1852*; reprinted with present title *1867* (*1868*),
1869, etc.

> When I shall be divorced, some ten years hence,
> From this poor present self which I am now;
> When youth has done its tedious vain expense
> Of passions that for ever ebb and flow;
>
> 5   Shall I not joy youth's heats are left behind,
> And breathe more happy in an even clime?

¶ 45. *3. tedious vain expense*] Perhaps echoing Shakespeare, Sonnet cxxxi
1–2,

> The expense of spirit in a waste of shame
> Is lust in action ...

5. youth's heats] Cp. 'Tristram and Iseult' iii 133–6 (p. 221 below),

> And yet, I swear, it angers me to see

6*

Ah no, for then I shall begin to find
A thousand virtues in this hated time!

10   Then I shall wish its agitations back,
And all its thwarting currents of desire;
Then shall I praise the heat which then I lack,
And call this hurrying fever, generous fire;

And sigh that one thing only has been lent
To youth and age in common – discontent.

> *How this fool passion gulls men potently;*
> *Being, in truth, but a diseased unrest,*
> *And an unnatural overheat at best.*

9–12. In 'Youth and Calm' 22–3 (p. 225 below), youth

> *. . . hears a voice within it tell:*
> Calm's not life's crown, though calm is well . . .

but here there is more bitterness and less resignation. Until we are free of youth's 'hurrying fever' we shall not really feel that there is anything to be said in its favour. When we do feel it, it will already be too late, and our 'calm' will be riddled with discontent.

46 The World's Triumphs

Date of composition unknown, but (?) 1849–50: see headn. to 'Youth's Agitations' (p. 145 above) for its appearance on the Yale MS. list of poems to be composed in 1849. The title refers to the world that triumphs over idealism and youthful enthusiasm, i.e. the 'monstrous, dead, unprofitable world' of 'Written in Emerson's Essays' (p. 52 above). See A.'s comment in the Yale MS., 'Nothing makes me more despise the world than the homage it pays to experience . . . it generally implies only the total absence of all youth and richness of soul, and the presence of a dead *fais la negative* callosity.'
Published as 'Sonnet' *1852*; reprinted with present title *1853* (*1854, 1857*), *1869*, etc.

> So far as I conceive the world's rebuke
> To him addressed who would recast her new,
> Not from herself her fame of strength she took,
> But from their weakness who would work her rue.

¶ 46. *4. weakness*] baseness *MS.* A.'s autograph is on the inside cover of his copy of vol. iii of Eckermann's *Gespräche mit Goethe* (Magdeburg, 1848) – see *Commentary* 50.

5   'Behold,' she cries, 'so many rages lulled,
So many fiery spirits quite cooled down;
Look how so many valours, long undulled,
After short commerce with me, fear my frown!

    'Thou too, when thou against my crimes wouldst cry,
10   Let thy foreboded homage check thy tongue!'
The world speaks well; yet might her foe reply:
'Are wills so weak? – then let not mine wait long!

    'Hast thou so rare a poison? – let me be
Keener to slay thee, lest thou poison me!'

10. homage] treason MS.

47 Empedocles on Etna

A DRAMATIC POEM

Written 1849–52, but – since perhaps completed much earlier than publication in Oct. 1852 – exact period of composition unknown. In Feb. or March 1849 A. wrote to his mother, 'I had thoughts of publishing another volume of short poems next spring [1850], and a tragedy I have long had in mind, the spring after [1851] . . . which however will not be a very quick affair' (quoted by Mrs. A. in a letter to Tom A. March 1849, Mrs. H. Ward, *A Writer's Recollections* (1918) 43). This projected tragedy on the subject of Lucretius – whom A. was reading seriously from 1845 – at one time included stanzas that later became 'Empedocles on Etna' I ii 397–410 (see *Commentary* 293). A.'s letter bears on the interpretation of the Yale list of poems to compose in 1849 (undated, but after Oct. 1848), which begins 'Chew Lucretius' (? the tragedy for 1851) and continues with a numbered list of suggestions for other poems (? the proposed 1850 collection of shorter pieces), the first being 'Empedocles – refusal of limitation by the religious sentiment' – a description that fits the philosophical chant of 'Empedocles on Etna' I ii 77–426 but not A.'s completed 'dramatic poem'. Plausibly then the original poem outgrew A.'s first conception (drawing on material intended for 'Lucretius') and between Feb. or March and June 1849 A. therefore decided to give it dramatic form – see J. C. Shairp's letter to Clough 30 June 1849, 'He [A.] was working at an "Empedocles" – which seemed to be not much about the man who leapt into the crater – but his name and outward circumstances are used for the drapery of his own thoughts. I wish Matt would give up that old greek form . . .' (*Correspondence of A.H.C.* i 270). At the same time A. made (1) notes on the life of Empedocles from the introduction to S. Karsten's *Philosophorum Grae-*

corum Veterum . . . Operum Reliquiae ii (1838) 3–78 (these notes are reproduced *Commentary* 289–90) and (2) the following analysis of his pro-
tagonist's character and motives (preserved in the Yale MS.):

'He is a philosopher.

He has not the religious consolation of other men, facile because
adapted to their weaknesses, or because shared by all around and charg-
ing the atmosphere they breathe.

He sees things as they are – the world as it is – God as he is: in their
stern simplicity.

~~The sight is a severe and mind-tasking one:~~ to know the mysteries
which are communicated to others by fragments, in parables.

But he started towards it in hope: his first glimpses of it filled him
with joy; he had friends who shared his hope and joy and communicated to him theirs: even now he does not deny that the sight is
capable of affording rapture and the purest peace.

But his friends are dead: the world is all against him, and in-
credulous of the truth: his mind is overtasked by the effort to hold fast
so great and severe a truth in solitude: the atmosphere he breathes not
being modified by the presence of human life, is too rare for him. He
perceives still the truth of the truth, but cannot be transported and
rapturously agitated by his [*for* its] grandeur: his spring and elasticity
of mind are gone: he is clouded, oppressed, dispirited, without hope
and energy.

Before he becomes the victim of depression and overtension of
mind, to the utter deadness to joy, grandeur, spirit, and animated life,
he desires to die; to be reunited with the universe, before by exaggerating his human side he has become utterly estranged from it.'

With this analysis cp. the description of the 'modern feeling' in Lucretius –
see 'On the Modern Element in Literature' (1857), *Complete Prose Works*
ed. R. H. Super i (1960) 32–4 and particularly, 'The predominance of
thought . . . in the unsound, in the over-tasked, in the over-sensitive . . .
has produced a state of feeling unknown to less enlightened but perhaps
healthier epochs – the feeling of depression, the feeling of *ennui*' (*loc. cit.*
32); and for the further identification of Empedocles-Lucretius with
Obermann see 'Empedocles on Etna' I i 151–3 and *n*. (p. 155 below) and
Sainte-Beuve's 1832 essay on Senancour, which is included in *Portraits
Contemporains* i (1845):

'Dans son pèlerinage à la Dent du Midi, assis sur le plateau de granit,
au-dessus de la région des sapins, au niveau des neiges éternelles . . .
Oberman me figure exactment ce sage de Lucrèce qui habite

Edita doctrina sapientum templa serena,

temple, en effet, tout serein et glacé . . . S'il s'élancait, s'il disparaissait
alors, ce serait presque en Dieu, comme Empédocle à l'Etna.'

For A.'s recognition of Empedocles as a modern consciousness see also the

1853 Preface, '. . . we hear already the doubts, we witness the discouragement, of Hamlet and of Faust' (p. 591 below); and on I ii as 'modern thought', II [i] as 'modern feeling' – a distinction intended by A. – see W. E. Houghton's interpretation of the poem in *Vict. Stud.* i (1958) 311–36. The main sources of A.'s ideas are to be found in Empedocles, Lucretius, Epictetus, M. Aurelius, Carlyle's *Sartor Resartus*, Senancour's *Obermann*; the songs of Callicles draw on Pindar, Hesiod and Ovid; the choice of dramatic form and the evolution of the action were determined by imitation of Byron's *Manfred* – see my note in *N & Q* ns. ix (1962) 300–3. Published *1852*; reprinted entire ('. . . at the request of a man of genius . . . Mr. Robert Browning' – A.'s note) *1867 (1868)*, *1869*, etc. For the reasons A. gave for suppressing the poem in 1853 see *1853* Preface (pp. 590–2 below).

PERSONS

EMPEDOCLES
PAUSANIAS, *a Physician.*
CALLICLES, *a young Harp-player.*

The Scene of the Poem is on Mount Etna; at first in the forest region, afterwards on the summit of the mountain.

ACT I. SCENE I

Morning. A Pass in the forest region of Etna.

CALLICLES

(Alone, resting on a rock by the path.)
The mules, I think, will not be here this hour;
They feel the cool wet turf under their feet
By the stream-side, after the dusty lanes

¶ 47. *Persons and Scene.* Callicles is A.'s own conception – no hint of the name or character occurs in Karsten's introduction ('De Empedoclis Vita et Studiis'). The three scenes of the poem are set in the cool forest region of Etna in the early morning (I i), on the boundary of the forest region and the unsheltered upper slopes at noon (I ii), on the barren summit of the mountain at evening (II [i]). Callicles is seen only in I i; Empedocles is alone in II [i]. The journey to the summit is the journey from youth to middle age, from elasticity of spirit to world-weariness, from a proper balance of man's mental powers to his 'enslavement' by thought. Cp. Yale MS., 'I cannot conceal from myself the objection . . . that the service of reason is freezing to feeling . . . & feeling and the religious mood are eternally the deepest being of man, the ground of all joy and greatness for him.'

In which they have toiled all night from Catana,
5   And scarcely will they budge a yard. O Pan,
How gracious is the mountain at this hour!
A thousand times have I been here alone,
Or with the revellers from the mountain-towns,
But never on so fair a morn; the sun
10   Is shining on the brilliant mountain-crests,
And on the highest pines; but farther down,
Here in the valley, is in shade; the sward
Is dark, and on the stream the mist still hangs;
One sees one's footprints crushed in the wet grass,
15   One's breath curls in the air; and on these pines
That climb from the stream's edge, the long grey tufts,
Which the goats love, are jewelled thick with dew.
Here will I stay till the slow litter comes.
I have my harp too – that is well. Apollo!
20   What mortal could be sick or sorry here?
I know not in what mind Empedocles,
Whose mules I followed, may be coming up,
But if, as most men say, he is half mad
With exile, and with brooding on his wrongs,
25   Pausanias, his sage friend, who mounts with him,
Could scarce have lighted on a lovelier cure.
The mules must be below, far down. I hear
Their tinkling bells, mixed with the song of birds,
Rise faintly to me – now it stops! Who's here?
Pausanias! and on foot? alone?

Pausanias

30   And thou, then?
I left thee supping with Peisianax,
With thy head full of wine, and thy hair crowned,

I i *20. sick or sorry*] Cp. 'Pagan and Mediaeval Religious Sentiment',
E in C I (1865), *Works* iii 237, 'Well, the sentiment of the "religion of
pleasure" has much that is natural in it . . . to live by it one must never
be sick or sorry, and the old, ideal, limited, pagan world never . . . *was*
sick or sorry, never at least shows itself to us sick or sorry . . .'
I i *23–4.* 'He travelled in the East, to Greece and Olympia . . . Returning
to Sicily, he found the aristocrats uppermost, the children of his early
foes; he was repulsed [by] them and coming to Syracuse, abode in the
house of Pisianax a wealthy man . . .' – A.'s notes on Karsten's introduction
(*Commentary* 290).
I i *31–43.* Freely developing *Karsten* ii 34–5, 'Heraclides Ponticus prodit,
eum, postquam exanimem illam mulierem vitae reddidisset, sacrificium
instituisse apud agrum nobilis cujusdam viri, Pisianactis nomine, quo

Touching thy harp as the whim came on thee,
And praised and spoiled by master and by guests
35   Almost as much as the new dancing-girl.
Why hast thou followed us?

Callicles

                    The night was hot,
And the feast past its prime; so we slipped out,
Some of us, to the portico to breathe –
Peisianax, thou know'st, drinks late; and then,
40   As I was lifting my soiled garland off,
I saw the mules and litter in the court,
And in the litter sate Empedocles;
Thou, too, wast with him. Straightway I sped home;
I saddled my white mule, and all night long
45   Through the cool lovely country followed you,
Passed you a little since as morning dawned,
And have this hour sate by the torrent here,
Till the slow mules should climb in sight again.
And now?

Pausanias

            And now, back to the town with speed!
50   Crouch in the wood first, till the mules have passed;
They do but halt, they will be here anon.
Thou must be viewless to Empedocles;
Save mine, he must not meet a human eye.
One of his moods is on him that thou know'st;
I think, thou wouldst not vex him.

Callicles

55   No – and yet
I would fain stay, and help thee tend him. Once
He knew me well, and would oft notice me;
And still, I know not how, he draws me to him,

---

quidam ex ejus amicis invitati erant, inter quos etiam Pausanias . . . Peractis
epulis, reliquos somni capiendi causa digressos passim recubuisse, Empedoclem solum in loco ubi accubuisset remansisse. Mane autem quum
ceteri surrexissent, illum non esse inventum.'
I i *52. viewless*] Invisible. A poeticism used by Shakespeare, Milton and
Keats among other poets.

And I could watch him with his proud sad face,
60   His flowing locks and gold-encircled brow
And kingly gait, for ever; such a spell
In his severe looks, such a majesty
As drew of old the people after him,
In Agrigentum and Olympia,
65   When his star reigned, before his banishment,
Is potent still on me in his decline.
But oh! Pausanias, he is changed of late;
There is a settled trouble in his air
Admits no momentary brightening now,
70   And when he comes among his friends at feasts,
'Tis as an orphan among prosperous boys.
Thou know'st of old he loved this harp of mine,
When first he sojourned with Peisianax;
He is now always moody, and I fear him;
75   But I would serve him, soothe him, if I could,
Dared one but try.

Pausanias

                   Thou wast a kind child ever!
He loves thee, but he must not see thee now.
Thou hast indeed a rare touch on thy harp,
He loves that in thee, too; there was a time
80   (But that is passed), he would have paid thy strain
With music to have drawn the stars from heaven.
He hath his harp and laurel with him still,
But he has laid the use of music by,
And all which might relax his settled gloom.
85   Yet thou may'st try thy playing, if thou wilt –
But thou must keep unseen; follow us on,
But at a distance! in these solitudes,
In this clear mountain-air, a voice will rise,
Though from afar, distinctly; it may soothe him.

I i 59–63. Cp. *Karsten* ii 30–1, 'Affectabat tragicum quemdam fastum et dignitatem: inerat severitas in vultu, in verbis gravitas, habitus semper aequalis, austerus, luxuriae reprehensor; idem vero in corporis cultu magnificus: prodeuntem asseclarum vel pedissequorum turba comitabatur; indutus erat veste purpurea … comam alebat prolixam: quae omnia erant opulentiae vel dignitatis signa … Denique ita se gerebat, ut regiae ac paene divinae dignitatis speciem prae se ferret.'

I i 85–98. The Abbot's proposal to follow Manfred at a distance and endeavour to save him – see *Manfred* III i 160–71 – probably suggested to A. the shadowing of Empedocles by Callicles.

90   Play when we halt, and, when the evening comes
         And I must leave him (for his pleasure is
         To be left musing these soft nights alone
         In the high unfrequented mountain-spots),
         Then watch him, for he ranges swift and far,
95   Sometimes to Etna's top, and to the cone;
         But hide thee in the rocks a great way down,
         And try thy noblest strains, my Callicles,
         With the sweet night to help thy harmony!
         Thou wilt earn my thanks sure, and perhaps his.

Callicles

100   More than a day and night, Pausanias,
         Of this fair summer-weather, on these hills,
         Would I bestow to help Empedocles.
         That needs no thanks; one is far better here
         Than in the broiling city in these heats.
105   But tell me, how hast thou persuaded him
         In this his present fierce, man-hating mood,
         To bring thee out with him alone on Etna?

Pausanias

         Thou hast heard all men speaking of Pantheia,
         The woman who at Agrigentum lay
110   Thirty long days in a cold trance of death,
         And whom Empedocles called back to life.
         Thou art too young to note it, but his power
         Swells with the swelling evil of this time,
         And holds men mute to see where it will rise.
115   He could stay swift diseases in old days,
         Chain madmen by the music of his lyre,

I i *108–11*. Cp. *Karsten* ii 24–5, 'Fertur igitur Agrigenti fuisse mulier quaedam, cujus etiam nomen meminere, – Hermippus Pantheam appellatam tradidit, – quae per complures dies continuos (secundum Diogenem triginta; secundum Plinium probabilius, septem) sine respiratione et arteriarum pulsu mansisset, hoc uno cadaveri dissimilis, quod circa medias corporis partes caloris quiddam superesset: huic mulieri a medicis desperatae et jam conclamatae Empedocles spiritum et salutem reddidit.'
I i *115*. Cp. *Karsten* ii 19, 'Maxime vero celebratus est ob rerum naturalium scientiam et medicae artis peritiam . . .'
I i *116*. Cp. *Karsten* ii 25–6, 'Nam quum adolescens quidam furibundus stricto in illius hospitem gladio irrueret, patrem suum, quem ille judex lectus capitis condemnaverat, ulturus, jamque in eo esset ut eum feriret, fertur Empedocles, qui forte aderat, statim canendi modum inflexisse, et cantum exorsus dulcem et placabilem, illius iram temperasse . . .'

Cleanse to sweet airs the breath of poisonous streams,
And in the mountain-chinks inter the winds.
This he could do of old; but now, since all
120 Clouds and grows daily worse in Sicily,
Since broils tear us in twain, since this new swarm
Of sophists has got empire in our schools
Where he was paramount, since he is banished
And lives a lonely man in triple gloom –
125 He grasps the very reins of life and death.
I asked him of Pantheia yesterday,
When we were gathered with Peisianax,
And he made answer, I should come at night
On Etna here, and be alone with him,
130 And he would tell me, as his old, tried friend,
Who still was faithful, what might profit me;
That is, the secret of this miracle.

Callicles

Bah! Thou a doctor! Thou art superstitious.
Simple Pausanias, 'twas no miracle!
135 Pantheia, for I know her kinsmen well,
Was subject to these trances from a girl.
Empedocles would say so, did he deign;
But he still lets the people, whom he scorns,
Gape and cry *wizard* at him, if they list.
140 But thou, thou art no company for him!
Thou art as cross, as soured as himself!
Thou hast some wrong from thine own citizens,
And then thy friend is banished, and on that,
Straightway thou fallest to arraign the times,
145 As if the sky was impious not to fall.

I i *117.* Cp. *Karsten* ii 21-2, 'Alterum exemplum ... scientiae rerum naturalium hoc est, quod e Diodoro Ephesio Diogenes refert. Quum Selinuntios ex amnis circumfluentis foetore pestilentia vel tabes invasisset, qua homines perirent ... Empedoclem tale excogitasse mali remedium: duos vicinos amnes suo sumptu in fluvium immisisse, quorum commixtione factum, ut aqua dulcesceret et pestilentia cessaret.'
I i *118.* Cp. *Karsten* ii 20, 'Probabilior et simplicior est Plutarchi narratio: Empedoclem montis hiatum, quo graves et pestiferi austri flatus in campos immitterentur, obstruxisse, eoque pestilentiam avertisse creditum.'
I i *133-4* and below *159-60.* Callicles is as convinced as the author of *Literature and Dogma* (1873) that 'miracles do not happen'.
I i *138-9.* Cp. *Karsten* ii 27-8, 'Augurem et γόητα, id est magum, fuisse, fama increbuit, idque non post mortem ejus, sed jam vivo illo videtur pervulgatum.'

The sophists are no enemies of his;
I hear, Gorgias, their chief, speaks nobly of him,
As of his gifted master, and once friend.
He is too scornful, too high-wrought, too bitter.
150 'Tis not the times, 'tis not the sophists vex him;
There is some root of suffering in himself,
Some secret and unfollowed vein of woe,
Which makes the time look black and sad to him.
Pester him not in this his sombre mood
155 With questionings about an idle tale,
But lead him through the lovely mountain-paths,
And keep his mind from preying on itself,
And talk to him of things at hand and common,
Not miracles! thou art a learned man,
160 But credulous of fables as a girl.

Pausanias

And thou, a boy whose tongue outruns his knowledge,
And on whose lightness blame is thrown away.
Enough of this! I see the litter wind
Up by the torrent-side, under the pines.
165 I must rejoin Empedocles. Do thou
Crouch in the brushwood till the mules have passed;
Then play thy kind part well. Farewell till night!

SCENE II

*Noon. A Glen on the highest skirts of the woody region
of Etna.*

EMPEDOCLES – PAUSANIAS

Pausanias

The noon is hot. When we have crossed the stream,
We shall have left the woody tract, and come

I i *147–8.* Gorgias is mentioned as the most famous pupil of Empedocles, *Karsten* ii 56.

I i *151–3.* Cp. A. on Senancour, 'Obermann' (1869), *Neiman* 161, 'But a root of failure, powerlessness, and ennui, there certainly was in the constitution of Senancour's own nature; so that, unfavourable as may have been his time, we should err in attributing to any outward circumstances the whole of the discouragement by which he is pervaded.' See also the remarks on Byron's heroes in *On the Study of Celtic Literature* (1867), *Works* v 129, '...not so much in collision with outward things, as breaking on some rock of revolt and misery in the depths of their own nature; Manfred, self-consumed, fighting blindly and passionately with I know not what...'

        Upon the open shoulder of the hill.
        See how the giant spires of yellow bloom
5   Of the sun-loving gentian, in the heat,
        Are shining on those naked slopes like flame!
        Let us rest here; and now, Empedocles,
        Pantheia's history!

                          [*A harp-note below is heard.*

Empedocles

                Hark! what sound was that
        Rose from below? If it were possible,
10   And we were not so far from human haunt,
        I should have said that some one touched a harp.
        Hark! there again!

Pausanias

                'Tis the boy Callicles,
        The sweetest harp-player in Catana.
        He is for ever coming on these hills,
15   In summer, to all country-festivals,
        With a gay revelling band: he breaks from them
        Sometimes, and wanders far among the glens.
        But heed him not, he will not mount to us;
        I spoke with him this morning. Once more, therefore,
20   Instruct me of Pantheia's story, Master,
        As I have prayed thee.

Empedocles

                That? and to what end?

I ii *4–5*. A. is recalling the Alpine setting of *Obermann*. Cp. 'Obermann Once More' 21–2 (p. 520 below).

> *The gentian-flowered pass, its crown*
> *With yellow spires aflame . . .*

I ii *8. Stage direction.* Cp. stage direction, *Manfred* I ii 47, 'The Shepherd's pipe in the distance is heard.'

I ii *14–16.* These lines, repeating the sense of I i 7–8, connect Callicles with the Youth of 'The Strayed Reveller' (p. 65 above), who is also a poet of 'natural magic'.

I ii *19–21.* Cp. *Karsten* ii 25 (speaking of Pantheia's cure), 'Morbi ejus curandi rationem etiam Pausaniae medico familiari monstrasse vel explicuisse dicitur.'

Pausanias

It is enough that all men speak of it.
But I will also say, that when the Gods
Visit us as they do with sign and plague,
25 To know those spells of thine which stay their hand
Were to live free from terror.

Empedocles

Spells? Mistrust them!
Mind is the spell which governs earth and heaven.
Man has a mind with which to plan his safety;
Know that, and help thyself!

Pausanias

But thine own words?
30 'The wit and counsel of man was never clear,
Troubles confound the little wit he has.'
Mind is a light which the Gods mock us with,
To lead those false who trust it.

[*The harp sounds again.*

Empedocles

Hist! once more!
Listen, Pausanias! – Ay, 'tis Callicles;
35 I know these notes among a thousand. Hark!

Callicles
(*Sings unseen, from below*)

The track winds down to the clear stream,
To cross the sparkling shallows; there
The cattle love to gather, on their way
To the high mountain-pastures, and to stay,
40 Till the rough cow-herds drive them past,
Knee-deep in the cool ford; for 'tis the last
Of all the woody, high, well-watered dells
On Etna; and the beam
Of noon is broken there by chestnut-boughs
45 Down its steep verdant sides; the air
Is freshened by the leaping stream, which throws
Eternal showers of spray on the mossed roots

I ii *30–1.* Cp. Empedocles, *Karsten* ii 88, 'For scant means of obtaining knowledge are scattered through the limbs, and many evils break in to blunt the edge of careful thought.'
I ii *36–76.* Reprinted *1855* as 'The Harp-player on Etna. I. The Last Glen'.

       Of trees, and veins of turf, and long dark shoots
       Of ivy-plants, and fragrant hanging bells
50   Of hyacinths, and on late anemones,
       That muffle its wet banks; but glade,
       And stream, and sward, and chestnut-trees,
       End here; Etna beyond, in the broad glare
       Of the hot noon, without a shade,
55   Slope behind slope, up to the peak, lies bare;
       The peak, round which the white clouds play.

       In such a glen, on such a day,
       On Pelion, on the grassy ground,
       Chiron, the aged Centaur lay,
60   The young Achilles standing by.
       The Centaur taught him to explore
       The mountains; where the glens are dry
       And the tired Centaurs come to rest,

I ii 51. *muffle*] See A.'s letter 5 July 1865, 'The plain of Lombardy . . . refreshed my eyes, which were weary of the rocky, parched ground of Italy proper, for the vegetation of the south . . . is all *above* the ground in the branches and leaves of the trees, and not muffling and cooling the ground itself in the way I love . . .' (*L* i 286); and for one of several uses in the poems cp. 'The Scholar-Gipsy' 69 (p. 336 below),

      And watch the warm, green-muffled Cumner hills . . .

I ii 57–76. Like Empedocles Chiron was famed as a teacher and healer. The traditional lore taught to Achilles contrasts with the philosophical instruction about to be given to Pausanias. For the significance of this traditional lore see Edgar Quinet, *Le Génie des Religions* (1842), *Œuvres Complètes* (Paris, 1857) iii 123–4, 'Avant d'être le héros de sa race, Achille reçoit dans le sein des forêts les instructions du Centaure . . . Il apprend du vieillard contemporain du chaos, non pas seulement l'invention de l'arc et de la flèche, mais aussi la tradition et le mystère des premiers jours du monde. Tout peuple reçoit de même; en secret, les enseignements de Chiron.' There are accounts of the education of Achilles in Statius, *Achilleid* ii 86–167 and Pindar, *Nemean Odes* iii 53–63, but these are not A.'s sources. With ll. 71–5 cp. Homer's song in Chénier's 'L'Aveugle' 157–94 and especially 163–5, 169, 190,

      D'abord le roi divin, et l'Olympe, et les cieux,
      Et le monde, ébranlés d'un signe de ses yeux,
      Et les Dieux partagés en une immense guerre . . .

      Et les héros armés, brillant dans les campagnes . . .

      Et puis les demi-dieux et les champs d'asphodèle . . .

And where the soaking springs abound
65   And the straight ashes grow for spears,
And where the hill-goats come to feed,
And the sea-eagles build their nest.
He showed him Phthia far away,
And said: O boy, I taught this lore
70   To Peleus, in long distant years!
He told him of the Gods, the stars,
The tides; and then of mortal wars,
And of the life which heroes lead
Before they reach the Elysian place
75   And rest in the immortal mead;
And all the wisdom of his race.

The music below ceases, and EMPEDOCLES *speaks, accompanying
himself in a solemn manner on his harp.*

The out-spread world to span
A cord the Gods first slung,
And then the soul of man
80   There, like a mirror, hung,
And bade the winds through space impel the gusty toy.

Hither and thither spins
The wind-borne, mirroring soul,
A thousand glimpses wins,
85   And never sees a whole;
Looks once, and drives elsewhere, and leaves its last
[employ.

I ii *77–426*. Empedocles's attempt to free Pausanias from superstitious
fears is so far Lucretian, but this long philosophical chant – although it
marries classical and modern ideas of various kinds, sometimes incompatibly
– is primarily stoical in its insistence on recognizing and accepting the
limits of human freedom.
I ii *77. out-spread world*] howling void *1852*.
I ii *80. like a mirror*] A stock image, but perhaps suggested by *Obermann*
(Lettre xlviii) ii 19, 'Le métal que l'art a poli reçoit l'image d'une partie
de l'univers; nous la recevons comme lui. – Mais il n'a pas le sentiment de
ce contact.'
I ii *81. toy*] Cp. *Obermann* (Lettre xli) i 165, ' . . . jouet lamentable d'une
destinée que rien n'explique, l'homme abandonnera sa vie aux hasards et
des choses et des temps'.
I ii *82–6*. Cp. Empedocles, *Karsten* ii 88, 90, 'Struggling for a brief span of
existence that is not life, doomed to swift death, they fly up and are carried
away like smoke, each one convinced only of that on which he has chanced

       The Gods laugh in their sleeve
       To watch man doubt and fear,
       Who knows not what to believe
90   Since he sees nothing clear,
    And dares stamp nothing false where he finds nothing sure.

       Is this, Pausanias, so?
       And can our souls not strive,
       But with the winds must go,
95   And hurry where they drive?
    Is fate indeed so strong, man's strength indeed so poor?

       I will not judge. That man,
       Howbeit, I judge as lost,
       Whose mind allows a plan,
100   Which would degrade it most;
    And he treats doubt the best who tries to see least ill.

       Be not, then, fear's blind slave!
       Thou art my friend; to thee,
       All knowledge that I have,
105   All skill I wield, are free.
    Ask not the latest news of the last miracle,

       Ask not what days and nights
       In trance Pantheia lay,
       But ask how thou such sights
110   May'st see without dismay;
    Ask what most helps when known, thou son of Anchitus!

       What? hate, and awe, and shame
       Fill thee to see our time;

---

as he is driven to and fro, and vainly claiming that he has grasped the
Whole.' A.'s 'glimpses' and 'sees' are suggested by Karsten's Latin translation of the original Greek: '. . . tantum habentes perspectum quantum
cuique assequi licuit, in omnes partes se versantes; universum vero se
perspexisse frustra quis gloriatur . . .'
I ii *101. who tries to see least ill*] i.e. who, following the less 'degrading'
alternative, assumes that man has a limited freedom of action.
I ii *111. what most helps when known*] Glossed by l. 216 below,

   How man may here best live no care too great to explore . . .

– the fundamental preoccupation of Epictetus and of Marcus Aurelius.
I ii *113, 115–6. time . . . out of chime . . . chance*] day . . . in dismay . . . time
1852; world . . . rudely hurl'd . . . time *1867–77.*

Thou feelest thy soul's frame
115   Shaken and out of chime?
What? life and chance go hard with thee too, as with us;

Thy citizens, 'tis said,
Envy thee and oppress,
Thy goodness no men aid,
120   All strive to make it less;
Tyranny, pride, and lust, fill Sicily's abodes;

Heaven is with earth at strife,
Signs make thy soul afraid,
The dead return to life,
125   Rivers are dried, winds stayed;
Scarce can one think in calm, so threatening are the Gods;

And we feel, day and night,
The burden of ourselves —
Well, then, the wiser wight
130   In his own bosom delves,
And asks what ails him so, and gets what cure he can.

The sophist sneers: Fool, take
Thy pleasure, right or wrong.
The pious wail: Forsake
135   A world these sophists throng.
Be neither saint nor sophist-led, but be a man!

I ii *122–6*. The miracles attributed to Empedocles – cp. I i 108–111, 117–18. He is mocking Pausanias.

I ii *127–8*. Cp. A.'s *1853* Preface (p. 591 below), 'What those who are familiar only with the great monuments of early Greek genius suppose to be its exclusive characteristics have disappeared; the calm, the cheerfulness, the disinterested objectivity have disappeared: the dialogue of the mind with itself has commenced ...'

I ii *129–30*. A. is more sceptical about reaching the 'genuine self' in 'The Buried Life' 55–6,

> And many a man in his own breast then delves
> But deep enough, alas! none ever mines ...

The source of the image is probably M. Aurelius vii 59 tr. G. Long (1875 ed.) 140, 'Look within. Within is the fountain of good, and it will ever bubble up, if thou wilt ever dig', but see also Carlyle, *Past and Present* (1843), *Works* ed. H. D. Traill x 26, 'If thou ask me again, ... What is to be done? allow me to reply ... Thou shalt descend into thy inner man, and see if there be any traces of a soul there.'

I ii *136*. Cp. M. Aurelius ii 5 ed. *cit.* 79, 'Every moment think steadily as a Roman and a man to do what thou hast in hand ...'

These hundred doctors try
To preach thee to their school.
We have the truth! they cry;
140   And yet their oracle,
Trumpet it as they will, is but the same as thine.

Once read thy own breast right,
And thou hast done with fears;
Man gets no other light,
145   Search he a thousand years.
Sink in thyself! there ask what ails thee, at that shrine!

What makes thee struggle and rave?
Why are men ill at ease?
'Tis that the lot they have
150   Fails their own will to please;
For man would make no murmuring, were his will obeyed.

And why is it, that still
Man with his lot thus fights?
'Tis that he makes this *will*
155   The measure of his *rights*,
And believes Nature outraged if his will's gainsaid.

I ii *146. Sink in thyself!*] Cp. 'The Youth of Man' 116–18 (p. 254 below),

> *Sink, O youth, in thy soul!*
> *Yearn to the greatness of Nature;*
> *Rally the good in the depths of thyself.*

I ii *147–50.* Cp. Carlyle's translation (1824) of *Wilhelm Meister* ii ch. 2, *Works* ed. *cit.* xxiii 112, 'What is it that keep men in continual discontent and agitation? It is, that they cannot make realities correspond with their conceptions . . .' (passages neighbouring this are used by A. in 'Resignation' 144–69 – see p. 89 above and *n.*). The notion is again Stoic. Cp. Epictetus, *Enchiridion* viii tr. G. Long (1877) 382, 'Seek not that the things which happen should happen as you wish; but wish the things which happen to be as they are, and you will have a tranquil flow of life.'
I ii *151.* The Yale MS. has a variant of this line (unrecorded *1950*),

> *For man would ask no questions were his wish obeyed.*

I ii *152–6.* Cp. A.'s note (Yale MS.), 'All men have equal rights, therefore All men should have equal enjoyment. Oh! A man has *a right* to what he can get – and *then* – why, *necessity is laid upon him* to forego all . . .

Couldst thou, Pausanias, learn
How deep a fault is this;
Couldst thou but once discern
160   Thou hast no *right* to bliss,
No title from the Gods to welfare and repose;

Then thou wouldst look less mazed
Whene'er of bliss debarred,
Nor think the Gods were crazed
165   When thy own lot went hard.
But we are all the same — the fools of our own woes!

For, from the first faint morn
Of life, the thirst for bliss
Deep in man's heart is born;
170   And, sceptic as he is,
He fails not to judge clear if this be quenched or no.

Nor is the thirst to blame.
Man errs not that he deems
His welfare his true aim,
175   He errs because he dreams
The world does but exist that welfare to bestow.

Epicureanism is Stoical, and there is no theory of life but is.' This note is
connected with the second of two rejected stanzas in the Yale MS.:

> *That each man's lot is that*
> *Which he can win or keep*
> *Nor does Heaven toil thereat*
> *To make him laugh or weep;*
> *Learn that men will not and gods cannot help thy state.*

I ii *160*. Cp. Carlyle, *Sartor Resartus* (1838), *Works* ed. *cit.* i 153, 'Foolish
soul! What Act of Legislature was there that *thou* shouldst be Happy?'
I ii *172–4*. A., unlike Carlyle, thinks happiness a proper aim for man, but
with the Stoics and Spinoza he holds that his direct aim should be to live in
conformity with nature and so contentedly.
I ii *175–6*. Cp. Lucretius, *De Rerum Natura* v 156–7, 164–5 (of the gods),

> *dicere porro hominum causa voluisse parare*
> *praeclaram mundi naturam . . .*

> *cetera de genere hoc adfingere et addere, Memmi,*
> *desiperest . . .*

We mortals are no kings
For each of whom to sway
A new-made world up-springs,
180   Meant merely for his play;
No, we are strangers here; the world is from of old.

In vain our pent wills fret,
And would the world subdue.
Limits we did not set
185   Condition all we do;
Born into life we are, and life must be our mould.

Born into life! man grows
Forth from his parents' stem,
And blends their bloods, as those
190   Of theirs are blent in them;
So each new man strikes root into a far fore-time.

I ii *177–86.* Cp. A.'s prose summary of his argument in the Yale MS.:
   'We have a will;
   we find we cannot freely give it scope;
   we are irritated, and account for it on different theories
            into which we carry our irritation.
   But look at the matter calmly.
   We arrive, a new force, in a *schon* existent world of forces.
   Our force can only have play so far as these other forms will let it . . .'
and for these ideas see Spinoza, *Ethics* Pt. iv appendix, *Works* tr. R. H. M.
Elwes (1891) ii 242–3, 'But human power is extremely limited, and is
infinitely surpassed by the power of external causes; we have not, therefore, an absolute power of shaping to our use those things which are without us. Nevertheless, we shall bear with an equal mind all that happens to
us . . . remembering that we are a part of universal nature and that we
follow her order.' Spinoza's ideas accord with Stoic teaching – see Epictetus, *Discourses* i ch. 26 ed. *cit.* 77, '. . . the law of life, that we must act
conformably to nature . . .'
I ii *177–81.* Cp. 'In Utrumque Paratus' 36–42 (p. 56 above) and 'The
Youth of Man' 25–6 (p. 251 below),
            We are young and the world is ours,
            Man, man is the king of the world . . .
I ii *184–5.* Cp. 'To a Republican Friend, 1848: Continued' 5–8 (p. 103
above),
            Seeing this vale, this earth, whereon we dream,
            Is on all sides o'ershadowed by the high
            Uno'erleaped Mountains of Necessity,
            Sparing us narrower margin than we deem.
I ii *187–96.* Added *1867.*

Born into life! we bring
A bias with us here,
And, when here, each new thing
195   Affects us we come near;
To tunes we did not call our being must keep chime.

Born into life! in vain,
Opinions, those or these,
Unaltered to retain
200   The obstinate mind decrees;
Experience, like a sea, soaks all-effacing in.

Born into life! who lists
May what is false hold dear,
And for himself make mists
205   Through which to see less clear;
The world is what it is, for all our dust and din.

Born into life! 'tis we,
And not the world, are new;
Our cry for bliss, our plea,
210   Others have urged it too –
Our wants have all been felt, our errors made before.

No eye could be too sound
To observe a world so vast,
No patience too profound
215   To sort what's here amassed;
How man may here best live no care too great to explore.

But we – as some rude guest
Would change, where'er he roam,
The manners there professed
220   To those he brings from home –
We mark not the world's course, but would have *it* take
                        [*ours.*

I ii *197–201.* These lines follow ll. 202–6 in *1852.* Cp. A.'s note (Yale MS.),
'The Spirit of the world enounces the problems which this or that generation of Men is to work: men do not fix for themselves.'

I ii *203, 205. hold dear . . . clear*] maintain . . . plain *1852.*

I ii *221. course . . . take*] ways . . . learn *1852.*

I ii *217–20.* Cp. the cancelled motto to 'The Future' (p. 263 below) and
the Yale MS. note, 'Nature has long since kept this inn, the Earth, and
seen so many successive floods of guests with their fashions and ridicul-
ousnesses that no swagger of any new comer can impose upon her.'

          The world's course proves the terms
          On which man wins content;
          Reason the proof confirms –
225   We spurn it, and invent
     A false course for the world, and for ourselves, false
                                                  [powers.

          Riches we wish to get,
          Yet remain spendthrifts still;
          We would have health, and yet
230   Still use our bodies ill;
     Bafflers of our own prayers, from youth to life's last
                                                  [scenes.

          We would have inward peace,
          Yet will not look within;
          We would have misery cease,
235   Yet will not cease from sin;
     We want all pleasant ends, but will use no harsh means;

          We do not what we ought,
          What we ought not, we do,
          And lean upon the thought
240   That chance will bring us through;
     But our own acts, for good or ill, are mightier powers.

          Yet, even when man forsakes
          All sin – is just, is pure,
          Abandons all which makes
245   His welfare insecure –
     Other existences there are, that clash with ours.

See similar images in Epictetus, *Discourses* i ch. 24, ii ch. 23 ed. *cit.* 72, 186.
I ii *222–5. world's course proves . . . the proof . . . it . . . A false course for
the world, and for*] world proclaims . . . its voice . . . them . . . False weakness in the world, and in *1852.*
I ii *222–3.* Senancour also feeds A.'s Stoicism – cp. *Obermann* (Lettre
xli) i 160, 'Nul individu ne saurait arrêter le cours universel, et rien n'est
plus vain que la plainte des maux attachés nécessairement à notre nature.'
ii *237–8.* Cp. General Confession, *The Book of Common Prayer,* 'We have
left undone those things which we ought to have done; And we have
done those things which we ought not to have done . . .'
I ii *241.* Cp. A.'s note (Yale MS.), 'We learn late the truth of *Cause and
Effect*: that this or that operation will bring forth this or that result, and not
another: that a certain merit will not have a *heterogeneous* reward: that
there is no pity – no compromise.'

Like us, the lightning-fires
Love to have scope and play;
The stream, like us, desires
250   An unimpeded way;
Like us, the Libyan wind delights to roam at large.

Streams will not curb their pride
The just man not to entomb,
Nor lightnings go aside
255   To give his virtues room;
Nor is that wind less rough which blows a good man's
                               [barge.

Nature, with equal mind,
Sees all her sons at play;
Sees man control the wind,
260   The wind sweep man away;
Allows the proudly-riding and the foundering bark.

And, lastly, though of ours
No weakness spoil our lot,
Though the non-human powers
265   Of Nature harm us not,
The ill deeds of other men make often *our* life dark.

What were the wise man's plan?
Through this sharp, toil-set life,
To work as best he can,
270   And win what's won by strife.
But we an easier way to cheat our pains have found.

Scratched by a fall, with moans
As children of weak age
Lend life to the dumb stones
275   Whereon to vent their rage,
And bend their little fists, and rate the senseless ground;

I ii 252–6. Cp. Spinoza, *Ethics* Pt. i appendix, *Works* ed. *cit.* ii 76, 'Experience day by day protested and showed by infinite examples, that good and evil fortunes fall to the lot of pious and impious alike.'
I ii 261. *foundering*] founder'd *1852–69*.
I ii 266. Cp. A.'s note, 'The confusion and sinfulness of men which *we* are avoiding will continue to throw obstacles in our way even when we are cured' (Yale MS., immediately following sentences quoted in *n.* to I ii 177–86).

So, loth to suffer mute,
We, peopling the void air,
Make Gods to whom to impute
280   The ills we ought to bear;
With God and Fate to rail at, suffering easily.

Yet grant – as sense long missed
Things that are now perceived,
And much may still exist
285   Which is not yet believed –
Grant that the world were full of Gods we cannot see;

All things the world which fill
Of but one stuff are spun,
That we who rail are still,
290   With what we rail at, one;
One with the o'erlaboured Power that through the
        breadth and length

Of earth, and air, and sea,
In men, and plants, and stones,
Hath toil perpetually,
295   And travails, pants, and moans;
Fain would do all things well, but sometimes fails in
                                [strength.

And patiently exact
This universal God
Alike to any act
300   Proceeds at any nod,
And quietly declaims the cursings of himself.

This is not what man hates,
Yet he can curse but this.
Harsh Gods and hostile Fates
305   Are dreams! this only is –
Is everywhere; sustains the wise, the foolish elf.

I ii 287–301. Cp. A.'s notes (Yale MS.), (1) 'A God identical with the world
and with the sum of being and force therein contained: not exterior to it,
possessing being and force exterior to it, and determining it à son gré'; (2)
'We learn not to *abuse* or *storm at* the Gods or Fate: knowing this mere
madness: as there is nothing wilfully operating against us – the only object
of anger: and the power we would curse is the same with ourselves: the
same with the tongue employed to articulate the curse. God patiently
lends himself to curse himself.'
I ii 295. *travails, pants*] struggles, pants *1852–68*; travails, strives *1869*.
I ii 297, 301. *patiently . . . quietly*] punctually . . . patiently *1852*.

Nor only, in the intent
To attach blame elsewhere,
Do we at will invent
310   Stern Powers who make their care
To embitter human life, malignant Deities;

But, next, we would reverse
The scheme ourselves have spun,
And what we made to curse
315   We now would lean upon,
And feign kind Gods who perfect what man vainly tries.

Look, the world tempts our eye,
And we would know it all!
We map the starry sky,
320   We mine this earthen ball,
We measure the sea-tides, we number the sea-sands;

We scrutinise the dates
Of long-past human things,
The bounds of effaced states,
325   The lines of deceased kings;
We search out dead men's words, and works of dead
        men's hands;

We shut our eyes, and muse
How our own minds are made.
What springs of thought they use,
330   How rightened, how betrayed –
And spend our wit to name what most employ unnamed.

But still, as we proceed
The mass swells more and more
Of volumes yet to read,
335   Of secrets yet to explore.
Our hair grows grey, our eyes are dimmed, our heat is
        tamed;

I ii *332–6*. Cp. 'The Second Best' 5–8 (p. 278 below),

> *But so many books thou readest,*
> *But so many schemes thou breedest,*
> *But so many wishes feedest,*
>   *That thy poor head almost turns.*

7 + M.A.

We rest our faculties,
And thus address the Gods:
'True science if there is,
340   It stays in your abodes!
Man's measures cannot mete the immeasurable All,

'You only can take in
The world's immense design.
Our desperate search was sin,
345   Which henceforth we resign,
Sure only that your mind sees all things which befall.'

Fools! That in man's brief term
He cannot all things view,
Affords no ground to affirm
350   That there are Gods who do;
Nor does being weary prove that he has where to rest.

Again. Our youthful blood
Claims rapture as its right;
The world, a rolling flood
355   Of newness and delight,
Draws in the enamoured gazer to its shining breast;

Pleasure, to our hot grasp,
Gives flowers after flowers;
With passionate warmth we clasp
360   Hand after hand in ours;
Nor do we soon perceive how fast our youth is spent.

At once our eyes grow clear!
We see, in blank dismay,
Year posting after year,
365   Sense after sense decay;
Our shivering heart is mined by secret discontent;

I ii 341. *mete the immeasurable All*] span the illimitable All *1852*. The later reading may glance at Carlyle, *Sartor Resartus* (1838), *Works* ed. *cit.* i 205, 'Such a minnow is Man; his Creek this Planet Earth; his Ocean the immeasurable All . . .'

I ii 356. *the enamoured gazer*] A pertinent allusion. The gazer's delight depends on his 'youthful blood' and is in this sense narcissistic.

I ii 362-6. Autobiographical. A. felt acutely the passage of time and the loss of youth — cp. his letter of 25 Jan. 1851 to his sister 'K' (already quoted in headn. to 'Youth's Agitations', p. 145 above) and of 9 April 1852 to Clough, 'How life rushes away, and youth. One has dawdled and scrupled and fiddle faddled – and it is all over' (*CL* 120).

Yet still, in spite of truth,
In spite of hopes entombed,
That longing of our youth
370   Burns ever unconsumed,
Still hungrier for delight as delights grow more rare.

We pause; we hush our heart,
And thus address the Gods:
'The world hath failed to impart
375   The joy our youth forebodes,
Failed to fill up the void which in our breasts we bear.

'Changeful till now, we still
Looked on to something new;
Let us, with changeless will,
380   Henceforth look on to you,
To find with you the joy we in vain here require!'

Fools! That so often here
Happiness mocked our prayer,
I think, might make us fear
385   A like event elsewhere;
Make us, not fly to dreams, but moderate desire.

And yet, for those who know
Themselves, who wisely take
Their way through life, and bow
390   To what they cannot break,
Why should I say that life need yield but *moderate* bliss?

A Moderate
Hope d
Aim

Shall we, with temper spoiled,
Health sapped by living ill,
And judgment all embroiled
395   By sadness and self-will,
Shall *we* judge what for man is not true bliss or is?

I ii *386*. Cp. 'The Second Best' 1–4 (p. 278 below),

> *Moderate tasks and moderate leisure,*
> *Quiet living, strict-kept measure*
> *Both in suffering and in pleasure –*
> *'Tis for this thy nature yearns . . .*

and Carlyle's famous recipe for content, *Sartor Resartus* (1838), *Works* ed. *cit.* i 152–3, 'So true it is . . . that *the Fraction of Life can be increased in value not so much by increasing your Numerator as by lessening your Denominator.*'

             Is it so small a thing
             To have enjoyed the sun,
             To have lived light in the spring,
400   To have loved, to have thought, to have done;
     To have advanced true friends, and beat down baffling
                                        [foes –

             That we must feign a bliss
             Of doubtful future date,
             And, while we dream on this,
405   Lose all our present state,
     And relegate to worlds yet distant our repose?

             Not much, I know, you prize
             What pleasures may be had,
             Who look on life with eyes
410   Estranged, like mine, and sad;
     And yet the village-churl feels the truth more than you,

             Who's loth to leave this life
             Which to him little yields –
             His hard-tasked sunburnt wife,
415   His often-laboured fields,
     The boors with whom he talked, the country-spots he
                                    [knew.

             But thou, because thou hear'st
             Men scoff at Heaven and Fate,
             Because the Gods thou fear'st
420   Fail to make blest thy state,
     Tremblest, and wilt not dare to trust the joys there are!

             I say; Fear not! Life still
             Leaves human effort scope.
             But, since life teems with ill,
425   Nurse no extravagant hope;
     Because thou must not dream, thou need'st not then
       despair!

I ii *397–411.* An early draft of these stanzas is among A.'s materials for his projected 'Lucretius' (*Commentary* 294).
I ii *401. baffling foes*] Cp. *Manfred* I i *19–20,*

> *I have had my foes,*
> *And none have baffled, many fallen before me . . .*

I ii *409–16.* Cp. *Obermann* (Lettre xviii) i 74–5, ' . . . il est en moi une inquiétude qui ne me quittera pas . . . Plus heureux, sans doute, celui qui coupe du bois, qui fait du charbon . . . il chante en travaillant.'

A long pause. At the end of it the notes of a harp below are
again heard, and CALLICLES *sings : —*

Far, far from here,
The Adriatic breaks in a warm bay
Among the green Illyrian hills; and there
430   The sunshine in the happy glens is fair,
And by the sea, and in the brakes.
The grass is cool, the sea-side air
Buoyant and fresh, the mountain flowers
More virginal and sweet than ours.
435   And there, they say, two bright and aged snakes,
Who once were Cadmus and Harmonia,
Bask in the glens or on the warm sea-shore,
In breathless quiet, after all their ills;
Nor do they see their country, nor the place
440   Where the Sphinx lived among the frowning hills,
Nor the unhappy palace of their race,
Nor Thebes, nor the Ismenus, any more.

There those two live, far in the Illyrian brakes!
They had stayed long enough to see,
445   In Thebes, the billow of calamity
Over their own dear children rolled,
Curse upon curse, pang upon pang,
For years, they sitting helpless in their home,
A grey old man and woman; yet of old

I ii *427–60*. Printed separately as 'Cadmus and Harmonia' *1853 (1854, 1857)*. Lyrical relief after the philosopher's instruction of Pausanias. In general, Callicles's songs are intended 'to combine, to harmonise, to deepen the feelings excited' by the action and to provide 'relief and relaxation' from their intensity – see A.'s Preface to *Merope* (1858) on the 'grand effects' of the chorus in Greek tragedy (*Complete Prose Works* ed. R. H. Super i (1960) 61). The flight to Illyria and serpent-change of Cadmus and Harmonia are from Ovid, *Metamorphoses* iv 563–603; the wedding banquet from Pindar, *Pythian Odes* iii 86–96 – a passage quoted by A. in *On Translating Homer: Last Words* (1862), *Works* v 292. Empedocles is fleeing from men as Cadmus fled from Thebes.
I ii *436 Cadmus*] The founder of Thebes, to whom Zeus gave Harmonia for his wife.
I ii *445–7.* Cp. Sophocles, *Trachiniae* 112 ff., 'For as the tireless South or Northern blast / Billow on billow rolls o'er ocean wide, / So on the son of Cadmus follows fast / Sea upon sea of trouble . . .' (Loeb translation).
I ii *446. their own dear children*] Autonoe, Ino, Semele, Agave and Polydorus. For their misfortunes see Apollodorus, *Bibliotheca* iii 4.

450   The Gods had to their marriage come,
      And at the banquet all the Muses sang.

      Therefore they did not end their days
      In sight of blood; but were rapt, far away,
      To where the west-wind plays,
455   And murmurs of the Adriatic come
      To those untrodden mountain-lawns; and there
      Placed safely in changed forms, the pair
      Wholly forget their first sad life, and home,
      And all that Theban woe, and stray
460   For ever through the glens, placid and dumb.

                    Empedocles

      That was my harp-player again! – where is he?
      Down by the stream?

                    Pausanias

                    Yes, Master, in the wood.

                    Empedocles

      He ever loved the Theban story well!
      But the day wears. Go now, Pausanias,
465   For I must be alone. Leave me one mule;
      Take down with thee the rest to Catana.
      And for young Callicles, thank him from me;
      Tell him, I never failed to love his lyre –
      But he must follow me no more to-night.

I ii *450–1*. Cp. Pindar, *Pythian Odes* iii 86–93, 'But a life free from reverses
was the fate neither of Peleus ... nor of godlike Cadmus. Yet we learn
that they attained the highest happiness of all mortal men, in that they
heard the Muses of the golden snood singing on mount Pelion, and in
seven-gated Thebes, what time Cadmus took to wife Harmonia ... And
the gods banqueted with them ...'
I ii *457–60*. An echo, with a significant alteration, of Ovid, *Metamorphoses*
iv 600–3,

          et subito duo sunt iunctoque volumine serpunt,
          donec in adpositi nemoris subiere latebras,
          nunc quoque nec fugiunt hominem nec vulnere laedunt,
          quidque prius fuerint, placidi meminere dracones ...

A. thinks the snakes would be unhappy if they did not

          Wholly forget their first sad life, and home ...

Pausanias

470 Thou wilt return to-morrow to the city?

Empedocles

Either to-morrow or some other day,
In the sure revolutions of the world,
Good friend, I shall revisit Catana.
I have seen many cities in my time,
475 Till mine eyes ache with the long spectacle,
And I shall doubtless see them all again;
Thou know'st me for a wanderer from of old.
Meanwhile, stay me not now. Farewell, Pausanias!

He departs on his way up the mountain.

Pausanias (alone)

I dare not urge him further – he must go;
480 But he is strangely wrought! I will speed back
And bring Peisianax to him from the city;
His counsel could once soothe him. But, Apollo!
How his brow lightened as the music rose!
Callicles must wait here, and play to him;
485 I saw him through the chestnuts far below,
Just since, down at the stream. Ho! Callicles!

He descends, calling.

ACT II

Evening. The Summit of Etna.

EMPEDOCLES

Alone! –
On this charred, blackened, melancholy waste,
Crowned by the awful peak, Etna's great mouth,
Round which the sullen vapour rolls – alone!
5 Pausanias is far hence, and that is well,
For I must henceforth speak no more with man.
He hath his lesson too, and that debt's paid;

I ii 471–6. A reference to reincarnation. See *n.* to II [i] 368 (p. 190 below).
II [i] This scene formally resembles *Manfred* I ii (M. soliloquising and con-
templating suicide on the Jungfrau). Empedocles's 'discouragement' has
parallels with other expressions of romantic melancholy, e.g. Coleridge's
'Dejection', but A.'s main debt is probably to Obermann on his desponding
side – see especially the 'suicide' letter (xli), *Obermann* i 155–74.

And the good, learned, friendly, quiet man
May bravelier front his life, and in himself
10   Find henceforth energy and heart. But I –
The weary man, the banished citizen,
Whose banishment is not his greatest ill,
Whose weariness no energy can reach,
And for whose hurt courage is not the cure –
15   What should I do with life and living more?

No, thou art come too late, Empedocles!
And the world hath the day, and must break thee,
Not thou the world. With men thou canst not live,
Their thoughts, their ways, their wishes, are not thine;
20   And being lonely thou art miserable,
For something has impaired thy spirit's strength,
And dried its self-sufficing fount of joy.

II [i] *11–15*. Cp. Coleridge, 'Dejection' 21–3,

> *A grief without a pang, void, dark, and drear,*
> *A stifled, drowsy, unimpassioned grief,*
> *Which finds no natural outlet, no relief . . .*

but cp. also *Obermann* (Lettre xli) i 156, 'Ce n'est point dans le malheur que je songerais à rejeter la vie. La résistance éveille l'âme . . . on peut se plaire dans son énergie . . . Mais ce sont les embarras, les ennuis, les contraintes, l'insipidité de la vie, qui me fatiguent . . . quelle considération peut soutenir l'homme qui n'attend rien? Je suis las de mener une vie si vaine . . .'; and *Manfred* I ii 25–7,

> *If it be life to wear within myself*
> *This barrenness of Spirit, and to be*
> *My own Soul's sepulchre . . .*

II [i] *18–19*. Obermann's perpetual complaint. Cp. *Obermann* (Lettre xxii) i 91, 'Je suis seul . . . me voilà dans le monde, errant, solitaire, au milieu de la foule qui ne m'est rien.'

II [i] *21–2*. The 'something' is identified as 'the gradual furnace of the world'

> *Which kills in us the bloom, the youth, the spring . . .*

> *By drying up our joy in everything . . .*

in 'Tristram and Iseult' iii 119–26 (p. 221 below), but see ll. 235–75 below where the hostility of the age, the loss of youth and the tyranny of the 'imperious lonely thinking-power' (l. 376) are all implicated. The 'fount of joy' is also a 'spring of hope' (l. 317 below) and in 'The Progress of Poesy' 1–4 (p. 540 below) the poetic source:

Thou canst not live with men nor with thyself –
O sage! O sage! Take then the one way left;
25   And turn thee to the elements, thy friends,
Thy well-tried friends, thy willing ministers,
And say: Ye helpers, hear Empedocles,
Who asks this final service at your hands!
Before the sophist-brood hath overlaid
30   The last spark of man's consciousness with words –
Ere quite the being of man, ere quite the world
Be disarrayed of their divinity –
Before the soul lose all her solemn joys,
And awe be dead, and hope impossible,
35   And the soul's deep eternal night come on –
Receive me, hide me, quench me, take me home!

———

> *Youth rambles on life's arid mount,*
> *And strikes the rock, and finds the vein,*
> *And brings the water from the fount,*
> *The fount which shall not flow again.*

For aridity elsewhere in A. see Wordsworth's praise in 'Memorial Verses'
54–7 (p. 229 below),

> *Our youth returned; for there was shed*
> *Our spirits that had long been dead,*
> *Spirits dried up and closely furled,*
> *The freshness of the early world . . .*

and cp. *Obermann* (Lettre xv) i 72, 'Mon cœur . . . est flétri et desséché . . .
Je suis éteint, sans être calmé.'

II [i] 23. Expanded ll. 198–234 below.

II [i] 25–6. Cp. Empedocles, *Karsten* ii 96, 'Hear first the four roots of all
things: fire and water and earth and the immense height of air: for from
these come all things that are or have been or shall be.' A. has copied out
the Greek of this fragment in the Yale MS.

II [i] 27. *helpers*] servants *1852–81*.

II [i] 29–32. Cp. A.'s letters 23 Sept. 1849, 'My dearest Clough these are
damned times – everything is against one – the height to which knowledge
has come, the spread of luxury, our physical enervation, the absence of
great *natures*, the unavoidable contact with millions of small ones, news-
papers, cities . . . our own selves, and the sickening consciousness of our
difficulties . . .' (*CL* 111); and 7 June 1852, 'I am sure however that in the
air of the present times il nous manque d'aliment, and that we deteriorate
in spite of our struggles . . .' (*CL* 123).

II [i] 36. Cp. *Manfred* I ii 109,

> – *Earth! take these atoms!*

7*

He advances to the edge of the crater. Smoke and fire break
forth with a loud noise, and CALLICLES *is heard below*
singing : –

The lyre's voice is lovely everywhere:
In the court of Gods, in the city of men,
And in the lonely rock-strewn mountain-glen,
40   In the still mountain air.

Only to Typho it sounds hatefully;
To Typho only, the rebel o'erthrown,
Through whose heart Etna drives her roots of stone
To imbed them in the sea.

45   Wherefore dost thou groan so loud?
Wherefore do thy nostrils flash,
Through the dark night, suddenly,
Typho, such red jets of flame?
Is thy tortured heart still proud?
50   Is thy fire-scathed arm still rash?
Still alert thy stone-crushed frame?
Doth thy fierce soul still deplore
Thine ancient rout by the Cilician hills,

II [i] *37–88.* Printed separately *1855* as 'The Harp-player on Etna. II.
Typho'. Freely imitating in subject Pindar, *Pythian Odes* i *1–28* but
fashioned to suggest the symmetry of a Greek tragic chorus – see *Baum*
125, 'The metre of the Song is balanced like strophe and antistrophe: two
quatrains followed by two groups of twenty [-two] lines matching both in
rime scheme and line length'; A. regrets in the Preface to *Merope* (1858)
that Milton adopted in the choruses of *Samson Agonistes* a 'relaxed form of
the later Greek tragedy' (*Complete Prose Works* ed. *cit.* i 61). Empedocles
interprets the myth ll. 89–107 below.
II [i] *37–40.* Cp. Pindar, *Pythian Odes* i 1–4 'O golden lyre, that art owned
alike by Apollo and by the violet-tressed Muses! thou lyre, which the
footstep heareth, as it beginneth the gladsome dance; lyre, whose notes the
singers obey, whenever, with thy quivering strings, thou preparest to
strike up the prelude of the choir-leading overture!'
II [i] *41–4.* Cp. Pindar, *Pythian Odes*: 13–20, 'But all the beings that Zeus
hath not loved, are astonished, when they hear the voice of Pierides . . .
whereof is he who lieth in dread Tartarus, that foeman of the Gods,
Typhon with his hundred heads, who was nurtured of old by the famed
Cilician cave, though now the steep shores above Cyme, and Sicily too,
lieth heavy on his shaggy breast, and the column that soareth to heaven
crusheth him, even snow-clad Etna . . .'

And that cursed treachery on the Mount of Gore?
55   Do thy bloodshot eyes still weep
The fight which crowned thine ills,
Thy last mischance on this Sicilian deep?
Hast thou sworn, in thy sad lair,
Where erst the strong sea-currents sucked thee down,
60   Never to cease to writhe, and try to rest,
Letting the sea-stream wander through thy hair?
That thy groans, like thunder pressed,
Begin to roll, and almost drown
The sweet notes whose lulling spell
65   Gods and the race of mortals love so well,
When through thy caves thou hearest music swell?

But an awful pleasure bland
Spreading o'er the Thunderer's face,

II [i] 54. 'Mount Haemus, so called, said the legend, from Typho's blood spilt on it in his last battle with Zeus, when the giant's strength failed, owing to the Destinies having a short time before given treacherously to him, for his refreshment, perishable fruits. See Apollodorus, *Bibliotheca*, book i, chap. vi.' Arnold's note added *1885*.

II [i] 55. *still weep*] still see *1852*, *1867*; still flee *1869*. Baum notes a discrepancy between the two verse-paragraphs (ll. 45–66, 67–88) in the final text, in that – if the paragraphs are divided into groups of 7, 6, 6 and 3 lines – l. 55 (the c-rhyme of the first 6-line group) does not rhyme with l. 47 (the c-rhyme of the 7-line group) in the first paragraph as do the corresponding lines (ll. 69 and 77) in the second paragraph. But the readings of *1852*, *1867*, *1869* show that the rhyme once existed. It was probably removed inadvertently when A. had forgotten the full sophistication of his original scheme.

II [i] 57. Thy last defeat in this Sicilian sea? *1852–69*.

II [i] 60. *rest*] sleep *1852–69*.

II [i] 62. *thunder pressed*] thunder deep *1852–69*.

II [i] 67–83. Cp. Pindar, *Pythian Odes* i 5–12, 'Thou abatest even the warring thunderbolt of everlasting flame; and the eagle, king of birds, sleepeth on the sceptre of Zeus, while his swift pinions twain are drooping, and a darksome mist is shed over his bending head, sweetly sealing his eyelids . . . For even the stern god of war setteth aside his rude spears so keen, and warmeth his heart in deep repose; and thy shafts of music soothe even the minds of the deities . . .' A. also remembers in ll. 74–9 Gray's imitation of Pindar's eagle, 'The Progress of Poesy' 20–4,

    Perching on the scept'red hand
    Of Jove, thy magic lulls the feather'd king
    With ruffled plumes, and flagging wing:

When the sound climbs near his seat,
70   The Olympian council sees;
As he lets his lax right hand,
Which the lightnings doth embrace,
Sink upon his mighty knees.
And the eagle, at the beck
75   Of the appeasing, gracious harmony,
Droops all his sheeny, brown, deep-feathered neck,
Nestling nearer to Jove's feet;
While o'er his sovran eye
The curtains of the blue films slowly meet.
80   And the white Olympus-peaks
Rosily brighten, and the soothed Gods smile
At one another from their golden chairs,
And no one round the charméd circle speaks.
Only the loved Hebe bears
85   The cup about, whose draughts beguile
Pain and care, with a dark store
Of fresh-pulled violets wreathed and nodding o'er;
And her flushed feet glow on the marble floor.

Empedocles

He fables, yet speaks truth!
90   The brave, impetuous heart yields everywhere
To the subtle, contriving head;
Great qualities are trodden down,
And littleness united
Is become invincible.

Cf Yeats

Quench'd in dark clouds of slumber lie
The terror of his beak, and light'nings of his eye.

II [i] *90–1*. Cp. 'The Scholar-Gipsy' 205 (p. 342 below),

Its [modern life's] heads o'ertaxed, its palsied hearts . . .

II [i] *90. impetuous heart*] impetuous hand *1852*.
II [i] *92–4*. Cp. A.'s letter 7 June 1852, 'Au reste, a great career is hardly
possible any longer . . . I am more and more convinced that the world
tends to become more comfortable for the mass, and more uncomfortable
for those of any natural gift or distinction – and it is as well perhaps that it
should be so . . .' (*CL* 122) and Carlyle, 'Signs of the Times' (1829), *Crit.
and Miscell. Essays, Works* ed. cit. xxvii 61, 'No individual now hopes to
accomplish the poorest enterprise single-handed . . . In these days, more em-
phatically than ever, "to live, signifies to unite with a party, or to make one".'

95   These rumblings are not Typho's groans, I know!
         These angry smoke-bursts
         Are not the passionate breath
         Of the mountain-crushed, tortured, intractable Titan
         But over all the world   [king –
100   What suffering is there not seen
         Of plainness oppressed by cunning,
         As the well-counselled Zeus oppressed
         That self-helping son of earth!
         What anguish of greatness,
105   Railed and hunted from the world,
         Because its simplicity rebukes
         This envious, miserable age!

         I am weary of it.
         – Lie there, ye ensigns
110   Of my unloved preëminence
         In an age like this!
         Among a people of children,
         Who thronged me in their cities,
         Who worshipped me in their houses,
115   And asked, not wisdom,
         But drugs to charm with,
         But spells to mutter –
         All the fool's-armoury of magic! Lie there,
         My golden circlet,
120   My purple robe!

                Callicles (from below).

         As the sky-brightening south-wind clears the day,
         And makes the massed clouds roll,
         The music of the lyre blows away
         The clouds which wrap the soul.

II [i] *121–90*. Printed separately *1855* as 'The Harp-player on Etna. III.
Marsyas'. A. knew the story from Apollodorus, *Bibliotheca* i 4 (2) and
Ovid, *Metamorphoses* vi 383–95, but neither account mentions Pan's
jealousy or the presence of the Muses. The song, which consists metrically
of two matching quatrains followed by two passages of unequal length in
rhymed trochaic tetrameter, is about the price of being a poet – Empedocles,
like Marsyas, is Apollo's victim and finds the final price too high (cp.
Metamorphoses vi 385–6,

             '*quid me detrahis?*' *inquit;*
         '*a! piget, a! non est*' *clamabat* '*tibia tanti . . .*').

Callicles, like Olympus, has to stand helplessly by 'at his master's end'.

125   Oh! that Fate had let me see
That triumph of the sweet persuasive lyre,
That famous, final victory,
When jealous Pan with Marsyas did conspire;

When, from far Parnassus' side,
130   Young Apollo, all the pride
Of the Phrygian flutes to tame,
To the Phrygian highlands came;
Where the long green reed-beds sway
In the rippled waters grey
135   Of that solitary lake
Where Mæander's springs are born;
Whence the ridged pine-wooded roots
Of Messogis westward break,
Mounting westward, high and higher.
140   There was held the famous strife;
There the Phrygian brought his flutes,
And Apollo brought his lyre;
And, when now the westering sun
Touched the hills, the strife was done,
145   And the attentive Muses said:
'Marsyas, thou art vanquishéd!'
Then Apollo's minister
Hanged upon a branching fir
Marsyas, that unhappy Faun,
150   And began to whet his knife.
But the Mænads, who were there,
Left their friend, and with robes flowing
In the wind, and loose dark hair
O'er their polished bosoms blowing,
155   Each her ribboned tambourine
Flinging on the mountain-sod,
With a lovely frightened mien
Came about the youthful God.
But he turned his beauteous face
160   Haughtily another way,

II [i] *128. jealous Pan*] The inventor of the syrinx or shepherd's flute is jealous of the music of Apollo's lyre.

II [i] *131. Phrygian flutes*] Marsyas is always connected with Phrygia, where the flutes were used in the cult of Cybele.

II [i] *136–8.* The Maeander is a Phrygian river that in its lower course flows on the southern side of Mt. Messogis.

II [i] *148.* The fir was sacred to Pan.

From the grassy sun-warmed place
Where in proud repose he lay,
With one arm over his head,
Watching how the whetting sped.

165   But aloof, on the lake-strand,
Did the young Olympus stand,
Weeping at his master's end;
For the Faun had been his friend.
For he taught him how to sing,
170 And he taught him flute-playing.
Many a morning had they gone
To the glimmering mountain-lakes,
And had torn up by the roots
The tall crested water-reeds
175 With long plumes and soft brown seeds,
And had carved them into flutes,
Sitting on a tabled stone
Where the shoreward ripple breaks.
And he taught him how to please
180 The red-snooded Phrygian girls,
Whom the summer evening sees
Flashing in the dance's whirls
Underneath the starlit trees
In the mountain-villages.
185 Therefore now Olympus stands,
At his master's piteous cries
Pressing fast with both his hands
His white garment to his eyes,
Not to see Apollo's scorn;
190 Ah, poor Faun, poor Faun! ah, poor Faun!

Empedocles

And lie thou there,
My laurel bough!
Scornful Apollo's ensign, lie thou there!
Though thou hast been my shade in the world's heat –
195 Though I have loved thee, lived in honouring thee –
Yet lie thou there,
My laurel bough!

II [i] *165–8*. A. follows Ovid. In Apollodorus Olympus is the father of
Marsyas and is not mentioned as present at the contest with Apollo.
II [i] *190*. Hypermetrical.
II [i] *192. laurel bough*] Cp. *Karsten* ii 30–1, ' . . . Delphicam laurum sive
Apollinis infulam manu gerens . . .'

I am weary of thee.
I am weary of the solitude
200   Where he who bears thee must abide –
Of the rocks of Parnassus,
Of the gorge of Delphi,
Of the moonlit peaks, and the caves.
Thou guardest them, Apollo!
205   Over the grave of the slain Pytho,
Though young, intolerably severe!
Thou keepest aloof the profane,
But the solitude oppresses thy votary!
The jars of men reach him not in thy valley –
210   But can life reach him?
Thou fencest him from the multitude –
Who will fence him from himself?
He hears nothing but the cry of the torrents,
And the beating of his own heart.
215   The air is thin, the veins swell,
The temples tighten and throb there –
Air! air!

Take thy bough, set me free from my solitude;
I have been enough alone!

220   Where shall thy votary fly then? back to men?
But they will gladly welcome him once more,
And help him to unbend his too tense thought,
And rid him of the presence of himself,
And keep their friendly chatter at his ear,
225   And haunt him, till the absence from himself,

II [i] *198–219.* The solitude is that imposed on the Romantic poet by his
vocation. 'But can life reach him?' (l. 210) questions the Goethean view in
'Resignation' (echoed from *Wilhelm Meister*) that the poet is *happily* set
apart from the crowd – see *n.* to 'Resignation' 144–69 (p. 89 above).
II [i] *205.* Python, the dragon which guarded Delphi, was slain by Apollo.
II [i] *213.* See *Obermann* (Lettre xc) ii 230, 'La fuite de l'eau est comme la
fuite de nos années . . . le cours de l'eau restera, pour nous, l'image la plus
frappante de l'inexorable passage des heures.'
II [i] *220–9* Cp. 'Obermann' 93–6 (p. 134 above),

> *Ah! two desires toss about*
> *The poet's feverish blood.*
> *One drives him to the world without,*
> *And one to solitude . . .*

and *n.*

That other torment, grow unbearable;
And he will fly to solitude again,
And he will find its air too keen for him,
And so change back; and many thousand times
230   Be miserably bandied to and fro
Like a sea-wave, betwixt the world and thee,
Thou young, implacable God! and only death
Can cut his oscillations short, and so
Bring him to poise. There is no other way.

235   And yet what days were those, Parmenides!
When we were young, when we could number friends
In all the Italian cities like ourselves,
When with elated hearts we joined your train,
Ye Sun-born Virgins! on the road of truth.
240   Then we could still enjoy, then neither thought
Nor outward things were closed and dead to us;
But we received the shock of mighty thoughts
On simple minds with a pure natural joy;
And if the sacred load oppressed our brain,
245   We had the power to feel the pressure eased,
The brow unbound, the thoughts flow free again,
In the delightful commerce of the world.

II [i] *232–4. only death . . . to poise*] Contradicted by ll. 345–72 below. Even
death will not bring a man 'to poise' if mind has been his 'master part'.
II [i] *235–7.* Empedocles is an older Callicles. Neither has realized with
Wordsworth that of necessity

> *We Poets in our youth begin in gladness;*
> *But thereof in the end come despondency and madness . . .*
> ['Resolution and Independence' 48–9]

i.e. that the capacity for joy entails the capacity for suffering.
II [i] *235. Parmenides*] According to one tradition Empedocles had been his
pupil.
II [i] *238–9.* 'See the Fragments of Parmenides:

> κοῦραι δ' ὁδὸν ἡγεμόνευον
> ἡλίαδες κοῦραι, προλιποῦσαι δώματα νυκτός,
> εἰς φάος . . . '

A.'s note, first added *1867*. See *Karsten* i Pt. ii 28, 'The maidens of the sun,
leaving the halls of night, led the way to the light' and 56 (K'.s note),
'Ut vulgo veritas cum sole et luce comparari solet, sic Heliades, *Sole
natas*, appellat deas quae ad divinam veritatis lucem deducunt.'
II [i] *241. outward things*] Cp. Coleridge, 'Dejection' 45–6,

> *I may not hope from outward forms to win*
> *The passion and the life, whose fountains are within.*

We had not lost our balance then, nor grown
~~Thought's slaves, and dead to every natural joy.~~
250   The smallest thing could give us pleasure then –
The sports of the country-people,
A flute-note from the woods,
Sunset over the sea;
Seed-time and harvest,
255   The reapers in the corn,
The vinedresser in his vineyard,
The village-girl at her wheel.

Fullness of life and power of feeling, ye
~~Are for the happy,~~ for the souls at ease,
260   Who dwell on a firm basis of content!
But he, who has outlived his prosperous days –
But he, whose youth fell on a different world
From that on which his exiled age is thrown –
Whose mind was fed on other food, was trained
265   By other rules than are in vogue to-day –
Whose habit of thought is fixed, who will not change,
But, in a world he loves not, must subsist
In ceaseless opposition, be the guard
Of his own breast, fettered to what he guards,
270   That the world win no mastery over him –
Who has no friend, no fellow left, not one;
Who has no minute's breathing space allowed
To nurse his dwindling faculty of joy –
Joy and the outward world must die to him,
275   As they are dead to me.

II [i] 249. *Thought's slaves*] Cp. A.'s letter 12 Feb. 1853, 'There is a power of truth in your letter . . . yes – *congestion of the brain* is what we suffer from – I always feel it and say it – and cry for air like my own Empedocles . . .' (*CL* 130).

II [i] 251–7. Probably suggested by Chénier's 'L'Aveugle' 179–82,

> Puis aussi les moissons joyeuses, les troupeaux
> Bêlants ou mugissants, les rustiques pipeaux,
> Les chansons, les festins, les vendanges bruyantes,
> Et la flûte et la lyre, et les notes dansantes.

II [i] 261–75. Cp. 1853 Preface (p. 591 below), 'I intended to delineate the feelings of one of the last of the Greek religious philosophers, one of the family of Orpheus and Musaeus, having survived his fellows, living on into a time when the habits of Greek thought and feeling had begun fast to change, character to dwindle, the influence of the Sophists to prevail.'

A long pause, during which EMPEDOCLES *remains motionless, plunged in thought. The night deepens. He moves forward and gazes round him, and proceeds :* —

And you, ye stars,
Who slowly begin to marshal,
As of old, in the fields of heaven,
Your distant, melancholy lines !
280 Have you, too, survived yourselves ?
Are you, too, what I fear to become ?
You, too, once lived ;
You, too, moved joyfully
Among august companions,
285 In an older world, peopled by Gods,
In a mightier order,
The radiant, rejoicing, intelligent Sons of Heaven.
But now, ye kindle
Your lonely, cold-shining lights,
290 Unwilling lingerers
In the heavenly wilderness,
For a younger, ignoble world ;
And renew, by necessity,
Night after night your courses,
295 In echoing, unneared silence,
Above a race you know not —
Uncaring and undelighted,
Without friend and without home ;
Weary like us, though not
300 Weary with our weariness.

No, no, ye stars ! there is no death with you,
No languor, no decay ! languor and death,

II [i] *276–300.* Printed separately as 'The Philosopher and the Stars' *1855.*
II [i] *293–4.* A. is probably recalling Parmenides, *Karsten* i Pt. ii 44, 'Thou shalt know also the sky surrounding all things, whence it arose and how Necessity took and bound it so as to set a limit to the courses of the stars.'
II [i] *295.* In space so empty that it would echo like a bare room.
II [i] *301–2.* Cp. 'A Summer Night' 78–9 (p. 270 below),

> *Ye heavens, whose pure dark regions have no sign*
> *Of languor . . .*

and 'Self-Dependence' 21–3 (p. 143 above),

> *And with joy the stars perform their shining,*
> *And the sea its long-moon-silvered roll ;*
> *For self-poised they live . . .*

They are with me, not you! ye are alive –
Ye, and the pure dark ether where ye ride
305 Brilliant above me! And thou, fiery world,
That sapp'st the vitals of this terrible mount
Upon whose charred and quaking crust I stand –
Thou, too, brimmest with life! – the sea of cloud,
That heaves its white and billowy vapours up
310 To moat this isle of ashes from the world,
Lives; and that other fainter sea, far down,
O'er whose lit floor a road of moonbeams leads
To Etna's Liparëan sister-fires
And the long dusky line of Italy –
315 That mild and luminous floor of waters lives,
With held-in joy swelling its heart; I only,
Whose spring of hope is dried, whose spirit has failed,
I, who have not, like these, in solitude
Maintained courage and force, and in myself
320 Nursed an immortal vigour – I alone
Am dead to life and joy, therefore I read
In all things my own deadness.

A long silence. He continues :–

Oh, that I could glow like this mountain!
Oh, that my heart bounded with the swell of the sea!
325 Oh, that my soul were full of light as the stars!
Oh, that it brooded over the world like the air!

But no, this heart will glow no more; thou art
A living man no more, Empedocles!
Nothing but a devouring flame of thought –
330 But a naked, eternally restless mind!

After a pause : –

To the elements it came from
Everything will return –
Our bodies to earth,

II [i] *313. Liparëan sister-fires*] Stromboli is one of the volcanic Lipari
islands north-east of Sicily.
II [i] *315.* Cp. 'Sohrab and Rustum' 889–91 (p. 331 below),

> ... *and wide*
> *His luminous home of waters opens, bright*
> *And tranquil* ...

A. uses 'luminous' four times in poems written *c.* 1850–3, but nowhere
in his later verse. See *Parrish* 469.

Our blood to water,
335 Heat to fire,
Breath to air.
They were well born, they will be well entombed –
But mind? ...

And we might gladly share the fruitful stir
340 Down in our mother earth's miraculous womb;
Well would it be
With what rolled of us in the stormy main;
We might have joy, blent with the all-bathing air,
Or with the nimble, radiant life of fire.

345 But mind, but thought –
If these have been the master part of us –
Where will *they* find their parent element?
What will receive *them*, who will call *them* home?
But we shall still be in them, and they in us,
350 And we shall be the strangers of the world,
And they will be our lords, as they are now;
And keep us prisoners of our consciousness,
And never let us clasp and feel the All
But through their forms, and modes, and stifling veils.
355 And we shall be unsatisfied as now;
And we shall feel the agony of thirst,
The ineffable longing for the life of life
Baffled for ever; and still thought and mind
Will hurry us with them on their homeless march,
360 Over the unallied unopening earth,
Over the unrecognising sea; while air
Will blow us fiercely back to sea and earth,
And fire repel us from its living waves.

II [i] *344. nimble*] active *1852*.
II [i] *354.* The All is the noumenon behind phenomenal appearances. Kant
and the unknowability of the thing-in-itself (*Ding-an-sich*) are in the background here, but cp. Carlyle, *Sartor Resartus* (1838), *Works* ed. *cit.* i 43,
'Think well, thou too wilt find that Space is but a mode of our human
Sense, so likewise Time ...'; and 209, 'That the Thought-forms, Space
and Time, wherein, once for all, we are sent into this Earth to live, should
... usurp such sway over pure spiritual Meditation ... seems nowise [fit].'
II [i] *360–3.* Cp. Empedocles, *Karsten* ii 86, 'For the might of air drives
them to the sea, and the sea spews them out on the soil of the earth, and
earth throws them into the rays of the unwearied sun, and the sun into
the eddies of the air ...'

And then we shall unwillingly return
365   Back to this meadow of calamity,
        This uncongenial place, this human life;
        And in our individual human state
        Go through the sad probation all again,
        To see if we will poise our life at last,
370   To see if we will now at last be true
        To our own only true, deep-buried selves,
        Being one with which we are one with the whole
        Or whether we will once more fall away   [world;
        Into some bondage of the flesh or mind,
375   Some slough of sense, or some fantastic maze
        Forged by the imperious lonely thinking-power.
        And each succeeding age in which we are born
        Will have more peril for us than the last;
        Will goad our senses with a sharper spur,
380   Will fret our minds to an intenser play,
        Will make ourselves harder to be discerned.
        And we shall struggle awhile, gasp and rebel –

II [i] *365. meadow of calamity*] Cp. Empedocles, *Karsten* ii 88, 'meadow of
Ate'. K.'s Latin translation of the Greek is 'noxae pratum'.

II [i] *366 uncongenial place*] Cp. Empedocles, *Karsten* ii 86, 'joyless place'.
K. translates 'illaetabilis sedes'.

II [i] *368. sad probation*] Reincarnation is mentioned in several of the Fragments, but see 'De Empedoclis Philosophia', *Karsten* ii 508–9:

   'Daemonibus cognati et fatorum consortes sunt homines, i.e.
animae humanae, divina item stirpe oriundae, ob commissam vero
caedem a coelo in terram ut exsilium ejectae, corporeo vestimento
indutae et per ter dena annorum milia in varias corporum formas
migrare coactae.

   Itaque deplorabilis est, ex Empedoclis sententia, hominum sors: e
vivis mortales facti, cum luctu editi, in miseria vitam transigentes;
terra autem terrenaque regio . . . locus naturae nostrae contrarius,
antrum obscurum, malorum et miseriarum pratum.

   Mortales autem in hoc exsilio degentes coguntur in varias deinceps
animantum formas migrare, non solum hominum, sed etiam bestiarum
et arborum; quemadmodum ipse recordabatur, se quondam fuisse
marem et feminam et volucrem et piscem et arborem . . . Postquam
autem per constitutum temporis spatium circumacti fatales poenas
luerint et scelera expiaverint, postremo in praestantiores abeunt
naturas, vates, reges, cett. unde tandem ad coeleste evehuntur domi-
cilium . . .'

II [i] *371–2.* On the difficulty of knowing the buried self see 'The Buried
Life' (p. 271 below) and *n.* to I ii 129–30 (p. 161 above).

And we shall fly for refuge to past times,
Their soul of unworn youth, their breath of greatness;
385 And the reality will pluck us back,
Knead us in its hot hand, and change our nature.
And we shall feel our powers of effort flag,
And rally them for one last fight – and fail;
And we shall sink in the impossible strife,
And be astray for ever.

390   Slave of sense
I have in no wise been; but slave of thought?...
And who can say: I have been always free,
Lived ever in the light of my own soul? –
I cannot; I have lived in wrath and gloom,
395 Fierce, disputatious, ever at war with man,
Far from my own soul, far from warmth and light.
But I have not grown easy in these bonds –
But I have not denied what bonds these were.
Yea, I take myself to witness,
400 That I have loved no darkness,
Sophisticated no truth,
Nursed no delusion,
Allowed no fear!

And therefore, O ye elements! I know –
405 Ye know it too – it hath been granted me
Not to die wholly, not to be all enslaved.
I feel it in this hour. The numbing cloud
Mounts off my soul; I feel it, I breathe free.

II [i] *404–16.* Empedocles leaps to his death half-exultantly. See the Yale
MS. (summary of E.'s character and motives), 'Before he becomes the
victim of depression and overtension of mind, to the utter deadness to
joy, grandeur, spirit, and animated life, he desires to die; to be reunited
with the universe, before by exaggerating his human side he has become
utterly estranged from it.'

II [i] *407–8.* See II [i] 215–7 (p. 184 above),

> The air is thin, the veins swell,
> The temples tighten and throb there—
> Air! Air!

and cp. 'Revolutions' 20 (p. 281 below),

> The band will quit man's heart, he will breathe free ...

The images may have an autobiographical origin. A. suffered from a

Is it but for a moment?
410   – Ah, boil up, ye vapours!
Leap and roar, thou sea of fire!
My soul glows to meet you.
Ere it flag, ere the mists
Of despondency and gloom
415   Rush over it again,
Receive me, save me!

                              [*He plunges into the crater.*

                    Callicles

                  (*from below*)

Through the black, rushing smoke-bursts,
Thick breaks the red flame;
All Etna heaves fiercely
420   Her forest-clothed frame.

Not here, O Apollo!
Are haunts meet for thee.
But, where Helicon breaks down
In cliff to the sea,

425   Where the moon-silvered inlets
Send far their light voice
Up the still vale of Thisbe,
O speed, and rejoice!

----

congenital heart defect—see headn. to 'Mycerinus' (p. 26 above).
II [i] *417–68*. Reprinted *1855* as 'The Harp-player on Etna. IV. Apollo';
in *Selected Poems* (1878) as 'Apollo Musagetes'. The main part of the song
(ll. *437–68*) is adapted from the beginning of Hesiod's *Theogony*.
II [i] *417–20*. Cp. the Fourth Spirit's song, *Manfred* I i 88–95,

            Where the slumbering Earthquake
                Lies pillowed on fire,
            And the lakes of bitumen
                Rise boilingly higher;
            Where the roots of the Andes
                Strike deep in the earth,
            As their summits to heaven
                Shoot soaringly forth . . .

II [i] *427*. *Thisbe*] A Boeotian town between Mt. Helicon and the Gulf of
Corinth.

On the sward at the cliff-top
430   Lie strewn the white flocks,
On the cliff-side the pigeons
Roost deep in the rocks.

In the moonlight the shepherds,
Soft lulled by the rills,
435   Lie wrapped in their blankets
Asleep on the hills.

– What forms are these coming
So white through the gloom?
What garments out-glistening
440   The gold-flowered broom?

What sweet-breathing presence
Out-perfumes the thyme?
What voices enrapture
The night's balmy prime?

445   'Tis Apollo comes leading
His choir, the Nine.
– The leader is fairest,
But all are divine.

They are lost in the hollows!
450   They stream up again!
What seeks on this mountain
The glorified train?

They bathe on this mountain,
In the spring by their road;
455   Then on to Olympus,
Their endless abode.

II [i] *431–2*. Thisbe was famed for its wild pigeons.
II [i] *436–56*. Cp. Hesiod, *Theogony* 1–10, 'From the Heliconian Muses
let us begin to sing, who hold the great and holy mount of Helicon, and
dance on soft feet about the deep-blue spring ... and when they have
washed their tender bodies in Permessus or in the Horse's Springs or
Olmeius, make their fair lovely dances upon highest Helicon ... Thence
they arise and go abroad by night, veiled by thick mist, and utter their
song with lovely voice ...'

– Whose praise do they mention?
Of what is it told?
What will be for ever;
460   What was from of old.

First hymn they the Father
Of all things; and then,
The rest of immortals,
The action of men.

465   The day in his hotness,
The strife with the palm;
The night in her silence,
The stars in their calm.

II [i] 457–60. Cp. *Theogony* 36–9, 'Come thou, let us begin with the Muses who gladden the great spirit of their Father Zeus in Olympus with their songs, telling of things that are and that shall be and that were aforetime with consenting voice.'

II [i] *461–8*. Cp. *Theogony* 11–21, ' . . . praising Zeus the aegis-holder and queenly Hera of Argos who walks on golden sandals and the daughter of Zeus the aegis-holder bright-eyed Athene, and Phoebus Apollo, and Artemis who delights in arrows, and Poseidon the earth-holder who shakes the earth . . . Eos, and great Helius and bright Selene, Earth too, and great Oceanus, and dark Night, and the holy race of all the other deathless ones that are for ever . . .'; and 43–50, 'And they uttering their immortal voice, celebrate in song first of all the reverend race of the gods from the beginning . . . Then, next, the goddesses sing of Zeus, the father of gods and men . . . And again, they chant the race of men and strong giants . . .'

48 Tristram and Iseult

Exact period of composition unknown, but (?) drafted Sept. 1849–early 1850 and subsequently added to and revised before Oct. 1852): see A.'s letter to Herbert Hill 5 Nov. 1852 (printed by R. E. C. Houghton, *Times Lit. Supp.* 19 May 1932), 'I read the story of Tristram and Iseult some years ago at Thun in an article in a French Review on the romance literature: I had never met with it before, and it fastened upon me: when I got back to England I looked at the Morte d'Arthur and took what I could, but the poem was in the main formed, and I could not well disturb it.' This could refer to A.'s 1848 visit to Thun, but a tale of doomed love was more likely to fasten on him in 1849. Obviously 'formed' does not necessarily mean that any of the poem was written down at Thun, but it is nevertheless probable that A. took a rough draft of some of it home to England in Oct. 1849.

Sources are discussed *Commentary* 106–124 and *Baum* 35–57, but neither account is wholly reliable. A.'s letter to Clough 1 May 1853 identifies the French article which gave him the Tristram legend, but is misleading on the source of the tale of Merlin and Vivian: ' . . . my version of Tristram and Iseult comes from an article in the Revue de Paris, on Fauriel, I think: the story of Merlin is imported from the Morte d'Arthur' (*CL* 135–6). The article is Théodore de la Villemarqué's 'Les poèmes gallois et les romans de la Table-Ronde', the first instalment of which appeared *Revue de Paris* 3rd series xxiv (1841) 266–82 (A. used only this instalment and relied mainly on the summary of the Tristram legend on pp. 274–5), but the source of the Merlin episode is an earlier article by La Villemarqué, 'Visite au Tombeau de Merlin', *Revue de Paris* 2nd series xli (1837) 45–62 and especially 52–3. (There is no need to assume any borrowing from Louandre's 'L'Enchanteur Merlin', *Revue de Paris* 3rd series xvi (1840) 109–22, but it was probably read.) A. is indebted to Malory's *Le Morte Darthur* for background material and one or two phrases (see *nn.* below); and his letter to Swinburne 26 July 1882 (printed by E. Gosse, *Times Lit. Supp.* 12 Aug. 1920) – 'I suppose you have taken the *sails* as the issue of your story; a beautiful way of ending, which I should perhaps have used, had I known of it, but I did not' – shows that he did not consult J. Dunlop's *History of Fiction* (3rd ed. 1845), which contains the story of the sails, until 1853. The *1853* note, a patchwork of sentences from Dunlop's *History* (ed. *cit.* 85–7), was suggested by Froude – see A.'s letter to Clough 25 Aug. 1853, '[Froude] recommends prefacing Tristram and Iseult with an extract from Dunlop's Hist. of fiction to tell the story, in preference to telling it in my own words' (*CL* 140) – and, like the additions to the poem in *1853*, was part of A.'s attempt to meet the charge of obscurity made by Clough and others. 'Tristram and Iseult' is the first modern treatment of the Tristram legend in English. The oblique mode of storytelling in Pt. i, probably inspired by Byron's *The Giaour* (1813), also contributed to readers' difficulties. A.'s note from Dunlop is as follows:

'In the court of his uncle King Marc, the king of Cornwall, who at this time resided at the castle of Tyntagel, Tristram became expert in all knightly exercises. – The king of Ireland, at Tristram's solicitations, promised to bestow his daughter Iseult in marriage on King Marc. The mother of Iseult gave to her daughter's confidante a philtre, or love-potion, to be administered on the night of her nuptials. Of this beverage Tristram and Iseult, on their voyage to Cornwall, unfortunately partook. Its influence, during the remainder of their lives, regulated the affections and destiny of the lovers. –

After the arrival of Tristram and Iseult in Cornwall, and the nuptials of the latter with King Marc, a great part of the romance is occupied with their contrivances to procure secret interviews. – Tristram, being forced to leave Cornwall, on account of the displeasure of his uncle, repaired to Brittany, where lived Iseult with the White

Hands. – He married her – more out of gratitude than love. – Afterwards he proceeded to the dominions of Arthur, which became the theatre of unnumbered exploits.

Tristram, subsequent to these events, returned to Brittany, and to his long-neglected wife. There, being wounded and sick, he was soon reduced to the lowest ebb. In this situation, he despatched a confidant to the queen of Cornwall, to try if he could induce her to follow him to Brittany, etc.' – Dunlop's *History of Fiction*.

That the whole story developed a shadowy autobiographical significance for A. (with Marguerite and Frances Lucy Wightman as the 'two Iseults who did sway / Each her hour of Tristam's day') can hardly be doubted. For an interesting discussion of the use of colour in the poem see W. S. Johnson, *The Voices of Matthew Arnold* (New Haven, 1961) 95–101.

Published *1852*; reprinted with additions *1853* (*1854*, *1857*), *1869*, etc.

I TRISTRAM

For Tristram's life-story A. uses Malory and his own invention to fill out the following account in La Villemarqué's 'Les poèmes gallois et les romans de la Table-Ronde', *Revue de Paris* 3rd series xxiv (1841) 274–5:

'Tristan fait ses premières armes en Cornouailles, à la cour du roi March son oncle ... ayant reçu dans la cuisse un dard empoisonné, et ne trouvant pas en Cornouailles de médecin assez habile pour guérir sa blessure, il se déguise en joueur de harpe et se rend en Irlande. C'est là qu'il voit la belle Yseult, dont il fait, à son retour, un portrait si flatteur à son oncle, que le roi veut l'épouser. Tristan, chargé de la demander, part, déguisé en marchand, et il revient en Cornouailles avec la future du roi, quand, ayant porté par mégarde à ses lèvres et présenté à la princesse irlandaise une coupe contenant un philtre magique destiné à March et confié à Brangien, servante d'Yseult, ils sentent aussitôt l'amour couler dans leurs veines. Peu de jours après les noces, le sénéchal puis le nain s'aperçoivent de la liaison coupable de Tristan et d'Yseult, en informent le roi et lui ménagent l'occasion de les surprendre; mais Tristan déjoue leurs ruses. Enfin les deux amans sont pris ... [Yseult's 'innocence' is established by a trick.] Quoique l'innocence d'Yseult soit reconnue, son amant n'est point rappelé à la cour; il se retire dans la Petite-Bretagne et prend le parti de se marier à la fille d'Houel, roi du pays, qui porte aussi le nom d'Yseult. Toutefois c'est en vain qu'il essaie d'oublier son premier amour, c'est en vain qu'il court les aventures périlleuses; au lieu d'une distraction, il y trouve une blessure mortelle. La femme du roi March peut seule le guérir; il l'envoie chercher ...'

In La Villemarqué Tristan dies of chagrin when his wife deceitfully tells him that the Queen of Cornwall has refused to come. A. rejects this ending, making the second Iseult, whom he represents as the mother of two children by Tristram, a pattern of wifely patience and sympathy.

Tristram

Is she not come? The messenger was sure.
Prop me upon the pillows once again –
Raise me, my page! this cannot long endure.
– Christ, what a night! how the sleet whips the pane!
5   What lights will those out to the northward be?

The Page

The lanterns of the fishing-boats at sea.

Tristram

Soft – who is that, stands by the dying fire?

The Page

Iseult.

Tristram

Ah! not the Iseult I desire.

*   *   *   *

What Knight is this so weak and pale,
10   Though the locks are yet brown on his noble
Propped on pillows in his bed,   [head,
Gazing seaward for the light
Of some ship that fights the gale
On this wild December night?
15   Over the sick man's feet is spread

¶ 48. i 4. A reminiscence of Keats's 'The Eve of St. Agnes' 322–4,

> . . . the frost-wind blows
> Like Love's alarum pattering the sharp sleet
> Against the window-panes . . .

i 9–93. This and the later link-passages between Tristram's dreams are recited by a mediaeval Breton bard – see, for example, the invocations 'sweet angels' and 'sweet saints' (ll. 105, 142) and the appeal (ll. 274–5),

> To our lonely sea complain,
> To our forests tell thy pain!

A.'s narrator, here and in Pt. ii, speaks in what G. Saintsbury calls 'the equivalenced octosyllable of the Coleridgean stamp' – see *Matthew Arnold* (1899), 24.
i 9. An echo of Keats's 'La Belle Dame sans Merci' 5–6,

> O what can ail thee, Knight-at-arms!
> So haggard and so woe-begone?

A. had read the poem in R. Monckton Milnes's *Life of Keats* (1848).

A dark green forest-dress;
A gold harp leans against the bed,
Ruddy in the fire's light.
I know him by his harp of gold,
20   Famous in Arthur's court of old;
I know him by his forest-dress –
The peerless hunter, harper, knight,
Tristram of Lyoness.

What Lady is this, whose silk attire
25   Gleams so rich in the light of the fire?
The ringlets on her shoulders lying
In their flitting lustre vying
With the clasp of burnished gold
Which her heavy robe doth hold.
30   Her looks are mild, her fingers slight
As the driven snow are white;
But her cheeks are sunk and pale.
Is it that the bleak sea-gale
Beating from the Atlantic sea
35   On this coast of Brittany,
Nips too keenly the sweet flower?
Is it that a deep fatigue
Hath come on her, a chilly fear,
Passing all her youthful hour
40   Spinning with her maidens here,

19–23. An imitation of Byron, *The Giaour* 611–14, 619–20,

> *I know him by his pallid brow;*
> *I know him by the evil eye*
> *That aids his envious treachery;*
> *I know him by his jet-black barb . . .*

> *'Tis he! well met in any hour,*
> *Lost Leila's love – accursed Giaour!*

i 22. La Villemarqué mentions Tristram's skill with the harp, but see *Le Morte Darthur* viii ch. 3 ed. A. W. Pollard (1900) i 282, 'And so Tristram learned to be an harper passing all other . . . And after . . . he laboured ever in hunting and hawking, so that never gentlemen more, that ever we heard read of.'
i 25. After this line the following two lines in *1852*,

> *Never surely has been seen*
> *So slight a form in so rich a dress.*

i 30–1. First added *1853*.

Listlessly through the window-bars
Gazing seawards many a league,
From her lonely shore-built tower,
While the knights are at the wars?
45 Or, perhaps, has her young heart
Felt already some deeper smart,
Of those that in secret the heart-strings rive,
Leaving her sunk and pale, though fair?
Who is this snowdrop by the sea?
50 I know her by her mildness rare,
Her snow-white hands, her golden hair;
I know her by her rich silk dress,
And her fragile loveliness
The sweetest Christian soul alive,
55 Iseult of Brittany.

Iseult of Brittany? – but where
Is that other Iseult fair,
That proud, first Iseult, Cornwall's queen?
She, whom Tristram's ship of yore
60 From Ireland to Cornwall bore,
To Tyntagel, to the side
Of King Marc, to be his bride?
She who, as they voyaged, quaffed
With Tristram that spiced magic draught,
65 Which since then for ever rolls
Through their blood, and binds their souls,
Working love, but working teen?
There were two Iseults who did sway

i 50. *mildness rare*] golden hair *1852*.
i 51. First added *1853*.
i 56–82. First added *1853*. See A.'s letter to Clough 1 May 1853, 'If I
republish that poem I shall try to make it more intelligible: I wish I had
you with me to put marks against the places where something is wanted.
The whole affair is by no means thoroughly successful' (*CL* 135–6).
  60–1. The *1857* reading. In *1853, 1854*,

> To Tyntagil from Ireland bore,
> To Cornwall's palace, to the side . . .

This is one example of the minor textual changes that became necessary
in *1857* when A. discovered that Tyntagel is stressed on the second syllable.
i 65–7. Cp. La Villemarqué (cited headn. to Pt. i), '. . . ils sentent aussitôt
l'amour couler dans leurs veines . . .' and *Le Morte Darthur* viii ch. 24
ed. *cit.* i 319, 'But by that their drink was in their bodies, they loved either
other so well that never their love departed for weal neither for woe.'

Each her hour of Tristram's day;
70   But one possessed his waning time,
The other his resplendent prime.
Behold her here, the patient flower,
Who possessed his darker hour!
Iseult of the Snow-White Hand
75   Watches pale by Tristram's bed.
She is here who had his gloom,
Where art thou who hadst his bloom?
One such kiss as those of yore
Might thy dying knight restore!
80   Does the love-draught work no more?
Art thou cold, or false, or dead,
Iseult of Ireland?

   *   *   *   *

Loud howls the wind, sharp patters the rain,
And the knight sinks back on his pillows again.
85   He is weak with fever and pain,
And his spirit is not clear.
Hark! he mutters in his sleep,
As he wanders far from here,
Changes place and time of year,
90   And his closéd eye doth sweep
O'er some fair unwintry sea,
Not this fierce Atlantic deep,
While he mutters brokenly:—

Tristram

The calm sea shines, loose hang the vessel's sails;
95   Before us are the sweet green fields of Wales,
And overhead the cloudless sky of May.
'*Ah, would I were in those green fields at play,*
Not pent on ship-board this delicious day!
Tristram, I pray thee, of thy courtesy,
100   *Reach me my golden phial stands by thee,*
But pledge me in it first for courtesy.'

i *74*. This descriptive title for the second Iseult is not in La Villemarqué. A.
could have taken it from Malory's 'Isoud la Blanche Mains', but it occurs
only in the *1853* additions when he had met 'Yseult with the White
Hands' in Dunlop.
i *100 golden phial stands*] golden cup that stands *1852–81* (but in italics
from *1853*). La Villemarqué speaks of 'une coupe'; *Le Morte Darthur* viii
ch. 24 ed. *cit.* i 318 of 'a little flasket of gold'.

Ha! dost thou start? are thy lips blanched like mine?
Child, 'tis no true draught this, 'tis poisoned wine!
Iseult!...

*　　　　*　　　　*　　　　*

105   Ah, sweet angels, let him dream!
     Keep his eyelids! let him seem
     Not this fever-wasted wight
     Thinned and paled before his time,
     But the brilliant youthful knight
110   In the glory of his prime,
     Sitting in the gilded barge,
     At thy side, thou lovely charge,
     Bending gaily o'er thy hand,
     Iseult of Ireland!
115   And she too, that princess fair,
     If her bloom be now less rare,
     Let her have her youth again —
     Let her be as she was then!
     Let her have her proud dark eyes,
120   And her petulant quick replies —
     Let her sweep her dazzling hand
     With its gesture of command,
     And shake back her raven hair
     With the old imperious air!
125   As of old, so let her be,
     That first Iseult, princess bright,
     Chatting with her youthful knight
     As he steers her o'er the sea,
     Quitting at her father's will
130   The green isle where she was bred,
     And her bower in Ireland,
     For the surge-beat Cornish strand;
     Where the prince whom she must wed
     Dwells on loud Tyntagel's hill,
135   High above the sounding sea.
     And that potion rare her mother
     Gave her, that her future lord,
     Gave her, that King Marc and she,
     Might drink it on their marriage-day,
140   And for ever love each other —
     Let her, as she sits on board,
     Ah, sweet saints, unwittingly!
     See it shine, and take it up,

i 138. First added 1853.

8+M.A.

                    And to Tristram laughing say:
145   'Sir Tristram, of thy courtesy,
                    Pledge me in my golden cup!'
                    Let them drink it – let their hands
                    Tremble, and their cheeks be flame,
                    As they feel the fatal bands
150   Of a love they dare not name,
                    With a wild delicious pain,
                    Twine about their hearts again!
                    Let the early summer be
                    Once more round them, and the sea
155   Blue, and o'er its mirror kind
                    Let the breath of the May-wind,
                    Wandering through their drooping sails,
                    Die on the green fields of Wales!
                    Let a dream like this restore
160   What his eye must see no more!

                         Tristram

             Chill blows the wind, the pleasaunce-walks are drear –
             Madcap, what jest was this, to meet me here?
             Were feet like those made for so wild a way?
             The southern winter-parlour, by my fay,
165   Had been the likeliest trysting-place to-day!
             ' Tristram! – nay, nay – thou must not take my hand! –
             Tristram! – sweet love! – we are betrayed – out-planned.
             Fly – save thyself – save me! – I dare not stay.'
             One last kiss first! – ' *'Tis vain – to horse – away!'*

                 *   *   *   *

170   Ah! sweet saints, his dream doth move
                    Faster surely than it should,
                    From the fever in his blood!
                    All the spring-time of his love
                    Is already gone and past,
175   And instead thereof is seen
                    Its winter, which endureth still –
                    Tyntagel on its surge-beat hill,
                    The pleasaunce-walks, the weeping queen,
                    The flying leaves, the straining blast,
180   And that long, wild kiss – their last.

i *178–80.* A. is probably remembering the 'pleasaunce-walks' of the Hotel
Bellevue at Thun and his parting from Marguerite at the end of Sept.
1849.

And this rough December-night,
And his burning fever-pain,
Mingle with his hurrying dream,
Till they rule it, till he seem
185   The pressed fugitive again,
The love-desperate banished knight
With a fire in his brain
Flying o'er the stormy main.
– Whither does he wander now?
190   Haply in his dreams the wind
Wafts him here, and lets him find
The lovely orphan child again
In her castle by the coast;
The youngest, fairest chatelaine,
195   Whom this realm of France can boast,
Our snowdrop by the Atlantic sea,
Iseult of Brittany.
And – for through the haggard air,
The stained arms, the matted hair
200   Of that stranger-knight ill-starred,
There gleamed something, which recalled,
The Tristram who in better days
Was Launcelot's guest at Joyous Gard –
Welcomed here, and here installed,
205   Tended of his fever here,
Haply he seems again to move
His young guardian's heart with love;
In his exiled loneliness,
In his stately, deep distress,
210   Without a word, without a tear.
– Ah! 'tis well he should retrace
His tranquil life in this lone place;
His gentle bearing at the side
Of his timid youthful bride;
215   His long rambles by the shore
On winter-evenings, when the roar
Of the near waves came, sadly grand,
Through the dark, up the drowned sand,
Or his endless reveries
220   In the woods, where the gleams play
On the grass under the trees,
Passing the long summer's day

---

i *203*. Cp. *Le Morte Darthur* x ch. 52 ed. *cit.* ii 96, 'And so Sir Launcelot brought Sir Tristram and La Beale Isoud unto Joyous Gard, that was his own castle . . .'

              Idle as a mossy stone
              In the forest-depths alone,
225   The chase neglected, and his hound
              Couched beside him on the ground.
              – Ah! what trouble's on his brow?
              Hither let him wander now;
              Hither, to the quiet hours
230   Passed among these heaths of ours
              By the grey Atlantic sea;
              Hours, if not of ecstasy,
              From violent anguish surely free!

Tristram

              All red with blood the whirling river flows,
235   The wide plain rings, the dazed air throbs with blows.
              Upon us are the chivalry of Rome –
              Their spears are down, their steeds are bathed in foam.
              'Up, Tristram, up,' men cry, 'thou moonstruck knight!
              What foul fiend rides thee? On into the fight!'
240   – Above the din her voice is in my ears;
              I see her form glide through the crossing spears.
              Iseult! . . .

            *   *   *   *

              Ah! he wanders forth again;
              We cannot keep him; now, as then,
245   There's a secret in his breast
              Which will never let him rest.
              These musing fits in the green wood
              They cloud the brain, they dull the blood!
              – His sword is sharp, his horse is good;
250   Beyond the mountains will he see
              The famous towns of Italy,
              And label with the blessed sign

i *234–42.* Expanding La Villemarqué (see headn. to Pt. i above), 'Toutefois c'est en vain qu'il essaie d'oublier son premier amour, c'est en vain qu'il court les aventures périlleuses . . .' with the aid of Malory's account of King Arthur's struggle against 'Lucius the Emperor of Rome' (*Le Morte Darthur* v ed. *cit.* i 149–74). In Malory Tristram plays no part in these campaigns, which took place before he fled from Cornwall to Brittany.

i *250–3.* Cp. *Le Morte Darthur* v ch. 9 ed. *cit.* i 166, 'Now turn we unto King Arthur and his noble knights, which, after the great battle achieved against the Romans, entered into Lorraine, Brabant and Flanders, and sithen returned into Haut Almaine, and so over the mountains into Lombardy, and after, into Tuscany . . .'

The heathen Saxons on the Rhine.
At Arthur's side he fights once more
255   With the Roman Emperor.
There's many a gay knight where he goes
Will help him to forget his care;
The march, the leaguer, Heaven's blithe air,
The neighing steeds, the ringing blows –
260   Sick pining comes not where these are.
Ah! what boots it, that the jest
Lightens every other brow,
What, that every other breast
Dances as the trumpets blow,
265   If one's own heart beats not light
On the waves of the tossed fight,
If oneself cannot get free
From the clog of misery?
Thy lovely youthful wife grows pale
270   Watching by the salt sea-tide
With her children at her side
For the gleam of thy white sail.
Home, Tristram, to thy halls again!
To our lonely sea complain,
275   To our forests tell thy pain!

Tristram

All round the forest sweeps off, black in shade,
But it is moonlight in the open glade;
And in the bottom of the glade shine clear
The forest-chapel and the fountain near.
280   – I think, I have a fever in my blood;
Come, let me leave the shadow of this wood,
Ride down, and bathe my hot brow in the flood.
– Mild shines the cold spring in the moon's clear light;
God! 'tis *her* face plays in the waters bright.
285   'Fair love,' she says, 'canst thou forget so soon,
At this soft hour, under this sweet moon?'
Iseult!...

        *   *   *   *

i *276–87*. The incident is invented by A., but he took a hint from Malory –
see *Le Morte Darthur* ix chs. 26–7 ed. *cit.* i 397–8, 'And so . . . he saw a fair
well, and thither he rode to repose him, and tied his horse till a tree. And
then he pulled off his helm and washed his visage and his hands, and so he
fell asleep' and the earlier description of Tristram's madness in the wood
when he believes that La Beale Isoud is disloyal to him (ix chs. 18–20
ed. *cit.* i 380–6).

Ah, poor soul! if this be so,
Only death can balm thy woe.

290   The solitudes of the green wood
Had no medicine for thy mood;
The rushing battle cleared thy blood
As little as did solitude.
– Ah! his eyelids slowly break

295   Their hot seals, and let him wake;
What new change shall we now see?
A happier? Worse it cannot be.

Tristram

Is my page here? Come, turn me to the fire!
Upon the window-panes the moon shines bright;

300   The wind is down – but she'll not come to-night.
Ah no! she is asleep in Cornwall now,
Far hence; her dreams are fair – smooth is her brow.
Of me she recks not, nor my vain desire.
– I have had dreams, I have had dreams, my page,

305   Would take a score years from a strong man's age;
And with a blood like mine, will leave, I fear,
Scant leisure for a second messenger.
– My princess, art thou there? Sweet, do not wait!
To bed, and sleep! my fever is gone by;

310   To-night my page shall keep me company.
Where do the children sleep? kiss them for me!
Poor child, thou art almost as pale as I;
This comes of nursing long and watching late.
To bed – good night!

*   *   *   *

315   She left the gleam-lit fireplace,
She came to the bed-side;
She took his hands in hers – her tears
Down on his wasted fingers rained.
She raised her eyes upon his face –

320   Not with a look of wounded pride,
A look as if the heart complained –
Her look was like a sad embrace;
The gaze of one who can divine
A grief, and sympathise.

325   Sweet flower! thy children's eyes
Are not more innocent than thine.
But they sleep in sheltered rest,
Like helpless birds in the warm nest,
On the castle's southern side;

330   Where feebly comes the mournful roar
        Of buffeting wind and surging tide
        Through many a room and corridor.
        – Full on their window the moon's ray
        Makes their chamber as bright as day.
335   It shines upon the blank white walls,
        And on the snowy pillow falls,
        And on two angel-heads doth play
        Turned to each other – the eyes closed,
        The lashes on the cheeks reposed.
340   Round each sweet brow the cap close-set
        Hardly lets peep the golden hair;
        Through the soft-opened lips the air
        Scarcely moves the coverlet.
        One little wandering arm is thrown
345   At random on the counterpane,
        And often the fingers close in haste
        As if their baby-owner chased
        The butterflies again.
        This stir they have, and this alone;
350   But else they are so still!
        – Ah, tired madcaps! you lie still;
        But were you at the window now,
        To look forth on the fairy sight
        Of your illumined haunts by night,
355   To see the park-glades where you play
        Far lovelier than they are by day,
        To see the sparkle on the eaves,
        And upon every giant-bough
        Of those old oaks, whose wet red leaves
360   Are jewelled with bright drops of rain –
        How would your voices run again!
        And far beyond the sparkling trees
        Of the castle-park one sees
        The bare heaths spreading, clear as day,
365   Moor behind moor, far, far away,
        Into the heart of Brittany.
        And here and there, locked by the land,
        Long inlets of smooth glittering sea,
        And many a stretch of watery sand
370   All shining in the white moon-beams –
        But you see fairer in your dreams!

    What voices are these on the clear night-air?
    What lights in the court – what steps on the stair?

II ISEULT OF IRELAND

The meeting of the lovers at Tristram's deathbed is A.'s invention, but he had little talent for direct dramatization, and the choice of trochaic rhythm for the rhymed dialogue was perhaps an unsuccessful attempt to distance and to give an air of ritual to the scene – cp. W. S. Johnson, *The Voices of Matthew Arnold* (1961), 100, 'The lovers in their dialogue seem to be playing rôles (virtually operatic rôles) whereas the narrative and descriptive lines, closer to the rhythm of speech, reveal them more objectively and more movingly.' A. wrote to Herbert Hill 5 Nov. 1852 (see headn. to whole poem, p. 194 above), 'I am by no means satisfied with *Tristram* in the second part myself . . .', but his *1853* alterations were almost all in the second half of Pt. ii, i.e. in the descriptive passages that follow the *Liebestod*.

Tristram

Raise the light, my page! that I may see her.
    Thou art come at last, then, haughty Queen!
Long I've waited, long I've fought my fever;
    Late thou comest, cruel thou hast been.

Iseult

5   Blame me not, poor sufferer! that I tarried;
    Bound I was, I could not break the band.
Chide not with the past, but feel the present!
    I am here – we meet – I hold thy hand.

Tristram

Thou art come, indeed – thou hast rejoined me;
10   Thou hast dared it – but too late to save.
Fear not now that men should tax thine honour!
    I am dying: build (thou may'st) – my grave!

Iseult

Tristram, ah, for love of Heaven, speak kindly!
    What, I hear these bitter words from thee?
15   Sick with grief I am, and faint with travel –
    Take my hand – dear Tristram, look on me!

Tristram

I forgot, thou comest from thy voyage –
    Yes, the spray is on thy cloak and hair.
But thy dark eyes are not dimmed, proud Iseult!
20   And thy beauty never was more fair.

Iseult

Ah, harsh flatterer! let alone my beauty!
I, like thee, have left my youth afar.
Take my hand, and touch these wasted fingers –
See my cheek and lips, how white they are!

Tristram

25 Thou art paler – but thy sweet charm, Iseult!
Would not fade with the dull years away.
Ah, how fair thou standest in the moonlight!
I forgive thee, Iseult! – thou wilt stay?

Iseult

Fear me not, I will be always with thee;
30 I will watch thee, tend thee, soothe thy pain;
Sing thee tales of true, long-parted lovers,
Joined at evening of their days again.

Tristram

No, thou shalt not speak! I should be finding
Something altered in thy courtly tone.
35 Sit – sit by me! I will think, we've lived so
In the green wood, all our lives, alone.

Iseult

Altered, Tristram? Not in courts, believe me,
Love like mine is altered in the breast;
Courtly life is light and cannot reach it –
40 Ah! it lives, because so deep-suppressed!

What, thou think'st men speak in courtly chambers
Words by which the wretched are consoled?
What, thou think'st this aching brow was cooler,
Circled, Tristram, by a band of gold?

45 Royal state with Marc, my deep-wronged husband –
That was bliss to make my sorrows flee!
Silken courtiers whispering honied nothings –
Those were friends to make me false to thee!

Ah, on which, if both our lots were balanced,
50 Was indeed the heaviest burden thrown –
Thee, a pining exile in thy forest,
Me, a smiling queen upon my throne?

ii 45–8. First added *1853*. This stanza followed l. 40 *1853–69*.
8*

Vain and strange debate, where both have suffered,
  Both have passed a youth consumed and sad,
55 Both have brought their anxious day to evening,
  And have now short space for being glad!

Joined we are henceforth; nor will thy people,
  Nor thy younger Iseult take it ill,
That a former rival shares her office,
60   When she sees her humbled, pale, and still.

I, a faded watcher by thy pillow,
  I, a statue on thy chapel-floor,
Poured in prayer before the Virgin-Mother,
  Rouse no anger, make no rivals more.

65 She will cry: 'Is this the foe I dreaded?
  This his idol? this that royal bride?
Ah, an hour of health would purge his eyesight!
  Stay, pale queen! for ever by my side.'

Hush, no words! that smile, I see, forgives me.
70   I am now thy nurse, I bid thee sleep.
Close thine eyes – this flooding moonlight blinds
  Nay, all's well again! thou must not weep. [them! –

Tristram

I am happy! yet I feel, there's something
  Swells my heart, and takes my breath away.
75 Through a mist I see thee; near – come nearer!
  Bend – bend down! I yet have much to say.

Iseult

Heaven! his head sinks back upon the pillow –
  Tristram! Tristram! let thy heart not fail!
Call on God and on the holy angels!
80   What, love, courage! Christ! he is so pale.

Tristram

Hush, 'tis vain, I feel my end approaching!
  This is what my mother said should be,
When the fierce pains took her in the forest,
  The deep draughts of death, in bearing me.

ii 59. *a former*] an ancient *1852–3.*
ii 63. *in prayer*] in grief *1852–77.*
ii 84. *deep draughts of death*] A direct borrowing from *Le Morte Darthur*
viii ch. 1 ed. *cit.* i 279, 'And when she was far in the forest she might go no

85   'Son,' she said, 'thy name shall be of sorrow;
          Tristram art thou call'd for my death's sake.'
       So she said, and died in the drear forest.
          Grief since then his home with me doth make.

       I am dying. – Start not, nor look wildly!
90   Me, thy living friend, thou canst not save.
       But, since living we were ununited,
          Go not far, O Iseult! from my grave.

       Close mine eyes, then seek the princess Iseult;
          Speak her fair, she is of royal blood!
95   Say, I willed so, that thou stay beside me –
          She will grant it; she is kind and good.

       Now to sail the seas of death I leave thee –
          One last kiss upon the living shore!

---

farther, for she began to travail fast of her child. And she had many grimly throes; her gentlewoman helped her all that she might, and so by miracle of Our Lady of Heaven she was delivered with great pains. But she had taken such cold for the default of help that deep draughts of death took her . . .'

ii *85–7. Ibid.*, 'Ah, my little son, thou hast murdered thy mother . . . And because I shall die of the birth of thee, I charge thee, gentlewoman, that thou pray my lord . . . that when he is christened let call him Tristram, that is as much to say as a sorrowful birth. And therewith this queen gave up the ghost and died.'

ii *93. Close my eyes, then*] Rise, go hence, and *1852–77.*

ii *95. 1852–7,*

       Say, I charg'd her, that ye live together. . .

ii *97–100.* Replacing this stanza *1852*:

       Now stand clear before me in the moonlight.
       Fare, farewell, thou long, thou deeply lov'd!

               Iseult

       Tristram! – Tristram – stay – I come! Ah Sorrow –
       Fool! thou missest – we are both unmov'd!

Tristram is unmoved because he is dead, Iseult because at the moment of his death she feels nothing, and her own romantic words strike her as empty ('Fool! thou missest . . .'). But the last line is clumsy and ambiguous – it becomes a cynicism quite out of keeping with the rest of the scene if 'Fool' is taken as addressed to Tristram.

Iseult

Tristram! – Tristram! – stay – receive me with thee!
100   Iseult leaves thee, Tristram! never more.

*   *   *   *

You see them clear – the moon shines bright.
Slow, slow and softly, where she stood,
She sinks upon the ground; her hood
Had fallen back; her arms outspread
105   Still hold her lover's hand; her head
Is bowed, half-buried, on the bed.
O'er the blanched sheet her raven hair
Lies in disordered streams; and there,
Strung like white stars, the pearls still are,
110   And the golden bracelets, heavy and rare,
Flash on her white arms still.
The very same which yesternight
Flashed in the silver sconces' light,
When the feast was gay and the laughter loud
115   In Tyntagel's palace proud.
But then they decked a restless ghost
With hot-flushed cheeks and brilliant eyes,
And quivering lips on which the tide
Of courtly speech abruptly died,
120   And a glance which over the crowded floor,
The dancers, and the festive host,
Flew ever to the door.
That the knights eyed her in surprise,
And the dames whispered scoffingly:
125   'Her moods, good lack, they pass like showers!
But yesternight and she would be
As pale and still as withered flowers,
And now to-night she laughs and speaks
And has a colour in her cheeks;
130   Christ keep us from such fantasy!'

Yes, now the longing is o'erpast,
Which, dogged by fear and fought by shame
Shook her weak bosom day and night,
Consumed her beauty like a flame,

ii *101–11.* A subject for a Pre-Raphaelite painting.
ii *131–46.* First added in *1869.* In *1852* these lines were the first paragraph
of 'Lines written by a Death-bed', which may have formed part of an
early draft of 'Tristram and Iseult' – see headn. to 'Youth and Calm'
(p. 224 below).

135   And dimmed it like the desert-blast.
           And though the bed-clothes hide her face,
           Yet were it lifted to the light,
           The sweet expression of her brow
           Would charm the gazer, till his thought
140   Erased the ravages of time,
           Filled up the hollow cheek, and brought
           A freshness back as of her prime –
           So healing is her quiet now.
           So perfectly the lines express
145   A tranquil, settled loveliness,
           Her younger rival's purest grace.

           The air of the December-night
           Steals coldly around the chamber bright,
           Where those lifeless lovers be;
150   Swinging with it, in the light
           Flaps the ghostlike tapestry.
           And on the arras wrought you see

ii *136. bed-clothes*] curtains *1852, 1869–81*.
ii *146. younger rival's purest*] youngest rival's freshest *1852*; younger
rival's calmest *1869*.
ii *147–51.* Suggested by Byron's *The Siege of Corinth* (1816) 620–27,
            Like the figures on arras, that gloomily glare,
            Stirred by the breath of the wintry air
            So seen by the dying lamp's fitful light,
            Lifeless, but life-like, and awful to sight;
            As they seem, through the dimness, about to come down
            From the shadowy wall where their images frown;
            Fearfully flitting to and fro,
            As the gusts on the tapestry come and go . . .
A. included this passage in his selection *The Poetry of Byron* (1881).
ii *149.* First added *1853*.
ii *151. Flaps*] Shines *1852*.
ii *152–4.* Cp. Keats's 'The Eve of St. Agnes' 358–9,
            The arras, rich with horseman, hawk, and hound,
            Flutter'd in the besieging wind's uproar . . .
and Tennyson's 'The Palace of Art' (1832) 61–4,
            For some were hung with arras green and blue,
                Showing a gaudy summer-morn,
            Where with puff'd cheeks the belted hunter blew
                His wreathed bugle-horn.
Keats has the 'ghostlike tapestry' and the huntsman, but A.'s 'Tis noon
with him' (l. 155 in *1852*) and 'boisterous bugle-peal' (l. 177) point to the
reminiscence of Tennyson.

A stately Huntsman, clad in green,
And round him a fresh forest-scene.
155   On that clear forest-knoll he stays,
With his pack around him, and delays.
He stares and stares, with troubled face,
At this huge, gleam-lit fireplace,
At that bright, iron-figured door,
160   And those blown rushes on the floor.
He gazes down into the room
With heated cheeks and flurried air,
And to himself he seems to say:
'*What place is this, and who are they?*
165   *Who is that kneeling Lady fair?*
And on his pillows that pale Knight
Who seems of marble on a tomb?
How comes it here, this chamber bright,
Through whose mullioned windows clear
170   *The castle-court all wet with rain,*
The drawbridge and the moat appear,
And then the beach, and, marked with spray,
The sunken reefs, and far away
The unquiet bright Atlantic plain?

ii *155. On that clear forest-knoll*] 'Tis noon with him, and yet *1852*.
ii *156*. In *1852* this line ends with a comma and is followed by:

> *As rooted to the earth, nor sounds*
> *His lifted horn, nor cheers his hounds*
> *Into the tangled glen below.*
> *Yet in the sedgy bottom there*
> *Where the deep forest stream creeps slow*
> *Fring'd with dead leaves and mosses rare,*
> *The wild boar harbours close, and feeds.*

ii *157–60* In *1852* these lines follow l. 174.
ii *163–4*. First added *1853*.
ii *164–7*. For the connection of this picture with 'The Church of Brou'
iii (p. 300 below) see *Commentary* 115–16. Note that the 'Prophets, transfigured Saints, and Martyrs brave' (l. 20) look down on the tomb of the
'princely Pair' as the Huntsman looks down on the dead Tristram and
Iseult; the Duke has hunted 'the boar in the crisp woods till eve' (l. 11); the
Duke and Duchess ask, '*What is this? we are in bliss – forgiven – | Behold
the pavement of the courts of Heaven!* (ll. 30–1) as the Huntsman asks,
'*What place is this, and who are they?*' A. adopted italics for ll. 164–82 in
1853.
ii *174*. A rhythm obviously liked by A. Cp. 'To Marguerite – Continued'
24 (p. 125 above),

> *The unplumbed, salt, estranging sea.*

175   *– What, has some glamour made me sleep,*
       And sent me with my dogs to sweep,
       By night, with boisterous bugle-peal,
       Through some old, sea-side, knightly hall,
       Not in the free green wood at all?
180   *That Knight's asleep, and at her prayer*
       That Lady by the bed doth kneel –
       Then hush, thou boisterous bugle-peal!'
       – The wild boar rustles in his lair;
       The fierce hounds snuff the tainted air;
185   But lord and hounds keep rooted there.

       Cheer, cheer thy dogs into the brake,
       O Hunter! and without a fear
       Thy golden-tasselled bugle blow,
       And through the glades thy pastime take –
190   For thou wilt rouse no sleepers here!
       For these thou seest are unmoved;
       Cold, cold as those who lived and loved
       A thousand years ago.

ii *175–6. 1852,*

       Has then some glamour made him sleep,
       And sent him with his dogs to sweep . . .

ii *192–3.* The mediaeval Breton bard is speaking, and we are forced
to realize that Tristram and Iseult 'lived and loved / A thousand years ago'.
The change of perspective was probably suggested by the effect at the
end of Keats's 'The Eve of St. Agnes', especially ll. 370–1, 377–8,

       And they are gone: ay, ages long ago
       These lovers fled away into the storm.

       The Beadsman, after thousand aves told,
       For aye unsought for slept among his ashes cold.

III ISEULT OF BRITTANY

Apart from the tale of Merlin and Vivian Pt. iii is A.'s invention. It is
suggested *Commentary* 118 that it ended originally at what is now l. 63 –
A.'s autograph of this section is in the Yale MS. (for the variants, not
included in *1950*, see *nn.* below and *Commentary* 120–1) – and the editors
suppose that the Merlin-Vivian tale was an afterthought, citing A.'s letter
to Herbert Hill 5 Nov. 1852 (see headn. to whole poem, p. 194 above),
'The story of Merlin, of which I am particularly fond, was brought in on
purpose to relieve the poem, which would else I thought have ended too

sadly; but perhaps the new element introduced is too much.' It is more probable that the second Iseult's tale of Merlin was part of A.'s original conception. If Pt. iii was once shorter, ll. 112–50 – omitted *1853*, *1854* – may have been interpolated in the first draft. A.'s source for the Merlin-Vivian episode (of which he was 'particularly fond', probably because it recalled his own enchantment by Marguerite) is a passage in La Ville-marqué's 'Visite au Tombeau de Merlin', *Revue de Paris* 2nd series xli (1837) 52–3:

> 'Sire, fait Viviane, je veux que vous m'enseigniez comment je pourrais un homme enclore et enserrer, sans tour, sans mur, ni sans fer. – Quand Merlin l'entend, il branla la tête, et commença moult à soupirer, et Viviane lui demanda pourquoi il soupirait ainsi: Dame, répond Merlin, je sais bien que vous me voulez retenir; mais veuille ou non, me convient octroyer votre volonté ...
>
> Lors commença Merlin à deviser, et la damoiselle moult grande joie en eut, et lui montra plus grand semblant de l'aimer qu'elle n'avait fait auparavant, et tant qu'un jour advint qu'ils s'en allaient main à main par la forêt de Brocélian, et ils trouvèrent un buisson d'aubépine qui était tout chargé de fleurs, et ils s'assirent à l'ombre des aubépines, sur l'herbe verte, et jouèrent; et Merlin mit son chef au giron de la damoiselle, et elle le commença à tâtonner, tant qu'il s'endormit; puis se leva, et fit un cercle de sa guimpe autour du buisson et autour de Merlin, et commença ses enchantemens tels que lui-même lui avait appris, et fit neuf fois le cercle, et par neuf fois l'enchantement, et puis s'alla seoir auprès de lui, et lui mit la tête en son giron, et quand il se réveilla, il regarda autour de lui, et lui fut avis qu'il était enclos dans la plus forte tour du monde ...'

A year had flown, and o'er the sea away,
In Cornwall, Tristram and Queen Iseult lay;
In King Marc's chapel, in Tyntagel old –
There in a ship they bore those lovers cold.

iii *1–2*. *1852*,

> *A year had flown, and in the chapel old*
> *Lay Tristram and queen Iseult dead and cold.*

iii *3–4*. Added *1853* (in this form *1857*) when A. discovered from Dunlop that Tristram and Iseult had been buried in Cornwall – see *History of Fiction* (3rd ed. 1845) 87, 'The remains of Tristam and Yseult were embarked in a vessel, along with the sword, which was presented to the king of Cornwall ... He was melted with tenderness when he saw the weapon ... Marc ordered the lovers to be buried in his own chapel.'

5   The young surviving Iseult, one bright day,
    Had wandered forth. Her children were at play
    In a green circular hollow in the heath
    Which borders the sea-shore – a country path
    Creeps over it from the tilled fields behind.
10 The hollow's grassy banks are soft-inclined,
    And to one standing on them, far and near
    The lone unbroken view spreads bright and clear
    Over the waste. This cirque of open ground
    Is light and green; the heather, which all round
15 Creeps thickly, grows not here; but the pale grass
    Is strewn with rocks, and many a shivered mass
    Of veined white-gleaming quartz, and here and there
    Dotted with holly-trees and juniper.

iii 5. *The young surviving Iseult*] The year had travell'd round, and *Yale MS.*

iii 6. *Had wandered*] Drew Iseult *Yale MS.*

iii 7. *a green circular hollow*] that green circular opening *Yale MS.* Both phrases were suggested by La Villemarqué's description in his 'Visite au Tombeau de Merlin' of the Val-des-Fées as 'un immense amphithéâtre'. A. therefore knew – and had probably already decided to use – the tale of Merlin and Vivian when he began work on Pt. iii.

iii 9. In the *Yale MS.* 'fields' is written above 'land' and 'Steals' is an unadopted alternative to 'Creeps'.

iii 10. *Yale MS.*,

are

The opening's grassy banks were soft inclined . . .

Yet to one standing in it
Yet low – and from the bottom

iii 11. *And to one standing on them*] But their slope was not deep, and *Yale MS.*

iii 12. *spreads*] stretch'd *Yale MS.*

iii 13. *cirque*] ring *1852*. In the *Yale MS.* this line reads,

all the hollow
Over the waste: but where the open ground

light and green

iii 14. *light and green*] green and clear *Yale MS.* The following first attempt at ll. 14–15 has been cancelled:

leaves   encircling
First meets the fringing heath at once all round
The heather disappears . . .

Creeps

iii 15. *Creeps*] Blooms *Yale MS.*

iii 18. *Dotted*] Sprinkled *Yale MS.*

In the smooth centre of the opening stood
20   Three hollies side by side, and made a screen,
Warm with the winter-sun, of burnished green
With scarlet berries gemmed, the fell-fare's food.
Under the glittering hollies Iseult stands,
Watching her children play; their little hands
25   Are busy gathering spars of quartz, and streams
Of stagshorn for their hats; anon, with screams
Of mad delight they drop their spoils, and bound
Among the holly-clumps and broken ground,
Racing full speed, and startling in their rush
30   The fell-fares and the speckled missel-thrush
Out of their glossy coverts; but when now
Their cheeks were flushed, and over each hot brow,
Under the feathered hats of the sweet pair,
In blinding masses showered the golden hair –
35   Then Iseult called them to her, and the three
Clustered under the holly-screen, and she
Told them an old-world Breton history.

Warm in their mantles wrapped the three stood
Under the hollies, in the clear still air –   [there,
40   Mantles with those rich furs deep glistering
Which Venice ships do from swart Egypt bring.
Long they stayed still – then, pacing at their ease,
Moved up and down under the glossy trees.
But still, as they pursued their warm dry road,
45   From Iseult's lips the unbroken story flowed,
And still the children listened, their blue eyes
Fixed on their mother's face in wide surprise;
Nor did their looks stray once to the sea-side,

iii 19. *Yale MS.*,

> In the smooth centre
> Down in the middle of the hollow stood . . .

iii 20–2. *Yale MS.*,

> With scarlet berries bright the fellfare's food
> Three hollies side by side, and made a screen
> Where the sun's rays struck full and flash'd back keen.

The fell-fare, more commonly fieldfare, is a species of thrush.
iii 23. *glittering*] burnish'd *Yale MS.*
iii 25–6. *streams | Of stagshorn*] Streamers of fern.
iii 32. *were*] grew *Yale MS.* (written over 'were').
iii 40. *rich furs deep*] deep furs rich *Yale MS.*
iii 42. *ease*] eyes *Yale MS.* An obvious slip of the pen.
iii 43. *the*] their *Yale MS.*

Nor to the brown heaths round them, bright and wide,
50 Nor to the snow, which, though 'twas all away
From the open heath, still by the hedgerows lay,
Nor to the shining sea-fowl, that with screams
Bore up from where the bright Atlantic gleams,
Swooping to landward; nor to where, quite clear,
55 The fell-fares settled on the thickets near.
And they would still have listened, till dark night
Came keen and chill down on the heather bright;
But, when the red glow on the sea grew cold,
And the grey turrets of the castle old
60 Looked sternly through the frosty evening-air,
Then Iseult took by the hand those children fair,
And brought her tale to an end, and found the path,
And led them home over the darkening heath.

And is she happy? Does she see unmoved
65 The days in which she might have lived and loved
Slip without bringing bliss slowly away,
One after one, to-morrow like to-day?
Joy has not found her yet, nor ever will –
Is it this thought which makes her mien so still,
70 Her features so fatigued, her eyes, though sweet,
So sunk, so rarely lifted save to meet
Her children's? She moves slow; her voice alone
Hath yet an infantine and silver tone,
But even that comes languidly; in truth,
75 She seems one dying in a mask of youth.
And now she will go home, and softly lay
Her laughing children in their beds, and play
Awhile with them before they sleep; and then
She'll light her silver lamp, which fishermen
80 Dragging their nets through the rough waves, afar,
Along this iron coast, know like a star,
And take her broidery-frame, and there she'll sit
Hour after hour, her gold curls sweeping it;
Lifting her soft-bent head only to mind
85 Her children, or to listen to the wind.
And when the clock peals midnight, she will move
Her work away, and let her fingers rove
Across the shaggy brows of Tristram's hound
Who lies, guarding her feet, along the ground;

iii 49. *bright and*] warm and *Yale MS.*
iii 51. *the open heath, still*] th'open waste, white *Yale MS.*
iii 53. *Bore up*] Came in *Yale MS.*

90 Or else she will fall musing, her blue eyes
      Fixed, her slight hands clasped on her lap; then rise,
      And at her prie-dieu kneel, until she have told
      Her rosary-beads of ebony tipped with gold,
      Then to her soft sleep – and to-morrow 'll be
95 To-day's exact repeated effigy.

      Yes, it is lonely for her in her hall.
      The children and the grey-haired seneschal,
      Her women, and Sir Tristram's aged hound,
      Are there the sole companions to be found.
100 But these she loves; and noisier life than this
      She would find ill to bear, weak as she is.
      She has her children, too, and night and day
      Is with them; and the wide heaths where they play,
      The hollies, and the cliff, and the sea-shore,
105 The sand, the sea-birds, and the distant sails,
      These are to her dear as to them; the tales
      With which this day the children she beguiled
      She gleaned from Breton grandames, when a child,
      In every hut along this sea-coast wild.
110 She herself loves them still, and, when they are told,
      Can forget all to hear them, as of old.

      Dear saints, it is not sorrow, as I hear,
      Not suffering, which shuts up eye and ear
      To all that has delighted them before,
115 And lets us be what we were once no more.
      No, we may suffer deeply, yet retain
      Power to be moved and soothed, for all our pain,
      By what of old pleased us, and will again.

---

iii *112–50*. Omitted *1853*, *1854*. A. made an effort in ll. 133–50 to 'media-
evalize' these supposed reflections of the Breton narrator, but ll. 112–42
are clearly autobiographical. This would not have been obvious to the
poem's first readers, and the digression may have been omitted 1853–7
simply because A. thought it too long.

iii *112–26*. Cp. A.'s note in the Yale MS., 'The misery of the present age
is not in the intensity of men's suffering – but in their incapacity to suffer,
enjoy, feel at all, wholly and profoundly; in their having their susceptibility
eternally agacée by a continual dance of ever-changing objects . . . the
eternal tumult of the world mingling, breaking in upon, hurrying away
all. Deep suffering is the consciousness of oneself no less than deep enjoyment.'

       No, 'tis the gradual furnace of the world,
120 In whose hot air our spirits are upcurled
       Until they crumble, or else grow like steel –
       Which kills in us the bloom, the youth, the spring –
       Which leaves the fierce necessity to feel,
       But takes away the power – this can avail,
125 By drying up our joy in everything,
       To make our former pleasures all seem stale.
       This, or some tyrannous single thought, some fit
       Of passion, which subdues our souls to it,
       Till for its sake alone we live and move –
130 Call it ambition, or remorse, or love –
       This too can change us wholly, and make seem
       All which we did before, shadow and dream.

           And yet, I swear, it angers me to see
       How this fool passion gulls men potently;
135 Being, in truth, but a diseased unrest,
       And an unnatural overheat at best.
       How they are full of languor and distress
       Not having it; which when they do possess,
       They straightway are burnt up with fume and care,
140 And spend their lives in posting here and there
       Where this plague drives them; and have little ease,
       Are furious with themselves, and hard to please.
       Like that bald Cæsar, the famed Roman wight,

iii *119–22*. Cp. 'The Scholar-Gipsy' 142–5 (p. 339 below),

> For what wears out the life of mortal men?
>   'Tis that from change to change their being rolls;
>   'Tis that repeated shocks, again, again,
>   Exhaust the energy of strongest souls . . .

and, for the notion of the drying-up of feeling, 'Empedocles on Etna' II [i] 21–2 (p. 176 above),

> For something has impaired thy spirit's strength,
> And dried its self-sufficing fount of joy . . .

and 'Memorial Verses' 56 (p. 229 below),

> Spirits dried up and closely furled . . .

iii *122*. bloom] See *n.* to 'The Youth of Nature' 54 (p. 247 below).
iii *142*. *Are furious with themselves*] Can never end their tasks *1852*; Are fretful with themselves *1857*, *1869*.
iii *143–5*. See Suetonius, *De Vita Caesarum* i 7, 'Quaestori ulterior Hispania obvenit; ubi cum mandatu praetoris iure dicundo conventus circumiret Gadisque venisset, animadversa apud Herculis templum Magni

Who wept at reading of a Grecian knight
145 Who made a name at younger years than he;
Or that renowned mirror of chivalry,
Prince Alexander, Philip's peerless son,
Who carried the great war from Macedon
Into the Soudan's realm, and thundered on
150 To die at thirty-five in Babylon.

What tale did Iseult to the children say,
Under the hollies, that bright winter's day?

She told them of the fairy-haunted land
Away the other side of Brittany,
155 Beyond the heaths, edged by the lonely sea;
Of the deep forest-glades of Broce-liande,
Through whose green boughs the golden sunshine
    creeps,
Where Merlin by the enchanted thorn-tree sleeps.
For here he came with the fay Vivian,
160 One April, when the warm days first began.
He was on foot, and that false fay, his friend,
On her white palfrey; here he met his end,
In these lone sylvan glades, that April-day.
This tale of Merlin and the lovely fay
165 Was the one Iseult chose, and she brought clear
Before the children's fancy him and her.

Blowing between the stems, the forest-air
Had loosened the brown locks of Vivian's hair,
Which played on her flushed cheek, and her blue eyes
170 Sparkled with mocking glee and exercise.
Her palfrey's flanks were mired and bathed in sweat,
For they had travelled far and not stopped yet.
A brier in that tangled wilderness
Had scored her white right hand, which she allows
175 To rest ungloved on her green riding-dress;
The other warded off the drooping boughs.
But still she chatted on, with her blue eyes
Fixed full on Merlin's face, her stately prize.

Alexandri imagine ingemuit et quasi pertaesus ignaviam suam, quod
nihil dum a se memorabile actum esset in aetate, quam iam Alexander
orbem terrarum subegisset, missionem effligitavit.'
iii *149. the Soudan's realm*] The Persian empire of Darius.
iii *153–224.* See headn. to Pt. iii above for A.'s source.

Her 'haviour had the morning's fresh clear grace,
180   The spirit of the woods was in her face.
She looked so witching fair, that learned wight
Forgot his craft, and his best wits took flight;
And he grew fond, and eager to obey
His mistress, use her empire as she may.

185   They come to where the brushwood ceased, and day
Peered 'twixt the stems; and the ground broke away
In a sloped sward down to a brawling brook;
And up as high as where they stood to look
On the brook's farther side was clear, but then
190   The underwood and trees began again.
This open glen was studded thick with thorns
Then white with blossom; and you saw the horns,
Through last year's fern, of the shy fallow-deer
Who come at noon down to the water here.
195   You saw the bright-eyed squirrels dart along
Under the thorns on the green sward; and strong
The blackbird whistled from the dingles near,
And the weird chipping of the woodpecker
Rang lonelily and sharp; the sky was fair,
200   And a fresh breath of spring stirred everywhere.
Merlin and Vivian stopped on the slope's brow,
To gaze on the light sea of leaf and bough
Which glistering plays all round them, lone and mild,
As if to itself the quiet forest smiled.
205   Upon the brow-top grew a thorn, and here
The grass was dry and mossed, and you saw clear
Across the hollow; white anemones
Starred the cool turf, and clumps of primroses
Ran out from the dark underwood behind.
210   No fairer resting-place a man could find.
'Here let us halt,' said Merlin then; and she
Nodded, and tied her palfrey to a tree.

iii *179*. The description of Vivian recalls Marguerite – cp. 'Parting' 17–18
(p. 118 above),

> . . . *what voice is this I hear,*
> *Buoyant as morning, and as morning clear?*

iii *193. last year's fern*] the green fern *1852–77*. A correction for the sake of
botanical accuracy.
iii *198. weird*] light *1852–7*.
iii *202. light sea*] green sea *1852–77*.
iii *203. plays*] lay *1852–77*.

>   They sate them down together, and a sleep
>   Fell upon Merlin, more like death, so deep.
> 215 Her finger on her lips, then Vivian rose,
>   And from her brown-locked head the wimple throws,
>   And takes it in her hand, and waves it over
>   The blossomed thorn-tree and her sleeping lover.
>   Nine times she waved the fluttering wimple round,
> 220 And made a little plot of magic ground.
>   And in that daisied circle, as men say,
>   Is Merlin prisoner till the judgment-day;
>   But she herself whither she will can rove –
>   For she was passing weary of his love.

iii *224.* An echo of *Le Morte Darthur* iv ch. 1 ed. *cit.* i 103, 'And always Merlin lay about the lady to have her maidenhead, and she was ever passing weary of him . . .'

49 Youth and Calm

Date of composition unknown, but between Sept. 1849–Dec. 1851 if 'Lines written by a Death-bed' (of which 'Youth and Calm' formed part in *1852*) originally belonged, as I believe, to 'Tristram and Iseult' – cp. *Bonnerot* 85–6, '*Lines written by a Death-bed* appartiennent vraiment à *Tristram and Iseult* et ont, sans aucun doute, fait partie de la rédaction primitive du poème'; A.'s Arthurian romance was planned at Thun Sept. 1849 and composed between then and Oct. 1852, but the terminal date for the writing of 'Youth and Calm' is given by A.'s autograph of ll. 5–25, which is dated 28 Dec. 1851 in Rotha Quillinan's album (Wordsworth Museum, Grasmere). The speculative dating is supported by A.'s insertion of 'Lines written by a Death-bed' 1–16 virtually unaltered in Pt. ii of 'Tristram and Iseult' in *1869* to describe Iseult of Ireland (the description agrees with those at ii 21–4, 116–30). 'Youth and Calm', which is connected by theme with 'Youth's Agitations' (p. 145 above), was printed with it and 'Growing Old' (p. 538 below) in *1867*, and became an 'Early Poem' in *1877*.
Published as second paragraph of 'Lines written by a Death-bed' *1852*; with present title *1867*, *1869*, etc.

>   'Tis death! and peace, indeed, is here,
>   And ease from shame, and rest from fear.
>   There's nothing can dismarble now
>   The smoothness of that limpid brow.
> 5   But is a calm like this, in truth,
>   The crowning end of life and youth,
>   And when this boon rewards the dead,

Are all debts paid, has all been said?
And is the heart of youth so light,
10   Its step so firm, its eye so bright,
Because on its hot brow there blows
A wind of promise and repose
From the far grave, to which it goes;
Because it hath the hope to come,
15   One day, to harbour in the tomb?
Ah no, the bliss youth dreams is one
For daylight, for the cheerful sun,
For feeling nerves and living breath –
Youth dreams a bliss on this side death.
20   It dreams a rest, if not more deep,
More grateful than this marble sleep;
It hears a voice within it tell:
Calm's not life's crown, though calm is well.
'Tis all perhaps which man acquires,
25   But 'tis not what our youth desires.

¶ **49.** *11. hot brow*] hot hour *R.Q.'s Album.* Apart from this reading, the
texts of the *Album*, *1852* and *1867* do not differ significantly.
21. marble sleep] Cp. 'Tristram and Iseult' ii 165–7 (p. 214 above),

> *Who is that kneeling Lady fair?*
> *And on his pillows that pale Knight*
> *Who seems of marble on a tomb?*

and 'The Church of Brou' iii 16 (p. 301 below),

> *So sleep, for ever sleep, O marble Pair!*

23–5. Cp. Sainte-Beuve on the 'crise antérieure à toute maturité', 'M. de
Senancour' (1832), *Portraits Contemporains* i (1868 revised ed.) 168, '. . . il
devient plus calme, plus capable de cette régulière stabilité qui n'est pas le
bonheur au fond, mais qui le simule à la longue, même à nos propres
yeux'.

50 Memorial Verses

APRIL, 1850

Written *c.* 27 April 1850 (this date – of Wordsworth's burial at Grasmere –
being part of poem's title in the MS. in Yale Papers and in *Fraser's Magazine*)
at the request of Wordsworth's son-in-law, Edward Quillinan – see A.'s
letter to Clough (undated, but May 1850), 'I would fain see thee as I have
at Quillinan's sollicitation dirged W.W. *in the grand style* and need thy
rapture therewith' (*CL* 115). As combining elegy and literary criticism
cp. 'The Youth of Nature' (also on W.), 'Obermann', 'Haworth Churchyard' and 'Heine's Grave'. Wordsworth died 23 April 1850. For Quillinan

see headn. to A.'s 'Stanzas in Memory of Edward Quillinan' (p. 243 below);
and for his opinion of 'Memorial Verses' letter 16 Jan. 1851, *Correspondence
of H. C. Robinson with the Wordsworth Circle* ed. E. J. Morley (1927) ii 769,
'It is *very* classical, or it would not be M.A.'s ... It is a triple Epicede on
your Friends Wordsworth and Goethe, and on Byron who, I think, ... is
not tall enough for the other two ... But M. ~~Arnold~~ has a good deal of
poetry in him; and it will come out in spite of all the heathen Gods and
goddesses ...'
Published *Fraser's Magazine* June 1850; reprinted *1852, 1855, 1869*, etc.

> Goethe in Weimar sleeps, and Greece,
> Long since, saw Byron's struggle cease.
> But one such death remained to come;
> The last poetic voice is dumb –
5   We stand to-day by Wordsworth's tomb.
>
> When Byron's eyes were shut in death,
> We bowed our head and held our breath.
> He taught us little; but our soul
> Had *felt* him like the thunder's roll.
10   With shivering heart the strife we saw
> Of passion with eternal law;
> And yet with reverential awe
> We watched the fount of fiery life

¶ 50. *1–2.* Goethe died in 1832, Byron at Missolonghi in Greece in 1824.
5. We stand to-day by] We stand to-day at *MS., Fraser 1850*; What shall
be said o'er *1852–5.*
6–7. For other references to Byron in A.'s poetry see 'Courage' *17–24,*
'Stanzas from the Grande Chartreuse' 133–8 and 'Haworth Churchyard' 93–7 (pp. 142, 291 and 395 below), but his influence can be
traced in many poems. A.'s mature judgment on Byron as a poet can be
found in the essay cited in the next note.
8. taught us little] Cp. 'Byron', *E in C II* (1888), *Works* iv 136, 'Goethe
lays his finger on ... his [Byron's] real source of weakness both as a man
and as a poet. "The moment he reflects, he is a child," says Goethe; –
sobald er reflectirt ist er ein Kind".' At Oxford 'Goethe displaced Byron in
his [A.'s] poetical allegiance' (Tom Arnold, *Passages in a Wandering Life*
(1900) 57), probably at Carlyle's prompting – see *Sartor Resartus* (1838),
Works ed. H. D. Traill i 153, 'Close thy *Byron*; open thy *Goethe.*'
13. fount of fiery life] Cp. Byron, 'On this day I complete my thirty-sixth
year' 9–10,

> *The fire which on my bosom preys*
> *Is lone as some Volcanic isle ...*

For Byron's 'Titanism' see *On the Study of Celtic Literature* (1867), *Works*
v 129 (where A. quotes these verses), '... the Titanism of the Celt, his

Which served for that Titanic strife.

15   When Goethe's death was told, we said:
        Sunk, then, is Europe's sagest head.
        Physician of the iron age,
        Goethe has done his pilgrimage.
        He took the suffering human race,
20   He read each wound, each weakness clear;
        And struck his finger on the place,
        And said: *Thou ailest here, and here!*
        He looked on Europe's dying hour
        Of fitful dream and feverish power;
25   His eye plunged down the weltering strife,
        The turmoil of expiring life –
        He said: *The end is everywhere,*
        Art still has truth, take refuge there!
        And he was happy, if to know
30   Causes of things, and far below

---

passionate, turbulent, indomitable reaction against the despotism of fact;
and of whom does it remind us so much as of Byron?'
14. Which served] Suffic'd *MS.*; Which flow'd *Fraser 1850*.
15. When Goethe's death was told] When Goethe pass'd away *MS., Fraser*
1850.
19–22. Cp. 'The Scholar-Gipsy' 203 (p. 342 below),
                        ... *this strange disease of modern life* ...

and Carlyle, 'Characteristics' (1831), *Crit. and Miscell. Essays, Works* ed. *cit.*
xxviii 1–43, especially, 'If we now, with a practical medical view,
examine ... the Condition of our own Era ... the diagnosis ... is nowise
of a flattering sort ... On the outward, as it were Physical diseases of
Society, it were beside our purpose to insist here ... But alas, with us the
Spiritual condition of society is no less sickly ... the diseased self-conscious
state of Literature ...' (*loc. cit.* 18–24); and Goethe, Eckermann's *Conversations* under 2 April 1829 (Bohn's Library revised ed. (1883) 380), 'I call the
classic *healthy*, the romantic *sickly* ... Most modern productions are
romantic, not because they are new, but because they are weak, morbid,
and sickly; and the antique is classic, not because it is old, but because it is
strong, fresh, joyous, and healthy.'
25. weltering] seething *MS., Fraser 1850*.
29–33. An allusion to Virgil, *Georgics* ii 490–2,

                felix qui potuit rerum cognoscere causas
                atque metus omnis et inexorabile fatum
                subiecit pedibus strepitumque Acherontis avari.

Virgil is thinking of Lucretius. A.'s transition to Wordsworth is apt, as

His feet to see the lurid flow
Of terror, and insane distress,
And headlong fate, be happiness.

And Wordsworth! – Ah, pale ghosts, rejoice!
35   For never has such soothing voice
Been to your shadowy world conveyed,
Since erst, at morn, some wandering shade
Heard the clear song of Orpheus come
Through Hades, and the mournful gloom.
40   Wordsworth has gone from us – and ye,
Ah, may ye feel his voice as we!
He too upon a wintry clime
Had fallen – on this iron time
Of doubts, disputes, distractions, fears.
45   He found us when the age had bound
Our souls in its benumbing round;
He spoke, and loosed our heart in tears.
He laid us as we lay at birth
On the cool flowery lap of earth,
50   Smiles broke from us and we had ease;
The hills were round us, and the breeze
Went o'er the sun-lit fields again;

Virgil continues (l. 493, about his own poetry),

fortunatus et ille deos qui novit agrestes ...

43-4. Cp. Carlyle, 'Characteristics' (1831), *Works* ed. *cit.* xxviii 30,
'How changed in these new days ... Not Godhead, but an iron, ignoble
circle of Necessity embraces all things ... Doubt storms in ... through
every avenue; inquiries of the deepest, painfulest sort ... sceptical,
suicidal cavillings ...' A. added l. 44 in *1852*.
46. MS. and *Fraser 1850* read:

Our spirits in a brazen round ...

and follow this line with three lines discarded in 1852:

He tore us from the prison-cell
Of festering thoughts and personal fears,
Where we had long been doom'd to dwell.

48. He laid us as we lay] Once more we lay as erst *MS.*
49-57. Cp. 'Wordsworth', *E in C II* (1888), *Works* iv 112-14, 'Wordsworth's poetry is great because of the extraordinary power with which
Wordsworth feels the joy offered to us in nature ... Wordsworth's
poetry, when he is at his best, is inevitable, as inevitable as Nature herself.'
For A.'s recognition of Wordsworth's limitations, which could not be
expressed in a memorial panegyric, in a passage linking Wordsworth and
Goethe, cp. 'Obermann' 53-4 (p. 132 above).

Our foreheads felt the wind and rain.
Our youth returned; for there was shed
55   On spirits that had long been dead,
Spirits dried up and closely furled,
The freshness of the early world.

Ah! since dark days still bring to light
Man's prudence and man's fiery might,
60   Time may restore us in his course
Goethe's sage mind and Byron's force;
But where will Europe's latter hour
Again find Wordsworth's healing power?
Others will teach us how to dare,
65   And against fear our breast to steel;
Others will strengthen us to bear –
But who, ah! who, will make us feel?
The cloud of mortal destiny,
Others will front it fearlessly –
70   But who, like him, will put it by?

Keep fresh the grass upon his grave,
O Rotha, with thy living wave!
Sing him thy best! for few or none
Hears thy voice right, now he is gone.

54. *returned*] came back *MS., Fraser 1850*.
56. *dried up*] deep-crushed *MS., Fraser 1850*. With the *1852* reading cp.
'Empedocles on Etna' II [i] 21–2 (p. 176 above),

> For something has impaired thy spirit's strength,
> And dried its self-sufficing fount of joy . . .

and see *n.* to these lines.
57. Cp. 'The Youth of Nature' 53–5 (p. 247 below),

> But he was a priest to us all
> Of the wonder and bloom of the world,
> Which we saw with his eyes, and were glad.

63. *healing power*] The reference recalls ll. 17–22. Goethe diagnoses, but
Wordsworth heals.
72. The Rotha flows by Grasmere churchyard.

51 The River

Written Aug. 1850: 'Faded Leaves', the sequence of five poems (including
'The River') given this title *1855*, was inspired by a crisis in A.'s courtship of Frances Lucy Wightman in the late summer and autumn of 1850
(he met her first late 1849 or early 1850 and married her 10 June 1851); the

month of 'The River' is indicated in l. 2. For A.'s interest at this time in
Miss W. see Clough's letter to Tom A. 23 July 1850, 'Matt comes to
Switzerland in a month, after your sister's wedding. He is himself deep in
a flirtation with Miss Wightman, the d[aughter]r of the Judge. It is thought
it will come to something, for he has actually been to Church to meet her'
(*Correspondence of A.H.C.* i 286); and for a discreet reference to the crisis –
according to family tradition 'Justice Wightman, not sure that Arnold
was able to support a wife, had forbidden any further meeting of the two'
(*Commentary* 167) – see Tom A.'s obituary notice of M.A. (*Manchester
Guardian* 18 May 1888), 'It was not all prosperous sailing in his love . . .
and of one such counterblast which drove him out of England and towards
the Alps the lovely stanzas "Vain is the effort to forget" ['Faded Leaves.
IV. On the Rhine'] are the record.' A.'s holiday abroad in 1850 is also
connected with 'Calais Sands', which is dated Aug. 1850 in MS. and records A.'s sentimental delay at Calais to catch a glimpse of Miss W. with
her father before travelling on to the Rhine (see p. 233 below). 'Calais
Sands' belongs to 'Faded Leaves' between 'Separation' and 'On the Rhine',
but A. did not publish it until 1867, probably because it was too intimate
a self-revelation. 'The River' was abbreviated in 1852 for the same
reason. The order of the poems in 'Faded Leaves' is apparently chronological; I–IV were composed Aug.–Sept. 1850, V then or a little later. A.
often refers to Miss W. as 'F-L' in his 1851 diary and these initials may be
glanced at in the title 'Faded Leaves'.
Published in a shortened version *1852*; reprinted as 'Faded Leaves. I.
The River' *1855*, *1869*, etc.; printed from autograph now in the possession of Mrs. Barnett, with ll. 1–24 restored, in *Times Lit. Supp.* 28 March
1958 (where I have argued the case for restoration).

          On the broad-bosomed lordly Thames
          Down which we glide, the August sun
          In mellow evening splendour flames;
          Soon will our voyage all be done.

5   Wrapped in thy shawl, in still repose
          Back in the stern-seat soft-reclined,
          Round thy sweet form the cool air blows,
          And thy veil flutters in the wind.

          While I, crouched further yet astern,
10   Wait for the voice that flowed erewhile,
          Wait for the graceful head to turn,
          And lightly look, and gaily smile.

¶ 51. *1*. Sir William Wightman had a house by the river at Hampton-
on-Thames.
      While
9. *While*] But   *MS.*

But ah, the head keeps turned away;
I only see those fingers small
15   Flit charmingly in careless play
Through the green fringes of thy shawl.

Ah, let the harmless fringes float,
Let the shawl be; for it leaves bare
A lovely strip of thy soft throat
20   Gleaming between it and thy hair.

And see – for sleep his heavy balms
On all our tired crew outpours –
With half-shut eyes and languid arms
The rowers dip and lift their oars.

25   Still glides the stream, slow drops the boat
Under the rustling poplars' shade;
Silent the swans beside us float –
None speaks, none heeds; ah, turn thy head!

Let those arch eyes now softly shine,
30   That mocking mouth grow sweetly bland;
Ah, let them rest, those eyes, on mine!
On mine let rest that lovely hand!

My pent-up tears oppress my brain,
My heart is swollen with love unsaid.
35   Ah, let me weep, and tell my pain,
And on thy shoulder rest my head!

25. *Still glides the stream*] An echo of Wordsworth, 'The River Duddon'
(1820) xxxiv 5,

> *Still glides the Stream, and shall for ever glide* . . .

29–30. A. discovered archness and mockery in both Miss Wightman and
Marguerite. Cp. 'A Memory-Picture' 27–8 (p. 109 above),

> . . . *the archest chin*
> *Mockery ever ambushed in* . . .

and 'Parting' 39 (p. 119 above),

> *The lovely lips, with their arch smile* . . .

29. *softly*] softlier *MS.*
34. *swollen*] A monosyllable. The printed texts read 'swoln'.
35. *weep*] speak *MS.*

Before I die – before the soul,
Which now is mine, must re-attain
Immunity from my control,
40   And wander round the world again;

Before this teased o'erlaboured heart
For ever leaves its vain employ,
Dead to its deep habitual smart,
And dead to hopes of future joy.

41. o'erlaboured] o'eruséd *MS.*

52 Too Late

Written Aug. 1850: see headn. to 'The River' (p. 229 above); A.'s autograph is in the possession of Mr. A. Whitridge (facsimile in *UL* facing p. 17).
Published *1852*; reprinted as 'Faded Leaves. II. Too Late' *1855*, *1869*, etc.

Each on his own strict line we move,
And some find death ere they find love;
So far apart their lives are thrown
From the twin soul which halves their own.

5   And sometimes, by still harder fate,
The lovers meet, but meet too late.
– Thy heart is mine! – *True, true! ah, true!*
– Then, love, thy hand! – *Ah no! adieu!*

¶ 52. *4. halves*] i.e. is the other half of. A reference to Aristophanes's account of the origin of love in Plato's *Symposium*, but A. may also have had in mind Horace's *animae dimidium meae* (*Odes* I iii 8). Other lines in this ode are recalled in 'To Marguerite – Continued' (p. 123 above).

53 Separation

Written Aug. 1850: see headn. to 'The River' (p. 229 above); A.'s autograph (with minor variants from *1855*) is now in the possession of Mrs. Barnett.
Published as 'Faded Leaves. III. Separation' *1855*; reprinted *1869*, etc.

Stop! – not to me, at this bitter departing,
    Speak of the sure consolations of time!
Fresh be the wound, still-renewed be its smarting,
    So but thy image endure in its prime.

5   But, if the steadfast commandment of Nature
       Wills that remembrance should always decay –
    If the loved form and the deep-cherished feature
       Must, when unseen, from the soul fade away –

    Me let no half-effaced memories cumber!
10   Fled, fled at once, be all vestige of thee!
    Deep be the darkness and still be the slumber –
       Dead be the past and its phantoms to me!

    Then, when we meet, and thy look strays towards me,
       Scanning my face and the changes wrought there:
15   *Who, let me say, is this stranger regards me,*
       With the grey eyes, and the lovely brown hair?

the mighty
¶ 53. 5. *But, if the steadfast*] But if indeed the *MS.*

always
6. *always*] surely *MS.*
11. *darkness*] Silence *MS.*

when
13. *Then, when we meet, and thy look*] Then, if we meet, and thine Eye *MS.*
16. *lovely brown hair*] Cp. 'Calais Sands' 15–17 (p. 234 below),

    How sweetly would the fresh sea-breeze
    Shake loose some band of soft brown hair!

Miss Wightman's hair was brown; Marguerite's was 'ash-coloured' (see 'Parting' 37, p. 119 above).

54 Calais Sands

Written Aug. 1850: see title of MS. (now in possession of A.'s grandson, Mr. A. Whitridge), 'By the seaside near Calais. August. 1850'; much revised for publication in *1867*. For the 'story' behind the poem, which supplies a possible reason for the poem's exclusion from *1852*, see headn. to 'The River' (p. 229 above).
Published *1867*; reprinted (*1868*), *1869*, etc.

    A thousand knights have reined their steeds
    To watch this line of sand-hills run,
    Along the never-silent Strait,
    To Calais glittering in the sun;

¶ 54. 2. *watch*] see *MS.*
3. *Strait*] beach *MS.*
4. *glittering*] sparkling *MS.*

9+M.A.

5   To look tow'rd Ardres' Golden Field
                  Across this wide aërial plain,
                  Which glows as if the Middle Age
                  Were gorgeous upon earth again.

                  Oh, that to share this famous scene,
10   I saw, upon the open sand,
                  Thy lovely presence at my side,
                  Thy shawl, thy look, thy smile, thy hand!

                  How exquisite thy voice would come,
                  My darling, on this lonely air!
15   How sweetly would the fresh sea-breeze,
                  Shake loose some band of soft brown hair!

                  Yet now my glance but once hath roved
                  O'er Calais and its famous plain;
                  To England's cliffs my gaze is turned,
20   On the blue strait mine eyes I strain.

5. *look*] see *MS*. Ardres is a small town, ten miles south-east of Calais. Near it is the 'Field of the Cloth of Gold', the scene of the meeting between Henry VIII and Francis I of France in 1520.
6. *MS.*,
               Spread wide away the luminous plain...
See *n.* to 'Empedocles on Etna' II [i] 315 (p. 188 above).
9–10 *MS.*,
               Oh wert thou here! That I might turn
               And see upon the lovely sand...
11. *Thy lovely presence*] That slight sweet figure *MS.*
12. *MS.*,
               That shawl, – that step – that look – that hand!
14. *lonely*] quiet *MS.*
15. *sea-breeze*] sea-wind *MS.*
16. *loose some band*] back thy bands *MS.*; loose some lock *1867–9.*
17. *MS.*,
               Not once today these eyes have stay'd...
18. *O'er Calais and its famous*] On Calais and its shining *MS.*
19. *gaze*] look *MS.*
20. *MS.*,
               On the blue sea my gaze I strain.
In *1867–9* as final text with 'O'er' in place of 'On'.

Thou comest! Yes! the vessel's cloud
Hangs dark upon the rolling sea.
Oh, that yon sea-bird's wings were mine,
To win one instant's glimpse of thee!

25   I must not spring to grasp thy hand,
To woo thy smile, to seek thine eye;
But I may stand far off, and gaze,
And watch thee pass unconscious by,

And spell thy looks, and guess thy thoughts,
30   Mixed with the idlers on the pier.
Ah, might I always rest unseen,
So I might have thee always near!

To-morrow hurry through the fields
Of Flanders to the storied Rhine!
35   To-night those soft-fringed eyes shall close
Beneath one roof, my queen! with mine.

25. grasp] touch *MS.*
26. woo] catch *MS.*
28. watch] see *MS.*
29. And spell thy looks] And watch thy air *MS.*
34. storied] ancient *MS.*
35. soft-fringed] soft-veiled *MS.*

55 On the Rhine

Written Aug. or Sept. *1850*: see headn. to 'The River' (p. 229 above).
Published *1852*; reprinted as 'Faded Leaves. IV. On the Rhine' *1855, 1869,*
etc.

Vain is the effort to forget.
Some day I shall be cold, I know,
As is the eternal moonlit snow
Of the high Alps, to which I go –
5   But ah, not yet, not yet!

Vain is the agony of grief.
'Tis true, indeed, an iron knot
Ties straitly up from mine thy lot,
And were it snapped – thou lov'st me not!
10   But is despair relief?

¶ 55. 7–8. The 'iron knot' was A.'s poor prospects as private secretary to
Lord Lansdowne. Judge Wightman reconciled himself to his daughter's en-
gagement on 30 March 1851, a week after Lord Lansdowne had appointed
A. an Inspector of Schools (unpublished 1851 diary).

Awhile let me with thought have done.
And as this brimmed unwrinkled Rhine,
And that far purple mountain-line,
Lie sweetly in the look divine
15   Of the slow-sinking sun;

So let me lie, and, calm as they,
Let beam upon my inward view
Those eyes of deep, soft, lucent hue –
Eyes too expressive to be blue,
20   Too lovely to be grey.

Ah, Quiet, all things feel thy balm!
Those blue hills too, this river's flow,
Were restless once, but long ago.
Tamed is their turbulent youthful glow;
25   Their joy is in their calm.

56 Longing

Probably written Aug. or Sept. 1850, but perhaps as late as Nov.: see
headn. to 'The River' (p. 229 above); A. and Miss Wightman were
corresponding normally at the end of the year. For a facsimile of A.'s
autograph (now in the possession of Mr. A. Whitridge) see *UL* 16.
Published *1852*; reprint as 'Faded Leaves. V. Longing' *1855*, *1869*, etc.

Come to me in my dreams, and then
By day I shall be well again!
For then the night will more than pay
The hopeless longing of the day.

5   Come, as thou cam'st a thousand times,
A messenger from radiant climes,
And smile on thy new world, and be
As kind to others as to me!

Or, as thou never cam'st in sooth,
10   Come now, and let me dream it truth;
And part my hair, and kiss my brow,
And say: *My love! why sufferest thou?*

¶ 56. 8. *others as to*] all the rest as *1852*. A. restored the MS. reading in *1855*.
10. *dream*] deem MS.
12. *My love*] My friend MS.

> Come to me in my dreams, and then
> By day I shall be well again!
> *15*   For then the night will more than pay
> The hopeless longing of the day.

57   Urania

Date of composition unknown, but (?) summer *1850*. This poem and 'Euphrosyne', its constant companion-piece, seem to me by their position in *1852* (sandwiched between 'Faded Leaves' poems) and by their whole content and tone to belong to Miss Wightman rather than to Marguerite, but the opposite view is taken by some commentators.
Published as 'Excuse' *1852*; reprinted *1855*; with present title *1869*, etc.

> I too have suffered; yet I know
> She is not cold, though she seems so:
> She is not cold, she is not light;
> But our ignoble souls lack might.
>
> *5*   She smiles and smiles, and will not sigh,
> While we for hopeless passion die;
> Yet she could love, those eyes declare,
> Were but men nobler than they are.
>
> Eagerly once her gracious ken
> *10*   Was turned upon the sons of men;
> But light the serious visage grew –
> She looked, and smiled, and saw them through.
>
> Our petty souls, our strutting wits,
> Our laboured, puny passion-fits
> *15*   Ah, may she scorn them still, till we
> Scorn them as bitterly as she!

¶ *57. Title.* The Uranian Aphrodite is the goddess of ideal love.
1–8 and below *29–32*. The remote and apparently cold and disdainful Urania suggests A.'s characterisation of Miss W. to Wyndham Slade as '*die unerreichbare Schöne*' (the unattainable beauty) and his admission that at first he found something '*abstossend*' (disconcerting, repelling) in her manner (*Commentary* 169, quoting undated letter of 1850). See also Blanche Smith's remark to Clough 15 April 1852, 'I thought she was nice, but a little Belgravian' (*Correspondence of A.H.C.* ii 425 *fn.*).
1–4. Omitted *1869–81*.

Yet show her once, ye heavenly Powers,
One of some worthier race than ours!
One for whose sake she once might prove
20   How deeply she who scorns can love.

His eyes be like the starry lights –
His voice like sounds of summer nights –
In all his lovely mien let pierce
The magic of the universe!

25   And she to him will reach her hand,
And gazing in his eyes will stand,
And know her friend, and weep for glee,
And cry: *Long, long I've looked for thee.*

Then will she weep; with smiles, till then,
30   Coldly she mocks the sons of men.
Till then, her lovely eyes maintain
Their pure, unwavering, deep disdain.

17. *1852, 1855,*
     Yet oh, that Fate would let her see . . .
18. *worthier race than ours*] better race than we *1852*; worthier race than we
1855.
32. *pure*] gay *1852–5.*

58 Euphrosyne

Date of composition unknown, but (?) Aug. 1850: see headn. to 'Urania'
above; the final quatrain probably describes A.'s feelings in Aug. 1850 at
Miss Wightman's ready compliance with the enforced veto on their
meetings. Note that these lines cannot refer to Marguerite whose feeling
for A., to judge by the 'Switzerland' poems, was never one of 'indifference', and whom he may be said to have retreated from rather than failed
to win.
Published as 'Indifference' in *1852*; reprinted *1855*; with present title *1869,*
etc.

I must not say that thou wast true,
Yet let me say that thou wast fair;
And they, that lovely face who view,
Why should they ask if truth be there?

¶ 58. *Title. Euphrosyne* was one of the three Graces. The name itself
signifies joy in Greek.
4. *Why should they*] They will not *1852–5*; They should not *1869–81.*

5   Truth – what is truth? Two bleeding hearts,
    Wounded by men, by fortune tried,
    Outwearied with their lonely parts,
    Vow to beat henceforth side by side.

    The world to them was stern and drear,
10   Their lot was but to weep and moan.
    Ah, let them keep their faith sincere,
    For neither could subsist alone!

    But souls whom some benignant breath
    Hath charmed at birth from gloom and care,
15   These ask no love, these plight no faith,
    For they are happy as they are.

    The world to them may homage make,
    And garlands for their forehead weave;
    And what the world can give, they take –
20   But they bring more than they receive.

    They shine upon the world! Their ears
    To one demand alone are coy;
    They will not give us love and tears,
    They bring us light and warmth and joy.

25   It was not love which heaved thy breast,
    Fair child! – it was the bliss within.
    Adieu! and say that one, at least,
    Was just to what he did not win.

21. They shine] They smile *1852–69.*
25–8. 1869–81, *On one she smiled, and he was blest!*
       She smiles elsewhere – we make a din!
       But 'twas not love which heaved her breast,
       Fair child! – it was the bliss within.

59 Dover Beach

Date of composition unknown, but probably late June 1851 (although not published – cp. 'Calais Sands', p. 233 above – until *1867*): an early date for A.'s most famous lyric is indicated by the fact that the MS., a pencilled autograph of ll. 1–28 ending 'Ah love &c' (implying earlier composition of ll. 29–37), is on the back of a sheet of notes about Empedocles – these notes drawn from Karsten's *Philosophorum Graecorum Veterum . . . Operum Reliquiae* ii (1838) are undated but plausibly of 1849–50; the records of A.'s visits to Dover with his wife after his marriage on 10 June 1851 suggest

when the poem was actually written. A.'s published 1851 diary has no
entries at all 16 June–21 July, but the financial accounts for 19–30 June include 'Journey to Dover and back – £9–5–0' (pointing to a visit of two or
three days, perhaps 23–25 June). A. next spent a night at Dover on his
return from his delayed continental honeymoon on 8 Oct. Some critics
assume that ll. 1–28 were written at the time of A.'s Dover visit (whenever
this is supposed to have taken place) and that ll. 29–37 were rescued from
some discarded poem to complete the new lyric; more probably, ll. 29–37
were written at Dover in late June on A.'s first visit there after his marriage,
ll. 1–28 – which provide the setting for the final sentiment – added in
London shortly afterwards (it is unlikely that A. would have his notes from
Karsten with him on his first brief visit to Dover).

Concern with the decay of orthodox religious faith links 'Dover Beach'
with 'Stanzas from the Grande Chartreuse' (the latter poem being associated with A.'s honeymoon visit to the monastery on 7 Sept. 1851). Formally, 'Dover Beach' is a lyric consisting of four unequal verse-paragraphs
irregularly rhymed. Lines vary between two and five stresses, but more
than half the lines are five-stressed.

Published *1867*; reprinted (*1868*), *1869*, etc.

    The sea is calm to-night.
    The tide is full, the moon lies fair
    Upon the straits; on the French coast the light
    Gleams and is gone; the cliffs of England stand,
5   Glimmering and vast, out in the tranquil bay.
    Come to the window, sweet is the night-air!
    Only, from the long line of spray

¶ 59. *1–14.* The setting of sea and moonlight is from observation and in
any case typically Arnoldian, but A. is also recalling *Obermann* (Lettre iv)
i 22, '. . . je me plaçai sur le sable où venaient expirer les vagues. L'air était
calme . . . La lune parut; je restai long-temps. Vers le matin, elle répandait
sur les terres et sur les eaux l'ineffable mélancolie de ses dernières lueurs.
La nature paraît bien grande lorsque, dans un long recueillement on entend
le roulement des ondes sur la rive solitaire, dans le calme d'une nuit encore
ardente et éclairée par la lune qui finit.' This passage A. singled out as an
illustration of Senancour's 'poetic emotion and deep feeling for nature' in
his 1869 *Academy* article on *Obermann* (Neiman 162). In ll. 1–6 much of the
effectiveness of the description depends on the high proportion of mono-
syllables and the simplicity of the key epithets 'calm', 'fair', 'tranquil'.
In l. 6 the window is approached and the sweetness of the air felt before
the sound of the sea is first heard in the following lines.
3–4. the light | Gleams and is gone] The movement mimics the observation.
4. Gleams] Shines MS.
   sweet
6. sweet] hush'd MS.

Where the sea meets the moon-blanched land,
Listen! you hear the grating roar
10   Of pebbles which the waves draw back, and fling,
At their return, up the high strand,
Begin, and cease, and then again begin,
With tremulous cadence slow, and bring
The eternal note of sadness in.

15   Sophocles long ago
Heard it on the Ægæan, and it brought
Into his mind the turbid ebb and flow
Of human misery; we
Find also in the sound a thought,
20   Hearing it by this distant northern sea.

8. *Where the sea* ⟨Where the ebb *1867–77*. The earlier reading refers to the ebbing of successive waves (not of the tide), but A. restored 'sea' from the MS. because of possible confusion (in l. 2 'The tide is full . . .'). The reading 'land' is a late substitution for 'sand' (*MS.*, *1867–81*).

10. *draw*] suck *MS.*, *1867*.
                    barr'd
11. *high*] steep *MS.*
12. *Begin, and cease*] Cease and begin *MS.*
                    mournful
13. *tremulous cadence slow*] regular cadence slow *MS.* The positioning of the adjectives is a Miltonic Grecism – cp. 'vast edges drear' (l. 27) below).
14. *The eternal note of sadness*] The waves are the pulse of an alien mode of being, but inevitably they remind man of time and change. At Thiel Obermann felt that he had 'swallowed up ten years of his life at once' (reference in *n.* to ll. 1–14 above).
15–18. Sophocles was A.'s favourite Greek dramatist, but no passage in the plays is strictly applicable – see *Baum* 88, 'The alleged parallels simply do not meet the case; they are irrelevant.' Of those suggested the closest is *Trachiniae* 112 ff. (for a translation see *n.* to 'Empedocles on Etna' I ii 445–7, p. 173 above).
                    turbid
17. *turbid*] troubled *MS.*
19. Not strictly accurate. It is not in the ebb and flow of the waves, but in the sight of the full tide that A. finds his thought. But he then connects the imagined roar of the ebbing tide of faith with the actual sound of the waves carried up to him from the beach.
20. *this distant northern sea*] A. remembered this phrase in composing 'Stanzas from the Grande Chartreuse' 80–2 (p. 288 below),
  9*

The Sea of Faith
Was once, too, at the full, and round earth's shore
Lay like the folds of a bright girdle furled.
But now I only hear
25   Its melancholy, long, withdrawing roar,
Retreating, to the breath
Of the night-wind, down the vast edges drear
And naked shingles of the world.

Ah, love, let us be true
30   To one another! for the world, which seems
To lie before us like a land of dreams,
So various, so beautiful, so new,
Hath really neither joy, nor love, nor light,
Nor certitude, nor peace, nor help for pain;

> But as, on some far northern strand,
> Thinking of his own Gods, a Greek
> In pity and mournful awe might stand . . .

The Greek's musings over two dead faiths have the same elegiac tone as A.'s reflections at Dover.

21–5. Cp. 'Obermann Once More' 189–90 (p. 527 below),

> But slow that tide of common thought,
> Which bathed our life, retired . . .

girdle
23. girdle] garment MS. The sense of this, the one dubiously 'poetical' line in the poem, is not clear. Perhaps the girdle is meant to be visualized as a sash broad enough and soft enough to allow the appearance of parallel wrinkles, i.e. the successive waves.

24–8. Probably the most musically expressive passage in all A.'s poetry and a valid poetic equivalent for his feelings of loss, exposure and dismay.

I
24. I] We MS.
27. vast edges drear] See *n.* to l. 13 above.
29–34. The beauty of the moonlit scene, lingeringly recognized in l. 32, is a deceptive enchantment if it leads us to suppose that the universe is anything but indifferent to man. Cp. the lovers in 'The Youth of Man' 28–31 (pp. 251–2 below),

> Fools that these mystics are
> Who prate of Nature! for she
> Hath neither beauty, nor warmth,
> Nor life, nor emotion, nor power.

The lovers learn their mistake, but the two sets of assertions are not strictly parallel: in 'Dover Beach' the beauty of nature is fully recognized.

35 And we are here as on a darkling plain
Swept with confused alarms of struggle and flight,
Where ignorant armies clash by night.

35-7. A.'s source is Thucydides' description of the Battle of Epipolae (413 B.C.), *History of the Peloponnesian War* vii ch. 44, 'The Athenians were getting into a state of . . . great confusion and perplexity . . . in a battle by night . . . how could anyone know anything clearly? For though there was a bright moon, they could only see one another, as it is natural to do in moonlight – seeing before them the vision of a person but mistrusting their recognition of their own friends . . . the two sides were difficult to distinguish by reason of the outcries . . . the Athenians were trying to find their own comrades, and regarded as hostile what came from the opposite direction, even though it might be a party of friends belonging to the troops already in flight . . . And so finally, when once they had been thrown into confusion, coming into collision with their own comrades in many different parts of the army . . . they not only became panic-stricken but came to blows with one another . . .' (Loeb translation). A. probably knew this passage at Rugby (Dr. A. translated Thucydides' *History* in 3 vols., 1830–5), but the image of the 'night-battle' was a natural one to anyone who had read 'Greats' at Oxford. A. would have recognized Clough's use of it in *The Bothie of Toper-na-Fuosich* (1848) ix 51–4, but his own adoption of it is more likely to have been influenced by Newman's sermon of 6 Jan. 1839, *University Sermons* (1843) 193, 'Controversy, at least in this age, does not lie between the hosts of heaven, Michael and his angels on the one side, and the powers of evil on the other; but it is a sort of night battle, where each fights for himself, and friend and foe stand together.'

60 Stanzas in Memory of Edward Quillinan

Dated 27 Dec. 1851 in A.'s autograph in Rotha Quillinan's album (Wordsworth Museum, Grasmere). Edward Quillinan (1791–1851), minor poet and translator of Camoens, settled near Wordsworth in 1821 and married as his second wife Wordsworth's daughter Dora in 1841. It was at his house that A. met Charlotte Brontë with Harriet Martineau – see 'Haworth Churchyard' 4–8 (p. 390 below). The poem aims at a Wordsworthian simplicity of manner.
Published *1853*; reprinted (*1854, 1857*), *1869*, etc.

¶ 60. *Title.* Stanzas in Memory of the late Edward Quillinan, Esq. *1853–1869*.

I saw him sensitive in frame,
  I knew his spirits low;
And wished him health, success, and fame –
  I do not wish it now.

5   For these are all their own reward,
  And leave no good behind;
They try us, oftenest make us hard,
  Less modest, pure, and kind.

Alas! yet to the suffering man,
10   In this his mortal state,
Friends could not give what fortune can –
  Health, ease, a heart elate.

But he is now by fortune foiled
  No more; and we retain
15   The memory of a man unspoiled,
  Sweet, generous, and humane –

With all the fortunate have not,
  With gentle voice and brow.
– Alive, we would have changed his lot,
20   We would not change it now.

2. Dora's death in 1847 was a severe blow to her father and her husband.
For a while afterwards Wordsworth, who had not wanted Dora to marry,
could not bring himself to meet his son-in-law.
6. *good*] trace *R.Q.'s Album.*
10. *mortal*] living *R.Q.'s Album.*
15. *memory*] image *R.Q.'s Album.*

61 The Youth of Nature

Written between June 1850–Jan. 1852: Wordsworth died April 1850
and the 'pure June-night' (l. 6) must refer to 1850 since A. visited the Lake
District in the summer of this year but not in the summer of 1851, the year
of his marriage – see his letter to Wyndham Slade 15 Sept. 1852, 'Do you
remember sleeping at this little inn at the end of Wastwater two years
ago . . . ? I have just been looking at your name and mine written in the
Fremdenbuch in my hand' (*L* i 21); the entry under 4 Jan. in A.'s unpublished 1852 diary describes the poem's completion, '. . . windy bright day
– walked alone along Rydal and Grasmere during afternoon service.
finished Wordsworth's pindaric'. The term 'pindaric', also used of 'The
Youth of Man' (see headn., p. 250 below), is here applied by A. to a 'free'

unrhymed lyric made up of any number of verse-paragraphs, each paragraph having an unfixed number of lines. (In 'The Youth of Nature', 'The Youth of Man' and 'The Future', the only unrhymed lyrics of this type in *1852*, the line itself normally contains three stresses, but the number of syllables in a normal line varies between six and nine. A further variation is that lines with fewer or more than three stresses occur irregularly – most frequently in 'The Future', perhaps the last of the three pieces to be composed.) 'The Youth of Nature' and 'The Youth of Man' may be indicated by the entry 'world-religion stanzas' on a list of poems, undated but (?) 1851, found in the back of the second volume of A.'s copy of *Briefwechsel zwischen Schiller und Goethe* (Stuttgart and Tübingen, 1828) – for this list, 'a tentative table of contents' for *1852*, see *Commentary* 16–17; both poems celebrate Nature as a 'Power' in a way that may indicate a recent reading of *The Prelude* (1850), and both repudiate the Coleridgean view that '. . . in our life alone does Nature live'.

Published *1852*; reprinted *1855*, *1869*, etc.

> Raised are the dripping oars,
> Silent the boat! the lake,
> Lovely and soft as a dream,
> Swims in the sheen of the moon.
> The mountains stand at its head
> Clear in the pure June-night,
> But the valleys are flooded with haze.

5

¶ 61. *1–2.* A graceful allusion to Wordsworth's 'Remembrance of Collins' 17–18, 21–2,

> *Now let us, as we float along,*
> *For him suspend the dashing oar* . . .

> *How calm! how still! the only sound*
> *The dripping of the oar suspended!*

Wordsworth was alluding in his turn to Collins's 'Ode on the death of Mr. Thomson' 15–16,

> *And oft suspend the dashing Oar*
> *To bid his gentle Spirit rest!*

See W. E. Bezanson's 'Melville's Reading of Arnold's Poetry', *PMLA* lxix (1954) 378–9 for Melville's noting of these quotations in his copy of A.'s *Poems* (Boston, 1856) and his comment, 'How beautifully appropriate therefore this reminiscent prelude of Arnold concerning Wordsworth.'
2–9. The reference to Wordsworth, who is buried in the churchyard at Grasmere, suggests that his death was still recent. A.'s boat is out on the lake. If he looks in the direction of Ambleside, haze hides Rydal Water, but Fairfield rises on the left. A. was used to looking across at Fairfield from his home at Fox How.

Rydal and Fairfield are there;
In the shadow Wordsworth lies dead.
10   So it is, so it will be for aye.
Nature is fresh as of old,
Is lovely; a mortal is dead.

The spots which recall him survive,
For he lent a new life to these hills.
15   The Pillar still broods o'er the fields
Which border Ennerdale Lake,
And Egremont sleeps by the sea.
The gleam of The Evening Star
Twinkles on Grasmere no more,
20   But ruined and solemn and grey
The sheepfold of Michael survives;
And, far to the south, the heath
Still blows in the Quantock coombs,
By the favourite waters of Ruth.
25   These survive! – yet not without pain,
Pain and dejection to-night,
Can I feel that their poet is gone.

He grew old in an age he condemned.
He looked on the rushing decay
30   Of the times which had sheltered his youth;

15–17. The Pillar and Egremont are mentioned in Wordsworth's poem 'The Brothers' (1800). Egremont is a small town through which the river from Ennerdale Lake flows to the sea. For the Pillar see 'The Brothers' 366–8,

> *And in the midst is one particular rock*
> *That rises like a column from the vale,*
> *Whence by our shepherds it is called* THE PILLAR.

18. The Evening Star] The shepherd's cottage 'upon the forest-side in Grasmere Vale' in Wordsworth's poem 'Michael' (1800). See ll. 136–9,

> *And from this constant light, so regular,*
> *And so far seen, the House itself, by all*
> *Who dwelt within the limits of the vale,*
> *Both old and young, was named* THE EVENING STAR.

22–4. See Wordsworth's poem 'Ruth' (1800). Ruth lived on 'the Banks of Tone' (l. 214).
28–35. Wordsworth disapproved of the first Reform Act (1832) and in later years became an eccentric high Tory in his views, often clashing in argument with such Whig friends as Dr. Arnold and Crabb Robinson. He outlived all the other Romantic poets.

Felt the dissolving throes
Of a social order he loved;
Outlived his brethren, his peers,
And, like the Theban seer,
35   Died in his enemies' day.

Cold bubbled the spring of Tilphusa,
Copais lay bright in the moon,
Helicon glassed in the lake
Its firs, and afar rose the peaks
40   Of Parnassus, snowily clear;
Thebes was behind him in flames,
And the clang of arms in his ear,
When his awe-struck captors led
The Theban seer to the spring.
45   Tiresias drank and died.
Nor did reviving Thebes
See such a prophet again.

Well may we mourn, when the head
Of a sacred poet lies low
50   In an age which can rear them no more!
The complaining millions of men
Darken in labour and pain;
But he was a priest to us all
Of the wonder and bloom of the world,
55   Which we saw with his eyes, and were glad.
He is dead, and the fruit-bearing day
Of his race is past on the earth;
And darkness returns to our eyes.

36. *spring of Tilphusa*] Near Thebes.

41–5. After the Theban defeat in the war with the Epigoni Tiresias fled with the Thebans but was captured by his enemies. These lines give one account of his death. For another, see 'Fragment of an "Antigone"' 80–9 (p. 63 above).

53–5. Cp. A.'s praise of Wordsworth in 'Memorial Verses' 45–50 (p. 228 above).

54. *bloom*] A word that carries a high emotional charge for A. by its suggestion of an ephemeral delicacy and freshness. Cp. 'The Youth of Man' 40–2 (p. 252 below),

                 ... Time
      With the ceaseless stroke of his wings
      Brushed off the bloom from their soul ...

but the word is also used in 'Tristram and Iseult', 'Sohrab and Rustum', 'The Scholar-Gipsy', 'Thyrsis', 'Obermann Once More' and 'Growing Old'. See *Parrish* 79–80.

For, oh! is it you, is it you,
60   Moonlight, and shadow, and lake,
        And mountains, that fill us with joy,
        Or the poet who sings you so well?
        Is it you, O beauty, O grace,
        O charm, O romance, that we feel,
65   Or the voice which reveals what you are?
        Are ye, like daylight and sun,
        Shared and rejoiced in by all?
        Or are ye immersed in the mass
        Of matter, and hard to extract,
70   Or sunk at the core of the world
        Too deep for the most to discern?
        Like stars in the deep of the sky,
        Which arise on the glass of the sage,
        But are lost when their watcher is gone.

75   'They are here' – I heard, as men heard
        In Mysian Ida the voice
        Of the Mighty Mother, or Crete,
        The murmur of Nature reply –
        'Loveliness, magic, and grace,
80   They are here! they are set in the world,
        They abide; and the finest of souls
        Hath not been thrilled by them all,
        Nor the dullest been dead to them quite.
        The poet who sings them may die,
85   But they are immortal and live,
        For they are the life of the world.
        Will ye not learn it, and know,

59–74. A.'s question is whether he would experience the beauty of nature if a great poet had not revealed it to him (he is not asking here whether man 'invests' the world with beauty, as the rash young lovers assert in 'The Youth of Man' 26–37, pp. 251–2 below). Beauty is in some sense 'set in the world' as the stars are there even if, without a telescope, we cannot see them. Nature's reply to his question is (ll. 79–86) that the beauty in nature is experienced directly by all but in very different degrees, and that not even the greatest poet has appreciated it in full; and (ll. 103–6) that our knowledge and appreciation of nature depend on the extent to which we really know ourselves (i.e. the 'buried self').

76–7. Ida is both a mountain range in Mysia connected with the worship of Cybele (*Idaea Mater*) and a mountain in Crete where Rhea hid the infant Zeus to save him from Cronos. Rhea was identified by the Greeks of Asia Minor with the Asiatic 'Magna Mater'.

                When ye mourn that a poet is dead,
                That the singer was less than his themes,
90   Life, and emotion, and I?

                'More than the singer are these.
                Weak is the tremor of pain
                That thrills in his mournfullest chord
                To that which once ran through his soul.
95   Cold the elation of joy
                In his gladdest, airiest song,
                To that which of old in his youth
                Filled him and made him divine.
                Hardly his voice at its best
100   Gives us a sense of the awe,
                The vastness, the grandeur, the gloom
                Of the unlit gulph of himself.

                'Ye know not yourselves; and your bards –
                The clearest, the best, who have read
105   Most in themselves – have beheld
                Less than they left unrevealed.
                Ye express not yourselves; can you make
                With marble, with colour, with word,
                What charmed you in others re-live?
110   Can thy pencil, O artist! restore
                The figure, the bloom of thy love,
                As she was in her morning of spring?

92–8 Cp. Shelley, 'A Defence of Poetry' in *Peacock's Four Ages of Poetry*
. . . ed. H. F. B. Brett-Smith (Percy Reprints 3, 1921) 53–4, '. . . the mind
in creation is as a fading coal, which some invisible influence . . . awakens
to transitory brightness . . . but when composition begins, inspiration is
already on the decline, and the most glorious poetry that has ever been
communicated to the world is probably a feeble shadow of the original
conceptions of the poet . . .'
102. unlit gulph of himself] Cp. 'The Buried Life' 73 (p. 274 below),

                From the soul's subterranean depth . . .

and Victor Hugo's 'Tristesse d'Olympio' 129–21,

                Elle [*notre âme*] arrive à pas lents par une obscure rampe
                Jusqu'au fond désolé du gouffre intérieur;
                Et là, dans cette nuit qu'aucun rayon n'étoile . . .

Hugo's poem is from *Les Rayons et les Ombres* (1840).
110–14. A. is remembering Marguerite and his own 'A Memory-Picture'
(p. 107 above).

Canst thou paint the ineffable smile
Of her eyes as they rested on thine?
115   Can the image of life have the glow,
The motion of life itself?

'Yourselves and your fellows ye know not; and me,
The mateless, the one, will ye know?
Will ye scan me, and read me, and tell
120   Of the thoughts that ferment in my breast,
My longing, my sadness, my joy?
Will ye claim for your great ones the gift
To have rendered the gleam of my skies,
To have echoed the moan of my seas,
125   Uttered the voice of my hills?
When your great ones depart, will ye say:
All things have suffered a loss,
Nature is hid in their grave?

'Race after race, man after man,
130   Have thought that my secret was theirs,
Have dreamed that I lived but for them,
That they were my glory and joy.
– They are dust, they are changed, they are gone!
I remain.'

115–16. Nature expects the answer 'No', but see 'Epilogue to Lessing's
Laocoön' 129–52 (p. 513 below) where A. maintains that the poet, unlike
the painter or musician, 'must life's *movement* tell' (l. 140).
133–4. Perhaps a reminiscence of Shelley, 'Adonais' 460,

The One remains, the many change and pass . . .

Nature is 'the mateless, the one' above in l. 118.

62 The Youth of Man

Written between Jan.–Sept. 1852. The poem appears as 'Pindaric "sink
o youth in thy soul"' at the back of A.'s 1852 diary (*Note-books* 552) and
is a sequel to 'The Youth of Nature', which was completed 4 Jan. 1852 –
see headn. (p. 244 above) for this date and a comment on the form of both
poems.
Published *1852*; reprinted *1855*, *1869*, etc.

We, O Nature, depart,
Thou survivest us! this,
This, I know, is the law.
Yes! but more than this,
5 Thou who seest us die
Seest us change while we live;
Seest our dreams, one by one,
Seest our errors depart;
Watchest us, Nature! throughout,
10 Mild and inscrutably calm.

Well for us that we change!
Well for us that the power
Which in our morning-prime
Saw the mistakes of our youth,
15 Sweet, and forgiving, and good,
Sees the contrition of age!

Behold, O Nature, this pair!
See them to-night where they stand,
Not with the halo of youth
20 Crowning their brows with its light,
Not with the sunshine of hope,
Not with the rapture of spring,
Which they had of old, when they stood
Years ago at my side
25 In this self-same garden, and said:
'We are young and the world is ours;
Man, man is the king of the world!
Fools that these mystics are
Who prate of Nature! for she

¶ 62. *27.* Pausanias is warned against this view by Empedocles – see
'Empedocles on Etna' I ii 177–81 (p. 164 above),

> *We mortals are no kings*
> *For each of whom to sway*
> *A new-made world up-springs,*
> *Meant merely for his play;*
> *No, we are strangers here; the world is from of old.*

29–31. Cp. 'Dover Beach' 30–4 (p. 242 above),

> *...for the world, which seems*
> *To lie before us like a land of dreams,*
> *So various, so beautiful, so new,*
> *Hath really neither joy, nor love, nor light,*
> *No certitude, nor peace, nor help for pain ...*

30   Hath neither beauty, nor warmth,
      Nor life, nor emotion, nor power.
      But man has a thousand gifts,
      And the generous dreamer invests
      The senseless world with them all.
35   Nature is nothing; her charm
      Lives in our eyes which can paint,
      Lives in our hearts which can feel.'

      Thou, O Nature, wast mute,
      Mute as of old! days flew,
40   Days and years; and Time
      With the ceaseless stroke of his wings
      Brushed off the bloom from their soul.
      Clouded and dim grew their eye,
      Languid their heart – for youth
45   Quickened its pulses no more.
      Slowly, within the walls
      Of an ever-narrowing world,
      They drooped, they grew blind, they grew old.
      Thee and their youth in thee,
50   Nature! they saw no more.

      Murmur of living,
      Stir of existence,
      Soul of the world!
      Make, oh, make yourselves felt
55   To the dying spirit of youth!
      Come, like the breath of the spring!
      Leave not a human soul

32–7. A. is perhaps recalling Coleridge's 'Dejection' 47–54,

> *O Lady! we receive but what we give,*
> *And in our life alone does Nature live:*
> *Ours is her wedding garment, ours her shroud!*
>   *And would we aught behold, of higher worth,*
> *Than that inanimate cold world allowed,*
> *To the poor loveless ever-anxious crowd,*
>   *Ah! from the soul itself must issue forth*
> *A light, a glory, a fair luminous cloud . . .*

51–60. Reprinted separately as 'Richmond Hill' *1853*. Richmond Hill is close to Hampton-on-Thames, where A. often stayed in his father-in-law's house after his marriage. Complaints about the passing of youth are found in several of A.'s letters 1851–2 – see *n.* to 'Empedocles on Etna' I ii 362–6 (p. 170 above).

To grow old in darkness and pain!
Only the living can feel you,
60   But leave us not while we live!

Here they stand to-night –
Here, where this grey balustrade
Crowns the still valley; behind
Is the castled house, with its woods,
65   Which sheltered their childhood – the sun
On its ivied windows; a scent
From the grey-walled gardens, a breath
Of the fragrant stock and the pink,
Perfumes the evening air.
70   Their children play on the lawns.
They stand and listen; they hear
The children's shouts, and at times,
Faintly, the bark of a dog
From a distant farm in the hills.
75   Nothing besides! in front
The wide, wide valley outspreads
To the dim horizon, reposed
In the twilight, and bathed in dew,
Corn-field and hamlet and copse
80   Darkening fast; but a light,
Far off, a glory of day,
Still plays on the city spires;
And there in the dusk by the walls,
With the grey mist marking its course
85   Through the silent, flowery land,
On, to the plains, to the sea,
Floats the imperial stream.

Well I know what they feel!
They gaze, and the evening wind
90   Plays on their faces; they gaze –
Airs from the Eden of youth
Awake and stir in their soul;
The past returns – they feel
What they are, alas! what they were.
95   They, not Nature, are changed.
Well I know what they feel!

58. See 'The Youth of Nature' 51–2 (p. 247 above),
      The complaining millions of men
      Darken in labour and pain . . .

Hush, for tears
Begin to steal to their eyes!
Hush, for fruit
100   Grows from such sorrow as theirs!

And they remember,
With piercing, untold anguish,
The proud boasting of their youth.
And they feel how Nature was fair.
105   And the mists of delusion,
And the scales of habit,
Fall away from their eyes;
And they see, for a moment,
Stretching out, like the desert,
110   In its weary, unprofitable length,
Their faded, ignoble lives.

While the locks are yet brown on thy head,
While the soul still looks through thine eyes,
While the heart still pours
115   The mantling blood to thy cheek,
Sink, O youth, in thy soul!
Yearn to the greatness of Nature;
Rally the good in the depths of thyself!

112–18. Reprinted separately as 'Power of Youth' *1853.*
116–18. Cp. 'Empedocles on Etna' I ii 146 (p. 162 above),

   Sink in thyself! there ask what ails thee, at that shrine!

For A.'s Stoic notion of the 'buried self' see *n.* to 'Empedocles on Etna'
I ii 129–30 (p. 161 above); the 'depths of thyself' recalls the 'unlit gulph'
of 'The Youth of Nature' 102 (p. 249 above).

63 Lines written in Kensington Gardens

Date of composition unknown, but clearly 1849–52 and probably Spring
1852: for a similar invocation of Nature in connection with fears of having
missed 'life' (ll. 37–44) see 'The Youth of Man' (p. 250 above), which
belongs to 1852. The untitled and undated first draft of the poem in the
Yale MS. is reproduced *Commentary* 196–8, but its variant readings are
not included in *1950*. In A.'s final text the stanzas of the MS. appear in this
order: 1, 8, 3, 4, 5, 7, 12, 6, 9, 10, 11 (2 omitted). Published *1852*; reprinted *1867 (1868)*, *1869*, etc.

In this lone, open glade I lie,
Screened by deep boughs on either hand;
And at its end, to stay the eye,
Those black-crowned, red-boled pine-trees stand!

5   Birds here make song, each bird has his,
Across the girdling city's hum.
How green under the boughs it is!
How thick the tremulous sheep-cries come!

Sometimes a child will cross the glade
10   To take his nurse his broken toy;
Sometimes a thrush flit overhead
Deep in her unknown day's employ.

Here at my feet what wonders pass,
What endless, active life is here!

¶ 63. *2. deep boughs*] dark trees *MS., 1852.*
3. at its end] at its head *MS., 1852–68*; Where ends the glade *1869*.
4. black-crowned] dark-topp'd *MS.*, black-topp'd *1852*. After l. 4 the following stanza in *MS.* and *1852*:

> *The clouded sky is still and grey,*
> *Through silken rifts soft peers [winks MS.] the sun.*
> *Light the green-foliag'd [clear foliaged MS.] chestnuts play,*
> *The darker [massier MS.] elms stand grave and dun.*

5. MS., 1852,
> *The birds sing sweetly in these [their MS.] trees...*
7. The Yale MS. has 'between the stems' as an alternative reading to 'under the boughs'. For 'stems' meaning 'branches' see also 'Tristram and Iseult' iii 185–6 (p. 223 above),

> *They came to where the brushwood ceased, and day*
> *Peered 'twixt the stems ...*

9–11 MS.,
> *That child who darts across the glade*
> *Drags to his nurse his broken toy:*
> *The brown thrush crosses overhead ...*

13–16 MS.,
> *Here where I lie what marvels pass*
>   *active*
> *What swarming endless life is here:*
> *Buttercups, clover, daisies, grass,*
> *An air-stirr'd forest, fresh and clear.*

A. is echoing Werther's description of 'the swarming little world among the [grass-] stalks (*das Wimmeln der Kleinen Welt zwischen Halmen*)' in his

15   What blowing daisies, fragrant grass!
                An air-stirred forest, fresh and clear.

                Scarce fresher is the mountain-sod
                Where the tired angler lies, stretched out,
                And, eased of basket and of rod,
20   Counts his day's spoil, the spotted trout.

                In the huge world, which roars hard by,
                Be others happy if they can!
                But in my helpless cradle I
                Was breathed on by the rural Pan.

25   I, on men's impious uproar hurled,
                Think often, as I hear them rave,
                That peace has left the upper world
                And now keeps only in the grave.

                Yet here is peace for ever new!
30   When I who watch them am away,
                Still all things in this glade go through
                The changes of their quiet day.

                Then to their happy rest they pass!
                The flowers upclose, the birds are fed,

---

letter of 10 May 1771 – see Goethe's *Die Leiden des jungen Werther* (1774),
Werke (Cotta: Stuttgart and Tübingen) xvi (1828) 8. As he lies on the grass
Werther, like A., feels the presence of the 'Calm soul of all things'.

17. *Scarce fresher*] Not fresher *MS.*
18. *tired*] lone *MS.*
21–4. First inserted in the printed text in *1867*. In the Yale MS. this stanza
is written at the side of the page.
21. *MS.,*

                quick
        In the huge world that rumbles nigh
With the *1852* reading cp. 'Thyrsis' 234 (p. 508 below),

      – *Then through the great town's harsh, heart-wearying roar* . . .

24. *breathed*] looked *MS.*
25. *uproar*] tumult *MS.*
           sadly
26. *often*] sometimes *MS., 1852.*
28. *keeps*] dwells *MS.*
29. The Yale MS. has the reading of the text above

        But here this calm is nothing new . . .

32. *changes*] stages *MS.*
34. *upclose*] close *MS., 1852–67.*

35   The night comes down upon the grass,
            The child sleeps warmly in his bed.

            Calm soul of all things! make it mine
            To feel, amid the city's jar,
            That there abides a peace of thine,
40   Man did not make, and cannot mar.

                   sweetly
36. warmly] warmly *MS*. After l. 36 the Yale *MS.* has the following prose
argument: 'every day all these appear, live, go thro: their stages whether
I see them or no. I, in an unnatural state of effort and personal wrapped-
upedness, do not see them'.
37–44. With this Spinozist prayer to Nature (*Deus, sive Natura*) cp. 'The
Youth of Man' 51–60 (pp. 252–3 above) and especially 51–5, 59–60,

> *Murmur of living,*
> *Stir of existence,*
> *Soul of the World!*
> *Make, oh, make yourselves felt*
> *To the dying spirit of youth!*
>
> *Only the living can feel you,*
> *But leave us not while we live!*

As in other *1852* poems A. is in two minds. He wishes to be calm, but not
with the calm of nature (or he would hardly ask for the power to sympa-
thize with others). He wants feeling without agitation, calm without indifference, but in 'Youth's Agitations' (p. 145 above) he suspects that he
will be just as discontented with the calm in prospect as he is with the
disturbance of 'youth's hurrying fever'. And after the 'renunciation' of
1849 and the effort at self-mastery he is left knowing that he is growing
older and wondering whether life may not have passed him by.
37. Calm soul of all things] The *anima mundi* or *Weltseele* of ancient and
modern speculation (with much of which A. became familiar 1845–7 – see
my 'Three Early Diaries', *Vict. Stud.* ii (1959) 254–66, illustrating his
reading of Plato, Cudworth, Berkeley's *Siris*, Schelling, Creuzer, etc.). But
the idea is a commonplace in Pre-Romantic and Romantic nature poetry,
e.g. Wordsworth, *The Excursion* ix 1, 3–5, 13–15,

> *To every Form of being is assigned . . .*
>
> *An* active *Principle, howe'er removed*
> *From sense and observation, it subsists*
> *In all things . . .*
>
> *Spirit that knows no insulated spot,*
> *No chasm, no solitude; from link to link*
> *It circulates, the Soul of all the worlds.*

> The will to neither strive nor cry,
> The power to feel with others give!
> Calm, calm me more! nor let me die
> Before I have begun to live.

In the Yale MS. above this phrase is the abortive beginning, 'Spirit who must be here'.

39. abides] subsists *MS*. Cp. 'Resignation' 191–2 (p. 91 above),

> *That general life, which does not cease,*
> *Whose secret is not joy, but peace . . .*

43–4. The literal meaning of 'die' is present, but A. is thinking chiefly of 'the dying spirit of youth' and the loss of the ability to feel intensely – see *n.* to ll. 37–44 above and A.'s letter to Clough 19 Dec. 1851, 'But be bustling about it; we are growing old, and advancing towards the device-less darkness: it would be well not to reach it till we had at least tried *some* of the things men consider desirable' (*CL* 118). Cp. also 'Early Death and Fame' 16–17 (p. 398 below),

> *Give him emotion, though pain!*
> *Let him live, let him feel: I have lived.*

A.'s phrasing was suggested either by Senancour's description of the gravitation towards conventional life as youth dies – see *Obermann* (Lettre vii) i 44 *fn.*, 'Vous chercherez des délassemens; vous vous mettrez à table . . . Vous trouverez une sorte de mollesse dans votre ennui même, et vous passerez en oubliant que vous n'avez pas vécu . . .'; or directly by Rousseau, *Les Rêveries du Promeneur Solitaire* (1782) ed. M. Raymond (Geneva, 1948) 21, 'Je me disais en soupirant: qu'ai-je fait ici-bas. J'étais fait pour vivre, et je meurs sans avoir vécu.' A. entered this Rousseau quotation from the Seconde Promenade in his General Notebook No. 1 (*Note-books* 463).

64 Morality

Date of composition unknown, but (?) 1852 when A. was a married man working in disagreeable conditions as a school-inspector. His former admiration for the calm and detachment of nature – see 'Quiet Work' and 'Self-Dependence' (pp. 106 and 142 above) – has given place to admiration for man's efforts: as if the rigour of his new life demanded as compensation the discovery of a moral significance in the fact of struggle. Cp. A.'s letters to Clough 7 June 1852, 'I am sometimes in bad spirits . . . Still nothing can absolve us from the duty of doing all we can to keep alive our courage and activity'; and 28 Oct. 1852, 'I am not very well or in very good spirits, but I subsist . . . And after all there is so much to be done, if

one could but do it . . .' (*CL* 123, 124–5). The distance between A.'s two
attitudes suggests the violence done to his poetic self between 1849 and
1851 when he 'took refuge' in his 'morality and character' (for these expressions see his letter to his sister 'K' 25 Jan. 1851, *L* i 14).
Published *1852*; reprinted *1853* (*1854, 1857*), *1869*, etc.

> We cannot kindle when we will
> The fire which in the heart resides;
> The spirit bloweth and is still,
> In mystery our soul abides.
5   But tasks in hours of insight willed
>   Can be through hours of gloom fulfilled.
>
> With aching hands and bleeding feet
> We dig and heap, lay stone on stone;
> We bear the burden and the heat
10   Of the long day, and wish 'twere done.
>   Not till the hours of light return,
>   All we have built do we discern.
>
> Then, when the clouds are off the soul,
> When thou dost bask in Nature's eye,
15   Ask, how *she* viewed thy self-control,
>   Thy struggling, tasked morality –
>   Nature, whose free, light, cheerful air,
>   Oft made thee, in thy gloom, despair.

¶ 64. *3*. Cp. *John* iii 8, 'The wind bloweth where it listeth, and thou
hearest the sound thereof, but canst not tell whence it cometh, and whither
it goeth: so is every one that is born of the Spirit.'
9–10. An allusion to the Parable of the Labourers in the Vineyard, *Matthew*
xx 12, 'These last have wrought but one hour, and thou has made them
equal unto us, which have borne the burden and heat of the day.'
11. hours of light] The 'hours of insight' of l. 5, but A.'s failure to realize
the full meaning of his words suggests that those who have endured 'the
burden and the heat / Of the long day' have been working in darkness.
13. See A.'s letter to Clough 14 Dec. 1852, '. . . I doubt whether I shall ever
have heat and radiance enough to pierce the clouds that are massed round
me. Not in my little social sphere . . . but vis à vis of the world' (*CL* 126);
and also 'Memorial Verses' 68–70 (p. 229 above),

> *The cloud of mortal destiny,*
> *Others will front it fearlessly –*
> *But who, like him, will put it by?*

And she, whose censure thou dost dread,
20   Whose eye thou wast afraid to seek,
See, on her face a glow is spread,
A strong emotion on her cheek!
    'Ah, child!' she cries, 'that strife divine,
    Whence was it, for it is not mine?

25   'There is no effort on *my* brow –
I do not strive, I do not weep;
I rush with the swift spheres and glow
In joy, and when I will, I sleep.
        Yet that severe, that earnest air,
30   I saw, I felt it once – but where?

    'I knew not yet the gauge of time,   *By lote?*
Nor wore the manacles of space;
I felt it in some other clime,
I saw it in some other place.
35   'Twas when the heavenly house I trod,
And lay upon the breast of God.'

25–8. Cp. 'Quiet Work' 1–8 and 'Self-Dependence' 17–28 (pp. 106 and
143 above).
31–2. A reference to Kant's teaching that time and space are the formal
characters of sense-perception, but see *n.* to 'Empedocles on Etna' II [i]
354 (p. 189 above).

65 Progress

Date of composition unknown, but (?) 1852 from the new note of impatience – characteristic of all A.'s writing on religious subjects in the
1860s and 1870s – with liberal ideas in religion applied, in his opinion,
negatively and destructively; the poem represents 'the advanced thought
of 1852, particularly that of Renan, which aspired to keep the spirit of
Christianity without the specific articles of its creeds' (*Commentary* 191).
For A.'s attitude in the early 1850s see his letter to Clough 6 Sept. 1853,
'I would have others – most others stick to the old religious dogmas because I sincerely believe that this *warmth* is the great blessing, and this
frigidity the great curse – and on the old religious road they have still the
best chance of getting the one and avoiding the other' (*CL* 143); and the
undated (but probably earlier) note in the Yale MS., quoted in *n.* to ll. 31–2
below. There is no particular debt to Renan, but A.'s ideas may have been
influenced by Edgar Quinet's *Le Génie des Religions* (1842), which he seems

to have read while composing 'Empedocles on Etna' (see *n.* to I ii 57–76, p. 158 above). A.'s acquaintance with Quinet's writings at this time is proved by the use of another essay as the source for 'The Church of Brou' (p. 294 below).

Published *1852*; reprinted *1867* (*1868*), *1869*, etc.

> The Master stood upon the mount, and taught.
> He saw a fire in his disciples' eyes;
> 'The old law,' they cried, 'is wholly come to nought,
>   Behold the new world rise!'
>
> 5 'Was it,' the Lord then said, 'with scorn ye saw
> The old law observed by Scribes and Pharisees?
> I say unto you, see *ye* keep that law
>   More faithfully than these!
>
> 'Too hasty heads for ordering worlds, alas!
> 10 Think not that I to annul the law have willed;
> No jot, no tittle from the law shall pass,
>   Till all have been fulfilled.'
>
> So Christ said eighteen hundred years ago.
> And what then shall be said to those to-day,
> 15 Who cry aloud to lay the old world low
>   To clear the new world's way?
>
> 'Religious fervours! ardour misapplied!
> Hence, hence,' they cry, 'ye do but keep man blind!
> But keep him self-immersed, preoccupied,
> 20   And lame the active mind!'
>
> Ah! from the old world let some one answer give:
> 'Scorn ye this world, their tears, their inward cares?
> I say unto you, see that *your* souls live
>   A deeper life than theirs!'

¶ 65. *1–12*. See the Sermon on the Mount, *Matthew* v and especially 1–2, 17–18, 20, 'And seeing the multitudes, he went up into a mountain: and when he was set, his disciples came unto him: And he opened his mouth, and taught them . . . Think not that I am come to destroy the law, or the prophets: I am not come to destroy, but to fulfil. For verily I say unto you, Till heaven and earth pass, one jot or tittle shall in no wise pass from the law, till all be fulfilled . . . For I say unto you, That except your righteousness shall exceed the righteousness of the scribes and Pharisees, ye shall in no case enter into the kingdom of heaven.'

25   'Say ye: "The spirit of man has found new roads,
         And we must leave the old faiths, and walk there-
                 in"?
         Leave then the Cross as ye have left carved gods,
                 But guard the fire within!

         'Bright else and fast the stream of life may roll,
30   And no man may the other's hurt behold;
         Yet each will have one anguish – his own soul
                 Which perishes of cold.'

         Here let that voice make end; then, let a strain,
         From a far lonelier distance, like the wind
35   Be heard, floating through heaven, and fill again
                 These men's profoundest mind:

         'Children of men! the unseen Power, whose eye
         For ever doth accompany mankind,
         Hath looked on no religion scornfully
40   That men did ever find.

27-8. 1852,
               Quench then the altar fires of your old Gods!
                   Quench not the fire within!

31-2. See A.'s letter to Clough 6 Sept. 1853 (quoted in headn. above) and
note in Yale MS., 'I cannot conceal from myself the objection which really
wounds and perplexes me from the religious side is that the service of
reason is freezing to feeling, chilling to the religious mood. And feeling
and the religious mood are eternally the deepest being of man, the ground
of all joy and greatness for him.'

38-40. 1852,
               Ever accompanies the march of man,
               Hath without pain seen no religion die,
                   Since first the world began.

A.'s revision removes the 'march of man' cliché and the unintended
implication that the 'unseen Power' grieves over the disappearance of
crude forms of primitive worship. With A.'s whole stanza in its two versions cp. Quinet, *Le Génie des Religions* (1842), *Œuvres Complètes* (Paris,
1857) iii 13, 'Dans ce pèlerinage à travers les cultes du passé, errants d'autel
en autel, nous n'irons pas, infatués de la supériorité moderne, nous railler
de la misère des dieux abandonnés; au contraire, nous demanderons aux
vides sanctuaires s'ils n'ont pas renfermé un écho de la parole de vie . . .'
40. After this line the following extra stanza in *1852*:
               That man must still to some new worship press
               Hath in his eye ever but serv'd to show
               The depth of that consuming restlessness
                   Which makes man's greatest woe.

'Which has not taught weak wills how much they
    can?
Which has not fallen on the dry heart like rain?
Which has not cried to sunk, self-weary man:
    Thou must be born again!

45   'Children of men! not that your age excel
    In pride of life the ages of your sires,
    But that ye think clear, feel deep, bear fruit well,
      The Friend of man desires.'

42 fallen] A monosyllable.
44. See 'Obermann' 143–4 (p. 136 above) and *n.* quoting *John* iii, 3, 7.
47. But that ye think clear, feel deep] But that you too feel deeply *1852.*

66 The Future

Date of composition unknown, but (?) 1852 when A. completed 'The
Youth of Nature' and wrote 'The Youth of Man': see headnn. to both
these poems (pp. 244 and 250 above) for evidence of their dates, and the
headn. to 'The Youth of Nature' for a comment on the metrical form
shared by these three pieces, the only unrhymed lyrics of this type in *1852.*
For the appearance elsewhere in A.'s poetry of the 'river of Time' or
'stream of life' metaphor, which is used in 'The Future' to represent the
whole history of mankind, see the second part of *n.* to ll. 30–63 of 'The
Buried Life' (p. 273 below).
Published *1852*; reprinted *1853 (1854, 1857), 1869,* etc.

A wanderer is man from his birth.
He was born in a ship
On the breast of the river of Time;
Brimming with wonder and joy
5   He spreads out his arms to the light,
Rivets his gaze on the banks of the stream.

As what he sees is, so have his thoughts been.
Whether he wakes,
Where the snowy mountainous pass,

¶ 66. *Title.* Followed by this motto *1853, 1854:*

    For Nature hath long kept this inn, the Earth
    And many a guest hath she therein received –

The lines are A.'s own – see *n.* to 'Empedocles on Etna' I ii 217–20 (p. 165
above) quoting the prose note in the Yale MS. from which the motto
derives.

10   Echoing the screams of the eagles,
           Hems in its gorges the bed
           Of the new-born clear-flowing stream;
           Whether he first sees light
           Where the river in gleaming rings
15   Sluggishly winds through the plain;
           Whether in sound of the swallowing sea –
           As is the world on the banks,
           So is the mind of the man.

               Vainly does each, as he glides,
20   Fable and dream
           Of the lands which the river of Time
           Had left ere he woke on its breast,
           Or shall reach when his eyes have been closed.
           Only the tract where he sails
25   He wots of; only the thoughts,
           Raised by the objects he passes, are his.

           Who can see the green earth any more
           As she was by the sources of Time?
           Who imagines her fields as they lay
30   In the sunshine, unworn by the plough?
           Who thinks as they thought,
           The tribes who then roamed on her breast,
           Her vigorous, primitive sons?

           What girl
35   Now reads in her bosom as clear
           As Rebekah read, when she sate
           At eve by the palm-shaded well?
           Who guards in her breast
           As deep, as pellucid a spring
40   Of feeling, as tranquil, as sure?

36–7. Rebekah met Abraham's servant at the well and, at the wish of her
father and brother, returned with him to marry Abraham's son, Isaac –
see *Genesis* xxiv 1–67, and for the meeting at the well 11, 15, 'And he
made his camels to kneel down without the city by a well of water at the
time of the evening, even the time that women go out to draw water . . .
And it came to pass . . . that, behold, Rebekah came out . . . with her
pitcher upon her shoulder.' There is nothing in the story to justify A.'s
praise of Rebekah except her instant obedience.

                    What bard,
             At the height of his vision, can deem
             Of God, of the world, of the soul,
             With a plainness as near,
    45   As flashing as Moses felt
             When he lay in the night by his flock
             On the starlit Arabian waste?
             Can rise and obey
             The beck of the Spirit like him?

    50   This tract which the river of Time
             Now flows through with us, is the plain.
             Gone is the calm of its earlier shore.

41–9. Moses was keeping the flock of his father-in-law Jethro in the
Midian desert when he saw God in the burning bush (*Exodus* iii 1–6), but
A. is also recalling Carlyle's description of the wonder of the 'first Pagan
Thinker among rude men' in *Heroes and Hero-Worship* (1841), *Works* ed.
H. D. Traill v 7, 9, 'To the wild deep-hearted man all was yet new, not
veiled under names or formulas; it stood naked, flashing-in on him there,
beautiful, awful, unspeakable . . . The world, which is now divine only
to the gifted, was then divine to whosoever would turn his eye upon it.
He stood bare before it face to face . . . Canopus shining-down over the
desert . . . would pierce into the heart of the wild Ishmaelitish man . . .'
Moses is hardly a more fortunate example for A. than Rebekah – he does
not 'rise and obey / The beck of the Spirit' until he has exhausted all his
arguments for delay, and God has become angry and worked two miracles.
50–65. A. is probably remembering part of an unpublished poem by his
father, which may also have come into his mind at the end of 'The Buried
Life' (see *n.* to ll. 97–8, p. 275 below):

                    A straight embankéd Line
             Confines thee, wont to trace at Will erewhile
             Thine own free Margin; and the Haunts of Men
                    Thy spotless Waves defile.

                    Calmly thou flowest now;
             Singing no more, as erst, for mere Delight:
             But louder harsher sounds from Morn till Eve
                    Thy Banks affright.

                    .   .   .   .   .   .

                    Loud is that Din of Sounds,
             Gloomy and close the Dwellings whence they rise; –
             For Life and Freshness to the dreariest scenes
                    Thy Stream Supplies.

10+M.A.

Bordered by cities and hoarse
With a thousand cries is its stream.
55   And we on its breast, our minds
Are confused as the cries which we hear,
Changing and shot as the sights which we see.

And we say that repose has fled
For ever the course of the river of Time.
60   That cities will crowd to its edge
In a blacker, incessanter line;
That the din will be more on its banks,
Denser the trade on its stream,
Flatter the plain where it flows,
65   Fiercer the sun overhead.
That never will those on its breast
See an ennobling sight,
Drink of the feeling of quiet again.

But what was before us we know not,
70   And we know not what shall succeed.

Haply, the river of Time –
As it grows, as the towns on its marge
Fling their wavering lights
On a wider, statelier stream –
75   May acquire, if not the calm
Of its early mountainous shore,
Yet a solemn peace of its own.

And the width of the waters, the hush
Of the grey expanse where he floats,
Freshening its current and spotted with foam
80   As it draws to the Ocean, may strike

Cp. also 'A Dream' 36–7 (p. 346 below),

>   ... *us burning plains,*
> *Bristled with cities, us the sea received.*

57. *shot*] Wavering, i.e. as colours in shot silk.
78–82. Cp. the last stanza of Dr. Arnold's poem,

>   *No more at Distance now,*
> *The mighty Ocean calls thee to his Breast:–*
> *Soiled in God's Task, there wash thy Stains away –*
>   *God grants thee Rest.*

Peace to the soul of the man on its breast –
As the pale waste widens around him,
As the banks fade dimmer away,
85   As the stars come out, and the night-wind
Brings up the stream
Murmurs and scents of the infinite sea.

82. the man] Mankind living in 'as far as thought can reach', but see *Commentary* 201 for the view that A.'s figure breaks down in his final verse-paragraph and that he is now thinking of the end of an individual life.

67 A Summer Night

Date of composition unknown, but clearly 1849–52. The moonlit night of ll. 1–10 may well belong to May 1851 when after his engagement to Frances Lucy Wightman A. went several times late at night to gaze at her window in her father's house in Eaton Place (unpublished 1851 diary), but the setting and date of the earlier night (ll. 13–21) – which is referred to again in 'A Southern Night' 13–16 (p. 458 below) – are more doubtful. The suggestion that A. is recollecting Lake Thun and Marguerite seems to be ruled out by the spring-tide of ll. 16–17 (the Swiss lakes are not tidal). More probably A. is thinking of an earlier stage in his courtship of Miss Wightman at Calais in Aug. 1850 – see 'Calais Sands' and headn. to 'The River' (pp. 233 and 229 above) – but, if this is so, l. 21 involves a poetic licence. In style and the loose articulation of its parts this reflective lyric resembles 'The Buried Life' (p. 271 below).
Published *1852*; reprinted *1855, 1869,* etc.

In the deserted, moon-blanched street,
How lonely rings the echo of my feet!
Those windows, which I gaze at, frown,
Silent and white, unopening down,
5   Repellent as the world; but see,
A break between the housetops shows
The moon! and, lost behind her, fading dim
Into the dewy dark obscurity
Down at the far horizon's rim,
10   Doth a whole tract of heaven disclose!

¶ 67. *1. moon-blanched*] Cp. 'The Scholar-Gipsy' 9 (p. 334 below),

   Cross and recross the strips of moon-blanched green . . .

and 'Dover Beach' 8 (p. 241 above),

   Where the sea meets the moon-blanched land . . .

And to my mind the thought
Is on a sudden brought
Of a past night, and a far different scene.
Headlands stood out into the moonlit deep
15   As clearly as at noon;
The spring-tide's brimming flow
Heaved dazzlingly between;
Houses, with long white sweep,
Girdled the glistening bay;
20   Behind, through the soft air,
The blue haze-cradled mountains spread away.
That night was far more fair –
But the same restless pacings to and fro,
And the same vainly throbbing heart was there,
25   And the same bright, calm moon.

And the calm moonlight seems to say:
Hast thou then still the old unquiet breast,
Which neither deadens into rest,
Nor ever feels the fiery glow
30   *That whirls the spirit from itself away,*
But fluctuates to and fro,
Never by passion quite possessed
And never quite benumbed by the world's sway?
And I, I know not if to pray
35   Still to be what I am, or yield and be
Like all the other men I see.

24. *vainly throbbing heart*] agitated heart *1852.*
27–33. Cp. 'Empedocles on Etna' II [i] 220–34 (pp. 184–5 above) and
'Obermann' 93–6 (p. 134 above),

> *Ah! two desires toss about*
> *The poet's feverish blood.*
> *One drives him to the world without,*
> *And one to solitude.*

The divided self has neither the 'fiery glow' that enables the Romantic
poet to ignore his isolation, nor the deadness of feeling necessary to be
happy in the world. The alternative ways of life are illustrated in the
following two verse-paragraphs.
33. *benumbed*] Cp. 'Memorial Verses' 45–6 (p. 228 above),

> *. . . when the age had bound*
> *Our souls in its benumbing round . . .*

For most men in a brazen prison live,
Where, in the sun's hot eye,
With heads bent o'er their toil, they languidly
40   Their lives to some unmeaning taskwork give,
Dreaming of nought beyond their prison-wall.
And as, year after year,
Fresh products of their barren labour fall
From their tired hands, and rest
45   Never yet comes more near,
Gloom settles slowly down over their breast;
And while they try to stem
The waves of mournful thought by which they are press-
Death in their prison reaches them,   [ed,
50   Unfreed, having seen nothing, still unblest.

And the rest, a few,
Escape their prison and depart
On the wide ocean of life anew.
There the freed prisoner, where'er his heart
55   Listeth, will sail;
Nor doth he know how there prevail,
Despotic on that sea,

37–8. Cp. 'Growing Old' 23–4 (p. 539 below),

> . . . *immured*
> *In the hot prison of the present* . . .

and for 'brazen' see the earlier (1850) reading of 'Memorial Verses' 45–6,

> . . . *when the age had bound*
> *Our spirits in a brazen round* . . .

The prison image was probably suggested by Wordsworth, 'Immortality Ode' 67–8,

> *Shades of the prison-house begin to close*
> *Upon the growing Boy* . . .

51–73. The tone betrays some involuntary admiration for the Romantic poet-outlaw who prefers 'self-selected good', even if it entails destruction, to obedience to any law human or divine. The 'pale Master' driving before the storm on the 'Ocean of Life' (initial caps. thus *1852*, *1855*) is a doomed Titan, but A. is echoing, perhaps unconsciously, Shelley, 'Adonais' 488–492,

> . . . *my spirit's bark is driven*
> *Far from the shore, far from the trembling throng*
> *Whose sails were never to the tempest given;*
> *The massy earth and sphered skies are riven!*
> *I am borne darkly, fearfully, afar* . . .

Trade-winds which cross it from eternity.
Awhile he holds some false way, undebarred
60   By thwarting signs, and braves
The freshening wind and blackening waves.
And then the tempest strikes him; and between
The lightning-bursts is seen
Only a driving wreck,
65   And the pale master on his spar-strewn deck
With anguished face and flying hair
Grasping the rudder hard,
Still bent to make some port he knows not where,
Still standing for some false, impossible shore.
70   And sterner comes the roar
Of sea and wind, and through the deepening gloom
Fainter and fainter wreck and helmsman loom,
And he too disappears, and comes no more.

Is there no life, but these alone?
75   Madman or slave, must man be one?

Plainness and clearness without shadow of stain!
Clearness divine!
Ye heavens, whose pure dark regions have no sign
Of languor, though so calm, and, though so great,

74–5. Cp. A.'s letter to Clough 23 Sept. 1849, '. . . but for God's sake, let
us neither be fanatics nor yet chalf (*sic*) blown by the wind . . .' (*CL* iii);
and see also Vigny, 'Le Mont des Oliviers' (1844) 107–10,

> Pourquoi nul sentier entre deux larges voies,
> Entre l'ennui du calme et des paisibles joies
> Et la rage sans fin des vagues passions,
> Entre la lethargie et les convulsions . . .

and *Obermann* (Lettre xli) i 165, '. . . il cherche et s'égare, il végète et
s'endort'. Vigny's poem may be echoed again in 'The Buried Life' 54
(p. 274 below).
76–92. Cp. *Obermann* (Lettre xc) ii 231, 'Profondeurs de l'espace, serait-ce
en vain qu'il nous est donné de vous apercevoir? La majesté de la nuit
répète d'âge en âge: malheur à toute âme qui se complaît dans la servitude.'
The stars answer the question of ll. 74–5: man can learn from them
emotional detachment and to submit to the order of nature – cp. 'Quiet
Work' and 'Self-Dependence' (pp. 106 and 142 above).
77–8. Cp. 'Empedocles on Etna' II [i] 301–2 (p. 187 above),

> No, no, ye stars! there is no death in you,
> No languor, no decay . . .

and *n*.

80   Are yet untroubled and unpassionate;
      Who, though so noble, share in the world's toil,
      And, though so tasked, keep free from dust and soil!
      I will not say that your mild deeps retain
      A tinge, it may be, of their silent pain
85   Who have longed deeply once, and longed in vain –
      But I will rather say that you remain
      A world above man's head, to let him see
      How boundless might his soul's horizons be,
      How vast, yet of what clear transparency!
90   How it were good to abide there, and breath free;
      How fair a lot to fill
      Is left to each man still!

68 The Buried Life

Date of composition unknown, but clearly 1849–52. 'It bears obvious relation, in its opening motive, to the Marguerite series (cf. "Isolation: to Marguerite") and, in the second half, to "Dover Beach"' (*Commentary* 195).
Published *1852*; reprinted *1855*, *1869*, etc.

      Light flows our war of mocking words, and yet,
      Behold, with tears mine eyes are wet!
      I feel a nameless sadness o'er me roll.
      Yes, yes, we know that we can jest,
5   We know, we know that we can smile!
      But there's a something in this breast,
      To which thy light words bring no rest,
      And thy gay smiles no anodyne.
      Give me thy hand, and hush awhile,
10   And turn those limpid eyes on mine,
      And let me read there, love! thy inmost soul.

¶ 68. *2–3.* Cp. Tennyson, *The Princess* (1847) Pt. iv 'Tears, Idle Tears . . . I–2,

              Tears, idle tears, I know not what they mean,
              Tears from the depth of some divine despair . . .

8. anodyne] A.'s only other poetic use of this word is in 'The Scholar-Gipsy' 190 (p. 341 below),

              And all his hourly varied anodynes . . .

9–11. Cp. Keats, 'Ode on Melancholy' 19–20,

              Emprison her soft hand, and let her rave,
              And feed deep, deep upon her peerless eyes.

Alas! is even love too weak
To unlock the heart, and let it speak?
Are even lovers powerless to reveal
15   To one another what indeed they feel?
I knew the mass of men concealed
Their thoughts, for fear that if revealed
They would by other men be met
With blank indifference, or with blame reproved;
20   I knew they lived and moved
Tricked in disguises, alien to the rest
Of men, and alien to themselves – and yet
The same heart beats in every human breast!

But we, my love! – doth a like spell benumb
25   Our hearts, our voices? must we too be dumb?

Ah! well for us, if even we,
Even for a moment, can get free
Our heart, and have our lips unchained;
For that which seals them hath been deep-ordained!

30   Fate, which foresaw
How frivolous a baby man would be –
By what distractions he would be possessed,
How he would pour himself in every strife,
And well-nigh change his own identity –
35   That it might keep from his capricious play
His genuine self, and force him to obey

12–15. A. is less pessimistic than in 'Isolation. To Marguerite' 37–42 (p. 122 above) about the chance of understanding between lovers, but as the poem develops his main interest shifts to the possibility of self-knowledge at rare moments of happiness in love.

13. *unlock the heart*] The image is continued in ll. 28, '. . . have our lips unchained . . .' and 84, 'A bolt is shot back somewhere in our breast . . .'

21–2. Cp. 'Parting' 73–4 (p. 120 above),

> And what heart knows another?
> Ah! who knows his own?

29. Cp. 'To Marguerite – Continued' 22 (p. 125 above),

> A God, a God their severance ruled!

30–63. Some confusion here is due to the use cheek by jowl of two favourite ideas, namely, the river of life and the buried self. In ll. 38–40 the river is subterranean, and this agrees well enough with ll. 55–6 where shafts cannot be sunk deeply enough to reach the buried self or stream, but ll. 43–4 suggest that the everyday self is the surface of a stream broken by

Even in his own despite his being's law,
Bade through the deep recesses of our breast
The unregarded river of our life
40   Pursue with indiscernible flow its way;
And that we should not see
The buried stream, and seem to be
    Eddying at large in blind uncertainty,
Though driving on with it eternally.

45   But often, in the world's most crowded streets,
But often, in the din of strife,
There rises an unspeakable desire
After the knowledge of our buried life;
A thirst to spend our fire and restless force
50   In tracking out our true, original course;

eddies and the buried self the deeper levels of the same stream where the
direction of its flow is unmistakable. With ll. 43–4 cp. A.'s undated fragment, first printed in *St. Paul and Protestantism* (1870), *Works* ix 77,

> Below the surface-stream, shallow and light
> Of what we say we feel – below the stream,
> As light, of what we think we feel – there flows
> With noiseless current strong, obscure and deep,
> The central stream of what we feel indeed.

For the Stoic notion of an inner or buried self see *n.* to 'Empedocles on
Etna' I ii 129–30 (p. 161 above); for the river or stream of life see *n.* to
'To a Gipsy Child' 60 (p. 26 above) and cp. also 'In Utrumque Paratus'
11 (p. 55 above), 'Progress' 29 (p. 262 above) and 'A Dream' 31–2
(p. 345 below), but it is used to the greatest effect where the comparison
remains implicit at the end of 'Sohrab and Rustum' (ll. 875–92, pp. 330–1
below).

43–4. When he finally separated from Marguerite A. seems to have been
haunted by the distinction between our apparent freedom of behaviour
and the way in which it is really determined by forces beyond our control.
See 'Human Life' 13–30 and 'A Summer Night' 54–8 (pp. 140 and 269–
70 above).

43. Eddying] See *n.* to 'Rugby Chapel' 60 (p. 447 below).

45–6. Cp. Wordsworth, 'Tintern Abbey' 25–6,

> But oft, in lonely rooms, and 'mid the din
> Of towns and cities . . .

47. unspeakable desire] Cp. Milton, *Paradise Lost* iii 662–3,

> Unspeakable desire to see and know
> All these his wondrous works, but chiefly Man . . .

10*

A longing to inquire
Into the mystery of this heart which beats
So wild, so deep in us – to know
Whence our lives come and where they go.
55 And many a man in his own breast then delves,
But deep enough, alas! none ever mines.
And we have been on many thousand lines,
And we have shown, on each, spirit and power;
But hardly have we, for one little hour,
60 Been on our own line, have we been ourselves –
Hardly had skill to utter one of all
The nameless feelings that course through our
        breast,
But they course on for ever unexpressed.
And long we try in vain to speak and act
65 Our hidden self, and what we say and do
Is eloquent, is well – but 'tis not true!
And then we will no more be racked
With inward striving, and demand
Of all the thousand nothings of the hour
70 Their stupefying power;
Ah yes, and they benumb us at our call!
Yet still, from time to time, vague and forlorn,
From the soul's subterranean depth upborne
As from an infinitely distant land,
75 Come airs, and floating echoes, and convey
A melancholy into all our day.

54. See ll. 96–8 below and cp. Vigny, 'Le Mont des Oliviers' (1844) 129–30,

> Tout sera révélé dès que l'homme saura
> De quels lieux il arrive et dans quels il ira.

55. Cp. 'Empedocles on Etna' I ii 129–30 (p. 161 above),

> Well, then, the wiser wight
> In his own bosom delves . . .

and n.

57–60. A.'s prose argument of these lines is in the Yale MS.: 'We have been on a thousand lines and on each have shown spirit talent even geniality but hardly for an hour between birth and death have we been on our own one natural line, have we been ourselves, have we breathed freely.'
58. spirit and power] talent and power 1852–5.
67. And then we wish no more to be racked.
73. subterranean depth] Cp. 'The Youth of Nature' 101–2 (p. 249 above),

> The vastness, the grandeur, the gloom
> Of the unlit gulph of himself.

Only – but this is rare –
When a belovéd hand is laid in ours,
When, jaded with the rush and glare
80   Of the interminable hours,
Our eyes can in another's eyes read clear,
When our world-deafened ear
Is by the tones of a loved voice caressed –
A bolt is shot back somewhere in our breast,
85   And a lost pulse of feeling stirs again.
The eye sinks inward, and the heart lies plain,
And what we mean, we say, and what we would, we
    know.
A man becomes aware of his life's flow,
And hears its winding murmur; and he sees
90   The meadows where it glides, the sun, the breeze.

And there arrives a lull in the hot race
Wherein he doth for ever chase
That flying and elusive shadow, rest.
An air of coolness plays upon his face,
95   And an unwonted calm pervades his breast.
And then he thinks he knows
The hills where his life rose,
And the sea where it goes.

79–80 and *82* below. A.'s modern world is a sort of 'Waste Land', noisy,
hot, full of 'sick hurry' under a glaring noonday sun – see, for example,
'Tristram and Iseult' iii 119–26 (p. 221 above), 'A Summer Night' 37–50
(p. 269 above) and 'The Future' 58–68 (p. 266 above). His composite
image for happiness is antithetical: moonlight, water, trees, stillness and
calm.

88–90. When self-knowledge is momentarily achieved the buried stream
becomes an ordinary river.

97–8. A. may have had in mind some stanzas of an unpublished poem by his
father (dated Jan. 1839 in Mrs. A.'s domestic journal):

How still this upland Vale!
How clear, how peaceful is this infant Stream!
How blest in their untroubled Loneliness
    Its sparkling Waters seem!

Yonder in Distance far
How gleams beneath the Light the mighty Sea!
Eternal Life is there, eternal Power,
    Eternal Purity.

> *Between this upland Vale*
> *And yon far Ocean, canst thou nothing see?*
> *A wide Space parts the two – and there is set*
> *God's task for thee.*

For the full text of this poem, which may have indirectly inspired the coda
to 'Sohrab and Rustum', see Appendix B (p. 610 below); and for echoes
of other stanzas than those quoted above see *nn.* to 'The Future' 50–65,
78–82 (pp. 265, 266 above).

69 Self-Deception

Date of composition unknown, but clearly 1849–52. The 'master-feeling'
(ll. 23–4) that A. seeks to discover in himself recalls the remark in his
letter to Clough 23 Sept. 1849 that his 'one natural craving is not for profound thoughts, mighty spiritual workings etc. etc. but a distinct seeing of
my way as far as my own nature is concerned . . .' (*CL* 110). A. wrote to
F. T. Palgrave in 1869 that 'Self-Deception' was 'not a piece that [at] all
satisfies me' (*Russell* 43).
Published *1852*; reprinted *1855*, *1869*, etc.

> Say, what blinds us, that we claim the glory
> Of possessing powers not our share?
> – Since man woke on earth, he knows his story,
> But, before we woke on earth, we were.
>
> 5   Long, long since, undowered yet, our spirit
> Roamed, ere birth, the treasuries of God;
> Saw the gifts, the powers it might inherit,
> Asked an outfit for its earthly road.
>
> Then, as now, this tremulous, eager being
> 10   Strained and longed and grasped each gift it saw;
> Then, as now, a Power beyond our seeing
> Staved us back, and gave our choice the law.

¶ 69. *3–4*. The Yale MS. has an earlier version of these two lines on a page
that also contains part of an early draft of 'The Second Best' (p. 278
below):

> *We know our history since we woke on earth –*
> *But ere we woke, we were.*

5–12. The reminiscence of Plato's myth of Er in Bk. x of *The Republic* is
significantly altered by A. in ll. 9–12 (as noted *Bonnerot* 165 *fn.*). According
to Plato the souls to be reborn freely choose their future lives in strict order
of lot from the patterns laid before them; A. asserts that the choices are not
free and that the Power which sways them never satisfies wants in full.
9. tremulous, eager Being] Cp. Gray, 'Elegy written in a Country Churchyard' 86,

> *This pleasing anxious being . . .*

Ah, whose hand that day through Heaven guided
Man's new spirit, since it was not we?
15   Ah, who swayed our choice, and who decided
What our gifts, and what our wants should be?

For, alas! he left us each retaining
Shreds of gifts which he refused in full.
Still these waste us with their hopeless straining,
20   Still the attempt to use them proves them null.

And on earth we wander, groping, reeling;
Powers stir in us, stir and disappear.
Ah! and he, who placed our master-feeling,
Failed to place that master-feeling clear.

25   We but dream we have our wished-for powers,
Ends we seek we never shall attain.
Ah! *some* power exists there, which is ours?
Some end is there, we indeed may gain?

14. new] blank *1855*.
16. our gifts ... our wants] the parts ... the whole *1852*.
17–21. Cp. A.'s letter to his sister 'K' July (?) 1849 (misdated 1853), 'The
true reason why parts suit you while others do not is that my poems are
fragments – i.e. that I am fragments, while you are a whole; the whole
effect of my poems is quite vague & indeterminate – this is their weakness;
... and a person who has any inward completeness can at best only like parts
of them; in fact such a person stands firmly and knows what he is about
while the poems stagger weakly & are at their wits end' (*UL* 18).
21–2. The same thought is expressed in 'Despondency' 5–8 (p. 279 below)
and more fully in a note in the Yale MS. Men's unhappiness in the present,
says A., lies 'in their having a presentiment of all things, a possession of
none: in their having one moment the commencement of a feeling, at the
next the commencement of an imagination, at the next the commencement of a thought and the eternal tumult of the world mingling, breaking
in upon, hurrying away all'.
23–4. See headn. above and 'Self-Dependence' 1–2 (p. 142 above),

> *Weary of myself, and sick of asking*
> *What I am, and what I ought to be ...*

25–6. Cp. the comment in the Yale MS., 'Thou beholdest George Sand,
Musset, Bulwer, Jacobi etc., and wishest to get out and uttered like them,
even though like most of them in a false strain – but never.'

70 The Second Best

Date of composition unknown, but clearly 1849–52. It was classified as an
'Early Poem' in *1877*. The untitled and undated first draft is in the Yale
MS. and is reproduced *Commentary* 60–1, but its variant readings are not
included in *1950*.
Published *1852*; reprinted *1867* (*1868*), *1869*, etc.

         Moderate tasks and moderate leisure,
         Quiet living, strict-kept measure
         Both in suffering and in pleasure –
           'Tis for this thy nature yearns.

5   But so many books thou readest,
         But so many schemes thou breedest,
         But so many wishes feedest,
           That thy poor head almost turns.

         And (the world's so madly jangled,
10   Human things so fast entangled)
         Nature's wish must now be strangled
           For that best which she discerns.

         So it *must* be! yet, while leading
         A strained life, while overfeeding,
15   Like the rest, his wit with reading,
           No small profit that man earns,

¶ 70. *5–8.* Cp. 'Empedocles on Etna' I ii 332–5 (p. 169 above),

> But still, *as we proceed*,
> *The mass swells more and more*
> *Of volumes yet to read*,
> *Of secrets yet to explore . . .*

6. so many] The Yale MS. has 'such anxious' as an uncancelled alternative
to the reading of the text.
            furious
7. so many wishes] so many passions *Yale MS.*
10. Cp. 'Obermann' 83 (p. 133 above),

> – *The hopeless tangle of our age . . .*

The Yale MS. has this note from an unidentified source: 'Gott hat den
Menschen einfach gemacht; aber wie er gewickelt wird und sich verwickelt
ist sehr [? schwer] zu sagen' (God has made Man simple; but how he is
bound up and how he entangles himself is difficult to say).

Who through all he meets can steer him,
Can reject what cannot clear him,
Cling to what can truly cheer him;
20   Who each day more surely learns

That an impulse, from the distance
Of his deepest, best existence,
To the words, 'Hope, Light, Persistence,'
Strongly sets and truly burns.

17–20. Replacing this more autobiographical stanza in the Yale MS.,

Who from history's vague narrations,
From pretentious teas'd relations
Of man's mental operations
Turning sick and baffled learns . . .

With which cp. A.'s letter to Clough 1 May 1853, 'I feel immensely . . .
what I have (I believe) lost and choked by my treatment of myself and the
studies to which I have addicted myself' (*CL* 136). The studies referred to
were mainly in philosophy, and comparative religion.

21–3. Yale MS.,

That the one lore that's assuring
Is 'Persistance (sic) *all-enduring –'*
That man's spirit at its luring . . .

24. Strongly sets] Deeply stirs *MS.*; Strongly stirs *1852.*

71 Despondency

Date of composition unknown, but presumably 1849–52.
Published *1852*; reprinted *1855*, *1869*, etc.

The thoughts that rain their steady glow
Like stars on life's cold sea,
Which others know, or say they know –
They never shone for me.

5   Thoughts light, like gleams, my spirit's sky,
But they will not remain.
They light me once, they hurry by;
And never come again.

¶ 71. *2. life's cold sea*] Cp. 'To Marguerite – Continued' 1 (p. 124 above),
Yes! in the sea of life enisled . . .
and *n.*
5–8. Cp. 'Self-Deception' 21–2 (p. 277 above),
And on earth we wonder, groping, reeling;
Powers stir in us, stir and disappear . . .
and *n.*

72 Revolutions

Date of composition unknown, but presumably 1849–52. The central idea – that God's purpose in the world is the goal of history and that each civilization is an attempt to realize 'the order, which God meant should be' (l. 18) – is Hegel as interpreted by A. See Hegel's *Lectures on the Philosophy of History* (1837) tr. from 3rd German edition by J. Sibree, Bohn's Philosophical Library (1857) 82, 'The principles of the successive phases of Spirit that animate the Nations in a necessitated gradation, are themselves only steps in the development of the one universal Spirit, which through them elevates and completes itself to a self-comprehending *totality*.' It is not known when A. first read Hegel, but probably not later than 1847 when Tom A. took some work or works by Hegel with him to New Zealand (unpublished letter in the Bodleian Library, Tom A. to Clough Nov. 1847).
Published *1852*; reprinted *1855*, *1869*, etc.

> Before man parted for this earthly strand,
> While yet upon the verge of heaven he stood,
> God put a heap of letters in his hand,
> And bade him make with them what word he could.
>
> 5   And man has turned them many times; made Greece,
> Rome, England, France; yes, nor in vain essayed
> Way after way, changes that never cease!
> The letters have combined, something was made.
>
> But ah! an inextinguishable sense
> 10 Haunts him that he has not made what he should;
> That he has still, though old, to recommence,
> Since he has not yet found the word God would.
>
> And empire after empire, at their height
> Of sway, have felt this boding sense come on;
> 15 Have felt their huge frames not constructed right,
> And drooped, and slowly died upon their throne.

¶ 72. *13–16*. Cp. Hegel's *Lectures on the Philosophy of History* ed. *cit.* 82, 'The life of a people ripens a certain fruit; its activity aims at a complete manifestation of the principle which it embodies. But this fruit does not fall back into the bosom of the people that produced and matured it; on the contrary, it becomes a poison-draught to it ...'

One day, thou say'st, there will at last appear
The word, the order, which God meant should be.
 – Ah! we shall know *that* well when it comes near;
26 The band will quit man's heart, he will breathe free.

18. The word for Hegel was 'Freedom' (by which he meant the recognition
of necessity). See Hegel's *Lectures on the Philosophy of History* ed. *cit.* 20–1,
'The final aim [of the world's history] is God's purpose with the world;
but God is the absolutely perfect Being, and can, therefore, will nothing
other than himself – his own Will, The Nature of His Will – that is, His
Nature itself – is what we here call the Idea of Freedom.'
20. See *n.* to 'Empedocles on Etna' II [i] 407–8 (p. 191 above).

73 The Neckan

Date of composition unknown, but (?) *c.* Sept. 1852 – the poem, a companion-piece to 'The Forsaken Merman' (both pieces are printed together
in *1853* and all later editions), shows the influence of Heine, whom the
entry 'Heine's Gedichte' in A.'s 1852 diary shows that he planned to read
at Fox How in Sept. (*Note-books* 551). No single source has been identified
for ll. 17–40 of 'The Neckan', but such marriages, with the non-human
partner longing to possess a soul, are common in Scandinavian and German
folklore and form the subject of various tales and ballads (e.g. by Kerner,
Goethe, La Motte Fouqué in Germany). A.'s source for the story of the
Neck and the priest is Benjamin Thorpe's *Northern Mythology* (1851) ii
Scandinavian Popular Traditions and Superstitions 80:

'A priest riding one evening over a bridge, heard the most delightful tones of a stringed instrument, and on looking round, saw a young
man, naked to the waist, sitting on the surface of the water, with a red
cap and yellow locks . . . He saw that it was the Neck, and in his zeal
addressed him thus: – "Why dost thou so joyously strike thy harp?
Sooner shall this dried cane that I hold in my hand grow green and
flower, than thou shalt obtain salvation." Thereupon the unhappy
musician cast down his harp, and sat bitterly weeping on the water.
The priest then turned his horse, and continued his course. But lo!
before he had ridden far, he observed that green shoots and leaves,
mingled with most beautiful flowers, had sprung from his old staff . . .
He therefore hastened back to the mournful Neck, showed him the
green, flowery staff, and said: "Behold! now my old staff is grown
green and flowery like a young branch in a rose garden; so likewise
may hope bloom in the hearts of all created beings; for their Re-
deemer liveth!" Comforted by these words, the Neck again took his
harp, the joyous tones of which resounded along the shore the whole
livelong night.'

Note that in the Swedish tale the Neck is happy first and last, whereas A. makes him melancholic throughout – probably because of his wish to capture what he calls in his essay on Heine, *E in C I* (1865), *Works* iii 208, 'Heine's sweetest note . . . his plaintive note, his note of melancholy.' Earlier in this essay (p. 197) A. indicates his admiration for Heine's poetic form: 'The magic of Heine's poetic form is incomparable; he chiefly uses a form of old German popular poetry, a ballad-form which has more rapidity and grace than any of ours.' A. omits the miracle of the flowering staff in *1853* presumably for its apparent incompatibility with a melancholy ending. The *1869* additions admit the miracle but keep the mood of the original ending by making the Neckan less rejoiced over the news of his salvation than he is grieved by the thought of continued human unkindness.
Published *1853*; reprinted (*1854, 1857*), *1869*, etc.

In summer, on the headlands,
　　The Baltic Sea along,
Sits Neckan with his harp of gold,
　　And sings his plaintive song.

5　　　Green rolls beneath the headlands,
　　Green rolls the Baltic Sea;
And there, below the Neckan's feet,
　　His wife and children be.

He sings not of the ocean,
10　　Its shells and roses pale;
Of earth, of earth the Neckan sings,
　　He hath no other tale.

He sits upon the headlands,
　　And sings a mournful stave
15　Of all he saw and felt on earth
　　Far from the kind sea-wave.

¶ 73. *1–4.* Cp. Thorpe's *Northern Mythology* (1851) ii 78, 'The Neck appears . . . occasionally as a handsome youth, with yellow locks flowing over his shoulders and a red cap, sitting in a summer evening on the surface of the water with a golden harp in his hand.' A.'s poem is a song about a song in Heine's manner – see B. Fairley's *Heinrich Heine* (1954) 1–23 and especially 2, 3, 'It is in this way, by singing about song, that Heine achieves his effect . . . his mind readily created song within song as one of its ways of singing.'
16. kind] green *1853–7.*

Sings how, a knight, he wandered
   By castle, field, and town –
But earthly knights have harder hearts
20   Than the sea-children own.

Sings of his earthly bridal –
   Priest, knights, and ladies gay.
' –And who art thou,' the priest began,
   'Sir Knight, who wedd'st to-day?'

25   ' – I am no knight,' he answered;
   'From the sea-waves I come.'
The knights drew sword, the ladies screamed,
   The surpliced priest stood dumb.

He sings how from the chapel
30   He vanished with his bride,
And bore her down to the sea-halls,
    Beneath the salt sea-tide.

He sings how she sits weeping,
   'Mid shells that round her lie.
35   ' – False Neckan shares my bed,' she weeps;
   'No Christian mate have I.'

He sings how through the billows
   He rose to earth again,
And sought a priest to sign the cross,
40   That Neckan Heaven might gain.

He sings how, on an evening,
   Beneath the birch-trees cool,
He sate and played his harp of gold,
   Beside the river-pool.

45   Beside the pool sate Neckan –
   Tears filled his mild blue eye.
On his white mule, across the bridge,
   A cassocked priest rode by.

' – Why sitt'st thou there, O Neckan,
50   And play'st thy harp of gold?
Sooner shall this my staff bear leaves,
   Than thou shalt Heaven behold.'

46. *mild*] cold *1853–7*.

But, lo, the staff, it budded!
   It greened, it branched, it waved.
55   ' – O ruth of God,' the priest cried out,
   'This lost sea-creature saved!'

The cassocked priest rode onwards,
   And vanished with his mule;
But Neckan in the twilight grey
60   Wept by the river-pool.

He wept: 'The Earth hath kindness,
   The sea, the starry poles;
Earth, sea, and sky, and God above –
   But, ah, not human souls!'

65   In summer, on the headlands,
   The Baltic Sea along,
Sits Neckan with his harp of gold,
   And sings this plaintive song.

53–6. First added 1869.
61–4. First added 1869 (with 'said' for 'wept' in l. 61).

74 A Caution to Poets

Date of composition unknown, but by 14 Dec. 1852 when A. quoted it in
a letter to Clough with the comment, 'There is an oracular quatrain for
you, terribly true' (*CL* 126). The quatrain also appears undated in Yale
MS. with this prose argument, 'What it gave us no pleasure to conceive
or make, it will give the world no pleasure to contemplate.' A.'s position
is a refinement of Horace, *Ars Poetica* 101–3,

> *ut ridentibus arrident, ita flentibus adsunt*
> *humani vultus. si vis me flere, dolendum est*
> *primum ipsi tibi . . .*

as are Goethe's sentences (A.'s probable source) in 'Antik und Modern'
(1818), *Werke* (Cotta: Stuttgart and Tübingen) xxxix (1830) 76–7, '. . . we
may in general say that every artistic production puts us in the same state
of mind the author was in. If that state of mind was clear and bright, we
shall feel free; if it was narrow, timid and anxious, we shall feel constricted
in the same degree . . . every work will give us pleasure which the artist
produced with ease and facility.'
Published *1867*; reprinted (*1868*); without title *1869* (as prefatory poem to
vol. i); with title restored *1877*, etc.

What poets feel not, when they make,
    A pleasure in creating,
The world, in *its* turn, will not take
    Pleasure in contemplating.

75 Stanzas from the Grande Chartreuse

Date of composition unknown, but between 7 Sept. 1851–March 1855 (the limiting dates those of A.'s honeymoon visit to the Grand Chartreuse and of the poem's publication respectively); probably mainly written 1852 and revised 1853–5 (though incorporating some material which A. had planned to use in poems in 1849). In favour of 1852 are the entry 'The Chartreuse' in A.'s 1852 diary following the titles of two poems printed in *1852* (*Note-books* 552); the echoes of 'Tristram and Iseult' ii and 'The Church of Brou' i in ll. 181–6; the stanza, which is used elsewhere only in three poems of 1849–52 ('Isolation. To Marguerite', 'To Marguerite – Continued' and 'Morality'); above all, A.'s sympathy – which was less overt by the time of the *1853* Preface – with the romantic melancholy expressed. For the relationship between the finished poem, Carlyle's essay 'Characteristics' (which A. probably read first in 1847) and several entries in the Yale MS. list of poems to be composed in 1849 see *nn.* below. Published *Fraser's Magazine* April 1855; reprinted *1867* (*1868*), *1869*, etc.

Through Alpine meadows soft-suffused
    With rain, where thick the crocus blows,
Past the dark forges long disused,
    The mule-track from Saint Laurent goes.
5   The bridge is crossed, and slow we ride,
    Through forest, up the mountain-side.

The autumnal evening darkens round,
    The wind is up, and drives the rain;
While, hark! far down, with strangled sound
10   Doth the Dead Guier's stream complain,
    Where that wet smoke, among the woods,
    Over his boiling cauldron broods.

¶ 75. *Title*. A. visited the Grand Chartreuse with his wife on Sunday 7 Sept. 1851 on his way from Grenoble to Chambéry (unpublished 1851 diary). *To the Dead Guier's stream*] The Guiers Mort has its source near the Grande Chartreuse and unites with the Guiers Vif in the valley below.
12. boiling] black-worn *MS*. The location of the MS., if it still exists, is unknown, but see A. to J. W. Parker (editor of *Fraser's Magazine*) 20 March 1855, '. . . will you substitute *boiling* for *black-worn* as an epithet for the cauldrons of the Guiers Mort, in the last line of the second stanza of the Poem' (unpublished letter in Yale Papers).

Swift rush the spectral vapours white
Past limestone scars with ragged pines,
15   Showing – then blotting from our sight!
Halt – through the cloud-drift something shines!
High in the valley, wet and drear,
The huts of Courrerie appear.

Strike leftward! cries our guide; and higher
20   Mounts up the stony forest-way.
At last the encircling trees retire;
Look! through the showery twilight grey
What pointed roofs are these advance?
A palace of the Kings of France?

25   Approach, for what we seek is here!
Alight, and sparely sup, and wait
For rest in this outbuilding near;
Then cross the sward and reach that gate.
Knock; pass the wicket! Thou art come
30   To the Carthusians' world-famed home.

The silent courts, where night and day
Into their stone-carved basins cold
The splashing icy fountains play –
The humid corridors behold!
35   Where, ghostlike in the deepening night,
Cowled forms brush by in gleaming white.

27. *this outbuilding*] The old infirmary outside the main gate.

30. The first settlement was by St. Bruno, the founder of the Carthusians, in 1084. A.'s interest in the Grande Chartreuse may have been stimulated by Wordsworth's account in *The Prelude* (1850) vi 416–88 of his visit to the monastery in 1790.

31–6. Cp. A.'s discarded poem 'To Meta' 5–8, 15–16 (pp. 580–1 below),

> *Slowly, past the open spaces*
> *Of their cloister, see, they glide:*
> *Tears have washed their austere faces;*
> *Neither hate have they, nor fear, nor pride.*

> *Cool the murmur of the fountains*
> *Sinks and rises through this charmed arcade.*

'To Meta' is on the Yale MS. list of poems to be composed in 1849. A.'s interest in the contemplative life was natural to a poet who tended to see himself as an onlooker.

The chapel, where no organ's peal
Invests the stern and naked prayer –
With penitential cries they kneel
40   And wrestle; rising then, with bare
And white uplifted faces stand,
Passing the Host from hand to hand;

Each takes, and then his visage wan
Is buried in his cowl once more.
45   The cells! – the suffering Son of Man
Upon the wall – the knee-worn floor –
And where they sleep, that wooden bed,
Which shall their coffin be, when dead!

The library, where tract and tome
50   Not to feed priestly pride are there,
To hymn the conquering march of Rome,
Nor yet to amuse, as ours are!
They paint of souls the inner strife,
Their drops of blood, their death in life.

55   The garden, overgrown – yet mild,
See, fragrant herbs are flowering there!
Strong children of the Alpine wild
Whose culture is the brethren's care;
Of human tasks their only one,
60   And cheerful works beneath the sun.

Those halls, too, destined to contain
Each its own pilgrim-host of old,
From England, Germany, or Spain –
All are before me! I behold
65   The House, the Brotherhood austere!
– And what am I, that I am here?

40–42. Carthusians do not pass the Host from hand to hand or receive Holy Communion standing. A. is probably referring to the circulation of the tablet of the Pax (which is kissed by the officiating priest and then by the whole congregation). See *Catholic Encyclopaedia* under 'Pax' and *Commentary* 250–1.
47–8. A popular error. Carthusians are buried in their habits on a bare plank of wood.
56–60. A genteel reference to the manufacture of the famous liqueur.
66. Byronic apostrophe.

For rigorous teachers seized my youth,
And purged its faith, and trimmed its fire,
Showed me the high, white star of Truth,
70   There bade me gaze, and there aspire.
Even now their whispers pierce the gloom:
What dost thou in this living tomb?

Forgive me, masters of the mind!
At whose behest I long ago
75   So much unlearnt, so much resigned –
I come not here to be your foe!
I seek these anchorites, not in ruth,
To curse and to deny your truth;

Not as their friend, or child, I speak!
80   But as, on some far northern strand,
Thinking of his own Gods, a Greek
In pity and mournful awe might stand
Before some fallen Runic stone –
For both were faiths, and both are gone.

85   Wandering between two worlds, one dead,
The other powerless to be born,

67. *rigorous teachers*] Carlyle, Goethe, Senancour and Spinoza are certainly among those indicated.
68. *Fraser 1855,*

And prun'd its faith and quench'd its fire . . .

The 1855 versions of this and the following line are more candid.
69. *high, white*] pale cold *Fraser 1855.*
79–84. The 'fallen Runic stone' is almost certainly from Mallet's *Northern Antiquities*, which A. was reading for 'Balder Dead' in Dec. 1853 and Jan. 1854 (*Note-books* 554–5) but had also taken with him on his honeymoon journey abroad in Sept.–Oct. 1851. The Greek belongs to no specified period but is emancipated from Greek paganism (as A. feels himself to be from the Protestant Christianity in which he was educated). He laments over two dead faiths as A. regrets that the Protestant and Catholic forms of Christian orthodoxy are alike incredible.
85–8. An echo of Carlyle's 'Characteristics' (1831), *Crit. and Miscell. Essays* iii, *Works* ed. H. D. Traill xxviii 29–30, 32, 'Belief, Faith has wellnigh vanished from the world . . . For Contemplation and love of Wisdom, no Cloister now opens its religious shades; the Thinker must, in all senses, wander homeless . . . The doom of the Old has long been pronounced, and irrevocable; the Old has passed away: but, alas, the New appears not in its stead; the Time is still in pangs of travail with the New.'

With nowhere yet to rest my head,
Like these, on earth I wait forlorn.
Their faith, my tears, the world deride –
90 I come to shed them at their side.

Oh, hide me in your gloom profound,
Ye solemn seats of holy pain!
Take me, cowled forms, and fence me round,
Till I possess my soul again;
95 Till free my thoughts before me roll,
Not chafed by hourly false control!

For the world cries your faith is now
But a dead time's exploded dream;
My melancholy, sciolists say,
100 Is a past mode, an outworn theme –
As if the world had ever had
A faith, or sciolists been sad!

Ah, if it *be* passed, take away,
At least, the restlessness, the pain;
105 Be man henceforth no more a prey
To these out-dated stings again!
The nobleness of grief is gone –
Ah, leave us not the fret alone!

But – if you cannot give us ease –
110 Last of the race of them who grieve,
Here leave us to die out with these
Last of the people who believe!

The idea of the age as a spiritual No Man's Land was a commonplace in
A.'s circle – see Tom A.'s letter to Clough 16 April 1847, 'Our lot is cast
in an evil time; we cannot accept the present, and we shall not live to see
the future. It is an age of transition; in which the mass are carried hither
and thither by chimeras, while to the few . . . is left nothing but sadness
and isolation' (*Correspondence of A.H.C.* i 180).
87. Cp. *Matthew* viii 20, 'The foxes have holes, and the birds of the air
have nests; but the Son of man hath not where to lay his head.'
93. Fraser 1855,

> *Invest me, steep me, fold me round . . .*

99. sciolists say] A sciolist is a pretender to knowledge, a wiseacre. The
defective rhyme-word 'say' is found in all editions.
108. fret] pang *Fraser 1855.*

Silent, while years engrave the brow;
Silent – the best are silent now.

115 Achilles ponders in his tent,
The kings of modern thought are dumb;
Silent they are, though not content,
And wait to see the future come.
They have the grief men had of yore,
120 But they contend and cry no more.

Our fathers watered with their tears
This sea of time whereon we sail,
Their voices were in all men's ears
Who passed within their puissant hail.
125 Still the same ocean round us raves,
But we stand mute, and watch the waves.

113–14. Stoical silence. Cp. Vigny, 'La Mort du Loup' (Feb. 1843) 78,

> Seul le silence est grand; tout le reste est faiblesse . . .

and 'Le Mont des Oliviers' (June 1844) 146–9,

> Si le Ciel nous laissa comme un monde avorté,
> Le juste opposera le dédain à l'absence,
> Et ne répondra plus que par un froid silence
> Au silence éternel de la Divinité.

Vigny's poems appeared in *Revue des Deux Mondes* at the dates indicated in brackets. A. echoed 'Le Mont des Oliviers' in 'A Summer Night' 74–5 (p. 270 above), but the passage quoted here was not part of the text until 1862.

115. The reference is clumsy: it suggests that 'the best' are sulking as Achilles sulked apart until after the death of Patroclus.

116. The kings of modern thought] A borrowing from Shelley's 'Adonais' 430–1,

> . . . the kings of thought
> Who waged contention with their time's decay . . .

120. Cp. Vigny, 'La Mort du Loup' 85,

> Gémir, pleurer, prier, est également lâche.

122. sea of time] A variant of A.'s 'sea of life' metaphor, a favourite with him 1849–52 – see 'To Marguerite – Continued' 1, 'Human Life' 8, 27, 'A Summer Night' 53, 'Despondency' 2 (pp. 124, 140, 269, 279 above).

124. puissant] The epithet is used five times by A., but not before 1855 in other poems. See *Parrish* 624.

For what availed it, all the noise
And outcry of the former men?
Say, have their sons achieved more joys,
130   Say, is life lighter now than then?
The sufferers died, they left their pain –
The pangs which tortured them remain.

What helps it now, that Byron bore,
With haughty scorn which mocked the smart,
135   Through Europe to the Ætolian shore
The pageant of his bleeding heart?
That thousands counted every groan,
And Europe made his woe her own?

What boots it, Shelley! that the breeze
140   Carried thy lovely wail away,
Musical through Italian trees
Which fringe thy soft blue Spezzian bay?
Inheritors of thy distress,
Have restless hearts one throb the less?

145   Or are we easier, to have read,
O Obermann! the sad, stern page,
Which tells us how thou hidd'st thy head
From the fierce tempest of thine age
In the lone brakes of Fontainebleau,
150   Or chalets near the Alpine snow?

133–42. An echo of Carlyle's 'Characteristics' (1831), *Works* ed. *cit.*
xxviii 31, 'Behold a Byron, in melodious tones, "cursing his day"' . . .
Hear a Shelley filling the earth with inarticulate wail; like the infinite, inarticulate grief of forsaken infants.' A.'s familiarity with the passage is
confirmed by the entry 'Shelley–Spezzia – ah an eternal grief' in the Yale
MS. list of poems to be composed in 1849. For other references to Byron
in A.'s poems see 'Memorial Verses' 6–14 and *n.* to 6–7 (p. 266 above),
but the reference to Shelley is unique. The 'lovely wail' anticipates A.'s
comment on Shelley in 'Maurice de Guérin, *E in C I* (1865), *Works* iii 122
fn., 'It always seems to me that the right medium for Shelley's genius was
the sphere of music, not of poetry; the medium of sounds he can master, but
to master the more difficult medium of words he has neither intellectual
force enough nor sanity enough.'
145–50. See A.'s note on Senancour in headn. to 'Obermann' (p. 129
above).

Ye slumber in your silent grave!
The world, which for an idle day
Grace to your mood of sadness gave,
Long since hath flung her weeds away.
155   The eternal trifler breaks your spell;
But we – we learnt your lore too well!

Years hence, perhaps, may dawn an age,
More fortunate, alas! than we,
Which without hardness will be sage,
160   And gay without frivolity.
Sons of the world, oh, speed those years;
But, while we wait, allow our tears!

Allow them! We admire with awe
The exulting thunder of your race;
165   You give the universe your law,
You triumph over time and space!
Your pride of life, your tireless powers,
We laud them, but they are not ours.

We are like children reared in shade
170   Beneath some old-world abbey wall,
Forgotten in a forest-glade,
And secret from the eyes of all.
Deep, deep the greenwood round them waves,
Their abbey, and its close of graves!

175   But, where the road runs near the stream,
Oft through the trees they catch a glance
Of passing troops in the sun's beam –
Pennon, and plume, and flashing lance!
Forth to the world those soldiers fare,
180   To life, to cities, and to war!

151–6. Ye ... your ...] They ... their ... *Fraser 1855*.
157. Cp. Carlyle's 'Characteristics' (1831), *Works* ed. *cit.* xxviii 37, 'Deep
and sad as is our feeling that we yet stand in the bodeful Night; equally
deep, indestructible is our assurance that the Morning also will not fail.'
163–8. Only partly ironic, although the admiration is grudged. Cp. the
split nature of A.'s feelings about England's rôle in the world in 'Heine's
Grave' 70–96 (pp. 472–3 below).
168. *We laud them*] They awe us *Fraser 1855*; We mark them *1867–9*; We
praise them *1877–81*.
169. *in shade*] The shadow of Romantic melancholy.
173. *the greenwood*] Elsewhere A. uses the expression only in 'Tristram and
Iseult' (i 247, 290; ii 36, 179).

And through the wood, another way,
Faint bugle-notes from far are borne,
Where hunters gather, staghounds bay,
Round some fair forest-lodge at morn.
185   Gay dames are there, in sylvan green;
Laughter and cries – those notes between!

The banners flashing through the trees
Make their blood dance and chain their eyes;
That bugle-music on the breeze
190   Arrests them with a charmed surprise.
Banner by turns and bugle woo:
   Ye shy recluses, follow too!

O children, what do ye reply? –
'Action and pleasure, will ye roam
195   Through these secluded dells to cry
And call us? – but too late ye come!
Too late for us your call ye blow,
Whose bent was taken long ago.

181–6. Cp. 'Tristram and Iseult' ii 153–6, 186–9 (pp. 214–15 above)

> *A stately Huntsman, clad in green,*
> *And round him a fresh forest-scene.*
> *On that clear forest-knoll he stays,*
> *With his pack round him . . .*

> *Cheer, cheer thy dogs into the brake,*
> *O Hunter! and without a fear*
> *Thy golden-tasselled bugle blow,*
> *And through the glades thy pastime take . . .*

and 'The Church of Brou' i 9–12, 15–18 (p. 295 below),

> *Steeds are neighing, gallants glittering;*
>   *Gay, her smiling lord to greet,*
> *From her mullioned chamber-casement*
>   *Smiles the Duchess Marguerite . . .*

> *Now the autumn crisps the forest;*
>   *Hunters gather, bugles ring.*

> *Hounds are pulling, prickers swearing,*
>   *Horses fret, and boar-spears glance.*

The three passages were probably written within a short interval.
194–210. Italicized in 1855.

200
'Long since we pace this shadowed nave;
We watch those yellow tapers shine,
Emblems of hope over the grave,
In the high altar's depth divine;
The organ carries to our ear
Its accents of another sphere.

205
'Fenced early in this cloistral round
Of reverie, of shade, of prayer,
How should we grow in other ground?
How can we flower in foreign air?
– Pass, banners, pass, and bugles, cease;
210
And leave our desert to its peace!'

201. *hope over*] light above *Fraser 1855*.
210. *desert*] forest *Fraser 1855*. A significant alteration. By 1867 A. had
rejected 'the race of them who grieve' and had at least one foot in the
camp of the sciolists.

76 The Church of Brou

Date of composition unknown, but (?) 1852–3. Planned perhaps as early as
1851 – see the title 'La châtelaine architecte' in A.'s tentative list of poems
for *1852* (*Commentary* 16–17) – but probably not composed until late 1852
or early 1853; Pt. i 'The Castle' suggests the influence in metre and manner
of Heine's 'romances' (see headn. to 'The Neckan', p. 281 above, for A.'s
reading of Heine in Sept. 1852); Pt iii 'The Tomb' recalls in style and mood
'Tristram and Iseult' iii 152–94, which A. was revising after Oct. 1852 for
1853 (for these similarities see *n.* to 'Tristram and Iseult' ii 164–7, p. 214
above, and *Commentary* 115–16). A.'s single source was Edgar Quinet's
essay 'Des Arts de la Renaissance et de l'Église de Brou' in *Mélanges*
(1839), *Œuvres Complètes* (Paris 1857) vi 351–63. Quinet is sparing of historical detail, which explains some of A.'s factual inaccuracies, but the
failure to note Quinet's description of the flat marshy country in which
the church is situated and A.'s verbal closeness to his source in Pt. iii together argue that A. may have composed in 1852–3 from extracts made
earlier (? 1851) from Quinet's essay. The attraction that the essay had for
A. is indicated by two of Quinet's reflections (*Œuvres* ed. *cit.* vi 355, 361):
'. . . ce n'est pas seulement la duchesse et le duc de Savoie qui dorment là
dans ce cercueil, c'est l'ancienne foi; c'est l'ancien amour; c'est la poussière
de toutes les croyances tombées . . .' and '. . . l'idée que l'homme pût être
séparé par la mort de ce qu'il avait aimé n'avait pas encore approché de
l'âme humaine.'
A. wrote to F. T. Palgrave in 1869, 'In a succeeding edition, I am not at all
sure that I shall not leave out the second part of the "Church of Brou"'

(*Russell* 42), but the omission of Pts. i and ii in *1877* was because of their inaccuracies – see Sir Edward Cook's *Literary Recreations* (1919) *295n.* for A.'s admission of this to Oscar Browning – rather than from any strong sense of their inferiority to Pt. iii. The poem was restored to its original shape and classified as an 'Early Poem' in *1881*.

Published *1853*; reprinted (*1854*, *1857*), *1869*, *1881*, etc. In *1877* Pt. iii was reprinted as 'A Tomb among the Mountains'.

I
The Castle

Down the Savoy valleys sounding,
    Echoing round this castle old,
'Mid the distant mountain-chalets
    Hark! what bell for church is tolled?

5   In the bright October morning
        Savoy's Duke had left his bride.
    From the castle, past the drawbridge,
        Flowed the hunters' merry tide.

    Steeds are neighing, gallants glittering;
10   Gay, her smiling lord to greet,
    From her mullioned chamber-casement
        Smiles the Duchess Marguerite.

    From Vienna, by the Danube,
        Here she came, a bride, in spring.
15   Now the autumn crisps the forest;
        Hunters gather, bugles ring.

    Hounds are pulling, prickers swearing,
        Horses fret, and boar-spears glance.
    Off! – They sweep the marshy forests,
20   Westward, on the side of France.

¶ 76. i 6. *Savoy's Duke*] Philibert II of Savoy, left unnamed by Quinet. He died in 1504 of a disease contracted while hunting (*Commentary* 39).

i *12. Duchess Marguerite*] Marguerite d'Autriche (1480–1530) daughter of the Emperor Maximilian. She married Philibert II in 1501.

i *15–18.* Cp. 'Stanzas from the Grande Chartreuse' 181–6 and *n.* (p. 293 above).

i *17. prickers*] Mounted attendants at a hunt.

Hark! the game's on foot; they scatter!
  Down the forest-ridings lone,
Furious, single horsemen gallop –
  Hark! a shout – a crash – a groan!

25   Pale and breathless, came the hunters;
        On the turf dead lies the boar –
      God! the Duke lies stretched beside him,
        Senseless, weltering in his gore.

                *   *   *   *

      In the dull October evening,
30   Down the leaf-strewn forest-road,
      To the castle, past the drawbridge,
        Came the hunters with their load.

      In the hall, with sconces blazing,
        Ladies waiting round her seat,
35   Clothed in smiles, beneath the daïs
        Sate the Duchess Marguerite.

      Hark! below the gates unbarring!
        Tramp of men and quick commands!
      ' – 'Tis my lord come back from hunting – '
40   And the Duchess claps her hands.

      Slow and tired, came the hunters –
        Stopped in darkness in the court.
      ' – Ho, this way, ye laggard hunters!
        To the hall! What sport? What sport?'

45   Slow they entered with their master;
        In the hall they laid him down.
      On his coat were leaves and blood-stains,
        On his brow an angry frown.

      Dead her princely youthful husband
50   Lay before his youthful wife,
      Bloody, 'neath the flaring sconces –
        And the sight froze all her life.

                *   *   *   *

i 24. Only matched for clumsiness by 'Austerity of Poetry' 8 (p. 492 below),
        A prop gave way! crash fell a platform! lo . . .

In Vienna, by the Danube,
    Kings hold revel, gallants meet.
55   Gay of old amid the gayest
    Was the Duchess Marguerite.

In Vienna, by the Danube,
    Feast and dance her youth beguiled.
    Till that hour she never sorrowed;
60   But from then she never smiled.

'Mid the Savoy mountain valleys
    Far from town or haunt of man,
Stands a lonely church, unfinished,
    Which the Duchess Maud began;

65   Old, that Duchess stern began it,
    In gray age, with palsied hands;
But she died while it was building,
    And the Church unfinished stands –

Stands as erst the builders left it,
70   When she sank into her grave;
Mountain greensward paves the chancel,
    Harebells flower in the nave.

' – In my castle all is sorrow,'
    Said the Duchess Marguerite then;
75   'Guide me, some one, to the mountain!
    We will build the Church again.' –

Sandalled palmers, faring homeward,
    Austrian knights from Syria came.
' – Austrian wanderers bring, O warders!
80   Homage to your Austrian dame.'

From the gate the warders answered:
    ' – Gone, O knights, is she you knew!
Dead our Duke, and gone his Duchess;
    Seek her at the Church of Brou!'

---

i *61–4.* The Dukes of Savoy were also Counts of Bresse, and the church is in flat country close to the town of Bourg-en-Bresse. 'Maud' is A.'s invented name for the earlier duchess, who was Marguerite de Bourbon (Philibert II's mother). Quinet says (incorrectly), 'Deux ducs de Savoie meurent à la chasse dans les forêts des environs. La veuve du premier fait un vœu dont sa belle-fille hérite . . .' (*Œuvres* ed. *cit.* vi 360).

i *75. some one*] vassals *1853–7.*

11 + M.A.

85   Austrian knights and march-worn palmers
      Climb the winding mountain-way –
  Reach the valley, where the Fabric
      Rises higher day by day.

    Stones are sawing, hammers ringing;
90   On the work the bright sun shines,
  In the Savoy mountain-meadows,
      By the stream, below the pines.

  On her palfrey white the Duchess
      Sate and watched her working train –
95   Flemish carvers, Lombard gilders,
      German masons, smiths from Spain.

  Clad in black, on her white palfrey,
      Her old architect beside –
  There they found her in the mountains,
100   Morn and noon and eventide.

  There she sate, and watched the builders,
      Till the Church was roofed and done.
  Last of all, the builders reared her
      In the nave a tomb of stone.

105   On the tomb two forms they sculptured,
      Lifelike in the marble pale –
  One, the Duke in helm and armour;
      One the Duchess in her veil.

  Round the tomb the carved stone fretwork
110   Was at Easter-tide put on.
  Then the Duchess closed her labours;
      And she died at the St. John.

i *95–6.* Cp. Quinet, *Œuvres* ed. *cit.* vi 357, 'Les ouvriers arrivent de Toscane, de Nuremberg, d'Angleterre, de Suisse. Les Allemands apportent le génie du symbole et du mystère; les Italiens, les ornements de la renaissance; les Flamands, le goût des intérieurs domestiques; les Suisses des Alpes, l'industrie des détails et leurs rocs d'albâtre ciselés et brodés . . .'

i *98–100.* Cp. Quinet, *Œuvres* ed. *cit.* vi 360, 'Marguerite d'Autriche ne passera plus un jour sans broder et tisser ainsi le marbre de sa tombe . . . Elle conduit elle-même la main de son vieil architecte aveugle.'

i *104.* The tomb of the duchess is on the right of the choir.

i *105–8.* The effigies of the duke and duchess are on separate tombs.

II
The Church

Upon the glistening leaden roof
Of the new Pile, the sunlight shines;
    The stream goes leaping by.
The hills are clothed with pines sun-proof;
5   'Mid bright green fields, below the pines,
    Stands the Church on high.
What Church is this, from men aloof?
'Tis the Church of Brou.

    At sunrise, from their dewy lair
10   Crossing the stream, the kine are seen
    Round the wall to stray –
The churchyard wall that clips the square
Of open hill-sward fresh and green
    Where last year they lay.
15   But all things now are ordered fair
Round the Church of Brou.

On Sundays, at the matin-chime,
The Alpine peasants, two and three,
    Climb up here to pray;
20   Burghers and dames, at summer's prime,
Ride out to church from Chambery,
    Dight with mantles gay.
But else it is a lonely time
Round the Church of Brou.

25   On Sundays, too, a priest doth come
From the walled town beyond the pass,
    Down the mountain-way;
And then you hear the organ's hum,
You hear the white-robed priest say mass,
30   And the people pray.
But else the woods and fields are dumb
Round the Church of Brou.

ii *1–8.* In A.'s stanza the rhythm of Tennyson's 'The Lady of Shalott'
(1832; revised 1842) 'is suggested but not actually reproduced' (G. C.
Macaulay, *Poems by Matthew Arnold* (1896) 112).
ii *13. open hill-sward fresh*] shaven hill-sward trim *1853–7.*

And after church, when mass is done,
The people to the nave repair
35   Round the tomb to stray;
And marvel at the Forms of stone,
And praise the chiselled broideries rare –
    Then they drop away.
The princely Pair are left alone
40 In the Church of Brou.

III

The Tomb

So rest, for ever rest, O princely Pair!
In your high church, 'mid the still mountain-air,
Where horn, and hound, and vassals, never come.
Only the blessed Saints are smiling dumb,
5 From the rich painted windows of the nave,
On aisle, and transept, and your marble grave;
Where thou, young Prince! shalt never more arise
From the fringed mattress where thy Duchess lies,
On autumn-mornings, when the bugle sounds,
10 And ride across the drawbridge with thy hounds
To hunt the boar in the crisp woods till eve;
And thou, O Princess! shalt no more receive,
Thou and thy ladies, in the hall of state,
The jaded hunters with their bloody freight,
15 Coming benighted to the castle-gate.

ii *37. chiselled broideries rare*] See the phrase 'leurs rocs d'albâtre ciselés et brodés' in *n.* to i 95–6 above.

iii *1–15*. See Quinet, *Œuvres* ed. *cit.* vi 358, 360–1, 'Ah! que la vieille société se couche ici sans regret dans son tombeau! . . . Qu'il s'endorme pour jamais sur ce dur oreiller de marbre . . . Son lévrier fidèle à ses pieds ne se relèvera pas . . . [of the duchess] Et, quand le soir de sa vie arrive . . . elle vient, pieds nus, se coucher auprès de son époux . . . C'est de cette heure seulement que commence pour elle le vrai mariage dans son duché éternel. Les fanfares ne sonnent plus pour la chasse; son époux sur son cheval fougueux ne poursuit plus le sanglier dans la forêt; elle ne l'attendra plus vainement jusqu'à la nuit, en sanglotant à la fenêtre de sa tour.'

iii *16–46*. See Quinet, *Œuvres* ed. *cit.* vi 361, 'Les époux ont dépouillé leurs corps mortels qui gisent sur le pavé . . . Les voilà qui dorment leurs sommeils de marbre. Qui pourrait raconter leurs songes plus blancs que l'albâtre des tombeaux? Quand leurs froides paupières se soulèvent, ils voient les arceaux sur leurs têtes, la lumière transfigurée des vitraux, la Vierge et les Saintes immobiles à leurs places; et ils pensent en eux-mêmes: c'est ici l'éternité. Ils n'entendent pas l'orage qui ébranle au dehors la foi

So sleep, for ever sleep, O marble Pair!
Or, if ye wake, let it be then, when fair
On the carved western front a flood of light
Streams from the setting sun, and colours bright
20   Prophets, transfigured Saints, and Martyrs brave,
In the vast western window of the nave;
And on the pavement round the Tomb there glints
A chequer-work of glowing sapphire-tints,
And amethyst, and ruby – then unclose
25   Your eyelids on the stone where ye repose,
And from your broidered pillows lift your heads,
And rise upon your cold white marble beds;
And, looking down on the warm rosy tints,
Which chequer, at your feet, the illumined flints,
30   Say: *What is this? we are in bliss – forgiven –*
Behold the pavement of the courts of Heaven!
Or let it be on autumn nights, when rain
Doth rustlingly above your heads complain
On the smooth leaden roof, and on the walls
35   Shedding her pensive light at intervals
The moon through the clere-story windows shines,
And the wind washes through the mountain-pines.

---

sur son pilier; ils se prennent, malgré leurs durs chevets, à rêver de
duchés, de vassaux, de blasons qui rayonnent, de marguerites de marbre
qu'ils effeuillent dans leurs mains de marbre; et quand le vent fait gémir les
portes, ils murmurent entre eux: Qu'avez-vous, mon âme, pour soupirer
si haut? et quand la pluie creuse le toit sur leurs têtes, ils se disent:
Entendez-vous aussi sur votre dais la pluie de l'éternel Amour?'
iii *22–4* and below *28–9*. Besides Quinet's 'la lumière transfigurée des
vitraux' A. is thinking of Keats's 'The Eve of St. Agnes' 217-21,

> *Full on this casement shone the wintry moon,*
> *And threw warm gules on Madeline's fair breast,*
> *As down she knelt for heaven's grace and boon;*
> *Rose-bloom fell on her hands, together prest,*
> *And on her silver cross soft amethyst . . .*

Scott's 'foliaged tracery' in 'The Lay of the Last Minstrel' ii sect. 11,
one source of Keats's lines, probably supplied A. with his 'foliaged marble
forest' in l. 39 below.
iii *30–1*. A Miltonic allusion. Cp. *Paradise Lost* iii 515,

> *And waking cri'd, This is the Gate of Heav'n . . .*

Milton's reference is to Jacob's dream.
iii *37. washes through*] washes in *1853*; wails among *1854, 1857*; washes
'mid *1869, 1877*.

Then, gazing up 'mid the dim pillars high,
The foliaged marble forest where ye lie,
40   *Hush*, ye will say, *it is eternity!*
This is the glimmering verge of Heaven, and these
The columns of the heavenly palaces!
And, in the sweeping of the wind, your ear
The passage of the Angels' wings will hear,
45   And on the lichen-crusted leads above
The rustle of the eternal rain of love.

77 Sohrab and Rustum

AN EPISODE

Effective period of composition probably Dec. 1852–1 May 1853 (though planned and perhaps begun earlier); copied out by 3 Aug. and corrected for publication in Nov. 1853 (three portions of the corrected copy covering ll. 1–526 are known to exist). For the poem's origin see A.'s letter to Sainte-Beuve 6 Jan. 1854, '. . . c'est dans une de vos charmantes causeries que j'ai trouvé renseignements sur l'épisode de la mort de Sohrab, qui m'ont donné le courage de commencer enfin mon poème. J'en avais lu une notice très courte dans une note de l'histoire de Perse de Sir John Malcolm; et je conçus alors le dessein de le mettre en vers; mais je me vis aussitôt forcé d'y renoncer, faute des détails nécessaires . . .' (*Bonnerot* 518). The date of A.'s first sight of the story in Malcolm is unknown, but Sainte-Beuve's essay 'Le Livre des Rois, par Firdousi' appeared in the *Constitutionnel* 11 Feb. 1850 and was collected in *Causeries du Lundi* i (Paris, Dec. 1850), a copy of which (along with Homer's *Iliad*) A. seems to have taken on his delayed Continental honeymoon in Sept.–Oct. 1851 (unpublished 1851 diary); his provisional list of titles for *1852*, which includes 'The Death of Sohrab', probably dates from much the same time (*Commentary* 16–17). The entries 'Malcolm's Hist. of Persia vol. i' and 'Burnes's Bokhara ii' in A.'s diaries under Dec. 1852 and Jan. 1853 respectively (*Notebooks* 552, 553) argue that serious work on the poem was not begun or renewed until after the publication of *1852* in Oct.; it was completed by 1 May 1853 – see A.'s letter to Clough of this date, 'I have just got through a thing which pleases me more than anything I have yet done – but it is pain and grief composing with such interruptions as I have . . .' (*CL* 136) and his letter to his mother of May 1853, 'All my spare time has been spent on a poem which I have just finished, and which I think by far the best thing I have yet done . . . the story is a very noble and excellent one' (*L* i 30). For the poem's copying-out see A.'s letter to Clough 3 Aug. 1850, 'I have written out my Sohrab and Rustum, and like it less' (*CL* 139); and for the corrections in this copy see *nn.* below.

Sainte-Beuve's essay was A.'s main source, but Sir John Malcolm's *History of Persia* (1815) supplied background and the names of places and subsidiary characters not mentioned by Sainte-Beuve; other details, including the description of the Oxus, are from Alexander Burnes's *Travels into Bokhara* ... (1834), already drawn on by A. for 'The Sick King in Bokhara' and 'The Strayed Reveller' (the suggestion that some details are from *The Travels of Marco Polo* tr. H. Murray (Edinburgh, 1847) is unconvincing). Homeric imitation was inevitable in an 'episode' from an epic, but note that Sainte-Beuve refers to Firdausi as 'l'Homère de son pays'. The *Iliad* was on all A.'s monthly reading-lists from Dec. 1852 until June 1853.

'Sohrab and Rustum' illustrates the critical creed of the *1853* Preface, especially the emphasis on '. . . the all-importance of the choice of a subject; the necessity of accurate construction; and the subordinate character of expression' (Appendix A, p. 603 below); and A.'s satisfaction with it as 'naive' rather than 'sentimental' poetry (Schiller's terms) is evident in his letter to Clough 30 Nov. 1853, 'Homer *animates* – Shakespeare *animates* – in its poor way I think Sohrab and Rustum *animates* – the Gipsy Scholar at best awakens a pleasing melancholy. But this is not what we want' (*CL* 146). Modern criticism agrees with C. Patmore that 'the poem fixes our attention rather as a vivid reproduction of Homer's manner and spirit, than as a new and independent creation' (*North British Review* xxi (1854) 495); and many critics would argue that it is the poem's subjectivity that guarantees it a limited success – see, for example, *Trilling* 134–5, '. . . it is almost impossible not to find . . . at least a shadowy personal significance. The strong son is slain by the mightier father; and in the end Sohrab draws his father's spear from his own side to let out his life . . . We watch Arnold in his later youth and we must wonder if he is not, in a psychical sense, doing the same thing.' The early reviewers of *1853* were divided on the poem's merits, but the frequency of the epic similes was often objected to; *Blackwood's Magazine* lxxv (1854) 312 objected to the Oxus coda as 'not at all bad as a piece of versification, but utterly to be condemned in the place where it is introduced'.

A.'s note first appeared in *1854* and in its present form in *1869*. There was no note in *1853* or *1857*. In *1854*, in reply to J. D. Coleridge who had seen Sainte-Beuve's essay and complained in the *Christian Remembrancer* xxvii (1854) 322 that A. 'had not thought fit to offer a single syllable of acknowledgment to an author to whom he has manifestly been very largely indebted', A. gave a long extract from Sainte-Beuve (Appendix C, p. 612 below) with a summary of the story from Malcolm. A.'s *1869* note reads:

'The story of Sohrab and Rustum is told in Sir John Malcolm's *History of Persia*, as follows:

"The young Sohrab was the fruit of one of Rustum's early amours. He had left his mother, and sought fame under the banners of Afrasiab, whose armies he commanded, and soon obtained a renown beyond that of all contemporary heroes but his father. He had carried death and dismay into the ranks of the Persians, and had terrified the boldest warriors of that country, before Rustum encountered him, which at last that hero resolved to do, under a feigned name. They met three times. The first time they parted by mutual consent, though Sohrab had the advantage; the second, the youth obtained a victory, but granted life to his unknown father; the third was fatal to Sohrab, who, when writhing in the pangs of death, warned his conqueror to shun the vengeance that is inspired by parental woes, and bade him dread the rage of the mighty Rustum, who must soon learn that he had slain his son Sohrab. These words, we are told, were as death to the aged hero; and when he recovered from a trance, he called in despair for proofs of what Sohrab had said. The afflicted and dying youth tore open his mail, and showed his father a seal which his mother had placed on his arm when she discovered to him the secret of his birth, and bade him seek his father. The sight of his own signet rendered Rustum quite frantic; he cursed himself, attempting to put an end to his existence, and was only prevented by the efforts of his expiring son. After Sohrab's death, he burnt his tents and all his goods, and carried the corpse to Seistan, where it was interred; the army of Turan was, agreeably to the last request of Sohrab, permitted to cross the Oxus unmolested. To reconcile us to the improbability of this tale, we are informed that Rustum could have no idea his son was in existence. The mother of Sohrab had written to him her child was a daughter, fearing to lose her darling infant if she revealed the truth; and Rustum, as before stated, fought under a feigned name, an usage not uncommon in the chivalrous combats of those days."'

Published *1853*; reprinted (*1854, 1857*), *1869*, etc.

And the first grey of morning filled the east,
And the fog rose out of the Oxus stream.
But all the Tartar camp along the stream
Was hushed, and still the men were plunged in sleep;
5   Sohrab alone, he slept not; all night long
He had lain wakeful, tossing on his bed;

¶ 77. *1. grey of morning filled*] rays of morning streaked *MS.* (c). (This abbreviation is used throughout the notes to this poem to indicate a cancelled reading in A.'s fair copy.) With the cancelled reading cp. Milton, *Paradise Lost* iv 623,

To morrow ere fresh Morning streak the East . . .

3. Tartar camp] Sohrab is the champion of the Tartars in Malcolm, of the Turks in Sainte-Beuve.

6–10. See J. A. Froude's letter to Clough 22 Nov. 1853, 'I think he [A.] has overdone the plainness of expression which he so much studies, particularly in the beginning, and those repetitions of words (the word "tent" comes half a dozen times in the first 18 lines) however justified by Homer's example, certainly strike an English ear unpleasantly' (*Correspondence of A.H.C.* ii 467).

But when the grey dawn stole into his tent,
He rose, and clad himself, and girt his sword,
And took his horseman's cloak, and left his tent,
10   And went abroad into the cold wet fog,
Through the dim camp to Peran-Wisa's tent.
    Through the black Tartar tents he passed, which
Clustering like bee-hives on the low flat strand   [stood
Of Oxus, where the summer-floods o'erflow
15   When the sun melts the snows in high Pamere;
Through the black tents he passed, o'er that low strand
And to a hillock came, a little back
From the stream's brink – the spot where first a boat,
Crossing the stream in summer, scrapes the land.
20   The men of former times had crowned the top
With a clay fort; but that was fallen, and now
The Tartars built there Peran-Wisa's tent,
A dome of laths, and o'er it felts were spread.
And Sohrab came there, and went in, and stood
25   Upon the thick piled carpets in the tent,
And found the old man sleeping on his bed
Of rugs and felts, and near him lay his arms.
And Peran-Wisa heard him, though the step
Was dulled; for he slept light, an old man's sleep;
30   And he rose quickly on one arm, and said: –
    'Who art thou? for it is not yet clear dawn.
Speak! is there news, or any night alarm?'
    But Sohrab came to the bedside, and said: –
'Thou know'st me, Peran-Wisa! it is I.
35   The sun is not yet risen, and the foe
Sleep; but I sleep not; all night long I lie
Tossing and wakeful, and I come to thee.
For so did King Afrasiab bid me seek
Thy counsel, and to heed thee as thy son,

10. wet fog] dim air *MS.* (c).
11. dim] hush'd *MS.* (c).
12. black Tartar tents] Cp. Burnes, *Travels into Bokhara* (1834) ii 101, 'We
here saw … the wandering inhabitants, or Ilyats, of Khorasan, about a
thousand of whose black tents were scattered around.' A. puts the Ilyats
of Khorassan among the Persian forces, but describes them as Tartars
(ll. 136–8 below).
19. scrapes] meets *MS.* (c).
23–7. Cp. Burnes's *Travels* ii 59–60, 'The tent or khirgah was spacious …
The sides were of lattice-work, and the roof was formed of laths … The
floor was spread with felts and carpets.'
38–40. Peran-Wisa is the Nestor of the Tartar host.
11*

40   In Samarcand, before the army marched;
      And I will tell thee what my heart desires.
      Thou know'st if, since from Ader-baijan first
      I came among the Tartars and bore arms,
      I have still served Afrasiab well, and shown,
45   At my boy's years, the courage of a man.
      This too thou know'st, that while I still bear on
      The conquering Tartar ensigns through the world,
      And beat the Persians back on every field,
      I seek one man, one man, and one alone –
50   Rustum, my father; who I hoped should greet,
      Should one day greet, upon some well-fought field,
      His not unworthy, not inglorious son.
      So I long hoped, but him I never find.
      Come then, hear now, and grant me what I ask.
55   Let the two armies rest to-day; but I
      Will challenge forth the bravest Persian lords
      To meet me, man to man; if I prevail,
      Rustum will surely hear it; if I fall –
      Old man, the dead need no one, claim no kin.
60   Dim is the rumour of a common fight,
      Where host meets host, and many names are sunk;
      But of a single combat fame speaks clear.'
          He spoke; and Peran-Wisa took the hand
      Of the young man in his, and sighed, and said: –
65   'O Sohrab, an unquiet heart is thine!
      Canst thou not rest among the Tartar chiefs,
      And share the battle's common chance with us
      Who love thee, but must press for ever first,
      In single fight incurring single risk,
70   To find a father thou hast never seen?
      That were far best, my son, to stay with us
      Unmurmuring; in our tents, while it is war,
      And when 'tis truce, then in Afrasiab's towns.
      But, if this one desire indeed rules all,
75   To seek out Rustum – seek him not through fight!
      Seek him in peace, and carry to his arms,
      O Sohrab, carry an unwounded son!

59. Followed by this cancelled line in the MS.,

    But I shall conquer, that my heart forebodes.

A. deleted the line when he inserted ll. 86–7 below.

71–3. First added in *1854*.

74. But, if this one desire indeed] Or, if indeed this one desire *1853*. See A.'s
letter to Clough 30 Nov. 1853, 'I think "if indeed this one desire rules all"
is rather Tennysonian – at any rate it is not good' (*CL* 145).

But far hence seek him, for he is not here.
For now it is not as when I was young,
80   When Rustum was in front of every fray;
But now he keeps apart, and sits at home,
In Seistan, with Zal, his father old.
Whether that his own mighty strength at last
Feels the abhorred approaches of old age,
85   Or in some quarrel with the Persian King.
There go! – Thou wilt not? Yet my heart forebodes
Danger or death awaits thee on this field.
Fain would I know thee safe and well, though lost
To us; fain therefore send thee hence, in peace
90   To seek thy father, not seek single fights
In vain; but who can keep the lion's cub
From ravening, and who govern Rustum's son?
Go, I will grant thee what thy heart desires.'
    So said he, and dropped Sohrab's hand, and left
95   His bed, and the warm rugs whereon he lay;
And o'er his chilly limbs his woollen coat
He passed, and tied his sandals on his feet,
And threw a white cloak round him, and he took
In his right hand a ruler's staff, no sword;
100   And on his head he set his sheep-skin cap,
Black, glossy, curled, the fleece of Kara-Kul;
And raised the curtain of his tent, and called
His herald to his side, and went abroad.
    The sun by this had risen, and cleared the fog
105   From the broad Oxus and the glittering sands.
And from their tents the Tartar horsemen filed
Into the open plain; so Haman bade –
Haman, who next to Peran-Wisa ruled
The host, and still was in his lusty prime.
110   From their black tents, long files of horse, they
        streamed;

86-7. A later insertion in the MS. – see *n.* to l. 59 above.
100-1. A later insertion in the MS.
110-16. An imitation of *Iliad* ii 459-66, 'And as the many tribes of winged fowl, wild geese or cranes or long-necked swans on the Asian mead by the streams of Caystrius, fly this way and that, glorying in their strength of wing . . . even so their many tribes poured forth from ships and huts into the plain of Scamander, and the earth echoed wondrously beneath the tread of men and horses.' The Homeric simile introduces a roll-call of Greek chieftains as A.'s simile introduces a catalogue of the Tartar forces (ll. 117-35). Milton's influence in this passage is admitted in A.'s letter to J. D. Coleridge 22 Nov. 1853, 'Milton is a sufficiently great master to

As when some grey November morn the files,
In marching order spread, of long-necked cranes
Stream over Casbin and the southern slopes
Of Elburz, from the Aralian estuaries,
115   Or some frore Caspian reed-bed, southward bound
For the warm Persian sea-board – so they streamed.
The Tartars of the Oxus, the King's guard,
First, with black sheep-skin caps and with long spears;
Large men, large steeds; who from Bokhara come
120   And Khiva, and ferment the milk of mares.
Next, the more temperate Toorkmuns of the south,
The Tukas, and the lances of Salore,
And those from Attruck and the Caspian sands;
Light men and on light steeds, who only drink
125   The acrid milk of camels, and their wells.
And then a swarm of wandering horse, who came
From far, and a more doubtful service owned;
The Tartars of Ferghana, from the banks
Of the Jaxartes, men with scanty beards
130   And close-set skull-caps; and those wilder hordes
Who roam o'er Kipchak and the northern waste,
Kalmucks and unkempt Kuzzaks, tribes who stray
Nearest the Pole, and wandering Kirghizzes,
Who come on shaggy ponies from Pamere;
135   These all filed out from camp into the plain.
And on the other side the Persians formed;
First a light cloud of horse, Tartars they seemed,
The Ilyats of Khorassan; and behind,
The royal troops of Persia, horse and foot,
140   Marshalled battalions bright in burnished steel.
But Peran-Wisa with his herald came,
Threading the Tartar squadrons to the front,

imitate. The cranes are not taken direct from him [*Paradise Lost* vii 425–31]
as far as I can remember, but the passage is, no doubt, an imitation of his
manner. So with many others' (*Life of J.D.C.* i 210–11).

117–40. The proper names, which are used in the Miltonic manner for
their sound and suggestiveness, are from either Malcolm or Burnes.

119–21. Suggested by a careless reading of Burnes's *Travels* ii 19, 'I
believed that the Uzbeks and Toorkmuns drank mare's milk and fermented
liquors, but these are unknown in Bokhara, and only peculiar to Kuzzaks
and Kirgizzes, between that city and Russia.' Burnes adds that the Toorkmuns drink camel's milk.

131. roam o'er] A.'s three cancelled attempts at this phrase in the MS. were
successively: 'come from', 'dwell in', 'rove o'er'.

142. Threading] Swift through *MS.* 'Swift' replaces 'Slow' deleted.

And with his staff kept back the foremost ranks.
And when Feerood, who led the Persians, saw
145   That Peran-Wisa kept the Tartars back,
He took his spear, and to the front he came,
And checked his ranks, and fixed them where they
And the old Tartar came upon the sand   [stood.
Betwixt the silent hosts, and spake, and said: –
150   'Feerood, and ye, Persians and Tartars, hear!
Let there be truce between the hosts to-day.
But choose a champion from the Persian lords
To fight our champion Sohrab, man to man.'
As, in the country, on a morn in June,
155   When the dew glistens on the pearlèd ears,
A shiver runs through the deep corn for joy –
So, when they heard what Peran-Wisa said,
A thrill through all the Tartar squadrons ran
Of pride and hope for Sohrab, whom they loved.
160   But as a troop of pedlars, from Cabool,
Cross underneath the Indian Caucasus,
That vast sky-neighbouring mountain of milk snow;
Crossing so high, that, as they mount, they pass
Long flocks of travelling birds dead on the snow,
165   Choked by the air, and scarce can they themselves
Slake their parched throats with sugared mulberries –
In single file they move, and stop their breath,
For fear they should dislodge the o'erhanging snows –
So the pale Persians held their breath with fear.
170   And to Feerood his brother chiefs came up
To counsel; Gudurz and Zoarrah came,
And Feraburz, who ruled the Persian host

160–8. See Burnes's *Travels* ii 247–8, 'I have not spoken of the true mountain of Hindoo Koosh . . . This great peak is visible from Cabool, and entirely enveloped in milk-white snow . . . Its altitude must be considerable for the travellers complain of the difficulty of breathing, and carry sugar and mulberries with them, to ease their respiration . . . Thousands of birds are also found dead on the snow, for it is believed that they are unable to fly from the violence of the winds; but it is more probable that they are prevented by the rarity of the atmosphere . . . The greatest silence is preserved in crossing Hindoo Koosh; and no one speaks loud, or fires a gun, lest the reverberation cause a fall of snow.'
161. Cross] Climb *MS.* 'Climb' replaces 'Wind' deleted.
163–6. A later insertion in the MS., part of A.'s attempt to 'orientalise' his similes – see *n.* to ll. 286–8 below.
163. Crossing] Winding *MS., 1853–77.*
167. move] wind *MS.* 'Wind' replaces 'pass' deleted.

Second, and was the uncle of the King;
These came and counselled, and then Gudurz said: –
175   'Ferood, shame bids us take their challenge up,
Yet champion have we none to match this youth.
He has the wild stag's foot, the lion's heart.
But Rustum came last night; aloof he sits
And sullen, and has pitched his tents apart.
180   Him will I seek, and carry to his ear
The Tartar challenge, and this young man's name.
Haply he will forget his wrath, and fight.
Stand forth the while, and take their challenge up.'
        So spake he; and Ferood stood forth and cried: –
185   'Old man, be it agreed as thou hast said!
Let Sohrab arm, and we will find a man.'
        He spake: and Peran-Wisa turned, and strode
Back through the opening squadrons to his tent.
But through the anxious Persians Gudurz ran,
190   And crossed the camp which lay behind, and reached,
Out on the sands beyond it, Rustum's tents.
Of scarlet cloth they were, and glittering gay,
Just pitched; the high pavilion in the midst
Was Rustum's, and his men lay camped around.
195   And Gudurz entered Rustum's tent, and found
Rustum; his morning meal was done, but still
The table stood before him, charged with food –
A side of roasted sheep, and cakes of bread,
And dark green melons; and there Rustum sate
200   Listless, and held a falcon on his wrist,
And played with it; but Gudurz came and stood
Before him; and he looked, and saw him stand,
And with a cry sprang up and dropped the bird,
And greeted Gudurz with both hands, and said: –
205   'Welcome! these eyes could see no better sight.
What news? but sit down first, and eat and drink.'
        But Gudurz stood in the tent-door, and said: –
'Not now! a time will come to eat and drink,
But not to-day; to-day has other needs.
210   The armies are drawn out, and stand at gaze;
For from the Tartars is a challenge brought

178–9. Cp. Sainte-Beuve, 'Le Livre des Rois, par Firdousi', *Causeries du
Lundi* i (1850) 347, 'Roustem arrive pourtant; mais, mal accueilli par le
roi, il entre dans une colère d'Achille, et il est tout prêt à s'en retourner dans
sa tente.'
197. *food*] cates MS. (c).
198. *cakes*] loaves MS. (c).

To pick a champion from the Persian lords
To fight their champion – and thou know'st his name –
Sohrab men call him, but his birth is hid.
215 O Rustum, like thy might is this young man's!
He has the wild stag's foot, the lion's heart;
And he is young, and Iran's chiefs are old,
Or else too weak; and all eyes turn to thee.
Come down and help us, Rustum, or we lose!'
220 He spoke, but Rustum answered with a smile: –
'Go to! if Iran's chiefs are old, then I
Am older; if the young are weak, the King
Errs strangely; for the King, for Kai Khosroo,
Himself is young, and honours younger men,
225 And lets the agéd moulder to their graves.
Rustum he loves no more, but loves the young –
The young may rise at Sohrab's vaunts, not I.
For what care I, though all speak Sohrab's fame?
For would that I myself had such a son,
230 And not that one slight helpless girl I have –
A son so famed, so brave, to send to war,
And I to tarry with the snow-haired Zal,
My father, whom the robber Afghans vex,
And clip his borders short, and drive his herds,
235 And he has none to guard his weak old age.
There would I go, and hang my armour up,
And with my great name fence that weak old man,
And spend the goodly treasures I have got,
And rest my age, and hear of Sohrab's fame,
240 And leave to death the hosts of thankless kings,
And with these slaughterous hands draw sword no
    more.'

228. The MS. shows three cancelled attempts at this line:

　　(1) *What irks it me that men speak Sohrab's praise?*
　　(2) *I am not wrong'd when men speak Sohrab's praise*
　　(3) *For what care I, that Sohrab's fame quench theirs?*

230. See A.'s note from Malcolm (headn. above). Tamineh's ruse is not
mentioned by Sainte-Beuve.
231. *so famed*] A. hesitated between 'so famed' and 'so praised' as he
altered l. 228 above.
232. *snow-haired*] white-haired *MS.* (c).
233-5. An imitation of *Iliad* xxiv 486-9 (Priam to Achilles), 'Remember
thy father, O Achilles . . . whose years are even as mine, on the grievous
threshold of old age. Him fully likely the dwellers that be round about
are entreating evilly, neither is there any to ward from him ruin and
bane.'

He spoke, and smiled; and Gudurz made reply: –
'What then, O Rustum, will men say to this,
When Sohrab dares our bravest forth, and seeks
245 Thee most of all, and thou, whom most he seeks,
Hidest thy face? Take heed lest men should say:
Like some old miser, Rustum hoards his fame,
And shuns to peril it with younger men.'
And, greatly moved, then Rustum made reply: –
250 'O Gudurz, wherefore dost thou say such words?
Thou knowest better words than this to say.
What is one more, one less, obscure or famed,
Valiant or craven, young or old, to me?
Are not they mortal, am not I myself?
255 But who for men of nought would do great deeds?
Come, thou shalt see how Rustum hoards his fame!
But I will fight unknown, and in plain arms;
Let not men say of Rustum, he was matched
In single fight with any mortal man.'
260 He spoke, and frowned; and Gudurz turned, and
Back quickly through the camp in fear and joy – [ran
Fear at his wrath, but joy that Rustum came.
But Rustum strode to his tent-door, and called
His followers in, and bade them bring his arms,
265 And clad himself in steel; the arms he chose
Were plain, and on his shield was no device,
Only his helm was rich, inlaid with gold,
And, from the fluted spine atop, a plume
Of horsehair waved, a scarlet horsehair plume.
270 So armed, he issued forth; and Ruksh, his horse,
Followed him like a faithful hound at heel –
Ruksh, whose renown was noised through all the earth,
The horse, whom Rustum on a foray once
Did in Bokhara by the river find
275 A colt beneath its dam, and drove him home,
And reared him; a bright bay, with lofty crest,
Dight with a saddle-cloth of broidered green
Crusted with gold, and on the ground were worked
All beasts of chase, all beasts which hunters know.
280 So followed, Rustum left his tents, and crossed
The camp, and to the Persian host appeared.
And all the Persians knew him, and with shouts
Hailed; but the Tartars knew not who he was.

243–56. Cp. Sainte-Beuve, *op. cit.* 347, 'On ne le fléchit qu'en lui représentant que s'abstenir en une telle rencontre, ce serait paraître reculer devant
le jeune héros.'

And dear as the wet diver to the eyes
285   Of his pale wife who waits and weeps on shore,
By sandy Bahrein, in the Persian Gulf,
Plunging all day in the blue waves, at night,
Having made up his tale of precious pearls,
Rejoins her in their hut upon the sands –
290   So dear to the pale Persians Rustum came.
        And Rustum to the Persian front advanced,
And Sohrab armed in Haman's tent, and came.
And as afield the reapers cut a swath
Down through the middle of a rich man's corn,
295   And on each side are squares of standing corn,
And in the midst a stubble, short and bare –
So on each side were squares of men, with spears
Bristling, and in the midst, the open sand.
And Rustum came upon the sand, and cast
300   His eyes toward the Tartar tents, and saw
Sohrab come forth, and eyed him as he came.
        As some rich woman, on a winter's morn,
Eyes through her silken curtains the poor drudge
Who with numb blackened fingers makes her fire –
305   At cock-crow, on a starlit winter's morn,
When the frost flowers the whitened window-panes –
And wonders how she lives, and what the thoughts
Of that poor drudge may be; so Rustum eyed
The unknown adventurous youth, who from afar
310   Came seeking Rustum, and defying forth
All the most valiant chiefs; long he perused
His spirited air, and wondered who he was.
For very young he seemed, tenderly reared;
Like some young cypress, tall, and dark, and straight,

284. *diver*] fisher *MS.* (c).
285. *on shore*] ashore *MS.* (c).
286–8. *MS.* (c),

> *At twilight, on a stormy eve in March,*
> *Running fast homeward with the turn of tide*
> *Beaches the pinnace in a darkening cove . . .*

See A.'s letter to John Blackett 26 Nov. 1853 (replying to a complaint
about the similes), 'I can only say I took a great deal of trouble to orientalise them (the Bahrein diver was originally an ordinary fisher), because I
thought they looked strange, and jarred, if Western' (*L* i 32).
302–8. A vivid mid-Victorian image that A. failed to orientalize.
309. *from afar*] through the world *MS.* (c).
312. *spirited air*] face and air *MS.* (c).

315   Which in a queen's secluded garden throws
Its slight dark shadow on the moonlit turf,
By midnight, to a bubbling fountain's sound –
So slender Sohrab seemed, so softly reared.
And a deep pity entered Rustum's soul

320   As he beheld him coming; and he stood,
And beckoned to him with his hand, and said: –
   'O thou young man, the air of Heaven is soft,
And warm, and pleasant; but the grave is cold!
Heaven's air is better than the cold dead grave.

325   Behold me! I am vast, and clad in iron,
And tried; and I have stood on many a field
Of blood, and I have fought with many a foe –
Never was that field lost, or that foe saved.
O Sohrab, wherefore wilt thou rush on death?

330   Be governed! quit the Tartar host, and come
To Iran, and be as my son to me,
And fight beneath my banner till I die!
There are no youths in Iran brave as thou.'
   So he spake, mildly; Sohrab heard his voice,

335   The mighty voice of Rustum, and he saw
His giant figure planted on the sand,
Sole, like some single tower, which a chief
Hath builded on the waste in former years
Against the robbers; and he saw that head,
Streaked with its first grey hairs; hope filled his soul,

340   And he ran forward and embraced his knees,
And clasped his hand within his own, and said: –
   'O, by thy father's head! by thine own soul!
Art thou not Rustum? speak! art thou not he?'

345   But Rustum eyed askance the kneeling youth,
And turned away, and spake to his own soul: –

322–33. Taken from Mohl's translation of Firdausi quoted by Sainte-Beuve, *op. cit.* 348, 'O jeune homme si tendre! lui dit-il, la terre est sèche et froide, l'air est doux et chaud. Je suis vieux; j'ai vu maint champ de bataille, j'ai détruit mainte armée, et je n'ai jamais été battu ... Mais j'ai pitié de toi et ne voudrais pas t'arracher la vie. Ne reste pas avec les Turcs; je ne connais personne dans l'Iran qui ait des épaules et des bras comme toi.'
325. Tennysonian.
334–69. Expanding Sainte-Beuve, *op. cit.* 348, 'En entendant ces paroles qui semblent sortir d'une âme amie, le coeur de Sohrab s'élance, il a un pressentiment soudain; il demande ingénument au guerrier s'il n'est pas celui qu'il cherche, s'il n'est pas l'illustre Roustem. Mais le vieux chef, qui ne veut pas donner à ce jouvenceau trop d'orgueil, répond avec ruse qu'il n'est pas Roustem.'

'Ah me, I muse what this young fox may mean!
False, wily, boastful, are these Tartar boys.
For if I now confess this thing he asks,
350   And hide it not, but say: *Rustum is here!*
He will not yield indeed, nor quit our foes,
But he will find some pretext not to fight,
And praise my fame, and proffer courteous gifts,
A belt or sword perhaps, and go his way.
355   And on a feast-tide, in Afrasiab's hall,
In Samarcand, he will arise and cry:
"I challenged once, when the two armies camped
Beside the Oxus, all the Persian lords
To cope with me in single fight; but they
360   Shrank, only Rustum dared; then he and I
Changed gifts, and went on equal terms away."
So will he speak, perhaps, while men applaud;
Then were the chiefs of Iran shamed through me.'
        And then he turned, and sternly spake aloud: –
365   'Rise! wherefore dost thou vainly question thus
Of Rustum? I am here, whom thou hast called
By challenge forth; make good thy vaunt, or yield!
Is it with Rustum only thou wouldst fight?
Rash boy, men look on Rustum's face and flee!
370   For well I know, that did great Rustum stand
Before thy face this day, and were revealed,
There would be then no talk of fighting more.
But being what I am, I tell thee this –
Do thou record it in thine inmost soul:
375   Either thou shalt renounce thy vaunt and yield,
Or else thy bones shall strew this sand, till winds
Bleach them, or Oxus with his summer floods,
Oxus in summer wash them all away.'
        He spoke; and Sohrab answered, on his feet: –
380   'Art thou so fierce? Thou wilt not fright me so!
I am no girl, to be made pale by words.
Yet this thou hast said well, did Rustum stand
Here on this field, there were no fighting then.
But Rustum is far hence, and we stand here.
385   Begin! thou art more vast, more dread than I,
And thou art proved, I know, and I am young –
But yet success sways with the breath of Heaven.

355. *feast-tide*] feast day *1853–4*.
370–2. Dramatic irony.
381. Another instance of dramatic irony. Rustum thinks that he has a daughter (see l. 230 above).

        And though thou thinkest that thou knowest sure
        Thy victory, yet thou canst not surely know.
390   For we are all, like swimmers in the sea,
        Poised on the top of a huge wave of fate,
        Which hangs uncertain to which side to fall.
        And whether it will heave us up to land,
        Or whether it will roll us out to sea,
395   Back out to sea, to the deep waves of death,
        We know not, and no search will make us know;
        Only the event will teach us in its hour.'
            He spoke, and Rustum answered not, but hurled
        His spear; down from the shoulder, down it came,
400   As on some partridge in the corn a hawk,
        That long has towered in the airy clouds,
        Drops like a plummet; Sohrab saw it come,
        And sprang aside, quick as a flash; the spear
        Hissed, and went quivering down into the sand,
405   Which it sent flying wide; then Sohrab threw
        In turn, and full struck Rustum's shield; sharp rang,
        The iron plates rang sharp, but turned the spear.
        And Rustum seized his club, which none but he
        Could wield; an unlopped trunk it was, and huge,
410   Still rough – like those which men in treeless plains

390-7. See Harriet Martineau's comment in her review of *1853, Daily News* 26 Dec. 1853, 'There never was such a wave seen at Brighton, or elsewhere.' The image is connected with A.'s prose note (Yale MS.), 'We lie outstretched on a vast wave of this starlit sea of life, balancing backwards and forwards with it: we desire the shore, but we shall reach it only when our wave reaches it.'

400-2. Probably suggested by Achilles' pursuit of Hector, *Iliad* xxii 139-40, 'As a falcon in the mountains, swiftest of winged things, swoopeth lightly after a trembling dove . . .'

402-4. An imitation of *Iliad* xvi 610-13, 'But Meriones, looking steadily at him, avoided the spear of bronze; for he stooped forward, and the long spear fixed itself in the ground behind him, and the butt of the spear quivered.'

409. and huge] still rough *MS.* (c).

410. MS. (c),

        Like those which men who dwell in treeless plains . . .

410-15. A. is imitating Milton's description of Satan's spear, *Paradise Lost* i 292-4,

        His spear, to equal which the tallest Pine
        Hewn on Norwegian hills, to be the Mast
        Of some great Ammiral, were but a wand . . .

To build them boats fish from the flooded rivers,
Hyphasis or Hydaspes, when, high up
By their dark springs, the wind in winter-time
Hath made in Himalayan forests wrack,
415   And strewn the channels with torn boughs – so huge
The club which Rustum lifted now, and struck
One stroke; but again Sohrab sprang aside,
Lithe as the glancing snake, and the club came
Thundering to earth, and leapt from Rustum's hand.
420   And Rustum followed his own blow, and fell
To his knees, and with his fingers clutched the sand;
And now might Sohrab have unsheathed his sword,
And pierced the mighty Rustum while he lay
Dizzy, and on his knees, and choked with sand;
425   But he looked on, and smiled, nor bared his sword,
But courteously drew back, and spoke, and said: –
      'Thou strik'st too hard! that club of thine will float
Upon the summer-floods, and not my bones.
But rise, and be not wroth! not wroth am I;
430   No, when I see thee, wrath forsakes my soul.
Thou say'st, thou art not Rustum; be it so!
Who art thou then, that canst so touch my soul?
Boy as I am, I have seen battles too –
Have waded foremost in their bloody waves,
435   And heard their hollow roar of dying men;
But never was my heart thus touched before.
Are they from Heaven, these softenings of the heart?
O thou old warrior, let us yield to Heaven!
Come, plant we here in earth our angry spears,
440   And make a truce, and sit upon this sand,
And pledge each other in red wine, like friends,
And thou shalt talk to me of Rustum's deeds.

---

but his information is from Burnes, who speaks of cedars 'floated down
with the inundations of the river from the Hemilaya ... We saw a cedar-
tree lying on the banks of the Hydaspes, with a circumference of thirteen
feet' (*Travels* i 50).
411. build them boats] saw them planks MS. (c)
439–47. Developed from Mohl's translation of Firdausi quoted by Sainte-
Beuve, *op. cit.* 349, 'Jette cette massue et cette épée de la vengeance, jette
tout cet appareil d'un combat impie. Asseyons-nous tous deux à terre, et
adoucissons avec du vin nos regards courroucés. Faisons un traité en invoquant Dieu, et repentons-nous dans notre cœur de cette inimitié. Attends
qu'un autre se présente pour le combat ...' The combat takes place on
two days in Firdausi. Sohrab's speech is before its renewal on the second
day.

There are enough foes in the Persian host,
Whom I may meet, and strike, and feel no pang;
445   Champions enough Afrasiab has, whom thou
Mayst fight; fight *them*, when they confront thy spear!
But oh, let there be peace 'twixt thee and me!'
     He ceased, but while he spake, Rustum had risen,
And stood erect, trembling with rage; his club
450   He left to lie, but had regained his spear,
Whose fiery point now in his mailed right-hand
Blazed bright and baleful, like that autumn-star,
The baleful sign of fevers; dust had soiled
His stately crest, and dimmed his glittering arms.
455   His breast heaved, his lips foamed, and twice his voice
Was choked with rage; at last these words broke way:–
     'Girl! nimble with thy feet, not with thy hands!
Curled minion, dancer, coiner of sweet words!
Fight, let me hear thy hateful voice no more!
460   Thou art not in Afrasiab's gardens now
With Tartar girls, with whom thou art wont to dance;
But on the Oxus-sands, and in the dance
Of battle, and with me, who make no play
Of war; I fight it out, and hand to hand.
465   Speak not to me of truce, and pledge, and wine!
Remember all thy valour; try thy feints
And cunning! all the pity I had is gone;
Because thou hast shamed me before both the hosts
With thy light skipping tricks, and thy girl's wiles.'
470   He spoke, and Sohrab kindled at his taunts,
And he too drew his sword; at once they rushed
Together, as two eagles on one prey

451–3. A. combines two passages from Homer. See *Iliad* xxii 25–31, 'Him [Achilles] the old man Priam was first to behold with his eyes, as he sped all-gleaming over the plain, like to the star that cometh forth at harvest-time . . . Brightest of all is he, yet withal is he a sign of evil, and bringeth much fever upon wretched mortals' and 317–20, 'As a star goeth forth amid stars in the darkness of night . . . even so went forth a gleam from the keen spear that Achilles poised in his right hand, as he devised evil for goodly Hector.'

457–8. An imitation of *Iliad* xvi 617–18, 'Meriones, full soon, for all thou art a nimble dancer, would my spear have made thee to cease dancing for ever, had I but struck thee.'

471–4. Perhaps suggested by *Iliad* xvi 428–30 (the conflict of Patroclus and Sarpedon), 'And as vultures crooked of talon and curved of beak fight with loud cries upon a high rock, even so with cries rushed they one against the other.'

Come rushing down together from the clouds,
One from the east, one from the west; their shields
475   Dashed with a clang together, and a din
Rose, such as that the sinewy woodcutters
Make often in the forest's heart at morn,
Of hewing axes, crashing trees – such blows
Rustum and Sohrab on each other hailed.
48o   And you would say that sun and stars took part
In that unnatural conflict; for a cloud
Grew suddenly in Heaven, and darked the sun
Over the fighters' heads; and a wind rose
Under their feet, and moaning swept the plain,
485   And in a sandy whirlwind wrapped the pair.
In gloom they twain were wrapped, and they alone;
For both the on-looking hosts on either hand
Stood in broad daylight, and the sky was pure,
And the sun sparkled on the Oxus stream.
490   But in the gloom they fought, with bloodshot eyes
And labouring breath; first Rustum struck the shield
Which Sohrab held stiff out; the steel-spiked spear
Rent the tough plates, but failed to reach the skin,
And Rustum plucked it back with angry groan.
495   Then Sohrab with his sword smote Rustum's helm,
Nor clove its steel quite through; but all the crest
He shore away, and that proud horsehair plume,
Never till now defiled, sank to the dust;
And Rustum bowed his head; but then the gloom

474–9. An imitation of *Iliad* xvi 633–7 (the combat between Aeneas and Meriones), 'And from them – even as the din ariseth of woodcutters in the glades of a mountain, and afar is the sound heard thereof – so from them went up a clanging from the broad-wayed earth, a clanging of bronze and hide and well-wrought shields, as they thrust one at the other with swords and two-edged spears.'

480–9. An imitation of *Iliad* xvii 366–73 (the struggle for the body of Patroclus), 'So fought they . . . nor wouldst thou have deemed that sun and moon yet abode, for with darkness were they shrouded in the fight . . . But the rest of the Trojans and the well-greaved Achaeans fought at their ease under clear air, and over them was spread the piercing brightness of the sun, and on all the earth and the mountains was no cloud seen.'

484. *Under their feet, and moaning*] Eddying and moaning round, and MS.

497–8. An imitation of *Iliad* xvi 796–7 (Apollo strikes off the helmet of Patroclus), 'Not until that hour had the gods suffered that helm with plume of horsehair to be befouled with dust.'

498. MS.,

Never defac'd till now, sham'd to the dust . . .

500   Grew blacker, thunder rumbled in the air,
       And lightnings rent the cloud; and Ruksh, the horse,
       Who stood at hand, uttered a dreadful cry;
       No horse's cry was that, most like the roar
       Of some pained desert-lion, who all day
505   Hath trailed the hunter's javelin in his side,
       And comes at night to die upon the sand.
       The two hosts heard that cry, and quaked for fear,
       And Oxus curdled as it crossed his stream.
       But Sohrab heard, and quailed not, but rushed on,
510   And struck again; and again Rustum bowed
       His head; but this time all the blade, like glass,
       Sprang in a thousand shivers on the helm,
       And in the hand the hilt remained alone.
       Then Rustum raised his head; his dreadful eyes
515   Glared, and he shook on high his menacing spear,
       And shouted: *Rustum!* – Sohrab heard that shout,
       And shrank amazed; back he recoiled one step,
       And scanned with blinking eyes the advancing form;
       And then he stood bewildered; and he dropped
520   His covering shield, and the spear pierced his side.
       He reeled, and staggering back, sank to the ground;
       And then the gloom dispersed, and the wind fell,
       And the bright sun broke forth, and melted all
       The cloud; and the two armies saw the pair –
525   Saw Rustum standing, safe upon his feet,
       And Sohrab, wounded, on the bloody sand.
          Then, with a bitter smile, Rustum began: –
       'Sohrab, thou thoughtest in thy mind to kill
       A Persian lord this day, and strip his corpse,
530   And bear thy trophies to Afrasiab's tent.
       Or else that the great Rustum would come down
       Himself to fight, and that thy wiles would move
       His heart to take a gift, and let thee go.
       And then that all the Tartar host would praise
535   Thy courage or thy craft, and spread thy fame,

500. MS.,

          Grew deeper, thunder crash'd along the sky . . .

528–39. An imitation of the usual Homeric vaunt over the defeated. See, for example, Achilles to Hector, *Iliad* xxii 331–3, 335–6, 'Hector, thou thoughtest, I ween, while thou wast despoiling Patroclus, that thou wouldest be safe, and hadst no thought of me that was afar, thou fool . . . Thee shall dogs and birds rend in unseemly wise, but to him shall the Achaeans give burial.'

> To glad thy father in his weak old age.
> Fool, thou art slain, and by an unknown man!
> Dearer to the red jackals shalt thou be
> Than to thy friends, and to thy father old.'

540   And, with a fearless mien, Sohrab replied: –
> 'Unknown thou art; yet thy fierce vaunt is vain.
> Thou dost not slay me, proud and boastful man!
> No! Rustum slays me, and this filial heart.
> For were I matched with ten such men as thee,

545   And I were that which till to-day I was,
> They should be lying here, I standing there.
> But that belovéd name unnerved my arm –
> That name, and something, I confess, in thee,
> Which troubles all my heart, and made my shield

550   Fall; and thy spear transfixed an unarmed foe.
> And now thou boastest, and insult'st my fate.
> But hear thou this, fierce man, tremble to hear:
> The mighty Rustum shall avenge my death!
> My father, whom I seek through all the world,

555   He shall avenge my death, and punish thee!'
>   As when some hunter in the spring hath found
> A breeding eagle sitting on her nest,
> Upon the craggy isle of a hill-lake,
> And pierced her with an arrow as she rose,

541–55. An imitation of the dying speech of Patroclus, *Iliad* xvi 844–54, 'For this time, Hector, boast thou mightily . . . But if twenty such as thou had faced me, here would all have perished . . . Nay, it was baneful Fate and the son of Leto that slew me . . . And another thing will I tell thee, and do thou lay it to heart . . . even now doth death stand hard by thee, and mighty fate, that thou be slain beneath the hands of Achilles . . .'

554. Cp. 'Balder Dead' iii 109 and *n*. (p. 376 below).

556–75. A.'s most ambitious attempt at the long Miltonic simile. J. B. Broadbent sees a 'confluence of imitations' in this passage: 'To Milton Arnold owes "pinion" and the usage of "sole", and "out of his ken" has its colloquial quality elevated by Miltonic reminiscence . . . But the most pervasive influence is the Authorised Version: the rhythm of "And pierc'd her with an arrow as she rose", the phrasing of "Far off", "a great way off descries", and the last phrase "and knew him not"' ('Milton and Arnold', *Essays in Criticism* vi (1956) 406). This is helpful, but 'Far off' and 'a great way off descries' are A.'s recollection of *Paradise Lost* ii 636–7, 641–2,

> As when farr off at Sea a Fleet descri'd
> Hangs in the Clouds . . .
>
>   So seem'd
> Farr off the flying Fiend . . .

560   And followed her to find her where she fell
       Far off; anon her mate comes winging back
       From hunting, and a great way off descries
       His huddling young left sole; at that, he checks
       His pinion, and with short uneasy sweeps
565   Circles above his eyry, with loud screams
       Chiding his mate back to her nest; but she
       Lies dying, with the arrow in her side,
       In some far stony gorge out of his ken,
       A heap of fluttering feathers – never more
570   Shall the lake glass her, flying over it;
       Never the black and dripping precipices
       Echo her stormy scream as she sails by –
       As that poor bird flies home, nor knows his loss,
       So Rustum knew not his own loss, but stood
575   Over his dying son, and knew him not.
           But, with a cold incredulous voice, he said: –
       'What prate is this of fathers and revenge?
       The mighty Rustum never had a son.'
           And, with a failing voice, Sohrab replied:–
580   'Ah yes, he had! and that lost son am I.
       Surely the news will one day reach his ear,
       Reach Rustum, where he sits, and tarries long,
       Somewhere, I know not where, but far from here;
       And pierce him like a stab, and make him leap
585   To arms, and cry for vengeance upon thee.
       Fierce man, bethink thee, for an only son!
       What will that grief, what will that vengeance be?
       Oh, could I live, till I that grief had seen!
       Yet him I pity not so much, but her,
590   My mother, who in Ader-baijan dwells
       With that old king, her father, who grows grey
       With age, and rules over the valiant Koords.
       Her most I pity, who no more will see
       Sohrab returning from the Tartar camp,
595   With spoils and honour, when the war is done.
       But a dark rumour will be bruited up,
       From tribe to tribe, until it reach her ear;
       And then will that defenceless woman learn
       That Sohrab will rejoice her sight no more,
600   But that in battle with a nameless foe,
       By the far-distant Oxus, he is slain.'
           He spoke; and as he ceased, he wept aloud,
       Thinking of her he left, and his own death.
       He spoke; but Rustum listened, plunged in thought.
605   Nor did he yet believe it was his son

Who spoke, although he called back names he knew;
For he had had sure tidings that the babe,
Which was in Ader-baijan born to him,
Had been a puny girl, no boy at all –
610   So that sad mother sent him word, for fear
Rustum should seek the boy, to train in arms.
And so he deemed that either Sohrab took,
By a false boast, the style of Rustum's son;
Or that men gave it him, to swell his fame.
615   So deemed he; yet he listened, plunged in thought:
And his soul set to grief, as the vast tide
Of the bright rocking Ocean sets to shore
At the full moon; tears gathered in his eyes;
For he remembered his own early youth,
620   And all its bounding rapture; as, at dawn,
The shepherd from his mountain-lodge descries
A far, bright city, smitten by the sun,
Through many rolling clouds – so Rustum saw
His youth; saw Sohrab's mother, in her bloom;
625   And that old king, her father, who loved well
His wandering guest, and gave him his fair child
With joy; and all the pleasant life they led,
They three, in that long-distant summer-time –
The castle, and the dewy woods, and hunt
630   And hound, and morn on those delightful hills
In Ader-baijan. And he saw that Youth,
Of age and looks to be his own dear son,
Piteous and lovely, lying on the sand,
Like some rich hyacinth which by the scythe
635   Of an unskilful gardener has been cut,
Mowing the garden grass-plots near its bed,
And lies, a fragrant tower of purple bloom,
On the mown, dying grass – so Sohrab lay,
Lovely in death, upon the common sand.

623–31. A. bowdlerizes Sainte-Beuve's paraphrase of this part of the story
(*op. cit.* 344–6). Rustum sought the hospitality of the 'roi de Sémengan',
father of the beautiful Tehmimeh, when he had his horse stolen on a
hunting expedition. Tehmimeh offered herself to the hero 'ne souhaitant
rien plus que d'avoir un fils d'un homme tel que Roustem', but he felt
that there would be some breach of the laws of hospitality if he did not
marry her first. On the morning after the wedding-night Rustum deserted
his bride and returned to Persia.

634–8. Cp. Virgil's *Aeneid* ix 435–6 (the dying Euryalus),

       purpureus veluti cum flos succisus aratro
       languescit moriens . . .

640   And Rustum gazed on him with grief, and said: –
       'O Sohrab, thou indeed art such a son
       Whom Rustum, wert thou his, might well have loved.
       Yet here thou errest, Sohrab, or else men
       Have told thee false – thou art not Rustum's son.
645   For Rustum had no son; one child he had –
       But one – a girl; who with her mother now
       Plies some light female task, nor dreams of us –
       Of us she dreams not, nor of wounds, nor war.'
          But Sohrab answered him in wrath; for now
650   The anguish of the deep-fixed spear grew fierce,
       And he desired to draw forth the steel,
       And let the blood flow free, and so to die –
       But first he would convince his stubborn foe;
       And, rising sternly on one arm, he said: –
655   'Man, who art thou who dost deny my words?
       Truth sits upon the lips of dying men,
       And falsehood, while I lived, was far from mine.
       I tell thee, pricked upon this arm I bear
       That seal which Rustum to my mother gave,
660   That she might prick it on the babe she bore.'
          He spoke; and all the blood left Rustum's cheeks,
       And his knees tottered, and he smote his hand
       Against his breast, his heavy mailéd hand,
       That the hard iron corslet clanked aloud;
665   And to his heart he pressed the other hand,
       And in a hollow voice he spake, and said: –
          'Sohrab, that were a proof which could not lie!
       If thou show this, then art thou Rustum's son.'
          Then, with weak hasty fingers, Sohrab loosed
670   His belt, and near the shoulder bared his arm,
       And showed a sign in faint vermilion points
       Pricked; as a cunning workman, in Pekin,
       Pricks with vermilion some clear porcelain vase,
       An emperor's gift – at early morn he paints,
675   And all day long, and, when night comes, the lamp
       Lights up his studious forehead and thin hands –
       So delicately pricked the sign appeared
       On Sohrab's arm, the sign of Rustum's seal.

658–60. Sainte-Beuve says Rustum gave Sohrab's mother an onyx to be
placed in the hair of the daughter or on the arm of the son whom she would
bear (*op. cit.* 345–6), but A. is here closer to Malcolm's *History of Persia*
(1829 ed.) i 28, 'The afflicted and dying youth tore open his mail, and
showed his father a seal which his mother had placed on his arm when she
discovered to him the secret of his birth, and bade him seek his father.'

It was that griffin, which of old reared Zal,
680 Rustum's great father, whom they left to die,
A helpless babe, among the mountain-rocks;
Him that kind creature found, and reared, and loved –
Then Rustum took it for his glorious sign.
And Sohrab bared that image on his arm,
685 And himself scanned it long with mournful eyes,
And then he touched it with his hand and said: –
 'How say'st thou! Is that sign the proper sign
Of Rustum's son, or of some other man's?'
 He spoke; but Rustum gazed, and gazed, and stood
690 Speechless; and then he uttered one sharp cry:
O boy – thy father! – and his voice choked there.
And then a dark cloud passed before his eyes,
And his head swam, and he sank down to earth.
But Sohrab crawled to where he lay, and cast
695 His arms about his neck, and kissed his lips,
And with fond faltering fingers stroked his cheeks,
Trying to call him back to life; and life
Came back to Rustum, and he oped his eyes,
And they stood wide with horror; and he seized
700 In both his hands the dust which lay around,
And threw it on his head, and smirched his hair,
His hair, and face, and beard, and glittering arms;
And strong convulsive groanings shook his breast,
And his sobs choked him; and he clutched his sword,
705 To draw it, and for ever let life out.
But Sohrab saw his thought, and held his hands,
And with a soothing voice he spake, and said: –
 'Father, forbear! for I but meet to-day
The doom which at my birth was written down
710 In Heaven, and thou art Heaven's unconscious hand.
Surely my heart cried out that it was thou,
When first I saw thee; and thy heart spoke too,
I know it! but fate trod those promptings down
Under its iron heel; fate, fate engaged
715 The strife, and hurled me on my father's spear.
But let us speak no more of this! I find
My father; let me feel that I have found!
Come, sit beside me on this sand, and take

679–81. Zal was exposed to die because he was born white-haired.
684. *image*] figure *1853–77*.
708–10. Taken from Mohl's translation of Firdausi quoted by Sainte-Beuve, *op. cit.* 350, 'Mon sort était écrit au dessus de ma tête, et je devais mourir de la main de mon père.'

My head betwixt thy hands, and kiss my cheeks,
720   And wash them with thy tears, and say: *My son!*
Quick! quick! for numbered are my sands of life,
And swift; for like the lightning to this field
I came, and like the wind I go away –
Sudden, and swift, and like a passing wind.
725   But it was writ in Heaven that this should be.'
          So said he, and his voice released the heart
Of Rustum, and his tears broke forth; he cast
His arm round his son's neck, and wept aloud,
And kissed him. And awe fell on both the hosts,
730   When they saw Rustum's grief; and Ruksh, the horse,
With his head bowing to the ground and mane
Sweeping the dust, came near, and in mute woe
First to the one then to the other moved
His head, as if inquiring what their grief
735   Might mean; and from his dark, compassionate eyes,
The big warm tears rolled down, and caked the sand.
But Rustum chid him with stern voice, and said: –
          'Ruksh, now thou grievest; but, O Ruksh, thy feet
Should first have rotted on their nimble joints,
740   Or ere they brought thy master to this field!'
          But Sohrab looked upon the horse and said: –
'Is this, then, Ruksh? How often, in past days,
My mother told me of thee, thou brave steed,
My terrible father's terrible horse! and said,
745   That I should one day find thy lord and thee.
Come, let me lay my hand upon thy mane!
O Ruksh, thou art more fortunate than I;
For thou hast gone where I shall never go,
And snuffed the breezes of my father's home.
750   And thou hast trod the sands of Seistan,
And seen the River of Helmund, and the Lake
Of Zirrah; and the aged Zal himself
Has often stroked thy neck, and given thee food,
Corn in a golden platter soaked with wine,

722–4. The passage quoted in the previous note continues, 'Je suis venu comme le foudre, je m'en vais comme le vent.'

730–6. The horses of Achilles mourn similarly for Patroclus – see *Iliad* xvii 426–40 and especially 437 *ff.*, 'And hot tears ever flowed from their eyes to the ground, as they wept in longing for their charioteer, and their rich manes were befouled, streaming from beneath the yoke-pads beside the yoke on this side and on that.'

739. first] then *1853–81.*

740. Or ere they brought] When first they bore *1853–81.*

755 And said: *O Ruksh! bear Rustum well!* – but I
Have never known my grandsire's furrowed face,
Nor seen his lofty house in Seistan,
Nor slaked my thirst at the clear Helmund stream;
But lodged among my father's foes, and seen
760 Afrasiab's cities only, Samarcand,
Bokhara, and lone Khiva in the waste,
And the black Toorkmun tents; and only drunk
The desert rivers, Moorghab and Tejend,
Kohik, and where the Kalmucks feed their sheep,
765 The northern Sir; and this great Oxus stream,
The yellow Oxus, by whose brink I die.'
   Then, with a heavy groan, Rustum bewailed: –
'Oh, that its waves were flowing over me!
Oh, that I saw its grains of yellow silt
770 Roll tumbling in the current o'er my head!'
   But, with a grave mild voice, Sohrab replied: –
'Desire not that, my father! thou must live.
For some are born to do great deeds, and live,
As some are born to be obscured, and die.
775 Do thou the deeds I die too young to do,
And reap a second glory in thine age;
Thou art my father, and thy gain is mine.
But come! thou seest this great host of men
Which follow me; I pray thee, slay not these!
780 Let me entreat for them; what have they done?
They followed me, my hope, my fame, my star.
Let them all cross the Oxus back in peace.
But me thou must bear hence, not send with them,
But carry me with thee to Seistan,
785 And place me on a bed, and mourn for me,
Thou, and the snow-haired Zal, and all thy friends.
And thou must lay me in that lovely earth,
And heap a stately mound above my bones,
And plant a far-seen pillar over all.
790 That so the passing horseman on the waste
May see my tomb a great way off, and cry:
Sohrab, the mighty Rustum's son, lies there,

778-82. Cp. Sainte-Beuve, *op. cit.* 349, 'Le jeune homme meurt avec resignation, avec douceur ... en recommandant qu'on épargne après lui cette
armée qu'il a engagée dans une enterprise téméraire.'
783-9. For Sohrab's burial in Seistan see A.'s note from Malcolm (headn.
above). Mound and pillar (ll. 788-9) are from *Iliad* xvi 674-5, 'There
shall his kinsfolk give him burial with mound and pillar; for this is the due
of the dead.'

Whom his great father did in ignorance kill!
And I be not forgotten in my grave.'
795   And, with a mournful voice, Rustum replied : —
'Fear not! as thou hast said, Sohrab, my son,
So shall it be; for I will burn my tents,
And quit the host, and bear thee hence with me,
And carry thee away to Seistan,
800   And place thee on a bed, and mourn for thee,
With the snow-headed Zal, and all my friends.
And I will lay thee in that lovely earth,
And heap a stately mound above thy bones,
And plant a far-seen pillar over all,
805   And men shall not forget thee in thy grave.
And I will spare thy host; yea, let them go!
Let them all cross the Oxus back in peace!
What should I do with slaying any more?
For would that all whom I have ever slain
810   Might be once more alive; my bitterest foes,
And they who were called champions in their time,
And through whose death I won that fame I have —
And I were nothing but a common man,
A poor, mean soldier, and without renown,
815   So thou mightest live too, my son, my son!
Or rather would that I, even I myself,
Might now be lying on this bloody sand,
Near death, and by an ignorant stroke of thine,
Not thou of mine! and I might die, not thou;
820   And I, not thou, be borne to Seistan;
And Zal might weep above my grave, not thine;
And say: *O son, I weep thee not too sore,*
For willingly, I know, thou met'st thine end!
But now in blood and battles was my youth,
825   And full of blood and battles is my age,
And I shall never end this life of blood.'
      Then, at the point of death, Sohrab replied : —
'A life of blood indeed, thou dreadful man!
But thou shalt yet have peace; only not now,
830   Not yet! but thou shalt have it on that day,
When thou shalt sail in a high-masted ship,
Thou and the other peers of Kai Khosroo,
Returning home over the salt blue sea,
From laying thy dear master in his grave.'

815–19. An echo of David's lament 2 *Samuel* xviii 33, 'O my son Absalom, my son, my son Absalom! would God I had died for thee, O Absalom, my son, my son!'

835   And Rustum gazed in Sohrab's face, and said: –
    'Soon be that day, my son, and deep that sea!
    Till then, if fate so wills, let me endure.'
     He spoke; and Sohrab smiled on him, and took
    The spear, and drew it from his side, and eased
840   His wound's imperious anguish; but the blood
    Came welling from the open gash, and life
    Flowed with the stream; all down his cold white side
    The crimson torrent ran, dim now and soiled,
    Like the soiled tissue of white violets
845   Left, freshly gathered, on their native bank,
    By children whom their nurses call with haste
    Indoors from the sun's eye; his head drooped low,
    His limbs grew slack; motionless, white, he lay –
    White, with eyes closed; only when heavy gasps,
850   Deep heavy gasps quivering through all his frame,
    Convulsed him back to life, he opened them,
    And fixed them feebly on his father's face;
    Till now all strength was ebbed, and from his limbs
    Unwillingly the spirit fled away,
855   Regretting the warm mansion which it left,
    And youth, and bloom, and this delightful world.
     So, on the bloody sand, Sohrab lay dead;
    And the great Rustum drew his horseman's cloak
    Down o'er his face, and sate by his dead son.
860   As those black granite pillars, once high-reared

846. 1853–77,
     By romping children, whom their nurses call

847. Indoors from the sun's eye] From the hot fields [field *1869*] at noon *1853–69.*

853–6. Cp. *Iliad* xxii 361–3 (the death of Hector), 'Even as he thus spake the end of death enfolded him and his soul fleeting from his limbs was gone to Hades, bewailing her fate, leaving manliness and youth.'

855. warm mansion] A.'s phrase combines 'mansion' and 'warm precincts' from Gray's 'Elegy written in a Country Church-yard' – see ll. 41–2, 86–8,

     Can storied urn or animated bust
     Back to its mansion call the fleeting breath?

     [For who]
     This pleasing anxious being e'er resigned,
     Left the warm precincts of the chearful day,
     Nor cast one longing, ling'ring look behind?

856. bloom] See *n.* to 'The Youth of Nature' 54 (p. 247 above).

860–3. Perhaps suggested by E. Flandin's description of the broken col-
12+M.A.

By Jemshid in Persepolis, to bear
His house, now 'mid their broken flights of steps
Lie prone, enormous, down the mountain side –
So in the sand lay Rustum by his son.

865   And night came down over the solemn waste,
And the two gazing hosts, and that sole pair,
And darkened all; and a cold fog, with night,
Crept from the Oxus. Soon a hum arose,
As of a great assembly loosed, and fires

870   Began to twinkle through the fog; for now
Both armies moved to camp, and took their meal;
The Persians took it on the open sands
Southward, the Tartars by the river marge;
And Rustum and his son were left alone.

875   But the majestic river floated on,
Out of the mist and hum of that low land,
Into the frosty starlight, and there moved,
Rejoicing, through the hushed Chorasmian waste,
Under the solitary moon; he flowed

---

umns and basalt door-pillars of 'Tâkt-i-Djemchid' in two articles on the
ruins of Persepolis in *Revue des Deux Mondes* n.p. vii (1850) 114–41, 413–33.
868–74. A. is recalling the fires of the Trojan encampment by the Xanthus,
Iliad viii 542–65. Part of this passage he translated into English hexameters
– see *On Translating Homer* (1861), *Works* v 246 and p. 467 below.
875–92. A.'s most celebrated coda. The description of the Oxus, with its
implicit comparison of the course of the river to the course of a human
life, is drawn from Burnes's *Travels* ii 186–7, 'The Oxus rises in the table-
lands of Pamere, and is formed by a variety of rivulets which collect in that
elevated region of Asia ... It winds among mountains, and, approaching
within twenty miles of the town of Khoolloom ... passes about half a
degree to the north of Balkh. There are no hills between it and that ancient
city ... It here enters upon the desert by a course nearly N.W., fertilizes
a limited tract of about a mile on either side, till it reaches the territories of
Orgunje or Khiva, the ancient Kharasm, where it is more widely spread
by art, and is then lost in the sea of Aral. In the latter part of its course ...
it forms a swampy delta, overgrown with reeds and aquatic plants im-
pervious to the husbandman ...' For the significance of these lines see Maud
Bodkin's *Archetypal Patterns in Poetry* (1934) 66, 'Within the poetic vision
opened to the reader ... we can, I think, identify, as a single element, that
death-craving ... which appears to be a primary tendency of the organ-
ism ... Like the neurotic, the poet or his reader, dreaming on the river
that breaks at last into the free ocean, sees in this image his own life and
death ... in accordance with a deep organic need for release from conflict
and tension.'

880 Right for the polar star, past Orgunjè,
   Brimming, and bright, and large; then sands begin
   To hem his watery march, and dam his streams,
   And split his currents; that for many a league
   The shorn and parcelled Oxus strains along
885 Through beds of sand and matted rushy isles –
   Oxus, forgetting the bright speed he had
   In his high mountain-cradle in Pamere,
   A foiled circuitous wanderer – till at last
   The longed-for dash of waves is heard, and wide
890 His luminous home of waters opens, bright
   And tranquil, from whose floor the new-bathed stars
   Emerge, and shine upon the Aral Sea.

878. Chorasmian waste] Cp. Shelley's 'Alastor' 272–4,

> *At length upon the lone Chorasmian shore*
> *He paused, a wide and melancholy waste*
> *Of putrid marshes . . .*

and see *n.* to 'The Strayed Reveller' 183 (p. 72 above).
890–1. His luminous . . . tranquil] Cp. 'Empedocles on Etna' II [i] 315 (p. 188 above),

> *That mild and luminous floor of waters . . .*

891–2. H. F. Lowry compares Tennyson's 'Morte d'Arthur' 242–3,

> *And on a sudden, lo! the level lake,*
> *And the long glories of the winter moon . . .*

in a comment on A.'s letter to Clough 25 Nov. 1853, 'I think the likeness [i.e. between 'Sohrab and Rustum' and 'Morte d'Arthur'], where there is likeness (except in the two last lines which I own are a regular slip), proceeds from our both having imitated Homer' (*CL* 145).

78 The Scholar-Gipsy

Exact period of composition unknown, but almost certainly 1852–3 and perhaps May–Aug. 1853 (although A. knew the story of the scholar-gipsy in 1845 and by the autumn of 1848 had planned to write a poem about him). The story is from Joseph Glanvill's *The Vanity of Dogmatizing* (1661), which A. bought in 1844 (the date on his copy now in the Yale Collection) and probably read in 1845 (reading-list in unpublished 1845 diary); 'Thyrsis' 28–30 (p. 499 below) indicates that the figure of the scholar-gipsy had a special meaning for Arnold and Clough while they were still

¶ 78. *Title.* Glanvill refers to the 'Scholar-Gypsy' in the full passage which A. summarizes in his note.

at Oxford. The title 'The first mesmerist' on A.'s list of poems to be composed in 1849 (Yale MS.) proves that by late 1848 he saw the story as a poetic subject (note that in 1844–5 mesmerism was topical and greatly interested various members of A.'s family at Fox How and their neighbour Harriet Martineau); but the subsequent entry '? the wandering Mesmerist' on the list of poems for *1852* (*Commentary* 17) suggests that the poem had not been begun by late 1851 and also a doubt – not expressed about other pieces on this list which were in fact postponed until *1853* – about its completion for *1852*. J. P. Curgenven argues that the 1851 title '. . . is almost clinching evidence for "late" composition, pointing . . . to an intention . . . [still] to make magic a main interest . . . the final change of title corresponds in fact to a new orientation of theme that ensued when at last Arnold faced in earnest the business of composition . . .' ('The Scholar Gipsy: a study . . .', *Litera* ii (1955) 43). In support of May–Aug. 1853 as the effective period of composition note that (1) A. was busy with *1852* until Oct. 1852 and with 'Sohrab and Rustum' Dec. 1852–1 May 1853; (2) Keats, who influenced the stanza and style of 'The Scholar-Gipsy', is on A.'s reading-lists for June and Aug. 1853 (*Note-books* 553–4); (3) ll. 176–7 are quoted in a letter to Clough of 27 July 1853 (*CL* 138) as applicable to A.'s state of mind at the time.

In a letter to Clough of 30 Nov. 1853 A. ranked 'The Scholar-Gipsy' below 'Sohrab and Rustum' – see headn. to the latter poem (p. 303 above) and *CL* 146 – but his feeling for it when he forgot about the principles of the *1853* Preface is made clear in a letter to Tom A. of 15 May 1857, 'You alone of my brothers are associated with that life at Oxford, the *freest* and most delightful part, perhaps, of my life, when with you and Clough and Walrond I shook off all the bonds and formalities of the place, and enjoyed the spring of life and that unforgotten Oxfordshire and Berkshire country. Do you remember a poem of mine called "The Scholar Gipsy"? It was meant to fix the remembrance of those delightful wanderings of ours in the Cumner Hills . . .' (Mrs. H. Ward, *A Writer's Recollections* (1918) 54). This letter and A.'s classification of the poem as an elegy show that it should be read as a lament for youth and its wholeheartedness and energy, which are sapped by life in the world, i.e. the scholar-gipsy is a Callicles miraculously preserved from turning into an Empedocles. A. knows that such 'miracles do not happen', but to oppose the ideal and the actual is the method adopted here for a criticism of Victorian civilization (which is also a Romantic criticism of life for its failure to match expectation). For Clough's opinion of the poem see his letter 29 Nov. 1853 to C. E. Norton (on *1853*), '*He* is most ambitious about Sohrab and Rustum . . . I myself think that the Gipsy Scholar is best' (*Correspondence of A.H.C.* ii 467). In *The Common Pursuit* (1952) 29–30 F. R. Leavis has described it as 'a charming poem' that suffers from 'intellectual debility', but the charge is repudiated by three recent critics (who, however, differ widely – the last two totally – on the poem's interpretation): J. P. Curgenven, *Litera* ii (1955) 41–58 and iii (1956) 1–13, G. Wilson Knight, *RES* n.s. vi (1955) 53–62;

A. E. Dyson, *RES* n.s. viii (1957) 257–65. A.'s own note, a patchwork of sentences from Glanvill, is as follows:

'There was very lately a lad in the University at Oxford, who was by his poverty forced to leave his studies there; and at last to join himself to a company of vagabond gipsies. Among these extravagant people, by the insinuating subtilty of his carriage, he quickly got so much of their love and esteem as that they discovered to him their mystery. After he had been a pretty while well ['well' dropped inadvertently *1869* and the error left uncorrected in later editions] exercised in the trade, there chanced to ride by a couple of scholars, who had formerly been of his acquaintance. They quickly spied out their old friend among the gipsies; and he gave them an account of the necessity which drove him to that kind of life, and told them that the people he went with were not such impostors as they were taken for, but that they had a traditional kind of learning among them, and could do wonders by the power of imagination, their fancy binding that of others: that himself had learned much of their art, and when he had compassed the whole secret, he intended, he said, to leave their company, and give the world an account of what he had learned' – Glanvil's *Vanity of Dogmatizing*, 1661.

Published *1853*; reprinted (*1854, 1857*), *1869*, etc.

> Go, for they call you, shepherd, from the hill;
> Go, shepherd, and untie the wattled cotes!
> No longer leave thy wistful flock unfed,
> Nor let thy bawling fellows rack their throats,
> 5 Nor the cropped herbage shoot another head.
> But when the fields are still,
> And the tired men and dogs all gone to rest,
> And only the white sheep are sometimes seen

1–10. The stanza is original but influenced by the stanza of 'Ode to a Nightingale' (which Keats discovered while experimenting with the structure of the sonnet). A.'s stanza consists of the sestet followed by the first half of the octet of a Petrarchan sonnet, the sixth line being shortened from five to three stresses. Keats's 'Nightingale' stanza consists of a Shakespearian quatrain followed by a Petrarchan sestet, the eighth line being similarly shortened. On the comparative merits of the two stanzas see M. R. Ridley, *Keats' Craftsmanship* (1933) 208–9 and *Baum* 107–8. A. avoids a heavy pause at the end of l. 6 in the majority of his stanzas.
1. shepherd] Clough – cp. 'Thyrsis' 35 (p. 500 below),

> *Here, too, our shepherd-pipes we first assayed ...*

5. herbage] grasses *1853–81.*

Cross and recross the strips of moon-blanched green,
10   Come, shepherd, and again begin the quest!

Here, where the reaper was at work of late –
    In this high field's dark corner, where he leaves
        His coat, his basket, and his earthen cruse,
    And in the sun all morning binds the sheaves,
15   Then here, at noon, comes back his stores to use –
            Here will I sit and wait,
    While to my ear from uplands far away
        The bleating of the folded flocks is borne,
        With distant cries of reapers in the corn –
20   All the live murmur of a summer's day.

Screened is this nook o'er the high, half-reaped field,
    And here till sun-down, shepherd! will I be.
        Through the thick corn the scarlet poppies peep,
    And round green roots and yellowing stalks I see
25   Pale pink convolvulus in tendrils creep;
            And air-swept lindens yield
    Their scent, and rustle down their perfumed showers
        Of bloom on the bent grass where I am laid,
        And bower me from the August sun with shade;
30   And the eye travels down to Oxford's towers.

9. *moon-blanched*] Cp. 'A Summer Night' 1 (p. 267 above),

> *In the deserted, moon-blanched street . . .*

and *n.*
10. *begin the quest*] renew the quest *1853–7, 1877–81*. The present reading
was first adopted in *1869*. The quest is that of the scholar-gipsy – cp.
'Thyrsis' 201–2 (p. 507 below),

> *A fugitive and gracious light he seeks,*
> *Shy to illumine; and I seek it too . . .*

– but it is also a quest for the scholar-gipsy, i.e. for the simple integrity with
which he pursues his search. His search is for the truth that can be received
by the poetic imagination. The analogy between hypnotism and poetry is
suggested in A.'s note from Glanvill – the gipsies 'could do wonders by the
power of imagination, their fancy binding that of others.'
11–20. Keatsian influence without close verbal parallels.
21–3. A modulated echo of Keats's 'To Autumn' 16–17,

> *Or on a half-reap'd furrow sound asleep,*
> *Drows'd with the fume of poppies . . .*

25. *pink*] blue *1853–81*.

And near me on the grass lies Glanvil's book –
Come, let me read the oft-read tale again!
The story of the Oxford scholar poor,
Of pregnant parts and quick inventive brain,
35   Who, tired of knocking at preferment's door,
One summer-morn forsook
His friends, and went to learn the gipsy-lore,
And roamed the world with that wild brotherhood,
And came, as most men deemed, to little good,
40   But came to Oxford and his friends no more.

But once, years after, in the country-lanes,
Two scholars, whom at college erst he knew,
Met him, and of his way of life enquired;
Whereat he answered, that the gipsy-crew,
45   His mates, had arts to rule as they desired
The workings of men's brains,
And they can bind them to what thoughts they will.
'And I,' he said, 'the secret of their art,
When fully learned, will to the world impart;
50   But it needs heaven-sent moments for this skill.'

This said, he left them, and returned no more.
But rumours hung about the country-side,
That the lost Scholar long was seen to stray,
Seen by rare glimpses, pensive and tongue-tied,
55   In hat of antique shape, and cloak of grey,
The same the gipsies wore.

34–5. In Glanvill but omitted from A.'s note – cp. *The Vanity of Dogmatizing* (1661) 196, '. . . a Lad in the *University of Oxford*, who being of very pregnant and ready parts, and yet wanting the encouragement of preferment . . .'

50. *heaven-sent*] happy *1853*. On either reading the moments are those of poetic inspiration.

54. *Seen by rare glimpses*] The successive glimpses of the scholar-gipsy (ll. 57–130) were suggested by Gray's 'Elegy written in a Country Churchyard' 98–112, a passage describing how the country-folk see the poet in different places at different times of day. The poet and the country people who wonder about him both keep ('Elegy' 73),

Far from the madding crowd's ignoble strife . . .

and Gray's contrast between two ways of life has helped to shape A.'s poem. The same passage of the 'Elegy' is recalled by A. in 'Obermann' – see *n.* to ll. 171–4 (p. 137 above). Gray's 'Elegy' is in A.'s mind again at ll. 136–140 and perhaps also at l. 130 (p. 338 below).

>   Shepherds had met him on the Hurst in spring;
>   At some lone alehouse in the Berkshire moors,
>   On the warm ingle-bench, the smock-frocked boors
> 60   Had found him seated at their entering,

>   But, 'mid their drink and clatter, he would fly.
>   And I myself seem half to know thy looks,
>   And put the shepherds, wanderer! on thy trace;
>   And boys who in lone wheatfields scare the rooks
> 65   I ask if thou hast passed their quiet place;
>   Or in my boat I lie
>   Moored to the cool bank in the summer-heats,
>   'Mid wide grass meadows which the sunshine fills,
>   And watch the warm, green-muffled Cumner hills,
> 70   And wonder if thou haunt'st their shy retreats.

>   For most, I know, thou lov'st retiréd ground!
>   Thee at the ferry Oxford riders blithe,
>   Returning home on summer-nights, have met
>   Crossing the stripling Thames at Bab-lock-hithe,
> 75   Trailing in the cool stream thy fingers wet,
>   As the punt's rope chops round;
>   And leaning backward in a pensive dream,
>   And fostering in thy lap a heap of flowers
>   Plucked in shy fields and distant Wychwood
>   bowers,
> 80   And thine eyes resting on the moonlit stream.

>   And then they land, and thou art seen no more!
>   Maidens, who from the distant hamlets come
>   To dance around the Fyfield elm in May,
>   Oft through the darkening fields have seen thee roam,

57. *the Hurst*] Cumnor Hurst. Cp. 'Thyrsis' 216–17 (pp. 507–8 below),

>   *And this rude Cumner ground,*
>   *Its fir-topped Hurst . . .*

61. The scholar-gipsy is seen only in lonely places and only by the young and happy, the simple, and the innocent. Many epithets applied to the scenes in which he appears – e.g. lone, quiet, shy, retired – apply equally well to him, which is another way of saying that he is for A. 'un moyen d'animer le paysage' (*Bonnerot* 472).

69. *green-muffled*] See *n.* to 'Empedocles on Etna' I ii 51 (p. 158 above).

76. *punt's rope chops*] slow punt swings *1853–7*.

79. *Wychwood*] woodland *1853–4*.

85   Or cross a stile into the public way.
             Oft thou hast given them store
         Of flowers – the frail-leafed, white anemone,
             Dark bluebells drenched with dews of summer eves,
             And purple orchises with spotted leaves –
90   But none hath words she can report of thee.

         And, above Godstow Bridge, when hay-time's here
             In June, and many a scythe in sunshine flames,
             Men who through those wide fields of breezy grass
         Where black-winged swallows haunt the glittering
95   To bathe in the abandoned lasher pass,   [Thames,
                 Have often passed thee near
             Sitting upon the river bank o'ergrown;
                 Marked thine outlandish garb, thy figure spare,
             Thy dark vague eyes, and soft abstracted air –
100   But, when they came from bathing, thou wast gone!

         At some lone homestead in the Cumner hills,
             Where at her open door the housewife darns,
                 Thou hast been seen, or hanging on a gate
             To watch the threshers in the mossy barns.
105   Children, who early range these slopes and late
                 For cresses from the rills,
             Have known thee eying, all an April-day,
                 The springing pastures and the feeding kine;
                 And marked thee, when the stars come out and
                     shine,
110   Through the long dewy grass move slow away.

         In autumn, on the skirts of Bagley Wood –
             Where most the gipsies by the turf-edged way
                 Pitch their smoked tents, and every bush you see

88. *dews of summer eves*] Keatsian. Cp. 'Ode to a Nightingale' 49–50,

> *The coming musk-rose, full of dewy wine,*
>   *The murmurous haunt of flies on summer eves.*

95. *lasher*] A local word for a weir or, as here, for the pool below it.
101–4. A modulated echo of Keats's 'To Autumn' 12–15,

> *Who hath not seen thee oft amid thy store?*
>   *Sometimes whoever seeks abroad may find*
> *Thee sitting careless on a granary floor,*
>   *Thy hair soft-lifted by the winnowing wind . . .*

107. *eying*] watching *1853–7*; haunting *1869*.
   12*

With scarlet patches tagged and shreds of grey,
115   Above the forest-ground called Thessaly –
           The blackbird, picking food,
Sees thee, nor stops his meal, nor fears at all;
So often has he known thee past him stray,
Rapt, twirling in thy hand a withered spray,
120   And waiting for the spark from heaven to fall.

And once, in winter, on the causeway chill
     Where home through flooded fields foot-travellers go,
           Have I not passed thee on the wooden bridge,
     Wrapped in thy cloak and battling with the snow,
125   Thy face tow'rd Hinksey and its wintry ridge?
           And thou hast climbed the hill,
     And gained the white brow of the Cumner range;
           Turned once to watch, while thick the snowflakes
           The line of festal light in Christ-Church hall – [fall,
130   Then sought thy straw in some sequestered grange.

But what – I dream! Two hundred years are flown
     Since first thy story ran through Oxford halls,
           And the grave Glanvil did the tale inscribe
     That thou wert wandered from the studious walls
135   To learn strange arts, and join a gipsy-tribe;
           And thou from earth art gone
     Long since, and in some quiet churchyard laid –
           Some country-nook, where o'er thy unknown grave
           Tall grasses and white flowering nettles wave,
140   Under a dark, red-fruited yew-tree's shade.

120. *the spark from heaven*] A commonplace, but perhaps suggested by
Carlyle's 'Characteristics', *Crit. and Miscell. Essays* (1839), *Works* ed. H. D.
Traill xxviii 11, 'The lightning-spark of Thought, generated, or say rather
heaven-kindled, in the solitary mind.'
130. *sequestered*] The epithet occurs in Gray's 'Elegy' 75,

         Along the cool sequester'd vale of life . . .

131. *But what – I dream!*] Keatsian technique and an echo of 'Ode to a
Nightingale' 79,
              Was it a vision, or a waking dream?

Keats's return to everyday reality is the climax of his ode; A.'s similar
return marks the point at which he moves from pastoral description to the
criticism of modern life.
136–40. The quiet country churchyard and the 'yew-tree's shade' are from
Gray's 'Elegy' 13–15.

– No, no, thou hast not felt the lapse of hours!
  For what wears out the life of mortal men?
      'Tis that from change to change their being rolls;
      'Tis that repeated shocks, again, again,
145   Exhaust the energy of strongest souls
          And numb the elastic powers.
  Till having used our nerves with bliss and teen,
    And tired upon a thousand schemes our wit,
    To the just-pausing Genius we remit
150 Our worn-out life, and are – what we have been.

  Thou hast not lived, why should'st thou perish, so?
    Thou hadst *one* aim, *one* business, *one* desire;
      Else wert thou long since numbered with the dead!
    Else hadst thou spent, like other men, thy fire!
155   The generations of thy peers are fled,
            And we ourselves shall go;
      But thou possessest an immortal lot,
        And we imagine thee exempt from age
        And living as thou liv'st on Glanvil's page,
160   Because thou hadst – what we, alas! have not.

  For early didst thou leave the world, with powers
    Fresh, undiverted to the world without,

141. Cp. Keats's 'Ode to a Nightingale' 61–2,

>   *Thou wast not born for death, immortal Bird!*
>   *No hungry generations tread thee down . . .*

A. uses 'generations' in l. 155 below.
144–6. See A.'s letter to Clough of 27 July 1853 quoted in *n.* to l. 164 below.
147. teen] An archaism, here meaning 'grief' or 'woe'.
149. Genius] The tutelary spirit that accompanies a man throughout life.
152. See *n.* to l. 167 below.
161–2. Romantic *contemptus mundi.* The scholar-gipsy, like Keats in Shelley's 'Adonais', is secure from 'the contagion of the world's slow stain' (l. 356), and the world is seen as Keats saw it in 'Ode to a Nightingale' 23–4,

>   *The weariness, the fever, and the fret*
>   *Here, where men sit and hear each other groan . . .*

A.'s Romantic distrust of worldly experience is also expressed in the Yale MS.: 'Nothing makes me more despise the world than the homage it pays to experience . . . The feeling with wch a man of the world reads in books of sentiment and its gradual Suffocation in the world, after he himself has had his suffocated.'

Firm to their mark, not spent on other things;
Free from the sick fatigue, the languid doubt,
165   Which much to have tried, in much been baffled,
            brings.
         O life unlike to ours!
Who fluctuate idly without term or scope,
         Of whom each strives, nor knows for what he strives,
         And each half-lives a hundred different lives;
170   Who wait like thee, but not, like thee, in hope.

Thou waitest for the spark from heaven! and we,
         Light half-believers of our casual creeds,
         Who never deeply felt, nor clearly willed,
         Whose insight never has borne fruit in deeds,
175   Whose vague resolves never have been fulfilled;
            For whom each year we see
         Breeds new beginnings, disappointments new;
         Who hesitate and falter life away,
         And lose to-morrow the ground won to-day –
180   Ah! do not we, wanderer! await it too?

164. Cp. A.'s letter to Clough 27 July 1853, 'You will laugh if I tell you I am deplorably ennuyé. I seem to myself to have lost all ressort – [A. then quotes 'The Scholar-Gipsy' 176–7] One gets tired at last of one's own elasticity' (CL 138).
165. Cp. A.'s letter to his sister 'K' 2 May 1857, 'I shall be baffled, I daresay, as one continually is in so much' (L i 55).
167. fluctuate] Cp. 'A Summer Night' 27, 31–3 (p. 268 above),

> Hast thou then still the old unquiet breast . . .
>
> [Which] fluctuates to and fro,
> Never by passion quite possessed
> And never quite benumbed by the world's sway?

and A.'s letter to Clough 30 Nov. 1853 (in which he prefers 'Sohrab and Rustum' to 'The Scholar-Gipsy'), 'You certainly do not seem to me sufficiently to desire and earnestly strive towards – assured knowledge – activity – happiness. You are too content to fluctuate . . . That is why, with you, I feel it necessary to stiffen myself – and hold fast my rudder' (CL 146). The last phrase shows that A. saw himself as the 'grave Tyrian trader' (l. 232 below) flying from a threat to his peace of mind.
169. half-lives] The hyphen has been inserted.
173. Who never deeply felt] Cp. A.'s note in the Yale MS., 'The misery of the present age is . . . in [men's] incapacity to suffer, enjoy, feel at all, wholly and profoundly.'

Yes, we await it! – but it still delays,
   And then we suffer! and amongst us one,
      Who most has suffered, takes dejectedly
      His seat upon the intellectual throne;
185   And all his store of sad experience he
         Lays bare of wretched days;
      Tells us his misery's birth and growth and signs,
         And how the dying spark of hope was fed,
         And how the breast was soothed, and how the head,
190   And all his hourly varied anodynes.

   This for our wisest! and we others pine,
      And wish the long unhappy dream would end,
      And waive all claim to bliss, and try to bear;
   With close-lipped patience for our only friend,
195   Sad patience, too near neighbour to despair –
      But none has hope like thine!
      Thou through the fields and through the woods
         dost stray,
      Roaming the country-side, a truant boy,
      Nursing thy project in unclouded joy,
200   And every doubt long blown by time away.

182–90. For A.'s identification of the 'one' as Goethe see C. H. Leonard, 'Two Notes on Arnold', *MLN* xlvi (1931) 119 quoting *The Worcester Spy* (Massachusetts) of 29 Nov. 1883, 'Mr. Arnold said he had Goethe in mind when he wrote . . . The lines have been applied to many persons; but they were written just after Mr. Arnold had read Goethe's *Dichtung und Wahrheit*, and while he still felt the impression of its sadness.' But see *Commentary* 209–11 where the case for Tennyson is argued persuasively. Tennyson became Poet Laureate in Nov. 1850; ll. 185–90 are an apt description of *In Memoriam* (1850); 'intellectual throne' (l. 184) is borrowed from Tennyson's 'The Palace of Art' (l. 216).

185–6. The intellectual king laying bare his 'store of sad experience' is contrasted with the scholar-gipsy distributing his 'store of flowers' to the maidens who dance round the Fyfield elm (ll. 86–9 above). A. is echoing, probably unconsciously, 'To a Gipsy Child . . .' 33–4 (p. 25 above),

   . . . to hear some gray-haired King
   Unravel all his many-coloured lore . . .

190. anodynes] Perhaps suggested by Tennyson, *In Memoriam* v 7–8,

   The sad mechanic exercise,
   Like dull narcotics, numbing pain.

195. The kind of disquieting admission which A.'s poetic self was continually making to the annoyance of the moralist enclosed in the same skin.

O born in days when wits were fresh and clear,
　　And life ran gaily as the sparkling Thames;
　　　Before this strange disease of modern life,
　　With its sick hurry, its divided aims,
205　　　　Its heads o'ertaxed, its palsied hearts, was rife –
　　　Fly hence, our contact fear!
　　Still fly, plunge deeper in the bowering wood!
　　　Averse, as Dido did with gesture stern
　　　From her false friend's approach in Hades turn,
210　　Wave us away, and keep thy solitude!

　　Still nursing the unconquerable hope,
　　　Still clutching the inviolable shade,

201–2. The image of a golden age projected by the poet's own youthful experience of happiness. An acute sense of the special difficulties of Victorian times is needed to see the scholar-gipsy's seventeenth century as an era of 'the fond believing lyre' (Keats, 'Ode to Psyche' 37).

203. strange disease of modern life] See 'Memorial Verses' 19–22 (p. 227 above) and *n.* citing Carlyle and Goethe.

205. Its heads o'ertaxed, its palsied hearts] Cp. 'Empedocles on Etna II [i] 90–1,

> *The brave, impetuous heart yields everywhere*
> *To the subtle, contriving head . . .*

and II [i] 248–9,

> *We had not lost our balance then, nor grown*
> *Thought's slaves, and dead to every natural joy . . .*

(pp. 180 and 186 above). See, too, A.'s letter to Clough 12 Feb. 1853, 'Yes – *congestion of the brain* is what we suffer from – I always feel it and say it . . .' (*CL* 130).

207–9. See Virgil, *Aeneid* vi 469–73,

> *illa solo fixos oculos aversa tenebat*
> *nec magis incepto voltum sermone movetur,*
> *quam si dura silex aut stet Marpesia cautes.*
> *tandem corripuit sese atque inimica refugit*
> *in nemus umbriferum . . .*

211–12. Cp. 'A Summer Night' 68–9 (p. 270 above),

> *Still bent to make some port he knows not where,*
> *Still standing for some false, impossible shore.*

The echo shows A.'s indecision over Romantic attitudes. Resolution is approved in the scholar-gipsy, unwillingly admired but condemned in the Romantic rebel of 'A Summer Night'. The same image of sailing into the unknown is used for both the Romantic 'madman' and the 'grave Tyrian trader' who is the scholar-gipsy's representative – see 'A Summer Night' 54–73 and below ll. 242–7.

With a free, onward impulse brushing through,
By night, the silvered branches of the glade –
215   Far on the forest-skirts, where none pursue,
On some mild pastoral slope
Emerge, and resting on the moonlit pales
Freshen thy flowers as in former years
With dew, or listen with enchanted ears,
220   From the dark dingles, to the nightingales!

But fly our paths, our feverish contact fly!
For strong the infection of our mental strife,
Which, though it gives no bliss, yet spoils for rest;
And we should win thee from thy own fair life,
225   Like us distracted, and like us unblest.
Soon, soon thy cheer would die,
Thy hopes grow timorous, and unfixed thy powers,
And thy clear aims be cross and shifting made;
And then thy glad perennial youth would fade,
230   Fade, and grow old at last, and die like ours.

Then fly our greetings, fly our speech and smiles!
– As some grave Tyrian trader, from the sea,
Descried at sunrise an emerging prow
Lifting the cool-haired creepers stealthily,

217. pales] The stakes of a fence.
220. dingles] Wooded dells.
221–2. 'Feverish' and 'infection' insist again that modern life is a 'strange
disease'.
230. and die like ours] For A.'s feelings about the loss of youth see 'Empedocles on Etna' I ii 362–6 (p. 170 above) and *n.*; and *n.* to 'Lines written
in Kensington Gardens' 43–4 (p. 258 above).
232–50. G. Saintsbury claims that 'No ingenuity can work out the parallel
between the "uncloudedly joyous" scholar who is bid avoid the palsied,
diseased *enfants du siècle*, and the grave Tyrian who was indignant at the
competition of the merry Greek, and shook out more sail to seek fresh
markets' (*Matthew Arnold* (1899) 42), but E. K. Brown points out that
'The Tyrian trader's flight before the clamorous spirited Greeks is exactly
analogous to the scholar gipsy's flight before the drink and clatter of the
smock-frock'd boors or before the bathers in the abandoned lasher or
before the Oxford riders blithe. Both flights express a desire for calm, a
desire for aloofness. And little ingenuity is required to discover a similarity
between the gipsies and those "shy traffickers, the dark Iberians" to whom
the Tyrian trader flies. There is, at the least, a general relevance to the
character of the gipsy in the elaborate simile' (*Revue Anglo-Americaine* xii
(1934–5) 224–5). A. left the lines as they were written for *1853*.

235   The fringes of a southward-facing brow
                Among the Ægean isles;
        And saw the merry Grecian coaster come,
                Freighted with amber grapes, and Chian wine,
                Green, bursting figs, and tunnies steeped in brine –
240   And knew the intruders on his ancient home,

        The young light-hearted masters of the waves –
                And snatched his rudder, and shook out more sail;
                And day and night held on indignantly
                O'er the blue Midland waters with the gale,
245   Betwixt the Syrtes and soft Sicily,
                To where the Atlantic raves
        Outside the western straits; and unbent sails
                There, where down cloudy cliffs, through sheets of
                Shy traffickers, the dark Iberians come;   [foam,
250   And on the beach undid his corded bales.

246–50. From the association of the 'Tyrian trader' (l. 232) with Car-
thaginian trading-voyages (Carthage was founded as a Tyrian colony) A.
remembered Herodotus iv 196, 'The Carthaginians also relate the following: There is . . . a nation, beyond the Pillars of Hercules, which they
are wont to visit, where they no sooner arrive but forthwith they unlade
their wares, and, having disposed them after an orderly fashion along the
beach, leave them, and, returning aboard their ships, raise a great smoke.
The natives, when they see the smoke, come down to the shore, and, laying
out to view so much gold as they think the worth of the wares, withdraw to a distance. The Carthaginians upon this come ashore and
look. If they think the gold enough, they take it and go their way . . .'
(G. Rawlinson's 1858 translation). 'Shy traffickers' (l. 249) means 'shy in
their manner of trading' rather than 'shy to trade', but the noun itself is a
reminiscence of *Isaiah* xxiii 8, 'Tyre . . . whose traffickers are the
honourable of the earth.'

79 A Dream

Date of composition unknown, but clearly 1849–53. The unusual pictorial
vividness suggests that the poem may describe an actual dream. Martin and
Olivia are, if real, unidentified, but Martin may be Wyndham Slade if he
accompanied A. from Ischl to Thun in Sept. 1849 (see headn. to 'Meeting', p. 115 above). With its images of Swiss mountain freshness and of
the heat and noise of the 'cities of the plain' the poem reflects how
nostalgically A. looked back when he preferred duty to impulse at Thun
in 1849. 'A Dream', omitted from the collected editions of *1869*, *1877*,
was restored as an 'Early Poem' in *1881*.
Published *1853*; reprinted (*1854*, *1857*), *1881*, etc. ('Switzerland' 3 *1853–7*).

*Julian
and
Maddalo

Was it a dream? We sailed, I thought we sailed,
~~Martin and I, down a green Alpine stream,~~
Bordered, each bank, with pines; the morning sun,
On the wet umbrage of their glossy tops,
5   On the red pinings of their forest-floor,
Drew a warm scent abroad; behind the pines
The mountain-skirts, with all their sylvan change
Of bright-leafed chestnuts and mossed walnut-trees
And the frail scarlet-berried ash, began.
10   Swiss chalets glittered on the dewy slopes,
And from some swarded shelf, high up, there came,
Notes of wild pastoral music – over all
Ranged, diamond-bright, the eternal wall of snow.
Upon the mossy rocks at the stream's edge,
15   Backed by the pines, a plank-built cottage stood,
Bright in the sun; the climbing gourd-plant's leaves
Muffled its walls, and on the stone-strewn roof
Lay the warm golden gourds; golden, within,
Under the eaves, peered rows of Indian corn.
20   We shot beneath the cottage with the stream.
On the brown, rude-carved balcony, two forms
Came forth – Olivia's, Marguerite! and thine.
Clad were they both in white, flowers in their breast;
Straw hats bedecked their heads, with ribbons blue,
25   Which danced, and on their shoulders, fluttering,
        played.
They saw us, they conferred; their bosoms heaved,
And more than mortal impulse filled their eyes.
Their lips moved; their white arms, waved eagerly,
Flashed once, like falling streams; we rose, we gazed.
30   One moment, on the rapid's top, our boat
Hung poised – and then the darting river of Life

¶ 79. *3. Bordered, each bank, with pines*] Under o'erhanging pines *1853–7*.
9. scarlet-berried ash] The scarlet berries of the ash, like the harvested gourds
and Indian corn of ll. 17–19, are indications of late summer or autumn.
25. danced] wav'd *1853–7*.
26–7. A nicely mannered 'epic' touch – cp. Virgil's Sibyl, *Aeneid* vi 48–50,

> . . . *sed pectus anhelum,*
> *et rabie fera corda tument, maiorque videri*
> *nec mortale sonans . . .*

and Milton's description of the brothers, *Comus* (1637) 297,

> *Their port was more than human, as they stood . . .*

31. river of Life] For A.'s use of this metaphor in other poems see the second
half of *n.* to 'The Buried Life' 30–63 (p. 273 above).

    (Such now, methought, it was), the river of Life,
    Loud thundering, bore us by; swift, swift it foamed,
    Black under cliffs it raced, round headlands shone.
35   Soon the planked cottage by the sun-warmed pines
    Faded – the moss – the rocks; us burning plains,
    Bristled with cities, us the sea received.

32. First added 1881.
*36–7. Cp. 'The Future' 50–65 (p. 266 above) and n. – and especially 50–1,
53–4,*

> *This tract which the river of Time*
> *Now flows through with us, is the plain.*

> *Bordered by cities and hoarse*
> *With a thousand cries is its stream . . .*

80 Requiescat

Date of composition unknown, but (?) 1849–53. There is nothing that
enables us to identify the lady of the poem with an actual woman, and the
suggestion (*Sells* 127–8) that A. is imagining Marguerite's death is unsupported conjecture. The poem may be an exercise in the manner of
Wordsworth's 'A slumber did my spirit seal', and its dismissal in *1877* to
'Early Poems' perhaps indicates that A. thought less of it than do many of
his critics. In *1877* 'Requiescat' preceded 'Youth and Calm', but a
common autobiographical origin for the two pieces (both refer to a dead
woman) is ruled out if the latter (see headn. p. 224 above) was once part
of an early draft of 'Tristram and Iseult'.
Published *1853*; reprinted (*1854*, *1857*), *1869*, etc.

> Strew on her roses, roses,
>   And never a spray of yew!
> In quiet she reposes;
>   Ah, would that I did too!

5   Her mirth the world required;
>   She bathed it in smiles of glee.
> But her heart was tired, tired,
>   And now they let her be.

> Her life was turning, turning,
10   In mazes of heat and sound.
> But for peace her soul was yearning,
>   And now peace laps her round.

Her cabined, ample spirit,
It fluttered and failed for breath.

15   To-night it doth inherit
The vasty hall of death.

¶ 80. *13. cabined*] A Shakespearian echo. Cp. *Macbeth* III iv, 24,
But now I am cabin'd, cribb'd, confin'd, bound in . . .

81 Philomela

Date of composition unknown, but (?) 1852–3 : A. was often at his father-in-law's house at Hampton-on-Thames in 1852–3 (see *L* i 19, 30) – a setting suggested by ll. 10–12; if written in 1851 'Philomela' would probably have been included in *1852*. Note, however, that the Thames setting is not clearly indicated in A.'s untitled first draft, which is to be found – see *Commentary* 164 – on the flyleaf of a copy of Latham's *English Grammar* (1848). For the legend of Philomela see H. J. Rose, *A Handbook of Greek Mythology* (1928) 262–3 : '[Pandion] had two daughters, Philomela and Prokne. The latter married Tereus King of Thrace . . . But Tereus saw Philomela, fell violently in love with her, and seduced or raped her. Then, lest Prokne should know of it, he cut out Philomela's tongue and hid her away. She, however, managed to embroider an account of her woes on a piece of needle-work and to send it to her sister; the latter, in revenge, killed her own son Itys, and served him up at a banquet to his father. Tereus, on discovering what had happened, pursued Prokne and Philomela to kill them; but he was turned into a hoopoe, and the women respectively into a nightingale and a swallow . . . So the story is told by all Greek authors; the Latins make Philomela the nightingale, Prokne the swallow; but clearly the Greek account is better for it explains why the nightingale always sings mournfully (she is lamenting her child), and why the swallow chatters (she has no tongue, and keeps trying to tell her story).' In his first draft A. follows the Greek form of the legend and should have called his poem 'Procne' – see the lines, omitted in print,

> Dost thou still reach
> Thy husband, weak avenger, through thyself?

A. dropped these lines when he realized how firmly established was the identification of Philomela with the nightingale, but he did not otherwise change the story of his poem, which therefore implies that it was Procne who lost her tongue. Inadvertently then A. appears to follow the version of the tale preferred by R. Graves, *The Greek Myths* (1955) i 166-8. Against H. J. Rose and Sir James Frazer (Loeb ed. of Apollodorus ii 89–101) Graves holds that Apollodorus' statement that Procne became a nightingale is really 'a clumsy attempt to rectify a slip made by some Greek mythographer: that Tereus cut out Philomela's tongue, not Procne's.' Published *1853*; reprinted (*1854, 1857*), *1869*, etc.

Hark! ah, the nightingale –
The tawny-throated!
Hark, from that moonlit cedar what a burst!
What triumph ! hark! – what pain!

5   O wanderer from a Grecian shore,
   Still, after many years, in distant lands,
   Still nourishing in thy bewildered brain
   That wild, unquenched, deep-sunken, old-world
   Say, will it never heal?   [pain –
10   And can this fragrant lawn
   With its cool trees, and night,
   And the sweet, tranquil Thames,
   And moonshine, and the dew,
   To thy racked heart and brain
15   Afford no balm?

¶ 81. *2. tawny-throated*] inken throated MS.
3–13. These lines replace the following in the MS.:

> *Hast thou not yet poor bird*
> *Been help'd by slipping years*
> *At least to half forgetfulness*
>   *Of that old pain.*
> *Can change of scene, and night*
> *And moonlight, and the dew,*
>   *blanch'd song-stirr'd*
> *And these frail acacia boughs*
>   *light*
> *Through whose frail leaves, and showers*
> *Of blossom'd clusters pale,*
>   *by*
> *Thy voice in gushes comes . . .*

4. Cp. 'The Strayed Reveller' 210–11 (p. 72 above),

> *But oh, what labour!*
> *O prince, what pain!*

The echo, which can hardly be accidental, argues that the nightingale's song represents the triumph and pain of poetic creation and that ll. 10–15 below have an autobiographical tinge. See A.'s letter to his sister 'K' 6 Aug. 1858, '. . . to attain or approach perfection in the region of thought and feeling, and to unite this with perfection of form, demands not merely an effort and a labour, but an actual tearing of oneself to pieces, which one does not readily consent to (although one is sometimes forced to it) . . .' (*L* i 63).

    rack'd
14. racked] torn MS.

Dost thou to-night behold,
Here, through the moonlight on this English grass,
The unfriendly palace in the Thracian wild?
Dost thou again peruse
20   With hot cheeks and seared eyes
The too clear web, and thy dumb sister's shame?
Dost thou once more assay
Thy flight, and feel come over thee,
Poor fugitive, the feathery change
25   Once more, and once more seem to make resound
With love and hate, triumph and agony,
Lone Daulis, and the high Cephissian vale?
Listen, Eugenia –
How thick the bursts come crowding through the
30   Again – thou hearest?   [leaves!
Eternal passion!
Eternal pain!

16. to-night] still *MS.*
17. Replacing two lines in *MS.,*
                     terror
       With horror, from thy tree,
       On this fair western lawn. . .
19. again] still *MS.* Between ll. 19 and 20 this additional line in the *MS.,*
          In the white acacia flowers . . .
21. Followed in the MS. by these additional lines:
          Dost thou still reach
     Thy husband, weak avenger, thro thyself?
27. Daulis is in Phocis, through which the River Cephisus runs to Lake Copais. Thucydides (ii 29) says that Tereus ruled over a Thracian-occupied
Daulis and that the poets spoke of the nightingale as 'the Daulian bird'.
28. Listen] Hark, hark *MS.* A. had earlier used the name 'Eugenia' in
'Horatian Echo' (p. 57 above).
        Once more
30. Again] Again   *MS.*

82 Thekla's Answer

(*from Schiller*)

Date of composition unknown, but (?) 1852–3. The poem is a translation
in the original metre of 'Thekla: Eine Geisterstimme' (Thekla: A Spirit
Voice), which Schiller wrote to satisfy those who asked what became of
Thekla at the end of Act IV of *Wallensteins Tod* (1799).
Published *1853*; not reprinted by A.

Where I am, thou ask'st, and where I wended
   When my fleeting shadow passed from thee?
Am I not concluded now, and ended?
   Have not life and love been granted me?

5   Ask, where now those nightingales are singing,
   Who, of late, on the soft nights of May,
Set thine ears with soul-fraught music ringing –
   Only, while their love lived, lasted they.

Find I him, from whom I had to sever?
10   Doubt it not, we met, and we are one.
There, where what is joined, is joined for ever,
   There, where tears are never more to run.

There thou too shalt live with us together,
   When thou too hast borne the love we bore:
15   There, from sin delivered, dwells my Father,
   Tracked by Murder's bloody sword no more.

There he feels, it was no dream deceiving
   Lured him starwards to uplift his eye:
God doth match his gifts to man's believing;
20   Believe, and thou shalt find the Holy nigh.

All thou augurest here of lovely seeming
   There shall find fulfilment in its day:
Dare, O Friend, be wandering, dare be dreaming;
   Lofty thought lies oft in childish play.

¶ 82. *9.* Max Piccolomini, who broke with Wallenstein (Thekla's father)
because of his loyalty to the Emperor.
17–18. Wallenstein's belief in astrology is stressed throughout *The Piccolomini* and *The Death of Wallenstein*.

83 Balder Dead

Exact period of composition unknown, but (?) Dec. 1853–early Oct. 1854;
probably begun shortly after publication of *1853* in Nov. 1853 – see
'Mallet's Northern Antiquities' on A.'s reading-lists for Dec. 1853 and
Jan. 1854 (*Note-books* 554–5) and his letter to his sister 'K' 12 Dec. 1854
(misdated 1855), 'Mallet, however . . . and his version of the Edda, is all

the poem is based upon' (*L* i 48); and completed early in the following Oct. at Fox How – see A.'s letter to 'K' 10 Oct. 1854, 'I have just finished a poem which I think is better than Sohrab and Rustum, though here I do not think they consider it so . . .' (*UL* 25). The *1855* subtitle 'An Episode' (which was dropped in *1869*) links 'Balder Dead' with 'Sohrab and Rustum' – both are imitations of classical epic and illustrate the poetic creed of the *1853* Preface – but is here misapplied to a narrative consisting of a group of episodes. At A. P. Stanley's prompting A. contemplated adding to their number by writing 'a first book with an account of the circumstances of the death of Balder himself' (letter of 12 Dec. 1854 cited above), but the project was abandoned; the 'circumstances' became the substance of A.'s *1869* note, which is extracted from I. A. Blackwell's translation of the *Prose Edda*. (A.'s copy of Mallet's *Northern Antiquities* was of the 1847 English edition, in which Blackwell's translation first appeared.) For story and background A. drew heavily on the *Prose Edda*, but took only a few details from elsewhere in Mallet. His reading for Dec. 1853 and Feb.–April 1854 included much of Homer's *Iliad* and *Odyssey*, and under Sept. 1854 his diary has the entries 'read in Homer and Mallet's Northern Antiquities' and 'Aeneid. lib. vi' (*Note-books* 555–6). The *1855* text was little altered.

J. A. Froude's recommendation of subjects from Teutonic mythology in his review of *1853* (*Westminster Review n.s.* v (1854) 158–9) may have encouraged A. to go on with 'Balder Dead', but he was already familiar with Mallet in 1851 (unpublished 1851 diary) and even earlier had probably read Carlyle's brief synopsis of the Balder legend in *Heroes and Hero-Worship* (1841). F. Page claims (*Essays and Studies* (English Association) xxviii (1942) 65) that 'Arnold's attraction to Balder was his attraction to Falkland' and quotes in support A.'s 'Falkland', *Mixed Essays* (1879), *Works* x 212, 'Falkland has for the imagination the indefinable, the irresistible charm of one who is and must be, in spite of the choicest gifts and graces, unfortunate, – of a man in the grasp of fatality . . . [He] is surely and visibly touched by the finger of doom.' A.'s disappointment with his poem's reception is expressed in his 1869 letter to F. T. Palgrave, '"Balder" perhaps no one cares much for except myself; but I have always thought . . . that it has not had justice done to it; I consider that it has a natural *propriety* of diction and rhythm which is what we all prize so much in Virgil' (*Russell* 42), but T. S. Eliot's comment that A.'s poetry is 'academic poetry in the best sense; the best fruit which can issue from the promise shown by the prize-poem' (*The Use of Poetry and the Use of Criticism* (1933) 105) can be applied with justice to 'Balder Dead'. A.'s *1869* note is as follows:

> 'Balder the Good having been tormented with terrible dreams, indicating that his life was in great peril, communicated them to the assembled Æsir, who resolved to conjure all things to avert from him the threatened danger. Then Frigga exacted an oath from fire and

water, from iron, and all other metals, as well as from stones, earths, diseases, beasts, birds, poisons, and creeping things, that none of them would do any harm to Balder. When this was done, it became a favourite pastime of the Æsir, at their meetings, to get Balder to stand up and serve them as a mark, some hurling darts at him, some stones, while others hewed at him with their swords and battle-axes, for do what they would, none of them could harm him, and this was regarded by all as a great honour shown to Balder. But when Loki beheld the scene he was sorely vexed that Balder was not hurt. Assuming, therefore, the shape of a woman, he went to Fensalir, the mansion of Frigga. That goddess, when she saw the pretended woman, inquired of her if she knew what the Æsir were doing at their meetings. She replied, that they were throwing darts and stones at Balder without being able to hurt him.

"Ay," said Frigga, "neither metal nor wood can hurt Balder, for I have exacted an oath from all of them."

"What!" exclaimed the woman, "have all things sworn to spare Balder?"

"All things," replied Frigga, "except one little shrub that grows on the eastern side of Valhalla, and is called Mistletoe, and which I thought too young and feeble to crave an oath from."

As soon as Loki heard this he went away, and, resuming his natural shape, cut off the mistletoe, and repaired to the place where the gods were assembled. There he found Hodur standing apart, without partaking of the sports, on account of his blindness, and going up to him said, "Why dost thou not also throw something at Balder?"

"Because I am blind," answered Hodur, "and see not where Balder is, and have, moreover, nothing to throw with."

"Come, then," said Loki, "do like the rest, and show honour to Balder by throwing this twig at him, and I will direct thy arm towards the place where he stands."

Hodur then took the mistletoe, and, under the guidance of Loki, darted it at Balder, who, pierced through and through, fell down lifeless.' – *Edda.*

Published *1855*; reprinted *1869*, etc.

1. SENDING

The story of Hoder and the appearance of the dead Balder to Nanna in a dream – the latter incident suggested by the similar appearance of Patroclus to Achilles, *Iliad* xxiii – are A.'s and enable him to 'stress, above all, a Virgilian tenderness and a Virgilian pathos' (*Commentary* 92). In the *Prose Edda* (ch. 49) Hoder is unmentioned after Balder's death; Hermod responds at once to Frea's appeal for a volunteer to ride to Hel; Nanna dies of grief as her husband's body is placed on the funeral pyre.

So on the floor lay Balder dead; and round
Lay thickly strewn swords, axes, darts, and spears,
Which all the Gods in sport had idly thrown
At Balder, whom no weapon pierced or clove;
5   But in his breast stood fixed the fatal bough
Of mistletoe, which Lok the Accuser gave
To Hoder, and unwitting Hoder threw –
'Gainst that alone had Balder's life no charm.
     And all the Gods and all the Heroes came,
10   And stood round Balder on the bloody floor,
Weeping and wailing; and Valhalla rang
Up to its golden roof with sobs and cries;
And on the tables stood the untasted meats,
And in the horns and gold-rimmed skulls the wine.
15   And now would night have fall'n and found them yet
Wailing; but otherwise was Odin's will.
And thus the father of the ages spake: –
     'Enough of tears, ye Gods, enough of wail!
Not to lament in was Valhalla made.
20   If any here might weep for Balder's death,
I most might weep, his father; such a son
I lose to-day, so bright, so loved a God.
But he has met that doom, which long ago
The Nornies, when his mother bare him, spun,
25   And fate set seal, that so his end must be.
Balder has met his death, and ye survive –

¶ 83. i 6. *Lok the Accuser*] See *Prose Edda* ch. 33, Mallet's *Northern Antiquities*
(Bohn's Library ed. 1882) 422, 'There is another deity . . . whom some call
the calumniator of the gods . . . His name is Loki.'
i *11. Valhalla*] The Paradise of those who fall in battle; the hall where they
are entertained by Odin and the Aesir.
i *14. gold-rimmed skulls*] A. ignores Blackwell's note (*Mallet* ed. *cit.* 105) that
this is an error due to the mistranslation of a phrase meaning 'the curved
branches of the skull', i.e. drinking-horns made from antlers.
i *15–17.* An imitation of *Iliad* xxiii 154, 'And now would the light of the
sun have gone down upon their weeping, had not Achilles drawn nigh to
Agamemnon's side and said . . .'
i *18.* An echo of Milton's *Samson Agonistes* 1721,

       Nothing is here for tears, nothing to wail . . .

i *22. so bright, so loved a God*] Cp. i 126 and iii 64, below. An imitation of
similar descriptive labels in Homer, e.g. 'swift-footed Achilles', 'man-
slaying Hector', etc.
i *24. The Nornies*] The Norse Fates. See *Prose Edda* ch. 15, *Mallet* 412,
'These maidens fix the lifetime of all men, and are called Norns.'

Weep him an hour, but what can grief avail?
For ye yourselves, ye Gods, shall meet your doom,
All ye who hear me, and inhabit Heaven,
30   And I too, Odin too, the Lord of all.
But ours we shall not meet, when that day comes,
With women's tears and weak complaining cries –
Why should we meet another's portion so?
Rather it fits you, having wept your hour,
35   With cold dry eyes, and hearts composed and stern,
To live, as erst, your daily life in Heaven.
By me shall vengeance on the murderer Lok,
The foe, the accuser, whom, though Gods, we hate,
Be strictly cared for, in the appointed day.
40   Meanwhile, to-morrow, when the morning dawns,
Bring wood to the seashore to Balder's ship,
And on the deck build high a funeral-pile,
And on the top lay Balder's corpse, and put
Fire to the wood, and send him out to sea
45   To burn; for that is what the dead desire.'
      So spake the King of Gods, and straightway rose,
And mounted his horse Sleipner, whom he rode;
And from the hall of Heaven he rode away
To Lidskialf, and sate upon his throne,
50   The mount, from whence his eye surveys the world.
And far from Heaven he turned his shining orbs
To look on Midgard, and the earth, and men.

i *28–30.* The first of many allusions to Ragnarök (the Doom or Twilight of the Gods), of which Balder's death is a portent.
i *45. for that is what the dead desire*] Cp. *Iliad* xvi 675, '. . . for this is the due of the dead'.
i *46. 1855–69,*
                So having spoke, the King of Gods arose
i *49–50.* See *Prose Edda* ch. 9, *Mallet* 406, 'There is in that city [Asgard] a place called Hlidskjálf, and when Odin is seated there on his lofty throne he sees over the whole world.'
i *51–60.* Cp. *Iliad* xiii 1–9, 'Now Zeus . . . turned away his bright eyes, and looked afar, upon the land of the Thracian horsemen, and of the Mysians that fight in close combat, and of the lordly Hippemolgi that drink the milk of asses, and of the Abii, the most righteous of men. To Troy he no longer . . . turned his bright eyes, for he deemed not . . . that any of the immortals would draw nigh to aid either Trojans or Danaans.'
i *52. Midgard*] Sometimes the earth, but here 'Midgard fortress' (l. 141), the bulwark raised to protect earth from the giants. See *Prose Edda* ch. 8, *Mallet* 405.

And on the conjuring Lapps he bent his gaze
Whom antlered reindeer pull over the snow;
55   And on the Finns, the gentlest of mankind,
Fair men, who live in holes under the ground;
Nor did he look once more to Ida's plain,
Nor tow'rd Valhalla, and the sorrowing Gods;
For well he knew the Gods would heed his word,
60   And cease to mourn, and think of Balder's pyre.
    But in Valhalla all the Gods went back
From around Balder, all the Heroes went;
And left his body stretched upon the floor.
And on their golden chairs they sate again,
65   Beside the tables, in the hall of Heaven;
And before each the cooks who served them placed
New messes of the boar Serimner's flesh,
And the Valkyries crowned their horns with mead.
So they, with pent-up hearts and tearless eyes,
70   Wailing no more, in silence ate and drank,
While twilight fell, and sacred night came on.
    But the blind Hoder left the feasting Gods
In Odin's hall, and went through Asgard streets,
And past the haven where the Gods have moored
75   Their ships, and through the gate, beyond the wall;
Though sightless, yet his own mind led the God.
Down to the margin of the roaring sea
He came, and sadly went along the sand,
Between the waves and black o'erhanging cliffs
80   Where in and out the screaming seafowl fly;
Until he came to where a gully breaks
Through the cliff-wall, and a fresh stream runs down
From the high moors behind, and meets the sea.
There, in the glen, Fensaler stands, the house
85   Of Frea, honoured mother of the Gods,
And shows its lighted windows to the main.
There he went up, and passed the open doors;

i 53. *conjuring Lapps*] The Lapps are traditionally associated with witchcraft.
Cp. Shakespeare's *Comedy of Errors* IV iii 10–11,

> *Sure these are but imaginary wiles,*
> *And Lapland sorcerers inhabit here.*

i 67. *the boar Serimner's flesh*] See *Prose Edda* ch. 38, *Mallet* 429, 'But however great the band of men in Valhalla may be, the flesh of the boar
Saehrimnir will more than suffice for their sustenance. For although this
boar is sodden every morning he becomes whole again every night.'
i 68. *the Valkyries*] Etymologically, choosers of the slain. See ii 19–28
(p. 363 below) and *n.*

And in the hall, he found those women old,
The prophetesses, who by rite eterne
90   On Frea's hearth feed high the sacred fire
Both night and day; and by the inner wall
Upon her golden chair the Mother sate,
With folded hands, revolving things to come.
To her drew Hoder near, and spake, and said: –
95   'Mother, a child of bale thou bar'st in me!
For, first, thou barest me with blinded eyes,
Sightless and helpless, wandering weak in Heaven;
And, after that, of ignorant witless mind
Thou barest me, and unforeseeing soul;
100   That I alone must take the branch from Lok,
The foe, the accuser, whom, though Gods, we hate,
And cast it at the dear-loved Balder's breast
At whom the Gods in sport their weapons threw –
'Gainst that alone had Balder's life no charm.
105   Now therefore what to attempt, or whither fly,
For who will bear my hateful sight in Heaven?
Can I, O mother, bring them Balder back?
Or – for thou know'st the fates, and things allowed –
Can I with Hela's power a compact strike,
110   And make exchange, and give my life for his?'
        He spoke: the mother of the Gods replied: –
'Hoder, ill-fated, child of bale, my son,
Sightless in soul and eye, what words are these?
That one, long portioned with his doom of death,
115   Should change his lot, and fill another's life,
And Hela yield to this, and let him go!
On Balder Death hath laid her hand, not thee;
Nor doth she count this life a price for that.
For many Gods in Heaven, not thou alone,
120   Would freely die to purchase Balder back,
And wend themselves to Hela's gloomy realm.
For not so gladsome is that life in Heaven

---

i *93. revolving things to come*] A Virgilian tag. Frigga in the *Prose Edda* ch. 20 (*Mallet* 416) 'foresees the destinies of men, but never reveals what is to come'. The prophetesses and sacred hearth (ll. 89–91) are A.'s gift to Frea as the 'mother of the Gods'.

i *95. bale*] Evil or malign influence.

i *109–10* and *118* below. Cp. *Psalms* xlix 7, 'None of them can by any means redeem his brother, nor give to God a ransom for him.'

i *109. Hela's power*] Hela is the Norse goddess of the underworld, one of Loki's children. See ii 206–16 (pp. 369–70 below).

i *122–5.* Arnoldian rather than Eddic sentiment.

Which Gods and heroes lead, in feast and fray,
Waiting the darkness of the final times,
125   That one should grudge its loss for Balder's sake,
Balder their joy, so bright, so loved a God.
But fate withstands, and laws forbid this way.
Yet in my secret mind one way I know,
Nor do I judge if it shall win or fail;
130   But much must still be tried, which shall but fail.'
    And the blind Hoder answered her, and said: –
'What way is this, O mother, that thou show'st?
Is it a matter which a God might try?'
    And straight the mother of the Gods replied: –
135   'There is a road which leads to Hela's realm,
Untrodden, lonely, far from light and Heaven.
Who goes that way must take no other horse
To ride, but Sleipner, Odin's horse, alone.
Nor must he choose that common path of Gods
140   Which every day they come and go in Heaven,
O'er the bridge Bifrost, where is Heimdall's watch,
Past Midgard fortress, down to earth and men.
But he must tread a dark untravelled road,
Which branches from the north of Heaven, and ride
145   Nine days, nine nights, toward the northern ice,
Through valleys deep-engulphed, with roaring
       streams.
And he will reach on the tenth morn a bridge
Which spans with golden arches Giall's stream,
Not Bifrost, but that bridge a damsel keeps,
150   Who tells the passing troops of dead their way
To the low shore of ghosts, and Hela's realm.
And she will bid him northward steer his course.
Then he will journey through no lighted land,
Nor see the sun arise, nor see it set;
155   But he must ever watch the northern Bear,
Who from her frozen height with jealous eye

i *127. fate withstands*] Translating Virgil's *fas obstat* (*fata obstant*) – see, for example, *Aeneid* iv 440, vi 438.
i *141*. Bifrost is the rainbow. See *Prose Edda* ch. 13, *Mallet* 408, 'Hast thou not been told that the gods made a bridge from earth to heaven, and called if Bifröst?' For Heimdall, the warder of the gods, see *Prose Edda* ch. 26, *Mallet* 421.
i *143–73*. See *n.* to ii 78–178 (p. 365 below).
i *155–8*. An imitation of *Iliad* xviii 487–9, '... and the Bear ... that circleth ever in her place, and watcheth Orion, and alone hath no part in the baths of Ocean'.

Confronts the Dog and Hunter in the south,
And is alone not dipped in Ocean's stream.
And straight he will come down to Ocean's strand –
160   Ocean, whose watery ring enfolds the world,
And on whose marge the ancient giants dwell.
But he will reach its unknown northern shore,
Far, far beyond the outmost giant's home,
At the chinked fields of ice, the waste of snow.
165   And he must fare across the dismal ice
Northward, until he meets a stretching wall
Barring his way, and in the wall a grate.
But then he must dismount, and on the ice
Tighten the girths of Sleipner, Odin's horse,
170   And make him leap the grate, and come within.
And he will see stretch round him Hela's realm,
The plains of Niflheim, where dwell the dead,
And hear the roaring of the streams of Hell.
And he will see the feeble, shadowy tribes,
175   And Balder sitting crowned, and Hela's throne.
Then must he not regard the wailful ghosts
Who all will flit, like eddying leaves, around;
But he must straight accost their solemn queen,
And pay her homage, and entreat with prayers,
180   Telling her all that grief they have in Heaven
For Balder, whom she holds by right below;
If haply he may melt her heart with words,
And make her yield, and give him Balder back.'
                    She spoke; but Hoder answered her and said: –
185   'Mother, a dreadful way is this thou show'st;
No journey for a sightless God to go!'
                    And straight the mother of the Gods replied: –
'Therefore thyself thou shalt not go, my son.
But he whom first thou meetest when thou com'st
190   To Asgard, and declar'st this hidden way,

i *172. Niflheim*] The shadowy region of the dead; a synonym for Hel.
i *174. feeble, shadowy tribes*] Suggested by Homer's 'powerless heads of the
dead' (νεκύων ἀμενηνὰ κάρηνα) and 'tribes of the dead' (ἔθνεα νεκρῶν),
Odyssey xi 29, 34.
i *176-7.* A double reminiscence of Virgil's *Aeneid* vi 309–10,

> *quam multa in silvis autumni frigore primo*
> *lapsa cadunt folia . . .*

and Milton's *Paradise Lost* i 302–3,

> *Thick as Autumnal Leaves that strow the Brooks*
> *In* Vallombrosa . . .

Shall go; and I will be his guide unseen.'
　　She spoke, and on her face let fall her veil,
And bowed her head, and sate with folded hands,
But at the central hearth those women old,
195　Who while the Mother spake had ceased their toil,
Began again to heap the sacred fire.
And Hoder turned, and left his mother's house,
Fensaler, whose lit windows look to sea;
And came again down to the roaring waves,
200　And back along the beach to Asgard went,
Pondering on that which Frea said should be.
　　But night came down, and darkened Asgard streets.
Then from their loathéd feast the Gods arose,
And lighted torches, and took up the corpse
205　Of Balder from the floor of Odin's hall,
And laid it on a bier, and bare him home
Through the fast-darkening streets to his own house,
Breidablik, on whose columns Balder graved
The enchantments that recall the dead to life.
210　For wise he was, and many curious arts,
Postures of runes, and healing herbs he knew;
Unhappy! but that art he did not know,
To keep his own life safe, and see the sun.
There to his hall the Gods brought Balder home,
215　And each bespake him as he laid him down: —
　　'Would that ourselves, O Balder, we were borne
Home to our halls, with torchlight, by our kin,
So thou might'st live, and still delight the Gods!'
　　They spake; and each went home to his own house.
220　But there was one, the first of all the Gods
For speed, and Hermod was his name in Heaven;
Most fleet he was, but now he went the last,
Heavy in heart for Balder, to his house,
Which he in Asgard built him, there to dwell,

i *208-9*. Not in the *Prose Edda*, but A. noted the quotation from the *Háva-mál*, *Mallet* 372, 'If I see a man dead and hanging aloft on a tree, I engrave Runic characters so wonderful, that the man immediately descends and converses with me.'

i *212-13*. An allusion to *Matthew* xxvii 42 and *Mark* xv 31, 'He saved others; himself he could not save.' For a similar allusion see iii 484–6 (p. 386 below). The parallel between Balder and Christ may have been suggested to A. by Carlyle's *Heroes and Hero-Worship* (1841), *Works* ed. H. D. Traill v 18, 'Balder again, the White God, the beautiful, the just and benignant (whom the early Christian missionaries found to resemble Christ) . . .'

225 Against the harbour, by the city wall.
   Him the blind Hoder met, as he came up
   From the sea cityward, and knew his step;
   Nor yet could Hermod see his brother's face,
   For it grew dark; but Hoder touched his arm.
230 And as a spray of honeysuckle flowers
   Brushes across a tired traveller's face
   Who shuffles through the deep dew-moistened dust,
   On a May evening, in the darkened lanes,
   And starts him, that he thinks a ghost went by –
235 So Hoder brushed by Hermod's side, and said: –
    'Take Sleipner, Hermod, and set forth with dawn
   To Hela's kingdom, to ask Balder back;
   And they shall be thy guides, who have the power.'
    He spake, and brushed soft by, and disappeared.
240 And Hermod gazed into the night, and said: –
    'Who is it utters through the dark his hest
   So quickly, and will wait for no reply?
   The voice was like the unhappy Hoder's voice.
   Howbeit I will see, and do his hest;
245 For there rang note divine in that command.'
    So speaking, the fleet-footed Hermod came
   Home, and lay down to sleep in his own house;
   And all the Gods lay down in their own homes.
   And Hoder too came home, distraught with grief,
250 Loathing to meet, at dawn, the other Gods;
   And he went in, and shut the door, and fixed
   His sword upright, and fell on it, and died.
    But from the hill of Lidskialf Odin rose,
   The throne, from which his eye surveys the world;
255 And mounted Sleipner, and in darkness rode
   To Asgard. And the stars came out in heaven,
   High over Asgard, to light home the King.
   But fiercely Odin galloped, moved in heart;
   And swift to Asgard, to the gate, he came.
260 And terribly the hoofs of Sleipner rang
   Along the flinty floor of Asgard streets,
   And the Gods trembled on their golden beds
   Hearing the wrathful Father coming home –
   For dread, for like a whirlwind, Odin came.
265 And to Valhalla's gate he rode, and left
   Sleipner; and Sleipner went to his own stall;
   And in Valhalla Odin laid him down.

i 230–4. A.'s first epic simile of the type used so lavishly in 'Sohrab and Rustum'. Their number is reduced by half in the longer 'Balder Dead'.

But in Breidablik, Nanna, Balder's wife,
Came with the Goddesses who wrought her will,
270   And stood by Balder lying on his bier.
And at his head and feet she stationed Scalds
Who in their lives were famous for their song;
These o'er the corpse intoned a plaintive strain,
A dirge – and Nanna and her train replied.
275   And far into the night they wailed their dirge.
But when their souls were satisfied with wail,
They went, and laid them down, and Nanna went
Into an upper chamber, and lay down;
And Frea sealed her tired lids with sleep.
280   And 'twas when night is bordering hard on dawn,
When air is chilliest, and the stars sunk low;
Then Balder's spirit through the gloom drew near,
In garb, in form, in feature as he was,
Alive; and still the rays were round his head
285   Which were his glorious mark in Heaven; he stood
Over against the curtain of the bed,
And gazed on Nanna as she slept, and spake: –
      'Poor lamb, thou sleepest, and forgett'st thy woe!
Tears stand upon the lashes of thine eyes,
290   Tears wet the pillow by thy cheek; but thou,
Like a young child, hast cried thyself to sleep.
Sleep on; I watch thee, and am here to aid.
Alive I kept not far from thee, dear soul!
Neither do I neglect thee now, though dead.
295   For with to-morrow's dawn the Gods prepare
To gather wood, and build a funeral-pile
Upon my ship, and burn my corpse with fire,
That sad, sole honour of the dead; and thee
They think to burn, and all my choicest wealth,
300   With me, for thus ordains the common rite.
But it shall not be so; but mild, but swift,
But painless shall a stroke from Frea come,
To cut thy thread of life, and free thy soul,
And they shall burn thy corpse with mine, not thee.

282–3. An imitation of *Iliad* xxiii 65–7 (the appearance of the dead
Patroclus to Achilles), '. . . then there came to him the spirit of hapless
Patroclus, in all things like his very self, in stature and fair eyes and in voice,
and in like raiment was he clad withal . . .'
i 284–5. Balder is the sun-god. For the rays see *Prose Edda* ch. 22, *Mallet*
417, 'So fair and dazzling is he in form and features, that rays of light seem
to issue from him.' It is A. who converts them into a halo.
288. Cp. *Iliad* xxiii 69, 'Thou sleepest, and hast forgotten me, Achilles.'
13+M.A.

305   And well I know that by no stroke of death,
    Tardy or swift, would'st thou be loth to die,
    So it restored thee, Nanna, to my side,
    Whom thou so well hast loved; but I can smooth
    Thy way, and this, at least, my prayers avail.
310   Yes, and I fain would altogether ward
    Death from thy head, and with the Gods in Heaven
    Prolong thy life, though not by thee desired –
    But right bars this, not only thy desire.
    Yet dreary, Nanna, is the life they lead
315   In that dim world, in Hela's mouldering realm;
    And doleful are the ghosts, the troops of dead,
    Whom Hela with austere control presides.
    For of the race of Gods is no one there,
    Save me alone, and Hela, solemn queen;
320   And all the nobler souls of mortal men
    On battle-field have met their death, and now
    Feast in Valhalla, in my father's hall;
    Only the inglorious sort are there below,
    The old, the cowards, and the weak are there –
325   Men spent by sickness, or obscure decay.
    But even there, O Nanna, we might find
    Some solace in each other's look and speech,
    Wandering together through that gloomy world,
    And talking of the life we led in Heaven,
330   While we yet lived, among the other Gods.'
      He spake, and straight his lineaments began
    To fade; and Nanna in her sleep stretched out
    Her arms towards him with a cry – but he
    Mournfully shook his head, and disappeared.
335   And as the woodman sees a little smoke
    Hang in the air, afield, and disappear,
    So Balder faded in the night away.
    And Nanna on her bed sank back; but then
    Frea, the mother of the Gods, with stroke
340   Painless and swift, set free her airy soul,
    Which took, on Balder's track, the way below;
    And instantly the sacred morn appeared.

i *323–5*. Hela's subjects are 'all who die through sickness or old age' (*Prose Edda* ch. 34, *Mallet* 423).
i *331–7*. Imitating *Iliad* xxiii 99–101; 'So saying he reached forth with his hands, yet clasped him not; but the spirit like a vapour was gone beneath the earth, gibbering faintly.' Virgil's Eurydice (*Georgics* iv 499–500) and Anchises (*Aeneid* v 740) disappear 'ceu fumus in auras'.
i *339–40*. Cp. the 'gentle shafts of Artemis', *Odyssey* xi 172–3.

2. JOURNEY TO THE DEAD

Balder's prediction that the condition for his release will not be fulfilled is
A.'s invention. Hermod's journey and visit to Hel are from the *Prose Edda*
(mainly ch. 49) with some echoes of Odysseus' visit to Hades, *Odyssey* xi.
The preparations for Balder's funeral recall those for the funeral of Patroclus, *Iliad* xxiii.

> Forth from the east, up the ascent of Heaven,
> Day drove his courser with the shining mane;
> And in Valhalla, from his gable-perch,
> The golden-crested cock began to crow.
> 5   Hereafter, in the blackest dead of night,
> With shrill and dismal cries that bird shall crow,
> Warning the Gods that foes draw nigh to Heaven;
> But now he crew at dawn, a cheerful note,
> To wake the Gods and Heroes to their tasks.
> 10   And all the Gods, and all the Heroes, woke.
> And from their beds the Heroes rose, and donned
> Their arms, and led their horses from the stall,
> And mounted them, and in Valhalla's court
> Were ranged; and then the daily fray began.
> 15   And all day long they there are hacked and hewn,
> 'Mid dust, and groans, and limbs lopped off, and
>   blood;
> But all at night return to Odin's hall,
> Woundless and fresh; such lot is theirs in Heaven.
> And the Valkyries on their steeds went forth
> 20   Tow'rd earth and fights of men; and at their side
> Skulda, the youngest of the Nornies, rode;
> And over Bifrost, where is Heimdall's watch,
> Past Midgard fortress, down to earth they came;
> There through some battle-field, where men fall fast,
> 25   Their horses fetlock-deep in blood, they ride,
> And pick the bravest warriors out for death,

ii *5–7*. To announce Ragnarök – cp. iii 495–7 (p. 387 below). A detail
not in *Mallet*, but see *Elder Edda* (Völuspá st. 43).

ii *11–18*. See *Prose Edda* ch. 41, *Mallet* 432, 'Every day ... as soon as they
have dressed themselves they ride out into the court, and there fight until
they cut each other in pieces. This is their pastime, but when meal-tide
approaches they remount their steeds and return to drink in Valhalla.'

ii *19–28*. See *Prose Edda* ch. 36, *Mallet* 427, 'Odin sends them to every field
of battle, to make choice of those who are to be slain ... Gudur, Rota,
and the youngest of the Norns, Skuld, also ride forth to choose the slain
and turn the combat.'

Whom they bring back with them at night to Heaven
To glad the Gods, and feast in Odin's hall.
        But the Gods went not now, as otherwile,
30   Into the tilt-yard, where the Heroes fought,
To feast their eyes with looking on the fray;
Nor did they to their judgment-place repair
By the ash Igdrasil, in Ida's plain,
Where they hold council, and give laws for men.
35   But they went, Odin first, the rest behind,
To the hall Gladheim, which is built of gold;
Where are in circle ranged twelve golden chairs,
And in the midst one higher, Odin's throne.
There all the Gods in silence sate them down;
40   And thus the Father of the ages spake: –
        'Go quickly, Gods, bring wood to the seashore,
With all, which it beseems the dead to have,
And make a funeral-pile on Balder's ship;
On the twelfth day the Gods shall burn his corpse.
45   But Hermod, thou take Sleipner, and ride down
To Hela's kingdom, to ask Balder back.'
        So said he; and the Gods arose, and took
Axes and ropes, and at their head came Thor,
Shouldering his hammer, which the giants know.
50   Forth wended they, and drave their steeds before.
And up the dewy mountain-tracks they fared
To the dark forests, in the early dawn;
And up and down, and side and slant they roamed.
And from the glens all day an echo came

ii *32–4.* See *Prose Edda* ch. 15, *Mallet* 411, 'The third root of the ash [the
tree Igdrasil] is in heaven and under it is the holy Urdar-fount. 'Tis here
that the gods sit in judgment.'

ii *36. Gladheim*] See *Prose Edda* ch. 13, *Mallet* 409, 'This hall is the largest
and most magnificent in the universe, being resplendent on all sides, both
within and without, with the finest gold. Its name is Gladsheim.'

ii *47–69.* An imitation of *Iliad* xxiii 114–26 (the preparations for the
funeral of Patroclus), 'And they went forth bearing in their hands axes for
the cutting of wood and well-woven ropes, and before them went the
mules; and ever upward, downward, sideward, and aslant they fared. But
when they were come to the spurs of many-fountained Ida, forthwith they
set them to fell high-crested oaks . . . ; and with a mighty crash the trees
kept falling. Then the Achaeans split the trunks asunder and bound them
behind the mules, and these tore up the earth with their feet as they hasted
. . . through the thick underbrush. And all the woodcutters bare logs . . .
Then down upon the shore they cast them . . . where Achilles planned a
great barrow . . .'

55 Of crashing falls; for with his hammer Thor
    Smote 'mid the rocks the lichen-bearded pines,
    And burst their roots, while to their tops the Gods
    Made fast the woven ropes, and haled them down,
    And lopped their boughs, and clove them on the sward,
60 And bound the logs behind their steeds to draw,
    And drave them homeward; and the snorting steeds
    Went straining through the crackling brushwood down,
    And by the darkling forest-paths the Gods
    Followed, and on their shoulders carried boughs.
65 And they came out upon the plain, and passed
    Asgard, and led their horses to the beach,
    And loosed them of their loads on the seashore,
    And ranged the wood in stacks by Balder's ship;
    And every God went home to his own house.
70   But when the Gods were to the forest gone,
    Hermod led Sleipner from Valhalla forth
    And saddled him; before that, Sleipner brooked
    No meaner hand than Odin's on his mane,
    On his broad back no lesser rider bore;
75 Yet docile now he stood at Hermod's side,
    Arching his neck, and glad to be bestrode,
    Knowing the God they went to seek, how dear.
    But Hermod mounted him, and sadly fared
    In silence up the dark untravelled road
80 Which branches from the north of Heaven, and went
    All day; and daylight waned, and night came on.
    And all that night he rode, and journeyed so,

ii *78–178*. Developed from *Prose Edda* ch. 49, *Mallet* 448–9, 'For the space of nine days, and as many nights, he [Hermod] rode through deep glens so dark that he could not discern anything until he arrived at the river Gjöll, which he passed over on a bridge covered with glittering gold. Modgudur, the maiden who kept the bridge, asked him his name and lineage, telling him that the day before five bands of dead persons had ridden over the bridge, and did not shake it so much as he alone. "But," she added, "thou hast not death's hue on thee, why then ridest thou here on the way to Hel?" "I ride to Hel," answered Hermod, "to seek Baldur. Hast thou perchance seen him pass this way?" "Baldur," she replied, "hath ridden over Gjöll's bridge, but there below, towards the north, lies the way to the abodes of death." Hermod then pursued his journey until he came to the barred gates of Hel. Here he alighted, girthed his saddle tighter, and remounting, clapped both spurs to his horse, who cleared the gate by a tremendous leap without touching it. Hermod then rode on to the palace, where he found his brother Baldur occuping the most distinguished seat in the hall.'

Nine days, nine nights, toward the northern ice,
Through valleys deep-engulphed, by roaring streams.
85 And on the tenth morn he beheld the bridge
Which spans with golden arches Giall's stream,
And on the bridge a damsel watching armed,
In the strait passage, at the farther end,
Where the road issues between walling rocks.
90 Scant space that warder left for passers-by;
But as when cowherds in October drive
Their kine across a snowy mountain-pass
To winter-pasture on the southern side,
And on the ridge a waggon chokes the way,
95 Wedged in the snow; then painfully the hinds
With goad and shouting urge their cattle past,
Plunging through deep untrodden banks of snow
To right and left, and warm steam fills the air –
So on the bridge that damsel blocked the way,
100 And questioned Hermod as he came, and said: –
    'Who art thou on thy black and fiery horse
Under whose hoofs the bridge o'er Giall's stream
Rumbles and shakes? Tell me thy race and home.
But yestermorn, five troops of dead passed by,
105 Bound on their way below to Hela's realm,
Nor shook the bridge so much as thou alone.
And thou hast flesh and colour on thy cheeks,
Like men who live, and draw the vital air;
Nor look'st thou pale and wan, like men deceased,
110 Souls bound below, my daily passers here.'
    And the fleet-footed Hermod answered her: –
'O damsel, Hermod am I called, the son
Of Odin; and my high-roofed house is built
Far hence, in Asgard, in the city of Gods;
115 And Sleipner, Odin's horse, is this I ride.
And I come, sent this road on Balder's track;
Say then, if he hath crossed thy bridge or no?'
    He spake; the warder of the bridge replied: –
'O Hermod, rarely do the feet of Gods
120 Or of the horses of the Gods resound
Upon my bridge; and, when they cross, I know.
Balder hath gone this way, and ta'en the road

ii *101–10.* Suggested by Charon's speech, *Aeneid* vi 388–91,

> *quisquis es, armatus qui nostra ad flumina tendis,*
> *fare age, quid venias, iam istinc, et comprime gressum.*
> *umbrarum hic locus est, Somni Noctisque soporae;*
> *corpora viva nefas Stygia vectare carina.*

Below there, to the north, tow'rd Hela's realm.
From here the cold white mist can be discerned,
125 Nor lit with sun, but through the darksome air
By the dim vapour-blotted light of stars,
Which hangs over the ice where lies the road.
For in that ice are lost those northern streams,
Freezing and ridging in their onward flow,
130 Which from the fountain of Vergelmer run,
The spring that bubbles up by Hela's throne.
There are the joyless seats, the haunt of ghosts,
Hela's pale swarms; and there was Balder bound.
Ride on! pass free! but he by this is there.'
135   She spake, and stepped aside, and left him room.
And Hermod greeted her and galloped by
Across the bridge; then she took post again.
But northward Hermod rode, the way below;
And o'er a darksome tract, which knows no sun,
140 But by the blotted light of stars, he fared.
And he came down to Ocean's northern strand,
At the drear ice, beyond the giants' home.
Thence on he journeyed o'er the fields of ice
Still north, until he met a stretching wall
145 Barring his way, and in the wall a grate.
Then he dismounted, and drew tight the girths,
On the smooth ice, of Sleipner, Odin's horse,
And made him leap the grate, and came within.
And he beheld spread round him Hela's realm,
150 The plains of Niflheim, where dwell the dead,
And heard the thunder of the streams of Hell.
For near the wall the river of Roaring flows,
Outmost; the others near the centre run –
The Storm, the Abyss, the Howling, and the Pain;
155 These flow by Hela's throne, and near their spring.

ii *128–31.* See ii 152–5 below and *n.*
ii *138–42.* A. is recalling *Odyssey* xi 13–19, 'She [the ship of Odysseus]
came to deep-flowing Oceanus, that bounds the Earth, where is the land
and city of the Cimmerians, wrapped in mist and cloud. Never does the
bright sun look down on them . . . but baneful night is spread over
wretched mortals.'
ii *152–5.* See *Prose Edda* ch. 4, *Mallet* 401, 'Many ages before the earth was
made . . . was Niflheim formed, in the middle of which lies the spring
called Hvergelmir, from which flow twelve rivers, Gjöll being nearest to
the gate of the abode of death.' A.'s names are meant to recall the rivers of
Hades, but two are taken from Blackwell's glossary, which explains Gjöll
as 'sonorous, fulgid' (A.'s Roaring), Ylgr as 'the Howling'.

And from the dark flocked up the shadowy tribes;
And as the swallows crowd the bulrush-beds
Of some clear river, issuing from a lake,
On autumn-days, before they cross the sea;
160   And to each bulrush-crest a swallow hangs
Quivering, and others skim the river-streams,
And their quick twittering fills the banks and shores –
So around Hermod swarmed the twittering ghosts.
Women, and infants, and young men who died
165   Too soon for fame, with white ungraven shields;
And old men, known to glory, but their star
Betrayed them, and of wasting age they died,
Not wounds; yet, dying, they their armour wore,
And now have chief regard in Hela's realm.
170   Behind flocked wrangling up a piteous crew,
Greeted of none, disfeatured and forlorn –
Cowards, who were in sloughs interred alive;

ii *157–9*. Cp. *Aeneid* vi 310–12 (the dead thronging to Charon's boat),

> . . . *aut terram gurgite ab alto*
> *quam multa glomerantur aves, ubi frigidus annus*
> *trans pontum fugat* . . .

ii *161*. *Quivering*] Swinging *1855–81*.

ii *162*. *twittering*] The usual word for swallows, but cp. Keats's 'To Autumn' 33,

> *And gathering swallows twitter in the skies.*

ii *163*. *twittering ghosts*] An apt equivalent for Homer's τετριγυῖα ψυχὴ (*Iliad* xxiii 100–1).

ii *164–8*. Imitating *Odyssey* xi 38–41, '. . . brides, and unwedded youths, and toil-worn old men, and tender maidens with hearts yet new to sorrow, and many, too, that had been wounded with bronze-tipped spears, men slain in fight, wearing their bloodstained armour' and *Aeneid* vi 306–7,

> *matres atque viri, defuncta corpora vita*
> *magnanimum heroum, pueri innuptaeque puellae* . . .

ii *165*. *white ungraven shields*] Not in the *Prose Edda*, but see *Mallet* 167, 'When a young warrior was at first enlisted, they gave him a white and smooth buckler, which was called the "Shield of expectation". This he carried till, by some signal exploit, he had obtained leave to have proofs of his valour engraven on it.'

ii *172–5*. Not in the *Prose Edda*, but see *Mallet* 137, 'The laws of the ancient Danes . . . excluded them [cowards] from society . . . Among the Germans this was sometimes carried so far as to suffocate cowards in mud; after which they covered them over with hurdles; to show, says Tacitus, that . . . there are certain degrees of cowardice and infamy which ought to be buried in eternal silence.'

And round them still the wattled hurdles hung,
Wherewith they stamped them down, and trod them
175   To hide their shameful memory from men.   [deep,
But all he passed unhailed, and reached the throne
Of Hela, and saw, near it, Balder crowned,
And Hela set thereon, with countenance stern;
And thus bespake him first the solemn queen: –
180   'Unhappy, how hast thou endured to leave
The light, and journey to the cheerless land
Where idly flit about the feeble shades?
How didst thou cross the bridge o'er Giall's stream,
Being alive, and come to Ocean's shore?
185   Or how o'erleap the grate that bars the wall?'
     She spake; but down off Sleipner Hermod sprang,
And fell before her feet, and clasped her knees;
And spake, and mild entreated her, and said: –
     'O Hela, wherefore should the Gods declare
190   Their errands to each other, or the ways
They go? the errand and the way is known.
Thou know'st, thou know'st, what grief we have in
       Heaven
For Balder, whom thou hold'st by right below.
Restore him! for what part fulfils he here?
195   Shall he shed cheer over the cheerless seats,
And touch the apathetic ghosts with joy?
Not for such end, O queen, thou hold'st thy realm.
For Heaven was Balder born, the city of Gods
And Heroes, where they live in light and joy.
200   Thither restore him, for his place is there!'
     He spoke; and grave replied the solemn queen: –
'Hermod, for he thou art, thou son of Heaven!
A strange unlikely errand, sure, is thine.
Do the Gods send to me to make them blest?
205   Small bliss my race hath of the Gods obtained.
Three mighty children to my father Lok
Did Angerbode, the giantess, bring forth –
Fenris the wolf, the Serpent huge, and me.
Of these the Serpent in the sea ye cast,
210   Who since in your despite hath waxed amain,
And now with gleaming ring enfolds the world;
Me on this cheerless nether world ye threw,
And gave me nine unlighted realms to rule;
While on his island in the lake afar,

ii *206–16.* Based on *Prose Edda* ch. 34, *Mallet* 423–6.
  13*

215   Made fast to the bored crag, by wile not strength
        Subdued, with limber chains lives Fenris bound.
        Lok still subsists in Heaven, our father wise,
        Your mate, though loathed, and feasts in Odin's hall;
        But him too foes await, and netted snares,
220   And in a cave a bed of needle rocks,
        And o'er his visage serpents dropping gall.
        Yet he shall one day rise, and burst his bonds,
        And with himself set us his offspring free,
        When he guides Muspel's children to their bourne.
225   Till then in peril or in pain we live,
        Wrought by the Gods – and ask the Gods our aid?
        Howbeit, we abide our day; till then,
        We do not as some feebler haters do –
        Seek to afflict our foes with petty pangs,
230   Helpless to better us, or ruin them.
        Come then! if Balder was so dear beloved,
        And this is true, and such a loss is Heaven's –
        Hear, how to Heaven may Balder be restored.
        Show me through all the world the signs of grief!
235   Fails but one thing to grieve, here Balder stops!
        Let all that lives and moves upon the earth
        Weep him, and all that is without life weep;
        Let Gods, men, brutes, beweep him; plants and stones!
        So I shall know the lost was dear indeed,
240   And bend my heart, and give him back to Heaven.'
           She spake; and Hermod answered her, and said: –
        'Hela, such as thou say'st, the terms shall be.
        But come, declare me this, and truly tell:
        May I, ere I depart, bid Balder hail,
245   Or is it here withheld to greet the dead?'
           He spake, and straightway Hela answered him: –

ii *215–16.* The wolf Fenrir was flattered by the gods into allowing himself to be bound by a magic cord made by the Dark Elves.

ii *219–21.* See *Prose Edda* ch. 50, *Mallet* 449–51 for Loki's punishment. 'Netted snares' refers to his attempt to escape by turning himself into a salmon.

i *222–4.* Cp. iii 475–6 below. Muspell, the opposite of Niflheim, is 'a world too luminous and glowing to be entered by those who are not indigenous there' (*Prose Edda* ch. 4, *Mallet* 401).

ii *231–40.* See *Prose Edda* ch. 49, *Mallet* 449, 'Hela answered that it should now be tried whether Baldur was so beloved . . . "If therefore," she added, "all things in the world, both living and lifeless, weep for him, then shall he return to the Aesir, but if any one thing speak against him or refuse to weep, he shall be kept in Hel".'

'Hermod, greet Balder if thou wilt, and hold
Converse; his speech remains, though he be dead.'
      And straight to Balder Hermod turned, and spake: –
250 'Even in the abode of death, O Balder, hail!
Thou hear'st, if hearing, like as speech, is thine,
The terms of thy releasement hence to Heaven;
Fear nothing but that all shall be fulfilled.
For not unmindful of thee are the Gods,
255 Who see the light, and blest in Asgard dwell;
Even here they seek thee out, in Hela's realm.
And sure of all the happiest far art thou
Who ever have been known in earth or Heaven;
Alive, thou wast of Gods the most beloved,
260 And now thou sittest crowned by Hela's side,
Here, and hast honour among all the dead.'
      He spake; and Balder uttered him reply,
But feebly, as a voice far off; he said: –
      'Hermod the nimble, gild me not my death!
265 Better to live a serf, a captured man,
Who scatters rushes in a master's hall,
Than be a crowned king here, and rule the dead.
And now I count not of these terms as safe
To be fulfilled, nor my return as sure,
270 Though I be loved, and many mourn my death;
For double-minded ever was the seed
Of Lok, and double are the gifts they give.
Howbeit, report thy message; and therewith,
To Odin, to my father, take this ring,
275 Memorial of me, whether saved or no;
And tell the Heaven-born Gods how thou hast seen

ii 257–67. An imitation of *Odyssey* xi 482–91 (Odysseus and the ghost of
Achilles), '". . . than thou, Achilles, no man aforetime was more blessed
or shall be hereafter. For of old, when thou wast alive, we Argives honoured thee even as the gods, and now that thou art here, thou rulest
mightily among the dead . . ." So I spoke, and he straightway made
answer and said: "Nay, seek not to speak soothingly to me of death,
glorious Odysseus. I should choose, so I might live on earth, to serve as the
hireling of another, of some portionless man . . . rather than to be lord
over all the dead that have perished."'
ii 265. *serf*] slave *1855*.
ii 274. *take this ring*] In the *Prose Edda* Balder's funeral has already taken
place and Balder is returning the gold ring Draupnir which Odin had
thrown on the pyre and which had since acquired magical properties. A.
still has Odin throw a gold ring on the pyre (iii 172–3, p. 378 below),
but the detail is pointless.

Me sitting here below by Hela's side,
Crowned, having honour among all the dead.'
      He spake, and raised his hand, and gave the ring.
280   And with inscrutable regard the queen
Of Hell beheld them, and the ghosts stood dumb.
But Hermod took the ring, and yet once more
Kneeled and did homage to the solemn queen;
Then mounted Sleipner, and set forth to ride
285   Back, through the astonished tribes of dead, to Heaven.
And to the wall he came, and found the grate
Lifted, and issued on the fields of ice.
And o'er the ice he fared to Ocean's strand,
And up from thence, a wet and misty road,
290   To the armed damsel's bridge, and Giall's stream.
Worse was that way to go than to return,
For him; for others all return is barred.
Nine days he took to go, two to return,
And on the twelfth morn saw the light of Heaven.
295   And as a traveller in the early dawn
To the steep edge of some great valley comes,
Through which a river flows, and sees, beneath,
Clouds of white rolling vapours fill the vale,
But o'er them, on the farther slope, descries
300   Vineyards, and crofts, and pastures, bright with sun –
So Hermod, o'er the fog between, saw Heaven.
And Sleipner snorted, for he smelt the air
Of Heaven; and mightily, as winged, he flew.
And Hermod saw the towers of Asgard rise;
305   And he drew near, and heard no living voice
In Asgard; and the golden halls were dumb.
Then Hermod knew what labour held the Gods;
And through the empty streets he rode, and passed
Under the gate-house to the sands, and found
310   The Gods on the sea-shore by Balder's ship.

3. FUNERAL

Pt. 3 has three movements. In the first (ll. 1–212) Lok's mockery of Hermod and the lamentations of the gods by Balder's pyre are A.'s; the
funeral is developed from the *Prose Edda* (ch. 49) with some echoes of the
funeral of Patroclus, *Iliad* xxiii. In the second movement (ll. 213–372)
the council of the Aesir is A.'s – with the substance of Frea's description of
creation from the *Prose Edda* (chs. 7–9); the weeping of all things for Balder
is also from the *Prose Edda* (ch. 49). In the final movement (ll. 373–566)
Hermod's meeting with Hoder is A.'s; Hermod's account of Ragnarök
and Balder's prophecy of a world restored – though it is A. who places
these in their mouths – are from the *Prose Edda* (chs. 51 and 53 respectively).

The Gods held talk together, grouped in knots,
Round Balder's corpse, which they had thither borne;
And Hermod came down tow'rds them from the gate.
And Lok, the father of the serpent, first
Beheld him come, and to his neighbour spake: –
5   'See, here is Hermod, who comes single back
From Hell; and shall I tell thee how he seems?
Like as a farmer, who hath lost his dog,
Some morn, at market, in a crowded town –
10   Through many streets the poor beast runs in vain,
And follows this man after that, for hours;
And, late at evening, spent and panting, falls
Before a stranger's threshold, not his home,
With flanks a-tremble, and his slender tongue
15   Hangs quivering out between his dust-smeared jaws,
And piteously he eyes the passers-by;
But home his master comes to his own farm,
Far in the country, wondering where he is –
So Hermod comes to-day unfollowed home.'
20   And straight his neighbour, moved with wrath, re-
'Deceiver! fair in form, but false in heart!   [plied: –
Enemy, mocker, whom, though Gods, we hate –
Peace, lest our father Odin hear thee jibe!
Would I might see him snatch thee in his hand,
25   And bind thy carcase, like a bale, with cords,
And hurl thee in a lake, to sink or swim!
If clear from plotting Balder's death, to swim;
But deep, if thou devisedst it, to drown,
And perish, against fate, before thy day.'
30   So they two soft to one another spake.
But Odin looked toward the land, and saw
His messenger; and he stood forth, and cried.
And Hermod came, and leapt from Sleipner down,
And in his father's hand put Sleipner's rein,
35   And greeted Odin and the Gods, and said: –
'Odin, my father, and ye, Gods of Heaven!
Lo, home, having performed your will, I come.

iii *24–8.* The ordeal by water is from *Mallet* 132, 'Thus sometimes they
cast him [the accused] into a deep water, tied about with cords: if he sunk,
that is, if the genius of the water received him . . . , it declared him to be
innocent; if it rejected him, if he swam upon the surface, he was looked
upon as convicted of the crime.' A. reverses the interpretation.
iii *29.* Cp. *Aeneid* iv 696–7 (the death of Dido),

> *nam quia nec fato, merita nec morte peribat*
> *sed misera ante diem . . .*

Into the joyless kingdom have I been,
Below, and looked upon the shadowy tribes
40   Of ghosts, and communed with their solemn queen;
And to your prayers she sends you this reply:
Show her through all the world the signs of grief!
Fails but one thing to grieve, there Balder stops!
Let Gods, men, brutes, beweep him; plants and stones!
45   *So shall she know your loss was dear indeed,*
And bend her heart, and give you Balder back.'
        He spoke; and all the Gods to Odin looked;
And straight the Father of the ages said: –
        'Ye Gods, these terms may keep another day.
50   But now, put on your arms, and mount your steeds,
And in procession all come near, and weep
Balder; for that is what the dead desire.
When ye enough have wept, then build a pile
Of the heaped wood, and burn his corpse with fire
55   Out of our sight; that we may turn from grief,
And lead, as erst, our daily life in Heaven.'
        He spoke, and the Gods armed; and Odin donned
His dazzling corslet and his helm of gold,
And led the way on Sleipner; and the rest
60   Followed, in tears, their father and their king.
And thrice in arms around the dead they rode,
Weeping; the sands were wetted, and their arms,
With their thick-falling tears – so good a friend
They mourned that day, so bright, so loved a God.
65   And Odin came, and laid his kingly hands
On Balder's breast, and thus began the wail: –
        'Farewell, O Balder, bright and loved, my son!
In that great day, the twilight of the Gods,
When Muspel's children shall beleaguer Heaven,
70   Then we shall miss thy counsel and thy arm.'
        Thou camest near the next, O warrior Thor!
Shouldering thy hammer, in thy chariot drawn,

iii 52. See *n.* to i 45 (p. 354 above).
iii 61–2. *And thrice . . . Weeping*] Cp. *Aeneid* xi 188–90 (the funeral of
Pallas),

> *ter circum accensos cincti fulgentibus armis*
> *decurrere rogos, ter maestum funeris ignem*
> *lustravere in equis ululatusque ore dedere . . .*

iii 68–9. See *n.* to iii 474–81 (p. 386 below).
iii 71. This direct address to a character in the action is Homeric.
iii 72–3. Thor's chariot drawn by two goats is mentioned in the *Prose Edda*
ch. 21, *Mallet* 417.

Swaying the long-haired goats with silvered rein;
And over Balder's corpse these words didst say: –
75   'Brother, thou dwellest in the darksome land,
And talkest with the feeble tribes of ghosts,
Now, and I know not how they prize thee there –
But here, I know, thou wilt be missed and mourned.
For haughty spirits and high wraths are rife
80   Among the Gods and Heroes here in Heaven,
As among those whose joy and work is war;
And daily strifes arise, and angry words.
But from thy lips, O Balder, night or day,
Heard no one ever an injurious word
85   To God or Hero, but thou keptest back
The others, labouring to compose their brawls.
Be ye then kind, as Balder too was kind!
For we lose him, who smoothed all strife in Heaven.'
He spake, and all the Gods assenting wailed.
90   And Freya next came nigh, with golden tears;
The loveliest Goddess she in Heaven, by all
Most honoured after Frea, Odin's wife.
Her long ago the wandering Oder took
To mate, but left her to roam distant lands;
95   Since then she seeks him, and weeps tears of gold.
Names hath she many; Vanadis on earth
They call her, Freya is her name in Heaven;
She in her hands took Balder's head, and spake: –
'Balder, my brother, thou art gone a road
100   Unknown and long, and haply on that way
My long-lost wandering Oder thou has met,
For in the paths of Heaven he is not found.
Oh, if it be so, tell him what thou wast

iii 75–88. Thor's praise of Balder's mildness is A.'s. In the *Prose Edda* (ch. 49, *Mallet* 447–8) Thor loses his temper with the giantess who launches the death-ship and has to be prevented from cracking her skull with his hammer; he then kicks a dwarf into the fire. A. omits these incidents, as he ignores other grotesque elements in the Eddic story, e.g. the eight legs of Odin's horse Sleipnir.

iii 90–7. See *Prose Edda* ch. 35, *Mallet* 426, 'Freyja is ranked next to Frigga: she is wedded to ... Odur ... But Odur left his wife in order to travel into very remote countries. Since that time Freyja continually weeps, and her tears are drops of pure gold. She has a great variety of names ... She is thus called Mardöll, Horn, Gefn, and Syr, and also Vanadis.'

iii 98. As Andromache takes the dead Hector's head in her hands to begin the lament, *Iliad* xxiv 723–4.

To his neglected wife, and what he is,
105   And wring his heart with shame, to hear thy word!
For he, my husband, left me here to pine,
Not long a wife, when his unquiet heart
First drove him from me into distant lands;
Since then I vainly seek him through the world,
110   And weep from shore to shore my golden tears,
But neither god nor mortal heeds my pain.
Thou only, Balder, wast for ever kind,
To take my hand, and wipe my tears, and say:
Weep not, O Freya, weep no golden tears!
115   *One day the wandering Oder will return,*
Or thou wilt find him in thy faithful search
On some great road, or resting in an inn,
Or at a ford, or sleeping by a tree.
So Balder said; but Oder, well I know,
120   My truant Oder I shall see no more
To the world's end; and Balder now is gone,
And I am left uncomforted in Heaven.'
    She spake; and all the Goddesses bewailed.
Last from among the Heroes one came near,
125   No God, but of the hero-troop the chief –
Regner, who swept the northern sea with fleets,
And ruled o'er Denmark and the heathy isles,
Living; but Ella captured him and slew;
A king whose fame then filled the vast of Heaven,

---

iii *109.* An echo of Milton's *Paradise Lost* iv 271–2,

> *. . . which cost* Ceres *all that pain*
> *To seek her through the world . . .*

iii *112* and below *121–2.* Freya's praise of Balder's kindness and her grief that she will now be 'left uncomforted' parallel Helen's lament for Hector, who was always courteous to her, and her complaint that 'no longer have I anyone beside in broad Troy that is gentle to me or kind' (*Iliad* xxiv 774–5).

iii *124–52.* See Blackwell's supplementary ch. iv, *Mallet* 383–4, 'We must premise that Ragnar Lodbrok was a Danish king of the heroic period . . . In one of his numerous predatory expeditions . . . he is said to have been taken prisoner by Ella, a Northumbrian prince, thrown into a dungeon, and condemned to die by the bite of vipers. [His] death song is alleged to have been composed by him during his torments . . . In the first strophe Ragnar relates his expedition to Gothland. Thora, the daughter of a chieftain of that country, was detained in captivity by an enormous serpent, and was to become the reward of the daring champion who should deliver her. Ragnar undertook the task . . .' A footnote records that Ragnar's second wife was Aslauga.

130   Now time obscures it, and men's later deeds.
    He last approached the corpse, and spake, and said: –
      'Balder, there yet are many Scalds in Heaven
    Still left, and that chief Scald, thy brother Brage,
    Whom we may bid to sing, though thou art gone.
135   And all these gladly, while we drink, we hear,
    After the feast is done, in Odin's hall;
    But they harp ever on one string, and wake
    Remembrance in our soul of wars alone,
    Such as on earth we valiantly have waged,
140   And blood, and ringing blows, and violent death.
    But when thou sangest, Balder, thou didst strike
    Another note, and, like a bird in spring,
    Thy voice of joyance minded us, and youth,
    And wife, and children, and our ancient home.
145   Yes, and I, too, remembered then no more
    My dungeon, where the serpents stung me dead,
    Nor Ella's victory on the English coast –
    But I heard Thora laugh in Gothland Isle,
    And saw my shepherdess, Aslauga, tend
150   Her flock along the white Norwegian beach.
    Tears started to mine eyes with yearning joy.
    Therefore with grateful heart I mourn thee dead.'
      So Regner spake, and all the Heroes groaned.
    But now the sun had passed the height of Heaven,
155   And soon had all that day been spent in wail;
    But then the Father of the ages said: –
      'Ye Gods, there well may be too much of wail!
    Bring now the gathered wood to Balder's ship;
    Heap on the deck the logs, and build the pyre.'
160   But when the Gods and Heroes heard, they brought
    The wood to Balder's ship, and built a pile,
    Full the deck's breadth, and lofty; then the corpse
    Of Balder on the highest top they laid,
    With Nanna on his right, and on his left

---

iii *133. thy brother Brage*] Bragi is the Norse god of poetry and eloquence.
iii *143. minded us, and youth*] The meaning is clearly 'reminded us of youth',
but the reading of the text is in all editions.
iii *160–75.* An imitation of *Iliad* xxiii 161–77 (the funeral of Patroclus),
'Then . . . they heaped up the wood, and made a pyre of a hundred feet
this way and that, and on the topmost part thereof they set the dead man
. . . And thereon [Achilles] set two-handled jars of honey and oil, leaning
them against the bier; and four horses . . . he cast swiftly on the pyre . . .
Nine dogs had the prince, that fed beneath his table, and of these did
Achilles cut the throats of twain . . . and thereto he set the might of fire . . .'

165   Hoder, his brother, whom his own hand slew.
     And they set jars of wine and oil to lean
     Against the bodies, and stuck torches near,
     Splinters of pine-wood, soaked with turpentine;
     And brought his arms and gold, and all his stuff,
170   And slew the dogs who at his table fed,
     And his horse, Balder's horse, whom most he loved,
     And placed them on the pyre, and Odin threw
     A last choice gift thereon, his golden ring.
     The mast they fixed, and hoisted up the sails,
175   Then they put fire to the wood; and Thor
     Set his stout shoulder hard against the stern
     To push the ship through the thick sand; sparks flew
     From the deep trench she ploughed, so strong a God
     Furrowed it; and the water gurgled in.
180   And the ship floated on the waves, and rocked.
     But in the hills a strong east-wind arose,
     And came down moaning to the sea; first squalls
     Ran black o'er the sea's face, then steady rushed
     The breeze, and filled the sails, and blew the fire.
185   And wreathed in smoke the ship stood out to sea.
     Soon with a roaring rose the mighty fire,
     And the pile crackled; and between the logs
     Sharp quivering tongues of flame shot out, and leapt,
     Curling and darting, higher, until they licked
190   The summit of the pile, the dead, the mast
     And ate the shrivelling sails; but still the ship
     Drove on, ablaze above her hull with fire.
     And the Gods stood upon the beach, and gazed.
     And while they gazed, the sun went lurid down
195   Into the smoke-wrapped sea, and night came on.
     Then the wind fell, with night, and there was calm;
     But through the dark they watched the burning ship
     Still carried o'er the distant waters on,
     Farther and farther, like an eye of fire.

iii 173. *his golden ring*] See *n.* to ii 274 (p. 371 above).
iii. 175–9. *Thor . . . furrowed it*] The giantess Hyrrokin launches the ship in the *Prose Edda*, but the same effect is described.
iii 199. After this line the following lines in *1855,*

> *And as in the dark night a travelling man*
> *Who bivouacs in a forest 'mid the hills,*
> *Sees suddenly a spire of flame shoot up*
> *Out of the black waste forest, far below,*
> *Which woodcutters have lighted near their lodge*
> *Against the wolves; and all night long it flares: –*

200   And long, in the far dark, blazed Balder's pile;
But fainter, as the stars rose high, it flared,
The bodies were consumed, ash choked the pile.
And as, in a decaying winter-fire,
A charred log, falling, makes a shower of sparks –
205   So with a shower of sparks the pile fell in,
Reddening the sea around; and all was dark.
    But the Gods went by starlight up the shore
To Asgard, and sate down in Odin's hall
At table, and the funeral feast began.
210   All night they ate the boar Serimner's flesh,
And from their horns, with silver rimmed, drank mead,
Silent, and waited for the sacred morn.
    And morning over all the world was spread.
Then from their loathéd feast the Gods arose,
215   And took their horses, and set forth to ride
O'er the bridge Bifrost, where is Heimdall's watch,
To the ash Igdrasil, and Ida's plain;
Thor came on foot, the rest on horseback rode.
And they found Mimir sitting by his fount
220   Of wisdom, which beneath the ashtree springs;
And saw the Nornies watering the roots
Of that world-shadowing tree with honey-dew.
There came the Gods, and sate them down on stones;
And thus the Father of the ages said : –
225   'Ye Gods, the terms ye know, which Hermod
      brought.
Accept them or reject them! both have grounds.

iii 200. *1855*;
    So flar'd in the far darkness, Balder's pyre . . .
1869 substitutes 'show'd' for 'flar'd', 'pile' for 'pyre'.
iii *201. flared*] burn'd *1855.*
iii 207–12. Cp. Hector's funeral-feast, *Iliad* xxiv 801–3.
iii *215–23.* A. has confused Mimir's fount, which is in Jotunheim, with
the Urdar-fount, which is where the gods sit in judgment – see *n.* to ii
32–4 (p. 364 above). The Norns also live by the Urdar-fount.
iii *222. honey-dew*] See *Prose Edda* ch. 16, *Mallet* 413, 'The dew that falls
thence [from Igdrasil] on the earth men call honey-dew, and it is the food
of the bees.'
ii *225–53.* Cp. *Iliad* xxii 174–80 (Zeus and Athene), '"Nay then, come, ye
gods, bethink you and take counsel whether we shall save him from death,
or now at length shall slay him . . ." Then spake unto him the goddess . . .:
"O Father, Lord of the bright lightning and the dark cloud, what a word
hast thou said! A man that is mortal, doomed long since by fate, art thou
minded to deliver from dolorous death?"'

Accept them, and they bind us, unfulfilled,
To leave for ever Balder in the grave,
An unrecovered prisoner, shade with shades.
230   But how, ye say, should the fulfilment fail?
Smooth sound the terms, and light to be fulfilled;
For dear-beloved was Balder while he lived
In Heaven and earth, and who would grudge him
    tears?
But from the traitorous seed of Lok they come,
235   These terms, and I suspect some hidden fraud.
Bethink ye, Gods, is there no other way?
Speak, were not this a way, the way for Gods?
If I, if Odin, clad in radiant arms,
Mounted on Sleipner, with the warrior Thor
240   Drawn in his car beside me, and my sons,
All the strong brood of Heaven, to swell my train,
Should make irruption into Hela's realm,
And set the fields of gloom ablaze with light,
And bring in triumph Balder back to Heaven?'
245   He spake, and his fierce sons applauded loud.
But Frea, mother of the Gods, arose,
Daughter and wife of Odin; thus she said: –
    'Odin, thou whirlwind, what a threat is this!
Thou threatenest what transcends thy might, even
250   For of all powers the mightiest far art thou,   [thine.
Lord over men on earth, and Gods in Heaven;
Yet even from thee thyself hath been withheld
One thing – to undo what thou thyself hast ruled.
For all which hath been fixed, was fixed by thee.
255   In the beginning, ere the Gods were born,
Before the Heavens were builded, thou didst slay
The giant Ymir, whom the abyss brought forth,
Thou and thy brethren fierce, the sons of Bor,
And cast his trunk to choke the abysmal void.
260   But of his flesh and members thou didst build
The earth and Ocean, and above them Heaven.
And from the flaming world, where Muspel reigns,
Thou sent'st and fetched'st fire, and madest lights,
Sun, moon, and stars, which thou hast hung in
265   Dividing clear the paths of night and day.   [Heaven,
And Asgard thou didst build, and Midgard fort;

iii 255–78. Based on the creation myth in the *Prose Edda* chs. 7–9, *Mallet*
404–6.
iii 257. Ymir was formed from the abyss (Ginnungagap) where the cold of
Niflheim met the heat and light of Muspell (*Prose Edda* ch. 5, *Mallet* 402–3).

Then me thou mad'st; of us the Gods were born.
Last, walking by the sea, thou foundest spars
Of wood, and framed'st men, who till the earth,
270 Or on the sea, the field of pirates, sail.
And all the race of Ymir thou didst drown,
Save one, Bergelmer; he on shipboard fled
Thy deluge, and from him the giants sprang.
But all that brood thou hast removed far off,
275 And set by Ocean's utmost marge to dwell;
But Hela into Niflheim thou threw'st,
And gav'st her nine unlighted worlds to rule,
A queen, and empire over all the dead.
That empire wilt thou now invade, light up
280 Her darkness, from her grasp a subject tear?
Try it; but I, for one, will not applaud.
Nor do I merit, Odin, thou should'st slight
Me and my words, though thou be first in Heaven;
For I too am a Goddess, born of thee,
285 Thine eldest, and of me the Gods are sprung;
And all that is to come I know, but lock
In mine own breast, and have to none revealed.
Come then! since Hela holds by right her prey,
But offers terms for his release to Heaven,
290 Accept the chance; thou canst no more obtain.
Send through the world thy messengers; entreat
All living and unliving things to weep
For Balder; if thou haply thus may'st melt
Hela, and win the loved one back to Heaven.'
295   She spake, and on her face let fall her veil,
And bowed her head, and sate with folded hands.
Nor did the all-ruling Odin slight her word;
Straightway he spake, and thus addressed the Gods:
'Go quickly forth through all the world, and pray
300 All living and unliving things to weep
Balder, if haply he may thus be won.'
    When the Gods heard, they straight arose, and took
Their horses, and rode forth through all the world;
North, south, east, west, they struck, and roamed the
305 Entreating all things to weep Balder's death.   [world,
And all that lived, and all without life, wept.
And as in winter, when the frosts breaks up,
At winter's end, before the spring begins,
And a warm west-wind blows, and thaw sets in –
310 After an hour a dripping sound is heard
In all the forests, and the soft-strewn snow
Under the trees is dibbled thick with holes,

And from the boughs the snowloads shuffle down;
And, in fields sloping to the south, dark plots
315   Of grass peep out amid surrounding snow,
And widen, and the peasant's heart is glad –
So through the world was heard a dripping noise
Of all things weeping to bring Balder back;
And there fell joy upon the Gods to hear.

320   But Hermod rode with Niord, whom he took
To show him spits and beaches of the sea
Far off, where some unwarned might fail to weep –
Niord, the God of storms, whom fishers know;
Not born in Heaven; he was in Vanheim reared,
325   With men, but lives a hostage with the Gods;
He knows each frith, and every rocky creek
Fringed with dark pines, and sands where seafowl
      scream –
They two scoured every coast, and all things wept.
And they rode home together, through the wood
330   Of Jarnvid, which to east of Midgard lies
Bordering the giants, where the trees are iron;
There in the wood before a cave they came,
Where sate, in the cave's mouth, a skinny hag,
Toothless and old; she gibes the passers by.
335   Thok is she called, but now Lok wore her shape;
She greeted them the first, and laughed, and said: –
   'Ye Gods, good lack, is it so dull in Heaven,
That ye come pleasuring to Thok's iron wood?
Lovers of change ye are, fastidious sprites.
340   Look, as in some boor's yard a sweet-breath'd cow,

---

iii 323–5. See *Prose Edda* ch. 23, *Mallet* 418, 'He [Njörd] rules over the winds, and checks the fury of the sea and of fire, and is therefore invoked by seafarers and fishermen . . . Yet Njörd is not of the lineage of the Aesir, for he was born and bred in Vanaheim. But the Vanir gave him as a hostage to the Aesir . . .'

iii *327. where seafowl scream*] The phrase 'the screams of the sea-fowl' occurs in verses quoted in the same account of Njörd (*Mallet* 419).

iii *329–34.* See *Prose Edda* ch. 12, *Mallet* 408, 'A hag . . . dwells in a wood, to the eastward of Midgard, called Járnvid (the Iron wood) . . .'

iii *335–54.* See *Prose Edda* ch. 49, *Mallet* 449, 'As the messengers were returning . . . they found an old hag named Thaukt sitting in a cavern, and begged her to weep Baldur out of Hel. But she answered, "Thaukt will wail / With arid tears / Baldur's bale fire. / Nought, quick or dead, / By man's son gain I, / Let Hela hold what's hers." It was strongly suspected that this hag was no other than Loki himself.'

Whose manger is stuffed full of good fresh hay,
Snuffs at it daintily, and stoops her head
To chew the straw, her litter, at her feet –
So ye grow squeamish, Gods, and sniff at Heaven!'
345   She spake, but Hermod answered her and said: –
'Thok, not for gibes we come, we come for tears.
Balder is dead, and Hela holds her prey,
But will restore, if all things give him tears.
Begrudge not thine! to all was Balder dear.'
350   Then, with a louder laugh, the hag replied: –
'Is Balder dead? and do ye come for tears?
Thok with dry eyes will weep o'er Balder's pyre.
Weep him all other things, if weep they will –
I weep him not! let Hela keep her prey.'
355   She spake, and to the cavern's depth she fled,
Mocking; and Hermod knew their toil was vain.
And as seafaring men, who long have wrought
In the great deep for gain, at last come home,
And towards evening see the headlands rise
360   Of their dear country, and can plain descry
A fire of withered furze which boys have lit
Upon the cliffs, or smoke of burning weeds
Out of a tilled field inland; then the wind
Catches them, and drives out again to sea;
365   And they go long days tossing up and down
Over the grey sea-ridges, and the glimpse
Of port they had makes bitterer far their toil –
So the Gods' cross was bitterer for their joy.
        Then, sad at heart, to Niord Hermod spake: –
370   'It is the accuser Lok, who flouts us all!
Ride back, and tell in Heaven this heavy news;
I must again below, to Hela's realm.'
        He spoke; and Niord set forth back to Heaven.
But northward Hermod rode, the way below,
375   The way he knew; and traversed Giall's stream,
And down to Ocean groped, and crossed the ice,
And came beneath the wall, and found the grate
Still lifted; well was his return foreknown.
And once more Hermod saw around him spread
380   The joyless plains, and heard the streams of Hell.
But as he entered, on the extremest bound
Of Niflheim, he saw one ghost come near,
Hovering, and stopping oft, as if afraid –
Hoder, the unhappy, whom his own hand slew.

iii 360. ... *dear* ... *plain*] ... own ... clear 1855.

385 And Hermod looked, and knew his brother's ghost,
And called him by his name, and sternly said: –
'Hoder, ill-fated, blind in heart and eyes!
Why tarriest thou to plunge thee in the gulph
Of the deep inner gloom, but flittest here,
390 In twilight, on the lonely verge of Hell,
Far from the other ghosts, and Hela's throne?
Doubtless thou fearest to meet Balder's voice,
Thy brother, whom through folly thou didst slay.'
He spoke; but Hoder answered him, and said: –
395 'Hermod the nimble, dost thou still pursue
The unhappy with reproach, even in the grave?
For this I died, and fled beneath the gloom,
Not daily to endure abhorring Gods,
Nor with a hateful presence cumber Heaven;
400 And canst thou not, even here, pass pitying by?
No less than Balder have I lost the light
Of Heaven, and communion with my kin;
I too had once a wife, and once a child,
And substance, and a golden house in Heaven –
405 But all I left of my own act, and fled
Below, and dost thou hate me even here?
Balder upbraids me not, nor hates at all,
Though he has cause, have any cause; but he,
When that with downcast looks I hither came,
410 Stretched forth his hand, and with benignant voice,
Welcome, he said, *if there be welcome here,*
Brother and fellow-sport of Lok with me!
And not to offend thee, Hermod, nor to force
My hated converse on thee, came I up
415 From the deep gloom, where I will now return;
But earnestly I longed to hover near,
Not too far off, when that thou camest by;
To feel the presence of a brother God,
And hear the passage of a horse of Heaven,
420 For the last time – for here thou com'st no more.'
He spake, and turned to go to the inner gloom.
But Hermod stayed him with mild words, and said: –
'Thou doest well to chide me, Hoder blind!
Truly thou say'st, the planning guilty mind
425 Was Lok's; the unwitting hand alone was thine.
But Gods are like the sons of men in this –
When they have woe, they blame the nearest cause.
Howbeit stay, and be appeased! and tell:
Sits Balder still in pomp by Hela's side,
430 Or is he mingled with the unnumbered dead?'

And the blind Hoder answered him and spake: –
'His place of state remains by Hela's side,
But empty; for his wife, for Nanna came
Lately below, and joined him; and the pair
435 Frequent the still recesses of the realm
Of Hela, and hold converse undisturbed.
But they too, doubtless, will have breathed the balm,
Which floats before a visitant from Heaven,
And have drawn upward to this verge of Hell.'
440 He spake; and, as he ceased, a puff of wind
Rolled heavily the leaden mist aside
Round where they stood, and they beheld two forms
Make toward them o'er the stretching cloudy plain.
And Hermod straight perceived them, who they were,
445 Balder and Nanna; and to Balder said: –
'Balder, too truly thou foresaw'st a snare!
Lok triumphs still, and Hela keeps her prey.
No more to Asgard shalt thou come, n orlodge
In thy own house, Breidablik, nor enjoy
450 The love all bear toward thee, nor train up
Forset, thy son, to be beloved like thee.
Here must thou lie, and wait an endless age.
Therefore for the last time, O Balder, hail!'
He spake; and Balder answered him, and said: –
455 'Hail and farewell! for here thou com'st no more.
Yet mourn not for me, Hermod, when thou sitt'st
In Heaven, nor let the other Gods lament,
As wholly to be pitied, quite forlorn.
For Nanna hath rejoined me, who, of old,
460 In Heaven, was seldom parted from my side;
And still the acceptance follows me, which crowned
My former life, and cheers me even here.
The iron frown of Hela is relaxed
When I draw nigh, and the wan tribes of dead
465 Love me, and gladly bring for my award
Their ineffectual feuds and feeble hates –
Shadows of hates, but they distress them still.'
And the fleet-footed Hermod made reply: –
'Thou hast then all the solace death allows,
470 Esteem and function; and so far is well.
Yet here thou liest, Balder, underground,
Rusting for ever; and the years roll on,
The generations pass, the ages grow,

iii 451. *Forset, thy son*] For Forseti see *Prose Edda* ch. 22, *Mallet* 422.
iii 465 *Love*] Trust 1855.

And bring us nearer to the final day
475 When from the south shall march the fiery band
And cross the bridge of Heaven, with Lok for guide,
And Fenris at his heel with broken chain;
While from the east the giant Rymer steers
His ship, and the great serpent makes to land;
480 And all are marshalled in one flaming square
Against the Gods, upon the plains of Heaven,
I mourn thee, that thou canst not help us then.'
        He spake; but Balder answered him, and said: –
'Mourn not for me! Mourn, Hermod, for the Gods;
485 Mourn for the men on earth, the Gods in Heaven,
Who live, and with their eyes shall see that day!
The day will come, when fall shall Asgard's towers,
And Odin, and his sons, the seed of Heaven;
But what were I, to save them in that hour?
490 If strength might save them, could not Odin save,
My father, and his pride, the warrior Thor,
Vidar the silent, the impetuous Tyr?
I, what were I, when these can nought avail?
Yet, doubtless, when the day of battle comes,

iii *474–81*. See *Prose Edda* ch. 51, *Mallet* 452, 'Fenrir then breaks loose, and
the sea rushes over the earth, on account of the Midgard serpent turning
with great force, and gaining the land . . . But in this flood shall Naglfar
float, and the giant Hrym be its steersman . . . Amidst this devastation
heaven is cleft in twain, and the sons of Muspell ride through the breach
. . . Bifröst, as they ride over it, breaks to pieces. Then they direct their
course to the battlefield called Vigrid. Thither also repair the wolf Fenrir
and the Midgard serpent, and also Loki . . .'
iii *484–6*. An allusion to *Luke* xxiii 28–9, 'Daughters of Jerusalem, weep
not for me, but weep for yourselves, and for your children. For behold,
the days are coming, in the which they shall say, Blessed are the barren . . .'
For Balder as a surrogate for Christ see also *n.* to i 212–13 (p. 359 above).
iii *487. fall shall Asgard's towers*]. Asgard's towers shall fall *1855–69*. With
A.'s line cp. *Iliad* vi 488–9 (Hector to Andromache), '. . . the day shall
come when sacred Ilios shall be laid low, and Priam, and the people of
Priam . . .' For A.'s translation into English hexameters of the passage containing this sentence see *On Translating Homer* (1861), *Works* v 250–1 and
p. 467 below.
iii *492*. Vidar and Tyr are aptly associated with Thor. Vidar 'surnamed
the Silent' is 'almost as strong as Thor himself, and the gods place great
reliance on him in all critical conjunctures' (*Prose Edda* ch. 29, *Mallet* 422);
Tyr is 'the most daring and intrepid of all the gods' (*Prose Edda* ch. 25,
Mallet 420).

495　　And the two hosts are marshalled, and in Heaven
　　　The golden-crested cock shall sound alarm,
　　　And his black brother-bird from hence reply,
　　　And bucklers clash, and spears begin to pour –
　　　Longing will stir within my breast, though vain.
500　　But not to me so grievous, as, I know,
　　　To other Gods it were, is my enforced
　　　Absence from fields where I could nothing aid;
　　　For I am long since weary of your storm
　　　Of carnage, and find, Hermod, in your life
505　　Something too much of war and broils, which make
　　　Life one perpetual fight, a bath of blood.
　　　Mine eyes are dizzy with the arrowy hail;
　　　Mine ears are stunned with blows, and sick for calm.
　　　Inactive therefore let me lie, in gloom,
510　　Unarmed, inglorious; I attend the course
　　　Of ages, and my late return to light,
　　　In times less alien to a spirit mild,
　　　In new-recovered seats, the happier day.'
　　　　　He spake; and the fleet Hermod thus replied: –
515　　'Brother, what seats are these, what happier day?
　　　Tell me, that I may ponder it when gone.'
　　　　　And the ray-crownéd Balder answered him: –
　　　'Far to the south, beyond the blue, there spreads
　　　Another Heaven, the boundless – no one yet
520　　Hath reached it; there hereafter shall arise
　　　The second Asgard, with another name.
　　　Thither, when o'er this present earth and Heavens
　　　The tempest of the latter days hath swept,
　　　And they from sight have disappeared, and sunk,
525　　Shall a small remnant of the Gods repair;
　　　Hoder and I shall join them from the grave.

iii 496–7. See *n.* to ii 5–7 (p. 363 above).

iii 522–42. The prophecy of a 'second Asgard' is based on the *Prose Edda* ch. 53, *Mallet* 457, 'There will arise out of the sea . . . another earth most lovely and verdant, with pleasant fields where the grain shall grow unsown. Vidar and Váli shall survive . . . They shall dwell on the plain of Ida, where Asgard formerly stood. Thither shall come the sons of Thor, Módi and Magni . . . Balder and Hodur shall also repair thither from the abode of death (Hel). There shall they sit and converse together, and call to mind their former knowledge, and the perils they underwent . . . There too shall they find in the grass those golden tablets (orbs) which the Aesir once possessed.'

> There re-assembling we shall see emerge
> From the bright Ocean at our feet an earth
> More fresh, more verdant than the last, with fruits
> 530   Self-springing, and a seed of man preserved,
> Who then shall live in peace, as now in war.
> But we in Heaven shall find again with joy
> The ruined palaces of Odin, seats
> Familiar, halls where we have supped of old;
> 535   Re-enter them with wonder, never fill
> Our eyes with gazing, and rebuild with tears.
> And we shall tread once more the well-known plain
> Of Ida, and among the grass shall find
> The golden dice wherewith we played of yore;
> 540   And that will bring to mind the former life
> And pastime of the Gods, the wise discourse
> Of Odin, the delights of other days.
> O Hermod, pray that thou may'st join us then!
> Such for the future is my hope; meanwhile,
> 545   I rest the thrall of Hela, and endure
> Death, and the gloom which round me even now
> Thickens, and to its inner gulph recalls.
> Farewell, for longer speech is not allowed!'

iii *527–31*. A. remembered these lines in writing 'Obermann Once More' 285–6, 293–6 (pp. 531–2 below),

> *He breaks the winter of the past;*
> *A green, new earth appears.*
>
> *The world's great order dawns in sheen,*
> *After long darkness rude,*
> *Divinelier imaged, clearer seen,*
> *With happier zeal pursued.*

For the significance of this millenial vision to A. in 1865–6 see *nn.* to 'Obermann Once More' (p. 518 below), but it is not clear how much of this significance can be read back into 'Balder Dead'. The parallel between Balder and Christ suggests that already in 1854 the vision of a world restored may have expressed for A. something of his aspirations towards a new social order and a 'purified' undogmatic form of religion.

iii *530. a seed of man preserved*] Biblical, but also Miltonic. A. may be recalling Adam's joy at Noah's preservation, *Paradise Lost* xi 868–9,

> *. . . assur'd that Man shall live*
> *With all the Creatures, and their seed preserve.*

iii *548*. An allusion to *Aeneid* vi 466 (Aeneas to Dido),

> *. . . extremum fato, quod te adloquor, hoc est.*

He spoke, and waved farewell, and gave his hand
550 To Nanna; and she gave their brother blind
Her hand, in turn, for guidance; and the three
Departed o'er the cloudy plain, and soon
Faded from sight into the interior gloom.
But Hermod stood beside his drooping horse,
555 Mute, gazing after them in tears; and fain,
Fain had he followed their receding steps,
Though they to death were bound, and he to Heaven,
Then; but a power he could not break withheld.
And as a stork which idle boys have trapped,
560 And tied him in a yard, at autumn sees
Flocks of his kind pass flying o'er his head
To warmer lands, and coasts that keep the sun;
He strains to join their flight, and from his shed
Follows them with a long complaining cry –
565 So Hermod gazed, and yearned to join his kin.

At last he sighed, and set forth back to Heaven.

iii 559–64. A variation on a simile already used in 'Sohrab and Rustum' –
see ll. 111–16 (p. 308 above) and *n*.

84 Haworth Churchyard

APRIL, 1855

Written shortly after Charlotte Brontë's death (31 March) in April 1855:
title and A.'s unpublished letter 11 April 1855 to J. W. Parker jun., editor
of *Fraser's Magazine*, 'I am about a thing in memory of poor Charlotte
Brontë which I think may suit you when it is done, and which I should
like to appear at no great distance of time from her death . . . I shall not be
able to send it to you until the 23rd or 24th . . .' (Yale Papers); Harriet
Martineau's recovery from what had seemed in 1855 a mortal illness – see
ll. 30–3 – prevented A. from reprinting the poem in *1867* or *1869*, but
after her death in 1876 he included a much altered version in *1877*: nineteen
lines already removed from the original text for inclusion in *1867* as the
lyric 'Early Death and Fame' were not restored; a further forty-six lines
were dropped; a 14-line epilogue was added. There is no external evidence
to date these changes, but the resemblance between part of the epilogue
(ll. 135–8) and 'Rugby Chapel' 40–2 suggests that they were probably
made by 1860 (see headn. to 'Rugby Chapel', p. 444 below).

A. was in Haworth before the poem's composition on 6 May 1852 to
inspect the Wesleyan school (unpublished 1852 diary), but his mistake
about the Brontë graves (ll. 88–9) indicates that he did not visit the church

or churchyard – see his reply 1 June 1855 to a congratulatory letter from Mrs. Gaskell, 'I am almost sorry you told me about the place of their burial. It really seems to me to put the finishing touch to the strange cross-grained character of the fortunes of that ill-fated family that they should even be placed after death in the wrong, uncongenial spot' (*Bulletin of John Rylands Library* xix (1935) 135–6). In the same letter A. writes, 'I am afraid the metre in which the poem was composed must have interfered with many people's enjoyment of it: but I could not manage to say what I wished *as* I wished in any other metre.' For this metre, which is that of A.'s earlier 'pindarics', see headn. to 'The Youth of Nature' (p. 245 above); see also 'Rugby Chapel' and 'Heine's Grave' (pp. 444 and 469 below), later elegies which resemble 'Haworth Churchyard' in combining critical reflections with a 'composition of place'. For A.'s meeting with Charlotte Brontë and Harriet Martineau in Dec. 1850 see *nn*. below.

Published *Fraser's Magazine* May 1855; reprinted in revised form *1877*, etc.

> Where, under Loughrigg, the stream
> Of Rotha sparkles through fields
> Vested for ever with green,
> Four years since, in the house
> 5   Of a gentle spirit, now dead –
> Wordsworth's son-in-law, friend –
> I saw the meeting of two
> Gifted women. The one,

¶ 84. *1–2.* Fox How, A.'s home in the Lake District, is beside the Rotha and in the shadow of Loughrigg.

5–6. For Wordsworth's son-in-law Edward Quillinan see headn. to 'Stanzas in Memory of E.Q.' (p. 243 above).

7–8. 'Charlotte Brontë and Harriet Martineau'. A.'s *1877* note. The meeting took place 21 Dec. 1850 – see A.'s letter of this date to Frances Lucy Wightman, his future wife, 'At seven came Miss Martineau and Miss Brontë (Jane Eyre); talked to Miss Martineau (who blasphemes frightfully) about the prospects of the Church of England . . . talked to Miss Brontë (past thirty and plain, with expressive grey eyes though) of her curates, of French novels, and her education in a school at Brussels, and sent the lions roaring to their dens at half-past nine . . .' (*L* i 13). For Charlotte Brontë's impression of A. see her letter to James Taylor 15 Jan. 1851, 'Striking and prepossessing in appearance, his manner displeases from its seeming foppery . . . ere long a real modesty appeared under his assumed conceit, and some genuine intellectual aspirations . . . displaced superficial affectations. I was given to understand that his theological opinions were very vague and unsettled . . .' (C. K. Shorter's *Charlotte Brontë and her Circle* (1896) 459).

Brilliant with recent renown,
10   Young, unpractised, had told
With a master's accent her feigned
Story of passionate life;
The other, maturer in fame,
Earning, she too, her praise
15   First in fiction, had since
Widened her sweep, and surveyed
History, politics, mind.

The two held converse; they wrote
In a book which of world-famous souls
20   Kept the memorial; bard,
Warrior, statesman, had signed
Their names; chief glory of all
Scott had bestowed there his last
Breathings of song, with a pen
25   Tottering, a death-stricken hand.

Hope at that meeting smiled fair.
Years in number, it seemed,
Lay before both, and a fame

9–12. In 1850 Charlotte Brontë's most recent novel was *Shirley* (1849), but
A. is obviously referring to *Jane Eyre* (1847). In an unpublished letter from
India in Aug. 1848 A.'s brother William describes it as the 'book you were
all talking about when I left Home', i.e. in spring 1848.
13–17. Harriet Martineau (1802–76). She was known as a writer of 'useful'
fiction for adults and children when she settled near Ambleside in 1847,
but in ll. 15–17 A. glances at her *History of the Thirty Years' Peace* (1849),
which contains a tribute to Dr. Arnold, *Letters on the Laws of Man's Nature
and Development* (1851) and *Philosophy of Comte* (1853). The last two books
won her a reputation for unorthodoxy. To family complaints that his
poem seemed to approve her views A. replied characteristically that her
creed did not interest him, but that he admired her 'boldness in avowing
it' (L i 44).
19–20. Rotha Quillinan's album. A. had himself contributed to it in 1851
– see headnn. to 'Youth and Calm' and 'Stanzas in Memory of Edward
Quillinan' (pp. 224 and 243 above).
23–5. Scott's verses were written in the album, which then belonged to
Dora Wordsworth, at Abbotsford on 22 Sept. 1831. Scott himself observed that they would probably be his last verses. See *Wordsworth's
Poetical Works* ed. E. de Selincourt and H. Darbishire iii (1946) 526.
26. Replacing in *Fraser 1855,*

I beheld; the obscure
Saw the famous. Alas!

Heightened, and multiplied power.
30   Behold! The elder, to-day,
Lies expecting from death,
In mortal weakness, a last
Summons! the younger is dead!

First to the living we pay
35   Mournful homage; the Muse
Gains not an earth-deafened ear.

Hail to the steadfast soul,
Which, unflinching and keen,
Wrought to erase from its depth
Mist and illusion and fear!
Hail to the spirit which dared
Trust its own thoughts, before yet
Echoed her back by the crowd!
Hail to the courage which gave
45   Voice to its creed, ere the creed
Won consecration from time!

30–4. Harriet Martineau fell seriously ill early in 1855.
37–46. Cp. A.'s letter to his sister 'K' 7 May 1855, 'I think her character
to be a fine one, and her independence and efforts to be sincere with herself worthy of admiration. I am glad of an opportunity of expressing my
admiration at this time, when she has much to suffer – the more so as
speculations like those to which she had given herself are so utterly anti-
pathetic to me . . .' (UL 27).
46. Followed by these lines in *Fraser 1855*:

> *Turn, O Death, on the vile,*
> *Turn on the foolish the stroke*
> *Hanging now o'er a head*
> *Active, beneficent, pure!*
> [5]   *But, if the prayer be in vain –*
> *But, if the stroke must fall –*
> *Her, whom we cannot save,*
> *What might we say to console?*
>
> *She will not see her country lose*
> [10]   *Its greatness, nor the reign of fools prolong'd.*
> *She will behold no more*
> *This ignominious spectacle,*
> *Power dropping from the hand*
> *Of paralytic factions, and no soul*
> [15]   *To snatch and wield it: will not see*

Turn we next to the dead.
– How shall we honour the young,
The ardent, the gifted? how mourn?
50   Console we cannot, her ear
Is deaf. Far northward from here,
In a churchyard high 'mid the moors
Of Yorkshire, a little earth
Stops it for ever to praise.

55   Where, behind Keighley, the road
Up to the heart of the moors
Between heath-clad showery hills
Runs, and colliers' carts
Poach the deep ways coming down,
60   And a rough, grimed race have their homes.–
There on its slope is built
The moorland town. But the church
Stands on the crest of the hill,

_____

Her fellow-people sit
Helplessly gazing on their own decline.

Myrtle and rose fit the young,
Laurel and oak the mature.
[20]   *Private affections, for these,*
Have run their circle, and left
Space for things far from themselves,
Thoughts of the general weal,
Country, and public cares:
[25]   *Public cares, which move*
Seldom and faintly the depth
Of younger passionate souls
Plung'd in themselves, who demand
Only to live by the heart,
[30]   *Only to love and be lov'd.*

The references in ll. 9–17 of this cancelled passage indicate the state of
public feeling during the political crisis of early Feb. 1855. The Coalition
Ministry (Whigs and Peelites) resigned after being badly defeated on a vote
when they resisted a motion for a select committee to inquire into the conduct of the war in the Crimea. Lord Derby and Lord John Russell in turn
failed to form a new administration before Lord Palmerston succeeded on
6 Feb. His new Cabinet was a reshuffle of the old.
47. Inserted in *1877.*
59. *Poach*] Cut up and turn into mire.
14+M.A.

Lonely and bleak; at its side
65   The parsonage-house and the graves.

Strew with laurel the grave
Of the early-dying! Alas,
Early she goes on the path
To the silent country, and leaves
70   Half her laurels unwon,
Dying too soon! – yet green
Laurels she had, and a course
Short, but redoubled by fame.

And not friendless, and not
75   Only with strangers to meet,
Faces ungreeting and cold,
Thou, O mourned one, to-day
Enterest the house of the grave!

65. Followed by these lines in *Fraser 1855*:

> *See! in the desolate house*
> *The childless father! Alas –*
> *Age, whom the most of us chide,*
> *Chide, and put back, and delay –*
> [5]   *Come, unupbraided for once!*
> *Lay thy benumbing hand,*
> *Gratefully cold, on this brow!*
> *Shut out the grief, the despair!*
> *Weaken the sense of his loss!*
> [10]   *Deaden the infinite pain!*
>
> *Another grief I see,*
> *Younger: but this the Muse,*
> *In pity and silent awe*
> *Revering what she cannot soothe,*
> 15]   *With veil'd face and bow'd head,*
> *Salutes, and passes by.*

The references here are to the Rev. Patrick Brontë (ll. 1–10) and to his curate at Haworth, the Rev. A. B. Nicholls (ll. 11–16), whose marriage to Charlotte took place on 29 June 1854.
66. *laurel*] roses *Fraser 1855*.
73. For the nineteen lines following this line in *Fraser 1855* see 'Early Death and Fame' and *nn*. (p. 397 below).
78. *house of the grave*] Cp. *Merope* 390–1 (p. 410 below),

> *Behold, O King from the dark*
> *House of the grave, what we do!*

Those of thy blood, whom thou lov'dst,
80 Have preceded thee – young,
Loving, a sisterly band;
Some in art, some in gift
Inferior – all in fame.
They, like friends, shall receive
85 This comer, greet her with joy;
Welcome the sister, the friend;
Hear with delight of thy fame!

Round thee they lie – the grass
Blows from their graves to thy own!
90 She, whose genius, though not
Puissant like thine, was yet
Sweet and graceful; and she
(How shall I sing her?) whose soul
Knew no fellow for might,
95 Passion, vehemence, grief,
Daring, since Byron died,
That world-famed son of fire – she, who sank
Baffled, unknown, self-consumed;
Whose too bold dying song
100 Stirred, like a clarion-blast, my soul.

79–81. Emily died at Haworth 19 Dec. 1848, Anne at Scarborough 28 May 1849.
88–9. A false assumption by A. – see his letter to Mrs. Gaskell 1 June 1855 quoted in headn. above. Anne is buried at Scarborough. No grass blows between the Brontë graves at Haworth because Charlotte, Emily and Branwell are buried in a vault inside the church.
90–2. Anne Brontë.
92–6. Emily Brontë. For A.'s opinion of Byron see 'Memorial Verses' 6–14 (pp. 226–7 above) and *nn.*
99–100. 'See the last verses [lines *1877–81*] by Emily Brontë in *Poems by Currer, Ellis, and Acton Bell.*' A.'s *1877* note. 'No coward soul is mine' was not published in *Poems* (1846) but first appeared among the literary remains included by Charlotte Brontë in her 1850 ed. of *Wuthering Heights and Agnes Grey;* and it was obviously her note to this poem, 'The following are the last lines my sister Emily ever wrote', that made A. speak of a 'dying song'. ('No coward soul . . .' is dated 2 Jan. 1846, i.e. nearly three years before Emily's death.) The song was 'too bold' for A. presumably because of its blunt statement that 'the thousand creeds / That move men's hearts' are 'unutterably vain' (ll. 9–10).
100. Stirred] Shook *Fraser 1855, 1877–81.*

Of one, too, I have heard,
A brother – sleeps he here?
Of all that gifted race
Not the least gifted; young,
105   Unhappy, eloquent – the child
Of many hopes, of many tears.
O boy, if here thou sleep'st, sleep well!
On thee too did the Muse
Bright in thy cradle smile;
110   But some dark shadow came
(I know not what) and interposed.

Sleep, O cluster of friends,
Sleep! – or only when May,
Brought by the west-wind, returns
115   Back to your native heaths,
And the plover is heard on the moors,
Yearly awake to behold
The opening summer, the sky,
The shining moorland – to hear
120   The drowsy bee, as of old,
Hum o'er the thyme, the grouse
Call from the heather in bloom!
Sleep, or only for this
Break your united repose!

EPILOGUE

125   So I sang; but the Muse,
Shaking her head, took the harp –
Stern interrupted my strain,
Angrily smote on the chords.

April showers
130   Rush o'er the Yorkshire moors.

101–11. The references to Branwell are vague, but A. was writing before
the publication of Mrs. Gaskell's *Life of Charlotte Brontë* (1857).
105. *eloquent – the child*] beautiful; the cause *Fraser 1855*.
112–24. A. is remembering the last sentences of *Wuthering Heights*: 'I
sought, and soon discovered, the three headstones on the slope next the
moor ... I lingered round them, under that benign sky: watched the
moths fluttering among the heath and hare-bells; listened to the soft wind
breathing through the grass; and wondered how any one could ever
imagine unquiet slumbers for the sleepers in that quiet earth.'
125–38. Added in *1877*.

Stormy, through driving mist,
Loom the blurred hills; the rain
Lashes the newly-made grave.

135

Unquiet souls!
– In the dark fermentation of earth,
In the never idle workshop of nature,
In the eternal movement,
Ye shall find yourselves again!

135–7. Suggested by *Obermann* (Lettre lxxxv) ii 197–8, 'Une industrie céleste produit san relâche . . . si nous entrevoyons les mondes comme des sphères d'activité, comme des ateliers de régénération . . . cette fermentation silencieuse et terrible . . .' With A.'s lines cp. also 'Rugby Chapel' 40–2 (p. 446 below),

> *Somewhere, surely, afar*
> *In the sounding labour–house vast*
> *Of being, is practised that strength . . .*

85 Early Death and Fame

Written April 1855: see headn. to 'Haworth Churchyard' (p. 389 above). Published *Fraser's Magazine* May 1855 (as part of 'Haworth Churchyard'); reprinted as a separate poem with present title *1867* (*1868*), *1869*, etc.

For him who must see many years,
I praise the life which slips away
Out of the light and mutely; which avoids
Fame, and her less fair followers, envy, strife,
5 Stupid detraction, jealousy, cabal,
Insincere praises; which descends
The quiet mossy track to age.

But, when immature death
Beckons too early the guest
10 From the half-tried banquet of life,

¶ *85. 1. see*] live *Fraser 1855.*
2. I praise the life] That life is best *Fraser 1855.*
7. quiet mossy] The epithets were reversed in 1855.
10. The half-tried banquet of life] An echo of André Chénier's 'La Jeune Captive' 28,

> *Au banquet de la vie à peine commencé . . .*

For A.'s high opinion of Chénier see his statement reported by T. H. Ward, '. . . there is more in the one little volume of André Chénier than in the

> Young, in the bloom of his days;
> Leaves no leisure to press,
> Slowly and surely, the sweets
> Of a tranquil life in the shade –
> _15_   Fuller for him be the hours!
> Give him emotion, though pain!
> Let him live, let him feel: _I have lived._
> Heap up his moments with life!
> Triple his pulses with fame!

whole forty volumes of Hugo' (introduction to A.'s selected poems in appendix to 1894 ed. of T. H. Ward's _The English Poets_ iv 709).
13. _sweets_] sweet _Fraser 1855._
17. Cp. 'Lines written in Kensington Gardens' 43–4 (p. 258 above),

> . . . _nor let me die_
> _Before I have begun to live . . ._

19. _Triple_] Quicken _Fraser 1855._

86 Merope
A TRAGEDY

Exact period of composition unknown, but probably _c._ Oct. 1856–_c._ Oct. 1857: A.'s reading-lists show that his main poetic project in 1855, his tragedy on the subject of Lucretius, still preoccupied him Sept. 1856, but in Nov. and Dec. 1856 he was 'at Merope' (_Note-books_ 562). The play was probably finished by the end of Oct. 1857 since it was first announced for 5 Dec. 1857 (although actually published 29 Dec. with Preface dated 'London: December, 1857' and title-page dated 1858).
For A.'s choice of Merope as a subject, and his sources in Apollodorus and Hyginus, see his Preface, which also discusses the dramatic treatment of the story by Torelli, Maffei, Voltaire and Alfieri (he does not mention that Saint-Marc Girardin's _Cours de littérature dramatique_ i (1843), which he read in 1848, has a chapter headed 'De l'amour maternel – Mérope dans Torelli, Maffei, Voltaire et Alfieri' – see my article on A. and Girardin in _RES_ n.s. ix (1958) 291–2). A.'s declared intention, i.e. to give readers 'a specimen of the world created by the Greek imagination' (_L_ i 59), was not to be satisfied by a translation of an existing Greek tragedy, 'because no man can be penetrated by a subject which he does not conceive independently', nor even by an original play on a subject shared with a surviving Greek tragedy, because the existence of such a work would 'chill emulation' (_1858_ Preface, _Complete Prose Works_ ed. R. H. Super i (1960) 40), but these statements would be more convincing if he had not modelled _Merope_ so closely on Sophocles's _Electra_ (in both the action is of a son's return in disguise to exact vengeance for a father's death many years earlier) and had not tacitly admitted to his sister 'K' in a letter 6 Aug. 1858 (in which he

was still discussing the reception of his tragedy) that he undertook the pseudo-Greek *Merope* to avoid being 'penetrated' by a subject, 'People do not understand what a temptation there is . . . to transfer your operations to a region where form is everything. Perfection of a certain kind may there be attained . . . without knocking yourself to pieces' (*L* i 62–3). *Merope* is in fact evidence that the classicism of the *1853* Preface was at least in part an evasion of the anxieties of genuine poetic creation. The mixed reception of the tragedy by friends and reviewers shows A. on the defensive: 'As to Merope not exciting you – on the stage (for which these things are meant) I think the chief situations would excite you' (11 Jan. 1858, *UL* 37); 'Instead of reading it for what it is worth, everybody begins to consider whether it does not betray a design to substitute tragedies *à la Grecque* for every other kind of poetical composition in England' (3 Feb. 1858, *L* i 59); 'I am anxious to explain . . . that you are not the least bound to like her, as she is calculated rather to inaugurate my Professorship [of Poetry at Oxford – A. had been elected 5 May 1857] with dignity than to move deeply the present race of humans' (9 Feb. 1858, *L* i 60). Clough wrote to F. J. Child 16 April 1858, 'I cannot say that I received much natural pleasure from it when I read it' (*Correspondence of A.H.C.* ii 546), a temperate judgment endorsed by modern critical opinion.

There is an annotated edition of *Merope* by J. C. Collins (1906); the Preface is included in R. H. Super's *Complete Prose Works* i (1960) 38–64 and *nn.* 228–34; the 'Story of the Drama' below was intended by A. to explain the mythological and historical background and allusions. Annotation in this edition is restricted to (1) A.'s chief alterations of the *1858* text in *1885* and (2) the more important borrowings from Aeschylus, Sophocles and Euripides (which, further to economize space, are indicated but not quoted).

Published *1858*; reprinted (without the Preface and with 'Historical Introduction' retitled 'Story of the Drama') *1885*, etc.

STORY OF THE DRAMA

Apollodorus says: – 'Cresphontes had not reigned long in Messenia when he was murdered, together with two of his sons. And Polyphontes reigned in his stead, he, too, being of the family of Hercules; and he had for his wife, against her will, Merope, the widow of the murdered king. But Merope had 5 born to Cresphontes a third son, called Æpytus; him she gave to her own father to bring up. He, when he came to man's estate, returned secretly to Messenia, and slew Polyphontes and the other murderers of his father.'

¶ 86. *Story of the Drama.* The main differences from the 'Historical Introduction' in *1858* are the addition of A.'s translations of Apollodorus, *Bibliotheca* ii 8 (5) and Hyginus, *Fabulae* (ed. H. Rose (1933) no. 137) from the *1858* Preface (where they originally appeared in a slightly different form) and the omission of a short passage dealing with the death of Hercules. For the Pausanias reference (l. 111) see *Description of Greece* iv 3 (3–8).

Hyginus says: – 'Merope sent away and concealed her infant son. Polyphontes sought for him everywhere in vain. He, when he grew up, laid a
10 plan to avenge the murder of his father and brothers. In pursuance of this
plan he came to king Polyphontes and reported the death of the son of
Cresphontes and Merope. The king ordered him to be hospitably entertained, intending to inquire further of him. He, being very tired, went to
sleep, and an old man, who was the channel through whom the mother and
15 son used to communicate, arrives at this moment in tears, bringing word to
Merope that her son had disappeared from his protector's house, and was
slain. Merope, believing that the sleeping stranger is the murderer of her
son, comes into the guest-chamber with an axe, not knowing that he whom
she would slay was her son; the old man recognized him, and withheld
20 Merope from slaying him. The king, Polyphontes, rejoicing at the supposed
death of Æpytus, celebrated a sacrifice; his guest, pretending to strike the
sacrificial victim, slew the king, and so got back his father's kingdom.'

The events on which the action of the drama turns belong to the period
of transition from the heroic and fabulous to the human and historic age of
25 Greece. The doings of the hero Hercules, the ancestor of the Messenian
Æpytus, belong to fable; but the invasion of Peloponnesus by the Dorians
under chiefs claiming to be descended from Hercules, and their settlement
in Argos, Lacedæmon, and Messenia, belong to history. Æptyus is descended on the father's side from Hercules, Perseus, and the kings of Argos; on
30 the mother's side from Pelasgus, and the aboriginal kings of Arcadia.
Callisto, the daughter of the wicked Lycaon, and the mother, by Zeus, of
Arcas, from whom the Arcadians took their name, was the granddaughter
of Pelasgus. The birth of Arcas brought upon Callisto the anger of the
virgin-goddess Artemis, whose service she followed: she was changed into a
35 she-bear, and in this form was chased by her own son, grown to manhood.
Zeus interposed, and the mother and son were removed from the earth, and
placed among the stars. Callisto became the famous constellation of the
Great Bear; her son became Arcturus, Arctophylax, or Boötes. From this
son of Callisto were descended Cypselus, the maternal grandfather of
40 Æpytus, and the children of Cypselus, Laias and Merope.
The story of the life of Hercules, the paternal ancestor of Æpytus, is so
well known that there is no need to record it. The reader will remember
that, although entitled to the throne of Argos by right of descent from
Perseus and Danaus, and to the thrones of Sparta and Messenia by right of
45 conquest, Hercules yet passed his life in labours and wanderings, subjected
by the decree of fate to the commands of his kinsman, the feeble and malignant Eurystheus. At his death he bequeathed to his offspring, the Heracleidæ, his own claims to the kingdoms of Peloponnesus, and to the perse-
cution of Eurystheus. They at first sought shelter with Ceyx, king of Trachis;
50 he was too weak to protect them, and they then took refuge at Athens. The
Athenians refused to deliver them up at the demand of Eurystheus; he in-

vaded Attica, and a battle was fought near Marathon, in which, after
Macaria, a daughter of Hercules, had devoted herself for the preservation
of her house, Eurystheus fell, and the Heracleidæ and their Athenian pro-
55 tectors were victorious. The memory of Macaria's self-sacrifice was perpetu-
ated by the name of a spring of water on the plain of Marathon, the spring
Macaria. The Heracleidæ then endeavoured to effect their return to Peloponnesus. Hyllus, the eldest of them, inquired of the oracle at Delphi
respecting their return; he was told to return by the *narrow passage,* and in the
60 *third harvest.* Accordingly, in the third year from that time, Hyllus led an
army to the Isthmus of Corinth; but there he was encountered by an army
of Achaians and Arcadians, and fell in single combat with Echemus, king
of Tegea. Upon this defeat the Heracleidæ retired to northern Greece;
there, after much wandering, they finally took refuge with Ægimius, king
65 of the Dorians, who appears to have been the fastest friend of their house,
and whose Dorian warriors formed the army which at last achieved their
return. But, for a hundred years from the date of their first attempt, the
Heracleidæ were defeated in their successive invasions of Peloponnesus.
Cleolaus and Aristomachus, the son and grandson of Hyllus, fell in un-
70 successful expeditions. At length the sons of Aristomachus, Temenus,
Cresphontes, and Aristodemus, when grown up, repaired to Delphi and
taxed the oracle with the non-fulfilment of the promise made to their
ancestor Hyllus. But Apollo replied that his oracle had been misunderstood;
for that by the *third harvest* he had meant the third generation, and by the
75 *narrow passage* he had meant the straits of the Corinthian Gulf. After this
explanation the sons of Aristomachus built a fleet at Naupactus; and finally,
in the hundredth year from the death of Hyllus and the eightieth from the
fall of Troy, the invasion was again attempted and was this time successful.
The son of Orestes, Tisamenus, who ruled both Argo and Lacedæmon, fell
80 in battle; many of his vanquished subjects left their homes and took refuge
in Achaia.

The spoil was now to be divided among the conquerors. Aristodemus,
the youngest of the sons of Aristomachus, did not survive to enjoy his share.
He was slain at Delphi by the sons of Pylades and Electra, the kinsmen,
85 through their mother, of the house of Agamemnon, that house which the
Heracleidæ with their Dorian army had dispossessed. The claims of Aristodemus descended to his two sons, Procles and Eurysthenes, children under
the guardianship of their maternal uncle, Theras. Temenus, the eldest of
the sons of Aristomachus, took the kingdom of Argos. For the two remaining
90 kingdoms, that of Sparta and that of Messenia, his two nephews, who were
to rule jointly, and their uncle Cresphontes, had to cast lots. Cresphontes
wished to have the fertile Messenia, and induced his brother to acquiesce
in a trick which secured it to him. The lot of Cresphontes and that of his two
nephews were to be placed in a water-jar, and thrown out. Messenia was
95 to belong to him whose lot came out first. With the connivance of Temenus,
Cresphontes marked as his own lot a pellet composed of baked clay, as the

14*

lot of his nephews, a pellet of unbaked clay; the unbaked pellet was of course dissolved in the water, while the brick pellet fell out alone. Messenia, therefore, was assigned to Cresphontes.

100   Messenia was at this time ruled by Melanthus, a descendant of Neleus. This ancestor, a prince of the great house of Æolus, had come from Thessaly and succeeded to the Messenian throne on the failure of the previous dynasty. Melanthus and his race were thus foreigners in Messenia and were unpopular. His subjects offered little or no opposition to the invading

105 Dorians; Melanthus abandoned his kingdom to Cresphontes, and retired to Athens.

Cresphontes married Merope, whose native country, Arcadia, was not affected by the Dorian invasion. This marriage, the issue of which was three sons, connected him with the native population of Peloponnesus. He built

110 a new capital of Messenia, Stenyclaros, and transferred thither, from Pylos, the seat of government; he proposed, moreover, says Pausanias, to divide Messenia into five states, and to confer on the native Messenians equal privileges with their Dorian conquerors. The Dorians complained that his administration unduly favoured the vanquished people; his chief magnates,

115 headed by Polyphontes, himself a descendant of Hercules, formed a cabal against him, and he was slain with his two eldest sons. The youngest son of Cresphontes, Æyptus, then an infant, was saved by his mother, who sent him to her father, Cypselus, the king of Arcadia, under whose protection he was brought up.

120   The drama begins at the moment when Æpytus, grown to manhood, returns secretly to Messenia to take vengeance on his father's murderers. At this period Temenus was no longer reigning at Argos; he had been murdered by his sons, jealous of their brother-in-law, Deiphontes. The sons of Aristodemus, Procles and Eurysthenes, at variance with their uncle and

125 ex-guardian, Theras, were reigning at Sparta.

PERSONS OF THE DRAMA

LAIAS, *uncle of* ÆPYTUS, *brother of* MEROPE.
ÆPYTUS, *son of* MEROPE *and* CRESPHONTES.
POLYPHONTES, *king of* MESSENIA.
MEROPE, *widow of* CRESPHONTES, *the murdered king of* MESSENIA.
THE CHORUS, *of* MESSENIAN *maidens.*
ARCAS, *an old man of* MEROPE'S *household.*
MESSENGER.
GUARDS, ATTENDANTS, &c.

The scene is before the royal palace in STENYCLAROS, *the capital of* MESSENIA. *In the foreground is the tomb of* CRESPHONTES. *The action commences at daybreak.*

LAIAS.   ÆPYTUS

Laias

Son of Cresphontes, we have
   reached the goal
Of our night-journey, and thou
   see'st thy home.
Behold thy heritage, thy father's
   realm!
This is that fruitful, famed Messenian land,
5 Wealthy in corn and flocks, which,
   when at last
The late-relenting Gods with victory brought
The Heracleidæ back to Pelops'
   isle,
Fell to thy father's lot, the second
   prize.
Before thy feet this recent city
   spreads
10 Of Stenyclaros, which he built,
   and made
Of his fresh-conquered realm the
   royal seat,
Degrading Pylos from its ancient
   rule.
There stands the temple of thine
   ancestor,
Great Heracles; and, in that public place,
15 Zeus hath his altar, where thy
   father fell.
Southward and west, behold
   those snowy peaks,
Taygetus, Laconia's border-wall;
And, on this side, those confluent
   streams which make
Pamisus watering the Messenian
   plain;
20 Then to the north, Lycæus and
   the hills
Of pastoral Arcadia, where, a
   babe
Snatched from the slaughter of
   thy father's house,
Thy mother's kin received thee,
   and reared up.
Our journey is well made, the
   work remains
25 Which to perform we made it;
   means for that

Let us consult, before this palace
   sends
Its inmates on their daily tasks
   abroad.
Haste and advise, for day comes
   on apace.

Æpytus

O brother of my mother, guardian true,
30 And second father from that hour
   when first
My mother's faithful servant laid
   me down,
An infant, at the hearth of Cypselus,
My grandfather, the good Arcadian king –
Thy part it were to advise, and
   mine to obey.
35 But let us keep that purpose,
   which, at home,
We judged the best; chance finds
   no better way.
Go thou into the city, and seek out
Whate'er in the Messenian people
   stirs
Of faithful fondness for their former king
40 Or hatred to their present; in this
   last
Will lie, my grandsire said, our
   fairest chance.
For tyrants make man good
   beyond himself;
Hate to their rule, which else
   would die away,
Their daily-practised chafings
   keep alive.
45 Seek this! revive, unite it, give it
   hope;
Bid it rise boldly at the signal
   given.
Meanwhile within my father's
   palace I,
An unknown guest, will enter,
   bringing word
Of my own death – but, Laias,
   well I hope
50 Through that pretended death to
   live and reign.
         [THE CHORUS *comes forth.*

1–75. The opening scene is modelled on that of Sophocles's *Electra* 1–85, with
Aepytus and Laias in place of Orestes and his servant.
51–8. An adaptation of Aeschylus's *Choephoroe* 10–18.

Softly, stand back! – see, to these
  palace gates
What black procession slowly
  makes approach?
Sad-chanting maidens clad in
  mourning robes,
With pitchers in their hands, and
  fresh-pulled flowers –
55 Doubtless, they bear them to my
  father's tomb.

[MEROPE *comes forth.*

And look, to meet them, that one,
  grief-plunged Form,
Severer, paler, statelier than they
  all,
A golden circlet on her queenly
  brow!
O Laias, Laias, let the heart speak
  here –
60 Shall I not greet her? shall I not
  leap forth?

[POLYPHONTES *comes forth, following*
  MEROPE.

Laias

Not so! thy heart would pay its
  moment's speech
By silence ever after, for, behold!
The King (I know him, even
  through many years)
Follows the approaching Queen,
  who stops, as called.
65 No lingering now! straight to the
  city I;
Do thou, till for thine entrance to
  this house
The happy moment comes, lurk
  here unseen
Behind the shelter of thy father's
  tomb;
Remove yet further off, if aught
  comes near.
70 But, here while harbouring, on
  its margin lay,
Sole offering that thou hast, locks
  from thy head;
And fill thy leisure with an earnest prayer
To his avenging Shade, and to
  the Gods
Who under earth watch guilty
  deeds of men,
75 To guide our vengeance to a prosperous close.

[LAIAS *goes out.* POLYPHON-
  TES, MEROPE, *and* THE
  CHORUS *come forward. As they*

advance, ÆPYTUS, *who at first*
  conceals himself behind the tomb,
  moves off the stage.

Polyphontes (*To* THE CHORUS)

Set down your pitchers, maidens,
  and fall back!
Suspend your melancholy rites
  awhile;
Shortly ye shall resume them with
  your Queen.

(*To* MEROPE)

I sought thee, Merope; I find thee
  thus,
80 As I have ever found thee; bent
  to keep,
By sad observances and public
  grief,
A mournful feud alive, which else
  would die.
I blame thee not, I do thy heart
  no wrong!
Thy deep seclusion, thine un-
  yielding gloom,
85 Thine attitude of cold, estranged
  reproach,
These punctual funeral honours,
  year by year
Repeated, are in thee, I well believe,
Courageous, faithful actions,
  nobly dared.
But, Merope, the eyes of other
  men
90 Read in these actions, innocent
  in thee,
Perpetual promptings to rebellious hope,
War-cries to faction, year by year
  renewed,
Beacons of vengeance, not to be
  let die.
And me, believe it, wise men
  gravely blame,
95 And ignorant men despise me,
  that I stand
Passive, permitting thee what
  course thou wilt.
Yes, the crowd mutters that remorseful fear
And paralysing conscience stop
  my arm,
When it should pluck thee from
  thy hostile way.
100 All this I bear, for, what I seek, I
  know:

Peace, peace is what I seek, and
   public calm;
Endless extinction of unhappy
   hates,
Union cemented for this nation's
   weal.
And even now, if to behold me
   here,
105 This day, amid these rites, this
   black-robed train,
Wakens, O Queen! remembrance
   in thy heart
Too wide at variance with the
   peace I seek –
I will not violate thy noble grief,
The prayer I came to urge I will
   defer.

Merope

110 This day, to-morrow, yesterday,
   alike
I am, I shall be, have been, in my
   mind
Tow'rd thee; toward thy silence
   as thy speech.
Speak, therefore, or keep silence,
   which thou wilt.

Polyphontes

Hear me, then, speak; and let this
   mournful day,
115 The twentieth anniversary of
   strife,
Henceforth be honoured as the
   date of peace.
Yes, twenty years ago this day
   beheld
The king Cresphontes, thy great
   husband, fall;
It needs no yearly offerings at his
   tomb
120 To keep alive that memory in my
   heart –
It lives, and, while I see the light,
   will live.
For we were kinsmen – more than
   kinsmen – friends;
Together we had grown, together
   lived;
Together to this isle of Pelops
   came
125 To take the inheritance of Heracles,
Together won this fair Messenian
   land –
Alas, that, how to rule it, was our
   broil!

He had his counsel, party, friends
   – I mine;
He stood by what he wished for –
   I the same;
130 I smote him, when our wishes
   clashed in arms –
He had smit me, had he been as
   swift as I.
But while I smote him, Queen, I
   honoured him;
Me, too, had he prevailed, he
   had not scorned.
Enough of this! Since that, I have
   maintained
135 The sceptre – not remissly let it
   fall –
And I am seated on a prosperous
   throne;
Yet still, for I conceal it not, fer-
   ments
In the Messenian people what
   remains
Of thy dead husband's faction –
   vigorous once,
140 Now crushed but not quite lifeless
   by his fall.
And these men look to thee, and
   from thy grief –
Something too studiously, forgive
   me, shown –
Infer thee their accomplice; and
   they say
That thou in secret nurturest up
   thy son,
145 Him whom thou hiddest when
   thy husband fell,
To avenge that fall, and bring
   them back to power.
Such are their hopes – I ask not if
   by thee
Willingly fed or no – their most
   vain hopes;
For I have kept conspiracy fast-
   chained
150 Till now, and I have strength to
   chain it still.
But, Merope, the years advance;
   – I stand
Upon the threshold of old age,
   alone,
Always in arms, always in face of
   foes.
The long repressive attitude of
   rule
155 Leaves me austerer, sterner, than
   I would;

Old age is more suspicious than the free
And valiant heart of youth, or manhood's firm
Unclouded reason; I would not decline
Into a jealous tyrant, scourged with fears,
160　Closing in blood and gloom his sullen reign.
The cares which might in me with time, I feel,
Beget a cruel temper, help me quell!
The breach between our parties help me close!
Assist me to rule mildly; let us join
165　Our hands in solemn union, making friends
Our factions with the friendship of their chiefs.
Let us in marriage, King and Queen, unite
Claims ever hostile else, and set thy son –
No more an exile fed on empty hopes,
170　And to an unsubstantial title heir,
But prince adopted by the will of power,
And future king – before this people's eyes.
Consider him! consider not old hates!
Consider, too, this people, who were dear
175　To their dead king, thy husband – yea, too dear,
For that destroyed him. Give them peace! thou can'st.
O Merope, how many noble thoughts,
How many precious feelings of man's heart,
How many loves, how many gratitudes,
180　Do twenty years wear out, and see expire!
Shall they not wear one hatred out as well?

Merope
Thou hast forgot, then, who I am who hear,
And who thou art who speakest to me? I

Am Merope, thy murdered master's wife;
185　And thou are Polyphontes, first his friend,
And then . . . his murderer. These offending tears
That murder moves; this breach that thou would'st close
Was by that murder opened; that one child
(If still, indeed, he lives) whom thou would'st seat
190　Upon a throne not thine to give, is heir,
Because thou slew'st his brothers with their father.
Who can patch union here? What can there be
But everlasting horror 'twixt us two,
Gulfs of estranging blood? Across that chasm
195　Who can extend their hands? . . . Maidens, take back
These offerings home! our rites are spoiled to-day.

Polyphontes
Not so; let these Messenian maidens mark
The feared and blackened ruler of their race,
Albeit with lips unapt to self-excuse,
200　Blow off the spot of murder from his name –
Murder! – but what *is* murder? When a wretch
For private gain or hatred takes a life,
We call it murder, crush him, brand his name.
But when, for some great public cause, an arm
205　Is, without love or hate, austerely raised
Against a power exempt from common checks,
Dangerous to all, to be but thus annulled –
Ranks any man with murder such an act?
With grievous deeds, perhaps; with murder, no!
210　Find then such cause, the charge of murder falls –

Be judge thyself if it abound not
  here.
All know how weak the eagle,
  Heracles,
Soaring from his death-pile on
  Œta, left
His puny, callow eaglets; and
  what trials –
215 Infirm protectors, dubious oracles
Construed awry, misplanned invasions – wore
Three generations of his offspring
  out;
Hardly the fourth, with grievous
  loss, regained
Their father's realm, this isle,
  from Pelops named.
220 Who made that triumph, though
  deferred, secure?
Who, but the kinsmen of the
  royal brood
Of Heracles, scarce Heracleidæ
  less
Than they? these, and the Dorian
  lords, whose king
Ægimius gave our outcast house a
  home
225 When Thebes, when Athens
  dared not; who in arms
Thrice issued with us from their
  pastoral vales,
And shed their blood like water in
  our cause?
Such were the dispossessors; of
  what stamp
Were they we dispossessed? – of
  us I speak,
230 Who to Messenia with thy husband came;
I speak not now of Argos, where
  his brother,
Not now of Sparta, where his
  nephews reigned. –
What we found here were tribes
  of fame obscure,
Much turbulence, and little con-
  stancy,
235 Precariously ruled by foreign
  lords
From the Æolian stock of Neleus
  sprung,
A house once great, now dwindling in its sons.
Such were the conquered, such
  the conquerors; who
Had most thy husband's confidence? Consult

240 His acts! the wife he chose was –
  full of virtues –
But an Arcadian princess, more
  akin
To his new subjects than to us;
  his friends
Were the Messenian chiefs; the
  laws he framed
Were aimed at their promotion,
  our decline.
245 And, finally, this land, then half-
  subdued,
Which from one central city's
  guarded seat
As from a fastness in the rocks our
  scant
Handful of Dorian conquerors
  might have curbed,
He parcelled out in five confede-
  rate states,
250 Sowing his victors thinly through
  them all,
Mere prisoners, meant or not,
  among our foes.
If this was fear of them, it shamed
  the king;
If jealousy of us, it shamed the
  man.
Long we refrained ourselves, sub-
  mitted long,
255 Construed his acts indulgently,
  revered,
Though found perverse, the blood
  of Heracles;
Reluctantly the rest – but, against
  all,
One voice preached patience, and
  that voice was mine!
At last it reached us, that he, still
  mistrustful,
260 Deeming, as tyrants deem, our
  silence hate,
Unadulating grief conspiracy,
Had to this city, Stenyclaros,
  called
A general assemblage of the
  realm,
With compact in that concourse
  to deliver,
265 For death, his ancient to his new-
  made friends,
Patience was thenceforth self-
  destruction. I,
I his chief kinsman, I his pioneer
And champion to the throne, I
  honouring most

Of men the line of Heracles, preferred
270 The many of that lineage to the
one;
What his foes dared not, I, his
lover, dared;
I at that altar, where mid shouting crowds
He sacrificed, our ruin in his
heart,
To Zeus, before he struck his
blow, struck mine –
275 Struck once, and awed his mob,
and saved this realm.
Murder let others call this, if they
will;
I, self-defence and righteous execution.

Merope

Alas, how fair a colour can his
tongue,
Who self-exculpates, lend to foul-
est deeds!
280 Thy trusting lord didst thou, his
servant, slay;
Kinsman, thou slew'st thy kinsman; friend, thy friend –
This were enough; but let me tell
thee, too,
Thou hadst no cause, as feigned,
in his misrule.
For ask at Argos, ask in Lacedæmon,
285 Whose people, when the Heracleidæ came,
Were hunted out, and to Achaia
fled,
Whether is better, to abide alone,
A wolfish band, in a dispeopled
realm,
Or conquerors with conquered to
unite
290 Into one puissant folk, as he designed?
These sturdy and unworn Messenian tribes,
Who shook the fierce Neleidæ on
their throne,
Who to the invading Dorians
stretched a hand,
And half-bestowed, half yielded
up their soil –
295 He would not let his savage chiefs
alight,

A cloud of vultures, on this vigorous race,
Ravin a little while in spoil and
blood,
Then, gorged and helpless, be
assailed and slain.
He would have saved you from
your furious selves.
300 Not in abhorred estrangement let
you stand;
He would have mixed you with
your friendly foes,
Foes dazzled with your prowess,
well inclined
To reverence your lineage, more,
to obey;
So would have built you, in a few
short years,
305 A just, therefore a safe, supre-
macy.
For well he knew, what you, his
chiefs, did not –
How of all human rules the over-
tense
Are apt to snap; the easy-stretch-
ed endure,
O gentle wisdom, little understood!
310 O arts above the vulgar tyrant's
reach!
O policy too subtle far for sense
Of heady, masterful, injurious
men!
This good he meant you, and for
this he died!
Yet not for this – else might thy
crime in part
315 Be error deemed – but that pretence is vain.
For, if ye slew him for supposed
misrule,
Injustice to his kin and Dorian
friends,
Why with the offending father
did ye slay
Two unoffending babes, his
innocent sons?
320 Why not on them have placed the
forfeit crown,
Ruled in their name, and trained
them to your will?
Had *they* misruled? had *they* forgot
their friends,
Forsworn their blood? ungrate-
fully had *they*

284. *ask in Lacedaemon*] The *1858* reading. In *1885* 'asked' is a misprint.

Preferred Messenian serfs to
    Dorian lords?
325 No! but to thy ambition their
    poor lives
Were bar – and this, too, was
    their father's crime.
That thou might'st reign he died,
    not for his fault
Even fancied; and his death thou
    wroughtest chief!
For, if the other lords desired his
    fall
330 Hotlier than thou, and were by
    thee kept back,
Why dost thou only profit by his
    death?
Thy crown condemns thee, while
    thy tongue absolves.
And now to me thou tenderest
    friendly league,
And to my son reversion to thy
    throne!
335 Short answer is sufficient; league
    with thee,
For me I deem such impious; and
    for him
Exile abroad more safe than heir-
    ship here.

Polyphontes
I ask thee not to approve thy hus-
    band's death,
No, nor expect thee to admit the
    grounds,
340 In reason good, which justified my
    deed.
With women the heart argues,
    not the mind.
But, for thy children's death, I
    stand assoiled –
I saved them, meant them hon-
    our; but thy friends
Rose, and with fire and sword
    assailed my house
345 By night; in that blind tumult
    they were slain.
To chance impute their deaths,
    then, not to me.

Merope
Such chance as killed the father,
    killed the sons.

Polyphontes
One son at least I spared, for still
    he lives.

Merope
Tyrants think him they murder
    not they spare.

Polyphontes
350 Not much a tyrant thy free speech
    displays me.

Merope
Thy shame secures my freedom,
    not thy will.

Polyphontes
Shame rarely checks the genuine
    tyrant's will.

Merope
One merit, then, thou hast; exult
    in that.

Polyphontes
Thou standest out, I see, repellest
    peace.

Merope
355 Thy sword repelled it long ago,
    not I.

Polyphontes
Doubtless thou reckonest on the
    help of friends.

Merope
Not help of men, although, per-
    haps, of Gods.

Polyphontes
What Gods? the Gods of con-
    cord, civil weal?

Merope
No! the avenging Gods, who pun-
    ish crime.

Polyphontes
360 Beware! from thee upbraidings I
    receive
With pity, nay, with reverence;
    yet beware!

349. In the Preface (*Complete Prose Works* ed. R. H. Super i (1960) 44) A. acknowledges the imitation of Maffei's *Merope* (1713) I i 108–9,

    Ecco il don dei tiranni: a lor rassembra,
    Morte non dando altrui, di dar la vita.

I know, I know how hard it is to
    think
That right, that conscience point-
    ed to a deed,
Where interest seems to have en-
    joined it too.
365 Most men are led by interest; and
    the few,
Who are not, expiate the general
    sin,
Involved in one suspicion with
    the base.
Dizzy the path and perilous the
    way
Which in a deed like mine a just
    man treads,
370 But it is sometimes trodden, oh!
    believe it.
Yet how *canst* thou believe it?
    therefore thou
Hast all impunity. Yet, lest thy
    friends,
Emboldened by my lenience,
    think it fear,
And count on like impunity, and
    rise,
375 And have to thank thee for a fall,
    beware!
To rule this kingdom I intend;
    with sway
Clement, if may be, but to rule it
    – there
Expect no wavering, no retreat,
    no change.
And now I leave thee to these
    rites, esteemed
380 Pious, but impious, surely, if their
    scope
Be to foment old memories of
    wrath.
Pray, as thou pour'st libations on
    this tomb,
To be delivered from thy fostered
    hate,
Unjust suspicion, and erroneous
    fear.
    [POLYPHONTES *goes into the*
    palace. THE CHORUS *and*
    MEROPE *approach the tomb with*
    their offerings.

The Chorus
Draw, draw near to the tomb!
                [*strophe.*
385 Lay honey-cakes on its marge,

Pour the libation of milk,
Deck it with garlands of flowers.
Tears fall thickly the while!
390 Behold, O King from the dark
House of the grave, what we do!

O Arcadian hills   *antistrophe.*
Send us the Youth whom ye hide,
Girt with his coat for the chase,
395 With the low broad hat of the
    tanned
Hunter o'ershadowing his brow;
Grasping, firm, in his hand
Advanced, two javelins, not now
Dangerous alone to the deer!

Merope
400 What shall I bear, O lost   *str. 1*
Husband and King, to thy grave?
Pure libations, and fresh
Flowers? But thou, in the gloom,
Discontented, perhaps,
405 Demandest vengeance, not grief?
Sternly requirest a man,
Light to spring up to thy house?

The Chorus
Vengeance, O Queen, is his due,
His most just prayer; yet his [*str. 2*
    house –
If that might soothe him below –
410 Prosperous, mighty, came back
In the third generation, the way
Ordered by Fate, to their home;
And now, glorious, secure
415 Fill the wealth-giving thrones
Of their heritage, Pelops' isle.

Merope
Suffering sent them, Death *ant. 1*
Marched with them, Hatred and
    Strife
Met them entering their halls,
420 For from the day when the first
Heracleidæ received
That Delphic hest to return,
What hath involved them, but
    blind
Error on error, and blood?

The Chorus
425 Truly I hear of a Maid   *ant. 2*
Of that stock born, who bestowed
Her blood that so she might make

389–91. Suggested by Aeschylus's *Choephoroe* 333–4.

Victory sure to her race,
When the fight hung in doubt!
  but she now,
430 Honour'd and sung of by all,
Far on Marathon plain,
Gives her name to the spring
Macaria, blessed Child.

Merope
She led the way of death.   *str. 3*
And the plain of Tegea,
435 And the grave of Orestes –
Where, in secret seclusion
Of his unrevealed tomb,
Sleeps Agamemnon's unhappy,
440 Matricidal, world-faméd,
Seven-cubit-statured son –
Sent forth Echemus, the victor,
  the king,
By whose hand, at the Isthmus,
At the fate-denied straits,
445 Fell the eldest of the sons of
  Heracles,
Hyllus, the chief of his house.
Brother followed sister
The all-wept way.

The Chorus
Yes; but his seed still, wiser-
  counselled,
450 Sailed by the fate-meant Gulf to
  their conquest –
Slew their enemies' king, Tisamenus.
Wherefore accept that happier
  omen!
Yet shall restorer appear to the
  race.

Merope
Three brothers won the field,
455 And to two did Destiny   *[ant. 3*
Give the thrones that they con-
  quered,
But the third, what delays him
From his unattained crown? . . .
Ah Pylades and Electra,
460 Ever faithful, untired,

Jealous, blood-exacting friends!
Your sons leap upon the foe of
  your kin,
In the passes of Delphi,
In the temple-built gorge!
465 There the youngest of the band of
  conquerors
Perished, in sight of the goal.
Thrice son followed sire
The all-wept way.

The Chorus
Thou tellest the fate of the last
470 Of the three Heracleidæ.   *[str. 4*
Not of him, of Cresphontes thou
  shared'st the lot!
A king, a king was he while he
  lived,
Swaying the sceptre with pre-
  destined hand;
And now, minister loved,
Holds rule.

Merope
475   Ah me . . . Ah . . .

The Chorus
For the awful Monarchs below.

Merope
Thou touchest the worst of my ills.
Oh had he fallen of old   *[str. 5*
At the Isthmus, in fight with his
  foes,
480 By Achaian, Arcadian spear!
Then had his sepulchre risen
On the high sea-bank, in the sight
Of either Gulf, and remained
All-regarded afar,
485 Noble memorial of worth
Of a valiant Chief, to his own.

The Chorus
There rose up a cry in the streets
From the terrified people. *[ant. 4*
From the altar of Zeus, from the
  crowd, came a wail.

477. An echo of Sophocles's *Antigone* 858.
478–86. Suggested by Aeschylus's *Choephoroe* 345–53.
487–91. Suggested by the description of Agamemnon's death in *Electra* 193–
6.

490 A blow, a blow was struck, and he
  fell,
  Sullying his garment with dark-
  streaming blood;
  While stood o'er him a Form –
  Some Form

  Merope
  Ah me . . . Ah . . .

  The Chorus
  Of a dreadful Presence of fear.

  Merope
495 More piercing the second cry
  rang,   *ant. 5*
  Wailed from the palace within,
  From the Children . . . The Fury
  to them,
  Fresh from their father, draws
  near.
  Ah bloody axe! dizzy blows!
500 In these ears, they thunder, they
  ring,
  These poor ears, still! and these
  eyes
  Night and day see them fall,
  Fiery phantoms of death,
  On the fair, curled heads of my
  sons.

  The Chorus
505 Not to thee only hath come *str. 6*
  Sorrow, O Queen, of mankind.
  Had not Electra to haunt
  A palace defiled by a death un-
  avenged,

For years, in silence, devouring
  her heart?
510 But her nursling, her hope, came
  at last.
  Thou, too, rearest in hope,
  Far 'mid Arcadian hills,
  Somewhere, for vengeance, a
  champion, a light.
  Soon, soon shall Zeus bring him
  home!
515 Soon shall he dawn on this land!

  Merope
  Him in secret, in tears,   *str. 7.*
  Month after month, I await
  Vainly. For he, in the glens
  Of Lycæus afar,
520 A gladsome hunter of deer,
  Basks in his morning of youth,
  Spares not a thought to his home.

  The Chorus
  Give not thy heart to despair.
  No lamentation can loose [*ant. 6.*
525 Prisoners of death from the grave;
  But Zeus, who accounteth thy
  quarrel his own,
  Still rules, still watches, and num-
  b'reth the hours
  Till the sinner, the vengeance, be
  ripe.
  Still, by Acheron stream,
530 Terrible Deities throned
  Sit, and eye grimly the victim
  unscourged.
  Still, still the Dorian boy,
  Exiled, remembers his home.

505–6. A commonplace, but cp. *Electra* 153–4.
513. for vengeance, a champion] in safety, a nursling *1858.*
517–22. eplacing in *1858,*

> Month after month, through the slow-dragging year,
> Longing, listening, I wait, I implore.
> But he comes not. What dell,
> O Erymanthus! from sight
> Of his mother, which of thy glades
> O Lycaeus! conceals
> The happy hunter? He basks
> In youth's pure morning, nor thinks
> On the blood-stain'd home of his birth.

523, 525–6. An imitation of *Electra* 173–5.
531. 1858,

> Sit, and make ready the serpent, the scourge.

Merope

Him if high-ruling Zeus   *ant.* 7.
535 Bring to me safe, let the rest
Go as it will! But if this
Clash with justice, the Gods
Forgive my folly, and work
Vengeance on sinner and sin –
540 Only to me give my child!

The Chorus

Hear us and help us, Shade of our
King!   *str.* 8.

Merope

A return, O Father! give to thy
boy!   *str.* 9

The Chorus

Send an avenger, Gods of the
dead!   *ant.* 8.

Merope

An avenger I ask not – send me
my son!   *ant.* 9.

The Chorus

545 O Queen, for an avenger to ap-
pear,
Thinking that so I prayed aright,
I prayed;
If I prayed wrongly, I revoke the
prayer.

Merope

Forgive me, maidens, if I seem
too slack
In calling vengeance on a murderer's head.
550 Impious I deem the alliance
which he asks,
Requite him words severe for
seeming kind,

And righteous, if he falls, I count
his fall.
With this, to those unbribed
inquisitors
Who in man's inmost bosom sit
and judge,
555 The true avengers these, I leave
his deed,
By him shown fair, but, I believe,
most foul.
If these condemn him, let them
pass his doom!
That doom obtain effect, from
Gods or men!
So be it; yet will that more solace
bring
560 To the chafed heart of Justice
than to mine.
To hear another tumult in these
streets,
To have another murder in these
halls,
To see another mighty victim
bleed –
Small comfort offers for a woman
there!
565 A woman, O my friends, has one
desire:
To see secure, to live with, those
she loves.
Can vengeance give me back the
murdered? no!
Can it bring home my child? Ah,
if it can,
I pray the Furies' ever-restless
band,
570 And pray the Gods, and pray the
all-seeing sun:
'Sun, who careerest through the
height of Heaven,
When o'er the Arcadian forests
thou art come,

535–40. Replacing in *1858*,

> Bring to his mother, the rest I commit,
> Willing, patient, to Zeus, to his care.
> Blood I ask not. Enough,
> Sated, and more than enough,
> Are mine eyes with blood. But if this,
> O my comforters! strays
> Amiss from Justice, the Gods
> Forgive my folly, and work
> What they will! – but to me give my son!

571–8. An adaptation of Sophocles's *Ajax* 845–9.

And see'st my stripling hunter
   there afield,
Put tightness in thy gold-em-
   bosséd rein,
575 And check thy fiery steeds, and,
   leaning back,
Throw him a pealing word of
   summons down,
To come, a late avenger, to the
   aid
Of this poor soul who bare him,
   and his sire.'
If this will bring him back, be this
   my prayer!
580 But Vengeance travels in a
   dangerous way,
Double of issue, full of pits and
   snares
For all who pass, pursuers and
   pursued –
That way is dubious for a mother's
   prayer.
Rather on thee I call, Husband
   beloved –
585 May Hermes, herald of the dead,
   convey
My words below to thee, and
   make thee hear –
Bring back our son! if may be,
   without blood!
Install him in thy throne, still
   without blood!
Grant him to reign there wise and
   just like thee,
590 More fortunate than thee, more
   fairly judged!
This for our son; and for myself I
   pray,
Soon, having once beheld him, to
   descend
Into the quiet gloom, where thou
   art now.
These words to thine indulgent
   ear, thy wife,
595 I send, and these libations pour
   the while.
[*They make their offerings at the
tomb.* MEROPE *then turns to go
towards the palace.*

The Chorus
The dead hath now his offerings
   duly paid.
But whither go'st thou hence, O
   Queen, away?

589–90. Cp. Sophocles's *Ajax* 550–1.

Merope
To receive Arcas, who to-day
   should come,
Bringing me of my boy the annual
   news.

The Chorus
600 No certain news if like the rest it
   run.

Merope
Certain in this, that 'tis uncertain
   still.

The Chorus
What keeps him in Arcadia from
   return?

Merope
His grandsire and his uncles fear
   the risk.

The Chorus
Of what? it lies with them to
   make risk none.

Merope
605 Discovery of a visit made by
   stealth.

The Chorus
With arms then they should send
   him, not by stealth.

Merope
With arms they dare not, and by
   stealth they fear.

The Chorus
I doubt their caution little suits
   their ward.

Merope
The heart of youth I know; that
   most I fear.

The Chorus
610 I augur thou wilt hear some bold
   resolve.

Merope
I dare not wish it; but, at least, to
   hear
That my son still survives, in
   health, in bloom;

To hear that still he loves, still
   longs for, me,
Yet, with a light uncareworn
   spirit, turns
615 Quick from distressful thought,
   and floats in joy –
Thus much from Arcas, my old
   servant true,
Who saved him from these murderous halls a babe,
And since has fondly watched
   him night and day
Save for this annual charge, I
   hope to hear.
620 If this be all, I know not; but I
   know,
These many years I live for this
   alone.   [MEROPE *goes in.*

The Chorus
Much is there which the sea *str.* 1.
Conceals from man, who cannot
   plumb its depths.
Air to his unwinged form denies a
   way,
625 And keeps its liquid solitudes
   unscaled.
Even earth, whereon he treads,
So feeble is his march, so slow,
Holds countless tracts untrod.

But more than all unplumbed,
          [*ant.* 1.
630 Unscaled, untrodden, is the heart
   of man.
More than all secrets hid, the way
   it keeps.
Nor any of our organs so obtuse,
Inaccurate, and frail,
As those wherewith we try to test
635 Feelings and motives there.

Yea, and not only have we not
   explored   *str.* 2.
That wide and various world, the
   heart of others,
But even our own heart, that
   narrow world
Bounded in our own breast, we
   hardly know,
640 Of our own actions dimly trace
   the causes.
Whether a natural obscureness,
   hiding

That region in perpetual cloud,
Or our own want of effort, be the
   bar.

Therefore – while acts are from
   their motives judged, *ant.* 2.
645 And to one act many most unlike
   motives,
This pure, that guilty, may have
   each impelled –
Power fails us to try clearly if that
   cause
Assigned us by the actor be the
   true one;
Power fails the man himself to fix
   distinctly
650 The cause which drew him to his
   deed,
And stamp himself, thereafter,
   bad or good.

The most are bad, wise men have
   said.   *str.* 3.
Let the best rule, they say again.
The best, then, to dominion hath
   the right.
655 Rights unconceded and denied,
Surely, if rights, may be by force
   asserted –
May be, nay should, if for the
   general weal.
The best, then, to the throne may
   carve his way,
And strike opposers down,
660 Free from all guilt of lawlessness,
Or selfish lust of personal power;
Bent only to serve virtue,
Bent to diminish wrong.

And truly, in this ill-ruled world,
          [*ant.* 3,
665 Well sometimes may the good
   desire
To give to virtue her dominion
   due!
Well may he long to interrupt
The reign of folly, usurpation
   ever,
Though fenced by sanction of a
   thousand years!
670 Well thirst to drag the wrongful
   ruler down;
Well purpose to pen back
Into the narrow path of right

629–43. Cp. 'The Buried Life' 55–63 (p. 274 above).

The ignorant, headlong multi-
    tude,
Who blindly follow, ever,
675 Blind leaders, to their bane!

But who can say, without a fear:
                             [*str.* 4.
That best, who ought to rule, am I;
The mob, who ought to obey, are these;
I the one righteous, they the many bad?
680 Who, without check of conscience,
    can aver
That he to power makes way by
    arms,
Sheds blood, imprisons, banishes,
    attaints,
Commits all deeds the guilty
    oftenest do,
Without a single guilty thought,
685 Armed for right only, and the
    general good?

Therefore, with censure un-
    allayed,   *ant.* 4.
Therefore, with unexcepting ban,
Zeus and pure-thoughted Justice
    brand
Imperious self-asserting violence;
690 Sternly condemn the too bold
    man, who dares
Elect himself Heaven's destined
    arm;
And, knowing well man's inmost
    heart infirm,
However noble the committer be,
His grounds however specious
    shown,
695 Turn with averted eyes from
    deeds of blood.

Thus, though a woman, I was
    schooled   *epode.*
By those whom I revere.
Whether I learnt their lessons
    well,
Or, having learnt them, well
    apply
700 To what hath in this house
    befall'n,
If in the event be any proof,
The event will quickly show.
             [Æpytus *comes in.*

Æpytus
Maidens, assure me if they told
    me true
Who told me that the royal house
    was here.

The Chorus
705 Rightly they told thee, and thou
    art arrived.

Æpytus
Here, then, it is, where Poly-
    phontes dwells?

The Chorus
He doth; thou hast both house
    and master right.

Æpytus
Might some one straight inform
    him he is sought?

The Chorus
Inform him that thyself, for here
    he comes.

    [POLYPHONTES *comes forth,*
    with ATTENDANTS *and*
    GUARDS.

Æpytus
710 O King, all hail! I come with
    weighty news;
Most likely, grateful; but in all
    case, sure.

Polyphontes
Speak them, that I may judge
    their kind myself.

Æpytus
Accept them in one word, for
    good or bad:
Æpytus, the Messenian prince, is
    dead!

Polyphontes
715 Dead! – and when died he?
    where? and by what hand?
And who art thou, who bringest
    me such news?

713–14. The abrupt disclosure is Sophoclean – cp. *Electra* 673. Milton uses the
same device, *Samson Agonistes* 1570,

        Then take the worst in brief, Samson is dead.

Æpytus
He perished in Arcadia, where
    he dwelt
With Cypselus; and two days
    since he died.
One of the train of Cypselus am I.

Polyphontes
720 Instruct me of the manner of his
    death.

Æpytus
That will I do, and to this end I
    came.
For, being of like age, of birth not
    mean,
The son of an Arcadian noble, I
Was chosen his companion from a
    boy;
725 And on the hunting-rambles
    which his heart,
Unquiet, drove him ever to
    pursue
Through all the lordships of the
    Arcadian dales,
From chief to chief, I wandered at
    his side,
The captain of his squires, and his
    guard.
730 On such a hunting-journey, three
    morns since,
With beaters, hounds, and hunts-
    men, he and I
Set forth from Tegea, the royal
    town.
The prince at start seemed sad,
    but his regard
Cleared with blithe travel and
    the morning air.
735 We rode from Tegea, through the
    woods of oaks,
Past Arnê spring, where Rhea
    gave the babe

Poseidon to the shepherd-boys to
    hide
From Saturn's search among the
    new-yeaned lambs,
To Mantineia, with its unbaked
    walls;
740 Thence, by the Sea-God's
    Sanctuary and the tomb
Whither from wintry Mænalus
    were brought
The bones of Arcas, whence our
    race is named,
On, to the marshy Orchomenian
    plain,
And the Stone Coffins; then, by
    Caphyæ Cliffs,
745 To Pheneos with its craggy
    citadel.
There, with the chief of that hill-
    town, we lodged
One night; and the next day at
    dawn fared on
By the Three Fountains and the
    Adder's Hill
To the Stymphalian Lake, our
    journey's end,
750 To draw the coverts on Cyllenê's
    side.
There, on a high green spur
    which bathes its point
Far in the liquid lake, we sate,
    and drew
Cates from our hunters' pouch,
    Arcadian fare,
Sweet chestnuts, barley-cakes,
    and boar's-flesh dried;
755 And as we ate, and rested there,
    we talked
Of places we had passed, sport we
    had had,
Of beasts of chase that haunt the
    Arcadian hills,
Wild hog, and bear, and moun-
    tain-deer, and roe;

721–856. This fictitious account of the death of Aepytus corresponds to the
fictitious account of Orestes' death in Sophocles's *Electra* 680–763. See A.'s Preface,
'A noble and accomplished living poet, M. Manzoni, has . . . developed the thesis
of the importance to a poet of a basis of tradition . . . where driven to invent in
the false story told by Merope's son, as by Orestes in the *Electra*, of his own death,
I could not satisfy myself until I discovered in Pausanias [*Description of Greece* viii
22 (9)] a tradition . . . of an Arcadian hunter drowned in the lake Stymphalus,
down one of those singular Katabothra, or chasms in the limestone rock . . .'
(*Complete Prose Works* ed. *cit.* i 53). Orestes' fictitious death in the *Electra*, however, is not related by Orestes (as A. says), but by his servant. Topographical and
mythological details in A.'s lines are also taken from Pausanias viii.

Last of our quarters with the
      Arcadian chiefs.
760 For courteous entertainment,
      welcome warm,
    Sad, reverential homage, had our
      prince
    From all, for his great lineage and
      his woes;
    All which he owned, and praised
      with grateful mind.
    But still over his speech a gloom
      there hung,
765 As of one shadowed by impending
      death;
    And strangely, as we talked, he
      would apply
    The story of spots mentioned to
      his own;
    Telling us, Arnê minded him, he
      too
    Was saved a babe, but to a life
      obscure,
770 Which he, the seed of Heracles,
      dragged on
    Inglorious, and should drop at
      last unknown,
    Even as those dead unepitaphed,
      who lie
    In the stone coffins at Orcho-
      menus.
    And, then, he bade remember
      how we passed
    The Mantineän Sanctuary, forbid
775 To foot of mortal, where his
      ancestor,
    Named Æpytus like him, having
      gone in,
    Was blinded by the outgushing
      springs of brine.
    Then, turning westward to the
      Adder's Hill –
780 *Another ancestor, named, too, like me,*
    Died of a snake-bite, said he, *on that*
      brow;
    Still at his mountain-tomb men marvel,
      built
    Where, as life ebbed, his bearers laid
      him down.
    So he played on; then ended,
      with a smile:
785 *This region is not happy for my race.*
    We cheered him; but, that
      moment, from the copse
    By the lake-edge, broke the sharp
      cry of hounds;
    The prickers shouted that the
      stag was gone.

We sprang upon our feet, we
      snatched our spears,
790 We bounded down the swarded
      slope, we plunged
    Through the dense ilex-thickets to
      the dogs.
    Far in the woods ahead their
      music rang;
    And many times that morn we
      coursed in ring
    The forests round that belt
      Cyllenê's side;
795 Till I, thrown out and tired, came
      to halt
    On that same spur where we had
      sate at morn.
    And resting there to breathe, I
      watched the chase –
    Rare, straggling hunters, foiled
      by brake and crag,
    And the prince, single, pressing
      on the rear
800 Of that unflagging quarry and
      the hounds.
    Now in the woods far down I saw
      them cross
    An open glade; now he was high
      aloft
    On some tall scar fringed with
      dark feathery pines,
    Peering to spy a goat-track down
      the cliff,
805 Cheering with hand, and voice,
      and horn his dogs.
    At last the cry drew to the
      water's edge –
    And through the brushwood, to
      the pebbly strand,
    Broke, black with sweat, the
      antlered mountain-stag,
    And took the lake. Two hounds
      alone pursued,
810 Then came the prince; he shouted
      and plunged in.
    – There is a chasm rifted in the
      base
    Of that unfooted precipice, whose
      rock
    Walls on one side the deep
      Stymphalian Lake;
    There the lake-waters, which in
      ages gone
815 Washed, as the marks upon the
      hills still show,
    All the Stymphalian plain, are
      now sucked down.

A headland, with one aged plane-
tree crowned,
Parts from this cave-pierced cliff
the shelving bay
Where first the chase plunged in;
the bay is smooth,
820 But round the headland's point a
current sets,
Strong, black, tempestuous, to
the cavern-mouth.
Stoutly, under the headland's lee,
they swam;
But when they came abreast the
point, the race
Caught them as wind takes
feathers, whirled them round
825 Struggling in vain to cross it,
swept them on,
Stag, dogs, and hunter, to the
yawning gulf.
All this, O King, not piecemeal,
as to thee
Now told, but in one flashing
instant passed.
While from the turf whereon I
lay I sprang
830 And took three strides, quarry
and dogs were gone;
A moment more – I saw the
prince turn round
Once in the black and arrowy
race, and cast
An arm aloft for help; then sweep
beneath
The low-browed cavern-arch,
and disappear.
835 And what I could, I did – to call
by cries
Some straggling hunters to my
aid, to rouse
Fishers who live on the lake-side,
to launch
Boats, and approach, near as we
dared, the chasm.
But of the prince nothing remained, save this,
840 His boar-spear's broken shaft,
back on the lake
Cast by the rumbling subterranean stream;
And this, at landing spied by us
and saved,
His broad-brimmed hunter's hat,
which, in the bay,
Where first the stag took water,
floated still.

845 And I across the mountains
brought with haste
To Cypselus, at Basilis, this
news –
Basilis, his new city, which he
now
Near Lycosura builds, Lycaon's
town,
First city founded on the earth by
men.
850 He to thee sends me on, in one
thing glad,
While all else grieves him, that
his grandchild's death
Extinguishes distrust 'twixt him
and thee.
But I from our deplored mischance learn this:
The man who to untimely death
is doomed,
855 Vainly you hedge him from the
assault of harm;
He bears the seed of ruin in
himself.

The Chorus

So dies the last shoot of our royal
tree!
Who shall tell Merope this heavy
news?

Polyphontes

Stranger, this news thou bringest
is too great
860 For instant comment, having
many sides
Of import, and in silence best
received,
Whether it turn at last to joy or
woe.
But thou, the zealous bearer, hast
no part
In what it hath of painful,
whether now
865 First heard, or in its future issue
shown.
Thou for thy labour hast deserved
our best
Refreshment, needed by thee, as I
judge,
With mountain-travel and night-
watching spent.
To the guest-chamber lead him,
some one! give
870 All entertainment which a
traveller needs,

And such as fits a royal house to
 show;
To friends, still more, and
 labourers in our cause.

[ATTENDANTS *conduct* ÆPYTUS
                    within the palace.

The Chorus
The youth is gone within; alas!
 he bears
A presence sad for some one
 through those doors.

Polyphontes
875 Admire then, maidens, how in
 one short hour
The schemes, pursued in vain for
 twenty years,
Are – by a stroke, though un-
 desired, complete –
Crowned with success, not in my
 way, but Heaven's!
This at a moment, too, when I
 had urged
880 A last, long-cherished project, in
 my aim
Of peace, and been repulsed with
 hate and scorn.
Fair terms of reconcilement,
 equal rule,
I offered to my foes, and they
 refused;
Worse terms than mine they have
 obtained from Heaven.
885 Dire is this blow for Merope; and
 I
Wished, truly wished, solution to
 our broil
Other than by this death; but it
 hath come!
I speak no word of boast, but this
 I say:
A private loss here founds a
 nation's peace.
                [POLYPHONTES *goes out.*

The Chorus
890 Peace, who tarriest too long;   *str.*
Peace, with delight in thy train;
Come, come back to our prayer!

Then shall the revel again
Visit our streets, and the sound
895 Of the harp be heard with the
 pipe,
When the flashing torches appear
In the marriage-train coming on,
With dancing maidens and boys –
While the matrons come to the
 doors,
900 And the old men rise from their
 bench,
When the youths bring home the
 bride.

Not condemned by my voice *ant.*
He who restores thee shall be,
Not unfavoured by Heaven.
905 Surely no sinner the man,
Dread though his acts, to whose
 hand
Such a boon to bring hath been
 given.
Let her come, fair Peace! let her
 come!
But the demons long nourished
 here,
910 Murder, Discord, and Hate,
In the stormy desolate waves
Of the Thracian Sea let her leave,
Or the howling outermost main!
                [MEROPE *comes forth.*

Merope
A whisper through the palace
 flies of one
915 Arrived from Tegea with weighty
 news;
And I came, thinking to find
 Arcas here.
Ye have not left this gate, which
 he must pass;
Tell me – hath one not come? or,
 worse mischance,
Come, but been intercepted by
 the King?

The Chorus
920 A messenger, sent from Arcadia
 here,
Arrived, and of the King had
 speech but now.

890–913. Suggested, as A. indicates (*1858* Preface, *Complete Prose Works* ed. *cit.*
i 41), by the choral address to Peace in a surviving fragment of Euripides's *Cresphontes*, which he found in A. Nauck's *Tragicorum Graecorum Fragmenta* (Leipzig,
1856). The book was in A.'s library.

Merope
Ah me! the wrong expectant got
his news.

The Chorus
The message brought was for the
King designed.

Merope
How so? was Arcas not the
messenger?

The Chorus
925 A younger man, and of a different
name.

Merope
And what Arcadian news had he
to tell?

The Chorus
Learn that from other lips, O
Queen, than mine.

Merope
He kept his tale, then, for the
King alone?

The Chorus
His tale was meeter for that ear
than thine.

Merope
930 Why dost thou falter, and make
half reply?

The Chorus
O thrice unhappy, how I groan
thy fate!

Merope
Thou frightenest and confound'st
me by thy words.
O were but Arcas come, all would
be well!

The Chorus
If so, all's well: for look, the old
man speeds
935 Up from the city tow'rd this gated
hill.
[ARCAS *comes in.*

943. First added 1885.

Merope
Not with the failing breath and
foot of age
My faithful follower comes.
Welcome, old friend!

Arcas
Faithful, not welcome, when my
tale is told.
O that my over-speed and
bursting grief
940 Had on the journey choked my
labouring breath,
And locked my speech for ever in
my breast!
Yet then another man would
bring this news,
Wherewith from end to end
Arcadia rings. –
O honoured Queen, thy son, my
charge, is gone.

The Chorus
945 Too suddenly thou tellest such a
loss.
Look up, O Queen! look up, O
mistress dear!
Look up, and see thy friends who
comfort thee.

Merope
Ah...Ah...Ah me!

The Chorus
And I, too, say, ah me!

Arcas
Forgive, forgive the bringer of
such news!

Merope
950 Better from thine than from an
enemy's tongue.

The Chorus
And yet no enemy did this, O
Queen:
But the wit-baffling will and hand
of Heaven.

Arcas
No enemy! and what hast thou,
then, heard?
Swift as I came, hath falsehood
been before?

The Chorus

955 A youth arrived but now – the
     son, he said,
     Of an Arcadian lord – our
     prince's friend –
     Jaded with travel, clad in hunter's
     garb.
     He brought report that his own
     eyes had seen
     The prince, in chase after a
     swimming stag,
960 Swept down a chasm rifted in the
     cliff
     Which hangs o'er the Stymph-
     alian Lake, and drowned.

Arcas

     Ah me! with what a foot doth
     treason post,
     While loyalty, with all her speed,
     is slow!
     Another tale, I trow, thy messen-
     ger
965 For the King's private ear reser-
     ves, like this
     In one thing only, that the prince
     is dead.

The Chorus

     And how then runs this true and
     private tale?

Arcas

     As much to the King's wish,
     more to his shame.
     This young Arcadian noble,
     guard and mate
970 To Æpytus, the king seduced with
     gold,
     And had him at the prince's side
     in leash,
     Ready to slip on his unconscious
     prey.
     He on a hunting party two days
     since,
     Among the forests on Cyllenê's
     side,
975 Performed good service for his
     bloody wage;
     Our prince, and the good Laias,
     whom his ward
     Had in a father's place, he basely
     murdered.
     'Tis so, 'tis so, alas, for see the
     proof:

978–85. Replacing in *1858*,

          Take this for true, the other tale for feign'd.

                    The Chorus
          And this perfidious murder who reveal'd?

                    Arcas
          The faithless murderer's own, no other tongue.

                    The Chorus
          Did conscience goad him to denounce himself?

                    Arcas
          To Cypselus at Basilis he brought
          This strange unlikely tale, the prince was drown'd.

                    The Chorus
          But not a word appears of murder here.

                    Arcas
          Examin'd close, he own'd this story false.
          Then evidence came – his comrades of the hunt,
          Who saw the Prince and Laias last with him,
          Never again in life – next, agents, fee'd
          To ply 'twixt the Messenian king and him,
          Spoke, and reveal'd that traffic, and the traitor.
          So charg'd, he stood dumb-founder'd: Cypselus
          On this suspicion, cast him into chains.
          Thence he escap'd – and next I find him here.

                    The Chorus
          His presence with the King, thou mean'st, implies –

Uncle and nephew disappear;
their death
980 Is charged against this stripling;
agents, fee'd
To ply 'twixt the Messenian king
and him,
Come forth, denounce the traffic
and the traitor.
Seized, he escapes – and next I
find him here.
Take this for true, the other tale
for feigned.

The Chorus
985 The youth, thou say'st, we saw
and heard but now –

Arcas
He comes to tell his prompter he
hath sped.

The Chorus
Still he repeats the drowning story
here.

Arcas
To thee – that needs no Œdipus
to explain.

The Chorus
Interpret, then; for we, it seems,
are dull.

Arcas
990 Your King desired the profit of
his death,
Not the black credit of his
murderer.
That stern word '*murder*' had too
dread a sound
For the Messenian hearts, who
loved the prince.

The Chorus
Suspicion grave I see, but no firm
proof.

Merope
995 Peace! peace! all's clear. – The
wicked watch and work

While the good sleep; the work-
ers have the day.
Yes! yes! now I conceive the
liberal grace
Of this far-scheming tyrant and
his boon
Of heirship to his kingdom for my
son:
1000 He had his murderer ready, and
the sword
Lifted, and that unwished-for
heirship void –
A tale, meanwhile, forged for his
subject's ears –
And me, henceforth, sole rival
with himself
In their allegiance, me, in my
son's death-hour,
1005 When all turned tow'rds me, me
he would have shown
To my Messenians, duped, dis-
armed, despised,
The willing sharer of his guilty
rule,
All claim to succour forfeit, to
myself
Hateful, by each Messenian heart
abhorred.
1010 His offers I repelled – but what of
that?
If with no rage, no fire of righteous hate,
Such as ere now hath spurred to
fearful deeds
Weak women with a thousandth
part my wrongs,
But calm, but unresentful, I
endured
1015 His offers, coldly heard them,
cold repelled?
How must men think me abject,
void of heart,
While all this time I bear to linger
on
In this blood-deluged palace, in
whose halls
Either a vengeful Fury I should
stalk,
1020 Or else not live at all! – but here I
haunt,

996. After this line in *1858*,

     He who was sent hath sped, and now comes back,
     To chuckle with the sender o'er the game
     Which foolish innocence plays with subtle guilt.

1016. First added *1885*.

A pale, unmeaning ghost, power-
　　less to fright
Or harm, and nurse my longing
　　for my son,
A helpless one, I know it – but
　　the Gods
Have tempered me e'en thus,
　　and, in some souls,
1025 Misery, which rouses others,
　　breaks the spring.
And even now, my son, ah me!
　　my son,
Fain would I fade away, as I have
　　lived,
Without a cry, a struggle, or a
　　blow,
All vengeance unattempted, and
　　descend
1030 To the invisible plains, to roam
　　with thee,
Fit denizens, the lampless under-
　　world –
But with what eyes should I
　　encounter there
My husband, wandering with his
　　stern compeers,
Amphiaraos, or Mycenæ's king,
1035 Who led the Greeks to Ilium,
　　Agamemnon,
Betrayed like him, but, not like
　　him, avenged?
Or with what voice shall I the
　　questions meet
Of my two elder sons, slain long
　　ago,
Who sadly ask me, what, if not
　　revenge,
1040 Kept me, their mother, from their
　　side so long?
Or how reply to thee, my child
　　last-born,
Last-murdered, who reproach-
　　fully wilt say:
*Mother, I well believed thou lived'st
　　on*
In the detested palace of thy foe,
1045 *With patience on thy face, death in thy
　　heart,*
*Counting, till I grew up, the laggard
　　years,*
*That our joint hands might then
　　together pay*

*To our unhappy house the debt we
　　owe.*
*My death makes my debt void, and
　　doubles thine –*
1050 *But down thou fleest here, and leav'st
　　our scourge*
*Triumphant, and condemnest all
　　our race*
To lie in gloom for ever unappeased.
What shall I have to answer to
　　such words?
No, something must be dared;
　　and, great as erst
1055 Our dastard patience, be our
　　daring now!
Come, ye swift Furies, who to him
　　ye haunt
Permit no peace till your behests
　　are done;
Come, Hermes, who dost friend
　　the unjustly killed,
And canst teach simple ones to
　　plot and feign;
1060 Come, lightning Passion, that
　　with foot of fire
Advancest to the middle of a deed
Almost before 'tis planned; come,
　　glowing Hate;
Come, baneful Mischief, from thy
　　murky den
Under the dripping black Tartar-
　　ean cliff
1065 Which Styx's awful waters trickle
　　down –
Inspire this coward heart, this
　　flagging arm!
How say ye, maidens, do ye know
　　these prayers?
Are these words Merope's – is
　　this voice mine?
Old man, old man, thou hadst
　　my boy in charge,
1070 And he is lost, and thou hast that
　　to atone!
Fly, find me on the instant where
　　confer
The murderer and his impious
　　setter-on –
And ye, keep faithful silence,
　　friends, and mark
What one weak woman can
　　achieve alone.

1054-5. Echoing Electra's determination to take vengeance into her own hands
when she hears of the reported death of Orestes – see *Electra* 947 ff.
1056-66. Compare Sophocles's *Ajax* 835-44, but A. is also thinking of Lady
Macbeth (*Macbeth* I v 40-54).

Arcas
1075 O mistress, by the Gods, do
    nothing rash!

Merope
Unfaithful servant, dost thou, too,
    desert me?

Arcas
I go! I go! – The King holds
    council – there
Will I seek tidings. Take, the
    while, this word:
Attempting deeds beyond thy
    power to do,
1080 Thou nothing profitest thy
    friends, but mak'st
Our misery more, and thine own
    ruin sure.
                    [ARCAS *goes out.*

The Chorus
I have heard, O Queen, how a
    prince,   *str.* 1.
Agamemnon's son, in Mycenæ,
Orestes, died but in name,
1085 Lived for the death of his foes.

Merope
Peace!

The Chorus
What is it?

Merope
                    Alas,
Thou destroyest me!

The Chorus
                    How?

Merope
Whispering hope of a life
Which no stranger unknown,
1090 But the faithful servant and nurse,
Whose tears warrant his truth,
Bears sad witness is lost.

The Chorus
Wheresoe'er men are, there is
    grief.   *ant.* 1.
In a thousand countries, a
    thousand

1095 Homes, e'en now is there wail;
    Mothers lamenting their sons.

Merope
Yes –

The Chorus
Thou knowest it?

Merope
                    This,
Who lives, witnesses.

The Chorus
                    True.

Merope
But is it only a fate
1100 Sure, all-common, to lose
In a land of friends, by a friend,
One last, murder-saved child?

The Chorus
Ah me!   *str.* 2.

Merope
Thou confessest the prize
1105 In the rushing, thundering, mad,
Cloud-enveloped, obscure,
Unapplauded, unsung
Race of calamity, mine?

The Chorus
None can truly claim that
1110 Mournful preëminence, not
Thou.

Merope
Fate *gives* it, ah me!

The Chorus
Not, above all, in the doubts,
Double and clashing, that hang –

Merope
What then?   *ant.* 2.
1115 Seems it lighter, my loss,
If, perhaps, unpierced by the
    sword,
My child lies in his jagged
Sunless prison of rock,
On the black wave borne to and
    fro?

1077–8. Replacing the single line in *1858*,
          I go! I go! – yet, Queen, take this one word . . .

15+M.A.

The Chorus
1120 Worse, far worse, if his friend,
If the Arcadian within,
If –

Merope (with a start)
How say'st thou? within? . . .

The Chorus
He in the guest-chamber now,
Faithlessly murdered his friend.

Merope
1125 Ye, too, ye, too, join to betray,
then
Your Queen!

The Chorus
What is this?

Merope
Ye knew,
O false friends! into what
Haven the murderer had
dropped?
Ye kept silence?

The Chorus
In fear,
1130 O loved mistress! in fear,
Dreading thine over-wrought
mood,
What I knew, I concealed.

Merope
Swear by the Gods henceforth to
obey me!

The Chorus
Unhappy one, what deed
1135 Purposes thy despair?
I promise; but I fear.

Merope
From the altar, the unavenged
tomb,
Fetch me the sacrifice-axe!

[THE CHORUS *goes towards the
tomb of* CRESPHONTES, *and
their leader brings back the axe.*

O Husband, O clothed
1140 With the grave's everlasting,
All-covering darkness! O King,
Well-mourned, but ill-avenged!
Approv'st thou thy wife now?
The axe! – who brings it?

The Chorus
'Tis here!
1145 But thy gesture, thy look,
Appals me, shakes me with awe.

Merope
Thrust back now the bolt of that
door!

The Chorus
Alas! alas! –
Behold the fastenings withdrawn
1150 Of the guest-chamber door!
Ah! I beseech thee – with tears –

Merope
Throw the door open!

The Chorus
'Tis done! . . .
[*The door of the house is thrown
open: the interior of the guest-
chamber is discovered, with* ÆPY-
TUS *asleep on a couch.*

Merope
He sleeps – sleeps calm. O ye all-
seeing Gods!
Thus peacefully do ye let sinners
sleep,
1155 While troubled innocents toss,
and lie awake?
What sweeter sleep than this
could I desire
For thee, my child, if thou wert
yet alive?
How often have I dreamed of thee
like this,
With thy soiled hunting-coat, and
sandals torn,
1160 Asleep in the Arcadian glens at
noon,
Thy head drooped softly, and the
golden curls

1147–52 *and following stage direction.* Perhaps suggested by the servant's call to un-
bar the door and the subsequent discovery of the body of Aegisthus, Aeschylus's
Choephoroe 875 ff.

Clustering o'er thy white fore-
    head, like a girl's;
The short proud lip showing thy
    race, thy cheeks
Browned with thine open-air,
    free, hunter's life.
1165 Ah me!
And where dost thou sleep now,
    my innocent boy?
In some dark fir-tree's shadow,
    amid rocks
Untrodden, on Cyllenê's desolate
    side;
Where travellers never pass,
    where only come
1170 Wild beasts, and vultures sailing
    overhead.
There, there thou liest now, my
    hapless child!
Stretched among briars and
    stones, the slow, black gore
Oozing through thy soaked
    hunting-shirt, with limbs
Yet stark from the death-struggle,
    tight-clenched hands,
1175 And eyeballs staring for revenge
    in vain.
Ah miserable!
And thou, thou fair-skinned
    Serpent! thou art laid
In a rich chamber, on a happy
    bed,
In a king's house, thy victim's
    heritage;
1180 And drink'st untroubled slumber,
    to sleep off
The toils of thy foul service, till
    thou wake
Refreshed, and claim thy master's
    thanks and gold.
Wake up in hell from thine un-
    hallowed sleep,
Thou smiling Fiend, and claim
    thy guerdon there!
1185 Wake amid gloom, and howling,
    and the noise
Of sinners pinioned on the
    torturing wheel,
And the staunch Furies' never-
    silent scourge.
And bid the chief tormentors
    there provide
For a grand culprit shortly
    coming down.

1190 Go thou the first, and usher in thy
    lord!
A more just stroke than that thou
    gav'st my son
Take –
    [MEROPE *advances towards the*
    sleeping ÆPYTUS, *with the axe*
    uplifted. At the same moment
    ARCAS *re-enters.*

    Arcas (to the Chorus)
    Not with him to council did
    the King
Carry his messenger, but left him
    here.
    [*Sees* MEROPE *and* ÆPYTUS
O Gods! . . .

        Merope
        Foolish old man, thou
    spoil'st my blow!

        Arcas
What do I see? . . .

        Merope
1195   A murderer at death's door.
Therefore no words!

        Arcas
    A murderer? . . .

        Merope
        And a captive
To the dear next-of-kin of him he
    murdered.
Stand, and let vengeance pass!

        Arcas
        Hold, O Queen, hold!
Thou know'st not whom thou
    strik'st . . .

        Merope
    I know his crime.

        Arcas
Unhappy one! thou strik'st –

        Merope
1200   A most just blow.

        Arcas
No, by the Gods, thou slay'st —

1191–2. A.'s translation of a fragment of Euripides's *Cresphontes* – see *1858* Preface
(*Complete Prose Works* ed. *cit.* i 41) and *n.* to ll. 890–913 (p. 420 above).

Merope
Stand off!

Arcas
                    Thy son!

Merope
Ah! ...

[*She lets the axe drop, and falls insensible.*

Æpytus (awaking)
Who are these? What shrill,
    ear-piercing scream
Wakes me thus kindly from the
    perilous sleep
Wherewith fatigue and youth had
    bound mine eyes,
1205 Even in the deadly palace of my
    foe?
Arcas! Thou here!

Arcas (embracing him)
                    O my dear master! O
My child, my charge beloved,
    welcome to life!
As dead we held thee, mourned
    for thee as dead.

Æpytus
In word I died, that I in deed
    might live.
But who are these?

Arcas
1210   Messenian maidens, friends.

Æpytus
And, Arcas! – but I tremble!

Arcas
                    Boldly ask.

Æpytus
That black-robed, swooning
    figure? ...

Arcas
                    Merope.

Æpytus
O mother! mother!

Merope
Who upbraids me? Ah! ..
        [*seeing the axe.*

Æpytus
Upbraids thee? no one.

Merope
Thou dost well: but take ...

Æpytus
What wav'st thou off?

Merope
1215   That murderous axe away!

Æpytus
Thy son is here.

Merope
One said so, sure, but now.

Æpytus
Here, here thou hast him!

Merope
Slaughtered by this hand! ...

Æpytus
No, by the Gods, alive and like to
    live!

Merope
What, thou? – I dream –

Æpytus
May'st thou dream ever so!

Merope (advancing towards him)
My child? unhurt? ...

Æpytus
1220   Only by over joy.

Merope
Art thou, then, come? ...

Æpytus
                    Never to part again.

[*They fall into one another's arms.
Then* MEROPE, *holding* ÆPY-
TUS *by the hand, turns to* THE
CHORUS.

Merope
O kind Messenian maidens, O my
    friends,

1219–21. The recognition recalls Electra's recognition of Orestes, *Electra* 1222–6.

Bear witness, see, mark well, on
    what a head
My first stroke of revenge had
    nearly fallen!

The Chorus

1225 We see, dear mistress: and we say,
    the Gods,
As hitherto they kept him, keep
    him now.

Merope

O my son!   *str.*
I have, I have thee . . . the years
Fly back, my child! and thou
    seem'st
1230 Ne'er to have gone from these
    eyes,
Never been torn from this breast.

Æpytus

Mother, my heart runs over; but
    the time
Presses me, chides me, will not let
    me weep.

Merope

Fearest thou now?

Æpytus

1235 I fear not, but I think on my
    design.

Merope

At the undried fount of this breast,
A babe, thou smilest again.
Thy brothers play at my feet,
Early-slain innocents! near,
1240 Thy kind-speaking father stands.

Æpytus

Remember, to revenge his death I
    come!

Merope

Ah . . . revenge!   *ant.*
That word! it kills me! I see
Once more roll back on my house,
1245 Never to ebb, the accursed
All-flooding ocean of blood.

Æpytus

Mother, sometimes the justice of
    the Gods
Appoints the way to peace
    through shedding blood.

Merope

Sorrowful peace!

Æpytus

1250 And yet the only peace to us
    allowed.

Merope

From the first-wrought vengeance
    is born
A long succession of crimes.
Fresh blood flows, calling for
    blood.
Fathers, sons, grandsons, are all
1255 One death-dealing vengeful train.

Æpytus

Mother, thy fears are idle; for I
    come
To close an old wound, not to
    open new.
In all else willing to be taught, in
    this
Instruct me not; I have my lesson
    clear.
1260 Arcas, seek out my uncle Laias,
    now
Conferring in the city with our
    friends;
Here bring him, ere the king
    come back from council.
That, how to accomplish what
    the Gods enjoin,
And the slow-ripening time at last
    prepares,
1265 We two with thee, my mother,
    may consult;
For whose help dare I count on,
    if not thine?

Merope

Approves my brother Laias this
    intent?

Æpytus

Yes, and alone is with me here to
    share.

1251-2. Cp. Aeschylus's *Agamemnon* 758-60.

Merope
And what of thine Arcadian mate, who bears
1270 Suspicion from thy grandsire of thy death,
For whom, as I suppose, thou passest here?

Æpytus
Sworn to our plot he is; if false surmise
Fix him the author of my death, I know not.

Merope
Proof, not surmise, shows him in commerce close –

Æpytus
1275 With this Messenian tyrant – that I know.

Merope
And entertain'st thou, child, such dangerous friends?

Æpytus
This commerce for my best behoof he plies.

Merope
That thou may'st read thine enemy's counsel plain?

Æpytus
Too dear his secret wiles have cost our house.

Merope
1280 And of his unsure agent what demands he?

Æpytus
News of my business, pastime, temper, friends.

Merope
His messages, then, point not to thy murder?

Æpytus
Not yet, though such, no doubt, his final aim.

Merope
And what Arcadian helpers bring'st thou here?

Æpytus
1285 Laias alone; no errand mine for crowds.

Merope
On what relying, to crush such a foe?

Æpytus
One sudden stroke, and the Messenians' love.

Merope
O thou long-lost, long seen in dreams alone,
But now seen face to face, my only child!
1290 Why wilt thou fly to lose as soon as found
My new-won treasure, thy belovéd life?
Or how expectest not to lose, who com'st
With such slight means to cope with such a foe?
Thine enemy thou know'st not, nor his strength.
The stroke thou purposest is desperate, rash –
1295 Yet grant that it succeeds – thou hast behind
The stricken king a second enemy
Scarce dangerous less than him, the Dorian lords.
These are not now the savage band who erst
1300 Followed thy father from their northern hills,
Mere ruthless and uncounselled wolves of war,
Good to obey, without a leader nought.
Their chief hath trained them, made them like himself,
Sagacious, men of iron, watchful, firm,
1305 Against surprise and sudden panic proof.
Their master fall'n, these will not flinch, but band
To keep their master's power; thou wilt find
Behind his corpse their hedge of serried spears.
But, to match these, thou hast the people's love?

1310 On what a reed, my child, thou
        leanest there!
     Knowest thou not how timorous,
        how unsure,
     How useless an ally a people is
     Against the one and certain arm
        of power?
     Thy father perished in this
        people's cause,
1315 Perished before their eyes, yet no
        man stirred!
     For years, his widow, in their
        sight I stand,
     A never-changing index to
        revenge –
     What help, what vengeance, at
        their hands have I?
     At least, if thou wilt trust them,
        try them first.
1320 Against the King himself array
        the host
     Thou countest on to back thee
        'gainst his lords;
     First rally the Messenians to thy
        cause,
     Give them cohesion, purpose, and
        resolve,
     Marshal them to an army – then
        advance,
1325 Then try the issue; and not,
        rushing on
     Single and friendless, give to
        certain death
     That dear-beloved, that young,
        that gracious head.
     Be guided, O my son! spurn
        counsel not!
     For know thou this, a violent
        heart hath been
1330 Fatal to all the race of Heracles.

            The Chorus
     With sage experience she speaks;
        and thou,
     O Æpytus, weigh well her counsel
        given.

            Æpytus
     Ill counsel, in my judgment, gives
        she here,
     Maidens, and reads experience
        much amiss;
1335 Discrediting the succour which
        our cause

     Might from the people draw, if
        rightly used;
     Advising us a course which would,
        indeed,
     If followed, make their succour
        slack and null.
     A people is no army, trained to
        fight,
1340 A passive engine, at their
        general's will;
     And, if so used, proves, as thou
        say'st, unsure.
     A people, like a common man, is
        dull,
     Is lifeless, while its heart remains
        untouched;
     A fool can drive it, and a fly may
        scare.
1345 When it admires and loves, its
        heart awakes;
     Then irresistibly it lives, it works;
     A people, then, is an ally indeed –
     It is ten thousand fiery wills in
        one.
     Now I, if I invite them to run
        risk
1350 Of life for my advantage, and
        myself,
     Who chiefly profit, run no more
        than they –
     How shall I rouse their love, their
        ardour so?
     But, if some signal, unassisted
        stroke,
     Dealt at my own sole risk, before
        their eyes,
1355 Announces me their rightful
        prince returned –
     The undegenerate blood of
        Heracles –
     The daring claimant of a perilous
        throne –
     How might not such a sight as
        this revive
     Their loyal passion tow'rd my
        father's house,
1360 Kindle their hearts, make them
        no more a mob,
     A craven mob, but a devouring
        fire?
     Then might I use them, then, for
        one who thus
     Spares not himself, themselves
        they will not spare.

1360. 1858,
    Electrify their hearts? make them no more . . .

Haply, had but one daring soul
    stood forth
1365 To rally them and lead them to
    revenge,
When my great father fell, they
    had replied!
Alas! our foe alone stood forward
    then.
And thou, my mother, hadst thou
    made a sign –
Hadst thou, from thy forlorn and
    captive state
1370 Of widowhood in these polluted
    halls,
Thy prison-house, raised one
    imploring cry –
Who knows but that avengers
    thou hadst found?
But mute thou sat'st, and each
    Messenian heart
In thy despondency desponded
    too.
1375 Enough of this! – Though not a
    finger stir
To succour me in my extremest
    need;
Though all free spirits in this land
    were dead,
And only slaves and tyrants left
    alive;
Yet for me, mother, I had liefer
    die
1380 On native ground, than drag the
    tedious hours
Of a protected exile any more.
Hate, duty, interest, passion call
    one way;
Here stand I now, and the
    attempt shall be.

The Chorus
Prudence is on the other side; but
    deeds
1385 Condemned by prudence have
    sometimes gone well.

Merope
Not till the ways of prudence all
    are tried,
And tried in vain, the turn of
    rashness comes.
Thou leapest to thy deed, and
    hast not asked
Thy kinsfolk and thy father's
    friends for aid.

Æpytus
1390 And to what friends should I for
    aid apply?

Merope
The royal race of Temenus, in
    Argos –

Æpytus
That house, like ours, intestine
    murder maims.

Merope
Thy Spartan cousins, Procles and
    his brother –

Æpytus
Love a won cause, but not a
    cause to win.

Merope
1395 My father, then, and his Arcadian
    chiefs –

Æpytus
Mean still to keep aloof from
    Dorian broil.

Merope
Wait, then, until sufficient help
    appears.

Æpytus
Orestes in Mycenæ had no more.

Merope
He to fulfil an order raised his
    hand.

Æpytus
1400 What order more precise had he
    than I?

Merope
Apollo pealed it from his
    Delphian cave.

Æpytus
A mother's murder needed hest
    divine.

Merope
He had a hest, at least, and thou
    hast none.

Æpytus
The Gods command not where
    the heart speaks clear.

Merope

1405 Thou wilt destroy, I see, thyself
       and us.

Æpytus

O suffering! O calamity! how
    ten,
How twentyfold worse are ye,
    when your blows
Not only wound the sense, but
    kill the soul,
The noble thought, which is
    alone the man!
1410 That I, to-day returning, find
       myself
Orphaned of both my parents –
    by his foes
My father, by your strokes my
    mother slain!
For this is not my mother, who
    dissuades,
At the dread altar of her hus-
    band's tomb,
1415 His son from vengeance on his
       murderer;
And not alone dissuades him, but
    compares
His just revenge to an unnatural
    deed,
A deed so awful, that the general
    tongue
Fluent of horrors, falters to relate
    it –
1420 Of darkness so tremendous, that
       its author,
Though to his act empowered,
    nay, impelled,
By the oracular sentence of the
    Gods,
Fled, for years after, o'er the face
    of earth,
A frenzied wanderer, a God-
    driven man,
1425 And hardly yet, some say, hath
       found a grave –
With such a deed as *this* thou
    matchest mine,
Which Nature sanctions, which
    the innocent blood
Clamours to find fulfilled, which
    good men praise,
And only bad men joy to see
    undone!
1430 O honoured father! hide thee in
       thy grave
Deep as thou canst, for hence no
    succour comes;

Since from thy faithful subjects
    what revenge
Canst thou expect, when thus thy
    widow fails?
Alas! an adamantine strength
    indeed,
1435 Past expectation, hath thy
       murderer built;
For this is the true strength of
    guilty kings,
When they corrupt the souls of
    those they rule.

The Chorus

Zeal makes him most unjust; but,
    in good time,
Here, as I guess, the noble Laias
    comes.

Laias

1440 Break off, break off your talking,
       and depart
Each to his post, where the
    occasion calls;
Lest from the council-chamber
    presently
The King return, and find you
    prating here.
A time will come for greetings;
    but to-day
1445 The hour for words is gone, is
       come for deeds.

Æpytus

O princely Laias! to what
    purpose calls
The occasion, if our chief
    confederate fails?
My mother stands aloof, and
    blames our deed.

Laias

My royal sister? . . . but, without
    some cause,
1450 I know, she honours not the dead
       so ill.

Merope

Brother, it seems thy sister must
    present,
At this first meeting after absence
    long,
Not welcome, exculpation to her
    kin;
Yet exculpation needs it, if I seek,
1455 A woman and a mother, to avert
       Risk from ny new-restored, my
       only son?

Sometimes, when he was gone, I
  wished him back,
Risk what he might; now that I
  have him here,
Now that I feed mine eyes on that
  young face,
1460 Hear that fresh voice, and clasp
  that gold-locked head,
I shudder, Laias, to commit my
  child
To murder's dread arena, where I
  saw
His father and his ill-starred
  brethren fall!
I loathe for him the slippery way
  of blood;
1465 I ask if bloodless means may gain
  his end.
In me the fever of revengeful hate,
Passion's first furious longing to
  imbrue
Our own right hand in the detested blood
Of enemies, and count their
  dying groans –
1470 If in this feeble bosom such a fire
Did ever burn – is long by time
  allayed,
And I would now have Justice
  strike, not me.
Besides – for from my brother and
  my son
I hide not even this – the reverence deep,
1475 Remorseful, tow'rd my hostile
  solitude,
By Polyphontes never failed-in
  once
Through twenty years; his
  mournful anxious zeal
To efface me in the memory of
  his crime –
Though it efface not that, yet
  makes me wish
1480 His death a public, not a personal
  act,
Treacherously plotted 'twixt my
  son and me;
To whom this day he came to
  proffer peace,
Treaty, and to this kingdom for
  my son
Heirship, with fair intent, as I
  believe.
1485 For that he plots thy death,
  account it false;

           [*to* ÆPYTUS.
Number it with the thousand
  rumours vain,
Figments of plots, wherewith
  intriguers fill
The enforcéd leisure of an exile's
  ear.
Immersed in serious state-craft is
  the King,
1490 Bent above all to pacify, to rule,
Rigidly, yet in settled calm, this
  realm;
Not prone, all say, averse to
  bloodshed now.
So much is due to truth, even
  tow'rds our foe.
           [*to* LAIAS.
Do I, then, give to usurpation
  grace,
1495 And from his natural rights my
  son debar?
Not so! let him – and none shall
  be more prompt
Than I to help – raise his
  Messenian friends;
Let him fetch succours from
  Arcadia, gain
His Argive or his Spartan
  cousins' aid;
1500 Let him do this, do aught but
  recommence
Murder's uncertain, secret,
  perilous game –
And I, when to his righteous
  standard down
Flies Victory winged, and Justice
  raises *then*
Her sword, will be the first to bid
  it fall.
1505 If, haply, at this moment, such
  attempt
Promise not fair, let him a little
  while
Have faith, and trust the future
  and the Gods.
He may; for never did the Gods
  allow
Fast permanence to an ill-gotten
  throne.
1510 These are but woman's words –
  yet, Laias, thou
Despise them not! for, brother,
  thou and I
Were not among the feuds of
  warrior-chiefs,
Each sovereign for his dear-
  bought hour, born;

But in the pastoral Arcadia reared,
1515 With Cypselus our father, where we saw
The simple patriarchal state of kings,
Where sire to son transmits the unquestioned crown,
Unhacked, unsmirched, un-bloodied, and have learnt
That spotless hands unshaken sceptres hold.
1520 Having learnt this, then, use thy knowledge now.

The Chorus
Which way to lean I know not: bloody strokes
Are never free from doubt, though sometimes due.

Laias
O Merope, the common heart of man
Agrees to deem some deeds so dark in guilt,
1525 That neither gratitude, nor tie of race,
Womanly pity, nor maternal fear,
Nor any pleader else, shall be indulged
To breathe a syllable to bar revenge.
All this, no doubt, thou to thyself hast urged –
1530 Time presses, so that theme forbear I now;
Direct to thy dissuasions I reply.
Blood-founded thrones, thou say'st, are insecure;
Our father's kingdom, because pure, is safe.
True; but what cause to our Arcadia gives
1535 Its privileged immunity from blood,
But that, since first the black and fruitful Earth
In the primeval mountain-forests bore
Pelasgus, our forefather and mankind's,
Legitimately sire to son, with us,
1540 Bequeathes the allegiance of our shepherd-tribes,
More loyal, as our line continues more?

How can your Heracleidan chiefs inspire
This awe which guards our earth-sprung, lineal kings?
What permanence, what stability like ours,
1545 Whether blood flows or no, can yet invest
The broken order of your Dorian thrones,
Fixed yesterday, and ten times changed since then?
Two brothers, and their orphan nephews, strove
For the three conquered king-doms of this isle;
1550 The eldest, mightiest brother, Temenus, took
Argos; a juggle to Cresphontes gave
Messenia; to those helpless Boys, the lot
Worst of the three, the stony Sparta, fell.
August, indeed, was the found-ation here!
1555 What followed? His most trusted kinsman slew
Cresphontes in Messenia; Temenus
Perished in Argos by his jealous sons;
The Spartan Brothers with their guardian strive.
Can houses thus ill-seated, thus embroiled,
1560 Thus little founded in their subjects' love,
Practise the indulgent, bloodless policy
Of dynasties long-fixed, and honoured long?
No! Vigour and severity must chain
Popular reverence to these recent lines.
1565 Be their first-founded order strict maintained –
Their murdered rulers terribly avenged –
Ruthlessly their rebellious subjects crushed!
Since policy bids thus, what fouler death
Than thine illustrious husband's to avenge

1570 Shall we select? than Polyphontes,
    what
  More daring and more grand
    offender find?
  Justice, my sister, long demands
    this blow,
  And Wisdom, now thou see'st,
    demands it too.
  To strike it, then, dissuade thy
    son no more;
1575 For to live disobedient to these
    two,
  Justice and Wisdom, is no life at
    all.

The Chorus

  The Gods, O mistress dear! the
    hard-souled man,
  Who spared not others, bid not us
    to spare.

Merope

  Alas! against my brother, son,
    and friends,
1580 One, and a woman, how can I
    prevail?
  O brother, thou hast conquered;
    yet, I fear!
  Son! with a doubting heart thy
    mother yields;
  May it turn happier than my
    doubts portend!

Laias

  Meantime on thee the task of
    silence only
1585 Shall be imposed; to us shall be
    the deed.
  Now, not another word, but to
    our act!
  Nephew! thy friends are sounded,
    and prove true.
  Thy father's murderer, in the
    public place,
  Performs, this noon, a solemn
    sacrifice;
1590 Be with him – choose the moment
    – strike thy blow!
  If prudence counsels thee to go
    unarmed,

  The sacrificer's axe will serve thy
    turn.
  To me and the Messenians leave
    the rest,
  With the Gods' aid – and, if they
    give but aid
1595 As our just cause deserves, I do
    not fear.

[ÆPYTUS, LAIAS, *and* ARCAS
go out.

The Chorus

O Son and Mother,   *str.* 1.
Whom the Gods o'ershadow,
In dangerous trial,
With certainty of favour!
1600 As erst they shadowed
Your race's founders
From irretrievable woe;
When the seed of Lycaon
Lay forlorn, lay outcast,
1605 Callisto and her Boy.

What deep-grassed meadow
At the meeting valleys –   [*ant.* 1.
Where clear-flowing Ladon,
Most beautiful of waters,
1610 Receives the river
Whose trout are vocal,
The Aroanian stream –
Without home, without mother,
Hid the babe, hid Arcas,
1615 The nursling of the dells?

But the sweet-smelling myrtle,
    [*str.* 2.
And the pink-flowered oleander,
And the green agnus-castus,
To the west-wind's murmur,
1620 Rustled round his cradle:
And Maia reared him.
Then, a boy, he startled,
In the snow-filled hollows
Of high Cyllenê,
1625 The white mountain-birds;
Or surprised, in the glens,
The basking tortoises,
Whose striped shell founded
In the hand of Hermes
1630 The glory of the lyre.

1600–78. Callisto and Arcas are the legendary maternal ancestors of Aepytus. Merope's attempt to slay her son when she fails to recognize him asleep parallels Arcas's attempt to kill his mother when he fails to recognize her in the form of a mountain-bear.

1611. A detail from Pausanias, *Description of Greece* viii 21 (2).

But his mother, Callisto,   *ant.* 2.
In her hiding-place of the
    thickets
Of the lentisk and ilex,
In her rough form, fearing
1635 The hunter on the outlook,
Poor changeling! trembled.
Or the children, plucking
In the thorn-choked gullies
Wild gooseberries, scared her,
1640 The shy mountain-bear!
Or the shepherds, on slopes
With pale-spiked lavender
And crisp thyme tufted,
Came upon her, stealing
1645 At day-break through the dew.

Once, 'mid those gorges,   *str.* 3.
Spray-drizzled, lonely,
Unclimbed of man –
O'er whose cliffs the townsmen
1650 Of crag-perched Nonacris
Behold in summer
The slender torrent
Of Styx come dancing,
A wind-blown thread –
1655 By the precipices of Khelmos,
The fleet, desperate hunter,
The youthful Arcas, born of Zeus,
His fleeing mother,
Transformed Callisto,
1660 Unwitting followed –
And raised his spear.

Turning, with piteous,   *ant.* 3.
Distressful longing,
Sad, eager eyes,
1665 Mutely she regarded
Her well-known enemy.
Low moans half uttered
What speech refused her;
Tears coursed, tears human,
1670 Down those disfigured,
Once human cheeks.
With unutterable foreboding
Her son, heart-stricken, eyed her.
The Gods had pity, made them
    Stars.
1675 Stars now they sparkle
In the northern Heaven –
The guard Arcturus,
The guard-watched Bear.

So, o'er thee and thy child,   *epode.*
1680 Some God, Merope, now,
In dangerous hour, stretches his
    hand.

So, like a star, dawns thy son,
Radiant with fortune and joy.
              [POLYPHONTES *comes in.*

Polyphontes

O Merope, the trouble on thy
    face
1685 Tells me enough thou know'st the
    news which all
Messenia speaks! the prince, thy
    son, is dead.
Not from my lips should consol-
    ation fall;
To offer that, I come not; but to
    urge,
Even after news of this sad death,
    our league.
1690 Yes, once again I come; I will not
    take
This morning's angry answer for
    thy last.
To the Messenian kingdom thou
    and I
Are the sole claimants left; what
    cause of strife
Lay in thy son is buried in his
    grave.
1695 Most honourably I meant, I call
    the Gods
To witness, offering him return
    and power;
Yet, had he lived, suspicion,
    jealousy,
Inevitably had surged up,
    perhaps,
'Twixt thee and me – suspicion,
    that I nursed
1700 Some ill design against him;
    jealousy,
That he enjoyed but part, being
    heir to all.
And he himself, with the
    impetuous heart
Of youth, 'tis like, had never
    quite forgone
The thought of vengeance on me,
    never quite
1705 Unclosed his itching fingers from
    his sword.
But thou, O Merope, though
    deeply wronged,
Though injured past forgiveness,
    as men deem,
Yet hast been long at school with
    thoughtful time,
And from that teacher may'st
    have learned, like me,

1710 That all may be endured, and all
               forgiv'n –
           Have learned, that we must
               sacrifice the bent
           Of personal feeling to the public
               weal –
           Have learned, that there are
               guilty deeds, which leave
           The hand that does them
               guiltless; in a word,
1715 That kings live for their peoples,
               not themselves.
           This having known, let us a union
               found
           (For the last time I ask, ask
               earnestly)
           Based on pure public welfare; let
               us be
           Not Merope and Polyphontes,
               foes
1720 Blood-severed, but Messenia's
               King and Queen!
           Let us forget ourselves for those
               we rule!
           Speak! I go hence to offer
               sacrifice
           To the Preserver Zeus; let me
               return
           Thanks to him for our amity as
               well.

Merope
1725 Oh hadst thou, Polyphontes, still
               but kept
           The silence thou hast kept for
               twenty years!

Polyphontes
           Henceforth, if what I urge dis-
               please, I may.
           But fair proposal merits fair reply.

Merope
           And thou shalt have it! Yes,
               because thou *hast*
1730 For twenty years forborne to
               interrupt
           The solitude of her whom thou
               hast wronged –
           That scanty grace shall earn thee
               this reply.
           First, for our union. Trust me,
               'twixt us two

           The brazen-footed Fury ever
               stalks,
1735 Waving her hundred hands, a
               torch in each,
           Aglow with angry fire, to keep us
               twain.
           Now, for thyself. Thou com'st
               with well-cloaked joy,
           To announce the ruin of my
               husband's house,
           To sound thy triumph in his
               widow's ears,
1740 To bid her share thine unen-
               dangered throne.
           To this thou would'st have
               answer. Take it: Fly! ...
           Cut short thy triumph, seeming
               at its height;
           Fling off thy crown, supposed at
               last secure;
           Forsake this ample, proud
               Messenian realm;
1745 To some small, humble, and
               unnoted strand,
           Some rock more lonely than that
               Lemnian isle
           Where Philoctetes pined, take
               ship and flee!
           Some solitude more inaccessible
           Than the ice-bastioned Caucasian
               Mount
1750 Chosen a prison for Prometheus,
               climb!
           There in unvoiced oblivion sink
               thy name,
           And bid the sun, thine only
               visitant,
           Divulge not to the far-off world
               of men
           What once-famed wretch he
               there did espy hid.
1755 There nurse a late remorse, and
               thank the Gods,
           And thank thy bitterest foe, that,
               having lost
           All things but life, thou lose not
               life as well.

Polyphontes
           What mad bewilderment of grief
               is this?

Merope
           Thou art bewildered; the sane
               head is mine.

1734. The brazen-footed Fury] Sophoclean—see *Electra* 491.

Polyphontes
1760 I pity thee, and wish thee calmer
mind.

Merope
Pity thyself; none needs
compassion more.

Polyphontes
Yet, oh! could'st thou but act as
reason bids!

Merope
And in my turn I wish the same
for thee.

Polyphontes
All I could do to soothe thee has
been tried.

Merope
1765 For that, in this my warning,
thou art paid.

Polyphontes
Know'st thou then aught, that
thus thou sound'st the alarm?

Merope
Thy crime! that were enough to
make one fear.

Polyphontes
My deed is of old date, and long
atoned.

Merope
Atoned this very day, perhaps, it
is.

Polyphontes
1770 My final victory proves the Gods
appeased.

Merope
O victor, victor, trip not at the
goal!

Polyphontes
Hatred and passionate envy
blind thine eyes.

Merope
O Heaven-abandoned wretch,
that envies thee!

Polyphontes
Thou hold'st so cheap, then, the
Messenian crown?

Merope
1775 I think on what the future hath in
store.

Polyphontes
To-day I reign; the rest I leave to
Fate.

Merope
For Fate thou wait'st not long;
since, in this hour –

Polyphontes
What? for so far Fate hath not
proved my foe –

Merope
Fate seals my lips, and drags to
ruin thee.

Polyphontes
1780 Enough! enough! I will no longer
hear
The ill-boding note which frantic
hatred sounds
To affright a fortune which the
Gods secure.
Once more my friendship thou
rejectest; well!
More for this land's sake grieve I,
than mine own.
1785 I chafe not with thee, that thy
hate endures,
Nor bend myself too low, to make
it yield.
What I have done is done; by my
own deed,
Neither exulting nor ashamed, I
stand.
Why should this heart of mine set
mighty store
1790 By the construction and report of
men?
Not men's good word hath made
me what I am.
Alone I mastered power; and
alone,
Since so thou wilt, I dare
maintain it still.

[POLYPHONTES *goes out.*

The Chorus

Did I then waver   *str.* 1.
1795 (O woman's judgment!)
Misled by seeming
Success of crime?
And ask, if sometimes
The Gods, perhaps, allowed you,
1800 O lawless daring of the strong,
O self-will recklessly indulged?

Not time, not lightning,   *ant.* 1.
Not rain, not thunder,
Efface the endless
1805 Decrees of Heaven –
Make Justice alter,
Revoke, assuage her sentence,
Which dooms dread ends to
     dreadful deeds,
And violent deaths to violent
     men.

1810 But the signal example   *str.* 2.
Of invariableness of justice
Our glorious founder
Heracles gave us,
Son loved of Zeus his father – for
     he sinned,

1815 And the strand of Euboea,   *ant.* 2.
And the promontory of Cenæum,
His painful, solemn
Punishment witnessed,
Beheld his expiation – for he died.

1820 O villages of Œta   *str.* 3
With hedges of the wild rose!
O pastures of the mountain,
Of short grass, beaded with dew,
Between the pine-woods and the
     cliffs!
1825 O cliffs, left by the eagles,
On that morn, when the smoke-
     cloud
From the oak-built, fiercely-
     burning pyre,
Up the precipices of Trachis,
Drove them screaming from their
     eyries!
1830 A willing, a willing sacrifice on
     that day

Ye witnessed, ye mountain lawns,
When the shirt-wrapped, poison-
     blistered Hero
Ascended, with undaunted heart,
Living, his own funeral-pile,
1835 And stood, shouting for a fiery
     torch;
And the kind, chance-arrived
     Wanderer,
The inheritor of the bow,
Coming swiftly through the sad
     Trachinians,
Put the torch to the pile,
1840 That the flame towered on high
     ⹁ to the Heaven;
Bearing with it, to Olympus,
To the side of Hebe,
To immortal delight,
The labour-released Hero.

1845 O heritage of Neleus,   *ant.* 3.
Ill-kept by his infirm heirs!
O kingdom of Messenê,
Of rich soil, chosen by craft,
Possessed in hatred, lost in blood!
1850 O town, high Stenyclaros,
With new walls, which the victors
From the four-towned, mountain-
     shadowed Doris,
For their Heracles-issued princes
Built in strength against the
     vanquished!
1855 Another, another sacrifice on this
     day
Ye witness, ye new-built towers!
When the white-robed, garland-
     crowned Monarch
Approaches, with undoubting
     heart,
Living, his own sacrifice-block,
1860 And stands, shouting for a
     slaughterous axe;
And the stern, destiny-brought
     Stranger,
The inheritor of the realm,
Coming swiftly through the
     jocund Dorians,
Drives the axe to its goal.
1865 That the blood rushes in streams
     to the dust;

1810–44. Aepytus traces his descent from Hercules on his father's side.
1836. 'Poias, the father of Philoctetes. Passing near, he was attracted by the concourse round the pyre, and at the entreaty of Hercules set fire to it, receiving the
bow and arrows of the hero as his reward.' A.'s note first added 1885 (when he
removed the account of Hercules's death from the Story of the Drama).

Bearing with it, to Erinnys,
To the Gods of Hades,
To the dead unavenged,
The fiercely-required Victim.

1870 Knowing he did it, unknowing
          pays for it.   *epode.*
      Unknowing, unknowing,
      Thinking atoned-for
      Deeds unatonable,
      Thinking appeased
1875 Gods unappeasable,
      Lo, the ill-fated one,
      Standing for harbour
      Right at the harbour-mouth
      Strikes with all sail set
1880 Full on the sharp-pointed
      Needle of ruin!
              [*A* MESSENGER *comes in.*

                  Messenger
      O honoured Queen, O faithful
          followers
      Of your dead master's line, I
          bring you news
      To make the gates of this long-
          mournful house
1885 Leap, and fly open of themselves
          for joy.
              [*noise and shouting heard.*
      Hark how the shouting crowds
          tramp hitherward
      With glad acclaim! Ere they
          forestall my news,
      Accept it: – Polyphontes is no
          more.

                   Merope
      Is my son safe? that question
          bounds my care.

                  Messenger
1890 He is, and by the people hailed
          for king.

                   Merope
      The rest to me is little; yet, since
          that
      Must from some mouth be heard,
          relate it thou.

                  Messenger
      Not little, if thou saw'st what
          love, what zeal,

At thy dead husband's name the
    people show.
1895 For when this morning in the
    public square
I took my stand, and saw the
    unarmed crowds
Of citizens in holiday attire,
Women and children intermixed;
    and then,
Grouped round Zeus's altar, all
    in arms,
1900 Serried and grim, the ring of
    Dorian lords –
I trembled for our prince and his
    attempt.
Silence and expectation held us
    all;
Till presently the King came
    forth, in robe
Of sacrifice, his guards clearing
    the way
1905 Before him – at his side, the
    prince, thy son,
Unarmed and travel-soiled, just
    as he was.
With him conferring the King
    slowly reached
The altar in the middle of the
    square,
Where, by the sacrificing
    minister,
1910 The flower-dressed victim stood –
    a milk-white bull,
Swaying from side to side his
    massy head
With short impatient lowings.
    There he stopped,
And seemed to muse awhile, then
    raised his eyes
To heaven, and laid his hand
    upon the steer,
1915 And cried: *O Zeus, let what blood-
    guiltiness*
*Yet stains our land be by this blood
    washed out,*
*And grant henceforth to the Messen-
    ians peace!*
That moment, while with up-
    turned eyes he prayed,
The prince snatched from the
    sacrificer's hand
1920 The axe, and on the forehead of
    the King,
Where twines the chaplet, dealt
    a mighty blow

1876–81. An echo of Aeschylus's *Agamemnon* 1005–7.

Which felled him to the earth,
     and o'er him stood,
And shouted: *Since by thee defile-
     ment came,*
*What blood so meet as thine to wash it
     out?*
1925 *What hand to strike thee meet as mine,
     the hand*
*Of Æpytus, thy murdered master's
     son?*
But, gazing at him from the
     ground, the King . . .
Is it, then, thou? he murmured;
     and with that,
He bowed his head, and deeply
     groaned, and died.
1930 Till then we all seemed stone, but
     then a cry
Broke from the Dorian lords;
     forward they rushed
To circle the prince round – when
     suddenly
Laias in arms sprang to his
     nephew's side,
Crying: *O ye Messenians, will ye
     leave*
1935 *The son to perish as ye left the sire?*
And from that moment I saw
     nothing clear;
For from all sides a deluge, as it
     seemed
Burst o'er the altar and the
     Dorian lords,
Of holiday-clad citizens trans-
     formed
1940 To arméd warriors; I heard
     vengeful cries,
I heard the clash of weapons;
     then I saw
The Dorians lying dead, thy son
     hailed king.
And, truly, one who sees, what
     seemed so strong,
The power of this tyrant and his
     lords,
1945 Melt like a passing smoke, a
     nightly dream,
At one bold word, one enterpris-
     ing blow –
Might ask, why we endured their
     yoke so long;
But that we know how every
     perilous feat
Of daring, easy as it seems when
     done,
1950 Is easy at no moment but the
     right.

The Chorus

Thou speakest well; but here, to
     give our eyes
Authentic proof of what thou
     tell'st our ears,
The conquerors, with the King's
     dead body, come.

[Æpytus, Laias, *and* Arcas
come in with the dead body of
Polyphontes, *followed by a
crowd of the* Messenians.

Laias

Sister, from this day forth thou
     art no more
1955 The widow of a husband
     unavenged,
The anxious mother of an exiled
     son.
Thine enemy is slain, thy son is
     king!
Rejoice with us! and trust me,
     he who wished
Welfare to the Messenian state,
     and calm,
1960 Could find no way to found them
     sure as this.

Æpytus

Mother, all these approve me;
     but if thou
Approve not too, I have but half
     my joy.

Merope

O Æpytus, my son, behold,
     behold
This iron man, my enemy and
     thine,
1965 This politic sovereign, lying at our
     feet,
With blood-bespattered robes,
     and chaplet shorn!
Inscrutable as ever, see, it keeps
Its sombre aspect of majestic care,
Of solitary thought, unshared
     resolve,
1970 Even in death, that countenance
     austere!
So looked he, when to Stenyclaros
     first,
A new-made wife, I from Arcadia
     came,
And found him at my husband's
     side, his friend,

His kinsman, his right hand in
    peace and war,
1975 Unsparing in his service of his
    toil,
His blood – to me, for I confess it,
    kind;
So looked he in that dreadful day
    of death;
So, when he pleaded for our
    league but now.
What meantest thou, O Poly-
    phontes, what
1980 Desired'st thou, what truly
    spurred thee on?
Was policy of state, the ascend-
    ancy
Of the Heracleidan conquerors,
    as thou said'st,
Indeed thy lifelong passion and
    sole aim?
Or didst thou but, as cautious
    schemers use,
1985 Cloak thine ambition with these
    specious words?
I know not; just, in either case,
    the stroke
Which laid thee low, for blood
    requires blood;
But yet, not knowing this, I
    triumph not
Over thy corpse – triumph not,
    neither mourn –
1990 For I find worth in thee, and
    badness too.
What mood of spirit, therefore,
    shall we call
The true one of a man – what
    way of life
His fixed condition and perpetual
    walk?
None, since a twofold colour
    reigns in all.
1995 But thou, my son, study to make
    prevail
One colour in thy life, the hue of
    truth;
That justice, that sage order, not
    alone
Natural vengeance, may main-
    tain thine act,
And make it stand indeed the will
    of Heaven.

2000 Thy father's passion was this
    people's ease,
This people's anarchy, thy foe's
    pretence.
As the chiefs rule, my son, the
    people are.
Unhappy people, where the
    chiefs themselves
Are, like the mob, vicious and
    ignorant!
2005 So rule, that even thine enemies
    may fail
To find in thee a fault whereon to
    found,
Of tyrannous harshness, or
    remissness weak –
So rule, that as thy father thou be
    loved!
So rule, that as his foe thou be
    obeyed!
2010 Take these, my son, over thine
    enemy's corpse
Thy mother's prayers! and this
    prayer last of all:
That even in thy victory thou
    show,
Mortal, the moderation of a man.

Æpytus

O mother, my best diligence shall
    be
2015 In all by thy experience to be
    ruled
Where my own youth falls short!
    But Laias, now,
First work after such victory, let
    us go
To render to my true Messenians
    thanks,
To the Gods grateful sacrifice;
    and then,
2020 Assume the ensigns of my father's
    power.

The Chorus

Son of Cresphontes, past what
    perils
Com'st thou, guided safe, to thy
    home!
What things daring! what
    enduring!
And all this by the will of the
    Gods.

2021–3. Cp. *Electra* 1508–10.
2024. A.'s version of the last line (l. 1278) of Sophocles's *Trachiniae*.

87 Rugby Chapel

NOVEMBER, 1857

Exact period of composition unknown, but Nov. 1857–(?) *c.* May 1860: the title shows when the poem was conceived or begun; the resemblance in idea of ll. 153 ff. to 'The Lord's Messengers', which was written by May 1860 (see headn., p. 452 below), may imply that 'Rugby Chapel' was completed about the same time; A.'s letter to his mother 8 Aug. 1867 establishes that there was an interval between composition and publication, 'I knew ... that the Rugby Chapel Poem would give you pleasure: often and often it had been in my mind to say it to you' (*CL* 164). A. visited Rugby Nov. 1855 and 1856, but is not known to have been there in Nov. 1857: the date probably indicates a reading of *Tom Brown's Schooldays* (which was published April 1857, celebrates Dr. Arnold as a Carlylean 'Hero', and is a possible source of 'The Lord's Messengers'). A.'s statement in his letter 8 Aug. 1867 (already quoted above), 'It was Fitzjames Stephen's thesis, maintained in the Edinburgh Review, of Papa's being a narrow bustling fanatic, which moved me first to the poem' (*CL* 164) suggests that in recollection A. ran together two close and related events, i.e. his reading of T. Hughes's novel in Nov. 1857 and his reaction to Stephen's review of it in Jan. 1858 (*Edinburgh Review* cvii 172–93). The view of Dr. A. expressed in 'Rugby Chapel' was not, however, a response to the views of Hughes or Stephen, but had been formed earlier – see A.'s letter to his mother 27 Feb. 1855, 'But this is just what makes him great – that he was not only a good man saving his soul by righteousness, but that he carried so many others along with him in his hand, and saved them ... along with himself' (*L* i 42). The MS. in Yale Papers, a fair copy with a few variants from *1867*, is not in my opinion in A.'s hand.

For the poetic pattern that the elegy shares with 'Haworth Churchyard' and 'Heine's Grave' see headn. to the former (p. 390 above); for a note on the metre, headn. to 'The Youth of Nature' (p. 245 above).

Published *1867*; reprinted (*1868*), *1869*, etc.

> Coldly, sadly descends
> The autumn-evening. The field
> Strewn with its dank yellow drifts
> Of withered leaves, and the elms,

¶ 87. *1–13*. See headn. above for the visits to Rugby in 1855 and 1856 which may have contributed to these lines, but A. is probably recalling his own schooldays – cp. his letter to his brother Tom Dec. 1886, 'What a long way back it is to the school field at this season, and the withered elm leaves, and the footballs kicking about, and the November dimness over everything' (W. T. Arnold's 'Thomas Arnold the Younger', *Century Magazine* i (1903) 118).

5   Fade into dimness apace,
       Silent; hardly a shout—
       From a few boys late at their play!
       The lights come out in the street,
       In the school-room windows; but cold,
10   Solemn, unlighted, austere,
       Through the gathering darkness, arise
       The chapel-walls, in whose bound
       Thou, my father! art laid.

       There thou dost lie, in the gloom
15   Of the autumn evening. But ah!
       That word, *gloom*, to my mind
       Brings thee back, in the light
       Of thy radiant vigour, again;
       In the gloom of November we passed
20   Days not dark at thy side;
       Seasons impaired not the ray
       Of thy buoyant cheerfulness clear.
       Such thou wast! and I stand
       In the autumn evening, and think
25   Of bygone autumns with thee.

       Fifteen years have gone round
       Since thou arosest to tread,
       In the summer-morning, the road
       Of death, at a call unforeseen,
30   Sudden. For fifteen years,
       We who till then in thy shade
       Rested as under the boughs
       Of a mighty oak, have endured
       Sunshine and rain as we might,
35   Bare, unshaded, alone,
       Lacking the shelter of thee.

10. Similar groups of three epithets are found at ll. 35, 43, 139, 158, 160 below.

12–13. Dr. Arnold died 12 June and was buried in the school chapel at Rugby 17 June 1842.

14–22. The triple repetition of 'gloom' emphasizes the contrast with 'the light / Of thy radiant vigour', a phrase which is meant to be recalled at l. 191 below.

20. not dark] not of gloom MS., *1867–9.*

22. buoyant cheerfulness clear] Miltonic positioning of the adjectives. Cp. ll. 41, 70 below and also 'Dover Beach' 13, 28 (pp. 241, 242 above).

O strong soul, by what shore
Tarriest thou now? For that force,
Surely, has not been left vain!
40   Somewhere, surely, afar,
In the sounding labour-house vast
Of being, is practised that strength,
Zealous, beneficent, firm!

Yes, in some far-shining sphere,
45   Conscious or not of the past,
Still thou performest the word
Of the Spirit in whom thou dost live –
Prompt, unwearied, as here!
Still thou upraisest with zeal
50   The humble good from the ground,
Sternly repressest the bad!
Still, like a trumpet, dost rouse
Those who with half-open eyes
Tread the border-land dim
55   'Twixt vice and virtue; reviv'st,
Succourest! – this was thy work,
This was thy life upon earth.

37—43. A.'s intimations of immortality are always offered tentatively. Cp.
his attempt to console his sister 'K' (on the death of her father-in-law)
27 Feb. 1854, 'However, with them [the pure of heart] one feels – even I
feel – that for their purity's sake . . . they shall undoubtedly, in some sense
or other, see God' (*L* i 33); and see also *n.* to 'Immortality' 9–14 (p. 488
below), where A. entertains the idea of conditional survival.
41. sounding labour-house vast] Cp. 'Haworth Churchyard' 136 (p. 397
above),

> In the never idle workshop of nature . . .

and see *n.* to 'Haworth Churchyard' 135–7 for the passage of *Obermann*
echoed both there and here.
47. The phrase is capable of an orthodox Christian sense as an echo of *Acts*
xvii 28, 'For in him we live, and move, and have our being . . .', but cp.
'Heine's Grave' 214–17 (p. 478 below),

> What are we all, but a mood,
> A single mood, of the life
> Of the Spirit in whom we exist,
> Who alone is all things in one?

and *n.* to ll. 206–21 (also p. 478 below).

What is the course of the life
Of mortal men on the earth?
60   Most men eddy about
Here and there – eat and drink,
Chatter and love and hate,
Gather and squander, are raised
Aloft, are hurled in the dust,
65   Striving blindly, achieving
Nothing; and then they die –
Perish; and no one asks
Who or what they have been,
More than he asks what waves,
70   In the moonlit solitudes mild
Of the midmost Ocean, have swelled,
Foamed for a moment, and gone.

58–68. Cp. 'Epilogue to Lessing's Laocoön 169–70 (p. 514 below),

> *But ah! how few, of all that try*
> *This mighty march, do aught but die.*

The passage freely imitates part of a chorus in Milton's *Samson Agonistes* (which A. read while at work on *Merope*) – see especially ll. 667–70, 674–7,

> *God of our Fathers, what is man!*
> *That thou towards him with hand so various,*
> *Or might I say contrarious,*
> *Temperst thy providence through his short course . . .*

> *Nor do I name of men the common rout,*
> *That wandring loose about*
> *Grow up and perish, as the summer flie,*
> *Heads without name no more rememberd . . .*

60. eddy] A favourite word for purposeless activity – see l. 77 below and cp. also 'Resignation' 277 (p. 95 above),

> *In action's dizzying eddy whirled . . .*

'The Buried Life' 43 (p. 273 above),

> *Eddying at large in blind uncertainty . . .*

and 'Epilogue to Lessing's Laocoön' 157 (p. 513 below),

> *Yes! all this eddying, motley throng . . .*

63. Cp. Wordsworth's sonnet 'The world is too much with us . . .' 1–2,

> *The world is too much with us; late and soon,*
> *Getting and spending, we lay waste our powers . . .*

And there are some, whom a thirst
Ardent, unquenchable, fires,
75   Not with the crowd to be spent,
Not without aim to go round
In an eddy of purposeless dust,
Effort unmeaning and vain.
Ah yes! some of us strive
80   Not without action to die
Fruitless, but something to snatch
From dull oblivion, nor all
Glut the devouring grave!
We, we have chosen our path –
85   Path to a clear-purposed goal,
Path of advance! – but it leads
A long, steep journey, through sunk
Gorges, o'er mountains in snow.
Cheerful, with friends, we set forth –
90   Then, on the height, comes the storm.
Thunder crashes from rock
To rock, the cataracts reply,
Lightnings dazzle our eyes.
Roaring torrents have breached
95   The track, the stream-bed descends
In the place where the wayfarer once
Planted his footstep – the spray
Boils o'er its borders! aloft
The unseen snow-beds dislodge
100   Their hanging ruin; alas,
Havoc is made in our train!
Friends, who set forth at our side,
Falter, are lost in the storm.
We, we only are left!
105   With frowning foreheads, with lips
Sternly compressed, we strain on,
On – and at nightfall at last
Come to the end of our way,
To the lonely inn 'mid the rocks;
110   Where the gaunt and taciturn host
Stands on the threshold, the wind,
Shaking his thin white hairs –

83. Cp. *Paradise Lost* ii 259 (Christ's prophecy of 'ruining' his enemies),

  Death last, and with his Carcass glut the Grave . . .

109–12. Perhaps suggested by the 'ruined inn' and 'Wrinkled ostler, grim
and thin' in Tennyson's 'Vision of Sin' (1842) iii 17 and iv 1.

          Holds his lantern to scan
          Our storm-beat figures, and asks:
115   Whom in our party we bring?
          Whom we have left in the snow?

          Sadly we answer: We bring
          Only ourselves! we lost
          Sight of the rest in the storm.
120   Hardly ourselves we fought through,
          Stripped, without friends, as we are.
          Friends, companions, and train,
          The avalanche swept from our side.

          But thou would'st not *alone*
125   Be saved, my father! *alone*
          Conquer and come to thy goal,
          Leaving the rest in the wild.
          We were weary, and we
          Fearful, and we in our march
130   Fain to drop down and to die.
          Still thou turnedst, and still
          Beckonedst the trembler, and still
          Gavest the weary thy hand.

117–23. Cp. 'The Lord's Messengers' 13–14, 19–21 (p. 454 below),

          Some in the tumult are lost;
          Baffled, bewildered, they stray . . .

          Hardly, hardly shall one
          Come, with countenance bright,
          At the close of day, from the plain . . .

124–7. See A.'s letter to his mother 27 Feb. 1855 quoted in headn. above
and cp. also 'Marcus Aurelius', *E in C I* (1865). *Works* iii 399, 'Marcus
Aurelius saved his own soul by his righteousness, and he could do no more.
Happy they who can do this! but still happier, who can do more!' and
Culture and Anarchy (1869), *Works* vi 12, 'The individual is required, under
pain of being stunted and enfeebled in his own development if he disobeys,
to carry others along with him in his march to perfection . . .'
128–33. A. is recalling his father's behaviour on walks in the Lake District
and perhaps A. P. Stanley's account of these excursions in *Life of Thomas
Arnold* (1844) i 235, 'Most of all, perhaps, was to be observed his delight in
those long mountain-walks, when they would start with their provisions
for the day, himself the guide and life of the party, always on the look out
how best to break the ascent by gentle stages, comforting the little ones in
their falls, and helping forward those who were tired, himself always
keeping with the laggers, that none might strain their strength . . .'

If, in the paths of the world,
135   Stones might have wounded thy feet,
Toil or dejection have tried
Thy spirit, of that we saw
Nothing – to us thou wast still
Cheerful, and helpful, and firm!
140   Therefore to thee it was given
Many to save with thyself;
And, at the end of thy day,
O faithful shepherd! to come,
Bringing thy sheep in thy hand.

145   And through thee I believe
In the noble and great who are gone;
Pure souls honoured and blest
By former ages, who else –
Such, so soulless, so poor,
150   Is the race of men whom I see –
Seemed but a dream of the heart,
Seemed but a cry of desire.
Yes! I believe that there lived
Others like thee in the past,
155   Not like the men of the crowd
Who all round me to-day
Bluster or cringe, and make life
Hideous, and arid, and vile;
But souls tempered with fire,
160   Fervent, heroic, and good,
Helpers and friends of mankind.

Servants of God! – or sons
Shall I not call you? because
Not as servants ye knew
165   Your Father's innermost mind,

145–208. This version of Carlyle's doctrine of 'heroes' was probably
encouraged by the Carlylean tone of much of *Tom Brown's Schooldays* and
especially by Hughes's picture of Dr. Arnold as a hero and object of hero-
worship. For Carlyle's ideas, see *Heroes and Hero-Worship* (1841), *Works*
ed. H. D. Traill v 1, '... Universal history, the history of what man has
accomplished in this world, is at bottom the History of the Great Men who
have worked there. They were the leaders of men, these great ones ... all
things that we see standing accomplished ... are properly the outer
material result ... of Thoughts that dwelt in the Great Men sent into the
world.'

His, who unwillingly sees
One of his little ones lost –
Yours is the praise, if mankind
Hath not as yet in its march
170   Fainted, and fallen, and died!

See! In ~~the rocks of the world~~
Marches the host of mankind,
A ~~feeble, wavering line~~.
Where are they tending? – A God
175   Marshalled them, gave them their ~~goal~~.
Ah, but the way is so long!
Years they have been in the wild!
Sore thirst plagues them, the rocks,
Rising all round, overawe;
180   Factions ~~divide them,~~ their host
Threatens to break, to dissolve.
– Ah, keep, keep them combined!
Else, of the myriads who fill
That army, not one shall arrive;
185   Sole they shall stray; in the rocks
Stagger for ever in vain,
Die one by one in the waste.

Then, in such hour of need
Of your fainting, dispirited race,

166–7. An allusion to the Parable of the Lost Sheep, *Matthew* xviii 14, 'Even so it is not the will of your Father which is in heaven, that one of these little ones should perish.'

171–3. The march, which was the course of a single life in ll. 84–109 above, is now the march of mankind (which is also mentioned in 'Epilogue to Lessing's Laocoön' 170 – see quotation in *n*. to ll. 58–68 above).

174. A God] Some power. Cp. 'To Marguerite – Continued' 22 (p. 125 above),

A God, a God their severance ruled!

177. As were the Israelites before coming to the Promised Land.
186. Stagger] Labour *MS., 1867–9*; Batter *1877–81.*
188–91. Cp. 'The Lord's Messengers' 4–9,

Too long let we them groan;
Haste, arise ye, and go,
Carry my peace upon earth!

Gladly, they rise at his call,
Gladly obey his command,
Gladly descend to the plain.

190   Ye, like angels, appear,
          Radiant with ardour divine!
          Beacons of hope, ye appear!
          Languor is not in your heart,
          Weakness is not in your word,
195   Weariness not on your brow.
          Ye alight in our van! at your voice,
          Panic, despair, flee away.
          Ye move through the ranks, recall
          The stragglers, refresh the outworn,
200   Praise, re-inspire the brave!
          Order, courage, return.
          Eyes rekindling, and prayers,
          Follow your steps as ye go.
          Ye fill up the gaps in our files,
205   Strengthen the wavering line,
          Stablish, continue our march,
          On, to the bound of the waste,
          On, to the City of God.

208. *the City of God*] For A. not much more than a poetical way of saying
'righteousness'. See *Literature and Dogma* (1873), *Works* vii 371, 'The
world's chief nations have now all come . . . to reckon and profess themselves *born in Zion*, – born, that is, in the religion of Zion, *the city of
righteousness.*'

88 The Lord's Messengers

Date of composition unknown, but between Nov. 1857–May 1860: by its
view of 'men of genius' as sent into the world to help mankind the poem
is connected with the second half of 'Rugby Chapel', a poem which was
not begun before Nov. 1857 (headn., p. 444 above); A. returned the proof

¶ 88. *Title*. The earlier title, 'Men of Genius', is more in keeping with the
original first stanza (cancelled *1881*), which suggests Zeus overlooking the
Greeks and Trojans in the plain of Troy:

> Silent, *the Lord of the world*
> *Eyes from the heavenly height,*
> *Girt by his far-shining train,*
> *Us, who with banners unfurl'd*
> [5]   *Fight life's many-chanc'd fight*
> *Madly below, in the plain.*

With ll. 5–6 here cp. 'Palladium' 13–14 (p. 496 below),

> *We shall renew the battle in the plain*
> *To-morrow; red with blood will Xanthus be . . .*

of the poem to Thackeray 2 June 1860 (*Buckler* 16). The cancelled first
stanza's 'many-chanc'd fight ... in the plain' may be in part an Homeric
echo – see *n.* to Title above – but also occurs in the following passage
from *Tom Brown's Schooldays* (1857) ch. 7: '... we listened ... to a man
[Dr. Arnold] who we felt to be with all his heart and soul and strength
striving ... It was not the cold clear voice of one giving advice and
warning from serene heights, to those who were struggling and sinning
below, but the warm living voice of one who was fighting for us and by
our sides ... And so ... was brought home to the young boy ... that it
was no fool's or sluggard's paradise into which he had wandered ... but
a battle-field ordained from of old ...' (Everyman Library ed. (1944)
105). A. suppressed the poem after 1860 until *1881*, probably because of
its resemblances to 'Rugby Chapel' 153 ff. and 'Palladium'.
Published as 'Men of Genius' *Cornhill Magazine* July 1860; reprinted with
present title *1881*, etc.

> Thus saith the Lord to his own:
>   'See ye the trouble below?
>   Warfare of man from his birth!
> Too long let we them groan;
>   Haste, arise ye, and go,
>   Carry my peace upon earth!'
>
> Gladly they rise at his call,
>   Gladly obey his command,
>   Gladly descend to the plain.
> – Ah! How few of them all,
>   Those willing servants, shall stand
>   In the Master's presence again!
>
> Some in the tumult are lost;
>   Baffled, bewildered, they stray.
>   Some, as prisoners, draw breath.

5

10

15

2. *trouble*] battle *Cornhill 1860.*
3. *Cornhill 1860,*
> *Turmoil of death and of birth!*

10–24. For a more optimistic treatment of the idea of 'men of genius' as
helpers of mankind see 'Rugby Chapel' 153–208 (pp. 450–2 above), where
they appear like angels to inspirit an army on the march and are themselves superior to ordinary human weaknesses. Here A. argues that most
'men of genius' either die prematurely or lose their sense of vocation.
13–14. Cp. 'Rugby Chapel' 117–20 (p. 449 above),
> *Sadly we answer: We bring*
> *Only ourselves! we lost*

Some, unconquered, are crossed
(Not yet half through the day)
By a pitiless arrow of Death.

20   Hardly, hardly shall one
       Come, with countenance bright,
         At the close of day, from the plain;
His Master's errand well done,
Safe through the smoke of the fight,
       Back to his Master again.

—

Sight of the rest in the storm.
Hardly ourselves we fought through . . .

where, however, the lines apply to men of ability without the heroic qualities of genius.

16–18. Cornhill 1860,

Others – the bravest – are cross'd,
On the height of their bold-follow'd way,
By the swift-rushing missile of Death.

In both versions A. is probably thinking of his father, who died suddenly on the eve of his forty-seventh birthday.

22. An echo of the Parable of the Talents, *Matthew* xxv 21, 'Well done, thou good and faithful servant . . . enter thou into the joy of thy lord.'

89   Stanzas from Carnac

'Composed at Carnac, May 6, 1859' (*1867* title): the dating is confirmed by A.'s two letters of 8 May 1859 to his wife and mother (*L* i 81–4, 85–7), which continually recall the phrasing of the poem; A.'s autograph fair copy of 23 Oct. 1859 in his mother's domestic journal shows that the text was only slightly revised, at an unknown later date, for *1867*. A. was in France to study elementary education for the Newcastle Commission from mid-March to Aug. 1859 (except for brief visits to Holland and Switzerland, and a fortnight's holiday at Dover); news of the death of his younger brother William at Gibraltar – for whom see *n.* to l. 33 below – reached him in Paris 13 April (unpublished 1859 diary); his feelings found an outlet in two elegies – 'Stanzas from Carnac' and the later and more reflective 'A Southern Night' (p. 457 below).
Published as 'Stanzas composed at Carnac, May 6, 1859' *1867*; reprinted (*1868*), *1869*; with present title *1877*, etc.

Far on its rocky knoll descried
Saint Michael's chapel cuts the sky.
I climbed; beneath me, bright and wide,
Lay the lone coast of Brittany.

5   Bright in the sunset, weird and still,
It lay beside the Atlantic wave,
As though the wizard Merlin's will
Yet charmed it from his forest-grave.

Behind me on their grassy sweep,
10   Bearded with lichen, scrawled and grey,
The giant stones of Carnac sleep,
In the mild evening of the May.

No priestly stern procession now
Moves through their rows of pillars old;
15   No victims bleed, no Druids bow –
Sheep make the daisied aisles their fold.

From bush to bush the cuckoo flies,
The orchis red gleams everywhere;
Gold furze with broom in blossom vies,
20   The blue-bells perfume all the air.

¶ 89. *1–12.* Cp. A.'s letter to his wife 8 May 1859, 'The stones of Carnac
are very singular, but the chapel of St. Michel, on a hill between the stones
and the village of Carnac, I liked better still; the view over the stones and
the strange country of Morbihan (the little sea), on the spur of Carnac by
the sea . . .' (*L* i 82); and letter to his mother of the same date, 'I went to
Carnac to see the Druidical stones, which are very solemn and imposing.
The sea is close by . . .' (*L* i 85).
7–8. the wizard . . . / . . . charmed] th'enchanter . . . bound *MS.* For the
'forest-grave' see 'Tristram and Iseult' iii 153–8 (p. 222 above).
10. scrawled] old *MS.*
14. Moves] Streams *MS., 1867–81.*
16. daisied aisles] furze-grown nave *MS.*; furze-grown aisles *1867.*
19. Gold furze with broom] Gold broom with furze *MS., 1867.* Cp. A.'s
letter to his wife 8 May 1859, 'It is a very wild country – broom and furze,
broom and furze everywhere . . .' (*L* i 82); and letter to his mother of the
same date, 'One is haunted by the name *Plantagenet* . . . The moment one
enters Anjou . . . the broom begins, and Brittany seems all in flower with
it, with furze mixed' (*L* i 85).
20. blue-bells perfume] furze-scent perfumes *1868–77.*

And o'er the glistening, lonely land,
Rise up, all round, the Christian spires;
The church of Carnac, by the strand,
Catches the westering sun's last fires.

25   And there, across the watery way,
See, low above the tide at flood,
The sickle-sweep of Quiberon Bay,
Whose beach once ran with loyal blood!

And beyond that, the Atlantic wide!
30   All round, no soul, no boat, no hail;
But, on the horizon's verge descried,
Hangs, touched with light, one snowy sail!

Ah! where is he, who should have come
Where that far sail is passing now,
35   Past the Loire's mouth, and by the foam
Of Finistère's unquiet brow,

Home, round into the English wave?
– He tarries where the Rock of Spain

21–2. Cp. A. to his wife 8 May 1859, '. . . beautiful church towers rise on
all sides of you, for this is a land of churches' (L i 82).
25–8. Cp. A. to his mother 8 May 1859, 'The sea is close by, with the sickle-
shaped peninsula of Quiberon, where the emigrants landed and were
beaten by Hoche . . .' (L i 85). On 20 July 1795 General Hoche destroyed
at Quiberon an emigré expedition which had been equipped in England
and was bringing support to 'Loyalists' in the Vendée.
29–34. Cp. A. to his wife 8 May 1859, '. . . and beyond that the Atlantic.
All this at between six and seven on a perfectly still, cloudless evening in
May, with the sea like glass, and the solitude all round entire' (L i 83); and
to his mother on the same date, 'I thought of Willy . . . while I looked
over the perfectly still and bright Atlantic by Quiberon Bay, and saw the
sails passing in the distance where he would have passed had he lived to
come home' (L i 85).
32. snowy] distant MS.
33. 'The author's brother, William Delafield Arnold, Director of Public
Instruction in the Punjab, and author of Oakfield, or Fellowship in the East,
died at Gibraltar on his way home from India, April the 9th, 1859.' A.'s
1867 note. For further details of W. D. Arnold (1828–59) see n. to l. 47
below, nn. to 'A Southern Night' (pp. 458–9 below), and the full account
in F. J. Woodward's The Doctor's Disciples (1954) 180–227.
38. tarries] lingers MS.

Mediterranean waters lave;
40   He enters not the Atlantic main.

Oh, could he once have reached this air
Freshened by plunging tides, by showers!
~~Have felt this breath he loved, of fair~~
~~Cool northern fields, and grass, and flowers!~~

45   He longed for it – pressed on. In vain!
At the Straits failed that spirit brave.
~~The south was parent of his pain,~~
The south is mistress of his grave.

41–4. Cp. A. to his mother 8 May 1859, 'I had the climate of England, gray skies and cool air, and the gray rock of the north too, and the clear rushing water' (*L* i 85).
45. He longed for it – pressed on] He long'd it, he press'd on *MS.*
47. William A.'s wife, Frances Ann, died of dysentery at Kangra in the Punjab 24 March 1858, leaving her husband, who was absent on a tour of duty when she died, with four children under the age of seven to look after. The children, who were sent to England ahead of their father in Jan. 1859, were brought up by W. E. Forster and his wife, A.'s sister 'K'.

90 A Southern Night

Date of composition unknown, but almost certainly begun 20 or 21 May 1859, the only dates possible for A.'s unrecorded visit to Cette (he was in Carcassonne 19 May and Nîmes 22 May – see *Complete Prose Works* ed. R. H. Super ii (1962) 328 and *UL* 43–9); and probably completed in draft not long after this – a conjecture supported by (1) the allusion to 'Some youthful troubadour' (ll. 97–100): see A.'s letter to his sister 'K' 16 Feb. 1859, 'I shall try and give one lecture at Oxford before I go [to France], on the Troubadours' (*L* i 79); (2) the poem's expansion of A.'s reflections in a letter to his mother 14 April 1859, 'I, of whom he thought so far more than I deserved, and who showed him, poor boy, so far less tenderness than *he* deserved. How strange it seems that he should have overlived his first terrible illness when his wife was alive to nurse him ... And then that he should have overlived the misery of his poor wife's death to struggle through a year's loneliness, and then to die too. Poor Fanny, she at Dhurmsala, and he by the Rock of Gibraltar' (*L* i 79–80).
Published *Victoria Regia* 1861; reprinted *1867 (1868), 1869,* etc.
    16+M.A.

The sandy spits, the shore-locked lakes,   *Cagnul*
    Melt into open, moonlit sea;
The soft Mediterranean breaks
    At my feet, free.

5   Dotting the fields of corn and vine,
    Like ghosts the huge, gnarled olives stand.
Behind, that lovely mountain-line!
    While, by the strand,

Cette, with its glistening houses white,
10   Curves with the curving beach away
To where the lighthouse beacons bright
    Far in the bay.

Ah! such a night, so soft, so lone,
    So moonlit, saw me once of yore
15   Wander unquiet, and my own
    Vexed heart deplore.

But now that trouble is forgot;
    Thy memory, thy pain, to-night,
My brother! and thine early lot,
20   Possess me quite.

The murmur of this Midland deep
    Is heard to-night around thy grave,
There, where Gibraltar's cannoned steep
    O'erfrowns the wave.

25   For there, with bodily anguish keen,
    With Indian heats at last fordone,
With public toil and private teen –
    Thou sank'st, alone.

¶ 90. *1–12.* Cette (Sète) is a French seaport on the Gulf of Lions, eighteen
miles south-west of Montpellier. The older part of the town is on a tongue
of land separating the Mediterranean from the Lagoon of Thau.
13–16. 'See the poem, *A Summer Night* [p. 267 above]'. A.'s note first
added *1869.* The setting of the earlier moonlit night cannot be identified.
18–20. A. has a cross-reference in *1867* and subsequent editions to his note
to 'Stanzas from Carnac' 33 (p. 456 above). William A. died two days
after his thirty-first birthday.
25–8. See A.'s letter to his mother 14 April 1859 quoted in headn. above.
William A. first went out to India in 1848 as an ensign in the forces of the
East India Company. He was invalided home in Oct. 1852 and brought

30
Slow to a stop, at morning grey,
   I see the smoke-crowned vessel come;
Slow round her paddles dies away
    The seething foam.

A boat is lowered from her side;
   Ah, gently place him on the bench!
35
That spirit – if all have not yet died –
    A breath might quench.

Is this the eye, the footstep fast,
   The mien of youth we used to see,
Poor, gallant boy! – for such thou wast,
40
    Still art, to me.

The limbs their wonted tasks refuse;
   The eyes are glazed, thou canst not speak;
And whiter than thy white burnous
    That wasted cheek!

45
Enough! The boat, with quiet shock,
   Unto its haven coming nigh,
Touches, and on Gibraltar's rock
    Lands thee to die.

Ah me! Gibraltar's strand is far,
50
   But farther yet across the brine
Thy dear wife's ashes buried are,
    Remote from thine.

For there, where morning's sacred fount
   Its golden rain on earth confers,
55
The snowy Himalayan Mount
    O'ershadows hers.

---

his wife (whom he had married in April 1850) to Fox How. At the invitation of John Lawrence, then Chief Commissioner of the Punjab, he returned to India in 1855 to organize public education in the Punjab – a task which he continued to work at throughout the Indian Mutiny and only sought relief from when, after his wife's death, his own health began to break down towards the end of 1858.

26. *heats*] suns *VR 1861.*
27. *teen*] See *n.* to 'The Scholar-Gipsy' 147 (p. 339 above).
37. *the footstep fast*] the form alert *VR 1861.*
39. *wast*] wert *VR 1861.*
50–2. At Dharmsala in the Punjab.

Strange irony of fate, alas,
  Which, for two jaded English, saves,
When from their dusty life they pass,
60   Such peaceful graves!

In cities should we English lie,
  Where cries are rising ever new,
And men's incessant stream goes by –
    We who pursue

65 Our business with unslackening stride,
  Traverse in troops, with care-filled breast,
The soft Mediterranean side,
    The Nile, the East,

And see all sights from pole to pole,
70 And glance, and nod, and bustle by,
And never once possess our soul
    Before we die.

Not by those hoary Indian hills,
  Not by this gracious Midland sea
75 Whose floor to-night sweet moonshine fills,
    Should our graves be.

Some sage, to whom the world was dead,
  And men were specks, and life a play;
Who made the roots of trees his bed,
80   And once a day

With staff and gourd his way did bend
  To villages and homes of man,
For food to keep him till he end
    His mortal span

61–72. The light punctuation indicates English haste and hurry.
76–92. This picture of an Indian forest-sage was suggested by a reading of E. Burnouf's *Introduction à l'histoire de Bouddhisme indien* (Paris, 1844), which is quoted in 'On the Modern Element in Literature' (Nov. 1857), A.'s inaugural lecture as Professor of Poetry at Oxford. It appears on his reading-list for May 1857 as 'Le Bouddhisme' (*Note-books* 561) and again in his letter to his sister 'K' 1858 (probably Jan.), 'I must ask you to send me back my Bouddhisme to make a reference for my next lecture . . .' (*UL* 43).
82. *homes*] haunts *VR 1861*.

85 And the pure goal of being reach;
   Hoar-headed, wrinkled, clad in white,
  Without companion, without speech,
    By day and night

  Pondering God's mysteries untold,
90   And tranquil as the glacier-snows –
  He by those Indian mountains old
    Might well repose.

  Some grey crusading knight austere,
   Who bore Saint Louis company,
95 And came home hurt to death, and here
    Landed to die;

  Some youthful troubadour, whose tongue
   Filled Europe once with his love-pain,
  Who here outworn had sunk, and sung
100   His dying strain;

  Some girl, who here from castle-bower,
   With furtive step and cheek of flame,
  'Twixt myrtle-hedges all in flower
    By moonlight came

105 To meet her pirate-lover's ship;
   And from the wave-kissed marble stair
  Beckoned him on, with quivering lip
    And floating hair;

---

85. *the pure goal of being*] Deliverance from the cycle of births and deaths by the extinction of all desire; the Nirvana of the Buddhist and Mukti (liberation) of the Hindu.

86. *Hoar-headed*] Grey-headed *VR 1861, 1867–81*.

94. *Saint Louis*] Louis IX of France (1214–70), whom A. had been taught to admire by Dr. Arnold.

96. *Landed*] Touch'd shore *VR 1861*. Both readings link the crusading knight with William A. by echoing ll. 47–8 above.

97–100. An allusion prompted by A.'s work for his Oxford lecture on the Troubadours – see headn. above. The lecture was delivered 12 March 1859.

99. *outworn had*] outwearied *VR 1861, 1867–9*.

101–10. The Byronic romanticism of this vignette was outmoded even in 1859.

101. *castle-bower*] palace-bower *VR 1861*.

108. *floating*] unbound *1867*.

And lived some moons in happy trance,
110   Then learnt his death and pined away –
Such by these waters of romance
        'Twas meet to lay.

But you – a grave for knight or sage,
    Romantic, solitary, still,
115 O spent ones of a work-day age!
        Befits you ill.

So sang I; but the midnight breeze,
    Down to the brimmed, moon-charméd main,
Comes softly through the olive-trees,
120   And checks my strain.

I think of her, whose gentle tongue
    All plaint in her own cause controlled;
Of thee I think, my brother! young
        In heart, high-souled –

125 That comely face, that clustered brow,
    That cordial hand, that bearing free,
I see them still, I see them now,
        Shall always see!

And what but gentleness untired,
130   And what but noble feeling warm,
Wherever shown, howe'er inspired,
        Is grace, is charm?

What else is all these waters are,
    What else is steeped in lucid sheen,
135 What else is bright, what else is fair,
        What else serene?

Mild o'er her grave, ye mountains, shine!
    Gently by his, ye waters, glide!
To that in you which is divine
140   They were allied.

113. *knight*] Girl *VR 1861*.
131. *inspired*] attir'd *VR 1861, 1867*.

91 Saint Brandan

Date of composition unknown, but between late 1859–May 1860: A.'s source is a short passage from Renan's 'La poésie des races celtiques', originally published 1 Feb. 1854 in *Revue des Deux Mondes*, but first read by A. in *Essais de Morale et de Critique* (Paris, 1859) – see his letter to his sister 'K' 24 Dec. 1859, 'I thought the other day that I would tell you of a Frenchman whom I saw in Paris [in the summer of 1859], Ernest Renan ... The best book of his for you to read ... is his *Essais de Morale et de Critique*, lately published. I have read few things for a long time with more pleasure than a long essay with which the book concludes – "Sur la poésie des races celtiques"' (*L* i 111–12); A. wrote to J. W. Parker (editor of *Fraser's Magazine*) 1 June 1860, 'For some weeks past I have been intending to send you the accompanying lines, but have never found time to write them out till this morning' (unpublished letter in Yale Papers). The passage from Renan's essay used by A. is as follows: 'Ce sentiment [of pity for the weak and unfortunate] est un des plus profonds chez les peuples celtiques. Ils ont pitié même de Judas. Saint Brandan le rencontra sur un rocher au milieu des mers polaires: il passe là un jour par semaine pour se rafraîchir des feux de l'enfer; un drap qu'il avait donné en aumône à un lépreux est suspendu devant lui et tempère ses souffrances' (*Essais de Morale et de Critique* (1859) 394–5). A. changes the rock into an iceberg and reduces Judas's relief from one day a week to one hour annually at Christmas. His 1869 letter to F. T. Palgrave expresses dissatisfaction with the poem, '"St Brandan" ... is not a piece that [at] all satisfies me' (*Russell* 43). Published *Fraser's Magazine* July 1860; reprinted *1867* (*1868*), *1869*. etc.

> Saint Brandan sails the northern main;
> The brotherhoods of saint are glad.
> He greets them once, he sails again;
> So late! – such storms! The Saint is mad!
>
> 5　He heard, across the howling seas,
> Chime convent-bells on wintry nights;
> He saw, on spray-swept Hebrides,
> Twinkle the monastery-lights.
>
> But north, still north, Saint Brandan steered –
> 10　And now no bells, no convents more!
> The hurtling Polar lights are neared,
> The sea without a human shore.

¶ 91. *Title.* St. Brandan (*c.* 484–578) was the Benedictine Abbot of Clonfert, Galway. Renan describes the legend of his seven-year voyage in search of the Land of the Saints as 'l'expression la plus complète peut-être de l'idéal celtique' (*Essais* ed. *cit.* 446).

At last – it was the Christmas night;
Stars shone after a day of storm –
15   He sees float past an iceberg white,
And on it – Christ! – a living form.

That furtive mien, that scowling eye,
Of hair that red and tufted fell –
It is – Oh, where shall Brandan fly? –
20   The traitor Judas, out of hell!

Palsied with terror, Brandan sate;
The moon was bright, the iceberg near.
He hears a voice sigh humbly: 'Wait!
By high permission I am here.

25   'One moment wait, thou holy man!
On earth my crime, my death, they knew;
My name is under all men's ban –
Ah, tell them of my respite too!

'Tell them, one blessed Christmas-night –
30   It was the first after I came,
Breathing self-murder, frenzy, spite,
To rue my guilt in endless flame –

'I felt, as I in torment lay
'Mid the souls plagued by heavenly power,
35   An angel touch mine arm, and say:
Go hence and cool thyself an hour!

'"Ah, whence this mercy, Lord?" I said.
The Leper recollect, said he,
Who asked the passers-by for aid,
40   *In Joppa, and thy charity.*

'Then I remembered how I went,
In Joppa, through the public street,
One morn when the sirocco spent
Its storms of dust with burning heat;

15. *an iceberg white*] The iceberg was perhaps suggested by Renan's comment on the combination of the marvellous and the realistic in the legend
of St. Brandan, 'Au milieu de ces rêves apparaît . . . le sentiment pittoresque
des navigations polaires: la transparence de la mer, les aspects des banquises
et des îles de glace fondant au soleil . . .' (*Essais* ed. *cit.* 445).
18. *red*] black *Fraser 1860*.

45   'And in the street a leper sate,
         Shivering with fever, naked, old;
         Sand raked his sores from heel to pate,
         The hot wind fevered him five-fold.

         'He gazed upon me as I passed,
50   And murmured: *Help me, or I die!*
         To the poor wretch my cloak I cast,
         Saw him look eased, and hurried by.

         'Oh, Brandan, think what grace divine,
         What blessing must full goodness shower,
55   When fragment of it small, like mine,
         Hath such inestimable power!

         'Well-fed, well-clothed, well-friended, I
         Did that chance act of good, that one!
         Then went my way to kill and lie –
60   Forgot my good as soon as done.

         'That germ of kindness, in the womb
         Of mercy caught, did not expire;
         Outlives my guilt, outlives my doom,
         And friends me in the pit of fire.

65   'Once every year, when carols wake,
         On earth, the Christmas-night's repose,
         Arising from the sinners' lake,
         I journey to these healing snows.

         'I stanch with ice my burning breast,
70   With silence balm my whirling brain.
         O Brandan! to this hour of rest
         That Joppan leper's ease was pain.'

54. *full*] true *Fraser 1860, 1867.*
55. *When fragment of it small*] When semblance of it faint *Fraser 1860*; If
semblance of it faint *1867*; If fragment of it small *1868*.
56. *inestimable*] inalienable *Fraser 1860.*
60. *good*] deed *Fraser 1860.*
   16*

Tears started to Saint Brandan's eyes;
He bowed his head, he breathed a prayer –
75   Then looked, and lo, the frosty skies!
The iceberg, and no Judas there!

75. Replacing the following *Fraser 1860, 1867–9.*

When he look'd up – tenantless lies . . .

76. *and no Judas there!*] in the frosty air! *Fraser 1860, 1867–9*; and no tenant there! *1877.*

92 Translations from Homer

Date of composition unknown, but probably late 1860: the four passages were apparently specially translated for A.'s third Oxford lecture on Homer, which was completed by 18 Dec. 1860 and delivered 26 Jan. 1861 (*Complete Prose Works* ed. R. H. Super i (1960) 239) – see *On Translating Homer* (1861), *Works* v 245, 'I proceed at once to give you . . . one or two passages in which I have tried to follow those principles of Homeric translation which I have laid down' and *On Translating Homer: Last Words* (1862), *Works* v 323, 'From those perishable objects [the translations] I feel . . . a most Oriental detachment. You yourselves are witnesses . . . how humble a function I designed them to fill . . . I was thinking of the future translator of Homer, and trying to let him see . . . what I meant . . . by saying that this poetry was at once rapid in movement, plain in words and style, simple and direct in its ideas, and noble in manner.' The translations were projected and perhaps begun by 29 Oct. 1860 – see A.'s letter of that date to his mother, 'I shall give a few passages [of Homer] translated by myself to add practice to theory' (*L* i 126).
A.'s interest in the English hexameter as a medium for translating Homer was probably first aroused by Clough, whose earliest attempts to use it, however, did not please A. – see his letter of March 1849, 'Drat Hexameters. Try a bit in the metre I took for the sick king' (*CL* 104). By 1853 A. had made his own experiments with the English hexameter – see his letter to Clough 25 Aug. 1853, 'Did I tell you he [J. A. Froude] dislikes all Hexameters. I repeated to him some I thought my best – he said he thought they were as good as any, but not the thing' (*CL* 140). These hexameters may or may not have been Homeric translations, but the exchange between Froude and A. grew out of a discussion of C. Kingsley's unpublished 'Andromeda', an original poem in English hexameters (see *CL* 139).
Published in *On Translating Homer* 1861; not reprinted by A. in any collection of his poems.

I THE TROJAN CAMP

So shone forth, in front of Troy, by the bed of Xanthus,
Between that and the ships, the Trojans' numerous fires.
In the plain there were kindled a thousand fires: by each
There sate fifty men, in the ruddy light of the fire: [one
5 By their chariots stood the steeds, and champed the white
      barley
While their masters sate by the fire, and waited for
      Morning.

II ZEUS AND THE HORSES OF ACHILLES

And with pity the son of Saturn saw them bewailing,
And he shook his head, and thus addressed his own bosom: –
   'Ah, unhappy pair, to Peleus why did we give you,
To a mortal? but ye are without old age and immortal.
5 Was it that ye, with man, might have your thousands of
      sorrows?
For than man, indeed, there breathes no wretcheder
      creature,
Of all living things, that on earth are breathing and moving.'

II HECTOR TO ANDROMACHE

Woman, I too take thought for this; but then I bethink me
What the Trojan men and Trojan women might murmur,
If like a coward I skulked behind, apart from the battle.
Nor would my own heart let me; my heart, which has bid
      me be valiant
5 Always, and always fighting among the first of the Trojans,
Busy for Priam's fame and my own, in spite of the future.
For that day will come, my soul is assured of its coming,
It will come, when sacred Troy shall go to destruction,
Troy, and warlike Priam too, and the people of Priam.
10 And yet not that grief, which then will be, of the Trojans,
Moves me so much – not Hecuba's grief, nor Priam my
      father's,
Nor my brethren's, many and brave, who then will be lying
In the bloody dust, beneath the feet of their foemen –
As thy grief, when, in tears, some brazen-coated Achaian
15 Shall transport thee away, and the day of thy freedom be
      ended.

¶ 92. i 1–6. Iliad viii 560–5.
ii 1–7. Iliad xvii 441–7.
iii 1–25. Iliad vi 441–65.

Then, perhaps, thou shalt work at the loom of another, in
Or bear pails to the wells of Messeïs, or Hypereia,   [Argos,
Sorely against thy will, by strong Necessity's order.
And some man may say, as he looks and sees thy tears
20 *See, the wife of Hector, that great pre-eminent captain*   [falling:
Of the horsemen of Troy, in the day they fought for their city.
So some man will say; and then thy grief will redouble
At thy want of a man like me, to save thee from bondage.
But let me be dead, and the earth be mounded above me,
25 Ere I hear thy cries, and thy captivity told of.

IV ACHILLES AND XANTHUS

'Xanthus and Balius both, ye far-famed seed of Podarga!
See that ye bring your master home to the host of the
     Argives
In some other sort than your last, when the battle is ended;
And not leave him behind, a corpse on the plain, like
     Patroclus.'
5   Then, from beneath the yoke, the fleet horse Xanthus
          addressed him:
Sudden he bowed his head, and all his mane, as he bowed it,
Streamed to the ground by the yoke, escaping from under
     the collar;
And he was given a voice by the white-armed Goddess
     Hera.
'Truly, yet this time will we save thee, mighty Achilles!
10 But thy day of death is at hand; nor shall *we* be the reason –
No, but the will of Heaven, and Fate's invincible power.
For by no slow pace or want of swiftness of ours
Did the Trojans obtain to strip the arms from Patroclus;
But that prince among Gods, the son of the lovely-haired
     Leto,
15 Slew him fighting in front of the fray, and glorified Hector.
But, for us, we vie in speed with the breath of the West-
     Wind,
Which, men say, is the fleetest of winds; 'tis thou who art
     fated

iv *1–25. Iliad* xix 400–24. A.'s translation of these lines prompted him to
comment, 'I will make one general remark on the character of my own
translations . . . It is, that over the graver passages there is shed an air somewhat too strenuous and severe, by comparison with that lovely ease and
sweetness which Homer, for all his noble and masculine way of thinking,
never loses' (*On Translating Homer* (1861), *Works* v 255).

To lie low in death, by the hand of a God and a Mortal.'
    Thus far he; and here his voice was stopped by the Furies.
20 Then, with a troubled heart, the swift Achilles addressed
      him:
    'Why dost thou prophesy so my death to me, Xanthus?
    It needs not.
I of myself know well, that here I am destined to perish,
Far from my father and mother dear: for all that, I will not
Stay this hand from fight, till the Trojans are utterly
    routed.'
25 So he spake, and drove with a cry his steeds into battle.

93 Heine's Grave

Exact period of composition unknown, but between 14 Sept. 1858–19
April 1863; A. visited Heine's grave in Montmartre Cemetery 14 Sept.
1858 (unpublished 1858 diary), perhaps prompted by his reading of *Reisebilder* i 'Die Harzreise' (1824), a principal source of the elegy, in July 1858
(*Note-books* 563); the poem was begun before Jan. 1862 when the undeleted
entry 'finish "Heine's Grave"' appears on A.'s reading-lists (*Note-books*
566); and was completed 19 April 1863 (unpublished diary and *Note-books*
570), the final stages of composition overlapping A.'s preparation for his
Oxford lecture on Heine (delivered 13 June 1863). The poem was probably
begun either in Sept. 1858 or in 1860 when *Reisebilder* i again appears on
A.'s reading-lists among other 'Books for Summer' (*Note-books* 565).
Besides 'Die Harzreise' A. drew on other works by Heine (for details see
nn. below), and the picture of Heine on his 'mattress-grave' was undoubtedly influenced by Saint-René Taillandier's description in 'Poètes
contemporains de l'Allemagne: Henri Heine', *Revue des Deux Mondes*
nouvelle période xiv (1 April 1852) 5–36, which is accompanied by a
striking engraving of the dying poet. For a comment on the poetic pattern
common to 'Heine's Grave', 'Haworth Churchyard' and 'Rugby
Chapel' see headn. to 'Haworth Churchyard' (p. 390 above), which also
refers to A.'s use of the metre of the three elegies in earlier poems. In *1869*
'Heine's Grave' was classified as a lyric – perhaps to acknowledge that the
critical rather than the elegiac note is the dominant one – but in later
editions it was included among the elegies. That A.'s view of poetry is
restricted is well brought out by his keen enjoyment in his Oxford lecture
of Heine's wit and irony, and the feeling expressed in 'Heine's Grave'
103–20 that these qualities are out of place in serious poetry. On A.'s part
in the growth of Heine's English reputation see S. Liptzin, *JEGP* xliii
(1944) 317–25.
Published *1867*; reprinted (*1868*), *1869*, etc.

'*Henri Heine*' – 'tis here!
That black tombstone, the name
Carved there – no more! and the smooth,
Swarded alleys, the limes
5   Touched with yellow by hot
Summer, but under them still,
In September's bright afternoon,
Shadow, and verdure, and cool.
Trim Montmartre! the faint
10   Murmur of Paris outside;
Crisp everlasting-flowers,
Yellow and black, on the graves.

Half blind, palsied, in pain,
Hither to come, from the streets'
15   Uproar, surely not loth
Wast thou, Heine! to lie
Quiet, to ask for closed
Shutters, and darkened room,
And cool drinks, and an eased
20   Posture, and opium, no more;
Hither to come, and to sleep
Under the wings of Renown.

¶ 93. *1–3.* Heine died 17 Feb. 1856.
13–28. Probably suggested by C. Gleyre's portrait of the suffering Heine and Saint-René Taillandier's comment on it in 'Poètes contemporains de l'Allemagne', *Revue des Deux Mondes* n.p. xiv (1 April 1852) 8, 'En vain les années ont-elles suivi leur cours, en vain la souffrance, une souffrance affreuse, impitoyable, a-t-elle appesanti ses mains de plomb sur la fantaisie ailée . . . Voyez-le sur ce lit de douleur où un artiste éminent nous le représente ici, considérez cette tête fine et pensive . . . ce qui éclate dans la delicatesse du visage, dans le sourire des lèvres, dans ce regard à demi fermé où ne pénètre plus qu'un dernier rayon de lumière, c'est la séré-nité imperturbable, c'est la victoire de l'*humour* sur les plus cruelles souffrances.' (A.'s reading of Taillandier is proved by the quotation from this essay in one of his general note-books – see *Note-books* 479.) See, too, A.'s 'Heinrich Heine', *E in C I* (1865), *Works* iii 187, 'In May 1848 . . . he went out of doors for the last time, but his disease took more than eight years to kill him. For nearly eight years he lay helpless on a couch, with the use of his limbs gone, wasted almost to the proportions of a child . . . the sight of one eye lost, that of the other greatly dimmed . . . all this, and, besides this, suffering at short intervals paroxysms of nervous agony. I have said he was not pre-eminently brave; but in the astonishing force of spirit with which he retained his activity of mind, even his gaiety, amid all his suffering . . . he was truly brave.'

Ah! not little, when pain
Is most quelling, and man
25   Easily quelled, and the fine
Temper of genius so soon
Thrills at each smart, is the praise,
Not to have yielded to pain!
No small boast, for a weak
30   Son of mankind, to the earth
Pinned by the thunder, to rear
His bolt-scathed front to the stars;
And, undaunted, retort
'Gainst thick-crashing, insane,
35   Tyrannous tempests of bale,
Arrowy lightnings of soul.

Hark! through the alley resounds
Mocking laughter! A film
Creeps o'er the sunshine; a breeze
40   Ruffles the warm afternoon,
Saddens my soul with its chill.
Gibing of spirits in scorn
Shakes every leaf of the grove,
Mars the benignant repose
45   Of this amiable home of the dead.

Bitter spirits, ye claim
Heine? Alas, he is yours!
Only a moment I longed
Here in the quiet to snatch
50   From such mates the outworn
Poet, and steep him in calm.
Only a moment! I knew

26. *so soon*] alive *1867–9*.

27. *Thrills at each smart*] Quickest to ill *1867–9*.

29–32. George Eliot has the same comparison of the paralysed poet to a chained Titan – see 'German Wit: Heinrich Heine', *Impressions of Theophrastus Such, Essays and Leaves from a Note-book* (1888) 288. The essay originally appeared in the *Westminster Review* in Jan. 1856.

33–6. Perhaps suggested by Heine's *Ludwig Börne* (1840) ii (Helgoland 10 August), *Werke* ed. H. Friedmann (n.d.) xiv 59, 'Ach, lieber Herrgott, ich möchte donnern lernen, blitzen kann ich . . . (Ah, my dear God, I should like to learn to thunder; already I know how to hurl lightnings).' A. quotes from *Ludwig Börne* ii in his essay on Heine.

46. *Bitter spirits*] Probably Aristophanes and Voltaire, with both of whom Heine was often compared.

Whose he was who is here
Buried – I knew he was yours!
55   Ah, I knew that I saw
Here no sepulchre built
In the laurelled rock, o'er the blue
Naples bay, for a sweet
Tender Virgil! no tomb
60   On Ravenna sands, in the shade
Of Ravenna pines, for a high
Austere Dante! no grave
By the Avon side, in the bright
Stratford meadows, for thee,
65   Shakespeare! loveliest of souls,
Peerless in radiance, in joy.

What, then, so harsh and malign,
Heine! distils from thy life,
Poisons the peace of thy grave?

70   I chide with thee not, that thy sharp
Upbraidings often assailed
England, my country – for we,
Heavy and sad, for her sons,
Long since, deep in our hearts,
75   Echo the blame of her foes.
We, too, sigh that she flags;
We, too, say that she now –
Scarce comprehending the voice
Of her greatest, golden-mouthed sons
80   Of a former age any more –

62–4. Poetic licence. Shakespeare's grave is in the chancel of Holy Trinity Church, Stratford-on-Avon.

70–2. See, for example, *Reisebilder* iv 'Englische Fragmente' *passim* and A.'s 'Heinrich Heine', *E in C I* (1865), *Works* iii 179, '"I might settle in England", he says, in his exile, "if it were not that I should find there two things, coal-smoke and Englishmen; I cannot abide either." What he hated in the English was the "ächtbrittische Beschränkheit", as he calls it – the *genuine British narrowness*.' The last phrase is from 'Englische Fragmente' ch. 10.

73. *Heavy*] Fearful *1867–8*; Troublous *1869*.

77–84. Cp. *Culture and Anarchy* (1869), *Works* vi 16, 'If England were swallowed up by the sea tomorrow, which of the two, a hundred years hence, would most excite the love, interest, and admiration of mankind . . . the England of the last twenty years, or the England of Elizabeth, of a time of splendid spiritual effort . . . ?'

Stupidly travels her round
Of mechanic business, and lets
Slow die out of her life
Glory, and genius, and joy.

85   So thou arraign'st her, her foe;
        So we arraign her, her sons.

        Yes, we arraign her! but she,
        The weary Titan, with deaf
        Ears, and labour-dimmed eyes,
90   Regarding neither to right
        Nor left, goes passively by,
        Staggering on to her goal;
        Bearing on shoulders immense,
        Atlanteän, the load,
95   Wellnigh not to be borne,
        Of the too vast orb of her fate.

        But was it thou – I think
        Surely it was! – that bard
        Unnamed, who, Goethe said,
100   *Had every other gift, but wanted love;*
        Love, without which the tongue
        Even of angels sounds amiss?

        Charm is the glory which makes
        Song of the poet divine,
105   Love is the fountain of charm.

87–96. A. used these lines to complete his essay 'My Countrymen' (1866), which was collected in *Friendship's Garland* (1871).
94. Atlanteän] Atlas was condemned by Zeus to carry the globe on his shoulders for his part in the rebellion of the Titans.
97–100. Goethe was referring to Platen – see Eckermann's *Conversations of Goethe* (Bohn's Library revised ed. 1883) 164–5, 'We then mentioned one of our most modern German poets, Platen, who had lately gained a great name ... "We cannot deny," said Goethe, "that he has many brilliant qualities, but he is wanting in – *love.*" ' A. possessed the 1837 ed. of *Gespräche mit Goethe*, in which the poet is not identified by name.
101–2. An allusion to *1 Corinthians* xiii 1, 'Though I speak with the tongues of men and of angels, and have not charity, I am become as sounding brass, or a tinkling cymbal.'
103–20. A. is echoing his *1853* Preface (p. 591 below), 'It is demanded [of a poetic representation], not only that it shall interest, but also that it shall inspirit and rejoice the reader; that it shall convey a charm, and infuse

How without charm wilt thou draw,
Poet! the world to thy way?
Not by the lightnings of wit –
Not by the thunder of scorn!
110   These to the world, too, are given;
Wit it possesses, and scorn –
Charm is the poet's alone.
Hollow and dull are the great,
And artists envious, and the mob profane.
115   We know all this, we know!
Cam'st thou from heaven, O child
Of light! but this to declare?
Alas, to help us forget
Such barren knowledge awhile,
120   God gave the poet his song!

Therefore a secret unrest
Tortured thee, brilliant and bold!
Therefore triumph itself
Tasted amiss to thy soul.
125   Therefore, with blood of thy foes,
Trickled in silence thine own.
Therefore the victor's heart
Broke on the field of his fame.

Ah! as of old, from the pomp
130   Of Italian Milan, the fair

---

delight. For the Muses, as Hesiod says, were born that they might be "a forgetfulness of evils, and a truce from cares".'

116–17. O child / Of light] Heine is a 'child of light' because of his warfare
with the Philistines. See 'Heinrich Heine', *E in C I* (1865), *Works* iii 178,
'*Philistine* must have originally meant . . . a strong, dogged, unenlightened
opponent of the chosen people, of the children of the light.'

121–2. Taillandier (*loc. cit.* 35) says that Heine's was a 'sérénité incomplète
et fausse, qui bien souvent encore . . . laissait éclater subitement des
douleurs mal guéries'.

125–8. An allusion to Heine's 'Enfant Perdu' in the 'Lazarus' section of
Romanzero (1851) ii, *Werke* ed. *cit.* ii 213–14 and especially to ll. 20, 23–4,

> *Die Wunden klaffen – es verströmt mein Blut.*
>
> *Doch fall' ich unbesiegt, und meine Waffen*
> *Sind nicht gebrochen – Nur mein Herze brach.*

(My wounds gape and my blood flows . . . Yet I fall undefeated and my
arms are unbroken – only my heart broke.)

129–39. Suggested by *Reisebilder* i 'Die Harzreise', *Werke* ed. *cit.* vii 76,
'Only go and turn over that pretty "Luneburg Chronicle" in which the

Flower of marble of white
Southern palaces – steps
Bordered by statues, and walks
Terraced, and orange-bowers
135   Heavy with fragrance – the blond
German Kaiser full oft
Longed himself back to the fields,
Rivers, and high-roofed towns
Of his native Germany; so,
140   So, how often! from hot
Paris drawing-rooms, and lamps
Blazing, and brilliant crowds,
Starred and jewelled, of men
Famous, of women the queens
145   Of dazzling converse – from fumes
Of praise, hot, heady fumes, to the poor brain
That mount, that madden – how oft
Heine's spirit outworn
Longed itself out of the din,
150   Back to the tranquil, the cool
Far German home of his youth!

See! in the May-afternoon,
O'er the fresh, short turf of the Hartz,
A youth, with the foot of youth,
155   Heine! thou climbest again!

---

good old lords live again . . . and in the pleasant bearded faces you will
plainly read how often they have yearned from foreign lands for the kind
heart of their Hartz princess and the homely rustle of the Hartz woods –
aye, even from the citron-bearing and venomous southern realm into
which they and their successors were so often drawn by the desire to be
called Roman Emperors.' (Quotations from 'Die Harzreise' are taken from
R. McLintock's 1881 translation.)
140–51. Suggested by Heine's 'Anno 1839' 1–4 ('Romanzen' viii), *Neue
Gedichte* (1844), *Werke* ed. *cit.* ii 68,

> O Deutschland, meine ferne Liebe,
> Gedenk' ich deiner, wein' ich fast!
> Das muntre Frankreich scheint mir trübe,
> Das leichte Volk wird mir zur Last.

(O Germany, my distant love, I am near to weeping when I think of you.
Gay France seems sad and dull, the light folk are a burden to me.)
152–90. All the details are from 'Die Harzreise', but A. converts Heine into
a Romantic solitary by omitting both the humour and Heine's ready
enjoyment of chance company.

Up, through the tall dark firs
Warming their heads in the sun,
Chequering the grass with their shade –
Up, by the stream, with its huge
160   Moss-hung boulders, and thin
Musical water half-hid –
Up, o'er the rock-strewn slope,
With the sinking sun, and the air
Chill, and the shadows now
165   Long on the grey hill-side –
To the stone-roofed hut at the top!

Or, yet later, in watch
On the roof of the Brocken-tower
Thou standest, gazing! to see
170   The broad red sun, over field,
Forest, and city, and spire,
And mist-tracked stream of the wide,
Wide German land, going down
In a bank of vapours – again
175   Standest, at nightfall, alone!

Or, next morning, with limbs
Rested by slumber, and heart
Freshened and light with the May,
O'er the gracious spurs coming down

156–62. Cp. 'Die Harzreise', *Werke* ed. *cit.* vii 56–7, 'The mountain is
strewn with great blocks of granite . . . The golden sunbeams shot most
charmingly through the dense dark green of the pines . . . Swelling banks
of moss everywhere; for the stones are all grown over feet-deep with
moss . . . Delicious coolness and a dreamy murmur of unseen springs;
here and there one can see how the water is trickling, crystal clear, under
the stones . . .'
167–75. Heine was not alone. See 'Die Harzreise', *Werke* ed. *cit.* vii 61,
'While we were talking it began to grow dark; the wind became colder,
the sun sank lower, and the tower was filled with students, workmen on
their travels, and a few worthy citizens with their worthy wives and
daughters, who all came to see the sun set. For quite a quarter of an hour
all stood solemnly silent and watched the gradual descent of the glorious
fireball in the west.'
176–85. Heine made the descent towards Ilsenburg in a party of twenty
led by a guide, but for this description see 'Die Harzreise', *Werke* ed. *cit.*
vii 73, 'A host of other springs now hastily leapt from their concealment,
united with the one that appeared first, and soon formed an important
little brook, which, down numberless falls and by wondrous windings,

180   Of the Lower Hartz, among oaks,
     And beechen coverts, and copse
     Of hazels green in whose depth
     Ilse, the fairy transformed,
     In a thousand water-breaks light
185   Pours her petulant youth –
     Climbing the rock which juts
     O'er the valley, the dizzily perched
     Rock – to its iron cross
     Once more thou cling'st; to the Cross
190   Clingest! with smiles, with a sigh!

     Goethe, too, had been there.
     In the long-past winter he came
     To the frozen Hartz, with his soul
     Passionate, eager – his youth
195   All in ferment! – but he
     Destined to work and to live
     Left it, and thou, alas!
     Only to laugh and to die.

     But something prompts me: Not thus
200   Take leave of Heine! not thus
     Speak the last word at his grave!
     Not in pity, and not
     With half censure – with awe
     Hail, as it passes from earth
205   Scattering lightnings, that soul!

---

found its way down the mountain valley. It is now the Ilse – the sweet, the lovely Ilse. It flows through the heaven-blessed Ilsethal, along whose sides the mountains . . . are clothed to their feet, for the most part, with beeches, oak, and similar timber . . . Yes! the legend is right – the Ilse is a princess who runs laughing and blooming down the mountain . . . The tall beeches stand by like serious elders, smiling privily at the wilfulness of the lovely child.'

186–90. Heine grew giddy and clung for safety to the iron cross set on the granite cliff of the Ilsenstein – see 'Die Harzreise', *Werke* ed. *cit.* vii 76, 'I surely should have fallen with giddiness, but that in my dire distress I held fast to the iron cross. And I am sure no one will think the worse of me for doing so in such a critical moment.' The reference to the cross could hardly be more demure. A. heavyhandedly supplies the capital letter and the sigh.

191. 'See *Harzreise im Winter*, in Goethe's *Gedichte*.' A.'s note. Goethe visited the Brocken in the winter of 1777.

The Spirit of the world,
Beholding the absurdity of men –
Their vaunts, their feats – let a sardonic smile,
For one short moment, wander o'er his lips.
210   *That smile was Heine!* – for its earthly hour
The strange guest sparkled; now 'tis passed
      away.

That was Heine! and we,
Myriads who live, who have lived,
What are we all, but a mood,
215   A single mood, of the life
Of the Spirit in whom we exist,
Who alone is all things in one?

Spirit, who fillest us all!
Spirit, who utterest in each
220   New-coming son of mankind
Such of thy thoughts as thou wilt!
O thou, one of whose moods,
Bitter and strange, was the life
Of Heine – his strange, alas,
225   His bitter life! – may a life
Other and milder be mine!

May'st thou a mood more serene,

206–21. For a similar but earlier expression of pantheism see 'Empedocles on Etna' I ii 287–301 and *n.* quoting Yale MS. (p. 168 above), but A. may have been influenced here by Heine's praise of Spinoza in 'Zur Geschichte der Religion und Philosophie in Deutschland' (1835), which originally appeared in French as a series of three articles in *Revue des Deux Mondes* (1834) and formed the first part of *De l'Allemagne* in the French ed. of Heine's works. See the English translation by J. Snodgrass, *Religion and Philosophy in Germany* (1882) 77–8, 'God is identical with the world: he manifests himself in plants . . . in animals . . . But he manifests himself most gloriously in man . . . In man Deity reaches self-consciousness, and this self-consciousness Deity again reveals through man . . . in such wise that each man comprehends and represents but a portion of the God-universe; whereas collective humanity comprehends and represents in idea and in reality the whole God-universe.' The book appears as 'Heine's Germania' on A.'s reading-lists for 1862 (*Note-books* 568).
216. Spirit] Being *1867–9*. With the whole line cp. 'Rugby Chapel' 47 (p. 446 above),

      Of the Spirit in whom thou dost live . . .

Happier, have uttered in mine!
May'st thou the rapture of peace
230   Deep have embreathed at its core;
Made it a ray of thy thought,
Made it a beat of thy joy!

227–30. Cp. A.'s similar prayer in 'Lines written in Kensington Gardens'
37–40 (p. 257 above),

> *Calm soul of all things! make it mine*
> *To feel, amid the city's jar,*
> *That there abides a peace of thine,*
> *Man did not make, and cannot mar.*

94 The Terrace at Berne

Written 26 April–14 June 1863: the heading 'Composed Ten Years after
the Preceding' – first added *1869* (when the poem became the final piece
of the 'Switzerland' group) and retained in later collected editions – indicates that 'The Terrace at Berne' was conceived *c.* 29–30 June 1859 when
A. was in Berne very nearly ten years after his parting from Marguerite at
Thun, but the poem was not composed until 1863: see entries in unpublished 1863 diary 'begin Marguerite' (26 April), 'work at Marguerite'
(17, 24, 31 May), 'finish Marguerite' (14 June) and similar deleted entries
in A.'s reading-lists for April, May, June 1863 (*Note-books* 570–1); the
earlier entry 'Compose Marguerite' in April 1862 is undeleted – A.'s
intention probably being frustrated by difficulties with 'Heine's Grave'
(*Note-books* 567). The description of the poem as a 'mélange d'émotion
encore vive et de rancœur puritaine' (*Bonnerot* 71) is just.
Published *1867*; reprinted (*1868*), *1869*, etc. ('Switzerland' 8 *1869*; 7 *1877*,
etc.).

Ten years! and to my waking eye
Once more the roofs of Berne appear;
The rocky banks, the terrace high,
The stream! – and do I linger here?

5   The clouds are on the Oberland,
The Jungfrau snows look faint and far;
But bright are those green fields at hand,
And through those fields comes down the Aar,

And from the blue twin-lakes it comes,
10   Flows by the town, the churchyard fair;

¶ 94. *9. twin-lakes*] Lakes Thun and Brienz.

And 'neath the garden-walk it hums,
The house! – and is my Marguerite there?

Ah, shall I see thee, while a flush
Of startled pleasure floods thy brow,
15   Quick through the oleanders brush,
And clap thy hands, and cry: '*Tis thou!*

Or hast thou long since wandered back,
Daughter of France! to France, thy home;
And flitted down the flowery track
20   Where feet like thine too lightly come?

Doth riotous laughter now replace
Thy smile; and rouge, with stony glare,
Thy cheek's soft hue; and fluttering lace
The kerchief that enwound thy hair?

25   Or is it over? – art thou dead?
Dead! – and no warning shiver ran
Across my heart, to say thy thread
Of life was cut, and closed thy span!

Could from earth's ways that figure slight
30   Be lost, and I not feel 'twas so?
Of that fresh voice the gay delight
Fail from earth's air, and I not know?

Or shall I find thee still, but changed,
But not the Marguerite of thy prime?
35   With all thy being re-arranged,
Passed through the crucible of time;

With spirit vanished, beauty waned,
And hardly yet a glance, a tone,
A gesture – anything – retained
40   Of all that was my Marguerite's own?

11. *the garden-walk*] Of the Hotel Bellevue at Thun.
31. Cp. 'Parting' 17–18 (p. 118 above),

> But on the stairs what voice is this I hear,
> Buoyant as morning, and as morning clear?

I will not know! For wherefore try,
To things by mortal course that live,
A shadow durability,
For which they were not meant, to give?

45 Like driftwood spars, which meet and pass
Upon the boundless ocean-plain,
So on the sea of life, alas!
Man meets man – meets, and quits again.

I knew it when my life was young;
50 I feel it still, now youth is o'er.
– The mists are on the mountain hung,
And Marguerite I shall see no more.

41–4. The tortured word-order is inexcusable.

47. *sea of life*] See *n.* to 'To Marguerite – Continued' 1 (p. 124 above),
48. *1867–9,*

Man nears man, meets, and leaves again.

95 A Picture at Newstead

Written 21 June 1863: unpublished entry 'Compose sonnet on Newstead picture' in A.'s 1863 diary. For the identification of the picture as a Van Dyck portrait of the first Earl of Arundel (1585–1646) with one of his grandsons, and the suggestion that the story that struck A. may have been 'a local tradition, repeated by an attendant at the Abbey', see *Commentary* 137–8; the story is not in *A Souvenir of Newstead Abbey* (1874), which does, however, describe the Van Dyck erroneously as a portrait of the Earl of Arundel and his son. The date of A.'s visit to Newstead Abbey, the ancestral home of the Byron family in Nottinghamshire, is unknown.
In *1867* 'A Picture at Newstead' was the first of fourteen 'Italian' sonnets, which – from the known dates of three and highly probable dates of several other sonnets – were all written 1863–4 and printed in *1867* nearly or exactly in their order of composition. At least eight of the sonnets were written 21 June–25 Aug. 1863 (*Note-books* 571 and *Commentary* 135); the last four almost certainly belong to Aug.–Dec. 1864. The whole group – with the exception of the first 'Rachel' sonnet – does A. little poetic credit, but illustrates how difficult he found it to write poetry after 1860.
Published *1867*; reprinted (*1868*), *1869*, etc.

What made my heart, at Newstead, fullest swell?
'Twas not the thought of Byron, of his cry
Stormily sweet, his Titan-agony;
It was the sight of that Lord Arundel

5   Who struck, in heat, his child he loved so well,
And his child's reason flickered, and did die.
Painted (he willed it) in the gallery
They hang; the picture doth the story tell.

Behold the stern, mailed father, staff in hand!
10   The little fair-haired son, with vacant gaze,
Where no more lights of sense or knowledge are!

Methinks the woe, which made that father stand
Baring his dumb remorse to future days,
Was woe than Byron's woe more tragic far.

¶ 95. 3. *his Titan-agony*] For Byron as a Titan see 'Memorial Verses' 13–14
and *n.*, 'Haworth Churchyard' 96–7 (pp. 226–7 and 395 above). That he
should be more interested in Lord Arundel's remorse than in Lord Byron's
'cry' is A.'s snub to his own Romantic sympathies, but these sympathies
had drawn him to Newstead.

96 Rachel

I

Written 28 June 1863: one of the three sonnets on Rachel – it is natural to
assume the first – was written on this date (unpublished entry 'sonnet on
Rachel' in 1863 diary and *Commentary* 138); the second and third were
almost certainly two of the three sonnets A. is known to have completed
in July (*Note-books* 571). Rachel, the great French tragedienne, died 3 Jan.
1858 at the age of thirty-six. A.'s source for all three sonnets was A. de
Barréra's *Memoirs of Rachel* (1858), which he read in 1863 – his prose notes
paraphrasing and abbreviating passages from the *Memoirs* are in an unpublished general note-book at Yale (undated, but from other entries 1860–5).
A.'s enthusiasm for Rachel's acting sprang from seeing her in *Andromaque*
and *Phèdre* in London in July 1846; on the 29 Dec. following he arrived in
Paris and saw her ten times in plays by Racine, Corneille and other dramatists before returning to London on 11 Feb. 1847 (unpublished 1846–7
diaries). His account of these events thirty-three years later in 'The French
Play in London', *Irish Essays* (1882), *Works* xi 202 is faultily recollected,
but the essay proves that the impression Rachel made on him by her
'intellectual power' was deep and lasting.
Published *1867*; reprinted (*1868*), *1869*, etc.

In Paris all looked hot and like to fade.
Sere, in the garden of the Tuileries,
Sere with September, drooped the chestnut-trees.
'Twas dawn; a brougham rolled through the streets and
    made

5   Halt at the white and silent colonnade
Of the French Theatre. Worn with disease,
Rachel, with eyes no gazing can appease,
Sate in the brougham and those blank walls surveyed.

She follows the gay world, whose swarms have fled
To Switzerland, to Baden, to the Rhine;
Why stops she by this empty play-house drear?

Ah, where the spirit its highest life hath led,
All spots, matched with that spot, are less divine;
And Rachel's Switzerland, her Rhine, is here!

¶ 96. *1–8*. See Barréra's *Memoirs of Rachel* ii 304–5. A.'s summary of this
passage in his general note-book reads, 'On the morning of the 15th.
September she rose early, and, tormented by an anxious wish to see once
more a spot associated with the most memorable events of her life, she
was dressed long before the dawning of the tardy autumnal day. To all
remonstrances she replied that "she had a pilgrimage to perform." From
her house in the Place Royale she drove, passing by the Gymnase, to the
Théâtre Français, and ordering the carriage to stop before it, remained long
gazing at the house. A friend at last roused her from her meditations and
hurried her off. She leaned her head out of the window as long as the
building was in sight.'
2. Sere, in] Brown in *1867–9*.
3. Sere with] Brown with *1867—9*.
12–14. See *Bonnerot* 85, 'Il me semble qu'Arnold fait ici allusion à son propre
passé; il n y avait aucune nécessité de mentionner, par deux fois, la Suisse
et le Rhin, sinon pour le plaisir d'écrire . . . ces noms chéris de sa memoire
et d'affirmer, de facon indirecte et subtile, son attachement aux lieux où il
croyait vécu, lui aussi, "sa vie la plus pleine".' Switzerland and the Rhine
were associated respectively with Marguerite and with A.'s courtship of
his wife. It is the personal element that lifts this sonnet above the rest of the
1867 sonnets.

97 Rachel
II

Probably written July 1863; see headn. to previous poem.
Published *1867*; reprinted *(1868), 1869,* etc.

Unto a lonely villa, in a dell
Above the fragrant warm Provençal shore,
The dying Rachel in a chair they bore
Up the steep pine-plumed paths of the Estrelle,

5   And laid here in a stately room, where fell
The shadow of a marble Muse of yore,
The rose-crowned queen of legendary lore,
Polymnia, full on her death-bed. – 'Twas well!

The fret and misery of our northern towns,
10   In this her life's last day, our poor, our pain,
Our jangle of false wits, our climate's frowns,

Do for this radiant Greek-souled artist cease;
Sole object of her dying eyes remain
The beauty and the glorious art of Greece.

¶ 97. *1–8*. Cp. A.'s summary of *Memoirs of Rachel* ii 305–8, 'She was
carried in a chair from the station to the railway carriage, for she was no
longer able to walk. M. Sardou had lent her his villa in the South of France.
This villa is not at Cannes, but at Cannet, a little village in the environs, of
very difficult access. The road to it is from Cannes, and so difficult that
horses and carriages cannot pass, but the visitor has to walk or be carried
through the ravines and valleys. The house is spacious, beautifully situated
in an orange-grove, and well guarded from the wind . . . In the best
chamber – a spacious one with high snow-white walls, adorned with
friezes and sculptures in the antique style – the bed was also white and
seemed carved of stone. At the foot of the bed was a statute of Polyhymnia, wearing an expression of intense sadness; attired in long sweeping
robes that had a funereal aspect, she leaned on a pedestal that resembled a
tomb.'
8. Polymnia] Polymnia (Polyhymnia) was the Muse of mimic art.
11. Our jangle of false wits] Cp. 'The Second Best' 9–10 (p. 278 above),

          . . . *the world's so madly jangled,*
          Human things so fast entangled . . .

12. Greek-souled artist] See A.'s 'The French Play in London' (1879),
Works xi 204, 'One remark I will make, a remark suggested by the
inevitable comparison of Mdlle. Sarah Bernhardt with Rachel. One talks
vaguely of genius, but I had never till now comprehended how much of
Rachel's superiority was purely in intellectual power, how eminently this
power counts in the actor's art as in all art, how just is the instinct which
led the Greeks to mark with a high and severe stamp the Muses.'

98 Rachel
III

Probably written July 1863: see headn. to 'Rachel I' (p. 482 above).
Published *1867*; reprinted (*1868*), *1869*, etc.

Sprung from the blood of Israel's scattered race,
At a mean inn in German Aarau born,
To forms from antique Greece and Rome uptorn,
Tricked out with a Parisian speech and face,

5   Imparting life renewed, old classic grace;
Then, soothing with thy Christian strain forlorn,
A-Kempis! her departing soul outworn,
While by her bedside Hebrew rites have place –

Ah, not the radiant spirit of Greece alone
10   She had – one power, which made her breast its
         home!
In her, like us, there clashed, contending powers,

Germany, France, Christ, Moses, Athens, Rome.
The strife, the mixture in her soul, are ours;
Her genius and her glory are her own.

¶ 98. *2.* Cp. A.'s summary of *Memoirs of Rachel* i 7, 'She was born at a wretched little inn at Munf, Canton Aarau, Switzerland, on the 24th of March 1821.'
3–4. French classical tragedy. 'Tricked out' has a touch of hostility – cp. 'The French Play in London', *Irish Essays* (1882), *Works* xi 217, 'But the French had no Shakespeare to open their eyes to the insufficiencies of Corneille and Racine. Great artists like Talma and Rachel, whose power, as actors, was far superior to the power, as poets, of the dramatists whose works they were rendering ... themselves supported the poetry of the French classic drama rather than were supported by it.'
6–8. Cp. A.'s summary of *Memoirs of Rachel* ii 319, 324, 'The Jewish service for the dying was performed over her in her last moments, and she showed emotion at it ... But Rachel never gave signs of a preference for any particular creed; and so long as she had strength to read anything, her favourite book was the Imitation.' The *Imitation of Christ*, 'the most exquisite document after those of the New Testament, of all the documents the Christian spirit has ever inspired ...' ('Marcus Aurelius', *E in C* I (1865), *Works* x 378), is one of the most frequently quoted books in A.'s note-books.

99 East London

Date of composition unknown, but from position in *1867* and 'August' in
l. 1 probably written early Aug. 1863. For the identification of the preacher
(l. 5) as the Rev. William Tyler, a Congregational minister whom A. met
while inspecting schools in London's East End, see *Commentary* 141–2.
Published *1867*; reprinted (*1868*), *1869*, etc.

> 'Twas August, and the fierce sun overhead
> Smote on the squalid streets of Bethnal Green,
> And the pale weaver, through his windows seen
> In Spitalfields, looked thrice dispirited.
>
> 5   I met a preacher there I knew, and said:
> 'Ill and o'erworked, how fare you in this scene?'
> 'Bravely!' said he; 'for I of late have been
> 'Much cheered with thoughts of Christ, *the living*
>   *bread.*'
>
> O human soul! as long as thou canst so
> 10   Set up a mark of everlasting light,
> Above the howling senses' ebb and flow,
>
> To cheer thee, and to right thee if thou roam –
> Not with lost toil thou labourest through the night!
> Thou mak'st the heaven thou hop'st indeed thy
>   home.

¶ 99. *10–11*. These lines anticipate the central image of 'Palladium' (p. 494
below) and also recall 'Absence' 13–16 (p. 139 above),

> *I struggle towards the light; and ye,*
> *Once-longed-for storms of love!*
> *If with the light ye cannot be,*
> *I bear that ye remove.*

100 West London

Date of composition unknown, but (?) Aug. 1863: the poem is a companion piece to 'East London' and was probably composed about the same
time.
Published *1867*; reprinted (*1868*), *1869*, etc.

Crouched on the pavement, close by Belgrave Square,
A tramp I saw, ill, moody, and tongue-tied.
A babe was in her arms, and at her side
A girl; their clothes were rags, their feet were bare.

5   Some labouring men, whose work lay somewhere
           there,
Passed opposite; she touched her girl, who hied
Across, and begged, and came back satisfied.
The rich she had let pass with frozen stare.

     Thought I: 'Above her state this spirit towers;
10   She will not ask of aliens, but of friends,
     Of sharers in a common human fate.

     She turns from that cold succour, which attends
     The unknown little from the unknowing great,
     And points us to a better time than ours.'

101 The Better Part

Date of composition unknown, but from position in *1867* probably July or
Aug. 1863. The 'better part' is to choose to live virtuously simply because
this is to be 'human' rather than 'animal' – see *n*. to ll. 12–14 below. A
would find support for his view that humanity does not need to be cajoled
or frightened into virtue by supernatural rewards or punishments in
Marcus Aurelius, whom he was reading July–Sept. 1863 – see headn. to
'Worldly Place' (p. 489 below) and cp. Marcus Aurelius ix 42 tr. G. Long
(1875 ed.) 170, '. . . art thou not content that thou hast done something
conformable to thy nature, and dost thou seek to be paid for it, just as if
the eye demanded a recompense for seeing, or the feet for walking?'
Published as 'Anti-Desperation' *1867*; reprinted (*1868*); with present title
1869, etc.

     Long fed on boundless hopes, O race of man,
     How angrily thou spurn'st all simpler fare!
     'Christ,' some one says, 'was human as we are;
     No judge eyes us from Heaven, our sin to scan;

5   'We live no more, when we have done our span.'
     'Well, then, for Christ,' thou answerest, 'who can care?
     From sin, which Heaven records not, why forbear?
     Live we like brutes our life without a plan!'

¶ 101. *1. boundless hopes*] Of personal immortality.

So answerest thou; but why not rather say:
10   'Hath man no second life? – *Pitch this one high!*
Sits there no judge in Heaven, our sin to see?

'*More strictly, then, the inward judge obey!*
Was Christ a man like us? *Ah! let us try*
If we then, too, can be such men as he!'

12–14. Cp. *Culture and Anarchy* (1869), *Works* vi 11, 'Religion says: *The kingdom of God is within you*; and culture in like manner, places human perfection in an *internal* condition, in the growth and predominance of our humanity proper, as distinguished from our animality.'

102 Immortality

Date of composition unknown, but from position in *1867* probably July or Aug. 1863.
Published *1867*; reprinted (*1868*), *1869*, etc.

Foiled by our fellow-men, depressed, outworn,
We leave the brutal world to take its way,
And, *Patience, in another life,* we say,
The world shall be thrust down, and we up-borne.

5   And will not, then, the immortal armies scorn
The world's poor, routed leavings? or will they,
Who failed under the heat of this life's day,
Support the fervours of the heavenly morn?

No, no! the energy of life may be
10   Kept on after the grave, but not begun;
And he who flagged not in the earthly strife,

¶ 102. *9–14.* A. is playing with the idea of immortality for a selected few and extinction for the many – cp. 'Rugby Chapel' 40–3 (p. 446 above),

Somewhere, surely, afar
In the sounding labour-house vast
Of being, is practised that strength,
Zealous, beneficent, firm!

He had entertained something like the same idea much earlier – see his letter to Clough 29 Sept. 1848, 'Farewell, my love, to meet I hope at Oxford: not alas in heaven: tho: thus much I cannot but think: that our spirits retain their conquests; that from the height they succeed in raising themselves to, they can never fall. Tho: this uti possedetes principle may be compatible with entire loss of individuality and of the power to recognize one another' (*CL* 93).

From strength to strength advancing – only he,
His soul well-knit, and all his battles won,
Mounts, and that hardly, to eternal life.

103 Worldly Place

Written *c.* 25 Aug. 1863: the entry 'A man can even live well in a palace.
Long. 71' is in A.'s 1863 diary under this date (*Note-books* 19 and *Commen-
tary* 140) and refers to G. Long's translation *The Thoughts of the Emperor
M. Aurelius Antoninus* (1862), which is praised in A.'s essay 'Marcus
Aurelius', *E in C I* (1865), *Works* iii 377–416. The sonnet is a by-product
of A.'s reading for this essay, which was written July–Sept. 1863 (*Note-
books* 571–2).
Published *1867*; reprinted (*1868*), *1869*, etc.

Even in a palace, life may be led well!
So spake the imperial sage, purest of men,
Marcus Aurelius. But the stifling den
Of common life, where, crowded up pell-mell,

5   Our freedom for a little bread we sell,
And drudge under some foolish master's ken
Who rates us if we peer outside our pen –
Matched with a palace, is not this a hell!

¶ 103. *1.* See Marcus Aurelius v 16 tr. G. Long (1875 ed.) 112, 'Dye it [the
soul] with a continuous series of thoughts such as these: for instance, that
where a man can live, there he can also live well. But he must live in a
palace; – well then, he can also live well in a palace.'
3. Marcus Aurelius] Roman emperor (in succession to Antoninus Pius
161 A.D.) and Stoic moralist. A. characterizes him as 'wise, just, self-
governed, tender, thankful, blameless' in his essay (*Works* iii 416).
3–7. Cp. 'A Summer Night' 37–40 (p. 269 above),

> For most men in a brazen prison live,
> Where, in the sun's hot eye,
> With heads bent o'er their toil, they languidly
> Their lives to some unmeaning taskwork give . . .

A. is using Marcus Aurelius to help him to resign himself to the 'brazen
prison', i.e. his tedious life as a school-inspector. See A.'s letter to Lady de
Rothschild 14 Oct. 1864, 'I must go back to my charming occupation of
hearing students give lessons . . . Alluring, is it not? Twenty minutes each,
and the days of one's life are only threescore years and ten' (*L* i 242).

17 + M.A.

> *Even in a palace!* On his truth sincere,
> 10   Who spoke these words, no shadow ever came;
>   And when my ill-schooled spirit is aflame
>
>   Some nobler, ampler stage of life to win,
>   I'll stop, and say: 'There were no succour here!
>   The aids to noble life are all within.'

14. Cp., for example, Marcus Aurelius iv 3 ed. *cit.* 93, 'Men seek retreats for themselves . . . and thou too art wont to desire such things very much. But this is altogether a mark of the most common sort of men, for it is in thy power whenever thou shalt choose to retire into thyself.'

104 The Divinity

Date of composition unknown, but from position in *1867* perhaps the last sonnet written in the summer of 1863. A.'s source is a sentence in J. C. Morison's *The Life and Times of St. Bernard* . . . (1863) 465, '"Write it," replied Bernard, "with a pen of iron, and with the point of a diamond; nay, grave it in the flinty rock, that the Divine Essence, nature, form, deity, goodness, wisdom, virtue, power, magnitude, truly is God".' The book was marked as read in Feb. 1863 (*Note-books* 569), but A. could have written the sonnet in Aug. or Sept. from a prose note made in Feb. or from recollection of the passage.
Published *1867*; reprinted (*1868*), *1869*, etc.

>   'Yes, write it in the rock,' Saint Bernard said,
>   'Grave it on brass with adamantine pen!
>   'Tis God himself becomes apparent, when
>   God's wisdom and God's goodness are displayed,
>
> 5   'For God of these his attributes is made.'
>   Well spake the impetuous Saint, and bore of men
>   The suffrage captive; now, not one in ten
>   Recalls the obscure opposer he outweighed.
>
>   *God's wisdom and God's goodness!* – Ay, but fools
> 10   Mis-define these till God knows them no more.
>   *Wisdom and goodness, they are God!* – what schools

¶ 104. *8. the obscure opposer*] 'Gilbert de la Porrée, at the Council of Rheims, in 1148.' A.'s *1867* note. The dispute between Gilbert and St. Bernard, which turned on a charge that the former's views amounted to tritheism, did not really interest A. He fastened on a sentence that out of context might seem to support his own theological liberalism.

Have yet so much as heard this simpler lore?
This no Saint preaches, and this no Church rules;
'Tis in the desert, now and heretofore.

105 The Good Shepherd with the Kid

Written 27 Nov. 1864: unpublished entry 'Compose sonnet (Tertullian)'
in A.'s 1864 diary. A.'s source is A. F. Ozanam's *Les Poètes franciscains en
Italie au treizième siecle* (Paris, 1852) 20 *fn.*, 'Les peintures des catacombes
représentent quelquefois le Bon Pasteur chargé, non d'une brebis, mais
d'un chevreau ... Lorsqu'au second siècle, la secte des Montanistes refusait
à l'Église le droit de remettre les péchés commis après le baptême, les
catholiques leur opposaient l'exemple du Bon Pasteur rapportant la brebis
égarée. Mais Tertullien, qui venait de mettre sa fougueuse parole au
service de l'hérésie, reprochait aux catholiques de profaner ce parabole ...
"Le Christ, disait-il, ne sauve que la brebis, il est sans pitié pour les boucs."
L'Église répondit à cette doctrine désespérante en mettant un chevreau sur
les épaules du Pasteur éternel.' A. marked this book as read in 1864
(*Note-books* 576).
Published *1867*; reprinted (*1868*), *1869*, etc.

> He saves the sheep, the goats he doth not save.
> So rang Tertullian's sentence, on the side
> Of that unpitying Phrygian sect which cried:
> 'Him can no fount of fresh forgiveness lave,
>
> 5   Who sins, once washed by the baptismal wave.'
> So spake the fierce Tertullian. But she sighed,
> The infant Church! of love she felt the tide
> Stream on her from her Lord's yet recent grave.
>
> And then she smiled; and in the Catacombs,
> 10   With eye suffused but heart inspired true,
> On those walls subterranean, where she hid
>
> Her head 'mid ignominy, death, and tombs,
> She her Good Shepherd's hasty image drew –
> And on his shoulders, not a lamb, a kid.

¶ 105. *3. that unpitying Phrygian sect*] 'The Montanists.' A.'s note first
added *1869*. For Tertullian's support *c.* 206 A.D. of the ascetic exaggera-
tions that this second-century apocalyptic movement developed in Africa
see *Oxford Dictionary of the Christian Church* (1958) under 'Montanism'.
7–8. Cp. 'Obermann Once More' 146–8 (p. 526 below),

> ... the wave
> *Of love which set so deep and strong*
> *From Christ's then open grave.*

106 Austerity of Poetry

Date of composition unknown, but from position in *1867* and common
source with the previous poem (?) Nov.–Dec. 1864. A.'s source is A. F.
Ozanam's *Les Poètes franciscains en Italie au treizième siecle* (Paris, 1852)
170–1, 'Il arriva qu'un jour de l'année 1268, la ville de Todi célébrait des
jeux publics. La jeune épouse du jurisconsulte fut invitée; elle prit place sur
une estrade couverte de nobles femmes, pour jouir de la fête et pour en
faire le plus aimable ornement. Tout à coup l'estrade s'écroule . . . Jacques
se précipite, reconnaît sa femme parmi les victimes, l'enlève encore palpi-
tante, et veut la délivrer de ses vêtements. Mais elle, d'une main pudique,
repoussait les efforts de son mari, jusqu'à ce que, l'ayant portée dans un lieu
retiré, il put la découvrir enfin. Sous les riches tissus qu'elle portait, il
aperçut un cilice: au même instant, la mourante rendit le dernier soupir.'
A.'s reading of Ozanam was part of his preparations for his essay, 'Pagan
and Mediaeval Religious Sentiment', *E in C I* (1865), originally delivered
as a lecture 5 March 1864.
Published *1867*; reprinted (*1868*), *1869*, etc.

> That son of Italy who tried to blow,
> Ere Dante came, the trump of sacred song,
> In his light youth amid a festal throng
> Sate with his bride to see a public show.
>
> 5   Fair was the bride, and on her front did glow
> Youth like a star; and what to youth belong –
> Gay raiment, sparkling gauds, elation strong.
> A prop gave way! crash fell a platform! lo,
>
> 'Mid struggling sufferers, hurt to death, she lay!
> 10   Shuddering, they drew her garments off – and found
> A robe of sackcloth next the smooth, white skin.
>
> Such, poets, is your bride, the Muse! young, gay,
> Radiant, adorned outside; a hidden ground
> Of thought and of austerity within.

¶ 106. *1–2.* 'Giacopone di Todi.' A.'s *1867* note. Ozanam describes Giacopone (*c.* 1230–1306), who became a Franciscan after his wife's death
(*c.* 1268), as a precursor of Dante.

107 East and West

Date of composition unknown, but almost certainly 1864: its position in
1867 suggests that it was probably written Dec. 1864, but the use of an
unfamiliar Welsh legend may connect the sonnet with A.'s holiday in

North Wales in the previous Aug. – see his letter to his sister Frances Aug. 1864, 'The poetry of the Celtic race and its names of places quite over-powers me . . .' (*L* i 238). A.'s direct source is unknown, but he could have heard the legend – which he either misunderstood or altered to suit his purposes – in North Wales. The correct version is given by H. Wright in *MLR* xiii (1918) 324: 'Once a week Cybi and Seiriol used to meet in the middle of Anglesey at a place called Clorach near Llanerchymedd. At the present two springs, some ten yards apart, still exist there. One of them bears the name of Ffynnon Seiriol, the other that of Ffynnon Gybi . . . Seiriol, starting from Penmon towards Clorach, was travelling westwards and had the morning sun behind him. When returning home in the evening his face was once more turned from the sun. Hence in Welsh he is called *Seiriol wyn* or Seiriol the fair. Cybi, coming from Holyhead, faced the sun, and similarly on his homeward journey. In Welsh he is therefore styled *Cybi felyn* or Cybi the brown, that is, the sun-burnt . . .' Published *1867*; reprinted (*1868*), *1869*, etc.

> In the bare midst of Anglesey they show
> Two springs which close by one another play;
> And, 'Thirteen hundred years agone,' they say,
> 'Two saints met often where those waters flow.
>
> 5 'One came from Penmon westward, and a glow
> Whitened his face from the sun's fronting ray;
> Eastward the other, from the dying day,
> And he with unsunned face did always go.'
>
> *Seiriol the Bright, Kybi the Dark!* men said.
> 10 The seër from the East was then in light,
> The seër from the west was then in shade.
>
> Ah! now 'tis changed. In conquering sunshine bright
> The man of the bold West now comes arrayed;
> He of the mystic East is touched with night.

108 Monica's Last Prayer

Date of composition unknown, but almost certainly 1864: its position in *1867* suggests that it was probably written Dec. 1864, but – like the pre-vious sonnet, 'East and West' – it may be connected with A.'s summer holiday in North Wales; A. proposed to take 'St. Augustine' with him as holiday reading in Aug. 1864 (*Note-books* 574) and his *1869* note 'See St. Augustine's *Confessions*, book ix, chapter 11' indicates the sonnet's source. A. used the following passage: 'ego silebam et fletum frenabam. frater autem meus quiddam locutus est, quo eam non in peregre, sed in patriam

defungi tamquam felicius optaret. quo audito illa vultu anxio, reverberans
eum oculis, quod talia saperet, atque inde me intuens: "vide", ait, "quid
dicit". et mox ambobus: "ponite", inquit, "hoc corpus ubicumque: nihil
vos eius cura conturbet; tantum illud vos rogo, ut ad domini altare
memineritis mei, ubiubi fueritis". cumque hanc sententiam verbis quibus
poterat explicasset, conticuit et ingravescente morbo exercebatur'.
Published *1867*; reprinted (*1868*), *1869*, etc.

> 'Ah, could thy grave at home, at Carthage, be!'
> *Care not for that, and lay me where I fall!*
> *Everywhere heard will be the judgment-call;*
> *But at God's altar, oh! remember me.*

5   Thus Monica, and died in Italy.
    Yet fervent had her longing been, through all
    Her course, for home at last, and burial
    With her own husband, by the Libyan sea.

    Had been! but at the end, to her pure soul
10   All tie with all beside seemed vain and cheap,
    And union before God the only care.

    Creeds pass, rites change, no altar standeth whole.
    Yet we her memory, as she prayed, will keep,
    Keep by this: *Life in God, and union there!*

¶ 108. *5*. St. Monica, mother of St. Augustine, died at Ostia A.D. 387 when
she was about to return with him to Africa.
12. Cp. 'Obermann Once More' 229 (p. 529 below),

> *Your creeds are dead, your rites are dead . . .*

109 Palladium

Date of composition unknown, but not earlier than Sept. 1864 if, as seems
likely, the germ of the poem is the following phrase from E. Scherer's
Alexandre Vinet (Paris, 1853), '. . . ce palladium de l'humanité, de la verité,
de la vie, l'individualité . . .': A. read Scherer's book in Sept. 1864 and
planned to write on Vinet in 1865 (*Note-books* 574, 577); the phrase
quoted is underlined in A.'s copy, with the marginal comment, 'Yes –
l'individualité is all this . . .' (*Commentary* 190). The setting reflects A.'s

¶ 109. *Title.* The Palladium was the archaic wooden image of Pallas
preserved in the Trojan citadel as a pledge of the safety of Troy.

regular reading of Homer, but the battle tranquilly overlooked also recalls
Lucretius, *De Rerum Natura* ii 5–6,

> *suave etiam belli certamina magna tueri*
> *per campos instructa tua sine parte pericli . . .*

(part of a passage already imitated in 'Resignation' 164 ff., p. 90 above).
The Stoic notion of a self withdrawn from the struggle of warring im-
pulses occurs frequently in A.'s poetry and prose; with the image of the
Palladium above the battle compare A.'s note in Yale MS. (undated, but
probably 1849–52), 'Our remotest self must abide in its remoteness awful
and unchanged, presiding at the tumult of the rest of our being, changing
thoughts contending desires etc. as the moon over the agitations of the
Sea.'
Published *1867*; reprinted (*1868*), *1869*, etc.

> Set where the upper streams of Simois flow
> Was the Palladium, high 'mid rock and wood;
> And Hector was in Ilium, far below,
> And fought, and saw it not – but there it stood!

> 5   It stood, and sun and moonshine rained their light
> On the pure columns of its glen-built hall.
> Backward and forward rolled the waves of fight
> Round Troy – but while this stood, Troy could not
>   fall.

> So, in its lovely moonlight, lives the soul.
> 10   Mountains surround it, and sweet virgin air;
> Cold plashing, past it, crystal waters roll;
> We visit it by moments, ah, too rare!

8. *while this stood, Troy could not fall*] See Apollodorus, *Epitome* v 10,
'Helenus was forced to tell how Ilium could be taken, to wit, first if the
bones of Pelops were brought to them [the Greeks]; next, if Neoptolemus
fought for them; and third, if the Palladium, which had fallen from
heaven, were stolen from Troy, for while it was within the walls the city
could not be taken.'
9–11. A.'s ideal landscape to represent the soul's purity. With l. 9 cp.
'Empedocles on Etna' II [i] 392–3 (p. 191 above),

> *And who can say: I have been always free,*
> *Lived ever in the light of my own soul?*

12. Cp. 'The Buried Life' 77–90 (p. 275 above) and especially 77, 86,

> *Only – but this is rare . . .*

> *The eye sinks inward, and the heart lies plain . . .*

We shall renew the battle in the plain
To-morrow; red with blood will Xanthus be;
15   Hector and Ajax will be there again,
Helen will come upon the wall to see.

Then we shall rust in shade, or shine in strife,
And fluctuate 'twixt blind hopes and blind despairs,
And fancy that we put forth all our life,
20   And never know how with the soul it fares.

Still doth the soul, from its lone fastness high,
Upon our life a ruling effluence send.
And when it fails, fight as we will, we die;
And while it lasts, we cannot wholly end.

16. *Iliad* iii 154 ff.
17. *rust in shade*] A. uses 'rust' only here and in 'Balder Dead' iii 471–2
(p. 385 above),

> *Yet here thou liest, Balder, underground,*
> *Rusting for ever . . .*

18. *fluctuate*] Cp. 'The Scholar-Gipsy' 166–7 (p. 340 above),

> *O life unlike to ours!*
> *Who fluctuate idly without term or scope . . .*

and *n*. The word has the same unfavourable associations for A. as
'eddying'.
22. *effluence*] Used this once by A.

110 Thyrsis

A MONODY, *to commemorate the author's friend,*
ARTHUR HUGH CLOUGH, *who died at Florence,*
1861

Exact period of composition unknown, but projected 1862–3 and probably
mainly written 1864–5: the elegy was finished by late Jan. 1866 – see the
unpublished deleted entries in A.'s 1866 diary 'begin writing out poem' (23
and 25 Jan.) and 'send . . . poem' (26 Jan.) and his letter to his mother
3 Feb. 1866, 'I shall publish in April my poem about Clough, in *Macmillan*'

¶ 110. *Title*. A. is recalling the shepherd of this name in Virgil, *Eclogues* vii
(as the reference to rivalry with Corydon in l. 81 below indicates). The
name is also found in Theocritus, *Idylls* i.
Heading. The phrasing is intended to recall the heading of Milton's 'Lycidas': 'In this Monody the Author bewails a learned Friend, unfortunately

(*L* i 315) – but the dates of the poem's conception and of the main period of composition involve conjecture. The poem probably first took shape as an idea late March or early May 1862 when A. was in Oxford (*L* i 167, 169) – two months after Clough's death (13 Nov. 1861) A. had written to his widow 22 Jan. 1862, 'I shall take them [verses by C.] with me to Oxford, where I shall go alone after Easter; – and there, among the Cumner hills where we have so often rambled, I shall be able to think him over as I could wish' (*CL* 160). No progress with the elegy, however, was made in the first half of 1863 – see the undeleted entry 'Clough and Cumner Hill Side' in A.'s April reading-list and similar undeleted entries May and July (*Note-books* 570, 571); A.'s letter to his mother 25 April 1863 explains the failure in April, 'The weather was fine but with a detestable cold wind, so that a new poem about the Cumner hillside, and Clough in connexion with it, which I meant to have begun at Oxford this week, I could not begin. I have been accumulating stores for it, however' (*L* i 191), but throughout the summer A. was busy with other work in poetry and prose. The description of the mild 'winter-eve' (st. 2) suggests that the composition of 'Thyrsis' may have begun late Nov. or early Dec. 1863: A. was in Oxford to lecture on Joubert 28 Nov. 1863. Similarly, sts. 6–8 are likely to have been composed *c.* June 1864: A. was living at Woodford, Essex, May–July 1864 and wrote to his mother 7 April 1866 that these stanzas were 'reminiscences of Woodford' (*L* i 325). R. L. Brooks has shown that the identical deleted entries 'compose stanza' in A.'s 1865 diary under 22 and 29 Jan., 5 Feb., 26 March and 24 Dec. must refer to 'Thyrsis' (*RES* n.s. xiv (1963) 174). The record for 1865 is probably incomplete, and there are no corresponding entries for 1864, but the weight of evidence, external and internal, suggests that the poem was composed at intervals throughout 1864–5. A.'s 1866 reference to Theocritus, 'whom I have been much, reading during the two years this poem has been forming itself' (*L* i 325),

---

drown'd in his Passage from *Chester* on the *Irish* Seas, 1637 . . .' In *1867–8* only followed by this motto:

> *Thus yesterday, to-day, to-morrow come,*
> *They hustle one another and they pass;*
> *But all our hustling morrows only make*
> *The smooth to-day of God.*
>
> From Lucretius, *an unpublished Tragedy.*

The lines are without a particular application to 'Thyrsis', but by using them A. asserted a priority of claim to Lucretius as a poetic subject – see his letter to his mother 17 March 1866, 'I am rather troubled to find that Tennyson is at work on a subject, the story of the Latin poet Lucretius, which I have been occupied with for some twenty years. I was going to make a tragedy out of it, and the worst of it is that every one . . . will think I borrowed the subject from him' (*L* i 322). Tennyson's 'Lucretius' first appeared in *Macmillan's Magazine* May 1868.

17*

supports the idea of piecemeal composition 1864–5, but the only mention
of Theocritus in A.'s reading-lists between Clough's death and the publication of 'Thyrsis' is the deleted entry '(finish) Theocritus' in 1863
(*Note-books* 572).

A.'s *1867* note, 'Throughout this Poem there is reference to another piece,
The Scholar-Gipsy . . .', indicates the relationship between the two elegies,
which share the same stanza and are both influenced stylistically by Keats.
'Thyrsis' was praised by the reviewers; in the *Fortnightly Review* (Oct.
1867) Swinburne ranked it immediately after Milton's 'Lycidas' and
Shelley's 'Adonais' (see *Essays and Studies* (1875) 155–8); there are still
modern critics who prefer it to 'The Scholar-Gipsy'. For A.'s opinion see
his letter to J. C. Shairp 12 April 1866, '"Thyrsis" is a very quiet poem,
but I think solid and sincere. It will not be popular, however. It had long
been in my head to connect Clough with that Cumner country, and when
I began I was carried irresistibly into this form . . . one has the feeling, if
one reads the poem as a memorial poem, that not enough is said about
Clough in it . . . Still Clough *had* this idyllic side, too; to deal with this
suited my desire to deal again with that Cumner country: any way, only
so could I treat the matter this time' (*L* i 327). A.'s favourite stanzas were
'O easy access' (st. 10) and 'And long the way appears' (st. 15); he was
fond also of 'I know these slopes' (st. 12) and 'Where is the girl' (st. 13),
but this was 'because they bring certain places and moments before me'
(*L* i 325). A. claimed to have modelled his diction on Theocritus (*L* i 325),
but the debt to 'The Lament for Bion' is more obvious. (Moschus, to
whom 'The Lament' was then attributed, was read with Theocritus and
Bion in 1863 – see *Note-books* 572). For the topography of 'Thyrsis' see
Sir Francis Wylie's 'The Scholar-Gipsy Country', *Commentary* 351–73.
Published *Macmillan's Magazine* April 1866; reprinted *1867* (*1868*), *1869*,
etc. (Magazine publication in *Every Saturday* (U.S.A.) 10 March 1866 preceded first publication in England.)

> How changed is here each spot man makes or fills!
>   In the two Hinkseys nothing keeps the same;
>   The village street its haunted mansion lacks,
>   And from the sign is gone Sibylla's name,
> 5   And from the roofs the twisted chimney-stacks –
>   Are ye too changed, ye hills?
>   See, 'tis no foot of unfamiliar men
>   To-night from Oxford up your pathway strays!
>   Here came I often, often, in old days –
> 10   Thyrsis and I; we still had Thyrsis then.

1–10. For A.'s stanza see *n.* to 'The Scholar-Gipsy' 1–10 (p. 333 above).
2–4. See F. Wylie, 'The Scholar-Gipsy Country', *Commentary* 355–6.
Sybella Curr, who kept the Cross Keys inn in South Hinksey, died in 1860.
The 'haunted mansion' was in North Hinksey.

Runs it not here, the track by Childsworth Farm,
　　Past the high wood, to where the elm-tree crowns
　　　The hill behind whose ridge the sunset flames?
　　The signal-elm, that looks on Ilsley Downs,
15　　　The Vale, the three lone weirs, the youthful
　　　　Thames?
　　　　This winter-eve is warm,
　　Humid the air! leafless, yet soft as spring,
　　　The tender purple spray on copse and briers!
　　And that sweet city with her dreaming spires,
20　She needs not June for beauty's heightening,

Lovely all times she lies, lovely to-night! –
　　Only, methinks, some loss of habit's power
　　　Befalls me wandering through this upland dim.
　　Once passed I blindfold here, at any hour;
25　　　Now seldom come I, since I came with him.
　　　　That single elm-tree bright
　　Against the west – I miss it! is it gone?
　　　We prized it dearly; while it stood, we said,
　　Our friend, the Gipsy-Scholar, was not dead;
30　While the tree lived, he in these fields lived on.

Too rare, too rare, grow now my visits here,
　　But once I knew each field, each flower, each stick;
　　　And with the country-folk acquaintance made
　　By barn in threshing time, by new-built rick.

11. *Childsworth Farm*] So in the Ordnance Survey map of 1830, but more usually 'Chilswell Farm' (F. Wylie, *Commentary* 352–3).
16. *winter-eve*] See headn. above for A.'s presence in Oxford 28 Nov. 1863.
19–21. Cp. A.'s Preface to *E in C I* (1865), *Works* iii [11], 'Beautiful city! so venerable, so lovely, so unravaged by the fierce intellectual life of our century, so serene! . . . Adorable dreamer, whose heart has been so romantic!' In 'The Scholar-Gipsy' the Berkshire countryside provided an escape from Oxford; here Oxford and the Cumnor country are associated as an escape from the fierceness of the modern world.
26–30. The 'single elm-tree bright / Against the west' is the central symbol of 'Thyrsis' as the scholar-gipsy is of the earlier elegy. The search for the tree in the poem is a repetition of the scholar-gipsy's quest; A.'s sight of the tree (l. 160) and immediate recognition that he cannot reach it 'to-night' (l. 165) are a way of saying that the search for truth, however difficult, is not hopeless. On the 'quest' theme of the poem and the imagery connected with it see J. P. Curgenven, *Litera* vi (1959) 1–8.
34. *By barn in threshing-time*] Cp. 'The Scholar-Gipsy' 104 (p. 337 above),

　　　　To watch the threshers in the mossy barns.

35   Here, too, our shepherd-pipes we first assayed.
              Ah me! this many a year
          My pipe is lost, my shepherd's holiday!
              Needs must I lose them, needs with heavy heart
              Into the world and wave of men depart;
40   But Thyrsis of his own will went away.

          It irked him to be here, he could not rest.
              He loved each simple joy the country yields,
                  He loved his mates; but yet he could not keep,
              For that a shadow loured on the fields,
45   Here with the shepherds and the silly sheep.
                  Some life of men unblest
              He knew, which made him droop, and filled his head.
                  He went; his piping took a troubled sound
                  Of storms that rage outside our happy ground;
50   He could not wait their passing, he is dead.

          So, some tempestuous morn in early June,
              When the year's primal burst of bloom is o'er,
                  Before the roses and the longest day –
              When garden-walks and all the grassy floor
55   With blossoms red and white of fallen May
                  And chestnut-flowers are strewn –
              So have I heard the cuckoo's parting cry,
                  From the wet field, through the vexed garden-
                      trees,
                  Come with the volleying rain and tossing breeze:
60   *The bloom is gone, and with the bloom go I!*

35–7. Cp. Milton's similar use of the pastoral convention, 'Lycidas' 23–33.
35. *assayed*] Essayed.
41–50. Misleading as biography. Clough's social conscience (ll. 46–7) had
nothing directly to do with his leaving Oxford, and his poetry was no
more troubled after than before Oct. 1848 (when C. resigned his Oriel
fellowship because he feared 'that he could not honestly pursue Truth,
whilst under the fetters of Subscription to articles' – notes made 18 Oct.
1848 by the Provost of Oriel, E. Hawkins, *Correspondence of A.H.C.* i 221).
The dismissal of his friend's honesty as a kind of impatience betrays A.'s
hostility to an idealism less accommodating than his own.
51–80. See A.'s letter to his mother 7 April 1866, 'The cuckoo on the wet
June morning I heard in the garden at Woodford, and all those three
stanzas you like are reminiscences of Woodford' (*L* i 325).
57. *the cuckoo's parting cry*] An error. The cuckoo 'changes his tune' in
June, but does not migrate until August.
60. *bloom*] See *n.* to 'The Youth of Nature' 54 (p. 247 above).

Too quick despairer, wherefore wilt thou go?
   Soon will the high Midsummer pomps come on,
      Soon will the musk carnations break and swell,
   Soon shall we have gold-dusted snapdragon,
65   Sweet-William with his homely cottage-smell,
         And stocks in fragrant blow;
   Roses that down the alleys shine afar,
      And open, jasmine-muffled lattices,
         And groups under the dreaming garden-trees,
70   And the full moon, and the white evening-star.

He hearkens not! light comer, he is flown!
   What matters it? next year he will return,
      And we shall have him in the sweet spring-days,
   With whitening hedges, and uncrumpling fern,
75   And blue-bells trembling by the forest-ways,
         And scent of hay new-mown.
   But Thyrsis never more we swains shall see;
      See him come back, and cut a smoother reed,
         And blow a strain the world at last shall heed –
80   For Time, not Corydon, hath conquered thee!

63–8. A.'s version of the flower-sequence of the pastoral elegy—cp.
'Lycidas' 133–51.

69. dreaming garden-trees] Perhaps suggested by Keats's 'Hyperion' i 72,
74–5,

   As when upon a trancéd summer night

   Tall oaks, branch-charméd by the earnest stars,
   Dream, and so dream all night without a stir . . .

The whole stanza is Keatsian.

71–77. A free imitation of 'Lament for Bion' 99–104, 'Ay me! when the
mallows and the fresh green parsley and the springing crumpled anise
perish in the garden, they live yet again and grow another year; but we
men . . . soon as ever we be dead, unhearing there in a hole of the earth
sleep we both sound and long a sleep that is without end or waking' (Loeb
translation). A. has his own version of the last phrase in l. 169 below.

71. flown] gone *Macmillan 1866.*

78. a smoother reed] An oblique comment on Clough's poetry, which A.
always judged severely. See his letter 24 Feb. 1848, 'A growing sense of
the deficiency of the *beautiful* in your poems, and of this alone being
properly *poetical* . . . made me speak as I did' *(CL 66).*

80. Corydon] Corydon conquers Thyrsis in the singing-match in Virgil,
Eclogues vii. The name is also found in Theocritus, *Idylls* iv.

> Alack, for Corydon no rival now!
>   But when Sicilian shepherds lost a mate,
>   Some good survivor with his flute would go,
>   Piping a ditty sad for Bion's fate;
> 85   And cross the unpermitted ferry's flow,
>   And relax Pluto's brow,
>   And make leap up with joy the beauteous head
>   Of Proserpine, among whose crownéd hair
>   Are flowers first opened on Sicilian air,
> 90   And flute his friend, like Orpheus, from the dead.
>
>   O easy access to the hearer's grace
>   When Dorian shepherds sang to Proserpine!
>   For she herself had trod Sicilian fields,
>   She knew the Dorian water's gush divine,
> 95   She knew each lily white which Enna yields,
>   Each rose with blushing face;
>   She loved the Dorian pipe, the Dorian strain.

82-100. A passage inspired by 'Lament for Bion' 115-26, 'Could I but have gone down into Tartarus as Orpheus went . . . then perhaps would I also have come to the house of Pluto, that I might see thee . . . But all the same, I pray thee, chant some song of Sicily . . . unto the Maid; for she too is of Sicily, she too once sported on Etna's shores; she knows the Dorian music . . . Even as once she granted Orpheus his Eurydice's return, so likewise she shall give my Bion back unto the hills; and had but my pipe the power of his harp, I had played for this in the house of Pluto myself' (Loeb translation slightly modified).

84. Bion's fate] Bion is said to have died by poison – see 'Lament for Bion' 109-12.

86. relax] unbend *Macmillan 1866.*

88-9. The classic English reference to the myth is *Paradise Lost* iv 268-71,

> . . . *Not that faire field*
> *Of* Enna, *where Proserpin gathring flours*
> *Her self a fairer Floure by gloomie Dis*
> *Was gatherd . . .*

but 'each lily white' (l. 95 below) hints that A. is also thinking of Milton's original – see Ovid's *Metamorphoses* v 391-2, 395,

> *quo dum Proserpina luco*
> *ludit aut violas aut candida lilia carpit;*
>
> *paene simul visa est dilectaque raptaque Diti . . .*

90. like Orpheus] See 'Lament for Bion' 123-4 (quoted in *n.* to ll. 82-100 above) and Virgil, *Georgics* iv 454-503.

But ah, of our poor Thames she never heard!
Her foot the Cumner cowslips never stirred;
100   And we should tease her with our plaint in vain!

Well! wind-dispersed and vain the words will be,
  Yet, Thyrsis, let me give my grief its hour
    In the old haunt, and find our tree-topped hill!
Who, if not I, for questing here hath power?
105   I know the wood which hides the daffodil,
        I know the Fyfield tree,
I know what white, what purple fritillaries
  The grassy harvest of the river-fields,
  Above by Ensham, down by Sandford, yields,
110   And what sedged brooks are Thames's tributaries;

I know these slopes; who knows them if not I?
  But many a dingle on the loved hill-side,
    With thorns once studded, old, white-blossomed
        trees,
  Where thick the cowslips grew, and far descried
115   High towered the spikes of purple orchises,
        Hath since our day put by
  The coronals of that forgotten time;
    Down each green bank hath gone the ploughboy's
        team,
  And only in the hidden brookside gleam
120   Primroses, orphans of the flowery prime.

Where is the girl, who by the boatman's door,
  Above the locks, above the boating throng,
    Unmoored our skiff when through the Wytham
        flats,
  Red loosestrife and blond meadow-sweet among
125   And darting swallows and light water-gnats,
        We tracked the shy Thames shore?

106. Cp. 'The Scholar-Gipsy' 82–3 (p. 336 above),
              Maidens, who from the distant hamlets come
                  To dance around the Fyfield elm in May ...
109. Ensham] Eynsham.
111. A. rarely failed to re-visit his 'old haunts among the Cumner hills'
whenever he found himself in Oxford. For his undergraduate wanderings
see his letter to Tom A. of 15 May 1857 (quoted in headn. to 'The
Scholar-Gipsy', p. 332 above).
125. darting swallows] Cp. 'The Scholar-Gipsy' 94 (p. 337 above),
              Where black-winged swallows haunt the glittering Thames ...

Where are the mowers, who, as the tiny swell
Of our boat passing heaved the river-grass,
Stood with suspended scythe to see us pass?
130   They all are gone, and thou art gone as well!

Yes, thou art gone! and round me too the night
In ever-nearing circle weaves her shade.
I see her veil draw soft across the day,
I feel her slowly chilling breath invade
135   The cheek grown thin, the brown hair sprent with
grey;
I feel her finger light
Laid pausefully upon life's headlong train;
The foot less prompt to meet the morning dew,
The heart less bounding at emotion new,
140   And hope, once crushed, less quick to spring again.

And long the way appears, which seemed so short
To the less practised eye of sanguine youth;
And high the mountain-tops, in cloudy air,
The mountain-tops where is the throne of Truth,
145   Tops in life's morning-sun so bright and bare!
Unbreachable the fort

133 and below *161*. The image is from Collins's 'Ode to Evening' 39–40,

> *Thy dewy fingers draw*
> *The gradual dusky veil.*

137. pausefully] A neologism combining the two senses of 'purposefully'
and 'so as to induce a pause'.
141–5. A.'s uphill walk in search of the signal-elm suggests the image of
life as a climb towards truth set almost inaccessibly among mountain-tops.
Cp. the similar mountain ascent in 'In Utrumque Paratus' 15–21 (p. 55
above), and on the difficulty of reaching truth see also A.'s Preface to
E in C I (1865), *Works* iii [5], 'To try and approach truth on one side after
another . . . it is only thus, it seems to me, that mortals may hope to gain
any vision of the mysterious Goddess, whom we shall never see except in
outline . . .'
146–7. Cp. 'The Last Word' 13–16 (p. 542 below),

> *Charge once more, then, and be dumb!*
> *Let the victors, when they come,*
> *When the forts of folly fall,*
> *Find thy body by the wall!*

The struggle against folly and the pursuit of truth are distinct, but both
make the idea of rest welcome.

Of the long-battered world uplifts its wall;
　　And strange and vain the earthly turmoil grows,
　　And near and real the charm of thy repose,
150　And night as welcome as a friend would fall.

But hush! the upland hath a sudden loss
　　Of quiet! – Look, adown the dusk hill-side,
　　A troop of Oxford hunters going home,
　　As in old days, jovial and talking, ride!
155　　　From hunting with the Berkshire hounds they
　　　　　come.
　　　　Quick! let me fly, and cross
　　Into yon farther field! – 'Tis done; and see,
　　Backed by the sunset, which doth glorify
　　The orange and pale violet evening-sky,
160　Bare on its lonely ridge, the Tree! the Tree!

I take the omen! Eve lets down her veil,
　　The white fog creeps from bush to bush about,
　　　The west unflushes, the high stars grow bright,
　　And in the scattered farms the lights come out.
165　　　I cannot reach the signal-tree to-night,
　　　　　Yet, happy omen, hail!
　　Hear it from thy broad lucent Arno-vale
　　　(For there thine earth-forgetting eyelids keep
　　　The morningless and unawakening sleep
170　Under the flowery oleanders pale),

153–5. Cp. 'The Scholar-Gipsy' 72–3 (p. 336 above),

　　　　　　　　. . . Oxford riders blithe,
　　　　　Returning home on summer nights . . .

156. Quick! let me fly] As the scholar-gipsy is advised – 'The Scholar-Gipsy'
221, 231 (p. 343 above),

　　　　But fly our paths, our feverish contact fly!

　　　Then fly our greetings, fly our speech and smiles!

158–60. The climax of the poem, but so much colour is unusual for A.
166. happy omen] The tree still stands even if it cannot be reached at once.
See n. to ll. 26–30 above.
167. Arno-vale] Clough is buried in the Protestant cemetery at Florence.
169. An imitation of 'Lament for Bion' 104. The passage containing this
line is translated in n. to ll. 71–7 above.

Hear it, O Thyrsis, still our tree is there!
   Ah, vain! These English fields, this upland dim,
     These brambles pale with mist engarlanded,
   That lone, sky-pointing tree, are not for him;
175   To a boon southern country he is fled,
       And now in happier air,
   Wandering with the great Mother's train divine
     (And purer or more subtle soul than thee,
     I trow, the mighty Mother doth not see)
180   Within a folding of the Apennine,

   Thou hearest the immortal chants of old!
    Putting his sickle to the perilous grain
     In the hot cornfield of the Phrygian king,
   For thee the Lityerses-song again
185   Young Daphnis with his silver voice doth sing;
      Sings his Sicilian fold,
   His sheep, his hapless love, his blinded eyes –
    And how a call celestial round him rang,
    And heavenward from the fountain-brink he
      sprang,
190   And all the marvel of the golden skies.

175. boon] See *n.* to 'A Farewell' 81 (p. 128 above).

177. great Mother] Rhea was identified with the Asiatic 'Great Mother' by the Greeks of Asia Minor, but here A. is referring to Rhea's daughter, Demeter. Demeter and her daughter Persephone (Proserpine) were known as the Mother and the Maid (ἡ Μητὴρ καὶ ἡ κόρη).

178–9. A. had said it to Clough less flatteringly – see his letter 12 Feb. 1853, '. . . you are the most conscientious man I ever knew: but on some lines morbidly so . . .' (*CL* 130).

182–90. 'Daphnis, the ideal Sicilian shepherd of Greek pastoral poetry, was said to have followed into Phrygia his mistress Piplea, who had been carried off by robbers, and to have found her in the power of the king of Phrygia, Lityerses. Lityerses used to make strangers try a contest with him in reaping corn, and to put them to death if he overcame them. Hercules arrived in time to save Daphnis, took upon himself the reaping-contest with Lityerses, overcame him, and slew him. The Lityerses-song connected with this tradition was, like the Linus-song, one of the early plaintive strains of Greek popular poetry, and used to be sung by corn-reapers. Other traditions represented Daphnis as beloved by a nymph who exacted from him an oath to love no one else. He fell in love with a princess, and was struck blind by the jealous nymph. Mercury, who was his father, raised him to Heaven, and made a fountain spring up in the place from which he ascended. At this fountain the Sicilians offered yearly sacrifices.

There thou art gone, and me thou leavest here
  Sole in these fields! yet will I not despair.
  Despair I will not, while I yet descry
  'Neath the mild canopy of English air
195   That lonely tree against the western sky.
      Still, still these slopes, 'tis clear,
  Our Gipsy-Scholar haunts, outliving thee!
  Fields where soft sheep from cages pull the hay,
  Woods with anemones in flower till May,
200 Know him a wanderer still; then why not me?

  A fugitive and gracious light he seeks,
    Shy to illumine; and I seek it too.
  This does not come with houses or with gold,
  With place, with honour, and a flattering crew;
205   'Tis not in the world's market bought and sold –
      But the smooth-slipping weeks
  Drop by, and leave its seeker still untired;
  Out of the heed of mortals he is gone,
  He wends unfollowed, he must house alone;
210 Yet on he fares, by his own heart inspired.

  Thou too, O Thyrsis, on like quest wast bound;
  Thou wanderedst with me for a little hour!
    Men gave thee nothing; but this happy quest,
  If men esteemed thee feeble, gave thee power,
215   If men procured thee trouble, gave thee rest.
      And this rude Cumner ground,

See Servius, *Comment. in Virgil. Bucol.*, v 20 and viii 68.' A.'s note first added *1869*.

201. *A fugitive and gracious light*] A. is probably thinking of the scholar-gipsy as a sort of Joubert, i.e. as a man 'of extraordinary ardour in the search for truth' who has 'clearly seized the fine and just idea that beauty and light are properties of truth' ('Joubert', *E in C I* (1865), *Works* iii 306, 310). The French critic was fresh in A.'s mind when he began 'Thyrsis' – see headn. above and *Note-books* 572 for A.'s reading of the *Pensées* in Nov. 1863. A.'s own copy of Joubert was *Pensées, maximes, essais et correspondance* ed. P. Raynal (Paris, 1861).

203–5. Cp. A.'s tribute to Clough's integrity in *On Translating Homer: Last Words* (1862), *Works* v 326–7, 'In the saturnalia of ignoble personal passions, of which the struggle for literary success, in old and crowded communities, offers so sad a spectacle, he never mingled. He had not yet traduced his friends, nor flattered his enemies, nor disparaged what he admired, nor praised what he despised. Those who knew him well had the conviction that, even with time, these literary arts would never be his.'

Its fir-topped Hurst, its farms, its quiet fields,
 Here cam'st thou in thy jocund youthful time,
 Here was thine height of strength, thy golden
  prime!
220   And still the haunt beloved a virtue yields.

What though the music of thy rustic flute
 Kept not for long its happy, country tone;
 Lost it too soon, and learnt a stormy note
Of men contention-tossed, of men who groan,
225   Which tasked thy pipe too sore, and tired thy
   It failed, and thou wast mute!   [throat
 Yet hadst thou alway visions of our light,
  And long with men of care thou couldst not stay,
  And soon thy foot resumed its wandering way,
230   Left human haunt, and on alone till night.

Too rare, too rare, grow now my visits here!
 'Mid city-noise, not, as with thee of yore,
  Thyrsis! in reach of sheep-bells is my home.
 – Then through the great town's harsh, heart-
   wearying roar,
235   Let in thy voice a whisper often come,
   To chase fatigue and fear:
 Why faintest thou? I wandered till I died.   ⟶
 Roam on! The light we sought is shining still.
 Dost thou ask proof? Our tree yet crowns the hill,
240   *Our Scholar travels yet the loved hill-side.*

224. An echo of Keats's 'Ode to a Nightingale' 23–4,

> *The weariness, the fever, and the fret*
> *Here, where men sit and hear each other groan . . .*

226. Clough published no new poems in England after 1849. His *Amours
de Voyage* appeared only in the American *Atlantic Monthly* (Feb.–May 1858).

111   Epilogue to Lessing's Laocoön

Date of composition unknown, but perhaps between 1864–5: the
prominence of the critical element ties the poem to the 1860s; the double
reference in ll. 43–8 to the 'Lament for Bion' and to Theocritus, *Idylls* xi

¶ 111. *Title. Laokoon* is the most famous work of Gotthold Ephraim
Lessing (1729–81), the German critic and dramatist. A. describes it in a
letter to Clough (undated, but probably late 1848) as 'a little mare's nesty –

suggests that it was written after 1863 – when A. completed a reading of
Theocritus and 'Moschus' (*Note-books* 572) – and possibly in 1864–5,
when 'Thyrsis', which owes a large debt to these authors, was being composed. Lessing's *Laokoon* (1766) is A.'s source only in the sense that he, too,
rejects Horace's *Ut pictura, poesis* (*Ars Poetica* 361) and is interested in '*die
Grenzen der Malerei und Poesie*' (but A. adds music). Lessing's book is not
on A.'s reading-lists in the 1860s.
Published *1867*; reprinted (*1868*), *1869*, etc.

> One morn as through Hyde Park we walked,
> My friend and I, by chance we talked
> Of Lessing's famed Laocoön;
> And after we awhile had gone
> In Lessing's track, and tried to see
> What painting is, what poetry –
> Diverging to another thought,
> 'Ah,' cries my friend, 'but who hath taught
> Why music and the other arts
> Oftener perform aright their parts
> Than poetry? why she, than they,
> Fewer fine successes can display?
>
> 'For 'tis so, surely! Even in Greece,
> Where best the poet framed his piece,
> Even in that Phœbus-guarded ground
> Pausanias on his travels found
> Good poems, if he looked, more rare
> (Though many) than good statues were –
> For these, in truth, were everywhere.
> Of bards full many a stroke divine
> In Dante's, Petrarch's, Tasso's line,
> The land of Ariosto showed;
> And yet, e'en there, the canvas glowed
> With triumphs, a yet ampler brood,
> Of Raphael and his brotherhood.

(line numbers in margin: 5, 10, 15, 20, 25)

but very searching' (*CL* 97); he probably read it first in or shortly after
June 1847, the date of an unpublished commonplace book (in the possession of A. Whitridge) which contains among various passages translated
mainly from German authors a long extract from *Laokoon*; there is no
known record of a later reading.
12. *fine*] real *1867*.
16. *Pausanias on his travels*] Pausanias, a Greek of the second century A.D.,
wrote a *Description of Greece* in ten books (which A. drew on for local
colour in writing *Merope*).

And nobly perfect, in our day
Of haste, half-work, and disarray,
Profound yet touching, sweet yet strong,
Hath risen Goethe's, Wordsworth's song;
30   Yet even I (and none will bow
Deeper to these) must needs allow,
They yield us not, to soothe our pains,
Such multitude of heavenly strains
As from the kings of sound are blown,
35   Mozart, Beethoven, Mendelssohn.'

While thus my friend discoursed, we pass
Out of the path, and take the grass.
The grass had still the green of May,
And still the unblackened elms were gay;
40   The kine were resting in the shade,
The flies a summer-murmur made.
Bright was the morn and south the air;
The soft-couched cattle were as fair
As those which pastured by the sea,
45   That old-world morn, in Sicily,
When on the beach the Cyclops lay,
And Galatea from the bay
Mocked her poor lovelorn giant's lay.
'Behold,' I said, 'the painter's sphere!
50   The limits of his art appear.
The passing group, the summer-morn,
The grass, the elms, that blossomed thorn –
Those cattle couched, or, as they rise,
Their shining flanks, their liquid eyes –
55   These, or much greater things, but caught

29. Goethe and Wordsworth are also associated in 'Obermann' 49–56
(p. 132 above) and 'Memorial Verses' (p. 225 above).
43–8. A composite allusion. The lovelorn Polyphemus on the beach is from
Theocritus, but the cattle are owed to 'Lament for Bion' – see Theocritus,
Idylls xi 'The Cyclops' 7–16, ''Twas this [poetry and song] . . . that gave
best comfort to my countryman the Cyclops, when . . . Galatea was his
love . . . Time and again his sheep would leave the fresh green pasturage
and come back unbidden to fold, while their master must peak and pine
alone upon the wrack-strewn shore a-singing all the day long of Galatea,
sick at heart'; and 'Lament for Bion' 58–63, 'There's Galatea, too, weeps
for your music, the music that was erst her delight . . . For Cyclop's music
was all another thing; she shunned him . . . but she looked upon you more
gladly than upon the sea. And lo! now the waves are forgotten . . . but
your cows she tends for you still.'

Like these, and in one aspect brought!
In outward semblance he must give
A moment's life of things that live;
Then let him choose his moment well,
60   With power divine its story tell.'

Still we walked on, in thoughtful mood,
And now upon the bridge we stood.
Full of sweet breathings was the air,
Of sudden stirs and pauses fair.
65   Down o'er the stately bridge the breeze
Came rustling from the garden-trees
And on the sparkling waters played;
Light-plashing waves an answer made,
And mimic boats their haven neared.
70   Beyond, the Abbey-towers appeared,
By mist and chimneys unconfined,
Free to the sweep of light and wind;
While through their earth-moored nave below
Another breath of wind doth blow,
75   Sounds as of wandering breeze – but sound
In laws by human artists bound.
'The world of music!' I exclaimed: –
'This breeze that rustles by, that famed
Abbey recall it! what a sphere
80   Large and profound, hath genius here!
The inspired musician what a range,
What power of passion, wealth of change!
Some source of feeling he must choose   *pulse 1867*
And its locked fount of beauty use,
85   And through the stream of music tell
Its else unutterable spell;
To choose it rightly is his part,
And press into its inmost heart.

57–60. Cp. *Laokoon* ch. 3, 'If the Artist out of ever changing nature cannot
use more than a single moment, and the Painter especially can only use this
single moment with reference to a single point of view . . . then is it
certain that this single moment, and the single point of view of this single
moment, must be chosen which are most fruitful of effect' (tr. R. Phillimore, Morley's Universal Library ed. 70).
62. *the bridge*] Over the Serpentine in Hyde Park.
70. *the Abbey-towers*] Westminster Abbey.
83. *source*] pulse 1867.

'*Miserere, Domine!*
90   The words are uttered, and they flee.
Deep is their penitential moan,
Mighty their pathos, but 'tis gone.
They have declared the spirit's sore,
Sore load, and words can do no more.
95   Beethoven takes them then – those two
Poor, bounded words – and makes them new;
Infinite makes them, makes them young;
Transplants them to another tongue,
Where they can now, without constraint,
100   Pour all the soul of their complaint,
And roll adown a channel large
The wealth divine they have in charge.
Page after page of music turn,
And still they live and still they burn,
105   Eternal, passion-fraught, and free –
Miserere, Domine!'

Onward we moved, and reached the Ride
Where gaily flows the human tide.
Afar, in rest the cattle lay;
110   We heard, afar, faint music play;
But agitated, brisk, and near,
Men with their stream of life, were here.
Some hang upon the rails, and some
On foot behind them go and come.
115   This through the Ride upon his steed
Goes slowly by, and this at speed.
The young, the happy, and the fair,
The old, the sad, the worn, were there;
Some vacant, and some musing went,
120   And some in talk and merriment.
Nods, smiles, and greetings, and farewells!
And now and then, perhaps, there swells
A sigh, a tear – but in the throng
All changes fast, and hies along.
125   Hies, ah, from whence, what native ground?
And to what goal, what ending, bound?
'Behold, at last the poet's sphere⊦⎯⎯⎯⎯⎯➤
But who,' I said, 'suffices here?

95–106. The reference is to Beethoven's Missa Solemnis in D, op. 123.
107. *the Ride*] Rotten Row.

130
'For, ah! so much he has to do;
Be painter and musician too!
The aspect of the moment show,
The feeling of the moment know!
The aspect not, I grant, express
Clear as the painter's art can dress;
135
The feeling not, I grant, explore
So deep as the musician's lore –
But clear as words can make revealing,
And deep as words can follow feeling.

But, ah! then comes his sorest spell
140
Of toil – he must life's *movement* tell!
The thread which binds it all in one,
And not its separate parts alone.
The *movement* he must tell of life,
Its pain and pleasure, rest and strife;
145
His eye must travel down, at full,
The long, unpausing spectacle;
With faithful unrelaxing force
Attend it from its primal source,
From change to change and year to year
150
Attend it of its mid career,
Attend it to the last repose
And solemn silence of its close.

'The cattle rising from the grass
His thought must follow where they pass;
155
The penitent with anguish bowed
His thought must follow through the crowd.
Yes! all this eddying, motley throng
That sparkles in the sun along,
Girl, statesman, merchant, soldier bold,
160
Master and servant, young and old,

129–42. Cp. *Laokoon* ch. 4, 'Nothing . . . constrains the poet to concentrate his picture upon a single moment. He take up each of his actions as he likes from their very beginning and carries them through all possible changes to the very end' (tr. R. Phillimore, ed. *cit.* 74–5). Lessing holds that poetry differs from the plastic arts in being a progressive imitation of an action. A. expands the idea until it becomes the poet's duty to convey the movement of life itself.

145–52. A self-echo – cp. the description of the 'Eternal mundane spectacle' in 'Resignation' 164–90 (pp. 90–1 above). 'Source' (l. 148) and 'eddying' (l. 157 below) prepare for the explicit use of the 'stream of life' image in the last two verse-paragraphs (ll. 163–200).

157. eddying] See *n.* to 'Rugby Chapel' 60 (p. 447 above).

Grave, gay, child, parent, husband, wife,
He follows home, and lives their life.

'And many, many are the souls
Life's movement fascinates, controls;
165   It draws them on, they cannot save
Their feet from its alluring wave;
They cannot leave it, they must go
With its unconquerable flow.
But ah! how few, of all that try
170   This mighty march, do aught but die!
For ill-endowed for such a way,
Ill-stored in strength, in wits, are they.
They faint, they stagger to and fro,
And wandering from the stream they go;
175   In pain, in terror, in distress,
They see, all round, a wilderness.
Sometimes a momentary gleam
They catch of the mysterious stream;
Sometimes, a second's space, their ear
180   The murmur of its waves doth hear.
That transient glimpse in song they say,
But not as painter can portray –
That transient sound in song they tell,
But not, as the musician, well.
185   And when at last their snatches cease,
And they are silent and at peace,
The stream of life's majestic whole
Hath ne'er been mirrored on their soul.

169–70. Cp. 'Rugby Chapel' 58–72 and especially 58–9, 65–8 (p. 447 above),

> What is the course of the life
> Of mortal men on the earth?
>
> Striving blindly, achieving
> Nothing; and then they die –
> Perish; and no one asks
> Who or what they have been . . .

177–8. A. is remembering the secret stream of 'The Buried Life' (p. 271 above), which in the press of our usual activities we are prevented from knowing. Moments of creative inspiration are glimpses of the buried stream.

187–8. Cp. A.'s imitation of a fragment of Empedocles, 'Empedocles on Etna' I ii 82–5 and n. (p. 159 above).

'Only a few the life-stream's shore
190 With safe unwandering feet explore;
Untired its movement bright attend,
Follow its windings to the end.
Then from its brimming waves their eye
Drinks up delighted ecstasy,
195 And its deep-toned, melodious voice
For ever makes their ear rejoice.
They speak! the happiness divine
They feel, runs o'er in every line;
Its spell is round them like a shower –
200 It gives them pathos, gives them power.
No painter yet hath such a way,
Nor no musician made, as they,
And gathered on immortal knolls
Such lovely flowers for cheering souls.
205 Beethoven, Raphael, cannot reach
The charm which Homer, Shakespeare, teach.
To these, to these, their thankful race
Gives, then, the first, the fairest place;
And brightest is their glory's sheen,
210 For greatest hath their labour been.'

193–8. Cp. A.'s *1853* Preface (p. 592 below), '. . . it is not enough that the Poet should add to the knowledge of men, it is required of him also that he should add to their happiness. "All art," says Schiller, "is dedicated to Joy . . .".'
205–10. For another expression of A.'s view of poetry's superiority to the other arts see his Introduction to *The Hundred Greatest Men* (1879) i [1–3], 'And the poets are to pass first, Why? Because, of the various modes of manifestation through which the human spirit pours its force, theirs is the most adequate and happy . . .'

112 A Wish

Date of composition unknown, but probably 1865: see A.'s letter to his mother 4 Dec. 1865, 'I remember thinking in the Cemetery at Rome, how well to die in a place like Rome and be buried in peace, with only an acquaintance like Odo Russell to see one put into the earth. It is not death which is in my eyes hideous – but it is its ceremonial' (*Commentary* 200); A.'s visit to the English cemetery to see the graves of Keats and Shelley took place 5 June 1865 (*L* i 276–7).
Published *1867*; reprinted (*1868*), *1869*, etc.

I ask not that my bed of death
From bands of greedy heirs be free;
For these besiege the latest breath
Of fortune's favoured sons, not me.

5   I ask not each kind soul to keep
Tearless, when of my death he hears.
Let those who will, if any, weep!
There are worse plagues on earth than tears.

I ask but that my death may find
10   The freedom to my life denied;
Ask but the folly of mankind,
Then, then at last, to quit my side.

Spare me the whispering, crowded room,
The friends who come, and gape, and go;
15   The ceremonious air of gloom –
All, which makes death a hideous show!

Nor bring, to see me cease to live,
Some doctor full of phrase and fame,
To shake his sapient head, and give
20   The ill he cannot cure a name.

Nor fetch, to take the accustomed toll
Of the poor sinner bound for death,
His brother-doctor of the soul,
To canvass with official breath

25   The future and its viewless things –
That undiscovered mystery
Which one who feels death's winnowing wings
Must needs read clearer, sure, than he!

Bring none of these; but let me be,
30   While all around in silence lies,
Moved to the window near, and see
Once more, before my dying eyes,

¶ 112. *1–8.* A. is disagreeing with Byron's wish in 'Euthanasia' 5–8,

> *No band of friends or heirs be there*
> > *To weep, or wish, the coming blow:*
> *No maiden, with dishevelled hair*
> > *To feel, or feign, decorous woe.*

15–16. Cp. A.'s letter of 4 Dec. 1865 quoted in headn. above.
29–34. An echo of *Obermann* (Dernière Lettre) ii 246, 'Si j'arrive à la

Bathed in the sacred dews of morn
The wide aërial landscape spread –
35   The world which was ere I was born,
The world which lasts when I am dead;

Which never was the friend of *one*,
Nor promised love it could not give,
But lit for all its generous sun,
40   And lived itself, and made us live.

There let me gaze, till I become
In soul, with what I gaze on, wed!
To feel the universe my home;
To have before my mind – instead

45   Of the sick room, the mortal strife,
The turmoil for a little breath –
The pure eternal course of life,
Not human combatings with death!

Thus feeling, gazing, might I grow
50   Composed, refreshed, ennobled, clear;
Then willing let my spirit go
To work or wait elsewhere or here!

---

vieillesse, si, un jour, plein de pensées encore, mais renonçant à parler aux hommes, j'ai auprès de moi un ami pour recevoir mes adieux à la terre, qu'on place ma chaise sur l'herbe courte . . . sous le soleil, sous le ciel immense . . .' For A.'s familiarity with this passage see his letter to his wife 7 May 1877, 'I hope and trust he has got out – not getting out must be terrible. "When I am dying, *qu'on place ma chaise sur l'herbe courte*", says Obermann, and I quite share his feeling' (*L* ii 139–40).

43. Essentially the plea of 'Lines written in Kensington Gardens' 38–40 (p. 257 above),

> *To feel, amid the city's jar,*
> *That there abides a peace of thine,*
> *Man did not make, and cannot mar.*

51–2. With this muted hope of some form of survival cp. 'Haworth Churchyard' 136–8 (p. 397 above),

> *In the never idle workship of nature,*
> *In the eternal movement,*
> *Ye shall find yourselves again!*

and 'Rugby Chapel' 40–2 (p. 446 above),

> *Somewhere, surely, afar,*
> *In the sounding labour-house vast*
> *Of being, is practised that strength . . .*

113 Obermann Once More

Exact period of composition unknown, but probably Oct. 1865–March
1867: A. visited Vevey Sept. 1865 (*L* i 299) when in Switzerland for the
Taunton Commission; the entry 'begin Obermann' 1 Oct. and the appearance of *Obermann* on the reading-lists in his diaries for some three weeks
following 15 Nov. and again on 20 Jan. 1866 probably indicates when he
began to write 'Obermann Once More' (at a time when he was still busy
with 'Thyrsis' – see headn., p. 496 above), but composition must have
continued at intervals throughout 1866 since the poem was still unfinished
13 March 1867 – see A.'s letter of this date to A. Macmillan, 'I have nearly
done a poem I want to conclude my new volume with and then everything
will be finished and off my mind, down even to the four lines of introduction' (*Buckler* 33). The text was considerably revised after *1867* (particularly in *1877*).

A.'s answer to the epigraph's question is 'the service of reason and
nature' warmed by Christian feeling. 'Obermann Once More', his last
major poem, expresses the conviction that 'at the present moment two
things about the Christian religion must be clear ... One is, that men
cannot do without it; the other, that they cannot do with it as it is' (*God
and the Bible* (1875), *Works* viii [12]). As early as 1851–2 A. had wondered
whether religious warmth could be kept outside the old religious forms –
see 'Progress' 17–32 (pp. 261–2 above) and the Yale MS. note (quoted below), which also contains the parallel between the late Roman world and
the modern world found in 'Obermann Once More'. The parallel, which
is also used in 'On the Modern Element in Literature' (1857), *Complete
Prose Works* ed. R. H. Super i (1960) 18–37, derives from a way of looking
at history that A. inherited from his father – see, for example, 'The Social
Progress of States' (1830), *Miscellaneous Works of T. Arnold* (1845) 108–9,
'Thus the largest part of that history which we commonly call ancient is
practically modern, as it describes society in a state analogous to that in
which it now is ...' A.'s Yale MS. note (undated, but plausibly 1849–52)
is as follows:

> 'The Roman world perished for having disobeyed reason and nature.
> The infancy of the world was renewed with all its sweet illusions.
> But infancy and its illusions must for ever be transitory, and we are
> again in the place of the Roman world, our illusions past, debtors to the
> service of religion and nature.
> O let us beware how we again are false to them: we shall perish and

---

¶ 113. *Title*. In *1869* and later collected editions the poem followed
'Obermann' and had this second line of title: (COMPOSED MANY
YEARS AFTER THE PRECEDING).

the world will be renewed: but we shall leave the same question to be solved by a future age.

I cannot conceal from myself the objection which really wounds and perplexes me from the religious side is that the service of reason is freezing to feeling, chilling to the religious mood.

And feeling and the religious mood are eternally the deepest being of man, the ground of all joy and greatness for him.'

For A.'s note on Senancour, which first appeared attached to this poem in *1868*, see headn. to 'Obermann' (p. 129 above).
Published *1867*; reprinted (*1868*), *1869*, etc.

> *Savez-vous quelque bien qui console du regret d'un monde?*
> OBERMANN.

Glion? – Ah, twenty years, it cuts
All meaning from a name!
White houses prank where once were huts.
Glion, but not the same!

5   And yet I know not! All unchanged
The turf, the pines, the sky!
The hills in their old order ranged;
The lake, with Chillon by!

And, 'neath those chestnut-trees, where stiff
10   And stony mounts the way,
The crackling husk-heaps burn, as if
I left them yesterday!

Across the valley, on that slope,
The huts of Avant shine!
15   Its pines, under their branches, ope
Ways for the pasturing kine.

Motto. Obermann (Lettre xli) i 159.
1–8. 'Probably all who know the Vevey end of the Lake of Geneva will recollect Glion, the mountain-village above the castle of Chillon. Glion now has hotels, *pensions*, and villas; but twenty years ago it was hardly more than the huts of Avant opposite to it – huts through which goes that beautiful path over the Col de Jaman, followed by so many foot-travellers on their way from Vevey to the Simmenthal and Thun.' A.'s note first added *1868*. A. probably arrived at Thun in 1848 by the route mentioned. 'Twenty years' (l. 1) was a round figure in 1867.
16. pasturing] tinkling *1867–9*.

Full-foaming milk-pails, Alpine fare,
Sweet heaps of fresh-cut grass,
Invite to rest the traveller there
20   Before he climb the pass –

The gentian-flowered pass, its crown
With yellow spires aflame;
Whence drops the path to Allière down,
And walls where Byron came,

25   By their green river, who doth change
His birth-name just below;
Orchard, and croft, and full-stored grange
Nursed by his pastoral flow.

But stop! – to fetch back thoughts that stray
30   Beyond this gracious bound,
The cone of Jaman, pale and grey,
See, in the blue profound!

Ah, Jaman! delicately tall
Above his sun-warmed firs –
35   What thoughts to me his rocks recall,
What memories he stirs!

And who but thou must be, in truth,
Obermann! with me here?
Thou master of my wandering youth,
40   But left this many a year!

Yes, I forget the world's work wrought,
Its warfare waged with pain;
An eremite with thee, in thought
Once more I slip my chain,

21–2. 'The blossoms of the *Gentiana lutea.*' A.'s note first published in this form *1885*; in *1869* a similar note to 'Empedocles on Etna' I ii 4–5 and here a cross-reference. For A.'s identification of Empedocles and Obermann see headn. to 'Empedocles on Etna' (p. 149 above).
24. walls where Byron came] 'Montbovon. See Byron's Journal, in his *Works* [1832], vol. iii, p. 258. The river Saane becomes the Sarine below Montbovon.' A.'s *1867* note. Byron was with Hobhouse at Montbovon 19 Sept. 1816.
25–6. See previous note.
31. Jaman] See *n.* to 'Obermann' 114 (p. 135 above).

45 And to thy mountain-chalet come,
    And lie beside its door,
    And hear the wild bee's Alpine hum,
    And thy sad, tranquil lore!

    Again I feel the words inspire
50 Their mournful calm; serene,
    Yet tinged with infinite desire
    For all that *might* have been —

    The harmony from which man swerved
    Made his life's rule once more!
55 The universal order served,
    Earth happier than before!

    — While thus I mused, night gently ran
    Down over hill and wood.
    Then, still and sudden, Obermann
60 On the grass near me stood.

    Those pensive features well I knew,
    On my mind, years before,
    Imaged so oft! imaged so true!
    — A shepherd's garb he wore,

65 A mountain-flower was in his hand,
    A book was in his breast.
    Bent on my face, with gaze which scanned
    My soul, his eyes did rest.

51–2. The sentiment is pervasive in Senancour, but see *Obermann* (Lettre xxx) i 103–4, 'Nous imaginons, nous voyons une terre de paix, d'ordre, d'union, de justice, où tous sentent, veulent et jouissent avec la delicatesse qui fait les plaisirs, avec la simplicité qui les multiplie.'

53–6. Senancour thought that man had swerved from harmony because religion had sought to control human conduct by supernatural sanctions instead of trusting the 'tendency to order' which he held to be a basic human instinct. See *Obermann* (Lettre xliv) i 194 ff. and A.'s 1869 essay on *Obermann*, in which he says (summarizing Senancour's argument in the letter), 'Paganism and Christianity alike have tampered with man's mind and heart, and wrought confusion in them' (*Neiman* 158).

65–6. The flower is Obermann's poetic feeling for nature; the book, probably the 'Manuel de Pseusophanes', which Obermann says that he found written at the back of an old Plutarch. A. marked the 'Manuel' heavily in his own copy of *Obermann* (*Commentary* 266).

18+M.A.

'And is it thou,' he cried, 'so long
70   Held by the world which we
Loved not, who turnest from the throng
Back to thy youth and me?

'And from thy world, with heart oppressed,
Choosest thou *now* to turn?
75   Ah me! we anchorites read things best,
Clearest their course discern!

'Thou fledst me when the ungenial earth,
Man's work-place, lay in gloom.
Return'st thou in her hour of birth,
80   Of hopes and hearts in bloom?

'Perceiv'st thou not the change of day?
Ah! Carry back thy ken,
What, some two thousand years! Survey
The world as it was then!

75. *read things*] knew it *1867–9*.
76. *Clearest their*] Best can its *1867–9*.
78. *Man's work-place*] Thou soughtest *1867–9*.
79–80. The sanguine quality of A.'s meliorism in the 1860s was due to a
new confidence about the prospects of religious liberalism inside the
Church of England. See, for example, A.'s letter to F. Temple (who had
just been appointed Bishop of Exeter) 12 Oct. 1869, 'I rejoice in your move
. . . The times, in spite of all people say, are good and will be better; in the
seventeenth century I should certainly have been in orders, and I think, if
I were a young man now, I would take them. The future of the Church of
England depends entirely on itself . . . it may yet become far greater and
more national than it has ever been' (*Memoirs of Archbishop Temple* ed.
E. G. Sandford (1906) i 278–9). A. became more pessimistic with the
advance of Ritualism in the 1880s – see 'Westminster Abbey' 154–60
and *n.* (pp. 555–6 below).
81–4. *1867–9*,

> *Wellnigh two thousand years have brought*
> *Their load, and gone away,*
> *Since last on earth there lived and wrought*
> *A world like ours to-day.*

84. After this line the following stanza *1868–9*:

> *Like ours it look'd in outward air!*
> *But of that inward prize,*
> *Soul, that we take more count and care,* [*that than they we*
> *take more care 1868*]
> *Ah! there our future lies.*

85   'Like ours it looked in outward air.
        Its head was clear and true,
        Sumptuous its clothing, rich its fare,
        No pause its action knew;

        'Stout was its arm, each thew and bone
90   Seemed puissant and alive –
        But, ah! its heart, its heart was stone,
        And so it could not thrive!

        'On that hard Pagan world disgust
        And secret loathing fell.
95   Deep weariness and sated lust
        Made human life a hell.

        'In his cool hall, with haggard eyes,
        The Roman noble lay;

85–104. See A.'s Yale MS. note (quoted in headn. above) and 'On the
Modern Element in Literature' (1857), *Complete Prose Works* ed. R. H.
Super i (1960) 31–3, 'There is universally current, I think, a pretty correct
appreciation of the high development of the Rome of Cicero and Augus-
tus; no one doubts that material civilisation and the refinements of life
were widely diffused in it . . . The facts, the spectacle of this Roman world,
then, are immense: let us see how far the literature . . . has been adequate.
Let us begin with a great poet . . . Lucretius . . . Depression and ennui;
these are the characteristics stamped on how many of the representative
works of modern times! they are also the characteristics stamped on the
poem of Lucretius. One of the most powerful, the most solemn passages
of the work of Lucretius . . . is the well-known conclusion of the third
book. With what masterly touches he exhibits the lassitude, the incurable
tedium which pursue men in their amusements . . . [A. here translates *De
Rerum Natura* iii 1060–7, the passage imitated in ll. 97–100 below] Yes,
Lucretius is modern; but is he adequate? . . . Think of the varied, the
abundant, the wide spectacle of the Roman life of his day . . . From these
Lucretius withdraws himself . . . but there is no peace, no cheerfulness for
him either in the world . . . or in . . . solitude.'
89. thew] pulse *1867–8*.
97–100. Cp. Lucretius, *De Rerum Natura* iii 1060–67,
            exit saepe foras magnis ex aedibus ille,
            esse domi quem pertaesumst, subitoque revertit,
            quippe foris nilo melius qui sentiat esse.
            currit agens mannos ad villam praecipitanter,
            auxilium tectis quasi ferre ardentibus instans;
            oscitat extemplo, tetigit cum limina villae,
            aut abit in somnum gravis atque oblivia quaerit,
            aut etiam properans urbem petit atque revisit.

He drove abroad, in furious guise,
100   Along the Appian way.

'He made a feast, drank fierce and fast,
And crowned his hair with flowers –
No easier nor no quicker passed
The impracticable hours.

105   'The brooding East with awe beheld
Her impious younger world.
The Roman tempest swelled and swelled,
And on her head was hurled.

'The East bowed low before the blast
110   In patient, deep disdain;
She let the legions thunder past,
And plunged in thought again.

'So well she mused, a morning broke
Across her spirit grey;
115   A conquering, new-born joy awoke,
And filled her life with day.

'"Poor world," she cried, "so deep accursed,
That runn'st from pole to pole
To seek a draught to slake thy thirst –
120   Go, seek it in thy soul!"

'She heard it, the victorious West,
In crown and sword arrayed!
She felt the void which mined her breast,
She shivered and obeyed.

101–2. A. is echoing *De Rerum Natura* iii 912–13,

> ... *ubi discubuere tenentque*
> *pocula saepe homines et inumbrant ora coronis* ...

115. The joy of the Christian message. Cp. 'Pagan and Mediaeval Religious Sentiment', *E in C I* (1865), *Works* iii 241, 'It is this which made the fortune of Christianity, – its gladness, not its sorrow . . . its drawing from the spiritual world a source of joy so abundant that it ran over upon the material world and transfigured it.'

121–40. A. attributes the break-up of the old civilisation to its thirst for spiritual relief, but this is a 'poetic' account. For his sober judgment see the Preface to *God and the Bible* (1875), *Works* viii [24–5] 'The first Christians . . . had the multitude's appetite for miracles, the multitude's inexact

125 'She veiled her eagles, snapped her sword,
      And laid her sceptre down;
      Her stately purple she abhorred,
      And her imperial crown.

      'She broke her flutes, she stopped her sports,
130   Her artists could not please;
      She tore her books, she shut her courts,
      She fled her palaces;

      'Lust of the eye and pride of life
      She left it all behind,
135   And hurried, torn with inward strife,
      The wilderness to find.

      'Tears washed the trouble from her face!
      She changed into a child!
      'Mid weeds and wrecks she stood – a place
140   Of ruin – but she smiled!

---

observation and boundless credulity . . . if the old civilisation had not been
on the wane, if a supply of instructed . . . minds had continued, Christianity could not have established itself in the precise form it did. For its
establishment . . . the extinction of the old civilisation was necessary; – to
flood and drown all which this civilisation was, and thought, and knew,
with the barbarian nations of the north . . . The infancy of the world was
renewed, with all its sweet illusions.' The last sentence is taken unaltered
from A.'s Yale MS. note (quoted in headn. above).
129–40. Cp. Browning's 'Christmas-Eve' (1850) xi 54–93 and especially
54–67,

> *Oh, love of those first Christmas days!*
> *– Fanned so soon into a blaze,*
> *From the spark preserved by the trampled sect,*
> *That the antique sovereign Intellect*
> *Which then sat ruling in the world,*
> *Like a change in dreams, was hurled*
> *From the throne he reigned upon:*
> *You looked up and he was gone.*
> *Gone, his glory of the pen!*
> *– Love, with Greece and Rome in ken,*
> *Bade her scribes abhor the trick,*
> *Of poetry and rhetoric,*
> *And exult with hearts set free,*
> *In blessed imbecility . . .*

136. The Egyptian desert, birthplace of Christian monasticism.
139–40. Shelley modulated – see *n.* to ll. 292–6 (p. 532 below).

'Oh, had I lived in that great day,
How had its glory new
Filled earth and heaven, and caught away
My ravished spirit too!

145   'No thoughts that to the world belong
Had stood against the wave
Of love which set so deep and strong
From Christ's then open grave.

'No cloister-floor of humid stone
150   Had been too cold for me.
For me no Eastern desert lone
Had been too far to flee.

'No lonely life had passed too slow,
When I could hourly scan
155   Upon his Cross, with head sunk low,
That nailed, thorn-crownéd Man!

'Could see the Mother with her Child
Whose tender winning arts
Have to his little arms beguiled
160   So many wounded hearts!

'And centuries came and ran their course,
And unspent all that time
Still, still went forth that Child's dear force,
And still was at its prime.

165   'Ay, ages long endured his span
Of life – 'tis true received –
That gracious Child, that thorn-crowned Man!
– He lived while we believed.

'While we believed, on earth he went,
170   And open stood his grave.
Men called from chamber, church, and tent;
And Christ was by to save.

145–8. Preceded by ll. 149–52 *1867–9*.
154. *scan*] see *1867–9*.
155–6. *1867–9*,

> *That wan, nail'd Form, with head drooped low*
> *Upon the bitter tree . . .*

'Now he is dead! Far hence he lies
In the lorn Syrian town;
175   And on his grave, with shining eyes,
The Syrian stars look down.

'In vain men still, with hoping new,
Regard his death-place dumb,
And say the stone is not yet to,
180   And wait for words to come.

'Ah, o'er that silent sacred land,
Of sun, and arid stone,
And crumbling wall, and sultry sand,
Sounds now one word alone!

185   '*Unduped of fancy, henceforth man*
Must labour! – must resign
His all too human creeds, and scan
Simply the way divine!

'But slow that tide of common thought,
190   Which bathed our life, retired;
Slow, slow the old world wore to nought,
And pulse by pulse expired.

173. Now he is dead] But see A.'s letter to H. Dunn 12 Nov. 1867, 'M.
Sainte-Beuve writes to me from Paris: "C'est un Obermann transfiguré"
... But even transfiguré he retains ... an aridity and crudity in his
language which savours of the French Revolution ... and which certainly,
were I writing directly for myself, would not be mine ... That Christ is
alive is language far truer to my own feeling' (*Commentary* 271–2).
184. After this line the following stanza *1867–81*:

> *From David's lips this* [*that 1877–81*] *word did roll,*
> '*Tis true and living yet:*
> No man can save his brother's soul,
> Nor pay his brother's debt.

The reference is to *Psalms* xlix 7, quoted in *n.* to 'Balder Dead' i 109–10
(p. 356 above).
185. Unduped of fancy, henceforth] Alone, self-poised, henceforward *1867–
1881*. The whole stanza was first italicized in *1885*.
189–90. A self-echo. Cp. 'Dover Beach' 21–8 and especially 21–2, 24–5
(p. 242 above),

> *The Sea of Faith,*
> *Was once, too, at the full ...*
>
> *But now I only hear*
> *Its melancholy, long, withdrawing roar ...*

'Its frame yet stood without a breach
When blood and warmth were fled;
195   And still it spake its wonted speech –
But every word was dead.

'And oh, we cried, that on this corse
Might fall a freshening storm!
Rive its dry bones, and with new force
200   A new-sprung world inform!

'– Down came the storm! O'er France it passed
In sheets of scathing fire;
All Europe felt that fiery blast,
And shook as it rushed by her.

205   'Down came the storm! In ruins fell
The worn-out world we knew.
It passed, that elemental swell!
Again appeared the blue;

'The sun shone in the new-washed sky,
210   And what from heaven saw he?
Blocks of the past, like icebergs high,
Float on a rolling sea!

'Upon them plies the race of man
All it before endeavoured;
215   "Ye live," I cried, "ye work and plan,
And know not ye are severed!

'" Poor fragments of a broken world
Whereon men pitch their tent!
Why were ye too to death not hurled
220   When your world's day was spent?

201–4. First added *1868*. Cp. A.'s phrase 'the fiery storm of the French
Revolution' in his *1868* note on Senancour (headn. to 'Obermann', p. 129
above) and 'Obermann' 65–6 (p. 132 above),

> For though his manhood bore the blast
> Of a tremendous time . . .

209–12. Coleridgean. Cf. 'The Rime of the Ancient Mariner' 83–4 and
53–4,

> The Sun now rose upon the right:
> Out of the sea came he . . .
>
> And ice, mast-high, came floating by,
> As green as emerald.

     ' "That glow of central fire is done
     Which with its fusing flame
     Knit all your parts, and kept you one –
     But ye, ye are the same!

225   ' "The past, its mask of union on,
     Had ceased to live and thrive.
     The past, its mask of union gone,
     Say, is it more alive?

     ' "Your creeds are dead, your rites are dead,
230   Your social order too!
     Where tarries he, the Power who said:
     See, I make all things new?

     ' "The millions suffer still, and grieve,
     And what can helpers heal
235   With old-world cures men half believe
     For woes they wholly feel?

     ' "And yet men have such need of joy!
     But joy whose grounds are true;
     And joy that should all hearts employ
240   As when the past was new.

221–8. Here and in ll. 283–8 below A. is making a 'popular' use of familiar scientific ideas of the cooling of the earth from a molten mass and of the great ice-age. The 'glow of central fire' is the unifying belief of an age of faith. When the fire became extinct an ice-age succeeded. The French Revolution broke up the ice (ll. 211–12 above), but this was simply to remove a 'mask of union', i.e. to destroy the pretence that Europe still gave a real assent to its old social and religious beliefs. Only the sun at the appointed time (ll. 283–6 below) can melt all the ice and let the green earth beneath appear again. The sun stands for the intelligence at the service of the *Zeit-Geist*, which 'irresistibly changes the ideas current in the world' ('Dr. Stanley's Lectures on the Jewish Church' (1863), *Complete Prose Works* ed. R. H. Super iii (1962) 77). For A.'s use of the concept of the *Zeitgeist* see F. Neiman, *PMLA* lxxii (1957) 977–96.

232. An allusion to *Revelation* xxi 5, 'And he that sat upon the throne said, Behold, I make all things new'.

237–40. Senancour's doctrine. See *Obermann* (Lettre xxxviii) i 143, '. . . la destination de l'homme est d'accroître le sentiment de la joie, de féconder l'energie expansive, et de combattre, dans tout ce qui sent, le principe de l'avilissement et des douleurs'. The passage is copied out in A.'s 1866 note-book (*Note-books* 34).

18*

'"Ah, not the emotion of that past,
Its common hope, were vain!
Some new such hope must dawn at last,
Or man must toss in pain.

245   '"But now the old is out of date,
The new is not yet born,
And who can be *alone* elate,
While the world lies forlorn?"

'Then to the wilderness I fled.
250   There among Alpine snows
And pastoral huts I hid my head,
And sought and found repose.

'It was not yet the appointed hour.
Sad, patient, and resigned,
255   I watched the crocus fade and flower,
I felt the sun and wind.

'The day I lived in was not mine,
Man gets no second day.
In dreams I saw the future shine –
260   But ah! I could not stay!

'Action I had not, followers, fame;
I passed obscure, alone.
The after-world forgets my name,
Nor do I wish it known.

265   'Composed to bear, I lived and died,
And knew my life was vain,
With fate I murmur not, nor chide,
At Sèvres by the Seine

'(If Paris that brief flight allow)
270   My humble tomb explore!
It bears: *Eternity, be thou
My refuge!* and no more.

245–6. the old . . . / The new is] the past . . . / The future *1867–9*. The
revisions emphasize the echo of 'Stanzas from the Grand Chartreuse'
85–6 (p. 288 above),

> Wandering between two worlds, one dead,
> The other powerless to be born . . .

265. Composed to bear] Gloom-wrapped within *1867–9*.
268–72 See n. to 'Obermann' 161–4 (p. 137 above).

'But thou, whom fellowship of mood
    Did make from haunts of strife
275   Come to my mountain-solitude,
    And learn my frustrate life;

'O thou, who, ere thy flying span
    Was past of cheerful youth,
    Didst find the solitary man
280   And love his cheerless truth –

'Despair not thou as I despaired,
    Nor be cold gloom thy prison!
    Forward the gracious hours have fared,
    And see! the sun is risen!

285   'He breaks the winter of the past;
    A green, new earth appears.
    Millions, whose life in ice lay fast,
    Have thoughts, and smiles, and tears.

'What though there still need effort, strife?
290   Though much be still unwon?
    Yet warm it mounts, the hour of life!
    Death's frozen hour is done!

283–6. See *n.* to ll. 221–8 above and cp. *Culture and Anarchy* (1869), *Works* vi 8–9, '[Culture] needs times of faith and ardour, times when the intellectual horizon is opening and widening all round us, to flourish in. And is not the close and bounded intellectual horizon within which we have long lived and moved now lifting up . . .? But now . . . the iron force of exclusion of all which is new has wonderfully yielded.'

285. *1867–9*,

        He melts the icebergs of the past . . .

K. Tillotson suggests that the icebergs of the original reading (which picks up l. 211 above) may be an echo of Carlyle's *French Revolution* (1837) I iv ch. 4, *Works* ed. H. D. Traill ii 146, where the 'French noblesse' are 'alas, how changed from the old position; drifted down from their native latitude, like Arctic icebergs got into the Equatorial sea, and fast thawing there.'

286. Cp. *Revelation* xxi 1, 'And I saw a new heaven and a new earth . . .' and A.'s own picture of a world restored in 'Balder Dead' iii 527–9 (p. 388 above),

        There re-assembling we shall see emerge
        From the bright Ocean at our feet an earth
        More fresh, more verdant than the last . . .

289–92. First added *1877*.

'The world's great order dawns in sheen,
After long darkness rude,
295   Divinelier imaged, clearer seen,
With happier zeal pursued.

'With hope extinct and brow composed
I marked the present die;
Its term of life was nearly closed,
300   Yet it had more than I.

'But thou, though to the world's new hour
Thou come with aspect marred,
Shorn of the joy, the bloom, the power
Which best befit its bard –

305   'Though more than half thy years be past,
And spent thy youthful prime;
Though, round thy firmer manhood cast,
Hang weeds of our sad time,

'Whereof thy youth felt all the spell,
310   And traversed all the shade –
Though late, though dimmed, though weak, yet tell
Hope to a world new-made!

'Help it to fill that deep desire,
The want which racked our brain,

293–6. An allusion to Shelley's chorus in 'Hellas' 1060–5,

> The world's great age begins anew,
>   The golden years return,
> The earth doth like a snake renew
>   Her winter weeds outworn:
> Heaven smiles, and faiths and empires gleam,
> Like wrecks of a dissolving dream.

The echo of Shelley's first two lines is obvious, but 'Heaven smiles' and 'dissolving' have contributed to A.'s picture in ll. 283–6 above.

307–10. The best commentary on these lines is 'Stanzas from the Grande Chartreuse' 73–156 (pp. 288–92 above). The 'weeds of our sad time' (l. 308) were probably suggested by Shelley – see previous note.

313. fill that] reach our 1867–9.

314. want which racked] dream which fill'd 1867–9; want which crazed 1877–81.

315   Consumed our heart with thirst like fire,
        Immedicable pain;

        'Which to the wilderness drove out
        Our life, to Alpine snow,
        And palsied all our word with doubt,
320   And all our work with woe –

        'What still of strength is left, employ
        That end to help attain:
        One common wave of thought and joy
        Lifting mankind again!'

325   – The vision ended. I awoke
        As out of sleep, and no
        Voice moved; only the torrent broke
        The silence, far below.

        Soft darkness on the turf did lie.
330   Solemn, o'er hut and wood,
        In the yet star-sown nightly sky,
        The peak of Jaman stood.

        Still in my soul the voice I heard
        Of Obermann! – away
335   I turned; by some vague impulse stirred,
        Along the rocks of Naye

        Past Sonchaud's piny flanks I gaze
        And the blanched summit bare
        Of Malatrait, to where in haze
340   The Valais opens fair,

315. *Consumed our heart with*] Fix'd in our soul a *1867–9*; Consum'd our soul with *1877–81*.
316. *Immedicable pain*] Perhaps from 'l'irrémédiable ennui', *Obermann* (Lettre xli) i 165, but Milton has 'wounds immedicable', *Samson Agonistes* 620.
319. *word*] deed *1867–9*.
320. *work*] word *1867–9*.
323–4. Cp. *St. Paul and Protestantism* (1870), *Works* ix 65, where, in speaking of the 'wonder-working power of attachment' that St. Paul found in the life of Christ, A. says, 'The struggling stream of duty . . . was suddenly reinforced by the immense tidal wave of sympathy and emotion.'
323. *common*] mighty *1867–9*.
324. *again*] amain *1867–9*.

And the domed Velan, with his snows,
Behind the upcrowding hills,
Doth all the heavenly opening close
Which the Rhone's murmur fills;

345   And glorious there, without a sound,
Across the glimmering lake,
High in the Valais-depth profound,
I saw the morning break.

348. This daybreak is intended to recall that at the birth of Christianity
(ll. 113–16 above).

114 Persistency of Poetry

Probably written early *1867*: the quatrain occurs in A.'s 1867 note-book
(*Note-books* 45); A.'s letter to A. Macmillan 13 March 1867 (quoted in
headn. to 'Obermann Once More', p. 518 above) implies its recent
composition.
Published without title as prefatory poem *1867*; reprinted (*1868*), *1869*
(here as prefatory poem to vol. ii); with present title *1877*, etc.

Though the Muse be gone away,
Though she move not earth to-day,
Souls, erewhile who caught her word,
Ah! still harp on what they heard.

115 Bacchanalia; or, The New Age

Date of composition unknown, but probably between 1860–7: ll. 19–20
of Pt. ii recall 'the many-chanc'd fight in the plain' of the cancelled first
stanza of 'The Lord's Messengers' (p. 452 above) and 'the battle in the
plain' of 'Palladium' 13 (p. 496 above) – both these poems almost certainly
written in the 1860s when A. felt that a 'new age' was dawning: see, for
example, 'Obermann Once More' 281–312 (pp. 531–2 above). Mrs. H.
Ward's reference (*A Writer's Recollections* (1918) 244) to 'Bacchanalia' as
an 'early poem' is clearly mistaken, but the mistake would be a natural
one if i 1–19, a description of evening recalling the description of early
morning in 'Resignation' 170–85 (p. 91 above), were written much
earlier than the rest of the poem and possibly in 1853 – see *n.* to i 11–12
below.
Published *1867*; reprinted (*1868*), *1869*, etc.

I

The evening comes, the fields are still.
The tinkle of the thirsty rill,
Unheard all day, ascends again;
Deserted is the half-mown plain,
Silent the swaths! the ringing wain,
The mower's cry, the dog's alarms,
All housed within the sleeping farms!
The business of the day is done,
The last-left haymaker is gone.
And from the thyme upon the height,
And from the elder-blossom white
And pale dog-roses in the hedge,
And from the mint-plant in the sedge,
In puffs of balm the night-air blows
The perfume which the day forgoes.
And on the pure horizon far,
See, pulsing with the first-born star,
The liquid sky above the hill!
The evening comes, the fields are still.

Loitering and leaping,
With saunter, with bounds –
Flickering and circling
In files and in rounds –
Gaily their pine-staff green
Tossing in air,
Loose o'er their shoulders white
Showering their hair –

¶ 115. i 4. *half-mown plain*] new-reap'd grain *1867*. This and subsequent
changes in Pt. i were due to A.'s confusion of haymaking and harvest-time
in *1867*; elder-blossom and dog-roses (ll. 11–12) belong to the former.
i 5. *swaths*] sheaves *1867*.
i 6. *mower's cry*] reaper's cry *1867*.
i 9. *last-left haymaker*] last belated gleaner *1867*.
i *11–12*. Cp. A.'s letter to his mother about an evening walk near Louth in
July 1853, 'I have been shaking off the burden of the day by a walk to-night
along the Market Rasen road, over the skirts of the wolds between
hedges full of elder blossom and white roses' (*L* i 31). The letter, is dated
'Tuesday Night (1853)' only, but letter and entries in A.'s unpublished
1853 diary together show that the walk took place on 12 July. With i 12
cp. also 'Resignation' 178–9 (p. 91 above),

> *In the hedge straggling to the stream,*
> *Pale, dew-drenched, half-shut roses gleam . . .*

See! the wild Mænads
Break from the wood,
30   Youth and Iacchus
Maddening their blood.
See! through the quiet land
Rioting they pass –
Fling the fresh heaps about,
35   Trample the grass.
Tear from the rifled hedge
Garlands, their prize;
Fill with their sports the field,
Fill with their cries.

40   Shepherd, what ails thee, then?
Shepherd, why mute?
Forth with thy joyous song!
Forth with thy flute!
Tempts not the revel blithe?
45   Lure not their cries?
Glow not their shoulders smooth?
Melt not their eyes?
Is not, on cheeks like those,
Lovely the flush?
50   *– Ah, so the quiet was!*
So was the hush!

II

The epoch ends, the world is still.
The age has talked and worked its fill –
The famous orators have shone,
The famous poets sung and gone,
5   The famous men of war have fought,
The famous speculators thought,
The famous players, sculptors, wrought,
The famous painters filled their wall,
The famous critics judged it all.
10   The combatants are parted now –
Uphung the spear, unbent the bow,
The puissant crowned, the weak laid low.
And in the after-silence sweet,
Now strifes are hushed, our ears doth meet,
15   Ascending pure, the bell-like fame

i *30. Iacchus*] See *n.* to 'The Strayed Reveller' 38 (p. 67 above).
i *32. land*] corn *1867*.
i *34. fresh heaps*] piled sheaves *1867*.

Of this or that down-trodden name,
Delicate spirits, pushed away
In the hot press of the noon-day.
And o'er the plain, where the dead age
20   Did its now silent warfare wage –
O'er that wide plain, now wrapped in gloom,
Where many a splendour finds its tomb,
Many spent fames and fallen mights –
The one or two immortal lights
25   Rise slowly up into the sky
To shine there everlastingly,
Like stars over the bounding hill.
The epoch ends, the world is still.

            Thundering and bursting
30   In torrents, in waves –
            Carolling and shouting
            Over tombs, amid graves –
            See! on the cumbered plain
            Clearing a stage,
35   Scattering the past about,
            Comes the new age.
            Bards make new poems,
            Thinkers new schools,
            Statesmen new systems,
40   Critics new rules.
            All things begin again;
            Life is their prize;
            Earth with their deeds they fill,
            Fill with their cries.

45   Poet, what ails thee, then?
            Say, why so mute?
            Forth with thy praising voice!
            Forth with thy flute!
            Loiterer! why sittest thou
50   Sunk in thy dream?
            Tempts not the bright new age?
            Shines not its stream?
            Look, ah, what genius,
            Art, science, wit!
55   Soldiers like Cæsar,
            Statesmen like Pitt!
            Sculptors like Phidias,

ii *19–20*. For the resemblance of these lines to lines in 'The Lord's Messengers' and 'Palladium' see headn. (p. 534 above).

Raphaels in shoals,
Poets like Shakespeare –
60   Beautiful souls!
See, on their glowing cheeks
Heavenly the flush!
– *Ah, so the silence was!*
So was the hush!

65   The world but feels the present's spell,
The poet feels the past as well;
Whatever men have done, might do,
Whatever thought, might think it too.

ii *60*. Ironic. The expression, which was current when A. used it, derives
from Goethe's *Wilhelm Meisters Lehrjahre* (1795) vi 'Bekenntnisse einer
schönen Seele' (Confessions of a Beautiful Soul).
ii *67–8*. Adapting Terence, *Heautontimorumenos* I i 25,

Homo sum; humani nil a me alienum puto.

116 Growing Old

Date of composition unknown, but probably between 1864–7: the title is
a strong hint that the poem began as a sardonic comment on ll. 1–3 of
Browning's 'Rabbi Ben Ezra', which was first published in *Dramatis
Personae* (1864),

Grow old along with me
The best is yet to be,
The last of life, for which the first was made . . .

but A. also glances at Wordsworth's consolatory reflections on old age in
The Excursion ix (see *nn.* below). The unrhymed five-line stanza with lines
alternately of three and five stresses is original. For the tone of this and the
following five poems see *Trilling* 293, 'These new poems [in *1867*] do not
question but reply, do not hint but declare. A note of finality, even of
dismissal is here.' 'Growing Old' itself is perhaps the best illustration of
H. James's remark that A.'s poetic style shows 'a slight abuse of meagreness
for distinction's sake' (*English Illustrated Magazine* Jan. 1884; reprinted in
Literary Essays and Reviews by Henry James ed. A. Mordell (New York,
1957) 348).
Published *1867*; reprinted (*1868*), *1869*, etc.

What is it to grow old?
Is it to lose the glory of the form,
The lustre of the eye?
Is it for beauty to forgo her wreath?
5   – Yes, but not this alone.

Is it to feel our strength –
Not our bloom only, but our strength – decay?
Is it to feel each limb
Grow stiffer, every function less exact,
10   Each nerve more loosely strung?

Yes, this, and more; but not
Ah, 'tis not what in youth we dreamed 'twould be!
'Tis not to have our life
Mellowed and softened as with sunset-glow,
15   A golden day's decline.

'Tis not to see the world
As from a height, with rapt prophetic eyes,
And heart profoundly stirred;
And weep, and feel the fullness of the past,
20   The years that are no more.

It is to spend long days
And not once feel that we were ever young;
It is to add, immured
In the hot prison of the present, month
25   To month with weary pain.

¶ 116. *16–18*. Cp. Wordsworth's *The Excursion* ix 50–2, 55–8,

> *Yet I have thought that we might also speak,*
> *And not presumptuously, I trust, of Age*
> *As of a final EMINENCE . . .*

> *. . . a place of power,*
> *A throne that may be likened unto his,*
> *Who, in some placid day of summer, looks*
> *Down from a mountain-top . . .*

In the continuation of this passage Wordsworth refers to 'the mighty stream of tendency' (l. 87), a phrase that A. made his own in his religious work – see, for example, *St. Paul and Protestantism* (1870), *Works* ix 9 and *Literature and Dogma* (1873), *Works* vii 42.

19–20. An echo of Tennyson's 'Tears, idle tears . . .' 1, 3–5,

> *Tears, idle tears, I know what they mean . . .*

> *Rise in the heart, and gather to the eyes,*
> *In looking on the happy Autumn-fields,*
> *And thinking of the days that are no more.*

23–5. A self-echo – cp. 'A Summer Night' 37–40 (p. 269 above),

> *For most men in a brazen prison live,*
> *Where, in the sun's hot eye,*
> *With heads bent o'er their toil, they languidly*
> *Their lives to some unmeaning taskwork give . . .*

It is to suffer this,
And feel but half, and feebly, what we feel.
Deep in our hidden heart
Festers the dull remembrance of a change,
30   But no emotion – none.

It is – last stage of all –
When we are frozen up within, and quite
The phantom of ourselves,
To hear the world applaud the hollow ghost
35   Which blamed the living man.

31. last stage of all] Cp. *As You Like It* II vii 163–5,

> *Last scene of all*
> *That ends this strange eventful history*
> *Is second childishness and mere oblivion . . .*

117 The Progress of Poesy
A VARIATION

Date of composition unknown, but probably between 1864–7: A. wrote to George Smith 17 March 1864, 'I am a scanty spring, and nearly choked just now by all the rubbish that Mr. Lowe's Revised Code (I am a school-inspector) causes to be shot into me' (*Buckler* 17), but the development of the image may owe something to ll. 1367–71 of Browning's 'Mr. Sludge, "The Medium"', which was first published in *Dramatis Personae* (28 May 1864),

> *. . . Young, you've force*
> *Wasted like well-streams: old, – oh, then indeed,*
> *Behold a labyrinth of hydraulic pipes*
> *Through which you'd play off wondrous waterwork;*
> *Only, no water's left to feed their play.*

'The sub-title is no doubt meant to suggest a "variation" of the theme treated by Thomas Gray in his Pindaric Ode of the same title.' (*Commentary* 179).
Published *1867*; reprinted (*1868*), *1869*, etc.

> Youth rambles on life's arid mount,
> And strikes the rock, and finds the vein,
> And brings the water from the fount,
> The fount which shall not flow again.

¶ 117. *2. strikes the rock*] An echo of *Exodus* xvii 6, 'Behold, I will stand before thee there upon the rock in Horeb; and thou shalt smite the rock, and there shall come water out of it . . .'

5   The man mature with labour chops
       For the bright stream a channel grand,
       And sees not that the sacred drops
       Ran off and vanished out of hand.

       And then the old man totters nigh,
10   And feebly rakes among the stones.
       The mount is mute, the channel dry;
       And down he lays his weary bones.

118 A Nameless Epitaph
[I]

Date of composition unknown, but (?) 1864–7: from their position in *1867*
this and the following epitaph are other expressions of the bitterness found
in 'Growing Old', 'The Progress of Poesy' and 'The Last Word', all of
which were probably written 1864–7.
Published *1867*; reprinted (*1868*) only.

       This sentence have I left behind:
       An aching body, and a mind
       Not wholly clear, nor wholly blind,
       Too keen to rest, too weak to find,
5   That travails sore, and brings forth wind,
       Are God's worst portion to mankind.

119 A Nameless Epitaph
[II]

Date of composition unknown, but (?) 1864–7: see headn. to previous
poem.
Published after the preceding poem as '*Another*' *1867*; reprinted (*1868*);
with present title *1869*, etc.

       Ask not my name, O friend!
       That Being only, which hath known each man
       From the beginning, can
       Remember each unto the end.

120 The Last Word

Date of composition unknown, but almost certainly between 1864–7: a
dating suggested by (1) the parallel between ll. 13–16 and 'Thyrsis' 146–8
(pp. 504–5 above) – 'Thyrsis' was mainly written 1864–5; (2) A.'s concern

with warfare against the Philistine at the end of the Preface to *E in C I*
(1865), 'She [Oxford] will forgive me, even if I·have unwittingly drawn
upon her a shot or two aimed at her unworthy son . . . the cause in which
I fight is, after all, hers. Apparitions of a day, what is our puny warfare
against the Philistines, compared with the warfare which this queen of
romance has been waging against them for centuries . . . ?' (*Works* iii [12]
– A. was still busy with the Preface in Jan. 1865 (*L* i 246). A. was chiefly
indebted for his idea to Heine's 'Enfant Perdu' in *Romanzero* (1851),
which he had already echoed in 'Heine's Grave' 125–8 (p. 474 above), but
he probably also recalled Senancour's 'Périssons en résistant', which is
quoted in 'The Function of Criticism at the Present Time' (*Works* iii 30).
Senancour's phrase is from *Obermann* (Lettre xc) ii 231.
Published *1867*; reprinted (*1868*), *1869*, etc.

> Creep into thy narrow bed,
> Creep, and let no more be said!
> Vain thy onset! all stands fast.
> Thou thyself must break at last.
>
> 5   Let the long contention cease!
> Geese are swans, and swans are geese.
> Let them have it how they will!
> Thou art tired; best be still.
>
> They out-talked thee, hissed thee, tore thee?
> 10 Better men fared thus before thee;
> Fired their ringing shot and passed,
> Hotly charged – and sank at last.
>
> Charge once more, then, and be dumb!
> Let the victors, when they come,
> 15 When the forts of folly fall,
> Find thy body by the wall!

¶ 120. *12. sank*] broke *1867–9*.
13–16. Cp. 'Thyrsis' 146–8 (pp. 504–5 above),

> *Unbreachable the fort*
> *Of the long-battered world uplifts its wall;*
> *And strange and vain the earthly turmoil grows . . .*

121 Pis-Aller

Date of composition unknown, but metre and stanza are those of 'The
Last Word' above, which was probably written between 1864–7.
Published *1867*; reprinted (*1868*), *1869*, etc.

'Man is blind because of sin,
Revelation makes him sure;
Without that, who looks within,
Looks in vain, for all's obscure.'

5   Nay, look closer into man!
Tell me, can you find indeed
Nothing sure, no moral plan
Clear prescribed, without your creed?

'No, I nothing can perceive!
10   Without that, all's dark for men.
That, or nothing, I believe.' –
For God's sake, believe it then!

122 'Below the surface-stream . . .'

Date of composition unknown, but (?) Nov. 1869, the date of publication:
see A.'s letter to his mother 21 Feb. 1870, 'Tell Fan that the lines in my
second *Cornhill* article, "Below the surface stream", etc., are my own, and
I think them good' (*L* ii 28). The idea is a variation on the theme of the
buried stream of life – see 'The Buried Life' 39–44 (p. 273 above).
Published *Cornhill Magazine* Nov. 1869 (as part of 'St. Paul and Protestantism'); not reprinted by A.

Below the surface-stream, shallow and light,
Of what we *say* we feel – below the stream,
As light, of what we *think* we feel – there flows
With noiseless current strong, obscure and deep,
5   The central stream of what we feel indeed.

123 New Rome

LINES WRITTEN FOR MISS STORY'S ALBUM

Written in the latter half of April 1873: A. was in Rome with his family
in April 1873 and met William Wetmore Story – see his letter to his
mother 30 March 1873, 'The Storys (the American sculptor) are particularly kind. They are close by in the Barberini Palace' (*L* ii 96); A.'s note
'See *The Times* of April 15th', which accompanied 'New Rome' on its
first publication in June 1873, and his letter to his sister Frances 17 April
1873 (*L* ii 97) recording a visit on that day to the statues in the Vatican
Museum ('I could go there for ever, but the more they interest one, the
more it takes it out of one to look at them') indicate when in April this

'trifle ... which I think rather good' (A. to his brother Walter 5 May 1873, *L* ii 103) was composed. See *Commentary* 180–1 for extracts from *The Times* editorial of 15 April describing the Roman streets as 'narrow, irregular, tortuous, and dirty' and speaking patronisingly of the hotels as 'not, perhaps, the worst in Europe'. An early, probably the first, draft of the poem in an 1873 travel diary (formerly in the possession of Mrs. N. Thwaites) preserves some unimportant cancelled readings (for which see *1950* 214).

Published *Cornhill Magazine* June 1873; reprinted *1881*, etc.

> The armless Vatican Cupid
>   Hangs down his beautiful head;
> For the priests have got him in prison,
>   And Psyche long has been dead.
>
> 5   But see, his shaven oppressors
>   Begin to quake and disband!
> And *The Times*, that bright Apollo,
>   Proclaims salvation at hand.
>
> 'And what,' cries Cupid, 'will save us?'
> 10   Says Apollo: '*Modernise Rome!*
> What inns! Your streets, too, how narrow!
>   Too much of palace and dome!
>
> 'O learn of London, whose paupers
>   Are not pushed out by the swells!
> 15   Wide streets with fine double trottoirs;
>   And then – the London hotels!'
>
> The armless Vatican Cupid
>   Hangs down his head as before.
> Through centuries past it has hung so,
> 20   And will through centuries more.

124   Rome-Sickness

Date of composition unknown, but between 1873–5: the poem was probably solicited for a miscellany in aid of her charities by Mrs. Gould, an American lady whose work for Italian children seems to be glanced at in ll. 25–32, when A. was in Rome with his family in April 1873. (A.'s American acquaintances in Rome included William Wetmore Story and the U.S. Minister, Mr. Marsh – see *L* ii 96–7). Mrs. Gould died 31 Aug. 1875.

Published in *In Memoriam: A Wreath of Stray Leaves to the Memory of Emily Bliss Gould* (Rome, 1875); not reprinted by A.

To daily tasks we set our hand,
　　And oft the spirit, pent at home,
Breaks out and longs for Switzerland,
　　Longs oftener yet and pines for Rome.

5　　I passed to-day o'er Walton Heath –
　　The coming spring-time's earliest stir
Quickened and moved, a happy breath,
　　In moss, and gorse, and shining fir.

Fortunate firs! who never think
10　　How firs less cursed by Fortune's frown
O'er Glion fringe the mountain's brink,
　　Or dot the slopes to Vevey down.

I crossed St. George's Hill to-day –
　　There in the leaf-strewn copse I found
15　The tender foxglove-plants display
　　Their first green muffle on the ground.

They envy not, this tranquil brood,
　　The cyclamens whose blossoms fill
With fragrance all Frascati's wood
20　　Along the gracious Alban Hill!

Man only, with eternal bent
　　To come and go, to shift and range,
At life and living not content,
　　Chafes in his place, and pines for change.

¶ 124. 3. Switzerland appears, as it does in the first 'Rachel' sonnet (p. 483 above), only because it is A.'s 'land of heart's desire'. Cp. his revealing letter to his wife March 1853 (*L* i 26) quoted in headn. to 'Meeting' (p. 116 above).
5 and below 13. *Walton Heath . . . St. George's Hill*] Both within easy distance when A. moved from Harrow to Pains Hill Cottage at Cobham, Surrey in June 1873.
11–12. The country of *Obermann*.
6. *green muffle*] Cp. 'The Scholar-Gipsy' 69 (p. 336 above).

　　　And watch the warm, green-muffled Cumner hills . . .

and see *n*. to 'Empedocles on Etna' I ii 51 (p. 158 above).
18–20. See A.'s letter to his sister Frances 17 April 1873, 'At Frascati we got donkeys . . . and started for Tusculum. Directly we got clear of the villas we got into wood, and directly we got into the wood a feast of flowers began . . . Then the cyclamen, the purple one, covering all the ground' (*L* ii 98).

25   Yet happy – since his feverish blood
               Leaves him no rest, and change he will –
          When restlessness is restless good,
            Still mending, lessening, human ill!

          Unwearied, as from land to land
30   The incessant wanderer takes his way,
          To hold the light, and reach the hand
            To all who sink, to all who stray!

125   S.S. 'Lusitania'

Probably written Dec. 1878: A.'s third and then only surviving son, Richard Penrose A., travelled to Australia by the 'Lusitania' in the winter of 1878–9 (*Commentary* 328–9). The Dante reference is to *Inferno* xxvi 85–142. There are no reading-lists for 1878–9, but A. entered three quotations from the *Inferno* in his 1879 note-book (*Note-books* 320). Published *Nineteenth Century* Jan. 1879; not reprinted by A.

          I read in Dante how that hornéd light,
          Which hid Ulysses, waved itself and said:
          'Following the sun, we set our vessel's head
          To the great main; passed Seville on the right

5   'And Ceuta on the left; then southward sped.
          At last in air, far off, dim rose a Height.
          We cheered; but from it rushed a blast of might,
          And struck – and o'er us the sea-waters spread.'

          I dropped the book, and of my child I thought
10   In his long black ship speeding night and day
          O'er those same seas; dark Teneriffe rose, fraught

¶ 125. *1–8.* Cp. Dante's *Inferno* xxvi 85–6, 100, 110–11, 133–42, 'The greater horn of the ancient flame began to shake itself, murmuring . . . I put forth on the deep open sea . . . on the right hand, I left Seville; on the other, had already left Ceuta . . . when there appeared to us a Mountain, dim with distance; and to me it seemed the highest I had ever seen. We joyed, and soon our joy was turned to grief: for a tempest rose from the new land, and struck the forepart of our ship. Three times it made her whirl round with all the waters; at the fourth, made the poop rise up and the prow go down, as pleased Another, till the sea was closed above us' (J. A. Carlyle's 'Temple Classics' translation).

With omen; 'Oh! were that Mount passed', I say.
Then the door opens and this card is brought:
'Reached Cape Verde Islands, "Lusitania".'

14. The Cape Verde are off the west coast of Africa. Teneriffe, which is in
the Canary Islands, had therefore been passed safely.

126 Geist's Grave

Written 9–13 Nov. 1880: entries in A.'s unpublished 1880 diary (*Commentary* 313). Geist was a dachshund belonging to A.'s son Richard Penrose A. (then in Australia – see ll. 55–6 below and headn. to 'S.S. "Lusitania"' above). The poem was placed under 'Elegiac Poems' in *1881*, under 'Later Poems' in *1885* (when this category was first created).
Published *Fortnightly Review* Jan. 1881; reprinted *1881*, etc.

> Four years! – and didst thou stay above
> The ground, which hides thee now, but four?
> And all that life, and all that love,
> Were crowded, Geist! into no more?
>
> 5   Only four years those winning ways,
> Which make me for thy presence yearn,
> Called us to pet thee or to praise,
> Dear little friend! at every turn?
>
> That loving heart, that patient soul,
> 10   Had they indeed no longer span,
> To run their course, and reach their goal,
> And read their homily to man?
>
> That liquid, melancholy eye,
> From whose pathetic, soul-fed springs
> 15   Seemed surging the Virgilian cry,
> The sense of tears in mortal things –
>
> That steadfast, mournful strain, consoled
> By spirits gloriously gay,
> And temper of heroic mould –
> 20   What, was four years their whole short day?

¶ 126. *Title.* Geist had his name from A.'s pointed preaching of *Geist* (intelligence) to the English through the mouth of the 'Prussian savant' Arminius in *Friendship's Garland* (1871).
15–16. '*Sunt lacrimae rerum!*' A.'s note. See *Aeneid* i 462,

> sunt lacrimae rerum et mentem mortalia tangunt.

Yes, only four! – and not the course
Of all the centuries yet to come,
And not the infinite resource
Of Nature, with her countless sum

25   Of figures, with her fullness vast
Of new creation evermore,
Can ever quite repeat the past,
Or just thy little self restore.

Stern law of every mortal lot!
30   Which man, proud man, finds hard to bear,
And builds himself I know not what
Of second life I know not where.

But thou, when struck thine hour to go,
On us, who stood despondent by,
35   A meek last glance of love didst throw,
And humbly lay thee down to die.

Yet would we keep thee in our heart –
Would fix our favourite on the scene,
Nor let thee utterly depart
40   And be as if thou ne'er hadst been.

And so there rise these lines of verse
On lips that rarely form them now;
While to each other we rehearse:
Such ways, such arts, such looks hadst thou!

45   We stroke thy broad brown paws again,
We bid thee to thy vacant chair,
We greet thee by the window-pane,
We hear thy scuffle on the stair.

We see the flaps of thy large ears
50   Quick raised to ask which way we go;
Crossing the frozen lake, appears
Thy small black figure on the snow!

41–2. A. had not published a new collection of verse since *1867*. 'Later Poems' in *1885* consisted of elegies to a dachshund, a canary and a liberal Dean of Westminster.

Nor to us only art thou dear
Who mourn thee in thine English home;
55   Thou hast thine absent master's tear,
Dropped by the far Australian foam.

Thy memory lasts both here and there,
And thou shalt live as long as we.
And after that – thou dost not care!
60   In us was all the world to thee.

Yet, fondly zealous for thy fame,
Even to a date beyond our own
We strive to carry down thy name,
By mounded turf, and graven stone.

65   We lay thee, close within our reach,
Here, where the grass is smooth and warm,
Between the holly and the beech,
Where oft we watched thy couchant form,

Asleep, yet lending half an ear
70   To travellers on the Portsmouth road;
There build we thee, O guardian dear,
Marked with a stone, thy last abode.

Then some, who through this garden pass,
When we too, like thyself, are clay,
75   Shall see thy grave upon the grass,
And stop before the stone, and say:

People who lived here long ago
Did by this stone, it seems, intend
To name for future times to know
80   *The dachs-hound, Geist, their little friend.*

55–6. See headn. above.
65–72. The garden of A.'s home, Pains Hill Cottage, Cobham.

127 Westminster Abbey

JULY 25, 1881

(*The Day of Burial, in the Abbey, of* ARTHUR PENRHYN
STANLEY, *Dean of Westminster*)

Written 31 Oct.–16 Nov. and copied out 28 Nov. 1881: entries in A.'s
unpublished diary (*Commentary* 308–9). A.'s note to ll. 4–5 indicates the

¶ 127. *Title.* A. P. Stanley, biographer of Dr. Arnold and friend of the
whole Arnold family, died 18 July 1881. His devotion to Dr. A. began
when he was a prize pupil at Rugby.

source of the legend related in ll. 11–50 as Dudgale's *Monasticon Angli-canum*, but his comment in a letter to his sister 'K' 27 Dec. 1881, '. . . he himself [Stanley] would have taken great delight in the use I have made of a lovely legend of primitive Westminster' (*L* ii 195) is disingenuous: A. almost certainly met the legend first in Stanley's *Historical Memorials of Westminster Abbey* (1869) 19–21 and need not have consulted Dugdale until he compiled his note (the two versions of the story hardly differ, but 'Lambeth' and 'Thorney Isle' are mentioned only in Stanley). The legend allows A. to renew his old identification of light with the free intelligence and so enables him to picture Stanley in his Broad Church rôle as a light-bringer – see A.'s letter to Fontanès 20 Sept. 1872, 'Le Dean Stanley est le chef très brillant . . . de la minorité libérale du clergé anglicain' (*L* ii 88) – and to describe him as 'a child of light' in terms earlier applied to Joubert (see *n.* to ll. 71–80 below), but the final effect of the whole poem – with its Miltonic echoes and plethora of classical references – is one of laborious and unfeeling contrivance. A.'s stanza (aa³bccb⁵d³ede⁵) is original, but the movement of the first three lines obviously recalls the Hymn in Milton's 'On the Morning of Christ's Nativity' (the recollection perhaps suggested by Milton's light-imagery in the prologue 8–14). The text was revised for *1885*, but the changes made are not of much significance. A.'s note from Dugdale is as follows:

'Ailred of Rievaulx, and several other writers, assert that Sebert, king of the East Saxons and nephew of Ethelbert, founded the Abbey of Westminster very early in the seventh century.

Sulcardus, who lived in the time of William the Conqueror, gives a minute account of the miracle supposed to have been worked at the consecration of the Abbey.

The church had been prepared against the next day for dedication. On the night preceding, St. Peter appeared on the opposite side of the water to a fisherman, desiring to be conveyed to the farther shore. Having left the boat, St. Peter ordered the fisherman to wait, promis-ing him a reward on his return. An innumerable host from heaven accompanied the apostle, singing choral hymns, while everything was illuminated with a supernatural light. The dedication having been completed, St. Peter returned to the fisherman, quieted his alarm at what had passed, and announced himself as the apostle. He directed the fisherman to go as soon as it was day to the authorities, to state what he had seen and heard, and to inform them that, in corrobora-tion of his testimony, they would find the marks of consecration on the walls of the church. In obedience to the apostle's direction, the fisherman waited on Mellitus, Bishop of London, who, going to the church, found not only marks of the chrism, but of the tapers with which the church had been illuminated. Mellitus, therefore, desisted from proceeding to a new consecration, and contented himself with the celebration of the mass.' – Dugdale, *Monasticon Anglicanum* (edition of 1817), vol. i, pp. 265, 266. See also Montalambert, *Les Moines d'Occident*, vol. iii, pp. 428–32.

Published *Nineteenth Century* Jan. 1882; reprinted *1885*, etc.

> What! for a term so scant
> Our shining visitant
> Cheered us, and now is passed into the night?
> Couldst thou no better keep, O Abbey old,
> 5   The boon thy dedication-sign foretold,
> The presence of that gracious inmate, light?
> A child of light appeared;
> Hither he came, late-born and long-desired,
> And to men's hearts this ancient place endeared;
> 10   What, is the happy glow so soon expired?
>
> – Rough was the winter eve;
> Their craft the fishers leave,
> And down over the Thames the darkness drew.
> One still lags last, and turns, and eyes the Pile
> 15   Huge in the gloom, across in Thorney Isle,
> King Sebert's work, the wondrous Minster new.
> – 'Tis Lambeth now, where then
> They moored their boats among the bulrush stems;
> And that new Minster in the matted fen
> 20   The world-famed Abbey by the westering Thames.
>
> His mates are gone, and he
> For mist can scarcely see
> A strange wayfarer coming to his side –
> Who bade him loose his boat, and fix his oar,
> 25   And row him straightway to the further shore,
> And wait while he did there a space abide.
> The fisher awed obeys,
> That voice had note so clear of sweet command;
> Through pouring tide he pulls, and drizzling haze,
> 30   And sets his freight ashore on Thorney strand.

11–50. See A.'s note in headn. above.

11. Cp. Milton's 'Nativity Ode' 29,

> *It was the Winter wilde . . .*

20. *westering Thames*] A poeticism clumsily employed. 'Westering' means 'tending to the west', and A.'s phrase has to be translated as 'the Thames in the light of the setting (westering) sun.'

The Minster's outlined mass
Rose dim from the morass,
And thitherward the stranger took his way.
Lo, on a sudden all the Pile is bright!
35   Nave, choir and transept glorified with light,
While tongues of fire on coign and carving play!
And heavenly odours fair
Come streaming with the floods of glory in,
And carols float along the happy air,
40 As if the reign of joy did now begin.

Then all again is dark;
And by the fisher's bark
The unknown passenger returning stands.
O Saxon fisher! thou hast had with thee
45   *The fisher from the Lake of Galilee –*
So saith he, blessing him with outspread hands;
Then fades, but speaks the while:
At dawn thou to King Sebert shalt relate
How his St. Peter's Church in Thorney Isle
50 *Peter, his friend, with light did consecrate.*

Twelve hundred years and more
Along the holy floor
Pageants have passed, and tombs of mighty kings
Efface the humbler graves of Sebert's line,
55   And, as years sped, the minster-aisles divine
Grew used to the approach of Glory's wings.
Arts came, and arms, and law,
And majesty, and sacred form and fear;
Only that primal guest the fisher saw,
60 Light, only light, was slow to reappear.

The Saviour's happy light,
Wherein at first was dight
His boon of life and immortality,
In desert ice of subtleties was spent
65   Or drowned in mists of childish wonderment,
Fond fancies here, there false philosophy!
And harsh the temper grew
Of men with mind thus darkened and astray;
And scarce the boon of life could struggle through
70 For want of light which should the boon convey.

40. Cp. Milton's 'Nativity Ode' 63,
       His raign of peace upon the earth began.

Yet in this latter time
The promise of the prime
Seemed to come true at last, O Abbey old!
It seemed, a child of light did bring the dower
75   Foreshown thee in thy consecration-hour,
And in thy courts his shining freight unrolled:
Bright wits, and instincts sure,
And goodness warm, and truth without alloy,
And temper sweet, and love of all things pure,
80 And joy in light, and power to spread the joy.

And on that countenance bright
Shone oft so high a light,
That to my mind there came how, long ago,
Lay on the hearth, amid a fiery ring,
85   The charmed babe of the Eleusinian king –
His nurse, the Mighty Mother, willed it so.
Warm in her breast, by day,
He slumbered, and ambrosia balmed the child;
But all night long amid the flames he lay,
90 Upon the hearth, and played with them, and smiled.

But once, at midnight deep,
His mother woke from sleep,
And saw her babe amidst the fire, and screamed.
A sigh the Goddess gave, and with a frown
95   Plucked from the fire the child, and laid him down;
Then raised her face, and glory round her streamed.
The mourning-stole no more

71–80. Stanley was appointed Dean of Westminster 8 Nov. 1863. A.'s description of him as 'a child of light' recalls the characterisation of Joubert in *E in C I* (1865), *Works* iii 329-30, '. . . the peculiar beauty of Joubert . . . is not in what is exclusively intellectual, – it is in the union of *soul* with intellect . . . He is the most prepossessing and convincing of witnesses to the good of loving light. Because he sincerely loved light . . . he found light; his eye was single, and therefore his whole body was full of light. And because he was full of light, he was also full of happiness.'

76. A self-echo – see 'The Scholar-Gipsy' 250 (p. 344 above),

And on the beach undid his corded bales.

81–120. The extended classical parallel is frigid and artificial.

85. 'Demophoön, son of Celeus, King of Eleusis. See, in the *Homeric Hymns*, the *Hymn to Demeter*, 184-298.' A.'s note.

86. *the Mighty Mother*] Demeter. See *n.* to 'Thyrsis' 177 (p. 506 above).

97–8. Demeter was in mourning for Persephone, whom she was seeking, when Celeus received her hospitably (see l. 109 below).

19+M.A.

Mantled her form, no more her head was bowed;
But raiment of celestial sheen she wore,
100   And beauty filled her, and she spake aloud : –

'O ignorant race of man !
Achieve your good who can,
If your own hands the good begun undo ?
Had human cry not marred the work divine,
105   Immortal had I made this boy of mine;
But now his head to death again is due
And I have now no power
Unto this pious household to repay
Their kindness shown me in my wandering hour.'
110   – She spake, and from the portal passed away.

The Boy his nurse forgot,
And bore a mortal lot.
Long since, his name is heard on earth no more.
In some chance battle on Cithæron-side
115   The nursling of the Mighty Mother died,
And went where all his fathers went before.
– On thee too, in thy day
Of childhood, Arthur ! did some check have power,
That, radiant though thou wert, thou couldst but
120   Bringer of heavenly light, a human hour ?   [stay,

Therefore our happy guest
Knew care, and knew unrest,
And weakness warned him, and he feared decline.
And in the grave he laid a cherished wife,
125   And men ignoble harassed him with strife,
And deadly airs his strength did undermine.
Then from his Abbey fades
The sound beloved of his victorious breath;
And light's fair nursling stupor first invades,
130   And next the crowning impotence of death.

124. Lady Augusta Stanley died 1 March 1876.
125. See R. E. Prothero, *Life and Letters of Dean Stanley* (1909 single-volume ed.) 366, 372, 'So stormy was the atmosphere in which Stanley lived as Dean of Westminster, that it might be supposed to be the air he breathed most freely . . . From the very first Stanley's aims and opinions brought him into conflict with powerful tendencies of party feeling . . .'
126. deadly airs] Stanley died, as his wife had died in 1876, from a fever due to the insanitary condition of the Deanery. He had foolishly disregarded warnings that he was risking his life.

But hush! This mournful strain,
Which would of death complain,
The oracle forbade, not ill-inspired.
That Pair, whose head did plan, whose hands did
135   The Temple in the pure Parnassian gorge,   [forge
Finished their work, and then a meed required.
'Seven days', the God replied,
'Live happy, then expect your perfect meed!'
Quiet in sleep, the seventh night, they died.
140   Death, death was judged the boon supreme indeed.

And truly he who here
Hath run his bright career,
And served men nobly, and acceptance found,
And borne to light and right his witness high,
145   What could he better wish than then to die,
And wait the issue, sleeping underground?
Why should he pray to range
Down the long age of truth that ripens slow;
And break his heart with all the baffling change,
150   And all the tedious tossing to and fro?

For this and that way swings
The flux of mortal things,
Though moving inly to one far-set goal.
What had our Arthur gained, to stop and see,

131–40. More classical padding.

133. *not ill-inspired*] A Miltonism.

134–5. 'Agamedes and Trophonius, the builders of the temple of Apollo at Delphi. See Plutarch, *Consolatio ad Apollonium*, c. 14 [*Moralia* Loeb ed. ii 145].' A.'s note.

151–3. The idea of movement to a goal in spite of eddyings to and fro is expressed for the individual life in 'The Buried Life' 30–44 (pp. 272–3 above), but here A. is echoing Tennyson's *In Memoriam* (1850) cxxxi 155–6,

> And one far-off divine event
> To which the whole creation moves.

153. *far-set*] far-off *1882*.

154–60. A. is referring impatiently to the spread of Ritualism in the 1870s and 1880s – see 'The Church of England', *Last Essays* (1877), *Works* ix 367–8, 'However, a wave of religious reaction is evidently passing over Europe . . .' and 'A Liverpool Address' (1882), *Five Uncollected Essays of Matthew Arnold* (1953) 92, 'The movers of all those questions about apostolical succession, church, patristic authority, primitive usage, symbolism, postures, vestments – questions so passionately debated . . . – do they not all begin by taking for granted something no longer possible or receivable . . .'

155   After light's term, a term of cecity,
         A Church once large and then grown strait in soul?
                 To live, and see arise,
         Alternating with wisdom's too short reign,
                 Folly revived, re-furbished sophistries,
160   And pullulating rites externe and vain?

                 Ay me! 'Tis deaf, that ear
                 Which joyed my voice to hear;
         Yet would I not disturb thee from thy tomb,
                 Thus sleeping in thine Abbey's friendly shade,
165   And the rough waves of life for ever laid!
         I would not break thy rest, nor change thy doom.
                 Even as my father, thou –
         Even as that loved, that well-recorded friend –
                 Hast thy commission done; ye both may now
170   Wait for the leaven to work, the let to end.

                 And thou, O Abbey grey!
                 Predestined to the ray
         By this dear guest over thy precinct shed –
                 Fear not but that thy light once more shall burn,
175   Once more thine immemorial gleam return,
         Though sunk be now this bright, this gracious head!
                 Let but the light appear
         And thy transfigured walls be touched with flame –
                 Our Arthur will again be present here,
180   Again from lip to lip will pass his name.

155–70. *cecity . . . pullulating . . . let*] See A.'s letter to his sister Frances Jan.
1882, in which he defends 'cecity' as 'used by the great Hooker', 'pullu-
late' as 'used by the Cambridge Platonists a good deal', 'let' in the sense of
hindrance as 'thoroughly good English, being used several times by
Shakespeare' (*L* ii 197–8).
168. *well-recorded friend*] Alluding to Stanley's *The Life and Correspondence
of Thomas Arnold* (1844).
169. *Hast thy commission done*] Cp. 'The Lord's Messengers' 22 (p. 454
above),

         His Master's errand well done . . .

A. had recently revised the poem for inclusion in *1881*.
176. An echo of Milton's 'Lycidas' 167–9,

         Sunk though he be beneath the watry floor,
         So sinks the day-star in the Ocean bed,
         And yet anon repairs his drooping head . . .

128 Poor Matthias

Written 12–25 Oct. 1882: entries in A.'s unpublished 1882 diary (*Commentary* 313–14); see also A.'s letter to J. Morley 24 Oct. 1882, 'The "dirge" is as good as done – a simple thing enough, but honest' (*L* ii 207). For a parody, possibly by H. D. Traill, which amused A. see *L* ii 209. Published *Macmillan's Magazine* Dec. 1882; reprinted *1885*, etc.

> Poor Matthias! – Found him lying
> Fall'n beneath his perch and dying?
> Found him stiff, you say, though warm –
> All convulsed his little form?
> 5   Poor canary! many a year
> Well he knew his mistress dear;
> Now in vain you call his name,
> Vainly raise his rigid frame,
> Vainly warm him in your breast,
> 10   Vainly kiss his golden crest,
> Smooth his ruffled plumage fine,
> Touch his trembling beak with wine.
> One more gasp – it is the end!
> Dead and mute our tiny friend!
> 15   – Songster thou of many a year,
> Now thy mistress brings thee here,
> Says, it fits that I rehearse,
> Tribute due to thee, a verse,
> Meed for daily song of yore
> 20   Silent now for evermore.
>
> Poor Matthias! Wouldst thou have
> More than pity? claim'st a stave?
> – Friends more near us than a bird
> We dismissed without a word.
> 25   Rover, with the good brown head,
> Great Atossa, they are dead;
> Dead, and neither prose nor rhyme
> Tells the praises of their prime.
> Thou didst know them old and grey,
> 30   Know them in their sad decay.

¶ 128. *6. his mistress*] A.'s daughter Eleanor, the 'Nelly' of l. 191 below. *25–6.* Rover and Toss are also mentioned in 'Kaiser Dead' 65–6 (p. 564 below). 'Great Atossa' is a character in Pope's *Moral Essays* (Epistle ii 115–50), but A.'s Persian cat was aptly named after the historical Atossa, daughter of Cyrus the Great and wife of Darius.

Thou hast seen Atossa sage
Sit for hours beside thy cage;
Thou wouldst chirp, thou foolish bird,
Flutter, chirp – she never stirred!
35 What were now these toys to her?
Down she sank amid her fur;
Eyed thee with a soul resigned –
And thou deemedst cats were kind!
– Cruel, but composed and bland,
40 Dumb, inscrutable and grand,
So Tiberius might have sat,
Had Tiberius been a cat.

Rover died – Atossa too.
Less than they to us are you!
45 Nearer human were their powers,
Closer knit their life with ours.
Hands had stroked them, which are cold,
Now for years, in churchyard mould;
Comrades of our past were they,
50 Of that unreturning day.
Changed and aging, they and we
Dwelt, it seemed, in sympathy.
Alway from their presence broke
Somewhat which remembrance woke
55 Of the loved, the lost, the young –
Yet they died, and died unsung.

Geist came next, our little friend;
Geist had verse to mourn his end.
Yes, but that enforcement strong
60 Which compelled for Geist a song –
All that gay courageous cheer,
All that human pathos dear;
Soul-fed eyes with suffering worn,
Pain heroically borne,
65 Faithful love in depth divine –
Poor Matthias, were they thine?

Max and Kaiser we to-day
Greet upon the lawn at play;
Max a dachshound without blot –

47-55. Two of A.'s sons, Basil and Thomas, died in 1868; a third son, Trevenen William, in 1872.
58. See 'Geist's Grave' (p. 547 above).

70   Kaiser should be, but is not.
         Max, with shining yellow coat,
         Prinking ears and dewlap throat –
         Kaiser, with his collie face,
         Penitent for want of race.
75   – Which may be the first to die,
         Vain to augur, they or I?
         But, as age comes on, I know,
         Poet's fire gets faint and low;
         If so be that travel they
80   First the inevitable way,
         Much I doubt if they shall have
         Dirge from me to crown their grave.

             Yet, poor bird, thy tiny corse
         Moves me, somehow, to remorse;
85   Something haunts my conscience, brings
         Sad, compunctious visitings.
         Other favourites, dwelling here,
         Open lived to us, and near;
         Well we knew when they were glad,
90   Plain we saw if they were sad,
         Joyed with them when they were gay,
         Soothed them in their last decay;
         Sympathy could feel and show
         Both in weal of theirs and woe.

95   Birds, companions more unknown,
         Live beside us, but alone;
         Finding not, do all they can,
         Passage from their souls to man.
         Kindness we bestow, and praise,
100   Laud their plumage, greet their lays;
         Still beneath their feathered breast,
         Stirs a history unexpressed.
         Wishes there, and feelings strong,
         Incommunicably throng;
105   What they want, we cannot guess,
         Fail to track their deep distress –
         Dull look on when death is nigh,

70. See 'Kaiser Dead' 19–30 (p. 563 below).
86. *compunctious visitings*] An echo of *Macbeth* I v 44–5,

         Stop up the access and passage to remorse
         That no compunctious visitings of nature
         Shake my fell purpose . . .

Note no change, and let them die.
Poor Matthias! couldst thou speak,
110   What a tale of thy last week!
Every morning did we pay
Stupid salutations gay,
Suited well to health, but how
Mocking, how incongrous now!
115   Cake we offered, sugar, seed,
Never doubtful of thy need;
Praised, perhaps, thy courteous eye,
Praised thy golden livery.
Gravely thou the while, poor dear!
120   Sat'st upon thy perch to hear,
Fixing with a mute regard
Us, thy human keepers hard,
Troubling, with our chatter vain,
Ebb of life, and mortal pain --
125   Us, unable to divine
Our companion's dying sign,
Or o'erpass the severing sea
Set betwixt ourselves and thee,
Till the sand thy feathers smirch
130   Fallen dying off thy perch!

Was it, as the Grecian sings,
Birds were born the first of things,
Before the sun, before the wind,
Before the gods, before mankind,
135   Airy, ante-mundane throng --
Witness their unworldly song!
Proof they give, too, primal powers,
Of a prescience more than ours --
Teach us, while they come and go,
140   When to sail, and when to sow.
Cuckoo calling from the hill,
Swallow skimming by the mill,
Swallows trooping in the sedge,
Starlings swirling from the hedge,
145   Mark the seasons, map our year,
As they show and disappear.
But, with all this travail sage
Brought from that anterior age,
Goes an unreversed decree

131. *the Grecian*] Aristophanes. See *n.* to ll. 153-4 below.
143-4. First added *1885*.

150   Whereby strange are they and we,
        Making want of theirs, and plan,
        Indiscernible by man.

            No, away with tales like these
        Stol'n from Aristophanes!
155   Does it, if we miss your mind,
        Prove us so remote in kind?
        Birds! we but repeat on you
        What amongst ourselves we do.
        Somewhat more or somewhat less,
160   'Tis the same unskilfulness.
        What you feel, escapes our ken –
        Know we more our fellow men?
        Human suffering at our side,
        Ah, like yours is undescried!
165   Human longings, human fears,
        Miss our eyes and miss our ears.
        Little helping, wounding much,
        Dull of heart, and hard of touch,
        Brother man's despairing sign
170   Who may trust us to divine?
        Who assure us, sundering powers
        Stand not 'twixt his soul and ours?

            Poor Matthias! See, thy end
        What a lesson doth it lend!
175   For that lesson thou shalt have,
        Dead canary bird, a stave!
        Telling how, one stormy day,
        Stress of gale and showers of spray
        Drove my daughter small and me
180   Inland from the rocks and sea.
        Driv'n inshore, we follow down
        Ancient streets of Hastings town –
        Slowly thread them – when behold,
        French canary-merchant old
185   Shepherding his flock of gold
        In a low dim-lighted pen
        Scanned of tramps and fishermen!
        There a bird, high-coloured, fat,
        Proud of port, though something squat –
190   Pursy, played-out Philistine –
        Dazzled Nelly's youthful eyne.
        But, far in, obscure, there stirred

153–4. 'See *The Birds* of Aristophanes, 465–85.' A.'s note.
    19*

On his perch a sprightlier bird,
Courteous-eyed, erect and slim;
195   And I whispered: 'Fix on *him!*'
Home we brought him, young and fair,
Songs to trill in Surrey air.
Here Matthias sang his fill,
Saw the cedars of Pains Hill;
200   Here he poured his little soul,
Heard the murmur of the Mole.
Eight in number now the years
He hath pleased our eyes and ears;
Other favourites he hath known
205   Go, and now himself is gone.
– Fare thee well, companion dear!
Fare for ever well, nor fear,
Tiny though thou art, to stray
Down the uncompanioned way!
210   We without thee, little friend,
Many years have not to spend;
What are left, will hardly be
Better than we spent with thee.

199. See *n.* to 'Rome-Sickness' 5 (p. 545 above).
201. the Mole] A tributary of the Thames.
209. the uncompanioned way] A. is thinking of the *iter tenebricosum* travelled by Lesbia's sparrow – see Catullus iii 11.

129 Kaiser Dead

APRIL 6, 1887

A.'s last poem, written between April–June 1887: Kaiser, A.'s mongrel dachshund (who also appears in 'Poor Matthias' above) died 6 April 1887; the poem was published in the following July. A.'s stanza is from Burns and his treatment imitates that of the Elegy in Burns's 'The Death and Dying Words of Poor Mailie, the Author's only pet yowe' – see ll. 11–12 below and *n*.

Published *Fortnightly Review* July 1887; reprinted (after A.'s death) *1890*, etc.

What, Kaiser dead? The heavy news
Post-haste to Cobham calls the Muse,
From where in Farringford she brews
The ode sublime,

¶ 129. *3. Farringford*] Tennyson's home near Freshwater, Isle of Wight. In the 1880s Tennyson usually spent the summer at Aldworth, the winter at Farringford.

5   Or with Pen-bryn's bold bard pursues,
             A rival rhyme.

        Kai's bracelet tail, Kai's busy feet,
        Were known to all the village-street.
        'What, poor Kai dead?' say all I meet;
10   'A loss indeed!'
        O for the croon pathetic, sweet,
             Of Robin's reed!

        Six years ago I brought him down,
        A baby dog, from London town;
15   Round his small throat of black and brown
             A ribbon blue,
        And vouched by glorious renown
             A dachshound true.

        His mother, most majestic dame,
20   Of blood-unmixed, from Potsdam came;
        And Kaiser's race we deemed the same –
             No lineage higher.
        And so he bore the imperial name.
             But ah, his sire!

25   Soon, soon the days conviction bring.
        The collie hair, the collie swing,
        The tail's indomitable ring,
             The eye's unrest –
        The case was clear; a mongrel thing
30   Kai stood confessed.

        But all those virtues, which commend
        The humbler sort who serve and tend,
        Were thine in store, thou faithful friend.
             What sense, what cheer!
35   To us, declining tow'rds our end,
             A mate how dear!

5. *Pen-bryn's bold bard*] The popular poetaster Sir Lewis Morris (1833–1907), who styled himself 'Lewis Morris of Penbryn' on the title-page of *Songs Unsung* (1883) – see *Commentary* 316–7. Penbryn was the name of his house near Carmarthen.

11–12. Cp. Burns's 'Poor Mailie', Elegy 45–6,

> *Come, join the melancholious croon*
> *O' Robin's reed!*

For Max, thy brother-dog, began
To flag, and feel his narrowing span.
And cold, besides, his blue blood ran,
40   Since, 'gainst the classes,
He heard, of late, the Grand Old Man
          Incite the masses.

Yes, Max and we grew slow and sad;
But Kai, a tireless shepherd-lad,
45   Teeming with plans, alert, and glad
          In work or play,
Like sunshine went and came, and bade
          Live out the day!

50   Still, still I see the figure smart –
Trophy in mouth, agog to start,
Then, home returned, once more depart;
          Or pressed together
Against thy mistress, loving heart,
          In wintry weather.

55   I see the tail, like bracelet twirled,
In moments of disgrace uncurled,
Then at a pardoning word re-furled,
          A conquering sign;
Crying, 'Come on, and range the world,
60   And never pine.'

Thine eye was bright, thy coat it shone;
Thou hadst thine errands, off and on;
In joy thy last morn flew; anon,
          A fit! All's over;
65   And thou art gone where Geist hath gone,
          And Toss, and Rover.

Poor Max, with downcast, reverent head,
Regards his brother's form outspread;
Full well Max knows the friend is dead
70   Whose cordial talk,
And jokes in doggish language said,
          Beguiled his walk.

39–42. A facetious reference to the political excitement over the Franchise
Bill in 1884. Gladstone's moderation ensured the success of the bill, but
there was some heated talk of mob rule when Liberal supporters broke up
a Conservative meeting at Aston Park, Birmingham, in Oct. 1884.
65–6. See 'Poor Matthias' 43–58 (p. 558 above).

And Glory, stretched at Burwood gate,
Thy passing by doth vainly wait;
75   And jealous Jock, thy only hate,
The chiel from Skye,
Lets from his shaggy Highland pate
Thy memory die.

80   Well, fetch his graven collar fine,
And rub the steel, and make it shine,
And leave it round thy neck to twine,
Kai, in thy grave.
There of thy master keep that sign.
And this plain stave.

73. *Burwood*] An estate near A.'s cottage at Cobham.

JUVENILIA, UNFINISHED POEMS, AND FRAGMENTS

130 Lines written on the Seashore at Eagleshurst

JULY 12, 1836

Written on and shortly after 12 July 1836: see Mrs. A.'s unpublished letter to a sister (undated but clearly late July 1836) about a holiday visit to the Isle of Wight, 'Matt was missing [after breakfast]. It was suggested that he might have gone down to the shore, and this was in fact the case, but I do not think it would be guessed what he was doing there. I did not know till as we were driving along he put in at the carriage window a pencilled paper which proved that he had been poetizing. It was headed . . . [here title as above and ll. 1–20] I have not given all, but the rest is an after composition, and you have here enough to shew you his facility in thought and composition.' An autograph fair copy of the complete poem signed 'Matt, Arnold' is in Mrs. A.'s 1836 note-book (formerly in the possession of Miss Dorothy Ward). Stanza and diction suggest that A. had been reading Gray.

¶ 130. *Title.* Eaglehurst was the country seat on Southampton Water of Richard Lambart, seventh Earl of Cavan, whose second wife Lydia was Dr. A.'s sister.

First published (with one error of transcription – l. 33 'As though' for 'Although') in I. E. Sell's *Matthew Arnold and France* (1935).

Naiads were wont of old to dwell
Beneath the boundless ocean's swell,
And sport, midst halls of coral reared,
Where winds and angry waters feared
5   To force their rushing way;
And crowned with seaweed dance along
With bounding steps and mirth and song,
While each perchance presided o'er
Some favoured glen on wooded shore
10   With mild and gentle sway.

What naiad then, what nymph presides
To shelter thee from winds and tides,
To deck thy wooded cliff with flowers,
To revel mid thy sea-girt bowers
15   And haunts, O Eaglehurst?
If Thetis' self had deigned to prove
For some sweet spot peculiar love,
Sure thou wert worthy of her sway
Thus cradled in thy quiet bay,
20   By woodland fairies nursed.

What though the murmur of the sea
Beats gently on the sandy lea,
And ever restless fills the ear
With sounds which it is sweet to hear
25   On many a quiet shore.
Yet here it seems as if the wave
Were struggling with the sand to lave
The foot of yonder wooded cliff,
And then a barrier firm and stiff
30   Opposed the ocean's roar.

Still restlessly it struggles on
O'er seaweed fair, o'er shell and stone,
Although yon castled height looks down
And on the billows seems to frown
35   And bid the invader go.
But other scenes than castled towers,
The flowery fields, the woods and bowers,
Invite the intruder onward still,
But while his fancy takes its fill
40   His waves must roll below.

131 Lines written on first leaving home for a Public School

Written Sept. 1836: A. entered Winchester, his father's old school, as a Commoner on 31 Aug. 1836; the poem was written 'a few days later' – see N. Wymer's *Dr. Arnold of Rugby* (1953) 140. A fair copy signed 'M. Arnold' is in Mrs. A.'s 1836 note-book (after the signature she has added 'Age 13'). The lines suggest A.'s familiarity with Keble's *The Christian Year* (1827), parts of which he was learning by heart as a Sunday exercise from an early age. Keble was A.'s godfather.

First published (with two errors of transcription – l. 26 'allay' for 'alloy', l. 31 'with' for 'wch') in N. Wymer's *Dr. Arnold of Rugby* (1953).

> One step in life is taken,
> And we must hurry on
> And cheer our onward path as best we may;
> And if a moment's space we stay,
> 5   The world around seems all forsaken,
> And we, deserted and alone.
> But yet there gleams one ray of light
> To guide us through our trials here,
> To urge us fearlessly to fight our fight,
> 10 A spell our dreary path to cheer:
> More potent far than Eastern Talisman
> To cheer the drooping heart of man,
> The sound of home will cheer the mind when
>   naught beside it can.
>
> By every fond familiar face
> 15 That hitherto we know or love,
> By that long and last embrace
> Which e'en the roughest heart will move,
> By every kindred feeling that unites
> Our hearts with others and excites
> 20 E'en in this wilderness some thoughts of joy,
> When first we leave our early home
> Along the maze of life to roam,
> And stand dependent on ourselves alone
> To tread a path till now unknown –
> 25 Oh, stand a barrier 'gainst all ill
> And all that seeks our thoughts of good t'alloy;
> Be unto us a watchword on our way
> In darkest hour of night and in the bright noonday;
> Where'er our fancy strays be with us still.

¶ 131. *11. Eastern Talisman*] An allusion to Southey's *Thalaba* (1801).

30   Yet a still firmer pillar let us rear
        On which our sinking hopes to prop:
        Though all human aid forsake us
        And naught appears our way to cheer,
        Though conflicting passions shake us,
35   Do Thou, O Lord, be present still
        And aye direct us with Thy guiding hand,
        That, as we labour up life's toilsome hill,
        Or with a slower step descend, we may be found,
        Mid all the storms that shake the world around,
40   Not to have built our temple on the sand.

132 'Land of the East! Around thy shores are flung ...'

Probably written Christmas 1838 and copied out, with signature 'C.C.C.', for the Jan. 1839 number of the MS. *Fox How Magazine* (the family magazine produced twice a year by the Arnold children on holiday). All A.'s contributions to the *Fox How Magazine* have this signature (his family nickname was Crab).
Previously unpublished.

> *The Spirit of God was said during the Siege of Jerusalem by those who kept watch there to have departed from the Temple at night with a rushing noise.*

        Land of the East! Around thy shores are flung
        By fancy's hand the glittering stores of song.
        Around thy mouldering walls on Sion's hill
        The Almighty's viewless spirit lingers still.
5   Still on its height thy glorious temple stands
        (God's chosen place – if that were made with hands).

¶ 132. *Heading*. The four-year siege of Jerusalem by the Romans ended in the capture and destruction of the city A.D. 70. For the legend alluded to see Flavius Josephus, *The Jewish War* vi (Loeb ed. iii 463), 'Moreover, at the Feast which is called Pentecost, the priests in entering the inner court of the temple by night ... reported that they were conscious, first of a commotion and a din, and after that of a voice as of a host, "We are departing hence".'
4. *viewless*] Invisible. See *n.* to 'Empedocles on Etna' I i 52 (p. 151 above).
6. *if that were made with hands*] Cp. 2 *Corinthians* v 1, ... an house not made with hands, eternal in the heavens'.

Bethesda's pool beneath thy burning skies
Unruffled now by heavenly influence lies.
Yon holy mount where breathed a Saviour's prayer,
10 Yon spot that felt his agonizéd tear,
Each hallowed spot, or hill or vale, recall
Those days of old from time's encroaching thrall.
Calm is the touch and noiseless the decay
That sweeps the relics of the past away,
15 But frequent still before the entrancéd eye
Visions of long ago come fleeting by.
Oft o'er thy hills and glittering plains afar
Gleams the wild pomp of oriental war.
On Pisgah's height the inspired seer we see
20 Pierce the dim bounds of far futurity.
We mark Jehovah's Chosen People dwell
Beneath thy goodly tents, O Israel.
Or where the Avenging Angel's viewless sword
Silently smites each wild Assyrian horde.
25 While each dim vision of the past can tell
Thy palmy days of old, forsaken Israel.

But all is silent now. On Salem's hill
God's voice, that talked of old with man, is still.
'Mid the wild eddyings of the whirling storm
30 Sweeps past no more the Almighty's cloudgirt form,
But unrestrained, round yon beleaguered towers,
Borne on the threatening blast, destruction lours.
No more the voice of praise, the busy hum
Of many voices from thy temple, come.
35 The heathen's sword is in thy citadel,
And in thy palace doth the scorner dwell.
Lo, the triumphant Roman's conquering race

7–8. See *John* v 2–4. The first man to bathe in the pool after the angel
'troubled the water' was healed of any sickness.
11. *recall*] The MS. reading.
19. *the inspired seer*] Moses. See *Deuteronomy* xxxiv 1–4. From Pisgah Moses
was shown the Promised Land and was told that he would not live to enter
it.
23–4. An allusion to the destruction of Sennacherib's host. See 2 *Kings* xix
35, 'And it came to pass, that night, that the angel of the Lord went out, and
smote in the camp of the Assyrians an hundred fourscore and five
thousand.' A. would be familiar with Byron's 'The Destruction of Sennacherib' (1815).
30. *the Almighty's cloud-girt form*] Cp. *Exodus* xiii 21, 'And the Lord went
before them by day in a pillar of a cloud, to lead them the way.'
34. *come*] The MS. reading.

Pollute thine own Jehovah's resting-place.
Vanished thy glory, widowed thy estate.
40   Thine house is left unto thee desolate.

But hark – yon sound of rushing mighty wind.
Say, tells it naught to thy despairing mind?
God leaves his People desolate, forlorn,
Thy crown of glory withered, sere and torn.
45   From hill to hill, from plain to plain, it rings,
The dread departure of the King of Kings.
It gently sighed o'er Jordan's palmy lea
And o'er thy garden glades, Gethsemane,
And, as it breathed on far Gennesaret's sea,
50   Swept past thy guilty steep, dark Calvary.
It is not so. Hope still would picture dreams
Around thy balmy groves and murmuring streams:
That He, thy Saviour, Prophet, Priest and King,
Shall fold thee once again beneath his wing;
55   Again on Sion's height the Almighty dwell,
And God return to bless his Israel.

49. *Gennesaret's sea*] The Sea of Galilee.

133 'Alas, that race accursed . . .'

A.'s translation of *Aeneid* vii 293–319 probably made in the Christmas
holidays 1838 (perhaps as a holiday task) and copied out for *Fox How
Magazine* No. 3 (Jan. 1839). Juno, incensed by the favourable reception of
Aeneas by Latinus, is the speaker.
Previously unpublished.

Alas, that race accursed! those Fates of Troy
That, adverse still, forbid me to destroy!
Alas, they fell not on Sigea's plain,
But, still preserved, though captive burst their chain.
5   Troy's fall o'erwhelmed not them: mid fire and flood,
Mid war's embattled lines unharmed they stood.
What, hath my wrath departed from my breast,
Gorged with destruction, eager for its rest?
Nay! As they fled o'er ocean's billowy wave
10   In clouds I came to curse and not to save.
Yes, wind and wave all eager to destroy
Raged vainly 'gainst the charméd barks of Troy.
Vain were the Syrtes, vain was Scylla's cave,
In vain Charybdis tossed his whirling wave;

15   In Tiber's promised stream their vessels lie,
       Safe from my power and ocean's swelling high.
       Mars slew the Lapithae at will, and Heaven
       To stern Diana Calydon has given.
       Yes, those the Gods forbade not to destroy,
20   Though scarce so guilty as these sons of Troy.
       But we, the Thunderer's bride (whose fruitless wrath
       Hath tried each means to aid our vengeful path),
       Yes, we all-powerful, victors in the field,
       In might unconquered, to Aeneas yield.
25   But if my might sufficeth not, if Heaven
       Unto its mightiest sons no power hath given,
       Infernal Powers, assist my purpose well.
       If Heaven be unrelenting, aid me Hell!
       Yes, let the Latian sceptre glad his pride,
30   Yes, let him clasp Lavinia for his bride;
       But long delay shall heap those plains with dead,
       And death shall hover constant round his head.
       Be this thy marriage compact with thy sire –
       With seal of blood, in characters of fire.
35   And thou, fair maid, a dear-bought bride shall be
       By choicest blood of Troy and Italy,
       Purchased by ravaged lands and bloodstained sea.
       Bellona bears the marriage torch for thee!

134 Constantinople

Probably written summer 1839 and copied out for *Fox How Magazine* No. 4 (July 1839). At sixteen A. is already most at ease with an elegiac subject: this lament over Constantinople fallen to the Turks is a forerunner of the more skilful Byronic rhetoric of 'Alaric at Rome', the Rugby prize-poem of 1840. The eight-line stanza ending in an alexandrine (a⁵b³ab⁵ccd⁴d⁶) is probably original.
Previously unpublished.

    Oh, shed not on the dust whence life has fled
       The brightness of to-day;
    The halo lingering round the mighty dead
    Enshrines them with a more enduring ray;
5   More staid and sober is its hue,
       Its light more soft, its touch more true,
      Than the full sun's unsoftened glare
    To mar the mellowing touch that time hath printed there.

¶ 134. *8. To mar*] 'Which mars' would have made the sense clearer.

The sun that gilds the glorious eastern sky,
10   The giddy whirl of life,
The crowded street, the sound of joy or cry
Of restless labour and of human strife,
         The busy hum where men are met,
         The sparkling mosque or minaret –
15   Each sign of wealth and life and breath
Is but a glittering pall to hide the nakedness of death.

And thou, fair city, in thy spangled vest
       Of gay barbaric gold,
Doomed to obey thy stranger-lord's behest,
20   The Crescent's might triumphant to behold –
         The jewelled robe, the wild attire,
         The barbarous tongue, the eye of fire,
       Pledge of the children of a burning clime –
Float like a gaudy flower amid the weeds of time.

25   And still from year to year thy day of woe
       Returns in silent sorrow:
When thou didst gaze upon the gathering foe
In fearful trembling for that dread tomorrow,
         When through thine echoing Golden Horn
30   The gathering battle-cry was borne –
Until the unconquered Cross lay low
And wayward victory crowned the unbeliever's brow.

Burst forth in mourning for thy days of old
       And weep for those that are;
35   Clad be thy form in sackcloth's gloomiest fold
And ashes crown thine unadornéd hair;
         Sing out, thou ocean surge,
         Thy melancholy dirge,
To pour the sorrows of thy wailing tide
40   In fitting strains before thy long-neglected bride.

Oh, smile not on, thou glittering sun, for ever
       So beautifully bright;
Oh, flow not on, thou sparkling ocean river

---

16. Metrically irregular (as are ll. 23, 37–9 below).
24. *Float*] 'Floatest' or 'Dost float' is required (the subject being 'thou, fair city').
25. *day of woe*] Constantinople fell under Ottoman rule on 29 May 1453.

Serenely calm in darkness as in light.
45   Poetic fancy paints thy form
    In clouds and dreariness and storm,
    O'er faded flowers and glories gone
Brooding in joyless state, to stiffen into stone.

44. Serenely calm] A typically Arnoldian phrase anticipating 'Alaric at Rome' 100 (p. 7 above),

How calmly sad, how sadly beautiful . . .

and 'Cromwell' 186 (p. 20 above),

So sadly calm, so kingly, so serene . . .

135 The Incursion
A DRAMATIC FRAGMENT

Written at Christmas 1841 (in lively anticipation of his family's descent on Oxford at the beginning of the new term) and copied out in *Fox How Magazine* No. 9 (Jan. 1842). Dr. A., who had delivered his inaugural lecture as Professor of Modern History at Oxford 2 Dec. 1841, had taken lodgings in Beaumont Street to settle there with his family while giving a course of lectures in late Jan. and early Feb. 1842. A. was a freshman at Balliol – see Tom A.'s anecdote of his brother's behaviour at this time, *Passages in a Wandering Life* (1900) 55, 'My brother, in all the glory of a scholar's gown and three months' experience as a "University man", welcomed his rustic *geschwister* with an amused and superior graciousness. We visited him at his rooms in Balliol . . . When he had got us in, he is said to have exclaimed, "Thank God, you are in!" and when the visit was over, and he had seen the last of us out on the staircase, "Thank God, you are out!"'
Previously unpublished.

MEN		WOMEN
JENKINS	*Citizens of Oxford*	THE SPIRIT OF PROPRIETY
TOMKINS		

Place : Oxford

First Citizen
Jenkins, well met.

Second Citizen
    Tomkins, it is not well
With thy poor friend. Lo, how this bristling hair,
These cheeks of ghastly paleness, and this coat
Buttoned awry in mine excess of grief,

¶ *135. Title.* A facetious allusion to Wordsworth's *The Excursion* (1814).

5   Attest some grievous horror! What, well met?
       Well met in Oxford? Well met anywhere
       While every stone of our afflicted city
       Cries out for vengeance on this ruthless chief
       Who hath led hither his barbarian hordes
10   To brawl and riot in the heart of Oxford,
       This great and awful university?
       Well met at such a time? I tell thee, Tomkins,
       My appetite is gone, my peace is fled
       Since my sweet children in the Parks of late
15   Seeking fresh air and healthful exercise,
       Sedate and solemn as good children should,
       Were overthrown by two barbarians
       Young, stout and ruddy, with disordered dress;
       The one a boy of lungs unconquerable,
20   With coat all soiled and torn; a girl the other –
       If girl she could be called who had no sign
       Of girlish nature nor of feminine dress
       Save a brown garment half-way down her back,
       All loose and ill arranged. My frightened doves –
25   The very trousers on their startled legs
       Unfrilled, unstarched, in their excess of fear –
       Came running to their home, and there they lie
       In grievous perturbation and distress.

First Citizen

       Peace, peace, my poor sad friend, though at thy tale
30   The sympathetic tears bedew my eyes.
       Behold this female form, so pale, so wan,
       Threading with feeble steps the Cornmarket.
       Lo, here she comes –

Enter the SPIRIT OF PROPRIETY, *sick*

Spirit of Propriety

       A little further lead me, good my friends,
35   That I may gaze on High Street ere I die.
       Thou venerable pavement that so long
       Hast seen decorous undergraduates

19–24. A.'s brother and sister, William and Susan, aged thirteen and eleven
respectively.

34. Cp. Milton's *Samson Agonistes* 1–2,

> *A little onward lend thy guiding hand*
> *To these dark steps, a little further on . . .*

With solemn pace parading on thy stones,
What sights of horror hast thou late beheld!
40 From Beaumont Street the frighted citizens
Rush in disordered crowds, and the pale Proctor
Arrays his Bulldogs at the accursed house door
That holds this strange, unmannered family,
And vainly prays that its unruly inmates
45 Were subjected to his authority.
Negroes, they say, black as a starless night,
Haunt that unhappy region, and one form
More wondrous than my thought had e'er conceived,
For lo, it bears the likeness of a swine,
50 Well ringed, well bristled, with tight-curling tail
And loud and audible grunt . . .
All this I saw, and shuddered, and my heart
Grew cold within me, and I prayed to die.

Second Citizen

The Gods, my Tomkins, to mankind dispense
55 Most different gifts. Manners to some it gives,
Decorum, seemliness, propriety;
To others rude contempt of the wise rules
That decency hath laid upon mankind.
Now go we home and mourn this heavy day.

43. An echo of *As You Like It* II vii 164,

That ends this strange eventful history . . .

46–51. Referring to the family nicknames of A.'s younger brothers,
Edward and William. Edward was known as Pig or Swiney, William as
Nigger.

136 'Rude orator . . .'

Probably written 1843–4: this unfinished, rough draft, almost certainly an
undergraduate composition, is on p. 1 of Yale MS., which carries the
signature 'M. Arnold / Ball: Coll: / 1843'. The punctuation has been
corrected.
Published (with one error of transcription – l. 20 'peevish' for 'lavish')
Commentary (1940).

Rude orator,
Who, while I pondered on the lot of souls
Born reason's heirs and of that heritage
Made void, and held the sorrow and the joy
5 Within the balance of a slow suspense,

Didst force an audience ere I struck the scale
And dared pronounce it happy. What are these
Whereon thou buildest such a goodly pride,
Thy proofs, thy witness, and thy precedents,
10   That they should ease grave counsel of its care
And win deliberate reason to put on fear,
The credulous complexion of thy dreams?

— No lack of answer hast thou, O my heart.
For such a damning catalogue of ills
15   Thou dost allege for proof, such instances
Raked from the swarming gulf of sorrow's hell,
And to uphold thy desperate challenging
Invitest reason to forswear her state
Make cession of her sceptre, doom herself,
20   With such a lavish hardihood of scorn . . .

¶ 136. 7. it] After 'them' cancelled. 'It' refers to the 'lot of souls'.
12. dreams] 'Woe' in the margin is an uncancelled alternative.
16. gulf] Replacing the plural 'gulfs'.
18. Invitest reason] Faulty construction, but we should understand 'Dost so invite reason . . .'

137 Man's Works

Date of composition unknown, but from position in Yale Ms. (?) 1844.
Punctuation corrected and title supplied.
Previously unpublished.

What are man's works
Whereon he sets most store – his creeping temples,
His little fretted plots of garden ground,
His parcelled fields, his gewgaw palaces,
5   His puny parks, a play mocking his own state,
His trees, all their quaint skips and gambols gone,
Tortured in sullen clumps and modish rows
From the free use of nature – what are these,
The mighty Gods of his sweet workmanship,
10   Seen from the dizzy summit of an alp?

¶ 137. 5. a play mocking his own state] Over 'mock solemn as himself' uncancelled. The final reading reached by way of 'mocking his own sweet state' (with two indecipherable alternatives to 'sweet').
6. skips] Over 'tricks' uncancelled.
9. mighty . . . sweet] Over 'darling . . . dear' uncancelled.

138 'Night comes . . .'

From position in Yale MS. probably written 1844; quoted, with minor differences noted below, in A.'s letter to Clough Feb.–Mar. 1845 (*CL* 57). Punctuation corrected.
Previously unpublished in this form.

> Night comes; with Night comes Silence, hand in
>   hand;
> With Night comes Silence, and with that, Repose;
> And pillows on her drowsy breast and locks
> Within the marble prison of her arms
> The Poet's rash and feverish melancholy;
> Cuts short the feignings of fantastic grief,
> Freezes the false breath on the parted lips,
> And steals the shallow music of his tongue.

5

¶ 138. *3. drowsy*] Over 'cold white' uncancelled. *CL* has 'frozen'.
5. rash] Over 'fond' uncancelled. *CL* reads '"Usher's" rash'.
6. Originally followed l. 7.
7. false breath] Over 'sweet strain' (which is also the *CL* reading) cancelled. This alteration and that in the next line postdate A.'s letter.
8. shallow] Over 'honied' (which is also the *CL* reading).

139 'Say this of her . . .'

Probably written not long before 29 Sept. 1848, the date of A.'s letter to Clough containing these lines (*CL* 91–3); they are also found copied out at the back of A.'s copy of Gilbert Burnet's *Life of Matthew Hale* (see *CL* 94). Punctuation slightly altered.
Published *CL* (1932).

> Say this of her:
> The day was, thou wert not; the day will be,
> Thou wilt be most unlovely; shall I choose
> Thy little moment life of loveliness
> Betwixt blank nothing and abhorred decay
> To glue my fruitless gaze on, and to pine,

5

¶ 139. *1–10.* A.'s lines are an anti-pyretic for his reluctant romantic excitement at Thun in 1848. Cp. the resistance to the idea of romantic involvement in the part of the letter of 29 Sept. 1848 immediately preceding the poem: 'We know beforehand all they [women] can teach us: yet we are obliged to learn it directly from them. Why here is a marvellous thing' (*CL* 93).

Sooner than those twin reaches of great time
When thou art either nought, and so not loved,
Or somewhat, but that most unlovable,
10   That preface and post-scribe thee?

140 'Sacrilege ? – We kiss . . .'

From its position in Yale MS. (among notes for 'Empedocles on Etna')
probably *c.* 1849; perhaps a draft of a speech once intended for 'Lucretius'.
Punctuation slightly altered.
Previously unpublished.

Sacrilege ? – We kiss
Cheeks that decay to nourish us and thrive
Upon our fathers' ashes. Lust ? – We grow
By appetite. Injustice ? – We forgive
5   Or punish, and the cross-grained sentence twists
Into the avoided issue. Tyranny ? –
Wise men hold back their hand, and fools are crowned
For that forbearance: from that hour to them,
To them reluctant destiny consigns
10   The groaning nations; from that hour the chain
Is riveted; and history writes down slave
Against the name of man, and eating wounds
Widen in the world's heart – till misery
Breeds wrath, and wrath breeds change, and change,
          new love.

¶ 140. *2. nourish*] Over 'fatten' uncancelled.
7–8. . . . crowned/For] Over '. . . bred/By' cancelled.

141 'And every man relates . . .'

Date of composition unknown, but from its subject and position in Yale
MS. (?) 1849–50. The lines, a rough first draft, are perhaps worth preserving
for their autobiographical interest. Punctuation corrected.
Previously unpublished.

And every man relates
The history of his life
So far as he has yet gone,
And we hear him and perceive not
5   That his history still lacks
Its unguessed conclusion.

And every man has wandered,
    Every man wept,
    Every man raved,
10 Every man buried despondingly in his hands
    His burning brow,
    Even as I do.

And every man has found a home,
    Every man dried his tears,
15   Every man ceased his ravings,
Every man raised cheerfully his head,
    Looking forth upon life.
    Shall not I likewise?

Here and there are scattered their dwellings:
20   On rocks, by rivers,
    In cities, in fields,
Where they have struck root and planted themselves,
    Given over their wanderings.
'Long we wandered', they say, 'but now
25   We rest for ever.'

Who led you, O men, who counselled you?
    By this rock, by this river,
    In that city, on that field,
Wherefore did you strike root there and plant
      yourselves?
30   Why cease your wanderings?
Long you wandered, I know, but why
    Rest you now here?

You know not, you cannot answer.
One by one, over-wearied
35 You dropped down in your wanderings.
Where you dropped, there you remained;
    You awoke already rooted and planted there.
    'This is the place', you said,
'We sought in our wanderings. Here
40   Rest we for ever.'

¶ 141. *26. counselled*] Over 'planted' cancelled.
29. plant] planted *MS*.

This place, O men, you sought not,
    You chose it not beforehand:
Passing that way in your wanderings,
    You dropped down there.
45   For you alone is it a habitation,
        For you only.
    Well is it for you if you are well there.
        So much I say.

    I have not yet dropped down in my wanderings;
50   I wander still.
    Some time, perhaps, I too shall drop down
        In some other city.
    Tell me of your wanderings rather;
        Your rest for you,
55   Your wanderings for all men.

53–5. A. is badly cramped for space in the MS., but this appears to be the
intended lineation.

142 To Meta

Probably written 1849: from its position in Yale MS. and the entry 'To
Meta – the cloister and life liveable' on A.'s Yale MS. list of poems to
compose in 1849. The stanza is identical with that of 'The New Sirens'
(p. 33 above). Meta is probably a lay figure, but see *Commentary* 339 for
the suggestion that she may be A.'s sister 'K' and that the poem itself is
related in theme to 'Stanzas from the Grande Chartreuse' (p. 285 above).
Punctuation corrected.
Published *Commentary* (1940).

    Calmed by bitter disabusings
    Of all thirst of earthly things,
    Ah, they walk in starry musings
    Like stone-sculptured antique kings.
5   Slowly, past the open spaces,
    Of their cloister, see, they glide:
    Tears have washed their austere faces;
    Neither hate have they, nor fear, nor pride.

    See, one figure quits the mazes
10   Of that dusk slow-moving band,
    This way moves and pauses, gazing
    On the sweet and moon-bathed land.
    Softly gleam the far blue mountains,
    Dark the valley sleeps in shade,

15 Cool the murmur of the fountains
  Sinks and rises through this charmed arcade.

  Here where life and all things living
  Awe-struck fain would cease to be,
  Meta, with a vague misgiving
20 Your sweet eyes are turned on me.
  'Where', you whisper, 'is assurance
  Of a spirit softly clear,
  Of calm wishes, mild endurance,
  All the heart enjoins, but only here?'

25 Spare me, Meta. Question rather
  That lone gazer leaning near;
  Touch his robe and say, 'My father,
  Tell me, is it quiet here?
  Say, my father, does the tired
30 Restless heart in this retreat
  Learn to know what it desired,
  Knowing, clasp it and securely beat?'

  At your voice he rises slowly
  From the pillar where he leans,
35 In your gentle melancholy
  All your spirit's history gleans;
  Scans those parted lips, that purely
  Pleading gaze, that forehead clear,
  Signs the cross and answers, 'Surely
40 You say true, my daughter, peace is here.'

¶ 142. *15. Cool*] Over 'Calm' uncancelled.
16. charmed] Over 'cool' uncancelled.

143 The Pillars of the Universe

Date of composition unknown, but (?) 1849–52: 'apparently intended for a portion of one of the songs of Callicles in "Empedocles on Etna"' (*Commentary* 337). Punctuation corrected.
Published *Commentary* (1940).

  And that golden-fruited strand
  Near where Atlas hath his stand,
  Bearing on his shoulders broad

¶ 143. *1. golden-fruited strand*] A reference to Hera's golden apples. The Garden of the Hesperides was traditionally located on or near 'Mt. Atlas'.
2. Atlas] See *n.* to 'Heine's Grave' 94 (p. 473 above).

Earth, and heaven's star-spangled load,
5   In the farthest western wild;
There or eastward where up-piled
To maintain the Caspian free
From the fiercer Euxine sea,
In his wintry light austere
10   Great Elbruis whitens clear,
Prisoning in his rifted stones
The too-daring Titan's bones.

6. *There or*] Over 'Or far' uncancelled.
8. *fiercer*] Yale MS. has 'tyrannous', then 'fiercer' over 'encroaching'
uncancelled.
9. *wintry*] Yale MS. has 'snowy', then 'wintry' over 'roseate' cancelled.
10–12. One arm of the Elburz mountains runs parallel to the western shore
of the Caspian to join the Caucasus (where Prometheus was condemned
by Zeus to hang).
11. *rifted*] Over 'crevic'd' uncancelled.

144 Fragments

From various sources and usually of uncertain date. Fragments i–ii, v–viii,
xi are from Yale MS. (all probably 1843–8); iii, x are from *CL* (58, 85), ix
is from *L* (i 8) – all roughly dated by the letters in which they occur; iv
is from A.'s unpublished 1846 diary; xii is written out – see *Commentary*
347 – at the end of vol. i of A.'s copy of Herder's *Ideen zur Philosophie der
Geschichte der Menschheit* (Leipzig, 1828), which is on his reading-list for
1866 (*Note-books* 579).

(i)

The dropping patter of a child's small feet
Did fall like rain in the forsaken street.

(? 1844)

(ii)

To kindle with a storm of feignéd groans,
Or the quick marching motion of a rhyme,
The sickly dotage of a dying world,
Plying the lusty bellows of my wit
5   To keep its smouldering embers half alive.

(? 1844)

¶ 144. ii *1. storm of feignéd groans*] Over 'monstrous howl' cancelled.
ii *2. marching motion of a*] Over 'music of a jingling' cancelled.

(iii)

Ye too, who stand beside the hoary throne
Where Time, else dumb, hath signified his sway
To the blind slaves of power to make it known
Material grandeurs do in heaven decay,
5   Keep all, O keep, continual holiday!
And let . . .

(? 1844–5)

(iv)

They had not suffered, yet they said 'We love',
Said 'We are happy', yet could show no tears,
Were hopeful, having never yet despaired,
Had broke no vows, yet here they plighted one.

(1846)

(v)

Snow-vested knolls that mutely slope
Into the glassy frozen tarns . . .

(? 1847–8)

(vi)

That warm, south-scented and benignant breath
That bathes man's spirit like moonlight.

(? 1847–8)

(vii)

. . . some white soft-tissued cloud
Floating under the shrouded morn through heaven.

(? 1847–8)

(viii)

I believe
That in the solitudes beyond the stars
Where broods the uncompanioned life of God . . .

(? 1847–8)

v 1. *mutely*] Over 'whitely' uncancelled.
v 2. *Into*] Over 'Down to' uncancelled.
vi 2. *man's*] Over 'our' uncancelled.
vii 2. The reading 'shrouded' is doubtful.

(ix)

The clouds of sickness cast no stain upon
        Her valleys and blue hills:
The Doubt that assails all things never won
This faithful impulse of unfaithful wills.

                              (By May 1848)

(x)

. . . this little which we are
Swims on an obscure much we might have been.
                              (By July 1848)

(xi)

        . . . but while we plan,
Like all his fellows, with a bloody spur,
The breathless moment has shot by, wherein
We should be what we would be.

                              (? 1848)

(xii)

The everlasting substance of the hills
Hath frayed and slidden down, and we no more
Touch the same surface which our fathers trod.

    But she with prodigality brings forth
5   On every bank the virgin saxifrage,
    Waving her myriads of white fairy blooms,
    This morn, as ever . . .

                              (? 1866)

ix 3. *The Doubt that assails all things*] Probably suggested by Sainte-Beuve,
who speaks of Senancour's earlier atheism giving place to 'un doute
universel non moins accablant' in *Obermann* – see *Portraits Contemporains* i
(1868 revised ed.) 164. A. possessed the 1847 ed. of Sainte-Beuve's book.
xii 2. *we*] Over 'they' uncancelled.
xii 3. 'Touch' over 'have' cancelled and 'trod' over 'felt' and 'touched'
cancelled.

145 Fragments from 'Lucretius'

For a careful account of the whole history of 'Lucretius' see *Commentary*
340-5. Between 1845 and 1849 A. planned a tragedy on Lucretius, but in

1849 temporarily stopped work on the poem and used some of its materials for 'Empedocles on Etna' (see headn., p. 147 above). In 1855 he resumed reading for his tragedy (*Note-books* 557–8); on 29 Dec. 1855 he wrote to Wyndham Slade, 'I am full of a tragedy of the time of the end of the Roman Republic . . . It won't see the light, however, before 1857' (*L i* 49); and in March 1856 he was 'at Lucretius' (*Note-books* 559). The project was then dropped a second time (now to write *Merope*), and although A. again resumed reading for 'Lucretius' in 1858 (*Note-books* 564), it seems unlikely that he made any further progress with its composition. On 13 Jan. 1886, within a few months of retirement, he wrote to Goldwin Smith, 'One or two things in verse which all my life I have wished to do I am now probably too old to do well . . . One of them is a Roman play, with Clodius, Milo, Lucretius, Cicero, Caesar in it . . .' (*Goldwin Smith's Correspondence* ed. A. Haultain (1913) 182). For A.'s conception of Lucretius and his age see 'On the Modern Element in Literature' (1857), *Complete Prose Works* ed. R. H. Super i (1960) 31–4.

Fragment i below is from the Yale MS. and from its position may be dated 1849; fragments ii–viii probably belong to A.'s work on 'Lucretius' 1855–6; fragment ix may belong to the same period – for its use as a motto to 'Thyrsis' see *n.* on this matter (p. 497 above). The MS. of fragments ii–viii was formerly in the possession of A.'s grand-daughter, the late Mrs. Norman Thwaites, but its present location is unknown. The text in these instances is based on photostats of the MS. made before 1940. Fragments i and viii are printed for the first time.

(i)

For while we are, Lucretius, death is not,
And when death is, why, we have ceased to be –
So death can touch us never.

(ii)

Thou mirror that hast danced through such a world,
So manifold, so fresh, so brave a world,
That hast so much reflected, but, alas,
Retained so little in thy careless depths.

¶ 145. ii *1–4*. Cp. 'Empedocles on Etna' I ii 82–6 (p. 159 above),

> *Hither and thither spins*
> *The wind-borne, mirroring soul,*
> *A thousand glimpses wins,*
> *And never sees a whole;*
> *Looks once, and drives elsewhere, and leaves its last employ.*

20—M.A.

(iii)

It is a sad sight when the world denies
A gifted man the power to show his gift;
When he is tied and thwarted from his course;
When his fine genius foams itself away
5   Upon the reefs and sandbanks of the world,
And he dies fruitless, having found no field.
There is a sight more saddening yet, when all
Has been performed which can be, when the man
Has reached the limit of his utmost growth
10   Unthwarted, undiverted; when he stands,
Having been furthered to his very wish,
And stands – a failure: then, then happens, Oppius,
The true heart-breaking – baffled hope, and shame,
Sharp sense of deep self-ignorance, fear of looks
15   Of pitying friends, derisive enemies.
These, these are pangs which make the mind a hell,
And rend his heart who sees them.

(iv)

To me it seems as vain, Lucretius,
For any man to fret against his weakness
Of mental nature as for him to fret
Against a sickness or deformity.
5   Neither his mind nor body did he make,
Neither his mind nor body can he change.
Feeble he rests, if feeble he was born.
And wherefore then, if we can never change,
Are we dissatisfied with what we are?
10   The discontent itself is argument
That we were destined to a happier state.

iii *1–17.* Cp. A.'s prose argument for this passage: 'It is a sad thing to see a man who has been frittered away piecemeal by petty distractions, and who has never done his best. But it is still sadder to see a man who has done his best, who has reached his utmost limits – and finds his work a failure, and himself far less than he had imagined himself.'

iii *12. Oppius*] Presumably Gaius Oppius, Caesar's friend.

iv *7.* This reading over 'Both he must keep, torment him how as they may' uncancelled.

iv *8. if he can never change*] Over 'having no claim to more' uncancelled.

iv *9. are*] Replacing 'have' cancelled.

(v)

Ours is the reflex image of the world,
His is the prior pattern; he designed,
We but behold. He is the architect
In whose prophetic spirit lay the plan
Before a stone was lifted; and we, Memmius,
Are but the casual passers-by who come
In front of some great fane whereof we know
Nothing but that we see it. What respect
Of likeness or comparison can be
Betwixt such unlike powers?

5

10

(vi)

What are we all
But travellers in a hurry to arrive,
To whom their destination when 'tis reached
Soon seems as tedious as each tedious stage
They posted through to reach it?

5

(vii)

Many's the good
We prize not when 'tis present, but, when lost,
Desire it bitterly –

(viii)

The Spirit of Man
Moving over the face of the wide world,
Free, disengaged, beholding from a height,
Not hoodwinked in a dungeon – in one word
Active and glad, not suffering and cast-down,
Fills us below with joy to see its power.

5

v 2. *His is*] Over 'But His' uncancelled.
v 3. *behold*] Over 'survey' uncancelled.
v 4. The first version with 'capacious' for 'prophetic' and 'his' for 'the'
is uncancelled. The revised reading echoes Shakespeare's *Sonnets* cvii 1–2,

> . . . the prophetic soul
> *Of the wide world, dreaming on things to come* . . .

v 5. *Memmius*] Gaius Memmius, to whom Lucretius dedicated his *De
Rerum Natura*.
viii 1–2. An unconscious conflation of *Genesis* i 2, 'And the Spirit of God
moved upon the face of the waters' and Shakespeare's lines quoted in *n*. to
v 4 above. The MS. fragment begins with the cancelled word 'Sometimes'.
viii 3. *hoodwinked . . . – in one word*] Over 'new-bound . . . – finally'
(only the last word cancelled).

Which when we see, our spirits are released
Through new-awakéd consciousness of power
To float awhile, we too, through lucid air;
10   We too behold and act, not grope and feel,
We too lay hold on all things with our mind,
Not with our body; pain, therefore, and fear,
Which are the body's part, have passed away.

(ix)

Thus yesterday, to-day, to-morrow come,
They hustle one another and they pass;
But all our hustling morrows only make
The smooth to-day of God.

viii *8. Through*] Though *MS*. Earlier attempts at this line were 'Though
[*for* Through] consciousness of fellowship in power' uncancelled and 'As
conscious that what one is, all may be' cancelled.
viii *9. lucid air*] Replacing 'earth's thin air', which is over 'the clear
realms', both phrases uncancelled.
viii *11. lay*] Replacing 'take' cancelled.

Appendix A

THE CRITICAL PREFACES OF 1853 AND 1854

The *1853* Preface was written between 25 Aug. and 1 Oct. 1853; A. had decided to write a preface in May 1853 (*L* i 30), but it was not begun by 25 Aug. when he told Clough that in spite of J. A. Froude's disapproval 'I shall try my hand at it, at any rate, I think' (*CL* 141); A. dated the preface 'Fox How, Ambleside, October 1, 1853'. It appeared in *1853* and was reprinted in *1854*, *1857* along with the short *1854* Preface, which is dated 'London, June 1, 1854'. The prefaces were printed again in A.'s lifetime only in *Irish Essays* (1882), with the comment 'Some of the readers of my poetry have expressed a wish for their reappearance, and with that wish I here comply. Exactly as they stand, I should not have written them now; but perhaps they are none the worse on that account' (*Works* xi [5]).

Before publication A. was dissatisfied with the *1853* Preface for being 'far less *precise* than I had intended' (letter to Clough 10 Oct. 1853, *CL* 144), and the *1854* Preface is in part an acknowledgement that the earlier preface contained 'many things incompletely stated, many things which need qualification' (the chief of these being the failure to make it clear that the remarks on the choice of subjects in poetry applied to epic and dramatic poetry and not necessarily to lyric poetry). To his brother Tom in Tasmania A. wrote in an unpublished letter 28 March 1855, 'For the preface I doubt if you will care, not having much before your eyes the sins and offences at which it is directed: the fact being that we have numbers of young gentlemen with really wonderful powers of perception and expression, but to whom there is wholly wanting a "bedeutendes Individuum", so that their productions are most unedifying and unsatisfactory.' (Alexander Smith, whose poems Clough was kinder to than he was to A.'s in *North American Review* lxxvii (July 1853) 1–30, was certainly one of these 'young gentlemen', but A. was also thinking more generally of the 'Spasmodic' element in the accepted poetry of the day and of Keats's influence on poetic style.)

The contemporary reviewers of the *1853* Preface sharply separated what A. said about the importance of *Architectonicè* and 'the subordinate character of expression' (which on the whole they approved) from what he said on the choice of poetic subjects (which on the whole they disapproved); they were nearly unanimous on the excellence of A.'s prose style. G. Saintsbury at the end of the nineteenth century doubted 'whether he [A.] ever wrote better, either in sense or style' (*History of Criticism* 7th impression (1949) iii 516), but recent critics, while recognizing the historical importance of the preface, tend to regard it more warily as an expression of A.'s quarrel with himself about 'subjectivity' in poetry – see, for example, F. Kermode, *Romantic Image* (1957) 12–13, 'It was written by Arnold's spectre. Or perhaps we should say that the rejection [of 'Empedocles on Etna'] was the work of Arnold the Critic, who rightly distrusted poems which were victories to Arnold the poet, but messages of despair to one who saw the need to get poetry usefully working, leavening the lump.' The rejection of subjectivity was not simply, as Kermode suggests, the result of A.'s 'missionary' intentions as a critic of literature and society: it was also an active avoidance of the pains of poetic creation. The preface in fact represents a turning away from poetry that 'demands not merely an effort and a labour, but an actual tearing of oneself to pieces' in the attempt to 'approach perfection in the region of thought and feeling' and towards a kind of poetry in which 'form is everything' – see A.'s letter 6 Aug. 1858 (already quoted in part in headn. to *Merope*, p. 399 above), which contains these phrases and in which he adds, '. . . it is not so light a matter, when you have other grave claims on your powers, to submit voluntarily to the exhaustion of the best poetical production in a time like this . . . It is only in the best poetical epochs . . . that you can descend into yourself and produce the best of your thought and feeling naturally, and without an overwhelming and in some degree morbid effort' (*L* i 62–3). Goethe and Aristotle are the most important critical influences on the preface.

There is a valuable annotated edition of the *1853* and *1854* Prefaces by R. H. Super, *Complete Prose Works* i (1960) 1–17 and nn. 217–25. The fullest discussion of the background of the Prefaces is to be found in an excellent essay which appeared after this headn. was written – S. M. B. Coulling's 'Matthew Arnold's 1853 Preface: its origin and aftermath', *Vict. Stud.* vii (1964) 233–63. Two earlier essays still worth consulting are by H. W. Garrod (*RES* xvii (1941) 310–21) and J. D. Jump (*RES* xxv (1949) 61–4). Except as noted the text below follows *Irish Essays* (1882).

Preface to the First Edition of *Poems*
(1853)

In two small volumes of Poems, published anonymously, one in 1849 the other in 1852, many of the Poems which compose the present volume have already appeared. The rest are now published for the first time.

5   I have, in the present collection, omitted the poem from which the volume published in 1852 took its title. I have done so, not because

5–6. 'Empedocles on Etna'.

the subject of it was a Sicilian Greek born between two and three
thousand years ago, although many persons would think this a sufficient reason. Neither have I done so because I had, in my own opinion,
10 failed in the delineation which I intended to effect. I intended to
delineate the feelings of one of the last of the Greek religious philosophers, one of the family of Orpheus and Musaeus, having survived
his fellows, living on into a time when the habits of Greek thought and
feeling had begun fast to change, character to dwindle, the influence
15 of the Sophists to prevail. Into the feelings of a man so situated there
entered much that we are accustomed to consider as exclusively
modern; how much, the fragments of Empedocles himself which remain to us are sufficient at least to indicate. What those who are
familiar only with the great monuments of early Greek genius suppose
20 to be its exclusive characteristics, have disappeared; the calm, the
cheerfulness, the disinterested objectivity have disappeared: the dialogue of the mind with itself has commenced; modern problems have
presented themselves; we hear already the doubts, we witness the
discouragement, of Hamlet and of Faust.

25 The representation of such a man's feelings must be interesting, if
consistently drawn. We all naturally take pleasure, says Aristotle, in
any imitation or representation whatever: this is the basis of our love
of poetry; and we take pleasure in them, he adds, because all knowledge is naturally agreeable to us; not to the philosopher only, but to
30 mankind at large. Every representation therefore which is consistently
drawn may be supposed to be interesting, inasmuch as it gratifies this
natural interest in knowledge of all kinds. What is *not* interesting, is
that which does not add to our knowledge of any kind; that which
is vaguely conceived and loosely drawn; a representation which is
35 general, indeterminate, and faint, instead of being particular, precise,
and firm.

Any accurate representation may therefore be expected to be interesting; but, if the representation be a poetical one, more than this is
demanded. It is demanded, not only that it shall interest, but also
40 that it shall inspirit and rejoice the reader; that it shall convey a
charm, and infuse delight. For the Muses, as Hesiod says, were born
that they might be a 'forgetfulness of evils, and a truce from cares':

26–30. Cp. *Poetics* IV 2–4, 'The instinct of imitation is implanted in man
from childhood . . . through imitation he learns his earliest lessons; and no
less universal is the pleasure felt in things imitated . . . The cause of this
again is, that to learn gives the liveliest pleasure, not only to philosophers
but to men in general . . .' (tr. S. H. Butcher, *Aristotle's Theory of Poetry and
Fine Art* (3rd ed. 1902) 15).

41–2. See *Theogony* 53–5, 'Them in Pieria did Mnemosyne . . . bear of
union with the father, the son of Cronos, a forgetting of ills and a rest
from sorrow.'

and it is not enough that the Poet should add to the knowledge of
men, it is required of him also that he should add to their happiness.
45 'All art,' says Schiller, 'is dedicated to Joy, and there is no higher
and no more serious problem, than how to make men happy. The
right art is that alone, which creates the highest enjoyment.'

A poetical work, therefore, is not yet justified when it has been
shown to be an accurate, and therefore interesting representation; it
50 has to be shown also that it is a representation from which men can
derive enjoyment. In presence of the most tragic circumstances, represented in a work of art, the feeling of enjoyment, as is well known,
may still subsist; the representation of the most utter calamity, of the
liveliest anguish, is not sufficient to destroy it; the more tragic the
55 situation, the deeper becomes the enjoyment; and the situation is
more tragic in proportions as it becomes more terrible.

What then are the situations, from the representation of which,
though accurate, no poetical enjoyment can be derived? They are
those in which the suffering finds no vent in action; in which a
60 continuous state of mental distress is prolonged, unrelieved by incident, hope, or resistance; in which there is everything to be endured,
nothing to be done. In such situations there is inevitably something
morbid, in the description of them something monotonous. When
they occur in actual life, they are painful, not tragic; the representa-
65 tion of them in poetry is painful also.

To this class of situations, poetically faulty as it appears to me, that
of Empedocles, as I have endeavoured to represent him, belongs; and
I have therefore excluded the poem from the present collection.

And why, it may be asked, have I entered into this explanation
70 respecting a matter so unimportant as the admission or exclusion of
the poem in question? I have done so, because I was anxious to avow
that the sole reason for its exclusion was that which has been stated
above; and that it has not been excluded in deference to the opinion
which many critics of the present day appear to entertain against
75 subjects chosen from distant times and countries: against the choice,
in short, of any subjects but modern ones.

'The poet,' it is said, and by an intelligent critic, 'the poet who
would really fix the public attention must leave the exhausted past,

---

45-7. See the prefatory essay 'Über den Gebrauch des Chors in der
Tragödie' to *Die Braut von Messina* (1803), fourth paragraph.
57-62. A.'s own view, unsupported by Aristotle or Goethe. Goethe's
general objection to tragedy was that it unsettled the emotions and therefore hindered real self-development (see 'Nachlese zu Aristoteles Poetik',
Werke (Cotta: Stuttgart and Tubingen) xlvi (1833) 20).
77-80. 'In the *Spectator* of April 2, 1853 [p. 325]. The words quoted were
not used with reference to poems of mine.' A.'s note first added *1854*. The
words occur in a review of Edwin Arnold's *Poems Narrative and Lyrical*.

and draw his subjects from matters of present import, and *therefore*
80 both of interest and novelty.'
  Now this view I believe to be completely false. It is worth examining,
inasmuch as it is a fair sample of a class of critical dicta everywhere
current at the present day, having a philosophical form and air, but
no real basis in fact; and which are calculated to vitiate the judgment
85 of readers of poetry, while they exert, so far as they are adopted, a
misleading influence on the practice of those who make it.
  What are the eternal objects of poetry, among all nations and at all
times? They are actions; human actions; possessing an inherent
interest in themselves, and which are to be communicated in an in-
90 teresting manner by the art of the poet. Vainly will the latter imagine
that he has everything in his own power; that he can make an intrin-
sically inferior action delightful with a more excellent one by his
treatment of it. He may indeed compel us to admire his skill, but his
work will possess, within itself, an incurable defect.
95   The poet, then, has in the first place to select an excellent action;
and what actions are the most excellent? Those, certainly, which
most powerfully appeal to the great primary human affections: to those
elementary feelings which subsist permanently in the race, and which

---

See A.'s letter (undated, but Dec. 1853) to his sister 'K' (*UL* 22) for the
identification of the 'intelligent critic' as R. S. Rintoul, editor of the
Spectator.
77. intelligent] apparently intelligent *1853*.
86. make] write *1853–7*.
87–8. Cp. Aristotle, *Poetics* IX 9, '. . . the poet or "maker" should be the
maker of plots rather than of verses; since he is a poet because he imitates,
and what he imitates are actions' (Butcher ed. *cit.* 37).
90–4. See Goethe's *Dichtung und Wahrheit* (Pt. II) vii, *Werke* ed. *cit.* xxv
(1829) 104, '. . . no one will deny that genius, or cultivated artistic talent,
can by its method of treatment . . . render the most refractory subject
amenable. But . . . the result is rather an artistic feat than a work of art,
which latter should be based on a fitting subject . . .' (tr. M. S. Smith,
Bohn's Popular Library ed. i 249). A. echoes the same passage in the *1854*
Preface.
96–100. A.'s own view, which combines hints from Aristotle and Wordsworth. A. was probably influenced by the former's statements that a perfect tragedy should 'imitate actions which excite pity and fear' and that the
Greeks continually returned to a few significant actions of this kind
(*Poetics* XIII 2, 5: Butcher ed. *cit.* 45, 47; and for the quotation of the second
passage *n.* to ll. 164–7 below), but 'great primary human affections' recalls
Wordsworth's assertions that in his poems he had attempted to trace 'the
primary laws of our nature' and that 'the most valuable object of all
writing' included 'the great and universal passions of men', Preface to
Lyrical Ballads (1800), *Poetical Works* ed. E. de Selincourt ii (1946) 386, 398.
21 + M.A.

are independent of time. These feelings are permanent and the same;
100 that which interests them is permanent and the same also. The
modernness or antiquity of an action, therefore, has nothing to do
with its fitness for poetical representation; this depends upon its inherent qualities. To the elementary part of our nature, to our passions, that which is great and passionate is eternally interesting; and
105 interesting solely in proportion to its greatness and to its passion. A
great human action of a thousand years ago is more interesting to it
than a smaller human action of to-day, even though upon the representation of this last the most consummate skill may have been
expended, and though it has the advantage of appealing by its
110 modern language, familiar manners, and contemporary allusions, to
all our transient feelings and interests. These, however, have no right
to demand of a poetical work that it shall satisfy them; their claims
are to be directed elsewhere. Poetical works belong to the domain of
our permanent passions: let them interest these, and the voice of all
115 subordinate claims upon them is at once silenced.

Achilles, Prometheus, Clytemnestra, Dido – what modern poem
presents personages as interesting, even to us moderns, as these personages of an 'exhausted past'? We have the domestic epic dealing
with the details of modern life which pass daily under our eyes; we
120 have poems representing modern personages in contact with the
problems of modern life, moral, intellectual, and social; these works
have been produced by poets the most distinguished of their nation
and time; yet I fearlessly assert that *Hermann and Dorothea*, *Childe
Harold*, *Jocelyn*, *The Excursion*, leave the reader cold in comparison
125 with the effect produced upon him by the latter books of the *Iliad*, by
the *Oresteia*, or by the episode of Dido. And why is this? Simply because in the three last-named cases the action is greater, the personages nobler, the situations more intense: and this is the true basis of
the interest in a poetical work, and this alone.

130   It may be urged, however, that past actions may be interesting in
themselves, but that they are not to be adopted by the modern poet,
because it is impossible for him to have them clearly present to his
own mind, and he cannot therefore feel them deeply, nor represent
them forcibly. But this is not necessarily the case. The externals of a

---

116. Achilles from the *Iliad*; Prometheus from Aeschylus's *Prometheus
Bound*; Clytemnestra from the *Agamemnon* of Aeschylus; Dido from
Virgil, *Aeneid* iv.
123–4. The titles of modern poetic narratives by Goethe (1797), Byron
(1812–18), Lamartine (1835) and Wordsworth (1814).
134–43. Perhaps connected with Aristotle's remark that 'poetry tends to
express the universal, history the particular' (*Poetics* IX 3: Butcher ed. *cit.*
35), but cp. also Eckermann's *Conversations of Goethe* under 31 Jan. 1827,
'He [Manzoni] has too much respect for history, and ... is always adding

135 past action, indeed, he cannot know with the precision of a contemporary; but his business is with its essentials. The outward man of
Oedipus or of Macbeth, the houses in which they lived, the cere-
monies of their courts, he cannot accurately figure to himself; but
neither do they essentially concern him. His business is with their in-
140 ward man; with their feelings and behaviour in certain tragic situations, which engage their passions as men; these have in them nothing
local and casual; they are as accessible to the modern poet as to a
contemporary.

The date of an action, then, signifies nothing: the action itself, its
145 selection and construction, this is what is all-important. This the
Greeks understood far more clearly than we do. The radical difference between their poetical theory and ours consists, as it appears to
me, in this: that, with them, the poetical character of the action in
itself, and the conduct of it, was the first consideration; with us, atten-
150 tion is fixed mainly on the value of the separate thoughts and images
which occur in the treatment of an action. They regarded the whole;
we regard the parts. With them, the action predominated over the
expression of it; with us, the expression predominates over the action.
Not that they failed in expression, or were inattentive to it; on the
155 contrary, they are the highest models of expression, the unapproached
masters of the *grand style*. But their expression is so excellent because

notes to his pieces, in which he shows how faithful he has been to detail . . .
No poet has ever known the historical characters which he has painted;
if he had, he could scarcely have made use of them. The poet must know
what effects he wishes to produce, and regulate the nature of his characters
accordingly . . . What would be the use of poets, if they only repeated the
record of the historian? . . . Here, again . . . the Greeks were so great, that
they regarded fidelity to historic facts less than the treatment of them by
the poet' (Bohn's Library revised ed. (1883) 213–14).
148–9. Cp. Aristotle, *Poetics* VI 10, '. . . the incidents and the plot are the
end of a tragedy; and the end is the chief thing of all' (Butcher ed. *cit.* 27).
149–51. Cp. A.'s letter to Clough 28 Oct. 1852, 'More and more I feel
. . . that Keats and Shelley were on a false track when they set themselves
to reproduce the exuberance of expression, the charm, the richness of
images, and the felicity, of the Elizabethan poets. Yet critics cannot get to
learn this, because the Elizabethan poets are our greatest, and our canons of
poetry are founded on their works. They still think that the object of
poetry is to produce exquisite bits and images . . .' (*CL* 124).
156. grand style] A.'s first use of this expression, which he adopted from
Goethe – see 'Über die Parodie bei den Alten', *Werke* ed. *cit.* xlvi (1833) 7,
9–10, 'With the Greeks their work is all of one character and all in the
grand style (*im grossen Styl*) . . . The Greek poem [the *Iliad*] is in the grand
style [*im hohen Styl*], self-sufficient, making use only of what is essential, in
description and simile rejecting all decoration, resting upon a basis of

it is so admirably kept in its right degree of prominence; because it is
so simple and so well subordinated; because it draws its force directly
from the pregnancy of the matter which it conveys. For what reason
160 was the Greek tragic poet confined to so limited a range of subjects?
Because there are so few actions which unite in themselves, in the
highest degree, the conditions of excellence: and it was not thought
that on any but an excellent subject could an excellent poem be constructed. A few actions, therefore, eminently adapted for tragedy,
165 maintained almost exclusive possession of the Greek tragic stage. Their
significance appeared inexhaustible; they were as permanent problems, perpetually offered to the genius of every fresh poet. This too is
the reason of what appears to us moderns a certain baldness of expression in Greek tragedy; of the triviality with which we often re-
170 proach the remarks of the chorus, where it takes part in the dialogue:
that the action itself, the situation of Orestes, or Merope, or Alca-
maeon, was to stand the central point of interest, unforgotten,
absorbing, principal; that no accessories were for a moment to distract the spectator's attention from this; that the tone of the parts
175 was to be perpetually kept down, in order not to impair the grandiose
effect of the whole. The terrible old mythic story on which the drama
was founded stood, before he entered the theatre, traced in its bare
outlines upon the spectator's mind; it stood in his memory, as a group
of statuary, faintly seen, at the end of a long and dark vista: then came
180 the poet, embodying outlines, developing situations, not a word
wasted, not a sentiment capriciously thrown in: stroke upon stroke,
the drama proceeded: the light deepened upon the group; more and
more it revealed itself to the riveted gaze of the spectator: until at
last, when the final words were spoken, it stood before him in broad
185 sunlight, a model of immortal beauty.

   This was what a Greek critic demanded; this was what a Greek
poet endeavoured to effect. It signified nothing to what time an
action belonged. We do not find that the *Persae* occupied a particularly high rank among the dramas of Aeschylus, because it represen-
190 ted a matter of contemporary interest: this was not what a cultivated
Athenian required. He required that the permanent elements of his
nature should be moved; and dramas of which the action, though

---

traditional myth.' A. developed the idea of the grand style in *On Translating Homer* (1861) and *On Translating Homer: Last Words* (1862) – see
especially *Works* v 211–12, 287–92.
164–7. Cp. Aristotle, *Poetics* XIII 5, 'At first the poets recounted any
legend that came in their way. Now, the best tragedies are founded on the
story of a few houses, – on the fortunes of Alcmaeon, Oedipus, Orestes,
Meleager, Thyestes, Telephus, and those others who have done or suffered
something terrible' (Butcher ed. *cit.* 47).

taken from a long-distant mythic time, yet was calculated to accomplish this in a higher degree than that of the *Persae*, stood higher in his
195 estimation accordingly. The Greeks felt, no doubt, with their exquisite sagacity of taste, that an action of present times was too near them,
too much mixed up with what was accidental and passing, to form a
sufficiently grand, detached, and self-subsistent object for a tragic
poem. Such objects belonged to the domain of the comic poet, and
200 of the lighter kinds of poetry. For the more serious kinds, for *pragmatic*
poetry, to use an excellent expression of Polybius, they were more
difficult and severe in the range of subjects which they permitted.
Their theory and practice alike, the admirable treatise of Aristotle,
and the unrivalled works of their poets, exclaim with a thousand
205 tongues – 'All depends upon the subject; choose a fitting action,
penetrate yourself with the feeling of its situations; this done, everything else will follow.'

But for all kinds of poetry alike there was one point on which they
were rigidly exacting: the adaptability of the subject to the kind of
210 poetry selected, and the careful construction of the poem.

How different a way of thinking from this is ours! We can hardly
at the present day understand what Menander meant, when he told
a man who inquired as to the progress of his comedy that he had
finished it, not having yet written a single line, because he had con-
215 structed the action of it in his mind. A modern critic would have
assured him that the merit of his piece depended on the brilliant

200–1. Polybius speaks of 'pragmatic history' (πραγματικὴ ἱστορία),
i.e. history that aims to instruct and persuade by the example of real events,
but A. takes 'pragmatic poetry' from the heading 'Dilettantismus in der
pragmatischen Poesie' in Goethe's 'Über den sogennanten Dilettantismus
...' (1799), *Werke* ed. *cit.* xliv (1832) 279. A.'s translation of parts of this
work by Goethe is in an unpublished 1847 note-book now in the possession
of Mr. A. Whitridge.
205. Cp. Goethe, *Dichtung und Wahrheit* (Pt. II) vii, *Werke* ed *cit.* xxv
(1829) 104, 'For the significance of the subject treated is the Alpha and
Omega of art (*der innere Gehalt des bearbeiteten Gegenstandes ist der Anfang
und das Ende der Kunst*)' (tr. M. S. Smith, Bohn's Popular Library ed. i
249).
211–15. See Plutarch's *Moralia* 347 E–F, 'The story is told that one of
Menander's intimate friends said to him, "The Dionysian Festival is almost
here, Menander; haven't you composed your comedy?" Menander
answered, "By heaven, I have really composed the comedy: the plot's all
in order. But I still have to fit the lines to it." For even poets consider the
subject matter more necessary and vital than the words' (tr. F. C. Babbitt,
Loeb ed. iv 507).

things which arose under his pen as he went along. We have poems
which seem to exist merely for the sake of single lines and passages;
not for the sake of producing any total impression. We have critics
220 who seem to direct their attention merely to detached expressions, to
the language about the action, not to the action itself. I verily think
that the majority of them do not in their hearts believe that there is
such a thing as a total impression to be derived from a poem at all, or
to be demanded from a poet; they think the term a commonplace of
225 metaphysical criticism. They will permit the poet to select any action
he pleases, and to suffer that action to go as it will, provided he gratifies them with occasional bursts of fine writing, and with a shower of
isolated thoughts and images. That is, they permit him to leave their
poetical sense ungratified, provided that he gratifies their rhetorical
230 sense and their curiosity. Of his neglecting to gratify these, there is
little danger. He needs rather to be warned against the danger of
attempting to gratify these alone; he needs rather to be perpetually
reminded to prefer his action to everything else; so to treat this, as to
permit its inherent excellences to develop themselves, without inter-
235 ruption from the intrusion of his personal peculiarities; most fortunate, when he most entirely succeeds in effacing himself, and in
enabling a noble action to subsist as it did in nature.

But the modern critic not only permits a false practice; he absolutely prescribes false aims. 'A true allegory of the state of one's own

217–21. A. is thinking especially of the critic's praise of Alexander Smith's
A Life Drama (1853) in an unsigned article in *North British Review* xix
(Aug. 1853). He is less than fair to the writer of the article, who qualifies
his praise of the 'fine writing' of *A Life Drama* by saying that 'the great
fault of the poem is that it is composed of separate pieces, and does not
seem to be in itself, as a whole, a complete and coherent act of the imagination' (*loc. cit.* 338). A. identified the unknown critic as J. M. Ludlow –
see his letter to his sister 'K' 31 Oct. 1853, 'Ludlow . . . I believe is the author
of a precious piece of cant in the N. British which I have attacked in the
preface' (*UL* 20). This identification has been challenged by R. H. Super,
who points out that much of the article (not, however, the paragraphs on
Alexander Smith) was twice reprinted by David Masson in *Essays Bio-
graphical and Critical* (1856) and *Wordsworth, Shelley, Keats, and Other
Essays* (1874) – see S. M. B. Coulling, 'Matthew Arnold's 1853 Preface',
Vict. Stud. vii (1964) 236 *fn.*
239–41. See 'Theories of Poetry and a New Poet', *North British Review*
xix (Aug. 1853) 338. A. was peculiarly irritated, as the subsequent reference
to *Faust* shows, by the critic's assumption that he is expressing a Goethean
view of poetry illustrated at their different levels by both *Faust* and
Smith's *A Life Drama*. Against the writer of the article, who described
Goethe's view of lyric poetry fairly enough as 'the moods of its practi-
tioners objectivized as they rise' (*loc. cit.* 318), A. could set Eckermann's

240 mind in a representative history,' the poet is told, 'is perhaps the highest thing that one can attempt in the way of poetry.' And accordingly he attempts it. An allegory of the state of one's own mind, the highest problem of an art which imitates actions! No assuredly, it is not, it never can be so: no great poetical work has ever been pro-
245 duced with such an aim. *Faust* itself, in which something of the kind is attempted, wonderful passages as it contains, and in spite of the un-surpassed beauty of the scenes which relate to Margaret, *Faust* itself, judged as a whole, and judged strictly as a poetical work, is defective: its illustrious author, the greatest poet of modern times, the greatest
250 critic of all times, would have been the first to acknowledge it; he only defended his work, indeed, by asserting it to be 'something incommensurable'.

The confusion of the present times is great, the multitude of voices counselling different things bewildering, the number of existing works
255 capable of attracting a young writer's attention and of becoming his models, immense. What he wants is a hand to guide him through the confusion, a voice to prescribe to him the aim which he should keep in view, and to explain to him that the value of the literary works which offer themselves to his attention is relative to their power of helping
260 him forward on his road towards this aim. Such a guide the English writer at the present day will nowhere find. Failing this, all that can be looked for, all indeed that can be desired, is, that his attention should be fixed on excellent models; that he may reproduce, at any rate, something of their excellence, by penetrating himself with their works
265 and by catching their spirit, if he cannot be taught to produce what is excellent independently.

Foremost among these models for the English writer stands Shakespeare: a name the greatest perhaps of all poetical names; a name never to be mentioned without reverence. I will venture, how-

---

Conversations of Goethe under 24 Nov. 1824, 'The majority of our young poets ... have no fault but this, that their subjectivity is not important, and that they cannot find matter in the objective. At best, they only find a material ... which corresponds to their own subjectivity; but as for taking the material on its own account, when it is repugnant to their sub-jectivity, merely because it is poetical, such a thing is never thought of' (Bohn's Library revised ed. (1883) 97–8).

251–2. See Eckermann's *Conversations of Goethe* under 3 Jan. 1830, 'Faust ... is, however, quite incommensurable (*doch ganz etwas Inkommensura-beles*), and all attempts to bring it nearer to the understanding are in vain' (Bohn's Library revised ed. (1883) 422).

269–84. Cp. Eckermann's *Conversations of Goethe* under 25 Dec. 1825, 'He [Shakespeare] is even too rich and powerful. A productive nature ought not to read more than one of his dramas in a year if it would not be

270 ever, to express a doubt, whether the influence of his works, excellent
and fruitful for the readers of poetry, for the great majority, has been
of unmixed advantage to the writers of it. Shakespeare indeed chose
excellent subjects; the world could afford no better than Macbeth, or
Romeo and Juliet, or Othello: he had no theory respecting the neces-
275 sity of choosing subjects of present import, or the paramount interest
attaching to allegories of the state of one's own mind; like all great
poets, he knew well what constituted a poetical action; like them,
wherever he found such an action, he took it; like them, too, he found
his best in past times. But to these general characteristics of all great
280 poets he added a special one of his own; a gift, namely, of happy,
abundant, and ingenious expression, eminent and unrivalled: so
eminent as irresistibly to strike the attention first in him, and even to
throw into comparative shade his other excellences as a poet. Here
has been the mischief. These other excellences were his fundamental
285 excellences *as a poet*; what distinguishes the artist from the mere
amateur, says Goethe, is *Architectonicè* in the highest sense; that power
of execution, which creates, forms, and constitutes: not the profoundness of single thoughts, not the richness of imagery, not the abundance
of illustration. But these attractive accessories of a poetical work
290 being more easily seized than the spirit of the whole, and these
accessories being possessed by Shakespeare in an unequalled degree,
a young writer having recourse to Shakespeare as his model runs
great risk of being vanquished and absorbed by them, and, in conse-
quence, of reproducing, according to the measure of his power, these,
295 and these alone. Of this preponderating quality of Shakespeare's
genius, accordingly, almost the whole of modern English poetry has,

---

wrecked entirely . . . How many excellent Germans have been ruined by
him and Calderon. Shakespeare gives us golden apples in silver dishes'
(Bohn's Library revised ed. (1883) 163–4).
285–7. See Goethe's 'Über den sogennanten Dilettantismus . . .', *Werke*
ed. *cit.* xliv (1832) 271–2, 'What the dilettante wants at bottom is "Architectonicè" (*Architektonik*) in the highest sense, that power of execution,
which creates, forms, constitutes. Of this he has only a kind of foreboding,
but is in fact, as to this, always at the mercy of his materials, instead of
commanding them' (A.'s own translation from his unpublished 1847 note-
book – see *n.* to ll. *200–1* above).
289–95. See *n.* to ll. *269–84* above and cp. also A.'s letter to Clough (undated,
but after Sept. 1848), 'They [young Romantic poets of the Keatsian kind]
will not . . . understand that they must begin with an Idea of the world in
order not to be prevailed over by the world's multitudinousness . . . But
what perplexity Keats Tennyson et id genus omne must occasion to young
writers of the ὁπλίτης sort: yes and those d——d Elizabethan poets generally. Those who cannot read G[ree]k sh[ou]ld read nothing but Milton and
parts of Wordsworth' (*CL* 97).

it appears to me, felt the influence. To the exclusive attention on the part of his imitators to this it is in a great degree owing, that of the majority of modern poetical works the details alone are valuable, the
300 composition worthless. In reading them one is perpetually reminded of that terrible sentence on a modern French poet: – *il dit tout ce qu'il veut, mais malheureusement il n'a rien à dire.*

Let me give an instance of what I mean. I will take it from the works of the very chief among those who seem to have been formed
305 in the school of Shakespeare: of one whose exquisite genius and pathetic death render him for ever interesting. I will take the poem of *Isabella, or the Pot of Basil,* by Keats. I choose this rather than the *Endymion,* because the latter work (which a modern critic has classed with the *Fairy Queen!*), although undoubtedly there blows
310 through it the breath of genius, is yet as a whole so utterly incoherent, as not strictly to merit the name of a poem at all. The poem of *Isabella,* then, is a perfect treasure-house of graceful and felicitous words and images; almost in every stanza there occurs one of those vivid and picturesque turns of expression, by which the object is made to flash
315 upon the eye of the mind, and which thrill the reader with a sudden delight. This one short poem contains, perhaps, a greater number of happy single expressions which one could quote than all the extant tragedies of Sophocles. But the action, the story? The action in itself is an excellent one; but so feebly is it conceived by the poet, so loosely
320 constructed, that the effect produced by it, in and for itself, is absolutely null. Let the reader, after he has finished the poem of Keats, turn to the same story in the *Decameron:* he will then feel how pregnant and interesting the same action has become in the hands of a great artist, who above all things delineates his object; who subordi-
325 nates expression to that which it is designed to express.

I have said that the imitators of Shakespeare, fixing their attention

---

301-2. I have not traced this quotation, but the 'modern French poet' has been identified as Théophile Gautier by Sir Humphrey Milford in a note to the old Oxford Standard Authors *The Poems of Matthew Arnold, 1840–1867* (1909). A. probably met the 'terrible sentence' in a review of *Emaux et Camées* (1852).

304-5. Cp. A.'s essay on Keats (1880), *E in C II* (1888), *Works* iv 86, 'Nevertheless, let and hindered as he was, and with a short term and imperfect experience . . . Keats accomplished so much in poetry, that in one of the two great modes by which poetry interprets, in the faculty of naturalistic interpretation, in what we call natural magic, he ranks with Shakespeare.'

308-9. See 'Theories of Poetry and a New Poet', *North British Review* xix (Aug. 1853) 332, '. . . leisurely compositions of the sweet sensuous order such as Keats' *Endymion* and Spenser's *Faery Queene.*'

322. See Boccaccio's *Decameron,* the fifth novel of the fourth day.

21*

on his wonderful gift of expression, have directed their imitation to
this, neglecting his other excellences. These excellences, the fundamental excellences of poetical art, Shakespeare no doubt possessed
330 them – possessed many of them in a splendid degree; but it may perhaps be doubted whether even he himself did not sometimes give
scope to his faculty of expression to the prejudice of a higher poetical
duty. For we must never forget that Shakespeare is the great poet he is
from his skill in discerning and firmly conceiving an excellent action,
335 from his power of intensely feeling a situation, of intimately associating
himself with a character; not from his gift of expression, which rather
even leads him astray, degenerating sometimes into a fondness for
curiosity of expression, into an irritability of fancy, which seems to
make it impossible for him to say a thing plainly, even when the press
340 of the action demands the very directest language, or its level character the very simplest. Mr. Hallam, than whom it is impossible to find
a saner and more judicious critic, has had the courage (for at the
present day it needs courage) to remark, how extremely and faultily
difficult Shakespeare's language often is. It is so: you may find main
345 scenes in some of his greatest tragedies, *King Lear* for instance, where
the language is so artificial, so curiously tortured, and so difficult, that
every speech has to be read two or three times before its meaning can
be comprehended. This over-curiousness of expression is indeed but
the excessive employment of a wonderful gift – of the power of saying
350 a thing in a happier way than any other man; nevertheless, it is
carried so far that one understands what M. Guizot meant, when he

336–9. Cp. *On Translating Homer* (1861), *Works* v 223, 'Not a tragedy of
Shakespeare but contains passages in the worst of all styles, the affected
style . . .'
341–4. See Henry Hallam's *Introduction to the Literature of Europe in the
Fifteenth, Sixteenth, and Seventeenth Centuries* (1876 ed.) iii. 315–16, 'Besides
the blemishes in his plots . . . there are too many in his style. His conceits
and quibbles often spoil the effect of his scenes . . . Few will defend these
notorious faults. But is there not one, less frequently mentioned, yet of
more continual recurrence; the extreme obscurity of Shakespeare's diction? His style is full of new words and new senses . . . it is impossible to
deny that innumerable lines in Shakespeare were not more intelligible in
his time than they are at present.' Hallam's book was first published
1837–9.
351–3. A distortion of Guizot's words – see his *Shakspeare et son temps* (Paris,
1852) 114, 'De toutes les suppositions hasardées pour l'expliquer [the style
of Shakespeare's sonnets], une seule . . . a quelque vraisemblance. Dans un
temps où l'esprit, comme tourmenté de son inexpérience et de sa jeunesse,
essayait de toutes les formes, excepté de la simplicité . . . il se peut que . . .
le poète ait pris quelquefois, dans ces compositions légères, un rôle et un
langage de convention.' A copy of Guizot's book was in A.'s library.

said that Shakespeare appears in his language to have tried all styles
except that of simplicity. He has not the severe and scrupulous self-
restraint of the ancients, partly no doubt, because he had a far less
355 cultivated and exacting audience. He has indeed a far wider range
than they had, a far richer fertility of thought; in this respect he rises
above them. In his strong conception of his subject, in the genuine
way in which he is penetrated with it, he resembles them, and is unlike the moderns. But in the accurate limitation of it, the conscientious
360 rejection of superfluities, the simple and rigorous development of it
from the first line of his work to the last, he falls below them, and
comes nearer to the moderns. In his chief works, besides what he has
of his own, he has the elementary soundness of the ancients; he has
their important action and their large and broad manner; but he
365 has not their purity of method. He is therefore a less safe model; for
what he has of his own is personal, and inseparable from his own rich
nature; it may be imitated and exaggerated, it cannot be learned or
applied as an art. He is above all suggestive; more valuable, therefore,
to young writers as men than as artists. But clearness of arrangement,
370 rigour of development, simplicity of style – these may to a certain extent be learned; and these may, I am convinced, be learned best from
the ancients, who although infinitely less suggestive than Shakespeare,
are thus, to the artist, more instructive.

What, then, it will be asked, are the ancients to be our sole models?
375 the ancients with their comparatively narrow range of experience,
and their widely different circumstances? Not, certainly, that which
is narrow in the ancients, nor that in which we can no longer sympa-
thize. An action like the action of the *Antigone* of Sophocles, which
turns upon the conflict between the heroine's duty to her brother's
380 corpse and that to the laws of her country, is no longer one in which
it is possible that we should feel a deep interest. I am speaking too, it
will be remembered, not of the best sources of intellectual stimulus
for the general reader, but of the best models of instruction for the
individual writer. This last may certainly learn of the ancients, better
385 than anywhere else, three things which it is vitally important for him
to know: – the all-importance of the choice of a subject; the necessity
of accurate construction; and the subordinate character of expression. He will learn from them how unspeakably superior is the effect
of the one moral impression left by a great action treated as a whole,
390 to the effect produced by the most striking single thought or by the
happiest image. As he penetrates into the spirit of the great classical
works, as he becomes gradually aware of their intense significance,
their noble simplicity, and their calm pathos, he will be convinced that

391–6. The praise of the simplicity and calm of Greek art is Goethean.
See, for example, 'Antik und Modern' (1818), *Werke* ed. *cit.* xxxix 80–1,
'Clarity of vision, serenity of apprehension, ease of communication –

it is this effect, unity and profoundness of moral impression, at which
395 the ancient poets aimed; that it is this which constitutes the grandeur
of their works, and which makes them immortal. He will desire to
direct his own efforts towards producing the same effect. Above all,
he will deliver himself from the jargon of modern criticism, and
escape the danger of producing poetical works conceived in the spirit
400 of the passing time, and which partake of its transitoriness.

The present age makes great claims upon us: we owe it service, it
will not be satisfied without our admiration. I know not how it is,
but their commerce with the ancients appears to me to produce, in
those who constantly practise it, a steadying and composing effect
405 upon their judgment, not of literary works only, but of men and
events in general. They are like persons who have had a very weighty
and impressive experience; they are more truly than others under the
empire of facts, and more independent of the language current among
those with whom they live. They wish neither to applaud nor to
410 revile their age; they wish to know what it is, what it can give them,
and whether this is what they want. What they want, they know very
well; they want to educe and cultivate what is best and noblest in
themselves; they know, too, that this is no easy task – χαλεπὸν, as
Pittacus said, χαλεπὸν ἐσθλὸν ἔμμεναι – and they ask themselves
415 sincerely whether their age and its literature can assist them in the
attempt. If they are endeavouring to practise any art, they remember
the plain and simple proceedings of the old artists, who attained their
grand results by penetrating themselves with some noble and significant action, not by inflating themselves with a belief in the pre-
420 eminent importance and greatness of their own times. They do not
talk of their mission, nor of interpreting their age, nor of the coming

---

these are the qualities that delight us; and when we insist that they are all
to be found in the genuine Greek works of art, united with the noblest
subject-matter and most worthwhile content, with unfailing and perfect
execution, it can be seen why we always start from them and return to them
as a point of reference.'

413-14. See Diogenes Laertius, *Lives of the Philosophers* i (Life of Pittacus),
'It was a saying of his that it was a hard thing to be good, and this apo-
phthegm is quoted by Simonides ... Plato also mentions it in his Prota-
goras' (Bohn's Classical Library ed. 36). A. made use of Diogenes Laertius
in writing 'Empedocles on Etna' 1849–52.

420-2. Addressed to Alexander Smith. The bombastic passage which
annoyed A. is from the second scene of *A Life Drama* (fourth ed. 1856,
pp. 34–5) and is quoted in 'Theories of Poetry and a New Poet', *North
British Review* xix (Aug. 1853) 322:

> *My Friend! a Poet must ere long arise*
> *And with a regal song sun-crown this age,*

poet; all this, they know, is the mere delirium of vanity; their business
is not to praise their age, but to afford to the men who live in it the
highest pleasure which they are capable of feeling. If asked to afford
425 this by means of subjects drawn from the age itself, they ask what
special fitness the present age has for supplying them. They are told
that it is an era of progress, an age commissioned to carry out the
great ideas of industrial development and social amelioration. They
reply that with all this they can do nothing; that the elements they
430 need for the exercise of their art are great actions, calculated powerfully and delightfully to affect what is permanent in the human soul;
that so far as the present age can supply such actions, they will gladly
make use of them; but that an age wanting in moral grandeur can
with difficulty supply such, and an age of spiritual discomfort with
435 difficulty be powerfully and delightfully affected by them.

A host of voices will indignantly rejoin that the present age is
inferior to the past neither in moral grandeur nor in spiritual health.
He who possesses the discipline I speak of will content himself with
remembering the judgements passed upon the present age, in this
440 respect, by the two men, the one of strongest head, the other of widest
culture, whom it has produced; by Goethe and by Niebuhr. It will be
sufficient for him that he knows the opinions held by these two great

---

As a saint's head is with a halo crowned; –
A mighty Poet, whom this age shall choose
To be its spokesman to all coming times.
In the ripe full-blown season of his soul,
He shall go forward in his spirit's strength,
And grapple with the questions of all time,
And wring from them their meanings . . .

440–1. the two men . . . culture] the men of strongest head and widest
culture *1853–4, 1882*. A.'s return to the earlier reading in *Irish Essays* (1882)
was probably due to the use of *1853* or *1854* as a copy-text; the *1857*
reading is clearly preferable.

441. Niebuhr]. A. would be disposed to set a high value on Niebuhr's
judgment because of his father's 'sentiment of personal veneration' for the
German historian (Stanley's *Life of Thomas Arnold* (1844) i 45), but the
name might not have been coupled with Goethe's here if A. had not been
reading the *Life and Letters of B. G. Niebuhr* (1852) while he was busy with
the *1853* Preface (*Note-books* 551) and been struck by Niebuhr's pessimistic
letters in 1830 about the future of Europe.

442–3. For Goethe's opinion of the age and its literature see Eckermann's
Conversations of Goethe under 29 Jan. 1826, 'All eras in a state of decline and
dissolution are subjective . . . Our present time is retrograde (*rückschrei-*
tende), for it is subjective; we see this not merely in poetry, but also in
painting, and much besides. Every healthy effort, on the contrary, is

men respecting the present age and its literature; and that he feels
assured in his own mind that their aims and demands upon life were
445 such as he would wish, at any rate, his own to be; and their judge-
ment as to what is impeding and disabling such as he may safely follow. He will not, however, maintain a hostile attitude towards the
false pretensions of his age; he will content himself with not being
overwhelmed by them. He will esteem himself fortunate if he can
450 succeed in banishing from his mind all feelings of contradiction, and
irritation, and impatience; in order to delight himself with the contemplation of some noble action of a heroic time, and to enable
others, through his representation of it, to delight in it also.

I am far indeed from making any claim, for myself, that I possess
455 this discipline; or for the following poems, that they breathe its
spirit. But I say, that in the sincere endeavour to learn and practise,
amid the bewildering confusion of our times, what is sound and true
in poetical art, I seemed to myself to find the only sure guidance, the
only solid footing, among the ancients. They, at any rate, knew what
460 they wanted in Art, and we do not. It is this uncertainty which is dis-
heartening, and not hostile criticism. How often have I felt this when
reading words of disparagement or of cavil: that it is the uncertainty
as to what is really to be aimed at which makes our difficulty, not the
dissatisfaction of the critic, who himself suffers from the same un-
465 certainty. *Non me tua fervida terrent Dicta; ... Dii me terrent, et Jupiter hostis.*

Two kinds of *dilettanti*, says Goethe, there are in poetry: he who

---

directed from the inward to the outward world, as you will see in all great
eras ...' (Bohn's Library revised ed. (1833) 167) – a passage clearly relevant
to A.'s rejection of subjectivity in the *1853* Preface. Niebuhr's opinion of
the age is expressed most strongly in his letter to Savigny 16 Nov. 1830,
Life and Letters of B. G. Niebuhr (1852) ii 392, 'It is my firm conviction that
we, particularly in Germany, are rapidly hastening towards barbarism, and
it is not much better in France ... the end of the tale will be, despotism
enthroned amidst universal ruin. In fifty years, and probably much less,
there will be no trace left of free institutions ... throughout all Europe, at
least on the Continent.'
465. Virgil, *Aeneid* xii 894–5. *1853* reads *turbida* (for *fervida*), a mis-
quotation corrected in 1854.
466–71. Closely following 'Über den sogennanten Dilettantismus', *Werke*
ed. *cit.* xliv (1832) 291, 'Poetical Dilettantism may be of either of two
kinds. Either the man neglects the indispensable Mechanical Part, and
thinks he has done enough, if he shows Spirituality and Feeling: or he seeks
to arrive at Poetry merely by Mechanism, in which he can acquire an
artisan's readiness, and is without Soul and Matter. Both are bad, but the
first does most harm to Art and the last to himself' (A.'s own translation
in his unpublished 1847 note-book).

neglects the indispensable mechanical part, and thinks he has done
enough if he shows spirituality and feeling; and he who seeks to arrive
at poetry merely by mechanism, in which he can acquire an artisan's
470 readiness, and is without soul and matter. And he adds, that the first
does most harm to art, and the last to himself. If we must be *dilettanti*:
if it is impossible for us, under the circumstances amidst which we live,
to think clearly, to feel nobly, and to delineate firmly: if we cannot
attain to the mastery of the great artists – let us, at least, have so much
475 respect for our art as to prefer it to ourselves. Let us not bewilder our
successors; let us transmit to them the practice of poetry, with its
boundaries and wholesome regulative laws, under which excellent
works may again, perhaps, at some future time, be produced, not yet
fallen into oblivion through our neglect, not yet condemned and
480 cancelled by the influence of their eternal enemy, caprice.

Fox How, Ambleside,
  October 1, 1853.

Preface to Second Edition of *Poems*
(1854)

I have allowed the Preface to the former edition of these Poems to
stand almost without change, because I still believe it to be, in the
main, true. I must not, however, be supposed insensible to the force
of much that has been alleged against portions of it, or unaware that
5 it contains many things incompletely stated, many things which need
limitation. It leaves, too, untouched the question, how far, and in what
manner, the opinions there expressed respecting the choice of subjects apply to lyric poetry – that region of the poetical field which is
chiefly cultivated at present. But neither do I propose at the present
10 time to supply these deficiencies, nor indeed would this be the proper
place for attempting it. On one or two points alone I wish to offer,
in the briefest possible way, some explanation.

---

477. *regulative laws*] Also from Goethe (*loc. cit.* 287), 'Where Art itself has
no strict regulative laws (*kein rechtes Regulativ*) marked out . . .' (A.'s
translation).
6–8. This limitation of the 1853 Preface was pointed out by W. C. Roscoe
in Feb. 1854 – see *Prospective Review* x (1854) 111–12 and especially this
comment, 'Without venturing to contradict Aristotle, we may certainly
say that the poetic art is not limited to the representation of human actions
. . . We have poems to the Lesser Celandine, to a Mouse, to the Skylark –
nay, we have abundance of pieces which involve no picture of any thought
or sentiment of the poet himself, but are purely descriptive of natural
objects.'

An objection has been ably urged to the classing together, as subjects equally belonging to a past time, Oedipus and Macbeth. And it
15 is no doubt true that to Shakespeare, standing on the verge of the
middle ages, the epoch of Macbeth was more familiar than that of
Oedipus. But I was speaking of actions as they presented themselves
to us moderns: and it will hardly be said that the European mind,
in our day, has much more affinity with the times of Macbeth than
20 with those of Oedipus. As moderns, it seems to me, we have no longer
any direct affinity with the circumstances and feelings of either. As
individuals, we are attracted towards this or that personage, we have
a capacity for imagining him, irrespective of his times, solely according to a law of personal sympathy; and those subjects for which we
25 feel this personal attraction most strongly, we may hope to treat suc-
cessfully. Alcestis or Joan of Arc, Charlemagne or Agamemnon – one
of these is not really nearer to us now than another. Each can be made
present only by an act of poetic imagination; but this man's imagination has an affinity for one of them, and that man's for another.
30   It has been said that I wish to limit the poet in his choice of subjects
to the period of Greek and Roman antiquity; but it is not so. I only
counsel him to choose for his subjects great actions, without regarding
to what time they belong. Nor do I deny that the poetic faculty can
and does manifest itself in treating the most trifling action, the most

---

13–14. See *Spectator* 3 Dec. 1853, Supplement p. 5, 'Because the historical
Macbeth lived a thousand years ago, Mr. Arnold classes the Macbeth of
our great dramatist as a subject of the past, in the same sense as the mythic
legend of Oedipus, which belongs to an epoch . . . difficult to apprehend
even by close study of its fragments, quite impossible to present to oneself
as a concrete and living whole. With the exception of the objective form
given to the temptings of Macbeth's ambition, nothing in the thought or
passion of the play is alien from the spirit of modern life.'
19. in our day] since Voltaire *1854–7.*
26. Alcestis] Prometheus *1854, 1882.* A.'s return to the earlier reading in
Irish Essays (1882) destroys the balanced sequence of *1857* (two women followed by two men) and was probably inadvertent – see *n.* to *1853* Preface
440–1 (p. 605 above).
30–1. By various reviewers of *1853*, but A. was probably thinking particularly of the friendly notices in *Westminster Review* (Jan. 1854) and *Fraser's
Magazine* (Feb. 1854), which agreed that the poet might neglect modern
subjects and deal with the past, but reminded A. that Teutonic and Scandinavian legends were a part of heroic antiquity and had some claim on an
English poet. A. complied with these suggestions in writing 'Balder Dead'.
The writer in *Westminster Review* was J. A. Froude, who may also have
written the notice in *Fraser's Magazine.*
33–8. See *n.* to *1853* Preface 90–4 (p. 593 above) for the passage from
Goethe's *Dichtung und Wahrheit* echoed here.

35 hopeless subject. But it is a pity that power should be wasted; and
that the poet should be compelled to impart interest and force to his
subject, instead of receiving them from it, and thereby doubling his
impressiveness. There is, it has been excellently said, an immortal
strength in the stories of great actions; the most gifted poet, then, may
40 well be glad to supplement with it that mortal weakness, which, in
presence of the vast spectacle of life and the world, he must for ever
feel to be his individual portion.

Again, with respect to the study of the classical writers of antiquity;
it has been said that we should emulate rather than imitate them. I
45 make no objection; all I say is, let us study them. They can help to
cure us of what is, it seems to me, the great vice of our intellect,
manifesting itself in our incredible vagaries in literature, in art, in
religion, in morals: namely, that it is *fantastic*, and wants *sanity*.
Sanity – that is the great virtue of the ancient literature; the want of
50 that is the great defect of the modern, in spite of all its variety and
power. It is impossible to read carefully the great ancients, without
losing something of our caprice and eccentricity; and to emulate them
we must at least read them.

LONDON,
  June 1, 1854.

Appendix B

The following poem by Dr. Arnold is printed from his untitled autograph dated 'Fox How. January 13th., 1839' in Mrs. Arnold's domestic
journal.

> How still this upland Vale!
> How clear, how peaceful is this infant Stream!
> How blest in their untroubled Loneliness
> Its sparkling Waters seem!
>
> Yonder in Distance far
> How gleams beneath the Light the mighty Sea!
> Eternal Life is there, eternal Power,
> Eternal Purity.
>
> Could'st thou at once be there,
> O peaceful stream! thine were a wondrous Story:
> Here to have Rest and Pleasure for thy Lot,
> There, Rest and Glory
>
> Between this upland Vale
> And yon far Ocean, canst thou nothing see?
> A wide Space parts the two – and there is set
> God's Task for Thee.
>
> O rich and busy Land,
> Wide fruitful Fields, and many a crowded Town –
> Thither, O Stream, from this thy early Home,
> God calls thee down.
>
> Down with precipitous Fall
> From this thy upland Vale thou must be hurled;
> Chafing and restless, tossed and broken, reach
> That busy World.
>
> Soon from that wild Turmoil
> Escaped, with fuller and with calmer Flow,
> Lonely no more nor wandering, on thy Way
> I see thee go.

A straight embankéd Line
Confines thee, wont to trace at Will erewhile
Thine own free Margin; and the Haunts of Men
    Thy spotless Waves defile.

    Calmly thou flowest now;
Singing no more, as erst, for mere Delight:
But louder harsher sounds from Morn till Eve
    Thy Banks affright.

    So changed from what thou wast!
Curbed, soiled, and troubled! yet thou may'st not grieve,
Knowing their better Wisdom, who their Good
    Give, not receive.

    Better thy sullied Stream
Than thy clear Waters in thy upland Vale!
Better that ceaseless Din than thy blithe Song
    Answering the mountain Gale!

    Thy sullied Waters tell
Of others' Stains which thou hast wash'd away;
Thy straightened Course shows that where Duty calls
    Thou wilt not play.

    Loud is that Din of Sounds,
Gloomy and close the Dwellings whence they rise;
For Life and Freshness to the dreariest scenes
    Thy Stream supplies.

    No more at Distance now,
The mighty Ocean calls thee to his Breast:
Soiled in God's Task, there wash thy Stains away –
    God grants thee Rest.

Appendix C

ARNOLD'S NOTE ON 'SOHRAB AND RUSTUM'
IN 1854

A.'s *1869* note on 'Sohrab and Rustum' (for which see headn., p. 303 above) is abbreviated from his *1854* note, which, at the end of the quotation from Malcolm's *History of Persia*, continues as follows:

M. Sainte-Beuve, also, that most delightful of critics, in a notice of an edition of Ferdousi's great poem by M. Mohl now in course of publication at Paris, containing the original text and a prose translation, gives an analysis of this episode, with extracts from M. Mohl's translation, which I will quote at length: commencing from the point where Rustum leaves Tehmineh, the future mother of Sohrab, before the birth of her child; having given her an onyx with instructions to let the child wear it in her hair, if a girl, and on his arm, if a boy. Of M. Mohl's book itself I have not been able to obtain sight.

'Là-dessus Roustem part au matin, monté sur son cheval Raksch; il s'en retourne vers l'Iran, et, durant des années, il n'a plus que de vagues nouvelles de la belle Tehmineh et du fils qui lui est né; car c'est un fils et non une fille. Ce fils est beau et au visage brillant; on l'appelle Sohrab. "Quand il eut un mois, il était comme un enfant d'un an; quand il eut trois ans, il s'exerçait au jeu des armes, et à cinq ans il avait le cœur d'un lion. Quand il eut atteint l'âge de dix ans, personne dans son pays n'osait lutter contre lui." Il se distinguait, à première vue, de tous les Turcs d'alentour; il devenait manifeste qu'il était issu d'une autre race. L'enfant, sentant sa force, alla fièrement demander à sa mère le nom de son père, et, quand il le sut, il n'eut plus de cesse qu'il n'eût assemblé un armée pour aller combattre les Iraniens et se faire reconnaître du glorieux Roustem à ses exploits et à sa bravoure.

'Sohrab choisit un cheval assez fort pour le porter, un cheval fort comme un éléphant; il assemble un armée et se met en marche, non pour combattre son père, mais pour combattre et détrôner le souverain dont Roustem est le feudataire, et afin de mettre la race vaillante de Roustem à la place de ce roi déjà fainéant. C'est ici que l'action commence à se nouer avec un art et une habileté qui appartiennent au poëte. La solution fatale est à la fois entrevue et retardée moyennant des gradations qui vont la rendre plus dramatique. Roustem, mandé en toute hâte par le roi effrayé, ne s'empresse point d'accourir. A cette nouvelle d'une armée de Turcs commandée par un jeune homme si vaillant et si héroïque, il a l'idée d'abord que ce pourrait bien être son fils; mais non: ce rejeton de sa race est trop enfant, se dit-il, "et ses lèvres sentent encore le lait". Roustem arrive pourtant; mais, mal accueilli par le roi, il entre dans une colère d'Achille, et il est tout prêt à s'en retourner dans sa tente. On ne le fléchit qu'en lui représentant que s'abstenir en une telle rencontre, ce serait paraître reculer devant le jeune héros. Cependant les armées sont en présence. Roustem, de-guisé en Turc, s'introduit dans un château qu'occupe l'ennemi, pour juger de tout par lui-même. Il voit son fils assis à un festin : il l'admire, il le compare, pour la force et la beauté, à sa propre race; on dirait, à un moment, que le sang au-dedans va parler et lui crier : *C'est lui!* Le jeune Sohrab, de son côté, quand vient le matin, en présence de cette armée dont le camp se déploie devant lui, est avide de savoir si son noble père n'en est pas. Monté sur un lieu élevé, il se fait nommer par un prisonnier tous les chefs illustres dont il voit se dérouler les étendards. Le prisonnier les énumère avec complaisance et les lui nomme tous, tous excepté un seul, excepté celui, précisément, qui l'intéresse. Le prisonnier fait semblant de croire que Roustem n'est pas venu, car il craint que ce jeune orgueilleux, dans sa force indomptable, ne veuille se signaler en s'attaquant de préférence à ce chef illustre, et qu'il ne cause un grand malheur. Sohrab insiste et trouve étonnant qu'entre tant de chefs, le vaillant Roustem, le premier de tous, ait manqué cette fois à l'appel; il presse de questions le prisonnier, qui lutte de ruse, et qui s'obstine, sur ce point, à lui cacher la vérité; "Sans doute, réplique celui-ci, le héros sera allé dans le Zaboulistan, car c'est le temps des fêtes dans les jardins de roses." A quoi Sohrab, sentant bouillonner son sang, répond : "Ne parle pas ainsi, car le front de Roustem se tourne toujours vers le combat." Mais Sohrab a beau vouloir forcer le secret, la fatalité l'emporte : "Comment veux-tu gouverner ce monde que gouverne Dieu?" s'écrie le poëte. "C'est le Créateur qui a déterminé d'avance toutes choses. Le sort a écrit autrement que tu n'aurais voulu, et, comme il te mène, il faut que tu suives."

'Sohrab engage le combat; tout plie devant lui. Jamais nos vieux romans de chevalerie n'ont retenti de pareils coups d'épée. Les plus vaillants chefs reculent. Roustem est appelé; il arrive, il se trouve seul en présence de sons fils, et le duel va s'entamer. La pitié, tout à coup, saisit le vieux chef, en voyant ce jeune guerrier si fier, et si beau :

"'O jeune homme si tendre!" lui dit-il, "la terre est sèche et froide, l'air est doux et chaud. Je suis vieux; j'ai vu maint champ de bataille, j'ai détruit mainte armée, et je n'ai jamais été battu. . . . Mais j'ai pitié de toi et ne voudrais pas t'arracher la vie. Ne reste pas avec les Turcs; je ne connais personne dans l'Iran qui ait des épaules et des bras comme toi."

'En entendant ces paroles qui semblent sortir d'une âme amie, le cœur de Sohrab s'élance, il a un pressentiment soudain; il demande ingénument au guerrier s'il n'est pas celui qu'il cherche, s'il n'est pas l'illustre Roustem. Mais le vieux chef, qui ne veut pas donner à ce jouvenceau trop d'orgueil, répond avec ruse qu'il n'est pas Roustem, et le cœur de Sohrab se resserre aussitôt; le nuage qui venait de s'entr'ouvrir se referme, et la destinée se poursuit.

'Le duel commence: il n'est pas sans vicissitudes et sans péripéties singulières; il dure deux jours. Dès le premier choc, les épées des combattants se brisent en éclats sous leurs coups: "Quels coups! on eût dit qu'ils amenaient la Résurrection!" Le combat continue à coups de massue; nous sommes en plein âge héroïque. Le premier jour, le duel n'a pas de résultat. Après une lutte acharnée, les deux chefs s'éloignent, se donnant rendez-vous pour le lendemain. Roustem s'étonne d'avoir recontré pour la première fois son égal, presque son maître, et de sentir son cœur défaillir sans savoir pourquoi. Le second jour, au momente de reprendre la lutte, Sohrab a un mouvement de tendresse, et la nature, près de succomber, fait en lui comme un suprême effort. En abordant le vieux chef, il s'adresse à lui le sourire sur les lèvres et comme s'ils avaient passé la nuit amicalement ensemble:

'"Comment as-tu dormi?" lui demande-t-il, "comment t'es-tu levé ce matin? Pourquoi as-tu prépare ton cœur pour la lutte? Jette cette massue et cette épée de la vengeance, jette tout cet appareil d'un combat impie. Asseyons-nous tous deux à terre, et adoucissons avec du vin nos regards courroucés. Faisons un traité en invoquant Dieu, et repentons-nous dans notre cœur de cette inimitié. Attends qu'un autre se présente pour le combat, et apprête avec moi une fête. Mon cœur te communiquera son amour, et je ferai couler de tes yeux des larmes de honte. Puisque tu es né d'une noble race, fais-moi connaître ton origine; ne me cache pas ton nom, puisque tu vas me combattre: ne serais-tu pas Roustem?"

'Roustem, par sentiment d'orgueil, et soupçonnant toujours une feinte de la part d'un jeune homme avide de gloire, dissimule une dernière fois, et, dès ce moment, le sort n'a plus de trêve. Toutes les ruses de Roustem (et j'en supprime encore) tournent contre lui; il finit par plonger un poignard dans la poitrine de son fils, et ne le reconnaît que dans l'instant suprême. Le jeune homme meurt avec résignation, avec douceur, en pensant à sa mère, à ses amis, en recommandant qu'on épargne après lui cette armée qu'il a engagée dans une entreprise téméraire:

'"Pendant bien des jours, je leur ai donné de belles paroles, je leur ai donné l'espoir de tout obtenir; car comment pouvais-je savoir, ô héros illustre, que je périrais de la main de mon père?... Je voyais les signes que ma mère m'avait indiqués, mais je n'en croyais pas mes yeux. Mon sort était écrit au-dessus de ma tête, et je devais mourir de la main de mon père. Je suis venue comme la foudre, je m'en vais comme le vent; peut-être que je te retrouverai heureux dans le ciel!"

'Ainsi parle en expirant cet autre Hippolyte, immolé ici de la main de Thésée.'

A writer in the *Christian Remembrancer* (of the general tenour of whose remarks I have, assuredly, no right to complain) having made the discovery of this notice by M. Sainte-Beuve, has pointed out the passages in which I have made use of the extracts from M. Mohl's translation which it contains; has observed, apparently with blame, that I 'have not thought fit to offer a single syllable of acknowledgment to an author to whom I have been manifestly very largely indebted'; has complained of being 'under some embarrassment from not being sure how much of the treatment is Mr. Arnold's own'; and, finally, has suggested that 'the whole work of M. Mohl may have been used throughout, and the study of antiquity carried so far as simply to reproduce an ancient poem as well as an ancient subject'.

It would have been more charitable, perhaps, had the reviewer, before making this goodnatured suggestion, ascertained, by reference to M. Mohl's work, how far it was confirmed by the fact.

The reader, however, is now in possession of the whole of the sources from which I have drawn the story of *Sohrab and Rustum*, and can determine, if he pleases, the exact amount of my obligation to M. Mohl. But I hope that it will not in future be supposed, if I am silent as to the sources from which a poem has been derived, that I am trying to conceal obligations, or to claim an absolute originality for all parts of it. When any man endeavours to '*remanier et réinventer à sa manière*' a great story, which, as M. Sainte-Beuve says of that of *Sohrab and Rustum*, has '*couru le monde*', it may be considered quite certain that he has not drawn all the details of his work out of his own head. The reader is not, I think, concerned to ask, from what sources these have been drawn; but only how the whole work, as it stands, affects him. Real plagiarism, such as the borrowing without acknowledgment of passages from other English poets – real dishonesty, such as the endeavouring to pass off the mere translation of a poem as an original work – are always certain enough to be discovered.

I must not be led on, from defending the morality of my imitation, to defend at length its aesthetics; but I cannot forbear adding, that it would be a most unfortunate scruple which should restrain an author, treating matter of history or tradition, from placing, where he can, in the mouths of his personages the very words of the old chronicle, or romance, or poem (when the poem embodies, as that of Ferdousi, the tradition of a people); and which should lead him to substitute for these any '*eigene grossen Erfindungen*'. For my part, I only regret that I could not meet with a translation from Ferdousi's poem of the whole of the episode of *Sohrab and Rustum*; with a prose translation, that is: for in a verse translation no original work is any longer recognizable. I should certainly have made all the use I could of it. The use of the tradition, above everything else, gives to a work that *naïveté*, that flavour of reality and truth, which is the very life of poetry.

Appendix D

ARNOLD'S GREEK MOTTOES

The Greek mottoes which preface *The Strayed Reveller, and Other Poems* (1849), *Empedocles on Etna, and Other Poems* (1852), *Poems* Second Series (1855) and *Merope* (1858) have been forgotten by Arnold's commentators. They appeared originally without any indication of their origin, were omitted by A. in the collected editions of his poems in his lifetime, and have therefore been ignored in all subsequent collected editions except *The Poems of Matthew Arnold 1840–1867* (Oxford, 1909), which chose to print the poems in the chronological order of their publication. This edition, which did not identify or translate the mottoes, was superseded in 1950 by the present standard edition of the poems, *The Poetical Works of Matthew Arnold* (Oxford, 1950), and is now permanently out of print. The mottoes are reproduced below. I have added translations and details of their provenance.

1. *The Strayed Reveller, and Other Poems* (1849).

> ῎Α μάκαρ, ὅστις ἔην κεῖνον χρόνον ἴδρις ἀοιδῆς
> Μουσάων θεράπων, ὅτ᾿ ἀκείρατος ἦν ἔτι λειμών·
> νῦν δ᾿, ὅτε πάντα δέδασται, ἔχουσι δὲ πείρατα τέχναι,
> ὕστατοι ὥστε δρόμου καταλειπόμεθ᾿ –

These lines, as J. D. Coleridge pointed out in a review of *Poems* (1853) in *Christian Remembrancer* xxvii (April 1854) 310–33, are part of a fragment by Choerilus of Samos, but he had this information from A. himself – see A.'s letter 22 Nov. 1853 in E. H. Coleridge's *Life of J.D.C.* i 210–11. Coleridge translates: 'Yea, blessed is the servant of the Muses, who in days of old ere the meadow was mown, was skilled in song. But now, when all is apportioned and a bound is placed to the arts, we are left behind like stragglers who drop in at the tail-end of a race' (*op. cit.* i 212). A. copied out the whole fragment at an unknown date in one of his general note-books (*Note-books* 489). The editors of *Note-books*, who have traced the passage to H. Düntzer, *Die Fragmente der epischen Poesie der Griechen* (1840) 97, do not mention its connection with the *1849* motto. The fragment of Choerilus is quoted in part by Aristotle in *Rhetoric* iii 14 (4), where A. may have first come across it.

2. *Empedocles on Etna, and Other Poems* (1852).

> Σοφώτατον χρόνος · ἀνευρίσκει γὰρ πάντα

A saying attributed to Thales – see the 'Life of Thales' in Diogenes

Laertius, *Lives of the Philosophers* i, 'Time is the wisest of things, for it finds out everything' (C. D. Yonge's 1853 translation, Bohn's Library ed. 19). The motto has a particular application to the title-poem.

3. *Poems*, Second Series (1855).

$$ {}^{\epsilon}Ἡμεῖς\ δὲ\ κλέος\ οἷον\ ἀκούομεν,\ οὐδέ\ τι\ ἴδμεν $$

This line is part of the invocation of the Muses which introduces Homer's Catalogue of Ships – see *Iliad* ii 486, '. . . whereas we hear but a rumour and know not anything . . .' (Loeb ed. i 87). 'Balder Dead', which drew on the comparatively unfamiliar Scandinavian mythology, was the important new poem in *1855*.

4. *Merope* (1858).

$$ Φιλοκαλοῦμεν\ μετ'\ εὐτελείας $$

From the funeral oration of Pericles (431 B.C.) in Thucydides, *History* ii 40 (1), 'For we are lovers of beauty yet with no extravagance . . .' (Loeb ed. i 327). The motto is obviously relevant to A.'s 'classicism'.

Index of Titles and First Lines

(Titles are given in italic type. First lines normally in italic have been distinguished by an asterisk.)